ISBN 978-1-330-81854-1
PIBN 10109434

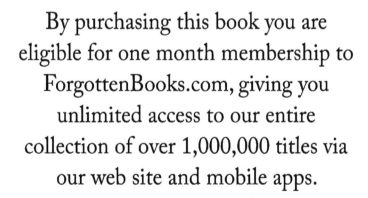

English
Français
Deutsche
Italiano
Español
Português

www.forgottenbooks.com

Mythology Photography **Fiction**
Fishing Christianity **Art** Cooking
Essays Buddhism Freemasonry
Medicine **Biology** Music **Ancient**
Egypt Evolution Carpentry Physics
Dance Geology **Mathematics** Fitness
Shakespeare **Folklore** Yoga Marketing
Confidence Immortality Biographies
Poetry **Psychology** Witchcraft
Electronics Chemistry History **Law**
Accounting **Philosophy** Anthropology
Alchemy Drama Quantum Mechanics
Atheism Sexual Health **Ancient History**
Entrepreneurship Languages Sport
Paleontology Needlework Islam
Metaphysics Investment Archaeology
Parenting Statistics Criminology
Motivational

THE

𝔗𝔥𝔢𝔬𝔩𝔬𝔤𝔦𝔠𝔞𝔩 𝔞𝔫𝔡 𝔐𝔦𝔰𝔠𝔢𝔩𝔩𝔞𝔫𝔢𝔬𝔲𝔰

WORKS,

&c.

OF

JOSEPH PRIESTLEY, LL. D. F. R. S. &c.

WITH

NOTES,

BY THE EDITOR.

---◆◆---

VOLUME IV.

Containing

A FREE DISCUSSION BETWEEN DR. PRICE AND DR. PRIESTLEY;

LETTERS

TO REV. J. BERRINGTON, DR. KENRICK, MR. J. WHITEHEAD, DR.
HORSLEY, REV. J. PALMER, AND JACOB BRYANT, ESQ.;

𝔈𝔬𝔩𝔩𝔦𝔫𝔰'𝔰 𝔍𝔫𝔮𝔲𝔦𝔯𝔶;

AND

LETTERS TO A PHILOSOPHICAL UNBELIEVER,

Part I. and II.

GEORGE SMALLFIELD, PRINTER, HACKNEY.

PREFACE

BY THE EDITOR.

THE first part of this Fourth Volume contains the remainder
of Dr. Priestley's Metaphysical Works, of which the earlier
parts appeared in the former Volume.

The *Free Discussion* has been often mentioned, and must
be always regarded, as a pleasing, though too rare an instance
of a dispute conducted with sufficient acuteness, on each
side, yet without the loss of good temper or the kindest
disposition towards his opponent, in the breast of either.
Mr. Morgan, in the *Memoirs* of his justly revered relation,
says, that " this metaphysical controversy was distinguished
from all others, in -one respect ; it neither disturbed the
friendship of the parties, nor abated the high opinion which
each entertained of his adversary's talents and integrity."
Those, indeed, who are least prepared to argue, in the
manner of Dr. Price, will, I am persuaded, be as ready as
any to do justice to his moral and intellectual attainments.
They will here admire his amiable solicitude not to fail in
the respectful treatment of his friendly opponent, who,
on his part, as is well known, was eager to testify a mutual
regard during his friend's life, and, till he followed him to
the grave, always cherished his memory.

Dr. Priestley has shewn, (p. 7,) how fully Dr. Price and
he agreed in the great objects of religion, which are essential
to " the general interests of virtue." Nor, I confess, am I
able to discover any important, if indeed any difference,
between the result of the Doctrine of Necessity, as held by
a Christian, and those views of divine determination which

I have quoted from the *Dissertations*, at p. 121. What could a Necessarian say more, than what Dr. Price there says, and every serious Christian, upon reflection, must admit, that God " is present in all minds," and that the " whole concatenation of events and causes, in consequence of which any agent finds himself, at any time, in any circumstances, should be considered as derived from him, and as having been in every part, the object of his superintending care"? I have sometimes thought that if, instead of early receiving, and approving through life the view of the divine dispensations ably maintained in Butler's Analogy, though substituting for the endless torments of a great part of mankind the comparatively merciful belief of their final destruction, Dr. Price had entertained the doctrine of Universal Restoration, that only *judge* which *ends the strife*, he would easily have admitted the Doctrine of Necessity. But *let every man be fully persuaded in his own mind.*

The Rev. J. Berrington, author of the *Letters on Materialism*, which gave occasion to the second article in this Volume, is well known by his publications on Theology and Literature. That gentleman had afterwards a very friendly personal intercourse with Dr. Priestley, at Birmingham, and received a testimony of good-will, as I have before expressed, in a Dedication of one of his last pieces published in America.

Dr. Kenrick, to whom the next *Letter* is addressed, is chiefly known as Editor of the *London Review*, which he conducted for a few years, but which was discontinued soon after his decease. Dr. K. had left his post as Critic and advanced as a Principal, availing himself, for this purpose, of the pages of his own Review, a conduct which was closely imitated afterwards by Mr. Badcock, who, however, at this period was contending on my Author's side; by ably shewing in *A slight Sketch of the Controversy*, that the only rational expectation of a future life was derived, not from natural appearances, but from the promise of the gospel.

The next *Letter* is addressed to Mr. Whitehead, of whose arguments Dr. Price has expressed some approbation, but whose manner he disapproves. Mr. W. became a physician in London, and was the friend and biographer of Mr. John Wesley. He began and closed his life among the *Methodists*, but was intermediately one of the Society of *Quakers*.

From the *Letter* to Dr. Horsley, it appears that the Author was now on friendly terms with his opponent, whom he probably met at the Royal Society. Dr. H. was, how-ever, soon to come forth against him as a *fierce polemic*, and in the plenitude of *archidiaconal* dignity.

The *Appendix* which follows, was originally at the end of the Second Edition of the *Illustrations*, and is now suitably annexed to the preceding *Letters*.

The Rev. John Palmer and Jacob Bryant, Esq., the *Letters* to whom form the next articles, opposed my Author's views of *Necessity*, while they themselves held opposite views of an important question, with which that doctrine is imme-diately connected. Mr. Palmer, like Socinus, seems to have considered the actions of intelligent agents as contingencies not knowable, and therefore, not subjects even of divine prescience. Mr. Bryant, on the other hand, like Dr. Price, fully admitted, what may be thought impossible for any serious Theist to dispute, the divine foreknowledge of every event. That Mr. Bryant, though a distinguished scholar, was unprepared for the discussion in which he now engaged, will, probably, appear from the passages of his Work which my Author has quoted.

I was induced to close these metaphysical pieces, with Dr. Priestley's Edition of Collins's *Inquiry*, from its present rareness, and the manner in which he considered that publi-cation, as part of his plan of illustrating the Doctrine of Necessity. In this republication, I have *distinguished* Collins's own notes, as I have also those of Dr. Price, annexed to the *Disscussion*.

In the case of Collins, as well as Hobbes, I found an

occasion, which I was by no means disposed to seek, of correcting the learned and pious Dr. Leland's representations of their opinions, in his *View of the Deistical Writers.* And, here, I cannot help expressing a wish that my justly valued friend, who once proposed an inquiry into the lives and writings of *Deists,* may find recovered health, and sufficient freedom from other important engagements, to pursue his design. He would probably lessen the number of *Deists,* and would, I am persuaded, do ample justice to those who remained.

In preparing for the Press the *Letters to a Philosophical Unbeliever,* having been favoured by a learned friend with the loan of the *Système de la Nature,* which I found a difficulty in procuring, I have annexed the originals, as *atheistical* curiosities, to the translations by my Author. Though the Letters, Part II. were written so long after the others, that the *History of the Corruptions of Christianity* intervened, I judged it best here to bring together every thing under the same appellation. In the very numerous quotations from *Dr. Lardner,* which I have endeavoured to render as accurate as possible, I thought it most convenient to refer to the volumes of the *Works,* which had not been published in a connected form, when Dr. Priestley wrote. The *History of the Corruptions of Christianity,* I propose for the succeeding Volume.

J. T. RUTT.

Clapton, March 27, 1818.

CONTENTS

OF THE FOURTH VOLUME.

———◆◆◆———

A FREE DISCUSSION, &c.

Page
THE DEDICATION   iii
THE INTRODUCTION   -   -   -   -   v

PART I.

Remarks by Dr. Price with Dr. Priestley's Replies concerning the Penetrability of Matter.

The First Communication   -   -   -   18
The Second Communication   -   -   -   26
The Third Communication   -   -   -   32
The Fourth Communication   '   -   33

PART II.

Of the Nature of Mind or Spirit.

The First Communication   -   35
Queries by Dr. Price   -   50
The Second Communication   -   -   -   51
The Third Communication   63

PART III.

Of the Doctrine of Necessity.

The First Communication   -   -   -   -   65
The Second Communication   -   -   66
The Third Communication   -   -   76
Queries addressed to Dr. Price   -   80

Additional Observations by Dr. Price.

Letter to Dr. Priestley   -   85
Sect.
  I. Of the Human Soul   -   87
 II. Of the Nature of Matter   90
III. Of the Doctrine of Necessity   -   -   92

Replies to Dr. Price's Additional Observations by Dr. Priestley.

Sect.	Page
I. Of the Human Soul -	100
II. Of the Nature of Matter	105
III. Of the Doctrine of Necessity	107
A Letter to Dr. Price - - - -	117
Note to Dr. Priestley -	120
Answer by Dr. Priestley -	121

LETTERS, &c.

To the Author of Letters on Materialism, and on Hartley's Theory of the Human Mind - -	122
Of the Doctrine of Necessity -	124
Of Materialism - - - -	125
Of Instinctive Principles - - - -	126
Misconstruction of Dr. Hartley's Meaning -	129
Misrepresentation - -	131
To Dr. Kenrick - - - -	138
To Mr. Whitehead -	144
To Dr. Horsley - -	150

APPENDIX.

Containing a farther Consideration of the Objection to the Doctrine of Necessity as favouring Indolence and Vice -	157

Letters to the Rev. Mr. John Palmer and Jacob Bryant, Esq. in Defence of the Illustrations of Philosophical Necessity   -   -   -   - | 165

Letter to the Rev. Mr. John Palmer | 167

Sect.	
I. Of the Argument for the Doctrine of Necessity from the Consideration of the Nature of Cause and Effect -	169
II. How far the Arguments for the Doctrine of Necessity are affected by the Consideration of the Soul being Material or Immaterial - - - -	171
III. Of Certainty and Necessity - -	175
IV. Of the Argument for the Doctrine of Necessity from the consideration of Divine Prescience - -	178
V. Of the Moral Tendency of the Doctrine of Necessity	186
VI. What makes Actions a Man's own, and depending on himself - - - -	193
VII. Of the Proper Object of this Controversy, and a Summary View of the Principal Sources of Mistake with respect to it - - - -	195
1. Of the Term Agent - - -	196
2. Of Responsibility - - -	197
3. Of the Prejudice arising from the Terms Machine and Necessity - - - -	198
The Conclusion - - -	201

Page

A Second Letter to the Rev. Mr. John Palmer 205

Sect

I. Of the Stating of the Question - - 206
II. Of Certainty, or Universality, as the Ground of con-
cluding that any thing is necessary - - 207
III. Of the Consequence of admitting the Certainty of Deter-
mination - - - 208
IV. Of the supposed Consciousness of Liberty - 211
V. Of the Difference between the Will and the Judgment 212
VI. Of the Argument from the supposed Consequences of
the Doctrine of Necessity - - - 214
VII. Of the Moral Influence of the Doctrine of Necessity 215
VIII. Miscellaneous Observations - - 216
IX. Queries addressed to Mr. Palmer 217
The Conclusion - - 222

*A Letter to Jacob Bryant, Esq. in Defence of
Philosophical Necessity.*

A Prefatory Letter - - - 224
Letter to Jacob Bryant, Esq. - 226
Sect.
I. Observations relating chiefly to Candour - 228
II. Of what relates to the proper Argument for the Doctrine
of Necessity - - - - 233
III. Of the Divine Prescience - - - - 244
IV. Of the Charge of Infidelity, and the Conclusion - 249

*A Philosophical Inquiry concerning Human Liberty, by
Anthony Collins, Esq. 1715. Republished with a
Preface, 1790* - - - 255

A Preface by the Editor - 257
The Author's Preface - - 264

A Philosophical Inquiry.

To Lucius - - - - - - 266
Introduction - - - ib.

The Question Stated.

First Argument, wherein our Experience is considered - 269
General Reflections on the Argument of Experience - 270
On Experience itself considered - - 277
Doing as we will - - - - 285
Second Argument, taken from the Impossibility of Liberty 286
Third Argument, taken from the Imperfection of Liberty - 288
The Perfection of Necessity - - - - 292
Fourth Argument, taken from the Consideration of the Divine
Prescience - - - - 295
Fifth Argument, taken from the Nature of Rewards and
Punishments - - - - 297

Page

Sixth Argument, taken from the Nature of Morality   -   298
Objections answered   -   -   -   -   299
The Opinions of the Learned concerning Liberty, &c.   -   305
The Author's Notion of Liberty   -   -   -   307
The seeming Inconsistence of the Divine Prescience with the
    Liberty of Man   -   -   -   -   308

LETTERS TO A PHILOSOPHICAL UNBELIEVER.   311

Dedication   -   -   -   -   -   313

PART I.

Letters to a Philosophical Unbeliever.

The Preface   -   -   -   -   317
Letter
  I. Of the Nature of Evidence   -   -   -   326
  II. Of the Direct Evidence for the Belief of a God   -   330
  III. Objections considered   -   -   -   333
  IV. Of the necessary Attributes of the Original Cause of all
      things   -   -   -   -   339
  V. The Evidence for the General Benevolence of the Deity   344
  VI. Arguments for the Infinite Benevolence of the Deity   351
  VII. The Evidence of the moral Government of the World,
      and the Branches of Natural Religion   -   -   357
  VIII. Of the Evidence for the future Existence of Man   -   363
  IX. An Examination of Mr. Hume's Dialogues on Natural
      Religion   -   -   -   -   367
  X. An Examination of Mr. Hume's Essay on a Particular
      Providence and a Future State   -   -   378
  XI. Of the *Systême de la Nature*   -   -   -   382
  XII. An Examination of some fallacious Methods of Demon-
      strating the Being and Attributes of God   -   389
  XIII. Of the Ideas of Cause and Effect, and the Influence of
      Mr. Hume's Opinion on this Subject, in the Argument
      for the Being of a God   -   -   -   398
  XIV. An Examination of Mr. Hume's Metaphysical Writings   400

Additional Letters to a Philosophical Unbeliever.

The Preface   -   -   -   -   -   412
Letter
  I. Of Mr. Hammon's Professions and Conduct, &c.   -   416
  II. Of the Proper Proof of the Existence of a God, as an
      Uncaused Being   -   -   -   -   422
  III. Concerning the Seat of that Intelligence which is con-
      spicuous in the Visible Universe   -   -   427
  IV. Of the Proof of the Being and Attributes of God, from
      Revelation   -   -   -   -   432
  V. Of the Moral Attributes of the Deity   -   -   435
  VI. Of the Moral Influence of Religion   -   -   437
  VII. Miscellaneous Observations   -   -   -   440

PART II.

Letters to a Philosophical Unbeliever.

Page

The Preface - - - - - 444

Letter

I. Of the Nature of Testimony - - - 453
II. Of the Evidence of Revelation - - 455
III. Of the Antecedent Probability of Divine Revelation 459
IV. Of the Nature of Prejudice for, or against Revelation 462
V. Of the Causes of Infidelity in Persons of a Speculative Turn of Mind - - - - 464
VI. Of the History of the Jewish Religion - - 468
VII. Of the Historical Evidence of the Truth of Christianity 475
VIII. Of the Causes of Infidelity in early Times - 480
IX. A more particular Account of the Nature of those Prejudices to which the Heathens were subject with respect to Christianity - - - - 489
X. Of the Different Foundations on which the Belief of Judaism or Christianity, and that of other Religions, stands - - - - - 494
XI. The Evidence of Judiasm and Christianity compared with that of Mahometanism, and of the Religion of Indostan 499
XII. Of the Nature of Idolatry, and the Attachment of the Heathens to it, as a Principal Cause of their Hatred of Christians - - - - 504
XIII. The Attachment of the Heathens to their Religion more particularly proved - - - - 511
XIV. Of the Objections to the Historical Evidence of Christianity in early Times - - - - 517
XV. Of other Objections to Christianity in early Times 527
XVI. Of the Two last Chapters of the First Book of Mr. Gibbon's History of the Decline and Fall of the Roman Empire - - - - 535

Free Discussion

OF THE

DOCTRINES OF MATERIALISM,

AND

PHILOSOPHICAL NECESSITY,

IN A

CORRESPONDENCE BETWEEN DR. PRICE AND DR. PRIESTLEY,

TO WHICH ARE ADDED,

BY DR. PRIESTLEY,

AN

Introduction,

Explaining the Nature of the CONTROVERSY, and LETTERS to several Writers
who have animadverted on his DISQUISITIONS RELATING TO MATTER
AND SPIRIT, or his TREATISE ON NECESSITY.

———◆———

Together let us beat this ample Field,
——————Be candid where we can,
But vindicate the Ways of God to Man.   POPE

———◆———

[First printed in 1778.]

JOHN LEE,* ESQ.

LINCOLN'S-INN.

———◆◆———

DEAR SIR,

I TAKE the liberty to present to you, not in the character of an *advocate*, but in that of a *friend*, and a *judge*, a production that is in part my own, and in part that of our common and excellent friend Dr. Price. Though you are employed in the practice of a particular profession, your education and studies have by no means been confined to it, but you have extended your inquiries to all subjects that are interesting to *men*, to *citizens* and to *Christians*.

My object in the present publication, as well as in those which have preceded it, is to overturn, as far as my endeavours can effect it, what I deem to be a prejudice of the greatest antiquity, and the deepest rooted, of any that have contributed to debase Christianity, and a corruption which, in this philosophical age, calls the loudest for reformation. And though this will necessarily destroy some flattering hopes respecting our prospects after death, they are such as are ill-founded ; and it will draw our attention more strongly to those *more certain*, though *more distant* prospects, that Christianity holds out to us.

Our friend, however, considers my endeavours in a light unfavourable and hostile to Christianity, and· overturning not supposed, but real foundations. As truth will finally prevail over all opposition, time (though we may not live to see the issue) will discover whether my zeal in attacking, or his in defending, is better founded ; and as our intentions, I believe, are equally upright, our discussion truly amicable,

---

* With whom, as Dr. Priestley relates in his *Memoirs*, he first became acquainted at Leeds. On Mr. L.'s zeal for the opening of *Essex-Street* Chapel, see Memoirs of Lindsey, pp. 109—111. This eminent lawyer, whose political connexion with Mr. Fox is well known, died 1793, aged 60.

B 2

and consequently *truth*, not *victory*, our object, it will be equally (or, to make allowance for a little human frailty, it will, I hope, be as near as possible equally) acceptable to us both, on which side soever it be found. You, who have an equal friendship for us both, will not, on this account, be biassed on one side more than on the other; and whichever way any of our friends incline, as we are confident we shall not lose their esteem, so, we can assure them, they will not lose ours.

Intricate as the discussion of such questions as these is, there is a peculiar pleasure attending the speculations; and from the relation they bear to the greatest of all objects, they have a dignity and sublimity in them, and eminently contribute to inspire a *serenity* and *elevation of mind*, which both improves and enlarges it, and thereby enables us to look down upon the trifling, but tormenting pursuits of a bustling world.

I have no occasion to describe to you the satisfaction that arises from the rational use of the human faculties, a freedom from vulgar and debasing prejudices, and the habitual contemplation of great and important subjects; and also from such a course of reading, and such a choice of company, as tends to keep up that *right bent*, and *firmness* of mind, which a necessary intercourse with the world would otherwise *warp* and *relax*. He who can have, and truly *enjoy*, the society of such men as Dr. Price, Mr. Lindsey, and Dr. Jebb, cannot envy the condition of princes. Such fellowship is the true balsam of life; its cement is infinitely more durable than that of the friendships of the world, and it looks for its proper *fruit*, and complete *gratification*, to the life beyond the grave.

I think myself happy in being able to call myself one of such a fraternity; and wishing to perpetuate, as far as may be in my power, the memory of such friendships, and especially that with yourself, which is now of long standing, and has been strengthened by a variety of ties, I subscribe myself,

Dear Sir,

Your countryman, friend, and fellow-christian,

J. PRIESTLEY.

Calne, Aug. 24, 1778.

INTRODUCTION.

THIS work, it will be owned, exhibits an uncommon, if not a singular spectacle, viz. that of two persons discussing, with the most perfect freedom and candour, questions which are generally deemed of the greatest consequence in practice, and which are certainly so in theory. The occasion of it was as follows:

When my *Disquisitions*, &c. was printed off, I put it, as I have observed, into the hands of several of my friends, both well and ill-affected to my general hypothesis, that I might take the advantage of their remarks, in an additional sheet of *Illustrations*, which is accordingly annexed to the first volume. Among others, Dr. Price was so obliging as to enter into a more particular discussion of several of the subjects of the work; and afterwards, imagining that I meant to write a direct answer to his remarks, he expressed a wish that I would .print them at large, together with any notice that I should think proper to take of them.

This, I told him, did not fall within my views with respect to that particular publication, but that I would take the liberty to propose another scheme, which I thought would correspond with both our views, and be useful to others who might wish to see the arguments on both sides freely canvassed, without the mixture of any thing personal, or foreign to the subject, which often constitutes a great part of the bulk of controversial writings, and tends to divert the mind from an attention to the real merits of the question in debate. It was, that he should re-write his remarks, after seeing what use I had already made of them in my sheet of *Illustrations;* that I would then reply to them distinctly, article by article, that he should remark, and I reply again, &c. till we should both be satisfied that we had done as much justice as we could to our several arguments, frankly acknowledging any mistakes we might be convinced of, and then publish the whole jointly.

To this proposal he cheerfully acceded, choosing only that the remarks he had already sent should serve as a basis, and that, to avoid repetitions, I might refer to my *Illustrations* in my first reply. He added, however, certain *Queries*, that by my answers to them he might perceive more distinctly in what respects my ideas really differed from his. Accordingly, I replied to his remarks, and answered his queries, with as much explicitness as I possibly could; and in the course of the correspondence proposed others to him with the same view, and likewise in order to bring into a small compass my objections to the commonly received hypothesis. In this manner, at our leisure, and without communicating with any third person, we exchanged our *remarks* and *replies*, till it appeared to us needless to advance any thing farther. In this state we submit the result of our discussion to the judgment of the public, wishing that they may attend to it with the same coolness and candour with which we ourselves have written.

Our readers will observe that this discussion respects all the subjects of my *Disquisitions*, except the doctrine of the *Pre-existence of Christ.* But though this be the point to which all that I have written tends, it being the capital inference that I make from the doctrines of *materialism*, *penetrability of matter* and *necessity*, (these being, in my idea, parts of the same system,) Dr. Price thought it was a subject that had been so much debated, that it would be needless to enter into it.

I will here acknowledge, that in proposing this scheme I was not without a farther view, which was, that, among so many angry opponents as I expected, I might secure a friendly one, and at the same time one who could not but be acknowledged to be as capable of doing ample justice to his argument as any writer of the age. I had pledged myself to go through with this business, replying to every thing that should appear deserving of notice; and it was much more agreeable to me to urge all that I had to say in letters to a candid friend, than in tart replies to an angry disputant. And I thought that, according to the law of arms, and modern honour, when I had fairly engaged with one antagonist on this score, I should be more easily excused encountering another. The reader, however, will find that I have not entirely availed myself of this privilege; for though I have not entered minutely into the argument, which would have been mere tautology, I have noticed such other opponents as have appeared since the publication of my work. And though I think I may now be excused from replying to any others in a separate publication, I will promise that, in any new edition either of the *Disquisitions* themselves, or of this work, I will take more or less notice of every thing that shall come out in the mean time, and that shall appear to myself and my friends to deserve it; and I will publish all such *additions* separately. To do more would, I think, be tedious with respect to the public, and unnecessary in itself.

As many persons unversed in controversies on the subject of religion (and I wish I could not say the same of some who are versed in them), will be apt to entertain a confused notion about the *nature* and *importance* of the questions that are here discussed, it may not be amiss to explain, with some distinctness, though it should be pretty much at large, what the nature and importance of them really are, and to give our readers a plain rule by which to form a judgment in other cases of a similar nature.

I must assume, as a maxim, that the object and end of all *speculation* is *practice*, and that, in matters of religion, opinions are on no other account worth contending for than as they influence the heart and the life. If this be allowed me, I think I can easily satisfy my readers, that they have no reason to be alarmed about the tendency or issue of this debate, notwithstanding all the clamour it has, in different ages, and even at present, excited.

That the general interests of virtue will be effectually secured by the belief of a *sufficient recompense in a future life*, for all that has been well or ill done in this, will hardly be denied. Now this is equally taken for granted both by Dr. Price and myself. We even believe this day of recompense to take place at the same period, viz. at the *general resurrection;* when " all that are in the graves shall hear the voice of the Son of Man, and shall arise; some to the resurrection of life, and others to the resurrection of condemnation."

The advantage, therefore, that either of our schemes can have over the other, must arise principally from the truth and consistency of such opinions as are used in support of the great doctrine of future retribution; on which account one of us may be supposed to give a more firm and unwavering assent to that practical doctrine, and to be in less danger of abandoning it. Or one set of opinions may be supposed to exhibit our Maker, or ourselves, in a light more proper to excite and keep up a just sense of devotion, consisting of the sentiments of love, reverence and trust in

God, and also to impress the mind with a stronger feeling of benevolence towards our fellow-creatures.

It must be added, also, that one set of moral and meta-physical principles, by exhibiting every thing about which we are conversant, and to which our speculations can extend, in such a manner as shall impress the mind with ideas of *simplicity*, *comprehensiveness*, *symmetry*, *beauty*, &c. may give the mind more pleasure in the contemplation of it, and consequently create a stronger attachment to it, and in some measure heighten the finer feelings of virtue.

But these are matters in which the bulk of mankind have certainly very little to do ; and as the effect of these views of things depends, in a great measure, upon our own *persuasion* concerning them, it cannot be easy to determine what system of speculative opinions has the most of these lesser advantages. We all claim them, and are too apt to think the system of our adversaries destitute of them ; so much so, that we often think it impossible to contemplate it with any degree of satisfaction, or without sensations of pain and disgust. Now the *fact* of this persuasion being generally *mutual* is a proof that there is a great deal of *imagination* in it. Why then should we dispute about these matters, with any other disposition, than that with which we usually discuss other subjects of *taste?* And we do not quarrel with our neighbours if they happen not to think as favourably of our houses, gardens, pictures, wives or children, as we do ourselves.

All that is worth considering, therefore, in this case, is, whether any of the opinions contended for by Dr. Price and myself will, if proved to be false, weaken our faith in the great doctrine of a future state of retribution, or indispose the heart to the love of God or of man.

Having stated these preliminaries, let us consider separately the nature and effects of the different opinions we hold with respect to the *penetrability of matter*, the *doctrine of the soul*, and of *philosophical necessity*.

That matter has, or that it has not, the property of *impenetrability*, has no aspect whatever with respect to morals and theology ; but as matter being supposed to be possessed of it, may be considered as an argument against its being endued with the properties of *perception* and *thought*, those different properties being apprehended to be incompatible.

But I think it will be generally acknowledged that there can be no objection to matter, as I describe and conceive of it, being capable of thought, so that one substance may admit of all the properties of man ; and its being favourable to this hypothesis is the circumstance that gives me a bias towards it: because it is with reluctance that I can admit the intimate union and mutual action of two substances, so different from one another as *matter* and *spirit* are defined to be, in the constitution of *one being*, i. e. *man*. To sup_pose man to be *all matter* or *all spirit*, will of itself be allowed to be an advantage in point of speculation, provided the thing itself be possible, and agreeable to appearances.

The proper advantage derived from the doctrine of *a soul*, or the hypothesis of the perceptive and thinking powers of man residing in a substance distinct from his body, is, that it will not be affected by the death of the body, but will pass into a state of recompense when the body is in the grave. This doctrine is, therefore, in fact nothing more than a pro_vision against a failure in the arguments for the scripture doctrine of the *resurrection of the dead*, and consequently does not affect a Christian, who, as such, firmly believes that doctrine.

On the contrary, the doctrine of a soul places the evidence of a future life on a foundation quite different from that on which revelation places it; which always represents the *resurrection of the dead* (founded on the promise of God, confirmed by the resurrection of Christ) as the object of all our future hopes, and never suggests the idea of the soul or the percipient and active part of man, being in one place and the body in another.

The doctrine of a soul is, indeed, generally represented as coming in aid of the Christian doctrine of a future life, and that would be the case if it supplied another argument for *the same thing ;* but here the things themselves are different: for the conscious state of the *separate soul* is not the resur_rection of the *whole man ;* and according to the Scripture, the rewards of virtue and the punishments of vice do not *commence* till the day of judgment; so that the Christian believes *one thing*, and the mere Theist *another.*

This, however, has nothing to do with any thing in debate between Dr. Price and myself; the difference between us being chiefly this : He supposes that the powers of percep_tion and thought reside in an immaterial substance, but that the exercise of these powers is made to depend on the organi_zation of the body ; whereas, I suppose these powers to reside in the organized body itself, and therefore *must* be suspended till the time when the organization shall be restored. This

I think can never be conceived to be a difference of much importance, all the *consequences* being the very same.

The consideration that baisses me as a Christian, exclusive of philosophical considerations, against the doctrine of a separate soul, is, that it has been the foundation of what appears to me to be the very grossest *corruptions of Christianity*, and even of that very *anti-christianism* that began to work in the apostles' times, and which extended itself so amazingly and dreadfully afterwards; I mean the oriental philosophy of the *pre-existence of souls*, which drew after it the belief of the pre-existence and divinity of Christ, the worship of Christ and of dead men, and the doctrine of purgatory, with all the Popish doctrines and practices that are connected with them and supported by them.

Among these I rank the doctrine of *atonement* for the sins of men by the sufferings or death of Christ. For I think it will be allowed, that had Christ never been considered as any other than a *mere man* (though the most distinguished prophet or messenger from God to man), it would never have been imagined that his sufferings could have had the effect that has been ascribed to them, and consequently the doctrine of the proper *placability*, and *free mercy* of God would not have been impeached. Also, what would it have signified to contend for the transmutation of bread and wine into the real body and blood of Christ, if Christ had been a mere man, and consequently his flesh and blood nothing-more than the flesh and blood of Moses, John the Baptist, or any other man?

As a *Christian*, therefore, and a *Protestant*, I am an enemy to the doctrine of a separate soul. One who believes in a soul *may not*, but one who disbelieves that doctrine, *cannot* be a Papist. At the same time I readily acknowledge that this bias may carry a man too far, even to reject doctrines essential to Christianity, though held by Papists. But this objection has no weight here.

I shall not enlarge upon this topic; but it would be easy to shew that almost every thing that has been represented as most absurd and mischievous in the faith of Christians, and what, of course, has been the cause or pretence of a great part of the infidelity of the philosophical world, in the present age, must be laid to the door of this one article.

It is evident, therefore, that a Christian has, at least, no reason to be biassed in favour of the doctrine of a soul, and may, without concern, leave it to philosophical discussion.

With those who do not believe the doctrine of an inter-mediate state, and myself, the difference between *a soul* and *no soul*, in my opinion, nearly vanishes; for, according to them, though it be a substance distinct from the body, it is altogether incapable of sensation or action but in conjunction with the body.

There only remains the doctrine of *necessity*, with respect to which the difference of opinion between Dr. Price and me can be thought of much importance. But even here our difference of opinion is not such as to effect our expec-tation of a future state of retribution; for whatever we ap-prehend to be the *foundation* or *ground* of future recompense, we equally believe both the *fact* and the *propriety* of it. To me it seems sufficient that men be *voluntary agents*, or that motives, such as hopes and fears, can influence them in a certain and mechanical manner to make it in the highest degree *right* and *wise* in the Divine Being to lay such motives before them, and consequently to place them in a state of moral discipline, or a state in which rewards and punish-ments are distributed so as to correspond to certain characters and actions. By this means, and by this means only, can his great object, the happiness of his intelligent offspring, be secured. And one principal reason why I reject the doctrine of philosophical liberty is, that exactly in the degree in which we suppose the mind *not* to be determined by motives, in that very degree do rewards and punishments lose their effect, and a man ceases to be a proper subject of moral discipline.

At the same time that I secure this great advantage, which is of a practical nature, I think it is a consideration greatly in favour of the doctrine of necessity, that, according to it, all *effects*, even those dependent on the volitions of men, have an *adequate cause* in their previous circumstances; which, being known, a being of competent understanding may certainly foresee the effect. On this scheme, therefore, there is a sufficient provision for a plan of *universal provi-dence* comprehending all events whatever, every thing being what God foresaw and intended, and which must issue as he wishes it to issue, i. e. as I suppose, in the greatest pos-sible happiness of his creation.

Upon this scheme, therefore, we have, as it appears to me, every motive that can possibly influence the mind of man to exert ourselves to the utmost to promote our own happiness and the happiness of others; at the same time that it lays the deepest foundation for the most entire submission to the will of God, and an unbounded confidence in his affection and providential care with respect to all things present, past and future. It also, in my opinion, takes away all possible ground for envy and hatred towards men, and thus gives the freest scope to the growth of universal benevolence and of all virtue.

In the eye of Dr. Price, however, this scheme, great and glorious as it appears to me, wears a very different aspect. He thinks we cannot justly be accountable for our conduct, and rewarded or punished for it, unless we be, in his sense of the word, *agents*, or the proper and ultimate causes of our own actions; that, therefore, since we are in a state of dis-cipline, and a future state of retribution will take place, we must be possessed of a power of proper *self-determination*, not subject to the controul of any being whatever; and that since God *does* govern the world, and has frequently fore-told events dependent upon the volitions of men, he must have a power, incomprehensible as it is to us, of foreseeing *such* events.

This difference, however, though real and important, has nothing to do with any thing that is within the apprehension of the bulk of mankind. Nay, the difference between the doctrines of *liberty* and *necessity* is what few writers appear truly to have apprehended. No Necessarian denies that, in a sufficiently proper sense, men have a power over their own actions, so that they can do what they please, and that with-out this power they could not be accountable beings, or the proper subjects of rewards or punishments.

The charge of *Atheism* has been so much hackneyed in religious controversy as to have passed almost into ridicule. It was the common charge against the primitive Christians, and has hardly ever failed to be urged, on one pretence or other, against every man who has dissented from the gene-rally received faith. But perhaps no character has suffered more generally, and at the same time more undeservedly on this account, than that of Mr. Hobbes, who, notwithstanding his heterodoxy in politics, appears to me, as far as I can judge from such of his writings as have fallen in my way, to have been no Atheist, but a sincere Christian, and a consci-entious good man.*

---

* See his Life, in the *Biographia Britannica.* (*P.*) IV. p. 2616, &c. See also the Author, on Hobbes, Vol. III p. 203, and the Note. Whatever views of divine revelation were entertained by this philosopher he has not always been fairly con-troverted. For instance, in the *Leviathan*, Pt. I. Ch. vi. is the following paragraph, described in the margin, as *Religion, Superstition, True Religion*, " Fear of power invisible, feigned by the mind, or imagined from tales, publicly allowed, *Religion*, not allowed, *Superstition*. And when the power imagined is truly such as we imagine, *True Religion*." Leviathan, fol. 1651. p. 26. Lord Clarendon professing to quote

The same tremendous cry of Atheism has not failed to be echoed against me also; but this cry has now been repeated so often that, like other echoes, the sound is become feeble, and is by no means so terrific as formerly. In this case, I think, there is something unusually absurd and ridiculous in the charge, because it supposes that less power is requisite to create and animate mere matter and even to make matter intelligent, than to give life and intelligence to a spiritual and immaterial substance; that the former may start up into being of itself, but that the latter requires an author.

If I were disposed to retort upon my adversaries, I would say that, a man who believes that *one effect* may exist without a cause (which I maintain to be the case with every person who denies the doctrine of necessity), may believe that any *other* effect, and consequently that *all* effects may exist without a cause, and therefore that the *whole universe* may have none. And what might I not say of the Scotch defenders of the doctrine of *instinctive principles of truth,* who, disclaiming *argument,* rest this most sacred article of all religion upon a fallacious *instinct;* and especially of Dr. Oswald, who even professedly, and at large, endeavours to invalidate the only proper argument for the being of God, viz. from effects to causes, and to prove it to be altogether inconclusive ?*

I am very far, however, from charging either the oppugners of the doctrine of necessity, my Scotch opponents, or Dr. Oswald himself, with *actual Atheism;* because, notwithstanding *atheistical conclusions* may be drawn from their principles, they themselves do not admit those conclusions, and I am satisfied that, were they convinced of the justness of those conclusions, they would readily abandon the principles from which they were drawn. I claim the same candid construc-

---

this passage, and even the page, charges the author with having " defined and described religion to be *Fear of Power invisible,* feigned by the mind, or *imagined from tales publicly allowed,*" (p. 26,) as if he had said nothing more. Lord C. adds, " all which I leave to his friends of the Universities." *Survey of the Leviathan,* Oxford, 1676, p. 21. I am sorry, in this view, to mention Dr. Leland. To prove that Hobbes " advanceth principles which evidently tend to subvert all religion," he says, " the account he gives of it is this, that *from the fear of power invisible, feigned by the mind or imagined from tales publicly allowed, ariseth religion, not allowed superstition,*" as if such were the whole account. See *View of the Deistical Writers,* Let. iii 2d Ed. I. p. 60. A *Christian* Necessarian and Materialist may smile at another proof of Hobbes's *deism* which presently occurs. " He takes pains in many of his works to prove man to be a necessary agent, and expressly asserts the materiality and mortality of the human soul; and he represents the doctrine concerning the distinction between soul and body in men, to be an error contracted by the contagion of the demonology of the Greeks." Ibid. p. 61.

* See " Remarks on Dr. Oswald's Appeal," in Vol. III. pp. 100—145.

tion for myself that I allow to-others. With the *reasonable*
and the. *candid* I shall have it, and as to the *uncandid*, I
thank.God it is of little consequence, except to themselves,
in what.light they consider me.

Dr. Price's. letter to me at the close of this Introduction,
and which he obligingly insists upon my publishing just as
he has sent it, shews that *all* those who even differ from me
the most in these speculative points, do not think so ill of
their necessary effects, with regard to *character* and *morals*.
Any testimony of mine in his favour, in return, would be
impertinent; or I should certainly, having much more reason for it, not express less esteem and good-will for him than
he has done for me. It is myself only who avow such unpopular opinions that stand in need of such a testimonial,
and, on this account, it shews considerable *courage in friendship* to act as Dr. Price has done.

If he will allow me to speak so freely, I would say, that I
see no reason for so particular an *apology* as he makes for a
seeming want of respect in his manner of writing, as I really
think he has nothing of this kind to apologize for. I am
certain I might with more reason apologize for the manner
in which I have expressed myself with respect to him. But,
in my opinion, it is perfectly consistent with candour, and
even with friendship, to express the strongest disapprobation
of any *opinions* whatever, and freely to say that we think
them *inconsistent, contradictory*, or even *absurd* or *dangerous*,
if, after an attentive consideration, they really do appear so
to us.

All that candour requires is, that we never impute to our
adversary a *bad intention*, or a *design to mislead*, and also
that we admit his *general good understanding*, though liable
to be misled by unperceived biasses and prejudices from the
influences of which the wisest and best of men are not
exempt. And where *particular friendship* is not concerned,
there certainly are occasions that will justify even great asperity, indignation or ridicule in controversial writing. This
is often the best method of repressing extreme conceit and
arrogance, joined, as it often is, with as great weakness in
supporting a bad cause, even when there is no proper want
of sincerity.

A man must be very criminal indeed, who can maintain
what he at the same time believes to be ill-founded. There
are very few, I hope, so much abandoned. But there may be
a great degree of guilt short of this. For the disposition may
be so vitiated by a wrong bias, that the most frivolous rea-

sons shall appear to have the force of demonstration when a favourite hypothesis is concerned, and arguments, in themselves the most perfectly conclusive, shall appear to have no weight at all when urged against it. The truly candid will consider not the *manner* of writing only, but also the *occasion* of it, and all the *circumstances* attending it. What can exceed the indignation and zeal with which Paul often writes, the severity with which the meek apostle John expresses himself, or the vehement invectives even of our Saviour himself on just provocation ?

The letters which I have addressed to my other opponents are written differently, according as I felt myself disposed towards them at the time of writing. I do not suspect that any thing will be objected to the manner in which I have expressed myself with respect to Dr. Kenrick, or Dr. Horsley; and my address to Mr. Whitehead is, I think, as respectful as he deserves. I had also addressed a letter to the anonymous author of *An Essay on the Immateriality and Immortality of the Soul;** but as I could not help treating him with a good deal of levity and contempt, I was advised by my friends not to insert it in the present publication, as not suiting the gravity with which the rest of the work is written.

Besides, I am not without hopes that this neglect may serve to keep back other equally ignorant and self-sufficient answerers, and thereby leave the field more open to the truly *able*, who are generally at the same time the most *candid*. And as the subject is of great importance, I still profess myself ready to argue it with any person who shall appear to me to have ability and learning equal to the discussion, and to such a one it would give me but little pain to make any concession or retractation, that I might be convinced was necessary. They must, however, go on other ground than that of Dr. Price, who has certainly done all possible justice to his argument.

It may be proper to observe, that in this publication I confine myself to the consideration of particular *objections* and *difficulties*, and that the proper arguments in support of my hypothesis are to be looked for in the *Disquisitions on Matter and Spirit*, and the *Treatise on Necessity*.

---

* Dr. Priestley, I apprehend, here refers to his Letter to " The Author of Letters on Materialism." It was annexed, with the other Letters, to the 2d Edition of the *Illustrations*. See this Volume *infra*.

A Letter from Dr. PRICE *to* Dr. PRIESTLEY.

Newington Green, May 14, 1778.

DEAR SIR,

I am obliged to you for sending me your last replies. I have read them with a desire to be as open as possible to conviction, and even not without wishing for an opportunity of shewing candour by retracting any mistakes into which I may have fallen. But more perhaps through a fault in me than in you, my views and sentiments continue the same.

I must leave you to manage the publication as you please. You must be sensible that my *first remarks* were written without the most distant view to publication; and this, I hope, will be an excuse for the incorrectnesses and want of order which will be found in them. There is also in some parts of these first remarks, a turn of expression which carries an appearance not sufficiently respectful, and which I should have avoided had I written them with a view to publication, and been more on my guard. I know your candour has engaged you to overlook this, but I cannot reflect upon it without some concern.

I shall be very happy should this publication answer any valuable ends; but I am afraid the discussion it contains will be too dry and metaphysical to be generally acceptable. Some good ends, however, it may probably answer. It will afford a proof that two persons may differ totally on points the most important and sacred, with a perfect esteem for one another; and it may likewise give a specimen of a proper manner of carrying on religious controversies.* There is nothing that offends me more than that acrimony of spirit with which controversies in general, and particularly religious ones, are commonly conducted. In religion there is nothing so essential as charity, candour and benevolence. How inexcusable then is that cruel zeal which some religious people indulge; and how melancholy is it to see them, in the very act of contending for religion, losing what is most valuable in religion! Will you give me leave, Sir, here to

---

* "Toute cette Correspondance, où deux *Ecclésiastiques,* tous deux *religieux,* qui se trouvent dans des idées diamétralement opposées sur un point si important de la *Théologie,* et qui ne se ménagent point en argumens, soutiennent néanmoins cette vive Controverse sans sortir un instant des égards que les hommes se doivent les uns aux autres, impriment en commun et restent amis, n'est pas seulement une réponse péremptoire à ceux qui prétendent qu'il faut cesser d'être *religieux* pour devenir *tolerant;* c'est un exemple à leur offrir." De Luc, on this Discussion, *Lettres,* I. pp. 318, 319. Advt. See Vol. III. p. 211, and the Notes.

add, that your opinions give a striking proof of a truth, which, could it be stamped on every human mind, would exterminate all bigotry and persecution ; I mean the truth, that worth of character, and true integrity, and consequently God's acceptance, are not necessarily connected with any particular set of opinions. Many think yours to be some of the most dangerous possible, and yet the person who holds them is known to be one of the best men in the world; and I ardently wish my soul may be united to his at the time when *all that are in their graves shall hear the voice of the son of man, and come forth ; they who have done good to the resurrection of life, and they who have done evil to the resurrection of damnation.* Our agreement in expecting this awful period makes it of little consequence in what we differ.*

With great respect and affection,

I am,

Dear Sir, ·

Ever yours,

RICHARD PRICE.

---

* To this conciliatory language of Dr. Priestley's friend, I cannot help adding the sentiments of a clergyman of the Church of England, whom I have mentioned in the Preface to the 3d Volume, and who appears to have differed from my author on the question of a *soul* more widely than even Dr. Price.

" With respect to the destination of a certain active, intelligent and moral principle within us, to an immortal life after this, I trust that you and I, Sir, concur in cherishing the same delightful hope. · I most cheerfully congratulate you upon this frame of mind without presuming to question, as your opponents have rashly done, the sincerity of your declarations." Baxter's "Evidence of Reason," &c., by Rev. J. Duncan, 1779. Dedication to Dr. Priestley, p. xvi.

REMARKS

BY

Dr. Price on several Passages in Dr. Priestley's

DISQUISITIONS ON MATTER AND SPIRIT,

WITH

DR. PRIESTLEY'S REPLIES.

———◆———

PART I.

Remarks concerning THE PENETRABILITY OF MATTER.

THE FIRST COMMUNICATION.

Dr. Price's Remark.

DR. PRIESTLEY observes in *Disquisitions, that it is asserted that matter is necessarily solid, and of itself destitute of all powers whatever, as those of attraction and repulsion, &c. or that matter is possessed of a* VIS INERTIÆ, *and indifferent to rest or motion but as it is acted upon by a foreign power*——*I do not wonder* (adds Dr. Priestley) *that the vulgar should have formed these notions, &c.* (Vol. III. p. 222.)

That matter is *inert,* or that it will continue in that state of rest or motion which it possesses till some foreign cause alters that state ; and that this alteration of state must be in proportion to the impressed force, &c. These positions are the foundation of all that is demonstrated by natural philosophers concerning the laws of the collision of bodies. They are, in particular, the foundation of *Sir Isaac Newton's* philosophy. The three laws of motion with which he begins his *Principia** have no meaning or evidence, if they are only *vulgar prejudices.* To me they appear to be *self-evident truths*——" That matter is of itself destitute of all powers," may be said with much more truth of matter according to Dr. Priestley's ideas of it, than of matter according to the

———
* See Vol. III. p. 236. Note.

common ideas. *Solid* matter has the power of acting on other matter by impulse, and the effects of this *action* in all cases have been demonstrated by mathematicians, particularly in the *laws* of motion and the corollaries at the beginning of the *Principia*. But unsolid matter, that is, matter which admits other matter into its place without resistance, cannot act at all by impulse; and this is the only way in which it is capable of acting.—See the next and some of the following remarks.

Answer, by Dr. Priestley.

All the laws relating to what has been called the *collision of bodies* are necessarily the very same, whether their separation from each other be supposed to take place at the point of contact, or at any given distance from it, occasioned by a power of repulsion, extending so far beyond the real surface. The *laws of motion* are only general rules, to which the facts relating to the approach of bodies to each other, and their receding from each other, are reducible, and are consistent with any *cause* of such approaching or receding.

Unsolid matter is here said to admit other matter into its place *without resistance;* but this is directly contrary to the hypothesis which makes matter to be a substance, which, though penetrable, is possessed of a power of repulsion, which, if an approaching body be not able to overcome, effectually prevents it from coming into its place. If it was not possible for matter to act but by impulse, it could not be true that rays of light are reflected from bodies at a distance from their surfaces, which Sir Isaac Newton has shewn to be the fact.

Dr. Price.—*Disquisitions.* The resistance of matter is never occasioned by its *solidity,* but by a *power of repulsion,* always acting at a real distance from the body. (Vol. III. p. 223.)

But suppose it solid or impenetrable, in the common sense, could we not conceive of its being brought into contact with other matter; and would there not then be resistance and action? Does Dr. Priestley here mean that one particle of matter can act upon another without contact and impulse; or in other words, that matter can *by its own proper agency,* attract or repel other matter which is at a distance from it? If this is true, a maxim hitherto universally received must be false, that *nothing can act where it is not.* If matter can act at the least distance from itself, it may at the greatest. Sir Isaac Newton, in his Letters to Dr. Bentley, calls the notion that matter possesses an innate power of attraction, or that it can act upon matter at a distance, and attract and repel by its own agency, " an absurdity into which he thought no one could possibly fall."—Shall I here beg leave to refer to what 1 have written on this subject in the *Dissertation on Providence?* (Ed. 4, p. 39, &c.)

ANSWER.—I do not say that, supposing matter to have solidity, it could not act upon other matter by impulse ; but that there is no evidence *from fact*, that resistance is ever occasioned by any thing absolutely impenetrable. It is undeniable, that, in *all known cases*, resistance is owing to some *other cause*, and therefore it is contrary to the acknowledged rules of philosophizing to suppose resistance in *any case* to be owing to this cause.

The difficulty respecting matter *acting where it is not* is precisely the same, whether it be supposed to be penetrable or impenetrable. Let any person explain how it is that the sun acts upon the earth, or how the parts of solid bodies are kept at a distance from each other *upon any hypothesis*. For a more particular discussion of this subject, I refer the reader to the sheet of *Illustrations* subjoined to the *Disquisitions.* *

At the close of this remark, Dr. Price refers me to his *Dissertation on Providence.* (P. 39, &c.) I have read the whole passage with care, but find nothing in it that appears to me to bear harder upon my hypothesis than on the common one. For it only shews, though in a very clear and masterly manner, that the present laws of nature require an *intelligence* and an *energy*, of which what we usually call matter is not capable. Now I certainly admit an intelligent and active cause in nature, and have no objection to supposing that this intelligent cause has even more to do in the execution of the laws of nature than Dr. Price is willing to allow.

DR. PRICE.—*Disquisitions.* The particles of light never impinge on any solid parts in passing through glass, &c. (Vol. III. p. 228.) How does this appear ? All the light never passes through glass. Part of it probably impinges, and is lost. This was Sir Isaac Newton's opinion. *Optics*, p. 241.

ANSWER.—That the particles of light never impinge on the solid part of glass, &c. is evident from none of them being

---

* See Sect. III. in Vol. III. p. 234.

observed to be deflected from their course after they have entered it, provided the substance be perfectly transparent. Newton's supposition of particles of light being lost by their impinging on the solid particles of bodies, is neither probable in itself, nor countenanced by any *fact.* The most probable effect of such impinging would be a reflexion, and not a cessation of motion.

DR. PRICE.—*Disquisitions.* " Matter has in fact no properties but those of attraction and repulsion." (Vol. III. p. 230.)

This is frequently asserted in the course of these *Disquisitions;* and matter is declared to be nothing but *powers.* And yet in p. 243, the property of *extension* is expressly ascribed to matter, *by which it occupies a certain portion of space.* And in p. 231, it is said to consist of *physical points* only, (that is, small parts of extension) *endued with powers of attraction and repulsion taking place at different distances.*——This is not consistent; but let us examine it particularly, and consider what matter is.

Matter, if it be any thing at all, must consist of solid particles or atoms occupying a certain portion of space, and therefore *extended*, but at the same time *simple* and *uncompounded*, and incapable of being resolved into any other smaller particles ; and it must be the different form of these *primary* particles and their different combinations and arrangement that constitute the different bodies and kinds of matter in the universe.——This seems to have been Sir Isaac Newton's idea of matter. See his *Optics*, p. 375, &c.

Mr. Baxter's notion that these particles are themselves composed of other particles which cohere by divine agency ; and for the same reason, these others of others still smaller which cohere by the same cause, and so on : this notion appears to me absurd. According to the account just given, each of these particles is a *monad* or a *solid continuum*, void of pore, and as such, endued with resistance and impenetrability, and capable of receiving and communicating motion by impulse, according to the laws of collision explained by *Keil, Newton* and others.

If this is not a right account, then matter must be either *mere* extension ; or it must be something more, which is entirely unknown to us. If the former is true, then matter is nothing but space. Instead of having pores, it is all pore. Like space, it must be necessary and infinite, and a vacuum must be impossible. This was Descartes's notion of matter, and also Spinoza's, who has founded upon it a system of atheism.

On the other hand, if it is asserted that the elementary parts of matter have in them something more than extension, but that this something not being *solidity*, is unknown to us, it will follow, that being ignorant what matter is, we cannot reason about it, or determine any more concerning it than that wanting solidity, it is incapable of acting or re-acting in any way on other matter.

It must not be said that the property which matter has more than extension, is a power of attracting and repelling. This would be saying that void space attracts and repels. Besides, it has been shewn that the particles of matter cannot, according to any conception of them, have such a power. When two particles not in contact are said to attract one another, all that is meant is, that there is some force that drives them towards one another, according to a certain law. That force, it is certain, cannot be their own force, for the reason already assigned. It must then be the *impulse* of surrounding particles, or (if that is not possible) some other *foreign* force. The power, therefore, of attraction and repulsion ascribed to matter, is demonstrably a *foreign* property. I say, *demonstrably;* for nothing can be demonstrated, if a position can be false which is implied in a maxim so clear as that, " nothing can act where it is not."

In short, matter according to the idea of it into which I am inquiring, being an *unknown extended something* which makes no opposition to any thing that would take its place, and not being capable of acting beyond the space which it occupies can have no powers. It can be of no use. It is as superfluous in nature as Dr. Priestley in p. 266, &c. represents matter to be according to Mr. Baxter's account.—But more than this may be said. From Dr. Priestley's account of matter it may be inferred, not only that it is of no use, but that it must be a *non-entity*. It has, he asserts repeatedly, no other property than the power of attracting and repelling; and the argument in *Disquisitions*, pp. 223, 224, obliges him to assert this. But it has been proved that this is a property that cannot belong to it. It must, therefore, be *nothing*.

Let it, however, be allowed the property of *extension*. If not *mere* extension, it must be something that has shape and form, and is circumscribed within a certain portion of space. It must, therefore, consist of parts. These parts must be held together by some power ; and the same must be true of the *parts* of these *parts*, and so on. But we cannot go on thus *in infinitum*. The existence of matter, therefore, is impossible.

Should it be said, in answer to this, that the primitive particles of matter may be extended and figured, and yet not be divisible, or want any attracting force to keep them from resolving themselves into nothing. Should this be said, I will say the same of a *solid continuum*, or the *monads* which constitute matter; and the argument in *Disquisitions*, p. 223, &c. will be overthrown.

But to return to the assertion that matter has no other property than the power of attraction and repulsion. All power is the power of something. What is that something in the present case?—Is it a power of attraction and repulsion only that perceives, thinks, reasons, &c.? Is it only powers that circulate in our veins, vibrate in the nerves, revolve round the sun, &c.? I will add what seems particularly worth Dr. Priestley's consideration. According to his own system, the attraction and repulsion of matter (performed with a skill that gives the world its order and beauty) cannot be its own actions. They must be the effects of some action upon it. But of what action are they effects? Let this be explained. If the effects of such action as that of ideas and motives on conscious and thinking beings, then, since all matter attracts and repels, all matter must be conscious and intelligent.

ANSWER.—It is very possible that, in defining matter in different places in a large treatise, with a view to different objects, I may sometimes have omitted some particulars to which it was not then necessary to attend. The complete definition is evidently this, viz. that *matter is an extended substance, possessed of certain powers of attraction and repulsion*.

That " matter wanting solidity must be incapable of acting or re-acting in any way on other matter" cannot be asserted, without taking it for granted, that a substance defined as matter is defined above, is in itself impossible. Now, it is rather extraordinary, that the only *proof* of impenetrability should be *actual impulse*, and yet that no clear case of actual impulse can be assigned ; and that a definition of matter framed purposely to correspond to *facts only*, should be deemed impossible, that is, *contrary to fact*.

The reasoning in this remark goes upon the idea that matter must be nothing at all, if it have not the property of *impenetrability*, a property which no one fact requires, and therefore which ought not to be admitted by any philosopher. It also seems to have arisen from a want of considering, that the term *thing*, or *substance*, signifies nothing more than that to which properties are ascribed, and is itself absolutely unknown, and incapable of suggesting any idea whatever. For when we exclude all properties, we, at the same time, exclude from our minds all idea of substance, and have nothing left to contemplate. Thus, a mass of gold is defined to be a substance of a certain length, breadth and thickness, of a certain colour, weight, &c. But take away all colour, weight, length, breadth, thickness, with every other sensible quality, and where is the substance of the gold? Impenetrability is only a property, or something that is *affirmed* concerning material substances, and therefore must not be affirmed without proof, any more than penetrability, or any other property. Now, what I demand, is, *a proof from fact*, that any material substance is impenetrable to other material substances. Till this be produced, I cannot, as a philosopher, admit that matter has such a property. On the contrary, analogy obliges me to suppose, that, since all the evidence of bodies being impenetrable, when rigorously examined, i. e. by actual experiments (as optical, electrical, &c.), appear to be cases in which bodies are prevented from coming into actual contact by *powers*, acting at a distance from their surfaces, that *all* resistance is of this kind only.

If the reasoning in the last part of this remark be just, it will not follow that, because all the powers of matter may be analyzed into modes of attraction and repulsion, all particular substances must have the very *same modes* of attraction and repulsion, and consequently that there is no difference between *acids* and *alkalis*, *metals* and *earths*, &c. The powers of perception and thought, in how great a degree soever they be unknown to us, may be the result of a certain state of the brain, and certain motions taking place within it, though they could not result from matter of a different form, texture, or consistence.

DR. PRICE.—*Disquisitions. Matter has no other* powers *than those " of attraction and repulsion."* (Vol. III. pp. 280, 296, 297.)

What is it that attracts and repels, and that is attracted and repelled? Till I am informed of this, no more is told me of matter, than would be told me of the inhabitants of *Jupiter*, by saying that they have no other powers than those of *moving*. (or rather *being moved*) *to* and *from* one another. And to make the idea of matter to consist in being thus moved, or to say that it has no other power or property, and at the same time to ascribe to it the powers of thought, sensation and reason—this seems to me indeed extraordinary.— How totally different are attraction and repulsion from perception, consciousness and judgment? What connexion can there be between them?

ANSWER.—It is impossible to know more of matter than can be inferred from the *phenomena* in which it is concerned. The relation that attractions and repulsions bear to several modes of thought, may be seen in *Hartley's Observations on Man*. But though the *mode* of the connexion be ever so much unknown, the *reality* of the connexion is evident from fact. Perception, and all the modes of thinking, as much depend upon the brain, as the power of giving a blow to a stick. Is not the *reality* of the union of the soul and body, on the common hypothesis, always asserted, without any person pretending to have the least idea of the *mode* of such an union?

DR. PRICE.—*Disquisitions*. " When we attempt to form an idea of the substance of matter, exclusive of the powers *of attraction and repulsion* which it has, and exclusive of the impenetrability which it has not,—absolutely nothing is left." (Vol. III. p. 297.) This is very true ; and the just conclusion from it is, that matter does not exist.

Exclusive of attraction and repulsion, it is here said, matter is absolutely nothing. But it has been demonstrated that it does not attract and repel, therefore it must be nothing. Besides, allow it the power of attracting and repelling, yet if, as here asserted, it is nothing but this power, it must be the power of nothing, and the very idea of it is a contradiction.—What a strange thing indeed is matter, according to Dr. Priestley's ideas ! Its essence, it seems, consists in impelling (without touching, or exerting any force that is conceivable) other matter *towards* itself and *from* itself. Take this away; set it at rest, or remove its neighbours, so as that it may have nothing to act upon, and it becomes nothing. The whole of it may be crowded into the very space that is now occupied by the smallest of its component parts, or into any compass not so little as a mathematical point; and in consequence of this, having nothing to attract or repel, it would be nothing.

ANSWER.—What a strange thing, indeed, is matter, according to Dr. Price's construction of my meaning ; but such matter as he here describes I never had in contemplation. The matter of which I treat is a substance possessed of certain powers of attraction and repulsion. These powers may be exerted more or less, or not at all, according to circumstances. To matter thus defined I cannot conceive that any of these remarks do in the least apply.

A QUERY BY DR. PRICE.—If matter is not solid exten-sion, what is it more than mere extension?

ANSWER.—If, as Dr. Clarke and Dr. Price suppose, *Spirit* be extended, but not solid, what is *that* more than mere extension? If Spirit can act upon matter, as they suppose, it must have the very power of attraction and repulsion with respect to matter that I ascribe to unsolid matter. If they choose to call my matter by the name of *Spirit*, I have no sort of objection. All that I contend for is, such a *conjunction of powers in the same thing*, or substance, by whatever term it be denominated, as we find by experience always go together, so as not to multiply substances without necessity.

THE SECOND COMMUNICATION.

OF THE NATURE OF MATTER, *containing Remarks by* DR. PRICE *on* DR. PRIESTLEY'S *Replies to the* FIRST COMMUNICATION; *with* DR. PRIESTLEY'S *Second Replies.*

DR. PRICE'S *Observations on the Reply,* p. 19.

THE laws of the collision of bodies, as determined by mathematicians, relate to two sorts of bodies, *elastic* and *unelastic*. The laws which govern the collisions of the latter suppose no repulsion between them, and are founded entirely on the consideration of matter as *solid* extension, and con-sequently *inert*, and endowed with all those properties ex-pressed by Sir Isaac Newton in his three laws of motion.— The laws also which govern the collisions of the latter sort of bodies, suppose matter to possess solidity, or a *momentum* in moving, proportioned to its quantity and velocity, inde-pendent of its power of repulsion.—For example, When an elastic body at rest is struck by another equal elastic body, the effect of the collision will be, that the latter will lose its whole motion, and the other move forward with the very velocity which the impelling body possessed before collision. But if both bodies were void of solidity, or nothing but figured and moveable extensions repelling one another, the impelling body would move *back*, and the other would move *forward*, as soon as they began to repel one another. It would be impossible for them to enter into the sphere of one another's repulsion, because they wanted that *solidity* which gives *momentum*.

It is not, in my opinion, consistent with Dr. Priestley's own system to intimate (as he seems to do in the passages in his *Disquisitions* to which I have referred in my first remark, p. 18,) that " matter possesses powers," and that it is a vulgar error to think it " indifferent to rest or motion but as it is acted upon by some foreign cause." If matter can move without being acted upon by a foreign cause, it must move itself; but this Dr. Priestley cannot allow. He must, therefore, say, that it is entirely a torpid and passive thing. This, without doubt, is the matter which is the object of natural philosophy; and it is this property that, in my opinion, forms one of the fundamental differences between it and spirit.

When I say that *unsolid* matter will admit other matter into its place " without resistance," I mean, " without any resistance given by itself;" and I suppose *contact*, which Dr. Priestley must grant to be at least *conceivable*. The resistance arising from repulsion, being always made at a distance, is not the resistance of the matter itself that is said to repel, but of some foreign cause ; and this I apprehend to be just as certain as that nothing can act on another thing without being present to it. When a ray of light is reflected from a body *before* contact, it is certainly not that body itself that reflects the light ; nor did Sir Isaac Newton, who discovered the fact, ever mean to assert this : on the contrary, he has called this an absurdity which no one can receive. He professes to have discovered only certain facts in the constitution of nature : the causes he has left others to investigate.

ANSWER.—I cannot conceive any difference between the case of *elastic* and *non-elastic* bodies, with respect to the hypothesis in question ; since whatever may be supposed concerning the parts of a *solid*, may be said concerning that *sphere of repulsion*, which, on the new hypothesis, is to be substituted in the place of such solid parts. It is denied that solidity is necessary to give *momentum*, since a sphere of resistance may, in certain circumstances, be as impenetrable as any supposed solid substance. It is not solidity, but the *resistance* occasioned by it, that is the immediate cause of *momentum*.

I readily admit the inaccuracy that Dr. Price observes. But I could not mean to give to a stone the self-determining power which I had denied to man. My meaning through the whole was, that matter, to be what it is, must be possessed of what has been denominated a *power*, viz. attraction, especially that of cohesion. All that I mean by a repulsion at a distance from the surface of a body, is that which Sir

Isaac Newton proves to be the case with respect to light ; so that whatever solution may be found for the difficulty in his case, will serve for mine.   His, too, is the case of an elastic substance.

Dr. Price's *Observations on the Reply*, p. 20.

Dr. Priestley, in his *Illustrations* (see the *Disquisitions*, Vol. III. p. 234), says, that *Newton* considered attraction and repulsion as " powers inhering *in* and properly belonging *to*" *matter*.   With great deference to Dr. Priestley's superior knowledge on this subject, I would observe, that I have never met with any assertion in Sir Isaac Newton's Works that can be fairly construed to imply this ; and that it is scarcely pos- sible that he should have used any expressions which will bear this interpretation, except when speaking loosely, and by way of accommodation to vulgar conceptions.   I have quoted a passage from the letters that passed between him and Dr. Bentley, in which he says the contrary very strongly. In the same letters he says to Dr. Bentley, " Pray don't ascribe the notion of *innate* gravity to me."   And, in an advertisement prefixed to his *Treatise on Optics*, he informs the public, that he had, in the second edition of this treatise, added a question concerning the cause of gravity, on purpose to shew that he did not take it to be an essential property of bodies.   And what he thought of the attraction or gravita- tion of matter he certainly thought likewise of its repulsion ; and would have acknowledged concerning the repulsion of that æther which (merely in the way of conjecture and illustration) he has supposed to be the cause of gravity.

Dr. Priestley here takes notice of the difficulty there is in accounting for the attractions and repulsions of bodies on *any hypothesis*.   But the maxim that " nothing can act where it is not," proves more than a difficulty in this case. It proves that, since these attractions and repulsions are always performed at a distance, and sometimes the *greatest* distance, from the surfaces of bodies, it is impossible they should be the actions of the bodies themselves ; and, conse- quently, that they are not properties inhering in bodies, or that belong to the nature of matter as matter.

If nothing can act where it is not, matter cannot attract or repel where it is not.   It cannot, therefore, have the *power* of attraction and repulsion ; and it must be an absurdity to include such a power in the definition of it, or to make it *an essential property* of matter.   In short, this seems to me the same absurdity, that it would be to ascribe to man, actions done by a higher order of beings; and when it is asked what he is, to describe or define him by these.

No light (see p. 20) that falls perpendicularly on an uniform transparent surface can be deflected in passing through it. But how does it appear that any substance can be made so transparent as to stop *none* of the light that enters it?

Dr. Price's *Observations on the Reply*, p. 23.

What has been said under the last head is all I would say with respect to the first part of this *Reply*. As to the latter part of it, I would observe, that we ascribe impenetrability or solidity to matter, partly because we find that we never can make one body occupy the place of another without removing it. The reason of this appears indeed in some instances to be, that they repel one another: but in most instances no such repulsion appears; and the true reason may be, that they are brought into contact, and will not penetrate one another in consequence of that essential property which we call *solidity*, and which we find ourselves under a necessity of ascribing to matter, in order to distinguish it from *mere extension*, or void space. Even in the collisions of elastic bodies, the probability is, that there is contact and impulse; and that the reason of their flying off from one another, or rebounding, is, that their parts, by impinging, are bent inwards, and afterwards unbent; agreeably to the reasonings of natural philosophers. I am, however, of opinion, that we derive our ideas of the solidity of bodies not so much from experience, as from another more important inlet of ideas, which I have endeavoured to explain in the first chapter of my *Treatise on Morals*. But I may be very wrong; and I refer all my disquisitions on these and other subjects to the candid attention of those who may think it worth their while to consider them.

When I say that "Matter, wanting solidity, must be incapable of acting or re-acting on other matter," I mean, by any action of its own. Two equal solid bodies moving towards one another in contrary directions, and with equal velocities, will meet and impinge and stop one another; but if *unsolid*, they would not act at all on one another, but pass through one another, just as if there had been nothing in their way. Dr. Priestley, in a subsequent Reply (see p. 25), says, if I understand him, that matter sometimes neither attracts nor repels, "according to circumstances." It is of *such* matter I here speak.—Sir Isaac Newton calls that *vis inertiæ* and *solidity*, which he says experience teaches us to ascribe to all bodies, even the minutest, *the foundation of all philosophy.* See his comment on his third rule of philosophizing.

DR. PRICE's *Observations on the Reply,* p. 25.

In the passage which has occasioned the remark to which Dr. Priestley makes this reply, it is said, that matter without the power of attraction and repulsion is nothing ; and in p. 19, he asserts, that this power is necessary to the very being of matter. I must insist upon it that matter cannot possess this power ; and that, consequently, according to Dr. Priestley's account of matter, it is *nothing.* Let it be as clearly proved that matter cannot possess *solidity,* and I will say the same of my own account of matter.

Dr. Priestley, in this reply, seems to acknowledge that, in particular circumstances, matter neither attracts nor repels : and it is very obvious that there must be such circumstances ; how then can attraction and repulsion be its essential property ? Would not one think that if it is essential to it to attract, it cannot be also essential to it to repel ? What is matter, when it neither attracts nor repels, different from void space ? I wish for a direct answer to this question. How does matter know *when,* and *where,* and with *what precise degree of force,* at different distances, to attract and repel other matter ? Or were there a possibility of its being *knowing* enough for this, how can it have the *power,* when perhaps the matter it is said to act upon is at the distance of millions of miles from it ? Even the Deity knows all things, and acts upon all things, only by being present with all things. " Deus est omnipresens (says Newton at the end of the *Principia*) non per *virtutem* solam, sed per *substantiam;* nam *virtus* sine *substantia* subsistere non potest." But I have perhaps repeated these arguments too often : and, however decisive they appear to me, I am afraid Dr. Priestley will think I mean to teaze him, and to wrangle with him. But I am as far as possible from having any such intention.

I am glad to learn from his Reply (p. 20), that he approves of the reasoning I have used, in the *Dissertation on Providence,* to prove that the laws of nature are derived from an intelligence, and a constant energy, of which matter is not capable. With this is connected a truth the most important and joyful of all truths : I mean, that there exists an All-wise Providence, or a benevolent and perfect direction of all events. Our agreement in these things should make us regard less our differences on other points.

In answer to a query of mine which follows this Reply, Dr. Priestley asks, p. 26, " If *spirit* be extended, what is it more than mere extension?" I answer, consciousness, perception, thought, &c. If this is likewise what matter is *more* than mere extension, then *matter* and *spirit* are the same; and our controversy is at an end. But the truth seems to be, that not extension, but solidity, inertness, figure, discerptibility, &c. are the properties which distinguish matter; and that, on the contrary, sensation, perception, simplicity, self-determination, judgment, &c. are the properties which distinguish spirit. I am entirely in the dark with respect to the *extension* of spirit, and therefore choose to enter into no dispute about it. All I am sure of, is, that it possesses locality. The *manner* I do not comprehend.

ANSWER.—If certain effects invariably take place in any case in which bodies are concerned, as on their mutual approach when placed at a given distance, the analogy of language requires us to say, that those bodies are possessed of the power of approaching or attracting one another. But by saying that bodies have certain properties, philosophers, I apprehend, only mean to express the unknown cause of the known effects. As to real *agency*, a Necessarian can allow of no more than one proper seat or source of it.

If, in any case, " no light can be deflected in passing through an uniformly transparent substance," whether we can by art make it perfectly so or not (p. 19), it is all that my hypothesis requires.

By matter attracting, or not attracting, I could only mean, either that, in certain circumstances, attraction and repulsion may be so balanced, as that no effect would be apparent, or that, leaving out the consideration of attraction of cohesion, there might be no foreign body to be attracted. Take away all attraction of cohesion, and let any person say whether any thing will be left to correspond to our common definition of matter; which is my ground for saying that, in that case, it will *cease to be.* There would, in that case, be an actual division *in infinitum.* Attraction and repulsion may be, and probably are, in reality, the same power; and some philosophers are inclined to think it to be the one, and some the other.

As to the question to which **Dr.** Price requires a direct

answer, viz. " How matter can *know* when and where to act," I reply, that the answer will be the very same as to this question : How do the rays of light, or the bodies to which they approach, know at what distance they are to begin to recede from each other ? Whatever shall be deemed a sufficient cause in this case, I shall admit to be sufficient in the other. In my hypothesis I only mean to combine known *facts*, without entering into the doctrine of *causes*.

Dr. Price says, that besides extension, spirit is possessed of *consciousness*, *perception*, &c. I answer, that besides extension body possesses a power of attraction, &c. He says, take away attraction, and what is *body* but mere extension ; I also say, take away consciousness, perception, &c. and what is *spirit* but mere extension ?

THE THIRD COMMUNICATION.

Of the Nature of Matter, *containing Remarks by* Dr. Price *on* Dr. Priestley's *Replies in the* Second Communication, (pp. 27, 31,) *with* Dr. Priestley's *third Replies*.

Matter that is not solid is the same with *pore :* it cannot therefore possess what natural philosophers mean by the *momentum* or *force of bodies*, which is always in proportion to the quantity of matter in bodies void of pore. *Momentum* is the cause of resistance, and not *vice versa*.

I must here repeat (See pp. 31, 32,) the following propositions, which I think have been demonstrated ; that matter has not the power of attracting and repelling.—That this power is the power of some foreign cause, acting upon matter according to stated laws—and that, consequently, attraction and repulsion not being actions, much less inherent qualities of matter, it ought not to be defined by them.

Answer.—I by no means allow, that though matter have not the property called *solidity* or *impenetrability*, it must be all *pore*, i. e. have no properties at all, or be nothing but empty space. If so, it would follow that *no substance* destitute of solidity can be any thing at all. Even every thing that has been called *spirit* would be a non-entity.

If what Dr. Price calls spirit, a substance without solidity, and consequently without *momentum*, can nevertheless act upon bodies ; e. g. the brain, surely the substances that I term material, though they be not impenetrable, may have the same power with respect to each other.

Article II. Every thing that exists must be defined by

its properties, or to speak more exactly, by the circumstances respecting it. Thus, if I describe a magnet, I must mention, as peculiar and *belonging* to it, the kinds of attraction and repulsion that take place when it is introduced, whether those attractions and repulsions, strictly speaking, necessarily accompany it, or be caused by the Deity or some intermediate unknown agent.

THE FOURTH COMMUNICATION.

OF THE NATURE OF MATTER, *by* DR. PRICE, *with* DR. PRIESTLEY'S *Answer.*

IT is, in my opinion, particularly incumbent on Dr. Priestley, to give a more explicit answer than he has yet given to the question, " What the true idea of matter is ;" or " what inherent and essential property it possesses that distinguishes it from mere space ?" I must repeat here what I have said in my first remarks, and insist upon it as of particular importance, that no answer is given to this question, by saying that matter is SOMETHING which is attracted and repelled ; or in other words, that it is *something* which is continually acted upon by a foreign force. What is it that is so acted upon ? Not mere space. That is absurd. Not a *solid* substance. There is no such thing according to Dr. Priestley. Not the subject of consciousness and thought. That would imply there is nothing but spirit in nature. The attractions and repulsions which take place between different bodies are only *external circumstances* which distinguish one parcel of matter from another, (a magnet, for instance, from other substances,) but they enter not into the idea of matter *as* matter. There are circumstances in which matter neither attracts nor repels ; as particularly in the limit between the sphere of attraction and repulsion.

But this leads me to the chief observation I intended to make. If I understand Dr. Priestley, all bodies at a small distance repel one another, so as to make contact between them impracticable. Within the sphere of repulsion, the *attraction of cohesion* takes place ; and this is the power which, according to Dr. Priestley, *unites* the parts of matter and gives it existence. But since matter is penetrable, will not this attraction drive all the parts of it into one another, and cause them to coalesce into nothing ? This effect must follow, unless there exists, beyond the sphere of attraction and nearer to matter, a second sphere of repulsion which again prevents contact. The argument which Dr. Priestley draws from the effect of cold in contracting bodies, and of heat in swelling them, makes it probable that this is his opinion. And, if true, the elementary parts of matter possess just the contrary principle to that which he asserts to be necessary to preserve their existence.

In short, since we cannot go on assigning a sphere of repulsion beyond a sphere of attraction, and a sphere of attraction beyond a sphere of repulsion *in infinitum ;* either no power at all acts on the elements of matter, or if a power does act, it must be either a power of attraction or a power of repulsion. Dr. Priestley asserts, that if no power at all acts to keep matter together, it must *crumble* into *nothing.* And it appears evident to me, that if a power of attracting acts, it must *contract* itself into nothing ; and that if a power of repulsion acts, it must *dissipate* itself into nothing.

What can be done in this dilemma ? The truth seems to be, that there is an absurdity in supposing the elements of matter to consist of parts actually distinct and separable, which require a foreign agency to unite them. For the same reason that these elements must consist of such parts, the elements of those elements must consist of such parts, and so on for ever. I have observed in my first remarks, that we must terminate in parts, each of which is a solid *continuum* incapable of division. Indeed, every real existence or substance must be a *monad.* We are sure this is true of the beings we are best acquainted with ; I mean *ourselves,* and all conscious and sentient beings. And if it be not true of matter, I know not what it is.

ANSWER.—With respect to the *definition of matter,* I really am not able to be more explicit than I have been. A definition of any particular *thing, substance* or *being,* (call it what you will,) cannot be any thing more than an enumeration of its known *properties ;* and in all cases whatever, as with respect to *matter, spirit,* &c. &c. if we take away all the known properties, nothing will be left, of which we can possibly have any idea at all ; every thing else being merely *hypothetical,* and the terms *substance, thing, essence,* &c. being, as I have observed, nothing more than a help to expression ; it being a convenience in speech to have certain words of this universal application.

Solid *atoms* or *monads of matter,* can only be hypothetical things ; and till we can either touch them or come at them some way or other, by actual experiment, I cannot be obliged to admit their existence. Admitting the existence of these solid atoms, they do not help us in the least to ex-plain any of the known properties of matter. All the *effects* are reducible to attractions or repulsions. Now what con-nexion *is* there between *solidity* and *attraction*, or even repulsion, at a distance from the surface of a body? And though resistance at the point of contact might be explained by it, no such thing as *real contact* can be *proved;* and most of the known repulsions in nature do certainly take place in *other circumstances*, and therefore must have some *other cause*.

In reply to Dr. Price, I must observe, that the limit be-tween a sphere of attraction and another of repulsion, can-not be a place where neither of these powers are exerted, but where they balance each other. It does not follow that because a beam is in equilibrio, there are no weights in the scales.

That there are spheres of attraction and repulsion within each other, is evident from fact, as in electricity, magnetism, &c.; nor can the cohesion of bodies, the parts of which (as is demonstrable from the phenomena of cold) do not actually touch each other, be explained without it. The parts of bodies must therefore attract each other at one distance and repel at another; and in the limit between both they must remain; and by this means bodies retain their form and texture.

PART II.

Of the Nature of MIND *or* SPIRIT.

THE FIRST COMMUNICATION,

By DR. PRICE, *with* DR. PRIESTLEY's *Answers.*

IN answer to the several arguments in the Disquisitions, Sect. IV. and V. (Vol. III. pp. 242—251,) it seems enough to say, that a *connexion* and *dependence* by no means prove *sameness*. We are conscious of the contrary in the present case. Seeing depends on our eyes, but *we* are not our eyes any more than the eye itself is the telescope through which it looks, or the artist is the tool which he uses.

ANSWER.—This is by no means a just state of the argument. I infer that the business of thinking is wholly carried on *in* and *by* the brain itself, because all the effects from which we infer the faculty of thinking, can be traced to the brain, and *no farther*. I conclude that the ultimate perceptive power relating to objects of sight is not in the eye, because though the eye be necessary to acquire ideas of sight, they remain *somewhere* when the eye is destroyed. But I have no reason whatever to refer this perceptive power to any thing beyond the brain, because when the brain is destroyed, there is, to all appearance, an end of all sensation and thought. To suppose that when the brain is destroyed the ideas remain in *something else*, is a mere hypothesis, unsupported by any fact whatever.

A philosopher supposes no more *causes* than are necessary to explain *effects*. He finds the business of thinking to be dependent upon the brain, and therefore he concludes that the brain itself is competent to this business whatever it be. To suppose any thing farther is mere hypothesis, and utterly unphilosophical. What I maintain then is, that, according to the established rules of philosophizing, we are not authorized to suppose any thing *within the brain* to be the seat of thought. If we do, we may just as well suppose it to reside in something within that, and in something again within that, and so on without end; just as the Indians are said to place the earth upon an elephant, the elephant upon a tortoise, and the tortoise on they knew not what.

DR. PRICE.—In the Disquisitions, (Vol. III. pp. 250, 292,) it is asserted, that ideas are certainly divisible. This seems to me very absurd. It would be as proper to assert ideas to be hard or round. The idea of an object is the apprehension, view, or notion of it; and how can this be divisible? Perception is a single and indivisible act. The object perceived may be divisible; but the *perception* of it by the mind cannot be so.

ANSWER.—What appears to Dr. Price to be *very absurd*, I cannot help thinking, after the most deliberate review, to be very certain and very clear. What correspondence can there be between an idea and its archetype, if the archetype consist of parts, and the idea have no parts? He seems to have been misled, by not distinguishing between the *power*, or rather the *act* of perception, and the thing (i. e. the *idea*) perceived. The object of perception he acknowledges to be divisible, but *the perception of it by the mind* cannot be so. True, because perception is either a faculty or an act of a faculty, to which divisibility is not applicable; but the thing about which the perceptive power is employed (which is not the object itself, but the idea or representation of it in the mind) must be as divisible as the archetype of that idea. If the mind be a simple and indivisible substance, it cannot be possessed of more than a single idea, and that the idea of something to which division is not applicable. However, I do not see why Dr. Price should object to a *repository of divisible ideas* in a mind which he supposes to be actually extended, and consequently to have room enough for that purpose.

DR. PRICE.—Disquisitions, (Vol. III. pp. 254, &c. 276, &c.). *Mr. Baxter*, and other ingenious men, have undoubtedly said a great deal that is very groundless about the union of the body to the soul; its being a clog; its leaving the soul more capable of exerting its powers when separated from it, &c. Were all that has been said on these subjects true, there would be no occasion for a resurrection. Nay, it would be a calamity, not a benefit. A false philosophy has, in this instance, contradicted nature and experience, as well as revelation. Thus far I agree entirely with Dr. Priestley; but some of the objections in Sect. VI. (Vol. III. p. 252,) have little weight with me, and cannot easily be answered on any hypothesis. If it must be taken for granted that brutes, or the sentient principles in brutes, are annihilated at death, as seems to be hinted sometimes by Dr. Priestley, I am afraid it will not easily be believed that the same is not true of men. And if true, there will be a complete end of us: a resurrection will be a contradiction. But it will come in my way to say more to this purpose.

ANSWER.—My only reason for not supposing that *brutes* will not survive the grave is, that there is no hint of it in revelation, where only it is that we are informed that *men* will rise again. It may, however, be true, though we have not been informed of it, and the analogy between men and other animals, makes it not very improbable.

DR. PRICE.—Disquisitions, (Vol. III. p. 259). Dr. Priestley here, and throughout a great part of this work, argues on the supposition, that according to the ideas of modern metaphysicians, spirit can have no relation to place, and is incapable of being present any where. This seems to me a mistake. I do not know what modern metaphysicians Dr. Priestley means, except the Cartesians. I am certain Dr. Clarke, and some others of the best modern writers, did not entertain these ideas of spirit. It is a maxim that cannot be disputed, that *time* and *place* are necessary to the existence of all things. Dr. Clarke has made use of this maxim, to prove that infinite space and duration are the essential properties of the Deity ; and I think he was right. Sir Isaac Newton thought in the same way, as appears from some passages at the end of his *Principia*, and in the queries at the end of his *Optics*. As far, therefore, as Dr. Priestley combats a notion of spirit that implies it has no relation to space, and exists no where, he combats an absurdity and contradiction which deserves no regard. What the nature is of the relation of spirit to place, or in what *manner* it is present in space, I am utterly ignorant. But I can be sure that, if it exists at all, it must exist *somewhere*, as well as in *some time*.

Dr. Clarke was not for excluding expansion from the idea of immaterial thinking substances. See his *First Defence of an Argument to prove the Immateriality and Natural Immortality of the Soul*, in answer to *Collins*. Has Dr. Priestley read this controversy ; or has he read the chapter on a Future State, with which *Butler's* Analogy begins? If he had, I fancy he would have writ differently in some parts of this book. Dr. Clarke is, without all doubt, the best and ablest of all writers, on the subjects of the Immateriality and Natural Immortality of the Soul, and also on *Liberty* and *Necessity*. What he says on these subjects in his *Demonstration of the Being and Attributes of God*, is but inconsiderable, compared with what he has said in his *Answer to Dodwell*, his *Controversies with Collins*, and the *Letters* between *him* and *Leibnitz*.

I think it of little consequence, whether it *can* or *cannot* be determined, whether the subject of consciousness and thought in man is matter, if by matter is meant not solid extension, but an unknown something that has a relation to place ; and it was hardly worth while to write a book to prove this.

Matter is incapable of consciousness and thought, not because it is *extended*, but because it is *solid* ; and, as such, inert and capable of being divided without being annihilated. *Solid extension*, and *perception, thought, volition*, &c. are totally different things ; and it is just as clear that the latter cannot be the figure, motion and arrangement of the parts of the former, as that any one thing cannot *be* another ; that a square, for instance, cannot *be*, or be *made to be*, sound or colour. Our ideas of *figured, extended, solid substances*, and of *conscious, perceiving, thinking substances*, are, according to

Mr. Locke's observation, equally clear and distinct. It seems, therefore, very unreasonable to confound them, or to talk of superadding one of them to the other.

Dr. Clarke makes use of the instance of *space*, to prove that there is no necessary connexion between extension and discerptibility. *Moveantur partes spatii de locis suis et movebuntur de seipsis. Newton's Princip. Lib.* I. *Schol. Defin.* 8.

ANSWER.—I consider Mr. Baxter as having been one of the most consistent of all the Immaterialists. That such a scheme as his is the only consistent one, is, I think, sufficiently proved by Dr. Watts. Some of his arguments I have referred to, (Vol. III. p. 368,) and other reasons for this opinion I have suggested, p. 260, &c.

If, as Dr. Clarke supposes, spirits have real extension, they must be of some shape, and therefore their relation to space cannot be a thing of which we are *utterly ignorant.* We may not know *where* they are, or *how much space* they occupy, (whether, for instance, *more* or *less* than the bodies they belong to,) but they must occupy *some space* as well as bodies.

I will farther observe, that if, according to Dr. Clarke, the Divine Being has infinite extension, and finite spirits a limited one, they must mutually penetrate each other ; and these spiritual substances being of *the same nature*, the difficulty attending it must be just as great as that which attends the mutual penetration of material substances.

I have carefully read all Dr. Clarke's metaphysical works, but thought it sufficient to quote his *Demonstration*, as the *best known* of all his writings, and containing a summary of his strongest arguments on all the topics that I have had occasion to discuss. I have also read *Butler's Analogy*, but this work does not stand so high with me as it does with Dr. Price. I did not think that, with respect to any thing that I have written, it was at all necessary to consider any passages of Dr. Clarke's other writings, or any of Butler's ; but if Dr. Price thinks otherwise, I will give particular attention to any thing, in either of them, that he shall be pleased to point out to me.

Dr. Price admits, that if matter be not solid and impenetrable, it may be capable of thought, but wonders that I should have written a book to prove this. My book was not written to prove this, but to prove that, whatever matter be, *thinking* is the result of a modification of it, or that this faculty does not belong to an invisible substance, different from the body, which I apprehend to have been the source of the greatest corruptions of the system of revelation. Effectually to explode this notion, originally borrowed from Heathenism, and thereby to discharge from Christianity many enormous errors that now disfigure it, and make it appear absurd in the present enlightened age of philosophy, appears to me to be rendering it the most important of all services. Whether I have in any measure *succeeded*, such, if I know my own heart, have been my views in writing both the *Disquisitions* themselves, and this defence of them.

I wish Dr. Price would inform me what is the connexion between, *a capacity of consciousness*, and *being indivisible without being annihilated*. Also, if spirits be extended, and something more than space, whether they may not be divisible and discerptible, as well as matter?

Dr. Hartley has shewn that all the faculties of the human mind may be the result of vibration, except that of *simple perception;* but this, though *different* from the other known properties of matter, may not be *incompatible* with them. The facts alleged in Sect. IV. (Vol. III. p. 242,) do, I apprehend, prove, that according to the established rules of philosophizing, it is a property that must *in fact* belong to the brain, whether we ever be able to conceive *how* it results from the structure of the brain, or not. In my opinion there is just the same reason to conclude that the brain *thinks*, as that it is *white* and *soft*.

Though Mr. Locke was of opinion that our ideas of thinking substances are as distinct as those of solid ones, he was likewise of opinion, that, for any thing that we know to the contrary, thinking *may* be the mere property of a solid substance.

Dr. Clarke should have shewn not only that *extension*, but that *a capacity of motion from place to place* is not necessarily connected with discerptibility. It appears to me very clear, that if a spirit be a thing that is extended and moveable, one part of it may be conceived to be moved, and the other part left behind, whether the property of *consciousness* would be destroyed in consequence of it, or not.

DR. PRICE.—In the Disquisitions, Dr. Priestley says, that " it is even demonstrable that matter is infinitely divisible." (Vol. III. p. 270.) Can he say that the being he calls 'him-*self* is likewise infinitely divisible ? What would be the result of such a division ? Would it not be an infinite number of *other* beings ? But does not this imply a contradiction ? Can there be such a thing as *half* a self? Or can the being I call *myself* be split into two *others?* Impossible! This would not be to *divide*, but to *annihilate* me. And the truth is, that in this case division cannot be imagined without annihilation. In another place Dr. Priestley intimates, that matter consists of *indivisible points*, (p. 233). How then can it be infinitely divisible ?

ANSWER.—The matter of which I consist may be divisible, though the *actual* division of it might so disarrange the parts of it, that the property of thinking (which is the result of a particular modification of them) would be destroyed. A whole brain may think, but half a brain may be incapable of it. I see no sort of difficulty in this case. Also, may not an extended spirit be conceived to be divided without annihilation, as well as an extended solid substance ? To the imagination it is equally easy.

DR. PRICE.—Disquisitions. *The " percipient power may as well belong to one system as to one atom."* (Vol. III. p. 286.) See likewise the answer to the fourth objection. *I am one person, but it does not follow that I cannot be divided : a sphere is one thing, but it does not follow that it consists of indivisible materials* (p. 283). But if matter consists of *indivisible points* (as is said in p. 233), and the soul is matter, then the soul consists of indivisible materials. But not to insist on this. Can any one believe of *himself* that he is one thinking being only as a great number of bodies forming a sphere are one sphere ? If this is true, he must be either the parts themselves that compose the sphere ; and if so, he is a *multitude* of beings ; or he must be their *sphericity ;* and if so, he is nothing but an *order* or *relation* of parts, and can never remain the same any longer than that order is preserved. As any change in the surface of a sphere would destroy the sphericity, and convert it into some other figure, so would any change in that *order* of parts which constitutes *myself*, destroy *me*, and convert me into some *other person.*

ANSWER.—If I say that matter consists of indivisible points, I use a common expression, though perhaps not a correct one. But as every sensible part of matter consists of an *infinity* of such points, it is plain that the substance can never be exhausted by any division. To infer from this, that the soul (consisting of matter) consists of an indivisible substance, seems to me to be a play upon words.

If a thinking being be a material substance of a particular texture and form, as I define it, it cannot follow, as is here asserted, that it is *a mere order or relation of parts*. A disarrangement of this texture would destroy all *power of thought,* but would not make *another person.*

Dr. Price.—Disquisitions. "*It must be impossible to say a priori, whether a single particle or a system of matter be the proper seat*" *of perception, but fact proves the latter.* (Vol. III. p. 285.) If a system of matter is the seat of per_ ception, then the system is the percipient being. But the percipient being is *one.* A system consists of *many* beings. It is inconceivable to me how any person can think that many substances united can be one substance, or that all the parts of a system can perceive, and yet no single part be a percipient being.

Answer.—A system, though consisting of many beings or things, is nevertheless but *one system.* A brain, though consisting of many parts, is but one brain ; and where can be the difficulty of conceiving that no single part of a brain should be a whole brain, or have the properties of a whole brain ?

Dr. Price.—Disquisitions, Sect. XII. (Vol. III. p. 296.) It seems evident that Dr. Priestley's principles go to prove, that the Deity is material, as well as all inferior beings. He would otherwise have no common property with matter, by which it would be possible for him to act upon it. But at the same time would there not be something shocking in saying of the Deity, that he is nothing but a power of attraction and repulsion ?

Answer.—By what construction am I made to assert that the Divine Essence is *material,* that is, of *the same kind of substance* with what we generally term *matter,* when I suppose it to have quite *different properties,* on account of which I expressly say, that it ought to have a quite *different name,* and not receive its denomination from the mere nega_ tion of the properties of matter, which is, in fact, no defini_ tion at all ? Let all beings and all things be defined by their *known properties,* and no mistake can possibly arise ; for then our knowledge and our language will always correspond to one another. It would certainly be something shocking to say that " the Deity is nothing but a power of attraction and repulsion," but it would be saying what is directly con- trary to the doctrine of my treatise, as must, I think, be obvious to the most superficial attention.

Dr. Price.—Disquisitions. I am surprised Dr. Priest- ley should here say, that it is almost universally acknow- ledged that, according to the Scriptures, " the Deity is—

incapable of local presence," when it is so well known that some of the first Christian writers have believed *infinite space* to be an attribute of the Deity.

ANSWER.—What I maintain is, that according to the only consistent scheme of immaterialism, the Divine Being, as well as other immaterial substances, has no *local presence*, and it is the opinion that till lately I held myself. That the Divine Being has a proper omnipresence, and consequently a proper extension, I now admit, but should not choose to say with any person, though ever so justly called the *first Christian writer in other respects*, that space is merely *an attribute of the Deity;* because, supposing that there was no Deity, space would still remain. It cannot be annihilated even in idea.

DR. PRICE.—Disquisitions. " *But till we know something positive concerning this supposed immaterial substance,*" &c. (Vol. III. p. 292.) What is similar to this may be more properly said of matter, according to Dr. Priestley's account of it. Whatever the soul is, it must, if it is to exist for ever, be somewhat so substantial as to have no tendency to decay, or wear out. But this cannot be true of any thing compounded.

ANSWER.—If, as Dr. Price supposes, a spiritual substance be extended, it must consist of an aggregation of parts, and therefore may be as liable to be dissolved as a homogeneous corporeal substance.

DR. PRICE.—When it is asserted that the soul is *naturally immortal*, the meaning is, that being a *substance* and not a *mode*, it will go on to exist, till by some positive act of the Creator it is annihilated. In the same sense it may be said of the *atoms*, or *elements* that compose our bodies, that they are naturally immortal: for it is, I think, a general truth, that only the power that brought any substance into being can put it out of being. Does Dr. Priestley deny the natural immortality of the soul in this sense? If he does, and if he really means when he says, " that the whole man becomes extinct at death," that death destroys or annihilates the thinking substance; and if also this is the dictate of nature and reason, then the doctrine of a resurrection is contradictory to nature and reason, and Dr. Priestley, by maintaining the natural mortality of the soul, injures revelation. But it is certain he means the contrary. He must therefore acknowledge, that death does not naturally destroy the soul; or, in other words, that it preserves its existence at death ; and that what then happens to it, can be no more than a suspension of the exercise of its faculties, or an *incapacitation* from which it will, by the power of Christ, be delivered at the resurrection. If he acknowledge this, he and I, and many other zealous immaterialists are agreed. If he does not mean this, the resurrection will be, not a *resurrection* but a *creation* of a new set of beings. If death annihilates us, there can be no future state. This is self-evident. A being who has lost his existence cannot be recovered. It is very improper here to mention the renewal of the flame of a candle after extinction ; for the substance of the candle is not affected by the extinction of the flame, just as the substance of the soul is not affected by the suspension of its powers at death. It should be considered also, that the flame of a candle, being nothing but a current of hot and shining vapour that is constantly passing away, like the water of a river, it never continues a moment the same ; and that, consequently, the *renewed* flame is properly a *new* and *different* flame.

ANSWER.—I am surprised at these conjectures concerning my meaning, which is, I think, always expressed with sufficient clearness, viz. that the faculty of thinking is the result of a certain arrangement of the parts of matter ; so that the disarrangement of them by death is neither the *extinction*, nor the *annihilation* of them, and the re-arrangement of them after death is (if any thing can be so called) a proper *resurrection*. It is as much so, as that of a seed sown in the ground, the *germ* of which does not perish, but rises again in the form of a new plant, though the greatest part of the bulk of the seed (being merely nutritious, and *extraneous matter*) does not properly rise again.

DR. PRICE.—If I understand what is said in the beginning of Sect. XVII. (Vol. III. p. 328,) on *Personal Identity*, the drift of it is to shew that a being may be the same with a *former* being, though their *substances*, and consequently all their *properties*, are different. It is likewise implied, that the men who are to be raised from death, will be the same with the men who have existed in this world, *only* as a river is called the same, because the water, though different, has followed other water in the same channel ; or, as a forest is called the same, because the present trees, though new, have been planted and grown up on the same spot, in the room of other trees which had been cut down and consumed. Did I believe this to be all the identity of man hereafter, I could not consider myself as having any concern in a future state.

The assertion that the man or the agent may be the same, though his substance, or every component part of him, is different, appears to me very extraordinary indeed. I am a different person from my neighbour, though organized in the same manner, because the organized matter is different. If, therefore, man after the resurrection will be, not only a different system of matter, but also a system of matter differently organized, and placed in a different world, what will there be to make him the same with man in this world? I think, therefore, that Dr. Priestley should, by all means, keep to what he advances towards the conclusion of this 17th Section, (p. 335). It is essential to his scheme to maintain the resurrection of the *same body*; or that the very matter that composes man at death, will be collected at the resurrection, and compose him again in another world, and for ever.

But what am I saying? Man a composition of substances! It is utterly impossible. The thinking substance would then be not *one being*, but a *multitude*; nor is it possible to evade this consequence; without denying that the soul is a substance, or any thing more than a modification of a substance, or an arrangement and order of the parts of substances. Can this be true? Is the subject of thought and perception; is what every one calls *himself*; not a *being*, and *one being*; but a mere result from the figure, motion, and order of a system of material beings? In short, if the soul is material, it must certainly be one of the primary atoms of matter. No where else in the corporeal world can we find any thing like that unity and substantiality which belong to the soul of man; and if it is an atom, it must have existed from the first creation of matter, unless there are new atoms created every time an animal is generated.

ANSWER.—In Sect. XVII. I professedly speculate upon principles that are not my own. It is intended to prove, that there may be such an *identity of person*, as will be a foundation for future *expectation*, *obligation*, &c., though every particle of the man should be changed. The reasoning in this Section I must take the liberty to say, I do not think to be invalidated by Dr. Price's remarks, though to him it appears so very extraordinary.

The remainder of this remark has been obviated again and again in the course of my work, and also in the preceding parts of this. What I call *myself* is an organized system of matter. It is not therefore, myself, but my *power of thought*, that is properly termed the result of figure, motion, &c.

DR. PRICE.—Disquisitions. *What is there in the matter that composes my body, that should attach me to it, more than to the matter that composes "the table on which I write?"* (Vol. III. p. 331.) This is a surprising question from Dr. Priestley. If the matter which composes my body is myself, I certainly have as much reason to prefer it to the matter of a table, as I have to prefer *myself* to a *table*. To assert, as Dr. Priestley does, that the matter of the body is the soul, and at the same time to suppose, as he does, in this 17th Section, that the soul may remain the same, though the whole matter of the body is changed, appears to me indeed so apparently inconsistent, that I cannot help suspecting I must greatly misunderstand him. Should he say, that the soul is not strictly the *matter* of the body, but the *organization* of that matter; this, as I have already observed more than once, is making the soul a modification, an order and juxta-position and connexion of parts, and not a *being*, or *substance*. But is it possible to conceive of any thing more substantial than the soul? Can there be a *being* in nature, if the sentient principle, the subject that feels pleasure and pain, that thinks and reasons, and loves and hates, is not a *being*? Suppose it, however, if you can, to be merely the organization of the body; would not a change in the matter of the body make *another* body? And would not *another* body make *another* soul, though the same organization should be preserved? If not, then may not I and Dr. Priestley be the same man, since the organization of our bodies is the same, and only the matter different? Would not, in short, any number of living bodies be one soul, one sentient principle, supposing their organization the same?

ANSWER.—The beginning of this remark relates to the speculation above-mentioned, which goes upon other principles than my own. To the question at the end of the remark, viz. "Would not any number of living bodies be one soul, one sentient principle, supposing their organization the same?" I answer, that different systems of matter, organized exactly alike, must make different beings, who

would feel and think exactly alike in the same circumstances. Their minds, therefore, would be exactly *similar*,
but *numerically different*.

DR. PRICE.—Disquisitions, (Vol. III. p. 309). It seems
to be hinted here, that the soul, after death, is as little of
a substance (that is, as truly nothing) as matter would be
without extension. It is added, *" If together with the*
opinion of the entire cessation of thought they will main-
tain the real existence of the soul, it must be for the sake
of hypothesis only, and for no real use whatever." Does
Dr. Priestley then really mean that the soul loses its existence at death?

How can it be said to be of no use to maintain the
existence of the soul after death, when without this, a
resurrection must be impossible?

ANSWER.—I say, that they who maintain the cessation
of thought after death, cannot maintain the separate existence of the soul, except for the sake of an hypothesis, and
for no real *use* whatever, for this plain reason, that, during
this entire cessation of thought, the soul is, in fact, of no use,
no phenomena indicating that any such thing exists. Had
not the persons who maintain such an insensible state of the
soul, believed a resurrection of the body, they would naturally have concluded that the soul, or the thinking part of
man, *ceased to be*, because its existence would never more
be manifested by any *effect*.

How is it true, that there can be no resurrection, unless
there be a soul distinct from the body? If the soul be the
same thing with the body, or a part of the body, may not the
body, or this part of it, rise again without the aid of *another*
substance? On the contrary, I think that a resurrection,
properly so called, (because this can be only a resurrection
of something that *had been dead*, viz. the body) is manifestly
useless, upon the supposition of there being a soul distinct
from the body; it being upon this hypothesis, the soul, and
not the body, that is the seat of all perception, and the
source of all action.

DR. PRICE.—Disquisitions. *" It was unquestionably the*
opinion of the apostles," that the *" thinking powers ceased*
at death." (Vol. III. p. 374.)

If, indeed, the apostles (as is here asserted too positively)
thought that the powers of sensation were destroyed at death,
or, as Dr. Priestley speaks in p. 387, that death is "the utter
extinction of all our percipient and intellectual powers;" if,
I say, the apostles thought thus, they believed a contradic-

tion in believing a resurrection. If these powers are not destroyed they must remain, and it can be only the *exercise* of them that ceases at death. Certainly Dr. Priestley should have guarded better his language on this subject, which is often such as implies that the soul loses its existence at death. Indeed, I never knew before that any believer in a future state could assert, not only that *thought* and *perception* cease at death, but that there is then a total extinction of the very *powers* themselves. In short, Dr. Priestley should be explicit in saying which it is he believes, the *sleep*, or the *non-existence* of the soul after death. There is no less than an infinite difference between these two things. The former may be the truth, and it implies the natural immortality of the soul; but if the latter is true, there is an end of all our hopes. Talking of the restoration of man after death, will be talking of the restoration of a non-entity. Dr. Priestley calls this, (in Disquisitions, p. 310,) an extraordinary assertion; but it appears to me self-evidently true. Of what use, Dr. Priestley asks, is an existence after death, without thought and perception? I have given a plain answer to this question. It is of infinite use, by making a future state, or a restoration of man, possible. Would it not be strange to say of a man who is fallen into a swoon, that since he is insensible it makes no difference whether he is in a swoon or dead? Would it not be proper to say in answer, that if he is only in a swoon he may recover, but if he is dead he will never recover? Just so; if a man at death is only *disabled*, he may be restored. But if this existence is gone, he never can be restored.

Answer.—I cannot help expressing my surprise at this remark. As far as I see, my language upon this subject is always uniform and strictly proper. I suppose that the powers of thought are not merely suspended, but are *extinct*, or *cease to be*, at death. To make my meaning, if possible, better understood, I will use the following comparison. The power of *cutting*, in a razor, depends upon a certain cohesion and arrangement of the parts of which it consists. If we suppose this razor to be wholly dissolved in any acid liquor, its power of cutting will certainly be *lost*, or *cease to be*, though no particle of the metal that constituted the razor be annihilated by the process; and its former *shape*, and *power of cutting*, &c., may be restored to it after the metal has been precipitated. Thus, when the body is dissolved by putrefaction, its power of thinking entirely ceases, but, no particle of the man being *lost*, as many of them as were essential to him, will, I doubt not, be collected and revivified at the resurrection, when the power of thinking will return of course. I do not, therefore, think that any thing that I have advanced implies that *the soul*, that is, *the man*, loses his *existence* at death, in any other sense than that the man loses his *power of thinking*.

I really do not know how I can be more explicit than I have been through the whole of my treatise on this subject, with respect to which *Dr. Price* complains that I am not explicit enough. The latter part of this remark I have replied to before.

DR. PRICE.—Disquisitions. " All the exertions—of the soul—are as much produced by *sensations and ideas* as any effect in nature can be said to be produced by its proper cause." They have "properly an impelling force." They are " moving powers." (Vol. III. p. 289.) An idea, therefore, is an *agent*, and the soul is passive under its action in the same manner as a ball is passive when impelled by another. But what is an idea? Nothing but a *perception* or *judgment* of the mind, that is, of the being that acts. How can this impel? What can it be more than the *occasion* of action?

There must be somewhere a *self-moving power*. For one thing cannot move another, and that another *in infinitum*. And if there is one self-moving power in nature, why may there not be many?

ANSWER.—*Dr. Price* should distinguish between a *perception* or *judgment*, which is an *act* of *the mind*, and the *idea* perceived and judged of by the mind, which must be different from the *mind itself*, or any of its *acts*. I maintain that ideas, whatever they be, have a proper *impelling power*, because men are invariably impelled to action in consequence of them; but as to a *self-motive power*, I deny that man has any such thing, for the reasons that are alleged in the *Treatise on Necessity*.

DR. PRICE.—Upon the whole, it may perhaps be possible to convince me that there is no such thing as *matter*, and *Dr. Priestley* has contributed a little to it; but I cannot be convinced that there is no such thing as *spirit*, meaning by spirit such a thinking intelligent nature as I feel myself to be. I am indeed full of darkness about myself; but in the midst of this darkness I am taught the following particulars by an irresistible consciousness which will not suffer me to doubt:

1. That I am a *being* or a *substance*, and not a *property*, or a mere *configuration of parts.*

2. That I am *one being*, and not *many* beings, or a *system.*

3. That I am a *voluntary agent*, possessed of powers of *self-motion*, and not a passive instrument.

4. That my senses and limbs, my eyes, hands, &c., are *instruments* by which I act and receive information ; and not *myself*, or *mine* and not *me.*

ANSWER.—If, by *spirit*, Dr. Price means nothing more than a thinking and an intelligent substance, I have the same consciousness of it that he has. I also believe with him that I am a *being* or *substance;* also that I am a *single being*, and a *voluntary agent*, though not possessed of a self-motive power ; and that my limbs and senses are instruments by which I act, and not *myself* or *me.* So that, if these be all the essential articles of *Dr. Price's* faith, and he seems to enumerate them as such, we are very nearly agreed, though in *words* we have differed so widely.

QUERIES *by* DR. PRICE.

1. Is not the *soul*, or what I call *myself*, a being or substance, and not merely a mode or accident ?

2. Does the soul lose its existence at death, or, am I, the subject of thought, reason, consciousness, &c., to be annihilated ?

3. If I am to lose my existence at death, will not my resurrection be the resurrection of a non-entity, and therefore a contradiction ?

4. If I am not to lose my existence at death, may it not be properly said that I am *naturally immortal?*

ANSWER.—I consider myself as a being consisting of what is called matter, disposed in a certain manner. At death the parts of this material substance are so disarranged, that the powers of perception and thought, which depended upon that arrangement, cease. At the resurrection they will be re-arranged, in the same, or a similar manner, as before, and consequently the powers of perception and thought will be restored. But this will require a miraculous interposition of Divine power, and therefore it cannot be said that thinking beings are *naturally* immortal, (i. e. as thinking beings,) though the parts that compose them are so.

THE SECOND COMMUNICATION,

Containing DR. PRICE'S *Observations on the Replies to the* FIRST COMMUNICATION, *with* DR. PRIESTLEY'S *Second Replies.*

Of the Nature of MIND *or* SPIRIT.

Observations on DR. PRIESTLEY'S *Reply,* p. 36.

WHEN the eye is destroyed we cannot see. So likewise when the brain is destroyed we cannot reason. If from hence it follows that it is the brain that reasons, why should it not also follow that it is the eye that sees? From the dependence of actual sensations and thought on the brain, we have, I think, no more reason to conclude that the brain is the mind, than a savage who had never heard the music of a harpsichord, and did not see the hand that played upon it, would have to conclude, that it played on itself, and was *the* musician; because he could trace all the sounds to the instrument, and found that when the strings were out of order, the music was disturbed or destroyed.

What experience teaches us, is, that the *exercise* of the mental powers *depends* on the brain and the nerves; not that the mind *is* the brain and the nerves. Common sense exclaims against such a conclusion as much as against concluding that there is pain in the point of a sword. We are sure the mind cannot be the brain, because the brain is an assemblage of beings. The mind is *one* being. Nothing seems to me more unphilosophical in this case than to rest our ideas on the organ, and to confound it with the being whose organ it is. This, I have said, is like thinking that a musical instrument plays on itself. But to go higher. It is not unlike resting our ideas in this visible world, and supposing it the same with that Deity who made, and actuates, and governs it. The laws of nature seem to terminate in matter. But is it philosophical, in order to avoid multiplying causes, to conclude they have no other cause than matter itself; and, with the French philosophers, to make *nature* the only Deity? In short, I am fully of opinion, that if that *mass of flesh and blood* which we call the *brain*, (no one part of which, or part of any part, touches another,) may be that sentient and intelligent being we call the *mind;* then that mass of corporeal substances which we call the *world,* may be *God;* and it must be unphilosophical to search farther than *itself* for its cause. Dr. Priestley, I know, is far from being sensible of this; but such indeed is the tendency of his principles and manner of reasoning. The very foundation of this atheistical conclusion is totally subverted by the demonstration which, I think, I have given, that the laws which govern matter, or its attractions and repulsions, are not the actions or properties of matter itself, but effects of the constant operation of a higher cause.

ANSWER, *by* DR. PRIESTLEY.

I cannot help expressing some surprise that my reasoning on this subject should not seem to be understood, and that such strange conclusions should be drawn from it. If, upon examination, nothing could be *found*, or *reasonably conjectured*, to move the strings of the harpsichord, it would be philosophical to conclude, that the cause of the music that came from it was *within itself.* But when we open it, and see the strings to be moved in such a manner as similar strings are never known to be moved but by *human means*, there is reason to conclude, from analogy, that these strings also are moved, though we do not see *how*, by the same, or a similar cause.

In like manner, when we see the parts of which the universe consists, to be arranged in such a manner, as, from analogy, we have reason to believe, that no other than an intelligent being could arrange them, we conclude that an intelligent being, visible or invisible, *has* arranged them.

I conclude, that there is nothing *within* the brain itself that is the cause of perception, because, for any thing that I know, perception may be the *property* of that material, as well as of any supposed immaterial substance; the relation of *perception* to *material* or *immaterial* substances being equally unknown. If the faculty of *playing could* be supposed to belong to the harpsichord, it would be unphilosophical to inquire for any *concealed musician;* so also if the power of arranging and moving the component parts of the universe *could* belong to themselves, it would be unphilosophical to inquire for a superintending mind, or God. But it is denied that the laws of nature do *seem* to terminate in the visible parts of the universe.

For the same reason that perception is ascribed to some immaterial substance within the brain, it seems to me that attraction ought to be ascribed to some immaterial substance within 'the earth,· the sun, &c., because, according to Dr. Price, *attraction* is a power quite foreign to the nature of matter, as well as *perception.*

DR. PRICE.—*Observations on* Dr. Priestley's *Reply,* pp. 36, 37. I had said that it is very absurd to imagine that ideas are divisible. Dr. Priestley here says, that after the most deliberate review, the contrary is very clear to him. Others must judge. What is the *idea* of an object? Is it not the *notion* or *conception* of the object? A line is infinitely divisible. Is the mind's *idea* or *conception* of a line, also infinitely divisible? But, I find *Dr. Priestley* thinks ideas to be the bodies themselves in miniature, which they represent, or models and delineations of external objects, distinct from the mind, but contained in it, like maps and globes in a chamber. And I suppose he will go so far as to ascribe all the properties of bodies to them, and particularly attraction and repulsion ; and maintain, that in volition they act upon and impel the mind containing them, as one body acts upon and impels another. The bare representation of such an opinion seems sufficient to confute it. But if not, it must be in vain to argue about it.

ANSWER.—If ideas be nothing distinct from the mind, or modifications of the mind, varying as their archetypes vary, a mind *with ideas,* and a mind without *ideas,* would be the same thing ; and if the ideas of compound objects be not compounded things, and consist of as many parts as the objects of which they are the ideas, I am unable to conceive any thing about ideas. That motions, or volitions of the mind, do depend upon ideas, or, in other words, that the mind is *influenced* or *acted upon* by them, is a certain *fact,* whether the representation confute itself or not. No person acquainted with the principles of *Hartley's Theory,* can be at a loss to know what I suppose ideas to be, and in what manner they operate.

DR. PRICE.—*Observations on* Dr. Priestley's *Reply,* pp. 39, 40. I have already said, that I know nothing of the extension of spirit. I only wish to distinguish on this subject between what is certain and what is uncertain. I think it *certain,* that whatever the subject of consciousness may be in other respects, it is incapable of being divided without being annihilated.

I do not expect that the chapter in *Butler's Analogy,* on a future State, which I have wished to recommend to Dr. Priestley's attention, can appear to him as weighty as it does to me. *Butler* and *Clarke* are with me two of the first of all writers. In the Disquisitions, (Vol. III. p. 369,) to which Dr. Priestley refers me, the contradictory account of spiritual beings, which makes them to exist no where, or to have no relation to place, is said to be " *the only consistent system of immaterialism,—*held by *Mr. Baxter,* and *all the most approved modern* writers on the subject." Can it be right to say this when there are such men as Dr. Clarke and Newton who have entertained different ideas, and extended them even to the Supreme Spirit ? I do not believe that even Mr. Baxter entertained any such notion. It is, however, the notion of spirit which is combated through the greatest part of Dr. Priestley's work.

Dr. Priestley's view in writing was, to prove that there is no distinction between matter and spirit, or between the soul and body; and thus to explode what he calls the heathenish system of Christianity, by exploding the doctrines of Christ's pre-existence and an intermediate state. But if, in doing this, it comes out that his account of matter does not answer to the common ideas of matter, or that it is not *solid* extension, but something *not solid* that exists in space, it agrees so far with spirit : and if such matter is, as he asserts, the only matter possible, what he has proved will be, not that we have no *souls* distinct from our *bodies,* but that we have no *bodies* distinct from our *souls.* Matter which possesses solidity, or impenetrability and inertness, is certainly the only matter that is the object of natural philosophy. This *Newton* has said, in a passage I have quoted from him " If such matter is impossible, it will follow that all in nature is spirit.

Dr. Priestley, in this reply, p. 40, mentions his *views.* They are, I doubt not, the purest and best possible. There is no one of whose heart I have a higher opinion. But at the same time my fixed apprehension is, that he is one of those great and good men who have pushed on too eagerly in the pursuit of truth, and who, in endeavouring to serve the best of all causes, have run upon bad ground; and, without knowing it, employed means of the most dangerous tendency.

ANSWER.—To this I have nothing particular to say. My quotations from various writers prove, that, besides the professed Cartesians, many other philosophers and metaphysicians have supposed that *spirit bears no relation to space.* Dr. Watts, without having ever been refuted that I know of, has shewn that this is the only consistent idea of an immaterial being. I have added some additional arguments to prove the same thing, and this was my own idea while, I held the doctrine of immaterialism. This idea, therefore, I have *chiefly* combated; but not this only, but also every other idea of immaterialism that I have met with, that appeared to me to deserve particular notice.

DR. PRICE.—*Observations on the Replies*, pp. 41 and 42. A thinking being, Dr. Priestley says, is " a material substance of a particular texture," not " a mere order or relation of parts." Does it not then follow, that the destruction of the order or texture of the parts, that is, their disarrangement, cannot be the destruction of the thinking being?

" A system," it is farther said, " though consisting of many *beings*, is but one *system;* and a brain, though consisting of many *parts*, is but one *brain;* no single part of which can be the whole." But it is self-evident that a system, consisting of many beings, though *one as a system*, in the same sense that an army is one as an army, must be a *multitude* of beings, and can no more be one being, than an army can be one man. In like manner, though a brain consisting of many material substances, not one of which, according to Dr. Priestley, is in contact with another, though I say such a brain may be one as a *brain*, it cannot certainly be one *substance*. But the soul is one *substance*, one being. This Dr. Priestley grants at the end of these replies, and it is impossible he should deny it. He cannot, therefore, think the brain to be the soul. All that he can believe is, that the soul's *thinking* depends on the order and texture of the brain. Experience proves this; and it is indeed, as I have before said, all that experience teaches us.

ANSWER.—I cannot see any thing in this remark that is not merely verbal. A man, in my idea, is *one thinking being*, and not two thinking beings, let this thinking being consist of as many substances, or *unthinking beings*, as any person pleases.

DR. PRICE.—*Observations on the Reply*, p. 42. " By what construction am I made to assert that the Divine Essence is material, that is, of the same kind of substance with what we generally term matter, when I suppose it to have *quite different properties*, &c. ?"

I have mentioned this only as an inference from Dr. Priestley's principles, and particularly from a principle which he has argued upon as a maxim, namely, " that no thing can act upon another without having *common properties* with it." If this is true, the Deity must have *common properties* with matter; and matter being a power of attrac-

tion and repulsion united to extension, the Deity must be
the same. If, in order to avoid this consequence, Dr.
Priestley should acknowledge this maxim not to be universally true, it will follow that spirit may act upon matter
without having any other common property with it than
being locally present to it, and one of his chief arguments
for the materiality of the soul will be given up.

Indeed, I cannot imagine how it is possible for him to
maintain this maxim without asserting the impossibility of
the *creation* of the world out of nothing: for what common
property can the Creator have with *nothing?* It would not
satisfy me to be told here, that the Divine nature possessing
peculiar properties, we can draw no argument from it. The
contrary is true in many cases: particularly in the following. The Deity acts on matter, without having any common
property with it; therefore such action is possible. The
Deity is an immaterial being; therefore immaterial beings
are possible: and the negation of matter is not the same with
the negation of all existence. In like manner, the Deity is
an intelligent being; therefore intelligent beings are possible. He possesses the powers of self-determination; therefore such powers are possible. He is an agent; therefore
there may be other agents. All these conclusions appear to
me to be just.

I have by no means designed to charge Dr. Priestley with
maintaining that the Deity is nothing but a power of attraction and repulsion. I only mean to say, that if the Deity
be a material being, and matter (as Dr. Priestley contends)
is nothing but such a power, then the Deity must also be
nothing but such a power. I know that Dr. Priestley asserts
the immateriality of the Deity. I only doubt about the
consistence of this with the other parts of his theory.

Dr. Priestley says, p. 43, that he does not choose to call
space an *attribute of the Deity*, because, supposing there was
no Deity, " space would still remain; it being impossible
to be annihilated even in idea."

According to Dr. Clarke, the impossibility of annihila-
ting even in idea, *space* and *time*, is the same with the
necessary existence of the Deity, whose attributes they are.
Instead therefore of saying, " was there no Deity space
would still remain," we should say, " space will still remain, and therefore the Deity will still remain; and his
non-existence cannot be imagined without a contradiction."
It appears to me, that whatever cannot be annihilated, even
in idea, must be an attribute of the Deity. This may be

applied not only to *space* and *time*, but to *truth, possibles,* &c., as I have done in my *Treatise on Morals. Eternity, immensity, infinite truth,* &c., cannot be *conceived* not to exist. All existence pre-supposes *their* existence: that is, there exists necessarily an eternal and omnipresent Intelligence, the parent of all things. I am afraid Dr. Priestley will not like this; but I am as much satisfied with it as he is with any part of Dr. Hartley's Theory.

ANSWER.—What is attraction or repulsion but a power of moving matter in a certain direction? If, therefore, the Deity *does* thus act upon matter, he must have that power, and therefore *one* property in common with matter, though he be possessed of ever so many *other* powers of which matter is incapable.

Dr. Price's argument, that because God is *a self-determining being*, there may be other self-determining beings, and because God is an *agent*, there may be other agents, &c. &c., may, I am afraid, carry us too far. For may it not be said also, that because God is a *self-existing being*, there may be other self-existent beings, and because God can *create out of nothing*, &c. &c., other beings may have the same powers?

I cannot, I own, see any thing conclusive in Dr. Price's argument for the being of a God, *a priori.* I do not see why it should be taken for granted, that " whatever cannot be annihilated, even in idea, must be an attribute of the Deity." This appears to me to be quite an arbitrary supposition. That *space, duration, truth, possibles,* &c., should be denominated *attributes,* sounds very harsh to me. If the infinite space occupied by the Deity be an attribute of his, I should think that the finite space, occupied by finite minds and things, should be called *their* attributes, and also the portions of duration to which they are co-existent, another of their attributes, &c., so that the same individual portions of space and time must be attributes both of the Deity and of created beings. Also, mere attributes of things cannot, in idea, be separated from them, whereas nothing is easier than to form the idea of *mere space,* without any thing to occupy it. But this is not my subject.

DR. PRICE.—*Observations on Reply,* p. 43. I must repeat here what I have already said, that I know no more of the extension of spirit, than that it possesses local presence, and is at the same time indiscerptible. Let any one reflect on himself, or on the immensity of the Divine Nature, and deny the possibility of this if he can.

Space, has parts, but they are only *assignable* parts. A separation of them from one another implies a contradiction.

ANSWER.—If a finite spirit occupy a finite portion of space, one part of that spirit may be *conceived* to be removed from another, as well as one part of solid matter from another; though this is not true of the Deity, who necessarily fills *all space.*

DR. PRICE.—*Observations on Reply,* p. 45. Dr. Priestley here says, that he intended in Sect. XVII. to prove, " that there may be such an identity of person as will be a foundation for future *expectation, obligation,* &c. though every particle of the man should be changed." In answer to this I have observed, that if every particle that constitutes the man is to be different at the resurrection, the *man* must be different ; and that, consequently, the men who exist in this world can have no such concern in what is to happen to the men who are to exist hereafter, as lays a foundation for expectation, obligation, &c. because. those men will not be *them,* but *other* men. In answer to this, Dr. Priestley must say, either that a man may be the same, though every particle that constitutes him is different ; or he must say, that men in this life are obliged to act with a view to *their own* existence in another life, though there is to be no such existence.

I am sensible that in this Section he reasons on the opinions of *others;* but, if in reasoning on these opinions, he attempts to prove what is plainly impossible, the reasoning must be so far wrong.

ANSWER.—I still say that I have nothing to add on this subject. I professedly argue on an hypothesis that is not my own, and submit the force of the argument to the judgment of the reader.

DR. PRICE.—*Observations on Reply,* p. 47. It is here said, that " if the cessation of thought at death is allowed, it can be of no use whatever to maintain the separate existence of the soul.". I have given what appears to me a full answer to this observation, by saying, that if the soul does not *exist* after death, there can be no *restoration* of it: and that, consequently, it must be of the utmost use to maintain that it does so exist, though perhaps in an *incapacitated* state. There is an infinite difference between the *annihilation* of the soul at death, and its *incapacitation*. One who believed the former could not possibly entertain the hope of a future state, but one who believes the latter, might reasonably entertain such a hope. He might think that a period would come when it should be restored. He might even think of men, as Dr. Priestley, Disquisitions, (Vol. III. p. 383,) seems to think of brutes, that their resurrection may be a part of the course of nature.

Dr. Priestley here adds, that "a resurrection is manifestly useless, if there is a soul distinct from the body." He well knows, that according to Mr. Locke, and many others, the future resurrection taught in the Scriptures, is to be the resurrection not of the *body*, but of the *soul*. It is to be the restoration of the *man* (incapacitated by the destruction of the organization by which he here acted, and received information) to the exercise of all his powers, in a new state of being, by furnishing him with another, and (if virtuous) a more durable and perfect organization. All then that can be said with any propriety, is, that a resurrection of the *same body* is useless, if there is a soul distinct from the body ; and, in saying this, some of the most zealous Christians and Immaterialists will agree with him.

ANSWER.—What I say of the resurrection being manifestly useless, if there be a soul distinct from the body, is upon the common hypothesis ; according to which the soul is the only source of action, and the body is so far from being necessary to its exertions as to be a *hindrance* to them. This is the original and genuine hypothesis of *a soul*, as a substance distinct from the body, though the phenomena have at length compelled those who cannot yet persuade themselves to give up the notion of a soul altogether, to acknowledge its necessary dependence upon the body, unaccountable as the mutual connexion and dependence of substances so very different in their nature must appear. It has been in consequence of finding more and more of the phenomena of the mind to depend upon the body, that myself and others conclude, that *every thing* belonging to man is corporeal. And I cannot help thinking that the general persuasion of the soul being incapable of any perception or action without the body, and therefore that all its faculties are in a perfectly dormant state from death to the resurrection, must gradually abate men's zeal in the defence of the doctrine of a soul, and prepare the way for the general belief, that the hypothesis is altogether unnecessary

DR. PRICE.—*Observations on Reply*, p. 46, *and the following.* In p. 46, at the top, Dr. Priestley says, "What I call myself, is, *an organized system of matter.*" Is not every atom of the matter that composes a *system*, a distinct *substance* or being? Does not, therefore, Dr. Priestley, here call himself a *system* of beings? But waving this, because perhaps it has been too often repeated, I will here beg leave to state, as briefly as I can, the whole question relating to the nature of the human soul and its mortality, according to my ideas. Should I be wrong in any instance, Dr. Priestley will, I hope, be so good as to set me right.

The soul, that is, the being that thinks and acts, must, if an organized system of matter, be either the material substances themselves which compose that system ; or it must be their organization, their texture, motion, arrangements, &c.

If the latter is true, it will follow:

1. That man is not a substance or a *being*, but a *mode*. For texture, motion, and arrangement of parts, are not substances, but modes of substances.

2. It must follow, that any number of men, having the same organization, have the same soul, or are the same men; just as points having the same arrangement round a centre, make the same figure.

3. It must follow, that the same systems of matter organized differently, will make different souls, or new men ; just as the same points, arranged differently round a centre, will make different figures.

Now it should be remembered, that at the resurrection, man being to live in a new state, the organization of his body must be new: and this, if man be that organization, must make a new man.

But I need not urge these consequences, because Dr. Priestley has allowed, that the man is the matter itself which constitutes the man, and not its form or arrangement: and two systems of matter organized alike, he expressly says, would make two men thinking, indeed, alike, but *numerically different*. The former, therefore, of the two accounts I have mentioned, must be his account of the soul of man, and it will follow from it—

1. That the man will always remain while the matter which constitutes him remains, however different its organization or arrangement may be.

2. That since death does not destroy the matter which constitutes man, it does not destroy the man ; and that, consequently, he goes on to exist after death, or is naturally immortal.

3. That in order to the resurrection of the same man, the same matter must arise ; and that for this reason, if the contrary is intended to be proved in *Disquisitions*, Sect. XVII. it cannot be right.

4. That it is no less possible for man to have existed *before*

his *birth*, than it is that he should *exist* after his *death*; and that, consequently, all the support to the Socinian scheme, which Dr. Priestley derives from his sentiments of ma. terialism, falls to the ground. Indeed, man must have existed, according to this account, before his birth, if the matter that constitutes him existed before his birth : and his birth, or rather his conception, could have been nothing but putting that matter together, or new arranging it after it had been disarranged in some former state.

But this leads me to the main inference from this account of the soul, namely, that the organization of the matter which constitutes man, since it is not the being that thinks, can only constitute actual thinking ; and, consequently, that it is only *actual thinking*, or the *exercise* of our powers, that depends on the bodily organization, and which can cease at death. Even his own simile in p. 48, implies that he means no more. For matter formed into a razor, would not lose its *existence*, but its *cutting power* only, by being disarranged. And, though, supposing the same matter formed into a *bul-let*, we should say the *razor* was destroyed, yet we should mean no more than that the matter which constituted it had assumed another shape, and could no longer cut. To this issue I wished to bring this dispute. Dr. Priestley agrees with me in believing that the soul does not lose its existence at death, p. 49. He, therefore, believes what I mean by the natural immortality of the soul : and I fancy he will go even farther with me, and allow that the being which thinks, can. not *then* cease to exist, without a positive act of the Creator to destroy it, like that which first brought it into existence. In return, I am ready to concede to Dr. Priestley, what he seems in p. 50, to give as the whole of his meaning, that " as *thinking* beings we are not immortal ;" that is, " that sometimes we fall into an *unthinking* state." Sound sleep may be such a state. *Death*, being the destruction of the whole machinery that connects us with this world, may be a more remediless state of the same kind ; and the chief dif. ference between these two states may be, that whereas there are *natural* and *ordinary* means by which we are recovered from the one, there may be no such means by which we can be recovered from the other. Dr. Priestley, indeed, seems to be doubtful about this. But does it not deserve his consideration, whether he has not, by expressing such a doubt, contradicted a sentiment on which he has laid great stress, namely, that " since man becomes extinct at death, our only hope of surviving the grave is derived from revela-tion" ? For if the resurrection may be, as he says, Disquisitions, (Vol. III. p. 383,) *within the proper course of nature;* that is, if there may be natural means by which the dead may be hereafter restored, why may there not be arguments from reason which make it probable that it is fact? He has mentioned, in the passage to which I have just referred, one argument which he thinks may lead to such a hope with respect to *brutes.* Why may there not be likewise arguments which, independent of revelation, may reasonably produce the same hope with respect to *men?*

I am of opinion, however, that all appearances are against the existence of any such *natural* and *ordinary* means ; and I will take this opportunity to add, that the scripture doctrine seems to be, that death is a distress in which our species has been involved by *extraordinary* causes, and from which we have obtained the hope of being saved by the most *extraordinary* means ; 1 mean, by the interposition of *Jesus Christ;* who, by taking upon him our nature, and *humbling himself to death,* has acquired the power of *destroying death,* and is on this account styled *the Saviour of the world.*

REPLY, p. 49.—" Dr. Price should distinguish," &c. With respect to what is here said by Dr. Priestley, I must refer to what I have said in pp. 36, 49, 53 ; and what will be said on the subject of the Doctrine of Necessity at the end of this correspondence.

ANSWER.—Admitting, as I do, that a man is a material system, so organized as to perceive and think, I must believe that the *materials* of which he is made had a pre-existence, and, consequently, those of *the man Jesus.* But this is certainly a very different *kind* of pre-existence, from that of those who make Christ, or rather the principal part of him, to have pre-existed in an active state, and to have afterwards entered into the embryo of the child of Mary. The belief that Christ was the maker of all things, the doctrine of a purgatory and the worship of the dead could never have arisen from my hypothesis ; but these, and many other corruptions of the Christian system, arose but too easily from the other. As a Christian, (though it is not every body that, like Dr. Price, has the candour to allow me to be one,) I think I have the greatest reason to be jealous of this kind of pre-existence, but none at all of the mere pre-existence of the parts of which men, animals, and even plants are composed.

1 am happy to concur with Dr. Price in the bulk of what he says under this head. My idea of the state of man between death and the resurrection, is, in fact, no way materially different from his. It is a state of *inaction* and *insensibility,* from which we shall not recover till the resurrection ;

which, whether it·will be brought about in a manner that may be said to be *within the laws of nature extensively* consi- *dered,* or not, I cannot tell, and I am sometimes inclined to one opinion, and sometimes to the other. · But though I should· decide for the former, the *evidence* for ·it is not so strong, but that I think myself justified in saying, " th t our only hope of surviving the grave is derived from revelation." For *hope* implies a *preponderance* of the arguments in favour of a desirable event, which preponderance of evidence *nature* does not appear to me to furnish. What the amount of that evidence, in my opinion, is, I have stated in my *Institutes of Natural and Revealed Religion.* (Vol. II. pp. 72—230.)

THE THIRD COMMUNICATION,

Containing Remarks by Dr. Price *on* Dr. Priestley's *Replies to the* Second Communication, *with* Dr. Priestley's Third *Replies.*

Observations on Dr. Priestley's *Reply,* p. 52.

Most certainly the attraction of the earth, the sun, the planets, &c. (see p. 53,) not being the action of the *matter itself* that is said to attract, ought to be ascribed to the action of some other substance *within* the earth, the sun and planets. Does not Dr. Priestley himself acknowledge this ? And does he not, by maintaining God to be the source of all the motions in the world, allow a *soul* to the *world,* though he will not to *men ?*

Answer, *by* Dr. Priestley.

My argument goes to prove, that for the same reason that *man* has been supposed to have a soul, every *particular sub- stance* to which any powers or properties are ascribed, may have *a separate soul* also.

Dr. Price.—*Ibid.* It is here said that *perception is the property of the brain.* I must again repeat, that the being that perceives is *one.* The brain consists of *many* substances. It is not, therefore, the brain that perceives. In p. 55, it is said, that though man " is one thinking being," he may con- sist of many " unthinking beings." Nothing can be more incomprehensible to me than this. Is it not the same with saying, that *many* beings who want reason, may make *one* being who has reason ? Or that a perfection may exist in the whole which does not exist in any of the parts ? If this can be true, why may not the component parts of this material world, though all of them separately unintelligent, make one supreme intelligent being?

ANSWER.—I find no difficulty in conceiving that *compound substances* may have properties which their *component parts* cannot have. But it does not, therefore, follow, that all the conjoined parts of any *particular whole*, e. g. *the universe*, can have the peculiar attributes of the being that we call *God;* though they may have various properties that cannot be affirmed of any of the parts separately taken.

DR. PRICE.—If I understand Dr. Priestley, he says in p. 57, that the Deity has a common property with matter, because, like matter, he has the power of attracting and repelling. But I have all along denied that matter has this power. According to Dr. Priestley himself, no being in nature *acts* but the Deity.

ANSWER.—If the supposed immaterial principle in man can really act upon the brain, it must necessarily be in the manner that we term attraction or repulsion : because these comprise all the possible affections of body ; and what may be predicated of a finite mind, in this respect, may also be predicated of the Infinite Mind.

DR. PRICE.—Does not Dr. Priestley's manner of arguing in p. 52, imply, that it is *possible* for a harpsichord to play on itself, and that there are circumstances in which it would be philosophical to draw this conclusion?

ANSWER.—My argument only proves, that, in certain *given*, but *impossible circumstances*, there could be no *apparent ground* to conclude that the music came from any thing but the harpsichord itself.

   "*What can we reason but from what we know ?*"

DR. PRICE.—It is said, in p. 53, that " if ideas be nothing distinct from the mind,—a mind with ideas, and a mind without ideas, would be the same thing." I maintain, that ideas are not distinct from the mind, but its conceptions ; or not themselves *things*, but *notions* of things. How does it follow from hence, that a mind with or without ideas, is the same? It would seem that this follows much more from the contrary assertion.

ANSWER.—By a *thing* I mean whatever has properties. Now ideas have many properties, and a mind may have ideas, or be without them. According to Dr. Hartley's Theory, however, ideas are only vibrations in the brain, which corresponds to what Dr. Price might call modifications of the mind ; so that on this subject our opinions are not materially, if at all, different.

PART III.

Of the Doctrine of NECESSITY.

THE FIRST COMMUNICATION.

QUERIES, BY DR. PRICE.

1. Do we not necessarily ascribe our volitions and actions to ourselves?
2. Do we not determine ourselves?
3. If we do not determine ourselves, are we not deceived when we ascribe our actions to ourselves, and for that reason reckon ourselves accountable for them?

ANSWER, BY DR. PRIESTLEY.

By the principle of association we do ascribe our volitions and actions to ourselves, and therefore we *necessarily* do so, but not in such a manner as to exclude *motives* from being necessary to every determination; and if we suppose that our volitions and actions have no cause foreign to themselves, that is, to our wills, we deceive ourselves, as in various other wrong judgments.

By being *liable to punishment* for our actions, and *accountable* for them, I mean its being wise and good in the Divine Being to appoint that certain sufferings should follow certain actions, provided they be *voluntary*, though *necessary* ones; such a connexion of voluntary actions and sufferings being calculated to produce the greatest ultimate good.

DR. PRICE.—Query 4. Does it follow from its being certain that we shall determine ourselves in a particular way, that we do not in that instance determine ourselves at all?

ANSWER.—I consider all self-determination, properly so called, as an impossibility, implying, that such a determination has, in fact, *no cause at all*. If the determination be *certain*, it must have a *certain or necessary cause* arising from views of things present to the mind. For the illustration of this argument, I refer to my *Treatise of* Necessity, Sect. II. (Vol. III. p. 462,) and to the " Letter to Dr. Horsley," *(infra)*.

THE SECOND COMMUNICATION.

On the Doctrine of NECESSITY.

Observations on DR. PRIESTLEY's *Answers to the* QUERIES *in* p. 65, *by* DR. PRICE.

IN order to bring the dispute between me and Dr. Priestley as much to a point as possible, and to discover how far we *agreed* and *differed*, I sent to him, after my first communication, on the nature of matter and spirit, and the immortality of the soul, the following queries :

1. Can any thing act on another without being *present* to it?

2. Can, therefore, matter act on other matter without contact and impulse?

3. Is not the *soul*, or what I call *myself*, a *being* or *substance;* and not merely a *mode* or *property?*

4. Does the soul lose its existence at death? Or am I, the subject of thought, reason, consciousness, &c. to be then annihilated?

5. If I am to lose my existence at death, will not my resurrection be the resurrection of a non-entity; and therefore impossible?

6. If I am not to lose my existence at death, may it not be properly said that I am naturally immortal?

7. Do we not necessarily ascribe our volitions or actions to ourselves?

8. Do we not determine ourselves?

9. If we do not determine ourselves, are we not deceived when we ascribe our actions to ourselves; and, for that reason, reckon ourselves accountable for them?

10. Does it follow from its being certain, in any instance, that we shall determine ourselves in a particular way, that we do not, in that instance, determine ourselves at all?

In answer to these queries, I wished for no more than a simple affirmation or negation ; thinking it would be a matter of some curiosity, should it appear that our minds were so differently framed, as that one of us would write a *yes* where the other would write a *no*. But I find that we are more nearly agreed than I expected. To the two first queries, Dr. Priestley has given no direct answer ; but what he has said in different places, seems to imply that he would agree with me in answering them in the negative. The 3d query he has, in p. 50, answered, as I should, in the affirmative; and the 4th and 6th in the negative. It appears, however, I think, that I had some reason for expecting that he would not grant the soul to be a *substance;* much less *one single substance.* For the obvious inference from hence, is, that the soul cannot be, either any system of substances, or the *organization* of any system ; and, therefore, not such an assemblage of substances as the brain, or the organization of the brain.

To the 7th query it appears also (see p. 65), that he answers in the affirmative, and yet that to the 8th he answers in the negative. In other words, he acknowledges that we necessarily ascribe our determinations to ourselves, but denies that we do *really* determine ourselves ; asserting, in answer to the 9th query, that we are deceived when we imagine that our volitions are not produced by a cause foreign to our wills, and *on that account* believe ourselves responsible for them ; all self-determination being impossible, and *accountableness* or liableness to punishment being only the connexion which Divine wisdom, in order to produce the greatest ultimate good, has established between certain *voluntary* though *necessary* actions and certain sufferings.

In several passages in my *Review of Morals* (pp. 301—304, and pp. 349—352, *2d edit.*), I have stated, in the best manner I am able, the question concerning Liberty and Necessity. Dr. Priestley, in his second volume, Sect. V. and VI. (Vol. III. pp. 480—492), has replied to what I have said in most of those passages, with *candour* and *ability :* but I cannot say that I think he has done it with *success.* He seems to misunderstand me, and, therefore, I will endeavour to give a more distinct account of my ideas on this subject. If they are wrong, I shall rejoice to see them proved to be so. If they are right, it will be easy to form a judgment of all Dr. Priestley's arguments in his second volume, and to determine how far we *agree* and *differ.*

After Dr. Clarke, I define Liberty to be " a power to act," or " a power of *self-motion* or self-determination." On this definition I would make the following obervations :

1. That liberty is common to all *animals,* as well as to all *reasonable beings;* every animal, as such, possessing powers of *self-motion* or *spontaneity.*

2. There are no *degrees* of liberty, because there is no medium between *acting* and *not acting,* or between possessing self-motive powers and not possessing them.

3. The liberty now defined is possible. One thing cannot

move another, and that another *in infinitum.* Somewhere
or other there must exist a power of beginning motion, that
is, of *self-motion.* This is no less certain than that, since
one thing cannot produce another, and that another *in infinitum,* there must be a *first* cause.

This argument seems to me decisive, not only for the
possibility, but the *actual existence* of liberty. But farther,
We are conscious of it in ourselves. I can say nothing to
convince a person who will declare that he believes *his* determinations do not originate *with himself,* or that he has
no power of moving or determining himself. It is another
question, whether he moves himself *with* or *without* a regard
to *motives.* Asserting self-determination with a regard to
motives, (and no one ever yet asserted the contrary,) is
asserting *self-determination,* and, therefore, it is the same
with asserting liberty. Dr. Priestley often says, that self-
determination implies an effect without a cause. But this
cannot be justly said. Does it follow that because I am
myself the cause, there is no cause?

4. This definition implies, that in our volitions, or determinations, we are not *acted upon. Acting* and being *acted
upon* are incompatible with one another. In whatever instances, therefore, it is truly said of us that we *act,* in those
instances we cannot be *acted upon.* A being in receiving a
change of its state, from the exertion of an adequate force,
is not an *agent.* Man, therefore, would not be an *agent,*
were all his volitions derived from any force, or the effects
of any mechanical causes. In this case it would be no more
true that he ever acts, than it is true of a ball that it *acts*
when *struck* by another ball. But the main observation I
would make is the following:

5. " The liberty now defined is consistent with acting
with a regard to motives." This has been already intimated;
but it is necessary it should be particularly attended to and
explained.

Supposing a power of self-determination to exist, it is by
no means necessary that it should be exerted without a regard
to any end or rule. On the contrary, it can never be exerted
without some view or design. Whoever acts, means to do
somewhat. This is true of the lowest reptile, as well as of
the wisest man. The power of determining ourselves, by
the very nature of it, wants an *end* and *rule* to guide it; and
no probability, or certainty, of its being exerted agreeably
to a rule, can have the least tendency to infringe or diminish
it. All that should be avoided here, is, the intolerable ab-

surdity of making our reasons and ends in acting the physical *causes* or *efficients* of action. This is the same with ascribing the action of walking, not to the feet (or the power which moves the feet), but to the eye, which only *sees the way*. The perception of a reason for acting, or the judgment of the understanding, is no more than seeing the way. It is the eye of the mind, which informs and directs; and what-ever *certainty* there may be that a particular determination will follow, such determination will be the *self-determination* of the mind, and not any change of its state stamped upon it, over which it has no power, and in receiving which, in-stead of being an *agent*, it is merely a *passive subject* of agency.

In a word. There is a distinction here of the last im-portance, which must never be overlooked. I mean the distinction so much insisted on by Dr. Clarke, between the *operation* of *physical causes*, and the *influence* of *moral rea-sons*. The views or ideas of beings may be the *account* or *occasions* of their acting; but it is a contradiction to make them the *mechanical efficients* of their actions. And yet I suspect that Dr. Priestley will avow this to be his opinion. Ideas he makes to be divisible and extended. He ascribes an impulsive force to them; and asserts that they act by mechanical laws on the mind, as one material substance acts upon another. See his *Replies*, pp. 36, 49, 53; and the *Disquisitions* (Vol. III. p. 250).

In order better to explain the distinction I have men-tioned, I will beg leave to give an account of the following particulars, in which it appears to me that *physical* and *moral* causes differ.

. 1. The one are *beings;* the others are only the *views* of beings.

.2. The one always *do*, and the other *may* produce a cer-tainty of event. But the certainties in these two cases differ essentially. It is, for instance, *certain* that a man dragged along like a piece of timber, will follow the superior force that acts upon him. It may be also *certain*, that a man invited by the hope of a reward, will follow a guide. But who sees not that these certainties, having different founda-tions, are of a totally different nature? In both cases the man might in common speech be said to *follow;* but his fol-lowing in the one case, however certain in event, would be *his own* agency: in the other case, it would be the agency of *another*. In the one case, he would really *follow;* but in the other case, being dragged, he could not properly be said to *follow*. In the one case, superior power moves him; in the other, he moves himself. In short, to ascribe a necessary and physical efficiency to motives, is (as Dr. Clarke has observed), the same with saying, that *an abstract notion can strike a ball.*

3. The certainty of event arising from the operation of *physical* causes is always equal and invariable; but the certainty of event arising from *moral* causes, that is, from the views and perceptions of beings, admits of an infinite variety of degrees, and sometimes passes into *probability* and *contingency.*

Supposing contrary reasons equally balanced in the mind, it may be *uncertain* how a being will act. If, for instance, a temptation to an act of wickedness comes in the way of a man whose love of virtue is nearly equal to the strength of his passions, it may be doubtful which way he will determine. If his love of virtue exceeds the influence of passion, there will be a *probability* of his acting virtuously, proportioned to the degree in which the love of virtue prevails within him: and it may be so prevalent as to make it *certain* that he will always follow his perceptions of virtue.

4. In the operation of physical causes, it is always implied that there is not in any sense a power to produce, or a possibility of producing, any other effect than that which is produced; but the contrary is true of effects dependent on the wills, and occasioned by the views of free agents. A benevolent man will *certainly* relieve misery when it falls in his way; but he has the *power* of not relieving it. On the contrary, a stone thrown from the hand *must* move. There is no sense in which it can be said, that it possesses the power of not moving in the precise direction in which it is thrown. The reason of this is, that the benevolent man *acts:* the stone only *suffers.* Were the determination to give relief in the former case, and the motions of the stone in the latter, both alike *sufferances* (if I may so speak), or both effects of a force which could not be resisted, they would be both alike void of all merit. A man at the bottom of St. Paul's *will* not jump *up:* a man at the top *will* not jump *down.* Both events may be *certain.* But a man at the bottom *cannot* jump up: a man at the top *can* jump down. And if in common speech we should say, in the latter case, that a man at the top *cannot* jump down, we should speak figuratively and improperly; meaning only that he certainly *will* not. Who can deny, even with respect to the Supreme Deity, that, however certain it may be that he will not make his

creation miserable, he has the power to do it? It is, indeed, on this power that all our notions of moral excellence in the actions of beings depend. Were the beneficence of a being no more *his* action or *self-determination*, than the falling of rain is the action or self-determination of rain, it would not be the object of moral approbation, or the ground of esteem and gratitude. (See *Review of Morals*, pp. 410—415, *2d edit.*). This leads me to observe, lastly,

6. That the *casuality* implied in the views and dispositions of beings is entirely consistent with moral obligation and responsibility; but that all effects brought about by mechanical laws are inconsistent with them. This appears sufficiently from the preceding observations.

Upon the whole; the question concerning Liberty is not, "Whether the views or ideas of beings *influence* their actions," but " what the *nature* of that *influence* is." That it is not any kind of *mechanical* or *physical* efficiency, appears to me palpably evident. But if I am mistaken in this opinion; and if, indeed, as Dr. Priestley maintains, man has no other liberty in following motives than water has in running down hill, or than the arms of a scale pressed by weights have in rising and falling; if, I say, this is the truth, man never *acts*. It is folly to applaud or reproach ourselves for our conduct; and there is an end of all moral obligation and accountableness. Dr. Priestley does not acknowledge these consequences. I think them clear to such a degree as not to admit of proper proof. The best that can be done in this case is, to state the question distinctly and intelligibly, and leave the decision to common sense.

In reviewing these papers I have found, that my desire to explain myself fully has led me to a redundancy of expression and many repetitions. Dr. Priestley will, I hope, excuse this. I refer myself to his candour, and choose now to withdraw from this controversy.—His first volume (III. 421,) concludes with some observations in defence of the *Socinian* scheme of Christianity. I will not enter into any debate with him on this subject. My opinion is, that the Socinian scheme degrades Christianity, and is by no means reconcileable to the Scriptures. But I know that some of the best men and wisest Christians have adopted it. Among these I reckon Dr. *Priestley*, Mr. *Lindsey*, and Dr. *Jebb;* and should it, contrary to my apprehensions, be the true Christian doctrine, I wish them all possible success in propagating it.

ANSWER.—On the subject of *Necessity* I have nothing material to add to what is contained in the second volume of my work; and I cannot help thinking, that if what I have there advanced be attended to, it will be sufficient to obviate the objections here urged by Dr. Price. But as he has been so obliging as to give his ideas with great frankness and distinctness on the subject, and I conceive this to be the only difference of real consequence between us, I shall so far repeat the substance of what I have said before, as may be necessary to reply with equal explicitness to what he has here observed.

If *self-motion*, or *self-determination*, properly so called, be essential to liberty, I must deny that man is possessed of it; and if this, and nothing else, must be called *agency*, I must deny that, *in this sense*, man is an agent; because every human volition is invariably directed by the circumstances in which a man is, and what we call *motives*. It appears to me that we have no more reason, *from fact and observation*, to conclude that a man can *move himself*, that is, that he can *will without motives*, than that a stone can move itself. And if the will is as invariably influenced by motives as the stone is influenced by gravity, it may just as well be said that the stone moves itself, though always according to the laws of gravity, as that the will, or the mind, moves itself, though always according to the motives; and whether these motives be called the *moral* or the *physical* causes of our volitions, is of no sort of signification; because they are the *only* and the *necessary* causes, just as much as gravity is the only and necessary cause of the motion of the stone. Let the mind act contrary to motives, or the stone move contrary to the laws of gravity, and I shall then, but not before, believe that they are *not* the only and necessary causes.

" The perception of reasons or motives Dr. Price calls the eye of the mind, which informs and directs;" but if the determination of the mind, which follows upon it, be invariably *according to* that perception, I must conclude that the nature of the mind is such, as that it *could not* act otherwise, and therefore that it has no self-determination properly so called. A power manifested by no effects, must be considered as merely imaginary, it being from *effects* alone that we arrive at the knowledge of *causes*.

Judging from facts, I must conclude that a proper *self-motion* can no more belong to man than *self-existence*. Indeed, we have no more idea of the nature of self-motion than we have of self-existence. Motion and existence cannot be eternally derived, and *actual existence* and *actual motion* necessarily lead us to some *self-existing*, and consequently *self-moving being.* Though the idea be ever so incomprehensible and confounding to our faculties, we must acquiesce in it; for to stop *short* of this, or go *beyond* it, is equally impossible.

The difference that Dr. Price and others make between *moral* and *physical* causes and effects, appears to me to be that which subsists between *voluntary* and *involuntary* causes and effects; and this is indeed a most important difference. Where involuntary motions are concerned, as in the case of a man dragged by force, it is absurd to use any reasoning or expostulation, or to apply rewards or punishments, because they can have *no effect;* but where voluntary motions are concerned, as in the case of a man who is at liberty to go where he pleases, and choose what company he pleases, &c., reasoning and expostulation, rewards and punishments, have the greatest *propriety,* because the greatest *effect;* for they are applied to, and influence or move the will, as much as external force moves the body.

It is on this circumstance, viz. *the influence of motives on the will,* that the whole of *moral discipline* depends; so that if the will of man were so formed, as that motives should have no influence upon it, he could not be the subject of moral government; because the hope of reward, and the fear of punishment, operate in no other manner than as *motives applied to the will.* And since the whole of moral government depends upon the distribution of rewards and punishments, what has been called *liberty,* or a power of acting independently of motives, is so far from being the only foundation of moral government, that it is absolutely inconsistent with it, as I have shewn at large in my second volume.

The ideas belonging to the terms *accountableness, praise and blame, merit and demerit,* all relate to the business of moral discipline, and therefore necessarily imply that men are influenced by motives, and act from *fixed principles* and *character;* though, on account of our not comprehending the doctrine of *causes,* and stopping where we ought not, we are generally under some mistake and misconception with respect to them. Therefore, to guard against all mistake, it may be more advisable that, in treating the subject philosophically, those words be disused. Every thing that really corresponds to them may be clearly expressed in different language, and all the *rules of discipline,* every thing in *practice,* on the part both of the *governor* and the *governed,* will stand just as before. To make my meaning intelligible, and shew that I do not advance this at random, I shall here endeavour to express in a strict and philosophical manner' the full import of all the terms above-mentioned.

.In common speech we say that we are *accountable creatures*, and *justly liable to rewards and punishments* for our conduct. The philosopher says, that *justice* .ought to be called *propriety* or *usefulness*, or a rule of conduct adapted to answer a good purpose, which in this case is the good of those who are the subjects of government or discipline ; and therefore, instead of saying, We are *justly liable to rewards or punishments*, he says, We are beings of such a constitution, that, to make us happy upon our observance of certain laws, and to make us suffer in consequence of our transgressing those laws, will have a good effect with respect both to our own future conduct and that of others ; i. e. tending to our own melioration, and operating to the melioration of others.

In common language we say a man is *praise-worthy*, and has *merit*. The philosopher says, that the man has acted from, or been influenced by good principles, or such principles as will make a man happy in himself, and useful to others ; that he is therefore a proper object of complacency, and fit to be made happy ; that is, the *general happiness* will be promoted by making him happy.

So also when, in common language, a man is said to be *blame-worthy* and to have *demerit*, the philosopher says, that he has acted from, or been influenced by bad principles, or such as will make a man unhappy in himself, and hurtful to others : that he is therefore a proper subject of aversion, and is fit to be made unhappy ; that is, the making him unhappy will tend to promote the general happiness.

Upon the whole, therefore, though the vulgar and philosophers use different language, they would see reason to *act* in the same manner. The governors will rule voluntary agents by means of rewards and punishments ; and the governed, being voluntary agents, will be influenced by the apprehension of them. It is consequently a matter of indifference in whatever language we describe actions and characters. If the common language be in some respects inconsistent with the doctrine of necessity, it is still more inconsistent with the doctrine of liberty, or the notion of our being capable of determining without regard to motives.

For the *effect* of the more exalted views of the philosophical Necessarian (as unspeakably superior to the more imperfect views of the vulgar), I refer to what I have said upon that subject in my second volume, (HI. pp. 506—509). . We are not, however, to expect that Necessarians should universally, and to the eye of the world, be better than other men. Even Christianity does not universally appear to this advantage in the lives of its professors. But of this I am persuaded, that if any man had strength of mind fully to comprehend the doctrine of necessity, and to keep his mind at all times under the influence of it, he would be much superior to the *mere Christian,* though not perhaps as much so as the Christian may be to the *mere virtuous Heathen.*

Before I conclude this subject, I cannot help noticing what appears to me to be an inconsistency in Dr. Price's account of his view of it. He says, p. 68, the " power of self-determination—can never be exerted without some view, or design," i. e. the will cannot be determined without motives, and " The power of determining ourselves, by the very nature of it, wants an *end* and *rule* to guide it." From this I should infer, that the end and rule by which the will was guided being given, the determination would be certain and invariable ; whereas, in another place, pp. 69, 70, he says, that " moral causes" only " may produce a certainty ;" and even, that " the certainty of event arising—from moral causes, that is, from the views and perceptions of beings, ad-mits of an infinite variety of degrees, and sometimes passes into *probability* and *contingency,*" p. 70. Also that in the operation of moral causes there is a possibility of producing any other effect than that which is produced.

Now that the will should, by the very nature of it, want an end and rule to guide it, and yet be capable of determin-ing not only *without,* but *contrary* to that rule, is, I think, inconsistent ; and yet upon this it is that the whole contro-versy hinges. If the will be always determined according to motives (whether it be alleged to be *by itself,* or *by the motives*), the determination is certain and invariable, which is all that I mean by *necessary ;* whereas, if it may determine *contrary to motives,* it is, *contingent* and uncertain ; which I maintain to be a thing as impossible as that, in any case whatever, an effect should arise without a cause ; and also to be a thing that is, in its nature, incapable of being the object of *fore-knowledge.* And yet, if there be any truth in the Scriptures, the Divine Being certainly foresees every determination of the mind of man.

THE THIRD COMMUNICATION.

Of the Doctrine of NECESSITY.

· DR. PRICE.—ON the subject of necessity I will only say farther, that notwithstanding what Dr. Priestley has said in his last reply, p. 71, &c.; I remain of opinion that self-determination and certainty of determination are perfectly consistent.—That a self-determining power which is under no influence from motives, or which destroys the use of discipline and the superintendency of Providence, has never been contended for, or meant by any advocates for liberty. And, that I am by no means sensible of any inconsistency between asserting that every being who acts at all must act for some end and with some view; and asserting, that a being may have the power of determining his choice to any one of different ends, and that when a regard to different ends is equal, *contingency* of event takes place. The controversy, however, does not according, to my views of it, hinge on the consideration last mentioned; but merely on this, whether man is a proper agent, or has a self-determining power or not. Beings may have a self-determining power, as, according to Dr. Priestley's concession, the Deity has; and yet they may be always guided, as the Deity certainly is, by a rule or end. I know Dr. Priestley will not allow me to argue thus from the Deity to inferior beings. But this method of arguing appears to me fair; and, in the present case, it seems decisive. It is only the *manner* in which God possesses his attributes that is incommunicable. We may justly say, God possesses power. Therefore he may give power. But we cannot, without a contradiction, say, God is self-existent; therefore, he may give self-existence: for this would be to say, that he can make a *derived* being *underived*. Nor can we say, God possesses infinite power; therefore he can communicate *infinite* power: for this would be to say, that he can make a being, who, as a creature, must be finite and dependent, infinite and independent. It might be shewn, that creation out of nothing implies infinite power, and therefore cannot be communicated.

Dr. Priestley will, I hope, allow me to add the following queries:

Is it not more honourable to the Deity to conceive of him, as the parent, guide, governor and judge of free beings formed after his own image, with powers of reason and self-deter-

mination, than to conceive of him, as the former and con-
ductor of a system of conscious machinery, or the mover and
controuler of an universe of puppets?

Can Dr. Priestley believe easily, that, in all those crimes
which men charge *themselves* with, and reproach *themselves*
for, God is the agent; and that (speaking philosophically)
they, in such instances, are no more *agents* than a *sword* is
an agent when employed to commit murder?

Is it surprising that few possess strength of mind enough
to avoid starting at such conclusions? I am, however, ready
to own the weight of some of the observations Dr. Priestley
has made to explain and soften them. And though I think,
that were they commonly received, they would be dreadfully
abused; yet I doubt not, but Dr. Priestley may be, as he
says he is, a better man for believing them.

But I must not go on. Were I to write all that offers itself,
I should fall into numberless tautologies; and there would
be no end of this controversy.

ANSWER.—I know very well that Dr. Price, and other
advocates for what is called philosophical free-will, do not
think that a self-determining power destroys the use of discipline, but I contend that it necessarily does so; I also
deny that, strictly speaking, there can be any such thing as
contingency, it always implying that there is *an effect without a cause;* and therefore, that a determination of the mind
in circumstances in which a regard to different objects is
equal, is an impossibility. This must be universal, and
consequently respect the supreme mind as well as others.
Those who speak with the greatest reverence of the Divine
Being, always suppose that he never acts but for some *end,*
and that the best, i. e. he acts according to some invariable
rule. But we soon lose ourselves in speculation concerning
the *first cause.*

In answer to the Queries, I reply, in general, that I cannot conceive any thing honourable to the Deity, because the
thing is *not possible in itself,* and if possible, not at all *beneficial to man,* in the supposition of his having endued us
with what is called *self-determination.* And though the doctrine of necessity may, like every thing the most true and
sublime, be exhibited in a ridiculous light, it is the only
system that is even *possible;* and in my opinion it is in the
highest degree *honourable,* both to the Universal Parent and
his offspring; the just contemplation of it being eminently
improving to the mind, and leading to the practice of every
thing great and excellent, as I think I have shewn in my
second volume, (Vol. III. Sect. IX. pp. 505—509).

It certainly sounds harsh to vulgar ears, to say that, " in all those crimes that men charge themselves with, and reproach themselves for, God is the agent ; and that—they in such instances, are in reality no more *agents*, than a *sword* is an agent when employed to commit murder." It does require *strength of mind* not to startle at such a conclusion ; but then it requires nothing but strength of mind ; i. e. such a view of things as shall carry us beyond *first* and *fallacious appearances*. And it requires, I think, but a small degree of sagacity to perceive that, whatever there is shocking in these conclusions, it is actually found, and under a very slight cover, in Dr. Price's own principles ; since, I believe, he admits that God foresees all the crimes that men would commit, and yet made man ; that he still has it in his power, in various ways, to prevent the commission of crimes, and yet does not choose to do it. If Dr. Price will answer a question that is frequently put by children, viz. "Papa, why does not God kill the Devil ?"—I will undertake to tell him why God *made* the Devil. Let him tell me why God *permits* vice, and I will tell him why he *appoints* it.

However, the very language that Dr. Price uses to make the doctrine of necessity appear horrid and frightful, is the very language of the Scriptures, in which wicked men are expressly called *God's sword*, and are said, in a great variety of phrases, to do *all his pleasure;* though, in a different sense, the very contrary expressions occur. The reply that Paul, Rom. ix. 18, makes to what might be objected to his saying, God " hath mercy on whom he will *have mercy*, and whom he will, he hardeneth," viz. ver. 18, " Thou wilt say then unto me, Why doth he yet find fault, for who hath resisted his will ?" savours more of the ideas of a Necessarian, than, I suspect, the abettors of the contrary doctrine can well bear ; ver. 20, 21, " Nay, but, O man, who art thou that repliest against God ? Shall the thing formed say to him that formed it, Why hast thou made me thus ? Hath not the potter power over the clay, of the same lump to make one vessel unto honour, and another unto dishonour ?"

I do not say it is impossible to explain this passage of scripture in a manner consistent with Dr. Price's opinions ; but I will say that, with less latitude of interpretation, I will undertake to explain every text that can be produced in favour of the Arian hypothesis, in a manner consistent with Socinianism.

Since, upon all schemes, it is a fact, that vice, as well as other evils, *does* and *must* exist, at least for a time ; is it not more honourable to the Universal Creator, and Supreme Ruler, to suppose that he *intended* it, as an instrument of virtue and happiness, rather than that, though he by no means chose it (as a thing that necessarily thwarted his views), it was not in his power to foresee or prevent it; but that he is content to make the best he can of it when it does happen, interposing from time to time to *palliate matters*, as *unforeseen emergencies* require? This, if it be possible in itself, is what we must acquiesce in, if we reject the doctrine of necessity. There is no other alternative.

I think it hardly possible that a person who believes in *contingencies* can have a steady faith in the doctrine of *divine prescience;* and to divest the Divine Being of this attribute, which in the Scriptures he claims as his distinguishing prerogative, is such a *lessening* and a *degradation* of God, respecting him too in his most important capacity, or that in which we are most concerned, viz. as *Governor of the Universe*, that every thing that Dr. Price can represent as the consequence of the doctrine of necessity appears to me as nothing in comparison with it.

But, as Dr. Price is fully sensible, we see things in very different lights; and it is happy for us that, in general, every light in which we view *our own principles* is more or less favourable to virtue. The Papist, I doubt not, thinks his mind powerfully and advantageously impressed with the idea of the sacramental elements being *the real body and blood of Christ;* the Trinitarian with the notion of *the Supreme God being incarnate;* and the Arian with his opinion, that it was the *Maker and Governor of the World that died upon the cross;* and numbers will say that Christianity is of no value, and, with Mr. Venn, that they would *burn their Bibles*, if these strange doctrines be not contained in them.

Dr. Price, however, does not *feel* that Christianity is degraded, *in his apprehension*, by considering these opinions as absurd or ill-founded, though he does think it degraded by the Socinian hypothesis. Neither do I think Christianity degraded, but, on the contrary, I think its effect upon the mind is much improved, and the wisdom and power of God more conspicuous, on the scheme which supposes that our Saviour was a *mere man, in all things like unto his brethren;* and that as by a *mere man came death*, so *by a mere man, also, comes the resurrection of the dead.* I cheerfully conclude with Dr. Price in saying, in his *letter* subjoined to the *Introduction*, "that our agreement in expecting this awful period makes it of little consequence in what we differ."

QUERIES ADDRESSED TO DR. PRICE.

Of the Penetrability of Matter.

1. Is it not a fact, that *resistance* is often occasioned, not by the contact of solid matter, but by a *power of repulsion* acting at a distance from the supposed substance, as in electricity, magnetism, optics, &c. ?

2. What is the effect of supposed *contact*, but another resistance ?

3. Is it not even certain, that this supposed contact cannot be *real contact*, since the particles that compose the most compact bodies, being capable of being brought nearer together by cold, appear not actually to touch one another ?

4. Since, therefore, there cannot be any evidence of impenetrability, but what results from the consideration of *contact*, and there is no *evidence* of any real contact; does not the doctrine of impenetrability stand altogether unsupported by any *fact*, and, therefore, must it not be unphilosophical to admit that it is any property of matter ?

Of the Soul.

1. If matter be not impenetrable, Dr. Price seems (if I may judge from what he says in p. 38) not unwilling; to admit that it may be endued with the properties of perception and thought. Since, therefore, *the uniform composition of the whole man* will be gained by the preceding hypothesis, is it not a consideration in favour of it ? It can only be a supposed *necessity* that could lead any person to adopt the hypothesis of *two substances* in the composition of *one being*, especially two substances so exceedingly heterogeneous as *matter* and *spirit* are defined to be.

2. Admitting matter to have the property of impenetrability, is there any reason to believe that the powers of perception and thought may not be superadded to it, but that we cannot *conceive* any connexion between the different properties of impenetrability and thought, or any relation they can bear to each other ?

3. Have we, in reality, any idea of a connexion between the property of perception, and extended substance, that is *not impenetrable ?*

4. If not, is it not more philosophical to suppose that the property of perception *may* be imparted to such a substance

as the body; it being certainly unphilosophical to suppose that man consists of *two kinds of substance*, when all the known properties and powers of man *may* belong to *one substance*.

5. If the soul of man be an extended substance, it is certainly in idea, and why may it not *in fact* be as discerptible as matter? If so, are all the parts into which it may be divided, thinking and conscious beings? If not, why may not a material being, possessed of thought, consist of material substances, not possessed of thought, as well as a spiritual one?

6. Whether is it more probable that God can endue organized matter with a capacity of thinking, or that an immaterial substance, possessed of that property, can be so dependent upon the body, as not to be capable of having a perception without it, so that even its peculiar power of *self-motion* cannot be exerted but in conjunction with the body?

7. If there can be any such thing as a proper connexion between material and immaterial substances, must not the former necessarily, according to the common hypothesis, impede the motions of the latter?

8. Is there, therefore, any proper medium between the hypothesis which makes man *wholly material*, and that which makes the body a clog upon the soul, and consequently the death of the body the freedom of the soul?

9. They who maintain the Arian hypothesis, believe that an immaterial spirit, similar to the human soul, is capable of the greatest exertions in a state independent of any connexion with body, at least such bodies as ours, They also suppose that between the death and the resurrection of our Lord, he possessed and exerted his original powers. Is it not then inconsonant to this system, to suppose that the human soul, which to all appearance is influenced by bodily affections exactly like the embodied soul of Christ, should be incapable of all sensation or action during the sleep or death of the body?

10. Consequently, does not every argument that proves the dependence of the soul on the body favour the Socinian hypothesis, by making it probable that the soul of Christ was equally dependent upon his body, and therefore was incapable of exertion *before* as well as *after* its union to it? In other words, that Christ had no proper existence before his birth?

Of the Doctrine of NECESSITY.

1. If any mental determination, or volition, be preceded by nothing, either within the mind itself, or external to it, but what might have existed without being followed by that determination, in what does that determination differ from *an effect without a cause?*

2. Admitting the possibility of such a determination, or a determination without any previous motive, with what propriety can it be the subject of praise or blame, there being no *principle* or *design* (which would come under the denomination of *motive*) from which the determination proceeded? How then can such a power of self-determination make us *accountable creatures*, or the proper objects of rewards and punishments?

3. If certain definite determinations of mind be always preceded by certain definite motives, or situations of mind, and the same definite motives be always followed by the same determinations, may not the determinations be properly called *necessary*, necessity signifying nothing more than the *cause of constancy?*

4. If certain determinations always follow certain states of mind, will it not follow, whether these determinations be called necessary or not, that no determination could have been *intended* or *expected*, by the Author of all things, to have been otherwise than it *has been, is,* or *is to be?* Since, in this case, they could not have been otherwise without a miracle.

5. If any event be properly *contingent*, i. e. if the determination does not depend upon the previous state of mind, is it possible that the most perfect knowledge of that mind, and of all the states of it, can enable a person to tell what the determination will be? In other words, is a contingent event the object of fore-knowledge, even to the Deity himself?

DR. PRICE.—In answer to Dr. Priestley's 4th *query, above,* and also to what he says in pp. 78, 79, &c. I readily admit that all events are such as the power of God (acting under the direction of infinite wisdom and goodness) either *causes* them to be, or *permits* them to be. I rejoice in this as the most agreeable and important of all truths; but I by no means think, with Dr. Priestley, that there is no difference between it, and God's *producing* all events. I scarcely think he would conclude thus in other cases. Are there not many instances in which Dr. Priestley would think it hard to be charged with *doing* what he only fore-sees, and, for the best reasons, thinks fit not to *hinder?*

Active and self-directing powers are the foundation of all morality, all dignity of nature and character, and the greatest possible happiness. It was, therefore, necessary such powers should be communicated ; and being communicated, it was equally necessary that scope, within certain limits, should be allowed for the exercise of them. Is God's *permitting* be-ings, in the use of such powers, to act wickedly, the same with being himself the agent in their wickedness ? Or can it be reasonable to say, that he *appoints* what cannot be done without breaking his laws, contradicting his will, and *abusing* the powers he has given ?

Were I to be asked such a question as that which Dr. Priestley (in p. 78) puts into the mouth of a child—" Why God made the Devil ?" or, " Why God does not confine or kill the Devil ?" I should probably answer, that God made the Devil good, but that he made himself a Devil ; and that a period is near when the Devil and all wicked beings will be destroyed ; but that, in the mean time, the mischief they do is not prevented by confining them, or taking away their power, for the same reason that a wise government does not prevent crimes by shutting men up in their houses, or that a parent does not prevent his children from doing wrong by tying up their hands and feet. I would, in short, lead the child to understand, if possible, that to prevent wickedness by denying a sphere of agency to beings, would be to pre-vent one evil by producing a greater.

The answer I would give to most of Dr. Priestley's other queries, may be easily collected from my former replies.

With respect to the last of them in particular, I cannot help observing, that it implies what I can by no means admit, that free agency is inconsistent with a dependence of our determinations on the state of our minds, and with a certainty of event. I think I have proved that our determinations may be *self*-determinations, and yet this be true of them.

The fore-knowlege of a *contingent* event carrying the ap-pearance of a contradiction, is indeed a difficulty ; and I do not pretend to be capable of removing it.

ANSWER.—I still cannot see any difference, with respect to *criminality*, between *doing* and *permitting* what may be prevented, even with respect to men, and much less with respect to the Deity ; and I should *not* think it hard to be charged with what I thought proper not to hinder. If I had,

G 2

as Dr. Price says, *the best reasons for it*, they would suffi-ciently justify me, and in both cases alike.

But men have only an imperfect controul upon each other, and the exertion of it is often difficult, or at least inconve-nient. We, therefore, make an allowance with respect to men, for which there is no reason with respect to God. He distinctly foresees every action of a man's life, and all the *actual consequences* of it. If, therefore, he did not think any particular man, and his conduct, proper for his plan of crea-tion and providence, he certainly would not have introduced him into being at all.

All that Dr. Price observes with respect to what he calls *active* and *self-directing powers*, I entirely approve; but I think the same conclusions will follow on the supposition of man and superior beings having what we call mere *voluntary powers*, liable to be influenced by the motives to which they will be exposed in the circumstances in which the Divine Being thinks proper to place them. It is this that I call *the foundation of morality;* and not to have given this power, or, by miraculous interposition, to controul it, would either be, as Dr. Price says, *to prevent smaller evils by producing greater*, or not to produce the greatest possible good. His reply to the child is the same that I make, but the question has a meaning to which the capacity of a child does not extend.

If Dr. Price admits, as, in this place he seems to do, that our determinations *certainly* depend upon the state of our minds, I shall have no objection to his calling us *free agents*. I believe we are so, in the popular sense of the words, and I think it perfectly consistent with all the *necessity* that I ascribe to man. When men say that they are *free*, they have no idea of any thing farther than a freedom from the controul of others, or what may be called *external force*, or causes of action not arising within themselves. *Internal causes* are never so much as thought of, and much less ex-pressly excluded, when they speak of this most perfect liberty.

ADDITIONAL OBSERVATIONS

BY

DR. PRICE,

ON A REVIEW OF THE WHOLE CONTROVERSY,

AND OF

DR. PRIESTLEY'S LETTERS AND ILLUSTRATIONS.

———◆◆◆———

LETTER TO DR. PRIESTLEY.

Newington-Green, Sept. 19, 1778.

DEAR SIR,

THE desire you have expressed that I would give you my sentiments of the Controversy between us, *on a view of the whole of it, as now printed*, has induced me once more to apply my thoughts to it. I have done this with care and attention; but am not sure that any thing which you will judge of great importance has occurred to me. It might, therefore, have been right to resolve to say no more; and, indeed, I am so much afraid of perplexing by a multiplicity of words, and of giving disgust by too many repetitions, that this would have been my resolution, had I not thought that the *Additional Observations*, which you will receive with this letter, contain some *new* matter, and place several of the arguments already insisted on in a light that may render them to some persons more intelligible and striking. I have now said the best I can; and I leave our readers to judge between us, hoping that, whether they decide in your favour or mine, they will be candid, and believe that we are both of us governed alike by a sincere love of truth and virtue. I feel deeply that I am in constant danger of being led into error by partial views, and of mistaking the suggestions of prejudice for the decisions of reason; and this, while it disposes me to be candid to others, makes me ardently wish that others would be candid to me.

I am, in a particular manner, sensible of my own blindness with respect to the nature of matter and spirit, and the faculties of the human mind. As far as I have gone in this dispute I am pretty well satisfied; but I cannot go much further.

You have asked me some questions (and many more may be asked me) which I am incapable of answering.

I cannot help taking this opportunity of repeating to you, that I dislike, more than I can easily express, the malevolence expressed by most of the writers against you. I have myself, as you well know, been long an object of abuse for a publication which I reckon one of the best actions of my life, and which events have fully justified. The consciousness of not deserving abuse has made me perfectly callous to it, and I doubt not but the same cause will render you so.

It is certain that, in the end, the interest of truth will be promoted by a free and open discussion of speculative points. Whatever will not bear this must be superstition and imposture. Instead, therefore, of being inclined to censure those who, with honest views, contribute to bring about such a discussion, we ought to thank and honour them, however mistaken we may think them, and however sacred the points of discussion may be reckoned. I wish I could see more of this disposition among the defenders of religion. I am particularly sorry to find that even Mr. Whitehead does not perfectly possess this temper. Had he avoided all uncandid insinuations, and treated you constantly with the same just respect that he does in general, his book in my opinion would have done him much honour.

Dr. Horsley is, I fancy, the only person who, in opposing your opinions, has discovered a just liberality. This is worthy of an able philosopher; and you have, therefore, very properly distinguished him from your other antagonists, by addressing him, in your letter to him, with particular respect. His method of arguing agrees very much with mine. There is, likewise, an agreement between some of Mr. Whitehead's arguments and those I have used. But this agreement has been accidental; for our correspondence was begun and finished long before I knew any thing of either Dr. Horsley's or Mr. Whitehead's publications.

Wishing you every possible blessing,

I am,

With the most affectionate respect,

Yours,

RICHARD PRICE.

ADDITIONAL OBSERVATIONS

BY

DR. PRICE.

————◆◆————

SECT. I. *Of the Human Soul.*

DR. PRIESTLEY acknowledges that the soul is a *single* being or substance. But at the same time he speaks of the *parts* of a soul; of its being a *system;* and, in p. 62, of the *materials* of which Christ consisted before his birth. Has he yet proved this to be consistent?* His doctrine is, that, as a number of corporeal substances put together in a particular manner, become, when put into motion, that *measurer of time* which we call a *clock* or a *watch;* so a number of corporeal substances put together in a particular manner in the brain, become *of course,* when circulation begins, that thinking being we call a *man.* And his doctrine further is, that both are alike machines, the operations of the one in measuring time, and of the other in thinking, perceiving, willing. &c. being equally brought about by mechanical laws, and the necessary result of particular motions and vibrations. This, I imagine, is as concise and just an account as can be given of his system. See, particularly, the 2nd Sect. of his *Additional Illustrations* (Vol. III. pp. 302—304).

Not to say any thing at present of the latter part of this system, I would beg leave again to remind him that, according to his own concession, it is *one* substance that *thinks;*

---

* " I believe I am a *being* or *substance;* also, that I am a *single* being; and that my limbs and senses are not *myself.*" P. 50. " Man, who is *one* being, is composed of *one kind* of substance, made of the dust of the earth." (Vol. III. p 276.) To the same purpose Dr Priestley says, that the " mind,—the subject of thought, is *one* thinking person or being," but afterwards (in the next page) he says, that the subject of thought is the body, "especially the brain;" and that its powers " inhere in *one kind* of substance." Ib. p. 294. These passages compared lead me to suspect, that when he says, in the first of them, that he is *one* being or substance, his meaning is, that he is *many* substances of *one kind* I can think of no other method of making these passages consistent. For I suppose he cannot possibly mean, that the mind, though one *being,* is many *substances.* This would imply, that a substance, numerically different from all others, is not a being. *(Price.)*

that, on the contrary, it is a number of substances that *mea-sure time;* and that, consequently, these cases cannot be parallel.

I know not how to believe Dr. Priestley will adhere to the only observation he has made in answer to this objection ; I mean, the observation (in p. 55), " that a *number* of un-thinking substances may make *one* thinking substance." Would he not wonder were I to maintain that a number of *un*learned men may make one learned *society ?* But what would he think were I to maintain, that a number of *un*-learned men may make one learned *man ?*

But dismissing this difficulty. According to Dr. Priestley, certain particles in the brain are the *subject* of thought and consciousness ; and their arrangement, order and motion, are *actual* thought and intelligence. These particles, it should be observed, must be some *definite* number : for were they an *indefinite* number, the *man,* or the *subject of thought,* could not continue always the same. Any particles added would *increase* the man, in proportion to the number added. Any taken away would *lessen* him, in proportion to the number taken away. Or, in other words, the man would become so far *different;* and so many particles might be added or taken away, as would make him, in any given proportion, a *different* or *another* being.

All this is manifestly absurd and contradictory. The soul we know, amidst all changes and through every period of its existence, maintains a precise and unvaried sameness and individuality. If, therefore, the soul is the brain, it must be, not that gross and ever-varying mass of substances commonly so called, but some certain *staminal* parts of it (see p. 48) which have existed from the first creation of matter,* but were put together at conception so as to form thought ; and which continue without increase or diminution during the life of man ; are only disarranged at death, will be put together again at the resurrection, so as to form an improved consciousness, and will remain precisely the same, except in their order and vibrations, through all eternity.

Can Dr. Priestley satisfy himself with such a notion of

· * When Dr. Priestley says, " I suppose *the sentient principle* in man to be the brain itself," (Letters to Kenrick, *ad fin.*) he means probably not the whole brain, but (agreeably to what is above observed) some *staminal* parts of it He sometimes, indeed, calls the *sentient principle* " a *result* from the organization of the brain ;" but his meaning must be, not that the soul itself is nothing but a *result* from the form and arrangement of the materials of the brain, for he has acknowlegded it to be a *substance,* p. 50, but that its consciousness and reason are such a result. See the reasoning, pp. 60, 61. It is not, he says, *myself,* but my *power of thought,* p. 46, that is the result of figure, motion, &c. *(Price.)*

the human soul ? Is it possible this should be a right account
of that simple and indivisible essence, which every man
calls *himself;* and of those faculties by which we investigate
truth, and are capable of growing for ever in knowledge and
bliss ? Does he, in particular, feel no difficulty in conceiving
that a number of particles, disposed in *one* order and moved
in *one* way, should be nothing but torpid matter ; but, disposed in *another* order and moved in *another* way, should
become perception, judgment and reason ? *

I must leave every one to make his own reflections on
what Dr. Priestley says (Vol. III. pp. 271, 272). I think
it scarcely worthy of him. Why might I not say that spirit
is not *extended ?* He says so, if I understand him, of matter ;
and yet maintains (ibid. p. 239), that it exists in place, pos-

---

* * Dr Priestley intimates, that the power of thinking may as well be the result of
the organization of the brain, is the attraction of iron be the result of the structure
of a magnet. (Vol. III. p. 303) But the attraction of iron by a magnet is the action,
not of the magnet itself, but of *another* cause It would be strange indeed if a mass
of matter could be so put together as to become capable of moving a body at a distance without touching it. The truth, in this case, seems to be, that there are causes
or powers in nature operating according to stated laws which unite themselves to
substances formed as iron and a magnet are, and drive them towards one another.
Perhaps, therefore, this fact might be mentioned as most similar to the union of a
soul to the brain in consequence of its organization. Some assert that magnetism
is caused by the emission of *effluvia,* or the intervention of a subtle fluid; and if
this is true, it is only an instance of the communication of motion by impulse from
matter to matter.

Dr. Priestley has observed, that a compound may have properties which the component parts have not. P. 64. This is true only of such properties as denote merely
an *order* or *relation* of parts For instance, though no *one* of the component parts
of a circle is *circular,* the whole compound is so. What can be plainer ? A number
of things may be ranged into the order of a circle, but one thing cannot. Does this
warrant us to conclude, that, though no one of the particles in a mass of matter is
conscious, yet all taken together may be so ? As well might we conclude, that
though no one of the particles moves, yet the whole compound may move. Such,
however, is the conclusion we are directed to draw by Dr. Priestley, and also by
Mr. Collins in his dispute with Dr. Clarke. In short, consciousness, not being a
mere order of parts, or an external denomination, but a quality *inhering* in its subject, it seems the plainest contradiction to say, that it can inhere in the *whole,* without inhering in the *parts*

I will beg leave to remark further, in this place, that Dr. Priestley's account
of the soul has no such tendency as he describes in the Introduction, pp. 9, 10 If
he is right, we shall, in the *future state,* have no separate souls. But this will give
us no reason for *then* concluding, that we had not pre-existed in a conscious and
active state Just as little reason, in my opinion, does it give us *now* for drawing
such a conclusion. But this observation may be carried much farther. Our existence after death, according to Dr Priestley, will be only the existence of the materials, separated and dispersed, of which we now consist But this is an existence
which belonged to us equally before we were born. Our *pre-existence,* therefore, is
no less certain than our *post-existence.* It is true, Dr. Priestley teaches, that
some time after death our scattered parts are to be brought into union, and to be
made again conscious. But will he say such an union might not have also taken
place some time or other before we were born Little then certainly is the support
which *Socinianism* receives from *Materialism.* See what is said to this purpose in
p. 71 The remembrance of pre-existence cannot be necessary ; or, if it is, Christ
might have possessed it. *(Price.)*

sesses a sphere of action, and is moveable. But I have repeatedly acknowledged my ignorance on this subject. I pretend to know no more than that, whatever my soul is in respect of *locality*, it is *indivisible*, the idea of a *part* of a self, or of a *self* divided into *two selves* being contradictory. Of this I think myself sure. See pp. 41, 53, 57.

Sect. II. *Of the Nature of Matter.*

Dr. Priestley denies that matter is impenetrable, because there is no experiment in which we are sure that we have found it to be so. I have given a reply to this in p. 25. What I would observe here is, that, according to Dr. Priestley's doctrine, there is also no experiment in which we have found that any one thing *causes* or *produces* another, the only proper cause in nature, as he asserts, being that power of the Deity which is not an object of our senses. When a body in motion gives motion to another, all that we observe (and all that is true, if Dr. Priestley is right) is a *conjunction*, not a *connexion* of two events, or one motion *going before* another, not one motion *producing* another; the body moved having really received its motion not from the *apparent*, but from an *invisible* cause. This, if I understand Dr. Priestley, is the truth in every instance. Even the determinations of the will are the actions of the Deity, and motives are properly no more than certain perceptions that constantly *precede* them. Since then experiments do not furnish us with the ideas of *causation* and *productive power*, how came we by these ideas? And how does Dr. Priestley know they have any existence? How, in particular, does he avoid the sceptical system which Mr. Hume has advanced in his Philosophical Essays, and which he founds entirely on this observation? I have shewn how I avoid it in my *Review* of the Difficulties in Morals, pp. 29, 30, &c.

In Vol. III. p. 238, Dr. Priestley repeats a former observation, namely, that it is no less proper to ask what remains of matter after solidity and extension are taken away, than to ask what remains of it after attraction and repulsion are taken away. I have answered, that solidity and extension are *inherent* properties; but that attraction and repulsion, signifying only *something that is done to matter*, convey no idea of it. Were he to ask me what *spirit* is, and I was to give him no other answer, than that it is *something* that is moved, he would probably be much dissatisfied.

In the first Section of the *Additional Illustrations*, Dr. Priestley has given a new account of matter, according to which it is only a number of centres of attraction and repulsion ; or, more properly, of centres (not divisible) to which divine agency is directed   (Vol. III. p. 230.)   I would here ask, wherein do such centres differ from mathematical points? Is not a mathematical point merely the *end* or *termination* of a line, as a line is the termination of a surface, and a surface of a solid ?   Can any one of these be conceived to subsist separately from the rest?   What conception can be formed of a point or centre which has no figure, nor is the termination of a line, but is capable of moving and being moved?   Is the whole universe nothing but a collection of such points acted upon by divine power?   Are these points *substances?*   If not, can they be *matter?*   Or can they be the *souls* of men?   Does not divine agency require an object different from itself to act upon ?   What then can Dr. Priestley mean when he intimates that there is nothing in nature but God's agency ?

At the beginning of this controversy, Dr. Priestley denied *solidity* to matter, but allowed it extension.   He seems now inclined to deny it *both*, and to be for reducing it (and consequently all sentient beings) to nothing but points to which God's agency (in attracting and repelling I know not what) is directed.

In Vol. III. p. 240, he observes, that since the constituent parts of matter do not touch one another, it can *do* nothing, (every thing being really done by divine power,) and consequently is of no use, and, if created, must have been created in vain.*   The obvious inference from hence is, that there is no such thing as matter.   And, accordingly, influenced by this reason, he says, that " it is nothing but the divine agency."   The whole creation, then, being matter, according to Dr. Priestley's doctrine, the whole creation is nothing but the divine agency ; and consequently it must be nothing at all.   For what idea can be formed of the *creation* of the divine agency, or of an agency that acts upon itself ?

But, perhaps, it is not proper to urge these objections, because Dr. Priestley in the very passage which contains this account of matter, asserts that though " every thing *is*

---

* Dr. Priestley intimates that he should prefer to his own hypothesis, an hypothesis, could he find it, " which should make provision for the use of created matter" without resolving it into the divine agency. (Vol. III. p 241.) I think I can inform him of such an hypothesis. *Solid* matter (that is, the matter hitherto believed in by all mankind) is capable of moving other matter by contact and impulse. It can, therefore, *do* somewhat, and be of use. Why then should he not admit it? *(Price.)*

the divine power,—and all action is his action," yet " every thing is not the *Deity himself;*" (Vol. III. p. 241,) and because, likewise, he has very candidly expressed a doubt whether he has not lost himself on this subject. (Ibid. p. 240.) It will, however, be proper to put him in mind (and I wish I could press it on his attention) that he ought not to lay so much stress as he does on the doctrine of materialism, till he is better able to inform us what matter is.

Sect. III.   *Of the Doctrine of Necessity.*

Dr. Priestley, in his letter to Dr. Horsley, endeavours to prove, that there is no difference between him and the Necessarians. His reason for this assertion is, that Dr. Horsley acknowledges a *certain*, and (in one sense) a *necessary* influence of motives on the will. Now, it should be recollected, that the whole controversy has been reduced to this short question—" Has man a power of *agency*, or *self-determination?* Dr. Priestley has denied this. He has maintained that such a power is an impossibility; (p. 65 and Vol. III. p. 220,) that we are mistaken when we refer our actions to ourselves; that our volitions are *perfectly mechanical things;* that motives influence *exactly as weights operate on a scale;** and that there is only *one agent* in nature.† It is only as far as he means to maintain such assertions that he opposes the doctrine of liberty as explained by Dr. Clarke and others.

The influence of motives has never been denied. The point in dispute is, the *nature* of that influence; and with respect to this, I have long ago observed, (see Review of Morals, p. 351, 2d edit.) that *no* influence of motives, which is short of making them *physical efficients* or *agents*, can clash with liberty. May I then ask him whether he still adheres to the assertions I have mentioned? If not, our controversy is at an end. But if he does, then he and I (and probably also he and Dr. Horsley) still differ. He should not say here, as he does, that, provided the influence of motives is

---

* See Treatise on Necessity, Dedication, (Vol. III p. 451,) and Illustrations, (pp. 475, 477, &c.) See likewise Vol. III. p. 520 . *(Price.)*

† Dr. Priestley has sometimes called man an *agent*. In Vol. III. p. 220, he says, that " man is a *voluntary agent*, though not possessed of a self-moving power." There seems to me an evident contradiction in these words. For an agent that does not put himself in motion, is an agent that is always acted upon, or an agent that never acts In p 84, he even allows that man may be called a *free* agent; but his meaning plainly is, that man is moved only by *internal* springs; and this no more makes him truly free than it makes a watch free. *(Price.)*

allowed, it makes no difference whether they influence in one way or in another, or whether we reckon them *physical causes* or *moral reasons*. This has been already answered in p. 69, &c. That kind of influence which I allow to motives implies, that man is a *self-moving* being. The other implies, that he is nothing but a machine. The one implies, that motives are only certain reasons on the view of which, or certain rules and perceptions according to which, the mind *determines itself*. The other implies, that they are *substances* which operate mechanically on the mind, and leave it no dominion over its determination. In short, the one is consistent with *moral agency;* the other, destroying *all* agency, destroys of course all *moral* agency. Is it possible there should be any greater difference? See p. 71.

I have in the course of this controversy sometimes appealed to common sense. Dr. Priestley will, I hope, allow me again to do this on the present occasion. Let us suppose a common man, who knows nothing of those refinements on plain points which have disgraced human learning, and turned so much of it into rank folly; let us, I say, suppose such a man asked whether, in all his actions, he does not determine himself? He would certainly answer, without hesitation, in the affirmative. Suppose him told, that he was mistaken; and that very wise men had discovered, that he no more determined himself in any of his actions than a stone determines itself when thrown from a hand. Would he not wonder greatly?

Suppose him farther asked, whether there is not a *certainty* that he would accept a good estate if it was offered to him fairly? He would answer in the affirmative. Suppose it objected to him, that there could be no such *certainty*, because, being a self-determiner, he would be free not to accept. Would there be a possibility of puzzling him by such an objection?

Dr. Priestley says, " that a determination of the mind in cases in which a regard to different motives is equal, is an impossibility."* The following case will prove the

---

* There are numberless cases in which there is a reason for acting *in general,* but no reason for any preference of one way of acting to another. It appears to me very wrong to say, that in these cases action becomes impossible. I may have a reason for going to a certain place, but it may be indifferent in which of two ways I go. Do I, in these circumstances, lose the power of going at all? Supposing the universe finite, it was indifferent where in infinite space it was placed. But was it, on this account, impossible to place it any where? Supposing it to consist of only two systems, there could have been no reason for placing one of them on *one* side of the other, rather than at an equal distance on the *opposite* side. But would it, on this account, have been impossible to create them?

contrary, and may, I hope, help a little to illustrate this subject.

Suppose an *agreeable* proposal made to a person which shocks his moral feelings, but which he must immediately resolve either to accept or not. If he *accepts*, he gratifies his passions. If he does not accept, he follows his sense of duty. This brings him into circumstances in which he must act upon a motive ; and also upon *one* or *other* of two given motives. Nothing is more conceivable, than that these motives may be equal in their influence. In that case, would determination be (as Dr. Priestley says) impossible? To say this, would be to say, that a person, when tempted, may neither comply with the temptation, nor reject it. Without all doubt, his power in such a situation is to do *either*, not to do *neither*.

In general, I would observe here that, in circumstances of temptation, there are always two motives which influence the will ; and that the essence of moral merit and demerit consists in the free resolution of the will (or in its *self-determination*) to act on one of them rather than on the other. Dr. Priestley, therefore, should not have said, that the doctrine of liberty implies that a man in acting wickedly or virtuously, acts without a motive. I cannot conceive of a more groundless assertion.

But let us again consider the case I have put.

Passion and interest draw us one way. Conscience and duty order us another. In these circumstances, we may determine as we *please*. Thus far Dr. Priestley and I would speak the same language, but we should mean differently. By determining *as we please*, he would mean our being subject, without the power of resistance, to the mechanical influence of that motive which happens to be strongest. But I should mean, our possessing a power to make *either* of the

In forming this earth, there could have been no reason against the transposition of any *similar* particles on its surface. Was it, therefore, impossible (as Mr. Leibnitz contended) that there should have been any such particles? See the beginning of Dr Clarke's, 3d, 4th, and 5th Replies in the collection of papers which passed between Dr Clarke and Mr. Leibnitz

When I say there are cases in which there can be no reason for any *preference* of one way of acting to another, I mean by *preference*, the judgment of the mind concerning the best way of acting I mention this because there is a *preference* included in the idea of volition ; and which signifies merely the determination to act in one way, and not in another. Preference in the former sense, is a perception of the understanding, and, therefore, *passive*. In the latter sense, it is the exertion of the self-moving faculty, and therefore *active*. These, though *commonly* united, are *often* separated ; and it is chiefly inattention to the difference between them, or the not distinguishing (as Dr. Clarke observes) between the *perceptive* and *active* faculties, that has produced the disputes about liberty and necessity. (*Price.*)

motives the strongest; that is, to make either of them the motive that *shall* prevail, and on which we *shall please* to determine. Unhappily for us, we are continually finding ourselves in these circumstances. Let every one examine himself, and consider which of these accounts is right. Has a man, urged by contrary inclinations, (by passion on one hand and a regard to virtue on the other) no controulling power over his inclinations to make one of them, preferably to the other, the inclination that he will follow. Or is he then exactly in the condition of a body impelled by contrary forces, which must be carried along by the strongest? If this is the truth, there is no *action* of the man, when a temptation overcomes him; nor consequently, if there is any meaning in words, can there be any guilt, or ill-desert. I entreat Dr. Priestley to remember, that this is the doctrine, and the *only* doctrine of necessity that I mean to oppose.

Dr. Priestley says, at the conclusion of his letter to Dr. Horsley, that there is no medium between acknowledging the will to be subject to the influence of motives, and asserting an effect without a cause; and that, consequently, " there is no choice but of the doctrine of necessity, or absolute nonsense." I am very sensible, that it is nonsense to deny the influence of motives, or to maintain that there are no fixed principles and ends by which the will is guided; but, at the same time, I must say, that this nonsense is scarcely equal to that of confounding *moral* with *physical* causes, making motives substances, asserting that we are not the causes of *our own* determinations, and denying that we are free merely because we have reasons for acting.

In *Disquisitions*, he says, that " in all cases where the principle of freedom from the certain influence of motives takes place, it is *exactly an equal chance* whether—rewards or punishments determine—or not. The self-determining power is not at all of the nature of any mechanical influence, that may be counteracted by influences equally mechanical." (Vol. III. p. 294.) Does not this imply, that if the will is not subject to a *mechanical* influence, it can be subject to *no* influence; and that, if there is not a *certainty* of its following a particular motive in any case, there cannot be even a *probability?*

Dr. Priestley lays great stress on the observation " that self-determination implies an effect without a cause." I have taken some notice of this objection in p. 68. It evidently implies that it is impossible a " self-moving power should be *itself* a cause," and " that there must be an endless progression of causes and effects without any first cause."* I cannot, therefore, but wonder at this objection; and I am disposed the more to wonder at it, because Dr. Priestley, though he urges it so repeatedly, has at the same time been so candid as to acknowledge that the Deity is a self-determining being. But in answer to this he observes, that the Deity is also *self-existent,* and that it does not follow, because he is so, that his creatures may be so. See what is said to this in pp. 56, 76. Let the impartial reader judge here. Would not one think that if God is a self-moving being, self-motion cannot imply an effect without a cause? And that, if our acting with a view to ends and reasons proves we do not begin motion in ourselves, it must much more prove the same of the Deity, and, consequently, that there can be no *beginner* of motion, or *first cause?* What analogy is there between saying " God is self-existent, (that is, *underived,*) therefore, his creatures may be so," and saying, " God is an *agent,* therefore, his creatures may be *agents"?* Did God's self-existence mean, that he is the cause of his own existence, or that he produced himself, it would be no less absurd to apply this attribute to him than to any other being ; but most certainly it has a very different meaning. It means, that being underived, he exists (as Dr. Clarke speaks) " by an absolute necessity in the nature of the thing ;" or (as I should choose to speak) that the *account* of his existence is the same with the account of the existence

---

* Mr. Leibnitz maintained, that in all cases of such absolute indifference as those referred to in the note, p. 94, there could be *no* determination of the will; because it would be a determination for which no reason could be given. Undoubtedly, says Dr. Clarke, in answering him, (see 3d Reply, Sect. 2d.) " Nothing is without a sufficient reason why it *is* rather than *not,* and why it is *thus* rather than otherwise. But in things in their own nature indifferent, mere will, without any thing external to influence it, is alone a sufficient reason; as in the instance of God's creating or placing a particle of matter in one place rather than in another, when all places are originally alike."

" A balance (5th Reply, 1st Sect) for want of having in itself a principle of action, cannot move at all when the weights are equal. But a free agent, when there appears two or more perfectly alike reasonable ways of acting, has still within itself, by virtue of its self moving principle a power of acting, and it may have very strong reasons for not forbearing to act at all, when yet there may be no possible reason to determine any particular way of doing the thing to be better than another. To affirm, therefore, that supposing two different ways of placing certain particles of matter were equally good and reasonable, God could neither wisely nor possibly place them in either of those ways for want of a sufficient weight to determine him which way he should choose, is making God not an active, but a passive being, which is not to be a God or governor at all." But the objection that liberty implies an effect without a cause, has been more particularly answered by Dr. Clarke, in his Remarks on Mr. Collins's *Philosophical Inquiry concerning Liberty.* It is, indeed, with some pain I reflect, that much of this discussion is little more than a repetition of Mr. Collins's objections on one side, and Dr. Clarke's Replies on the other. *(Price.)*

of space and duration, of the equality of the three angles of a triangle to two right angles, or of any abstract truth.

Dr. Priestley's arguments, in the 6th Section of his *Additional Illustrations*, (Vol. III. p. 516,) plainly lead to, and imply the following conclusions: That, since no action or event could possibly have been different from what it *has been, is,* or *will* be; and since there is but one cause, one will, one sole agent in nature; our proneness to look off from this one cause, and to refer our actions to ourselves, is an instance of vicious weakness in us, leading us to *idolize ourselves and others;* (ib. p. 519,) and that had we *fortitude* enough to conquer this weakness, and *wisdom* enough to lay aside all fallacious views, or were perfect philosophers and *necessarians,* we should ascribe to God our evil dispositions no less than our good ones, (ib. p. 522,) and consider ourselves as fellow-workers with him in our vices as well as our virtues; and, therefore, should never reproach ourselves for having done wrong, never think we have need of repentance, and never pray to God for pardon and mercy, or address him in any of the forms of confession and supplication.

If this is a just account, and *Dr. Priestley* really means to acknowledge these to be proper inferences from his doctrine, I must say that he cannot be sufficiently admired for his fairness in the pursuit of truth. He believes he has found it in the doctrine (the great and glorious doctrine, as he calls it) of necessity; and he follows it into all its consequences, however frightful, without attempting to evade or palliate them. For my own part, I feel here my own weakness. I shudder at these consequences, and cannot help flying from them. I think it impossible a doctrine should be true, from which such an apology for vice can be fairly deduced; and which opposes so strongly the constitution of nature and our necessary feelings, as not to be capable of being applied to practice, or even of being *believed* without particular fortitude. I am fully persuaded, however, that so sound is Dr. Priestley's constitution of mind, and so excellent his heart, that be can drink this deadly potion, and find it salutary. But such powers and such integrity are given to few.

I must farther confess to Dr. Priestley, that I am in some degree rendered averse to his doctrine by my pride. I had been used to think of my soul as so real and substantial, as to be the very principle that gives reality to the sensible qualities of bodies, and consequently to the whole dress of the external world ; as an essence of heavenly origin, incorporeal, uncompounded, self-determining, immortal, and indestructible; except by the power that created it ; possessed of faculties which (however· the exercise of them may be subject to interruptions) make it an image of the Deity, and render it capable of acting by the same rule with·him. of participating of his happiness, and of *living* for ever. and *improving* for ever under his eye and care. But if Dr. Priestley is right, my soul is literally the offspring of the earth ; a composition of dust ; incapable of all agency ; a piece of machinery moved by mechanical springs, and chained to the foot of fate ; all whose powers·of thought, imagination, reflection, volition, and reason, are no more than a *result* from the arrangement and play of a set of atoms, all unthinking and senseless.—What can be more humiliating than this account? How low does it bring the dignity of man! I cannot help feeling myself degraded by·it unspeakably! Were it to be received universally, it would, I am afraid, operate like a dead weight on the creation, breaking every aspiring effort, and producing universal abjectness. The natural effect of believing* that nothing is left to depend on ourselves, and that we can *do* nothing, must be concluding that we have *nothing to do;* and resolving to leave every thing to that Being who (as Dr. Priestley says, Vol. III. pp. 518, 523,) works *every thing in us, by us, and for us.*

That SELF-ANNIHILATION, therefore, which he mentions as one of the happy effects of his doctrine, is no great recommendation of it. On the contrary. That SELF-REVERENCE, which is taught by the opposite doctrine, inspiring high designs and a disdain of mean passions and vicious pursuits, is, in my opinion, a far more useful and noble principle.

Dr. Priestley takes notice of the serenity and joy which the doctrine of necessity inspires by causing us to view

---

* Dr. Priestley frequently speaks of the dependence of events on *ourselves;* but I cannot see the consistency of such language with his principles. Events, it is true, depend on our *determinations;* but our *determinations,* no more depending on *ourselves* than the motion of a wheel depends on *itself* when pushed by another wheel, no events derived from such determinations, can be properly said to depend on *ourselves.* Dr. Priestley's system allows no one to be the maker of his own *volitions.* How then can it, as he says it does, *Disquisitions,* (Vol. III. p. 503,) allow every one to be "the maker of his own *fortune*"? In truth, the use which he finds unavoidable of such expressions as these and many others implying liberty, is a strong argument against him. For it proves, that so incompatible is his system with the whole frame of *language* as well as *nature,* that it is impossible even to *speak* agreeably to it. *(Price.)*

every thing in a favourable light, by shewing us the hand of God in all occurrences, and by teaching us that there is nothing wrong in nature.   But these sources of joy are by no means confined to the doctrine of necessity.   The contrary doctrine supplies them on better ground, and with more safety and purity.   There are no ideas of free agency which do not allow of such a dependence of events on the circumstances of beings,. and the views presented to their minds as leaves room for *any* direction of events by superior wisdom. ᐧAnd though I believe that vice is an *absolute evil* productive of infinite losses to the individuals who practise it; and that the permission of it is to be accounted for chiefly by the impossibility of producing the greatest good without giving *active powers*,* and allowing scope for exercising them.   Though, I say, I believe this; yet I believe at the same time, that no event comes to pass which it would have been proper to exclude; and that, relatively to the divine plan and administration, *all is right.*†   Under this persuasion, I can view the course of events with satisfaction; and commit joyfully the disposal of my lot to that Self-existent Reason which governs all things; not doubting but that the order of nature is in every instance wise and good beyond the possibility of amendment; that infinitely more takes place in the creation than my warmest benevolence can wish for; and that, if I practise righteousness, I shall (according to the promise of God by Jesus Christ) rise again after sinking in death; and, together with all the upright of all nations and opinions, be at last happy for ever.

* ᐧSee p. 83.ᐧ The best that I can say on this subject, may be found in my Dissertation on Providence, Sect. iv. *Active* powers, *self-determining* powers, and *voluntary* powers, are, according to my ideas, the same. But according to Dr. Priestley, a *voluntary* power (or the power of willing) is a *passive* power. That is, it signifies only (like *moveableness* in bodies) the capacity of being acted upon, or the necessity of yielding to an impressed force. *(Price.)*

† "ᐧWere there no scope for action given beings, or had they no power over what comes to pass, there could be no such thing as a moral government in nature, there would be no room for *real* beneficence and the happiness connected with it, and the whole rational universe would be a system of conscious machinery, void of value and dignity. But then, surely, this does not oblige us to maintain that the Deity exercises no providence over the affairs of rational beings. The power which they have over events, with all its restrictions, was given by him; and all the particular exertions of it are under his direction " *Price on Providence,* Sect. iv. " Of the Objections against Providence," *Dissert.* Ed. 4, 1777, p. 94.

REPLIES

TO

D R. P R I C E ' S
ADDITIONAL OBSERVATIONS,

BY

DR. PRIESTLEY.

SECT. I. *Of the Human Soul.*

P. 87. I CANNOT see any real inconsistency between calling
the mind, or *the man, one being,* or even *one substance,*
and yet saying that this one substance, or being, consists of
many parts, each of which, separately considered, may likewise be called a distinct being, or substance ;* having again
and again observed, what I believe will be universally admitted, that by the words *being, substance,* or *thing,* we only
mean the unknown, and perhaps imaginary *support of properties,* some of which may belong to the parts, though others
may be peculiar to the whole.

Dr. Price, indeed, says, that " this is true only of such
properties as denote merely *an order or relation of parts,*" as
that " no one of the component parts of a circle is circular,"
though " the whole compound is so." P. 89, *note.* But I see
no reason for this limitation. It is well known that chemical
compounds have powers and properties which we could not
have deduced from those of their component parts, or their
new arrangement ; as the power of *aqua regia* to dissolve
gold, when neither the spirit of nitre, nor the spirit of salt,
of which it is composed, will do it. It may be said, that a

---

* That all the *unity* or *simplicity* of which we can be conscious with respect to
ourselves, is, that each person is *one,* and not *two* conscious intelligent beings; but
that consciousness can give us no information whatever concerning the *substance* to
which these powers belong, as whether it be *simple* or *complex, divisible* or *indivisible, &c.* has, I presume, been sufficiently shewn in the *Additional Illustrations*
under the article of *Consciousness,* especially Vol. III. p. 294; and yet this seems
to be the thing on which Dr. Price lays the greatest stress. *(P.)*

being of competent knowledge of the nature of gold, and that of the two acids, separately considered, might foretel that gold would be soluble in a mixture of them. But I also may say that 'a being of sufficient knowledge might have foretold, that when God had made a human body, even of the *dust of the earth*, or *mere matter*, the result of the animation of this organized system would have been his *feeling* and *thinking*, as well as his *breathing* and *walking ;* or, in the words of Moses, that when the mere *breath of life* was imparted, nothing more remained to be done to make a complete man. There was no *separate soul* to be communicated.

Even Dr. Price's own example, viz. that of *a clock,* or *watch,* will suit my purpose tolerably well. A watch, as he properly says, is a *time-measuring machine,* as man is a *thinking machine.* But what connexion is there between the ideas of the brass, or steel, &c. of which the watch is made, or even of the separate parts of which it consists, as the wheels, pinions, spring, or chain, &c. and the idea of *measuring time ?* Has not the whole, in this case, a property, or power, which does not, in the least degree, belong to any of the parts? Nay, the whole machine, when properly put together, has no more power of measuring time than any of its separate parts, or the rough materials of which they are made, till the spring is wound up; but then its power and office of measuring time takes place *of course.* Why then should it be thought not to be within the compass of Almighty power to form an organized body of mere matter, so that by simply giving it *life* the faculty of *thinking* shall be the necessary result ?

It is of no consequence, however, whether we be able to find any proper illustration of this case, or not, since, as I have shewn, both in the *Disquisitions,* and in the course of this correspondence, that it is as evident from fact, that the brain thinks, as that the magnet attracts iron. See p. 52, &c.

Dr. Price says, " The soul, we know, amidst all changes, and through every period of its existence, maintains a precise and unvaried sameness and individuality, p. 88 ; and he calls it a *simple and indivisible essence,* p. 90. Now I am satisfied that a man continues sufficiently the same being through the whole course of his life, and will be so after the resurrection ; but I do not think that our imperfect knowledge of the nature of organized bodies will authorize the very strong language above quoted. I consider *man* as preserving his individuality, or identity, in the same manner as a *tree* does ;

and if we consider the loss of memory, the change of disposition and character, and the impairing of all the human
faculties in old age, there will be no more argument from
fact of his having continued the same from his birth to his
death, than of an old, shattered and dismembered tree being
the same that it was when first planted, and during its vigour.

· · Dr. Price thinks, that what I have said on the subject of
extended spirit is *scarcely worthy of me.* P. 89. Now I
cannot help thinking that what I have advanced on that subject is both perfectly *just*, and likewise *proper.* In my *Disquisitions* I had considered principally the most refined and
proper kind of spiritualism, if I may use that expression, as
appearing to me to be the only consistent system ; according
to which, spirit has neither extension, nor relation to space.
This Dr. Price acknowledges to be *an absurdity and contradiction that deserves no regard.* He says, " That matter
is incapable of consciousness and thought, not because
it is *extended*, but because it is *solid*," p. 38 ; " That Dr.
Clarke," whose ideas he seems to adopt, " was not for excluding expansion from the idea of immaterial substances,"
ibid. ; and, together with myself and Dr. Clarke, he always
supposes the Divine essence to have proper extension, filling
all space.

It certainly then behoved me to examine this opinion of
extended human souls, and I think I have shewn it to be no
less absurd than the former. Dr. Price himself does not
choose to defend it, but rather seems willing to adopt a new
and middle opinion, supposing the soul to have *locality*
without *extension.* But this idea I have noticed, and I think
sufficiently, in my *Disquisitions* (Vol. III. pp. 368, 369),
referring to Dr. Watts, who confutes it more at large. I
presume, therefore, that *in no form whatever* can the hypothesis of a soul separate from the body be maintained.

As to what I advanced in my random speculation concerning the *centres of attraction and repulsion*, of which I
supposed that what we call *matter* might possibly consist,
it was a mere voluntary excursion into the regions of hypothesis. I do not at present see any thing amiss in it, but I
am confident that had I been more in earnest, and determined to abide by that hypothesis, there is nothing in it of
which Dr. Price could materially avail himself in support
of his doctrine of a separate soul.

The fact of the existence of *compound ideas* in the mind,
still appears to me decisive against the opinion of such an
absolute *simplicity* and *indivisibility* of its essence, as Dr.

Price contends for. See *Disquisitions* (Vol. III. p. 249), and this Correspondence, pp. 36, 53.

Since I wrote the *Additional Illustrations*, I have had the curiosity to make some inquiry into the actual state of opinions concerning the soul, and I see reason to think that, excepting Dr. Clarke, and perhaps a few others, the opinion that has most generally prevailed of late, is that which I have principally combated in my *Disquisitions*, viz. that it is a thing that has *no extension, or relation to space*. Dr. Watts asserts this opinion, and defends it very largely and ably *∗* against Mr. Locke; and it is the opinion that is advanced and proved, in all the forms of geometrical demonstration, by Dr. Doddridge in his *Lectures* (No. XCVI). These Lectures are now read in all our dissenting academies, where perhaps one half of the metaphysicians in the nation are formed; for the clergy of the established church do not, in general, seem to have so much of this turn. Now I do not remember that any of my fellow-students ever entertained a different idea, and many of us were very much intent upon metaphysical inquiries. We held very different opinions on other points, and were pretty eager disputants. I have also inquired of many other persons, and hitherto they have all told me, that their idea of spirit was that which I have considered. It will be observed, however, that all the arguments on which I lay the most stress respect the notion of a separate soul *in general*, without regard to any particular hypothesis about the nature of it.

Mr. Baxter seems to deny extension to spirits, but not *locality*, so that probably neither Dr. Price nor myself have been exactly right in our idea of his opinion. It rather seems to have been that middle opinion to which Dr. Price now reverts. As to the doctrine of immaterial spirits having real *size*, and consequently *form*, or *shape*, though I ought perhaps to have respected it more, as the opinion of so great a man as Dr. Clarke, I really considered it as an hypothesis universally abandoned, till Dr. Price's seeming avowal of it made me give it the degree of attention which I have done, and which produced what I have advanced on the subject in the *Additional Illustrations* to which he refers.

In his *Additional Observations*, Dr. Price suggests an idea of a soul, and of its union to the body, that I own I should not have expected from his general system; comparing it (as that to which, he says, it is " perhaps most similar")

∗ See his *Philosophical Essays*, No. VI. Sect. ii. Works, VL. pp. 540—543.

to those " causes or powers, in nature, operating according
to stated laws, which unite themselves to substances formed
as iron and a magnet are." P. 89, note.

Is then the soul nothing more than a *power* or *property*,
necessarily resulting from the organization of the brain?
This has been *my* idea, and not *his*. I therefore suppose
him to mean, that, whenever a body is completely organized,
there is a general law in nature, by which, without any particular interposition of the Deity, a soul immediately attaches
itself to it. But this supposes what Dr. Price will excuse
me for calling *a magazine of souls* ready formed for that purpose, or the pre-existence of all human souls ; which, indeed, was the original doctrine of a soul, and what I think
is necessary to make the system complete and consistent.

Dr. Price says, " Little certainly is the support which
Socinianism receives from *Materialism ;*" (ibid.) because the
resurrection being nothing more than the re-arrangement
of the same particles that composed a man before death, the
same may have composed a man in a state prior to his birth.

I answer, that this is certainly *possible*, and had I the same
authority for believing it, that I have to believe the resurrection, I should have admitted it ; but having no *evidence* at
at all for it, it is a notion so far within the region of mere
possibility, that it is in the highest degree incredible. For
none of the natural arguments for the future existence of
men, which are derived from the consideration of the moral
government of God, can be alleged in favour of a pre-existence of which we have no knowledge.

It is likewise possible that, in a former remote period,
not only myself, but every thing with which I am connected,
and the whole system of things, may have been just as it
now is ; that Dr. Price then wrote remarks on my *Disquisitions*, &c., and that I replied to him in a joint publication,
the very same as the present ; that there have been infinite
revolutions of the same system, and that there is an infinity
of them still to come ; which was the opinion of some of the
ancient philosophers.

But it is not the mere *possibility* of such a scheme that
can entitle it to any degree of credit. If, therefore, the
failure in the support that the doctrine of Materialism gives
to the doctrine of Socinianism be only in proportion to the
probability of the pre-existence of man on the system of
materialism (which excludes the notion of a separate soul),
I think it may be put down as an *evanescent quantity*, or
nothing at all. In other words, the doctrine of materialism

is a sufficient and effectual support of the Socinian hypothesis.

So much confidence have I in the tendency that the doctrine of materialism has to favour Socinianism, that I doubt not but the moment it is believed that men in general have no souls separate from their bodies, it will be immediately and universally concluded, that Christ had none. And as to the mere possibility of his and our *bodies* having had a pre-existence in an organized and thinking state, I should entertain no sort of apprehension about it. Or, if this odd opinion should gain ground, it will have nothing in it contrary to the *proper principle* of Socinianism, which is, that Christ was a *mere man*, having no natural pre-eminence over other men; but that all his extraordinary powers were derived from divine communications after his birth, and chiefly, if not wholly, after his baptism, and the descent of the Holy Spirit upon him. This kind of pre-existence can also afford no support to any other of those corruptions of Christianity which have been derived from the notion of a separate soul, such as the doctrine of *purgatory*, and the *worship of the dead*, &c. &c.

SECT. II. *Of the Nature of Matter.*

On what I advanced concerning the constitution of matter, as consisting of mere *centres of attraction and repulsion*, which I gave as a mere *random speculation*, and not at all necessary to my purpose, but according to which it may be said that every thing is the *divine agency*, Dr. Price asks, " Does not divine agency require an object different from itself to act upon?" p. 91; and, " What idea can be formed of the *creation* of the divine agency, or of an agency that acts upon itself?" Ibid.; I answer, that the difficulty consists in *terms* only; for that on the random hypothesis to which this argument refers, the *exertion of the divine agency* may properly enough be called *creation*, and the *modification* of that exertion, the *action* of the Deity upon that creation.

Dr. Price says, that " *solid matter can do somewhat*, and *be of use.*" Ibid. *note.* But is it not rather unfortunate for this hypothesis, and those who maintain it, that they are not able to say *what it does*, there being no *effect* or *appearance* in nature to the explication of which it is necessary; all that is *actually done*, where matter is concerned, being probably effected by something to which solidity cannot be ascribed. There is certainly no conceivable connexion between *solidity* and *attraction*. Solidity, indeed, might account for *resistance at the point of contact*, but I challenge any philosopher to stand forth, and produce but one clear instance of actual *unquestionable contact*, where matter is concerned. In most cases of repulsion it is undeniable ·that proper contact is not at all concerned, and therefore there can be no reason *from analogy* to lead us to conclude that it is, in *any case*, the proper cause of repulsion; but, on the contrary, that the true cause, as *certainly in most cases*, so *probably in all*, is something else. The case the most like to real contact is that of the component parts of solid bodies, as gold, &c., but even this cannot be any' thing more than a certain *near approach*, because they are brought *nearer* together by cold; and it will hardly be pretended that any body merely impinging against a piece of gold comes nearer to its substance than the distance at which its own component parts are placed from each other.

On this subject Dr. Price refers to what he has advanced p. 29. But all that he says there is, that, in some cases, the reason why bodies cannot be brought into contact *may be* their *solidity*, at the same time allowing that, in other cases, it is *certainly* a *repulsive power*. In the same Section he refers to his *Treatise on Morals* for another origin of the idea of solidity. But this I have fully considered in the third of the *Essays* prefixed to my edition of *Hartley's Theory of the Human Mind*. See particularly Vol. III. pp. 191, 192.

However, the whole of what I have advanced concerning *the penetrability of matter* is a thing on which I lay no great stress. I do not see any reason to be dissatisfied with it; but admitting matter to have all the solidity that is usually ascribed to it, I have no doubt of its being compatible with the powers of thought; all the phenomena demonstrating to me that man is a being composed of *one kind of substance*, and not of *two*, and these so heterogeneous to each other as has been generally supposed.

It is within the limits of this Section that Dr. Price puts the following question to me: " Since experiments do not furnish us with the ideas of *causation*, and *productive power*, how came we by these ideas, and how does Dr. Priestley know they have any existence? How, in particular, does he avoid the sceptical system which Mr. Hume has advanced?" P. 90.

I answer that my idea of *causation*, and of its origin in the mind, is, as far as I know, the very same with that of other persons; but we all distinguish between *primary* and *secon-*

dary causes, though speaking strictly and philosophically, we call secondary causes mere *effects,* and confine the term *cause* to the primary cause. Thus we say that the cause of moving iron is in the magnet, though the magnet is not the primary, but only the proximate, or secondary cause of that effect; deriving its power, and all' that can be said to belong to it from a higher cause, and ultimately from God, the original cause of all things. So also I formerly considered man as the original cause of his volitions and actions; till, on farther reflection, I saw reason to conclude that, like the magnet, he is no more than the proximate, immediate, or secondary cause of them; himself, his constitution, and circumstances, and consequently his actions, having a prior cause, viz. the same first cause from which the powers of the magnet, and all the powers in nature, are derived.

Sect. III. *Of the Doctrine of Necessity.*

On this subject Dr. Price refers me to the decisions of what he calls *common sense,* or the notions of the vulgar, (p. 93). These I have observed, as far as they go, are uniformly in favour of the doctrine of necessity. For if men were properly interrogated, they would admit all that I require in order to a proper demonstration of the doctrine; though, not being used to reflection, they do not *pursue* or even *apprehend* the consequences. See my *Treatise on Necessity,* Vol. III. p. 505.

As to the consistency of the *popular language* with the doctrine of necessity, I have again and again made observations upon it, which I think it unnecessary to repeat, in answer to the conclusion of Dr. Price's note, p. 98.

Dr. Price says, that he " cannot conceive of a more groundless assertion," than " that the doctrine of liberty implies that a man in acting wickedly or virtuously, acts without a motive," (p. 94). But after putting a case in which he supposes motives to be exactly equal, viz. the combination of *passion* and *interest* on one side, and of *conscience* and *duty* on the other, he makes liberty to consist in our possessing *a power of making either of them the motive that shall prevail.*

Now it appears to me to require very little power of analyzation to see that before the mind can decide to which of the motives it' shall give this preference, it must form a previous, real and most serious *determination,* and that this previous determination requires a motive as much as the final, determination itself, especially as Dr. Price expressly acknowledges that " it is nonsense, to deny the influence of motives, or to maintain that there are no fixed principles and ends by which the will is guided," (p. 95). In the case above mentioned I have the choice of two things, viz. either to give the preponderance to the *motives of interest,* or to *those of duty,* which, being by supposition exactly equal, are themselves out of the question, and therefore cannot at all contribute to the decision. Now this being a real determination of the mind, it must, by Dr. Price's own confession, require some motive or other.

This argument I own is quite new to me, and therefore I presume that it is, in part, the *new matter* which Dr. Price observes (p., 85) is contained in these *Additional Observations;* but I know he will excuse my frankness if I tell him, that it appears to me to be the last retreat of the doctrine of philosophical liberty, and not at all more tenable than any of those out of which it has been already driven. For when *all argument* fails, he will hardly take refuge in the *common sense* of my Scotch antagonists. I could say more on the subject of this new idea of *the mind choosing the motive on which it will decide,* but I think what I have now said may be sufficient.

I would take, this opportunity of observing that if the motives, in the case above-mentioned, be not of a *moral* nature, (and since both the motive of *interest* on one side, and that of *duty* on the other, are expressly excluded, every thing else of a moral nature seems to be excluded along with them) the determination cannot with propriety be denominated *moral,* or be said to be either *virtuous* or *vicious.*

. Dr. Price, on this occasion, supposes that a strict equality of motives is a very common case. I answer that we are, indeed, sometimes sensible of it, but that then the determination always remains in suspense. For it appears to me that, if we give attention to the state of our minds, we shall see reason enough to conclude that we never come to an actual determination without a sufficient preponderance of motive. And if we consider that the ,force of a motive depends upon *the state of the mind* to which, it is presented, as well as upon what it is in itself, that the state of mind is in perpetual fluctuation, and that the point of light in which we view the same thing is continually varying, we shall not be at all surprised that, in ordinary cases, when nothing of much consequence is depending, we determine with such readiness, and from motives so evanescent, that we are not able to trace the progress of our thoughts, so as distinctly to recollect the real causes of our choice, after the shortest interval of time. If it were possible to make a balance which should support a thousand pounds' weight, and yet turn with one thousandth part of a grain, would it be any wonder that a person should not be able easily to bring it to an equipoise? But what is even this to the exquisite structure of the mind?

Dr. Price acknowledges, as above, that " it is nonsense to deny the influence of motives, or to maintain that there are no fixed principles and ends by which the will is guided;" but at the same time he says " that this nonsense is scarcely equal to that of confounding *moral* with *physical causes*," (p. 95). Now if what I have said on this subject both in my *Treatise on Necessity*, and in my *Letter to Dr. Horsley* be not satisfactory, I shall despair of ever being able to give satisfaction with respect to any thing. I will even grant moral and physical causes to be as different, in their nature and operation, as Dr. Price himself can possibly suppose them to be; but if they be really *causes*, producing *certain effects*, that is, if we be so constituted, as that one definite determination shall always follow a definite state of mind, it must be true that, without a miracle, no volition, or action, could have been otherwise than it *has been*, *is*, or *is to be;* and this is all that, as a necessarian, I contend for. If any person can please himself with calling this *liberty*, or the result of the *mind's determining itself*, I have no sort of objection, because these are mere *words* and *phrases*.

Dr. Price calls the doctrine of necessity, according to which all events, moral as well as natural, are ultimately ascribed to God, a *deadly potion*, (p. 97,) and yet he hesitates not to say that he believes " no event comes to pass which it would have been proper to exclude, and that, relatively to the divine plan and administration, all is right," (p. 99). Now, between this doctrine, and those naked views of the doctrine of necessity at which Dr. Price is so much alarmed, I see no real difference. When a person can once bring himself to think that there is no wickedness of man which it would have been proper to exclude, and that the divine plan *requires* this wickedness, as well as every thing else that actually takes place (which is the purport of what Dr. Price advances, and very nearly his

own words) I wonder much that he should hesitate to admit
that the Divine Being might expressly *appoint* what it
would have been improper to exclude, what his plan absolutely required, and that without which the scheme could
not have been right, but must have been wrong.

May not this view of the subject, as given by Dr. Price,
be represented as an *apology for vice,* and a *thing to be
shuddered at,* and to be *fled from,* which is the language
that he uses, (p. 97,) with respect to the doctrine of necessity? If to make vice *necessary* be deadly poison, can that
doctrine be innocent which considers it as a thing that is
proper, and, relatively to the divine plan and administration,
right? The two opinions, if not the same, are certainly
very near *akin,* and must have the same kind of operation
and effect.

If Dr. Price will attend to *facts,* he may be satisfied that
it *cannot* require that great *strength* and *soundness of constitution* that he charitably ascribes to me, to convert the
doctrine of necessity, poison as he thinks it to be, into
wholesome nourishment, and that he must have seen it in
some very unfair and injurious light. I am far from being
singular in my belief of this doctrine. There are thousands,
I doubt not, who believe it as firmly as I do. A great
majority of the more intelligent, serious, and virtuous of my
acquaintance among men of letters, are necessarians; (as,
with respect to several of them, Dr. Price himself very well
knows) and we all think ourselves the better for it. Can
we *all* have this peculiar strength of constitution? It cannot
be surely deadly poison which so many persons take, not
only without injury, but with advantage, finding it to be,
as Dr. Price acknowledges with respect to myself, even
salutary. Ibid..

We are all, no doubt, constituted much alike, how different soever may be the opinions that we entertain concerning the principles of our common nature. I, therefore, infer
that Dr. Price himself, if it were possible for him to become
a necessarian, would think it not only a very harmless, but
a great and glorious scheme, worthy of a Christian divine
and philosopher, and that he would smile, as I myself now
do, at the notions which we first entertained of it.

Dr. Price also imagines that the belief of the doctrine
of necessity must " operate like a dead weight upon the
creation, breaking every aspiring effort, and producing
universal abjectness. The natural effect of believing
that nothing is left to depend on ourselves, and that we

can *do* nothing, must be concluding that we have nothing to do." P. 98.

But I have observed in my *Treatise on Necessity* that, in the only sense in which the consideration of it can operate as a motive of action, *every thing depends upon ourselves*, much more so than upon any other scheme ; (Vol. III. p. 502,) and therefore that the necessarian must feel himself more strongly impelled to an exertion of his faculties than any other man.

By a man's *making his own fortune*, I mean that his *success* depends upon his *actions*, as these depend upon his *volitions*, and his volitions upon the *motives* presented to him. Supposing a man, therefore, to have *propensities* and *objects of pursuit*, as his own happiness, &c. &c. of which no system of faith can deprive him, he will necessarily be roused to exert himself in proportion to the strength of his propensity, and his belief of the necessary connexion between his *end* and his *endeavours;* and nothing but such an opinion as that of philosophical liberty, which destroys that necessary connexion, can possibly slacken his endeavours.

With respect to this also, let Dr. Price consider whether his *theory* has any correspondence with *facts*. Let him consider those of his acquaintance who are necessarians. To say nothing of myself, who certainly, however, am not the most torpid and lifeless of all animals ; where will he find greater ardour of mind, a stronger and more unremitted exertion, or a more strenuous and steady pursuit of the most important objects, than among those of whom he knows to be necessarians? I can say with truth (and meaning no disparagement to Dr. Price, and many others, who, I believe, unknown to themselves, derive much of the excellence of their characters from principles very near akin to those of the doctrine of necessity), that I generally find *Christian necessarians* the most distinguished for active and sublime virtues, and more so in proportion to their steady belief of the doctrine, and the attention they habitually give to it. I appeal to every person who has read *Dr. Hartley's Observations on Man*, whether he can avoid having the same conviction with respect to him.

It is at *names* more than *things* that people in general are most frightened. Dr. Horsley is clearly a necessarian, in every thing but the name. He avows his belief that every determination of the mind certainly follows from previous circumstances, so that without a miracle, no volition or action could have been otherwise than it *has been*, *is*, or *is*

to be, and ,yet he disclaims the doctrine of necessity. Dr.
Price does not properly maintain the doctrine, but he stands
on the very brink of that tremendous precipice ; believing
that the mind cannot act without a motive, but thinking
to secure his liberty on the supposition that the mind (I
suppose, without any motive whatever) has the power of
choosing what motive it will act from ;· and believing with
the necessarian, that every thing is *as it should be,* and *as the
divine plan required it to be.*

Upon the whole, both he and Dr. Horsley appear to me
to want nothing more than what is called *courage* fully to
adopt and boldly defend the doctrine of necessity in *its
proper terms,* and to *its full extent.* - I well remember to
have had the same fears and apprehensions about the doctrine of necessity that they now express ; but being compelled by mere *force of argument,* to believe it to be *true,*
I was by degrees reconciled to it, and presently found that
there was nothing to be dreaded in it, but, on the contrary,
every thing that can give the greatest satisfaction to a well-
disposed mind, capable of any degree of comprehension or
extent of view. I think it much better, however, to admit
the doctrine of necessity explicitly, and with all its consequences, than be compelled to admit the same consequences
in other words, and in conjunction with principles that are
quite discordant with it.

To take off the dark cloud that Dr. Price has in these
last Observations thrown over the doctrine of necessity, I
shall not here repeat what I have on former occasions advanced in its favour, but shall leave it to make whatever
impression it may on our readers.

What Dr. Price says of *the soul,* that it is. " possessed of
faculties which make it an image of the Deity, and render
it capable of acting by the same rule with him, of participating of his happiness, and of living for ever, and improving
for ever under his eye and care," (p. 98,) I can say of *man.*
But I do not think that, for this purpose, it is at all necessary
that the mind should be *incorporeal, uncompounded* or *self-
determining,* arrogating to ourselves the attributes of *little
independent gods.* To whatever kind of substance, though
it should be the humblest *dust of the earth,* that the truly
noble prerogatives of man be imparted, it will appear to me
equally respectable. For it is not the *substance,* but the
properties, or *powers,* that make it so.

I also *reverence myself,* but not in the character of a being
self-determined, or *self-existent,* but as the rational offspring

of the first great and only proper cause of all things. By his power I am animated, by his wisdom I am conducted, and by his bounty I am made happy. It is only from the idea I have of my near relation to this great and glorious Being, and of my intimate connexion with him, that my exultation arises; far from founding it upon the idea that I have a will that is not ultimately his, or a single thought that he cannot controul. " Of him, and through him, and to him, are all things To him," therefore, and not to ourselves, " be glory."

Dr. Price lays great stress on the consideration of God being a *self-determining* and *self-moving* being, as a proof that man *may* be so too, (pp. 95 and 96 ;) and considering *self-determining* as equivalent to *self-moving*, and this is as equivalent to what we mean by a *self-existent*, or *first cause*, I have not objected to applying that appellation to the Divine Being; but I would observe, that in this I mean nothing more than to express my total want of conception concerning the *cause* or *reason* of the *existence*, and if I may so say, of the *original action*, of the Deity. For, considering the Divine Being as *actually existing*, I have no more idea of the possibility of his acting without a motive, (if there be any analogy between the divine mind and ours,) than of any created being doing so; and to ascribe this self-determining power to the Divine Being, meaning by it that *he acts without a motive*, or *reason*, is certainly so far from exalting the Deity, that we cannot form any idea of him more degrading. It is to divest him at once of all his moral perfections. For to act invariably from good principles, or motives, (in whatever it be that we make goodness or virtue to consist) is essential to moral excellence.

As to the *cause*, or *account*, as Dr. Price expresses it, of the divine existence, I profess to have no idea at all. That there must be a necessarily existing being, or a first cause, follows undeniably from the existence of other things; but the same disposition to inquire into the causes of things would lead us on *ad infinitum*, were it not that we see a manifest absurdity in it; so that, confounding as it is to the imagination, we are under an absolute necessity of acquiescing in the idea of a *self-existent being*.

Every thing that I have yet seen advanced with respect to the proper *cause*, or *reason* of the divine existence, appears to me either to suggest no ideas at all, or to give false ones. Dr. Clarke says, that *the Deity exists by an absolute necessity in the nature of things*, but this expression gives me no proper idea ;. for, exclusive of that necessity by which we are compelled to admit that such a being exists, which may be called necessity *a posteriori*, I am satisfied that no man, let his reasoning faculties be what they will, can have the least idea of any necessity. Of necessity *a priori* it is impossible we should know any thing. Let any person only exclude all idea of creation, which is not difficult, and consider whether in those circumstances he can discover a cause of any existence at all. To talk of *the nature of things* in this case, is to my understanding mere jargon, or a cloak for absolute ignorance.

Dr. Price himself does not seem to be satisfied with this explanation of the cause of the divine existence, and therefore suggests a different idea; saying that " the account of the divine existence is the same with the account of the existence of space and duration, of the equality of the three angles of a triangle to two right angles, or of any abstract truth;" (pp. 96, 97.) Now, as Dr. Clarke's language gives me no idea at all, this account appears to me to suggest a false one.

Though there may be the same necessity for the existence of the Deity, and for that of space or duration, we are not able to see it.* I can, in any case, form an idea of the non-existence both of all *effects* and of all *causes*, and consequently both of the creation and of the Creator, and of the non-existence of the latter just as easily as of that of the former : but still the ideas of *space* and *duration* remain in the mind, and cannot be excluded from it. To say that space is an *attribute of the Deity*, or that it necessarily implies and draws after it the idea of his existence, appears to me to have no foundation whatever, and to have been assumed without the least face of probability. For this I appeal to what passes in any person's mind.

Again, the reason of the divine existence, and that of an abstract truth, as that the three angles of a triangle are equal to two right angles, appear to me to have no sort of analogy. They agree in nothing but that both of them are true, but with respect to the *reason* or *cause of their being true*, no two things, in my opinion, can be more unlike.

An abstract truth is no *being, substance,* or *reality* whatever. It implies nothing more than the agreement of two ideas, whether the archetypes of those ideas have any exist-

* Corrected from the former Edition in the Author's Preface to " Letters to a

ence or not, and of this agreement we have the most perfect comprehension. Nothing can be more intelligible. Now, if our persuasion of this abstract truth was of the same nature with our persuasion concerning the existence of God, we should have the same perfect comprehension of the latter that we have of the former. But can any person seriously say this, when of the former we know *every thing*, and of the latter absolutely *nothing?* Let any person exclude from his mind all idea of the creation, and consider whether there be any thing left that will compel him to believe the existence of any *thing, being,* or *substance* whatever. A *creation* necessarily implies a *creator,* but if there be no creation, the only proof of the existence of a creator is cut off.

The cause of the existence of a *thing, substance,* or *being,* cannot, in the nature of things, be the same with that of a mere abstract hypothetical truth. The cause of a being, or substance, must be a being or substance also; and therefore, with respect to the Divine Being we are obliged to say that he has *no proper cause whatever.* The agreement of two ideas is a thing so very different in its nature from this, that the term *cause* is not even applicable to it; as, on the other hand, I see no meaning whatever in the word *account* as applicable to the divine existence. In this case there must either be *a cause,* or *no cause. Account,* here, is to me a word without meaning.

If by the word *account,* we mean the same with *reason,* the cases are clearly the farthest in the world from being parallel. If I be asked the reason why the three angles of a triangle are equal to two right angles, I answer, that the quantity of the three, and that of the two, is the same, or that the ideas, when rightly understood, exactly *coincide.* But if I be asked why the Divine Being exists (I say *why he exists,* not why I *believe* him to exist), can I satisfy any body, or myself, by saying that the two ideas in the proposition *God exists* are the same, or coincide? Is the idea of *God,* and that of mere *existence* the same idea? The two cases, therefore, have nothing in them at all parallel. How then can the *reason, account,* or *cause* of an *abstract truth,* be of *the same nature* with the reason, account, or cause of the *divine existence?*

————

I shall now conclude the whole controversy with mentioning what appear to me to be the things on which the principal arguments in each part of it turn, and the misconceptions that Dr. Price seems to me to have laboured under.

On the subject of the *penetrability of matter*, he has never produced what I have repeatedly called for, viz. *one case of real unquestionable contact*, without which the doctrine of proper impenetrability cannot be supported. And till this be produced, I am obliged to conclude, from analogy, that *all* resistance is owing to such causes as we both agree that, in *many*, if not in *most cases*, it does certainly arise from ; and this is not *solidity*, or impenetrability, but something very different from it.

With respect to the doctrine of *a soul*, Dr. Price appears to me to have been misled principally by his notion of the *absolute simplicity*, or *indivisibility* of the mind, or the thinking principle in man, as if it was a thing of which we could be *conscious;* whereas I think I have shewn sufficiently that we cannot be conscious of any thing relating to the *essence of the mind;* that we are properly conscious of nothing but what we *perceive*, and what we *do*. As to what we *are*, it is a thing that we must learn by way of *inference* and *deduction* from observations or consciousness ; and I think the *arguments* are decisively against such a simplicity and indivisibility as Dr. Price supposes.

On the subject of the doctrine of *necessity*, Dr. Price agrees with Dr. Horsley in admitting that our volitions *certainly* and invariably depend upon the preceding state of mind ; so that, without a miracle, there was a real necessity of every thing being as it *has been, is*, or *is to be ;* and imagines that the controversy depends on what I think to be the mere verbal distinction, of motives being the *moral*, and not the *physical causes* of our volitions and actions ; or, as he sometimes expresses himself, that it is not the motives that determine the mind, but that the mind determines itself according to the motives ; which I maintain to be the doctrine of necessity, only disguised in other words. Indeed, how any man can boast of his liberty, merely because he has a power of determining himself, when, at the same time, he knows that he cannot do it in any other than *in one precise and definite manner*, strictly depending upon the circumstances in which he is placed, and when he believes that, in no one action of his life, he could have determined otherwise than he has done, is to me a little difficult of comprehension.

As to *real liberty*, or the power of acting independently of motives, he expressly confines it to those cases in which the motives for and against any particular choice are *exactly equal*. Such cases, I think, seldom or never occur ; so that a man could have but few opportunities of shewing such a liberty as this. If they should occur, and any determination take place in those circumstances, it appears to me to be attended with the *absurdity* (as Dr. Price himself calls it) of determining without a motive ; and I should think that after supposing it possible that the mind might determine *without* a motive, it might also determine *contrary* to all motive. For the same constitution of mind that could enable it to do the one, would enable it to do the other.

A Letter *to* Dr. Price.

Dear Sir,

With this letter you will receive a few remarks on your *Additional Observations*, which I have read with that *attention* which every thing from you demands. That it has not been with *conviction*, your candour, I know, will not impute to any peculiar *obstinacy*, but to my unavoidably seeing the subjects of our discussion in a light different from that in which you see them. We have not the same idea of the nature of the human mind, or of the laws to which it is sub-ject, but we are both sufficiently aware of the force of *prejudice*, and that this may equally throw a bias on the side of *long established* or of *novel* opinions. Also, equally respect-ing the christian maxim of *doing to others as we would that others should do to us*, we are each of us ready to give to others that liberty which we claim ourselves ; while we equally reprobate those rash sentiments which proceed from a decision without a previous discussion of the reasons for and against a question in debate.

I am not a little proud of your commendation of me for my " fairness in the pursuit of truth," and following it " into all its consequences, however frightful, without attempting to evade or palliate them ;" (p. 97.) It is a conduct that I hope I shall always pursue, as the first of duties to that God who has given me whatever *faculties* I possess, and whatever *opportunity of inquiry* I have been favoured with ; and I trust I shall continue to pursue this conduct at all risks. As he is properly no Christian, who does not *confess Christ before men*, or who is *ashamed* of his religion in an unbe-lieving age, like the present ; this maxim, which the author of our religion inculcates with respect to Christianity in general, the reason of the thing requires that we extend to every thing that essentially affects Christianity.

So long, therefore, as I conceive the doctrine of a *separate soul,* to have been the true source of the grossest corruptions in the christian system, of that very *anti-christian system* which sprung up in the times of the apostles, concerning which they entertained the strongest apprehensions, and delivered, and left upon record, the most solemn warnings, I must think myself a very lukewarm and disaffected Christian if I do not bear my feeble testimony against it.

With respect to the private conduct of individuals, as affecting our happiness after death, I do not lay any stress upon this, or upon *any opinion whatever;* and there is no person of whose christian temper and conduct I think more highly than I do of yours, though you hold opinions the very reverse of mine, and defend them with so much zeal ; a zeal which, while you maintain the opinions at all, is certainly commendable. But with respect to the *general plan of Christianity*, the importance of the doctrines I contend for can hardly, in my opinion, be rated too high. What I contend for leaves nothing for the manifold corruptions and abuses of Popery to fasten on. Other doctrinal reformations are partial things, while this goes to the very root of almost all the mischief we complain of ; and, for my part, I shall not date the proper and complete downfall of what is called *antichrist,* but from the general prevalence of the doctrine of materialism.

This I cannot help saying appears to me to be that fundamental principle in true philosophy which is alone perfectly consonant to the doctrine of the Scriptures ; and being at the same time the only proper deduction from natural appearances, it must, in the progress of inquiry soon *appear to be so ;* and then, should it be found that an unquestionably true philosophy teaches one thing, and revelation another, the latter could not stand its ground, but must inevitably be exploded, as contrary to *truth and fact.* I therefore deem it to be of particular consequence, that philosophica unbelievers should be apprised in time, that there are Christians, who consider the *doctrine of a soul* as a tenet that is so far from being *essential* to the christian scheme, that it is a thing quite *foreign* to it, derived originally from Heathenism, discordant with the genuine principles of revealed religion, and ultimately subversive of them.

As to the doctrine of *necessity,* I cannot, after all our discussion, help considering it as *demonstrably true,* and the only possible foundation for the doctrines of a *Providence*, and the *moral government of God.*

Continuing to see things in this light, after the closest attention that I have been able to give to them, before, or in the course of our friendly debate (and you will pardon me, if I add, seeing this in a stronger light than ever), you will not be displeased with the *zeal* that I have occasionally shewn ; as I, on my part, entirely approve of yours, who consider yourself as defending important and long-received truth, against fundamental and most dangerous innovations.

We are neither of us so far blinded by prejudice as not to see, and acknowledge, the wisdom of constituting us in such a manner, as that every thing *new* respecting a subject of so much consequence as *religion*, should excite a great alarm and meet with great difficulty in establishing itself. This furnishes an occasion of a thorough examination and discussion of all new doctrines, in consequence of which they are either totally exploded, or more firmly established. The slow and gradual progress of Christianity, and also that of the reformation, is a circumstance that bids fairer for their perpetuity, than if they had met with a much readier reception in the world. You will allow me to indulge the hope of a similar advantage from the opposition that I expect to this article of reformation in the christian system, and that the truth I contend for will be the more valued for being dearly bought, and slowly acquired.

As to the *odium* that I may bring upon myself by the malevolence of my opposers, of which, in your letter to me, you make such obliging mention, I hope the same consciousness of not having deserved it, will support me as it has done you, when much worse treated than I have yet been, on an occasion on which you deserved the warmest gratitude of your country, whose interests you studied and watched over, whose calamities you foresaw, and faithfully pointed out ; and which might have derived, in various respects, the most solid and durable advantages from your labours. But we are no Christians, if we have not so far imbibed the principles and spirit of our religion, as even to *rejoice that we are counted worthy of suffering* in any good cause.

Here it is that, supposing me to be a defender of *christian truth*, my object gives me an advantage that your excellent *political writings* cannot give you. All your observations may be just, and your advice most excellent, and yet your country, the safety and happiness of which you have at heart, being in the hands of infatuated men, may go to ruin; whereas christian truth is a cause *founded upon a rock*, and though it may be overborne for a time, we are assured that the *gates of death shall not prevail against it.*

Having now, each of us, defended, in the best manner that we can, what we deem to be this important truth, we are, I doubt not, equally satisfied with ourselves, and shall cheerfully submit the result of our discussion to the judgment of our friends, and of the public, and to the final and infallible determination of the *God of all truth.*

I am, notwithstanding this, and every other possible difference in *mere opinion*, with the most perfect esteem,

Dear Sir,

Yours most affectionately,

J. PRIESTLEY.

Calne, Oct. 2, 1778.

NOTE *to* DR. PRIESTLEY.

DR. PRICE desires Dr. Priestley's acceptance of his gratitude for the expressions of his kindness and regard in the preceding letter; and assures him in return of his best wishes and ardent esteem. The controversy between them having grown much too tedious, he thinks there is a necessity of now dropping it. He cannot therefore persuade himself to enter farther into it; or to say any more than that his sentiments are undesignedly misrepresented, when, in p. 109, Dr. Priestley suggests, that he considers wickedness as *a thing that is proper*, and thinks the *plan of the Deity absolutely required it.* He has never meant to say more, than that the *permission* of wickedness is *proper;* and that (for the reasons mentioned in pp. 82, 83, 99) the divine plan required the communication of powers rendering beings capable of perversely *making themselves* wicked, by acting, not as the divine plan requires, (for this, he thinks, would be too good an excuse for wickedness) but, by acting in a manner that opposes the divine plan and will, and that would subvert the order of nature, and to which, on this account, punishment has been annexed.

ANSWER, *by* DR. PRIESTLEY.

DR. PRIESTLEY will always think himself happy in having an opportunity of expressing the very high and affectionate regard he entertains for Dr. Price, notwithstanding their difference of opinion on subjects of so much moment as those discussed in the present correspondence. He is confident that Dr. Price needs no assurance on the part of Dr. Priestley, that his sentiments have not been *knowingly* misrepresented ; but must take the liberty to say, that he cannot help considering the voluntary *permission* of evil, or the *certain cause* of it, by a Being who foresees it, and has sufficient power to prevent it, as equivalent to the express *appointment* of it.*

* The following passage from the *Dissertation on Providence*, will suitably conclude this *discussion*. It may, possibly, appear to some readers that Dr. Price was much nearer to his opponent in reality, than in his own apprehension. " In a word; the divine scheme is plainly, that events shall, to a certain degree, be what created agents make them. His will, in numberless cases, appears to be, that one being shall or shall not receive particular benefits, or suffer particular evils, as his fellow-beings shall please to determine. But then, this happens no farther than he knows to be best, and in no instances but such as he appoints. Every determination of every being, which would produce any degree of *wrong* suffering, or any event not consistent with a perfect order of administration, he will undoubtedly either prevent or over-rule in its consequences. He is present in all minds; and that whole concatenation of events and causes, in consequence of which any agent finds himself, at any time, in any circumstances, should be considered as derived from him, and as having been, in every part of it, the object of his superintending care. It would be denying the doctrine of Providence entirely, and making the universe in a manner forlorn and fatherless, to suppose that all that the Deity does is to endow beings with powers and affections, and then to turn them out into a wide theatre, there to scuffle as they can, and do what they please, without taking any care of them, or presiding over their affairs. We cannot be more sure of the moral perfections of the Deity than we are that this is false. Whatever evils there are in the world, they can be only such as he is pleased to admit into it. When he willed the existence of the present universe, he willed it as including every event which he foresaw would arise in it. All abuse of liberty and reason he does indeed disapprove and forbid, and will adequately punish. It is of essential malignity, and as far as it enters, tends to lay waste his works. But it can enter no further than he sees fit to suffer it. He had the best reasons for establishing at first those states and connexions of beings, from whence he knew it would spring. He can restrain and direct it as he pleases, and even turn it into an occasion of good." *Dissertations,* pp. 96—98.

LETTERS.

To the Author of

THE

LETTERS ON MATERIALISM,

TO

Dr. KENRICK, Mr. JOHN WHITEHEAD and Dr. HORSLEY.

To the Author of the LETTERS ON MATERIALISM *and on* HARTLEY'S THEORY OF THE MIND.[*]

SIR;

You have challenged me to the discussion of a variety of topics, some of which are the most difficult, sublime and important of any that lie within the reach of the human understanding ; and where the greatest men have expressed the greatest diffidence, you have written with the greatest possible confidence. Also, if your language be not ironical, you consider your antagonist as the most formidable combatant you could have to contend with. You have, on various occasions, expressed the highest opinion of my learning and abilities, and the strongest sense of my merit and services in the cause of literature, and where knowledge of the most valuable kind was concerned. To pass over what you say in general of my " eminent abilities and indefatigable labours in every learned and valuable pursuit," and also with respect to natural philosophy in particular, than which nothing finer can be said of any man, you are more particularly lavish of your encomiums upon me on the subject of my controversy with the Scotch defenders of the

---

[*] The author was the Rev. J. Berington. See Vol. III. pp. 215, 262, 268—270, 284—286 This letter was annexed to the *Illustrations of Necessity* in 1777, and in 1782 prefixed to the three following letters, which had been first published, with the Free Discussion, in 1778. See p. 15, *Note.*

doctrine of *Instinctive Principles of Truth*, in which I had occasion to introduce several of the opinions which have given you so much offence, and which you call upon me to defend.

As a prudent man, you certainly would not have provoked a combat in the very high tone in which you have done this, without the greatest certainty of success. You have, no doubt, therefore, in your own mind, *counted the cost* of the enterprise you have undertaken, and have already anticipated my confusion and your complete triumph.

Now it happens that so very great a philosopher, and so acute a metaphysician, as you represent me to be, and who has had the subjects on which you so boldly challenge me in contemplation from the time that I was capable of considering them at all, to the present time of my life, which is the memorable year *forty-five*, a period in which, at a medium, the human faculties may be deemed to have arrived at their very ἀκμή; a period in which we expect a due mixture of imagination and judgment, in which the ardour of youth is not extinguished, but improved into a manly vigour: it happens, I say, that, in these very advantageous circumstances, in which you and nature have placed me, after having had your Letters in my hands about twelve months, and having in that time exercised my faculties in a close attention to metaphysical subjects, as, I hope, my *Disquisitions on Matter and Spirit*, and the preceding treatise on *Philosophical Necessity* will prove, I do now, with great seriousness aver, that, in my opinion, hardly any of the works of the three Scotch writers, which you and I hold so cheap, is weaker in point of argument than yours. I barely except that of Dr. Oswald, who is certainly one of the most dogmatical and absurd of all writers

Farther, though, judging by facts, there is but little reason to expect that any man who has given to the public his opinion on any subject of importance, will ever retract it, I think I perceive marks of so much candour and ingenuousness in some parts of your Letters (though I own I perceive but few traces of those qualities in other places), that I do not absolutely despair of engaging you to *acknowledge*, that you have fallen into several very important mistakes ; at least, that your virulent censures of myself, and my opinions, are abundantly too severe. For this purpose, I shall lay before you a few plain considerations, to which I beg, in the first place, a very deliberate attention, and then an explicit answer. As I have already discussed sufficiently, as I think, at large, the principal points in debate between us, in the preceding treatises, I shall, in this letter, only briefly refer to them.

You will think it extraordinary that the first point I beg you would attend to, and be explicit upon, is, whether you do really hold any opinion different from mine, at least whether you do not acknowledge principles which necessarily, and not remotely, but *immediately*, draw after them the belief of all that I have contended for? And yet I am pretty confident that I can make this out to the satisfaction of others, and even to your own, with respect to the two great articles on which you arraign me, viz. the doctrines of *necessity* and of *materialism*.

Of the Doctrine of NECESSITY.

You expressly allow a *constant influence of motives to determine the will*. *The moral*, you say, *is as certain as is the physical cause;* (p. 171,) and you will not deny (for no man can do it) that the immediate consequence of this position is, that the Divine Being, who established this constant dependence of human volitions upon preceding motives and the state of mind, could not intend that any volition or choice, should have been otherwise than it has been, is, or is to be. You are, therefore, as much a necessarian as myself; and all your copious declamation upon this topic, concerning the great mischief done to morals and society, &c. &c. &c. affects yourself as much as it does me.

If the mind be, in fact, *constantly* determined by motives, I desire you would say candidly why you object to the mere term *necessity*, by which nothing is ever meant but the *cause of constancy*. As I have observed before, it is only because I see a stone fall to the ground *constantly*, that I infer it does so *necessarily*, or *according to some fixed law of nature;* and please to say whether you think it could happen, that the mind could be constantly determined by motives, if there be not a fixed law of nature, from which that constant determination results. Indeed, Sir, this is so very plain, that you must either avow yourself *a necessarian*, dreadfully as the term may sound in your ears, or adopt some quite new ground of defence, some new principles of human liberty, that is, some *other kind of liberty* than what you have yet contended for.

As far as the consequences of the *doctrine of necessity*

affect the Deity, you, who believe the divine prescience, make no scruple to admit them. You say, " Why a benevolent Creator gave free will to man, which he foresaw would be to his unhappiness and ruin, you can assign no other reason, than that such a being entered into his general plan of existence." P. 188.

You admit, therefore, that all the actual consequences of free will, the unhappiness and ruin of a great proportion of mankind, entered into the general plan of Providence, which is as much as saying that the plan required them, and could not proceed so well without them. And, if so, what objection can you have to the Divine Being having absolutely *decreed* them ? If his plan absolutely required these evils, it is plain, that, at any rate, he must introduce them. All the difference that there can possibly be between us is, that, according to you, the divine plan required *free will*, though necessarily attended with the evils you mention, and I say that his plan required *general* and *ultimate happiness*, though necessarily attended with the same evils. According to us both, the evils were necessarily, either to free will or to general happiness.

Of MATERIALISM.

The next great argument between us is, the uniform composition and materiality of the whole man. But, though you express the greatest abhorrence of this sentiment, I call upon you to shew that you yourself do not virtually admit it. You expressly declare for the doctrine of a proper *physical influence* between the mind and the body, as *the only philosophical notion*, and you maintain that the two substances *mutually act and re-act upon each other.* P. 76. Now this you explain on principles that most evidently set aside all distinction between matter and spirit, and make them to be as much of the same composition as I do myself. For you say that, " in order to this mutual action, spirit must be possessed of such inferior qualities, as are not unalliable with the more exalted species of matter." Now the most exalted species of matter possible must have length, breadth and thickness, and in the common opinion, *solidity*, or it would not be matter at all. And I call upon you to say whether those inferior qualities of spirit, by which it is capable of acting, and of being acted upon, by a substance that has no properties besides extension and solidity, must not be comprised under those of extension and solidity ? I will venture to say that you cannot name any other quality that will answer your purpose. In fact, therefore, you maintain exactly what I do, viz. that a substance possessed of the properties of matter may have those of perception and thought likewise. You may use a different language, but our ideas are the very same. I appeal to your own more mature reflections on the subject. I also desire you to explain how spirit, as you say, can *bear no relation to space*, (p. 76,) and yet be possessed of some properties in common with those of matter.

Besides ascribing to spirit the properties of matter, to confound them more effectually, you farther ascribe to matter the peculiar properties of spirit, for you give it an *active power*, which all other immaterialists, and indeed all consistent immaterialists, say is incompatible with their idea of matter. I desire you would tell me, therefore, why, if one species of active power (for you are not explicit enough to say *what kind* of active power you mean) may be imparted to matter, *another*, or *any other* species of it, may not? And what has the power of *thought* always been defined to be, but a particular species of active power?

These remarks, I will venture to say, are so very plain, that a much worse understanding than yours must be convinced of the justness of them, and a small degree of ingenuousness will produce an avowal of that conviction. These remarks also comprise all the great subjects on which we differ. As lesser matters, not worth repeating here, I desire you would say what you have to advance in defence of your notion of *space*, on which I have remarked, and what you mean by saying it is an " ideal phenomenon, arising from the external order of co-existing bodies." P. 58. To me the expression is absolute jargon. Tell me also what you have to reply to my answer to your argument on the subject of *attention*. P. 92.

I shall now advert to some other matters not discussed in either of the preceding treatises: and here, also, I have no doubt but that I shall make your mistakes and misrepresentations palpable even to yourself.

Of INSTINCTIVE PRINCIPLES.

What you say in order to prove that my own principles, or rather those of Dr. Hartley, are as unfriendly to the cause of truth as the doctrine of instinctive principles, is so exceedingly trifling and foreign to the purpose, that had I not seen it in the same book, I could not have persuaded myself that a person who joins me so very heartily as you do in my condemnation of that system, could possibly have written it.

You were " highly pleased," you say, " to see a doctrine so triumphantly thrown down from its usurped empire, which had, within a few years, gained an astonishing ascendancy over minds that should have been aware of its fallacy and erroneous principles;" (p. 8,) and upon many other occasions you express the strongest approbation of my services to the cause of truth on this account.

After this I might well be surprised to find myself accused of maintaining principles equally, or more unfavourable to the doctrine concerning *truth;* but I own I was still more surprised, when I perceived the foundation on which you advance this extraordinary charge, and that the only similarity you pretend to find between the doctrine of instinctive principles of truth and that of Dr. Hartley, is, that the assent to propositions is in both equally *necessary* and *infallible.* P. 122. " In both systems," you say, " belief, as well as every mental affection, is a necessary and mechanical effect." P. 123. The only difference, you say, " there is betwixt them seems to be, that Dr. Hartley admits of no effect for which he does not assign as the proper cause, some nervous vibration, whilst the Doctors, without any sufficient reason, are labouring to establish others which spring up immechanically, but however from some internal impulse. As far, therefore, as sensations, sensitive ideas, and their necessary Scotch adjuncts go, the dissimilarity of opinion is but trifling: they are all the effects of constitution, or pre-established laws." *Ibid.*

You also say, that " whenever any phenomenon of the human mind is explained by association, a cause is produced in its nature as impulsive and necessary as can possibly be the most unerring instinct; with this only difference, that your system must be productive of eternal discordance, and variety in opinions and feelings." P. 132.

Now surely, Sir, if you have read Mr. Locke, or indeed any other writer on the subject of the human mind, you must have found that, according to him, and all of them, how free soever man is described as *willing*, his *judgment* is always supposed to be necessary, or mechanical. Indeed, what is judgment, but the perception of the agreement or disagreement of ideas present to the mind? Now you expressly allow (indeed, with all the world) that the mind is passive in perception, that is, that all our perceptions must necessarily depend upon the objects present to us, and the state of the organs through which the ideas of them are transmitted. If I open my eyes, labouring under no disorder, and there be only a sheep before me, I cannot possibly see a horse; and if there be a young lamb accompanying the sheep, I necessarily *see*, and therefore *judge*, that the sheep is the bigger of the two. Now every other act of proper and simple judgment is as necessary and unavoidable, or in your own language, as much the *effect of constitution* and *established laws*, as this; and complex reasoning is all reducible to acts of simple judgment, as every logician knows. It is, therefore, impossible but that we must judge of all things as they appear to us, and it is this difference in the appearance of things that is the cause of the differences in the judgments that different men form of the same things. These are principles that you *must* admit, and therefore, all your violent declamation on the subject falls upon yourself, as well as on my devoted head.

Your censure of me on this subject is the more extraordinary, as upon another occasion, you complain of my principles as not sufficiently securing the assent to truth; for you say, " If every perception be factitious, then, in spite of all internal reasons and relations in the objects, our sentiments must widely deviate from, and the consequent actions be in direct opposition to, every thing that is right and virtuous. To obviate such deleterious effects, it appears that an all-wise Being must have provided some principle, *innate to our very constitutions*, whereby the charms of truth and virtue might be felt, and their respective rights immoveably fixed, in opposition to error and vice." P. 156.

Now really, Sir, notwithstanding your professed abhorrence of the principle of *instinctive belief*, I do not see of what other nature can be this principle of yours, which you say is *innate to our very constitutions*, and *by which the charms of truth and virtue may be felt, and their respective rights immoveably fixed, in opposition to error and vice*. I do not see how Messrs. Reid, Beattie and Oswald could have expressed their own meaning more properly, or that you can account for the actual prevalence of error and vice in the world, any better on your principles than they can on theirs. What then becomes of your vehement censures of me, as maintaining principles as subversive of truth as those of their reprobated system?

When, in favour of *your* instinctive principles of truth,

you object to mine of *association*, that they must be productive of *infinite discordancy, and variety of opinions and
feelings*, (p. 133,) you mention a remarkable fact, which, as
it appears to me, cannot be accounted for but upon the
principle of the association of ideas. This will, indeed,
fully account for the actual discordancy and variety of
opinions and feelings in the world, and in the most natural
manner; and these, I say, are inconsistent with any doctrine of instinctive principles of truth, whether maintained
by the Scotch Doctors, or by yourself.

Gross Misconstruction of Dr. Hartley's Meaning.

You sneer at me as a *rapid writer*, but rapid as my writings
have been, they appear *to my own review*, to have been sufficiently guarded. For, without excepting any thing *material*,
or any thing more than the slowest writers in general may
wish to correct and improve in their works, I do not know
of any thing that I now wish to have written otherwise than
it is. You, on the contrary, I presume, have written with
great caution, and have given sufficient time to your publication; and when, with all due precautions and advice of
friends, you sent it abroad, I dare say you judged it to be
superior to any opposition that it could meet with. But
notwithstanding this, I doubt not but after the perusal of
these remarks, if not before, you will see reason to wish you
had written many things otherwise than you have done;
and I do not mean with respect to the *manner* only, but the
matter too. Some of the instances I have already mentioned
will, I am persuaded, make you pause; but I shall proceed
to mention a few more, for which no apology can be made,
the blunders in point of reasoning being too gross for any
palliation; and yet I do not profess myself to be master of
any uncommon art of detecting sophistry. What ought to
make you blush the more, they relate to two very heavy
charges, one against Dr. Hartley, and the other against
myself.

Dr. Hartley, with great ingenuousness and truth, had
said, "However the necessarian may in theory ascribe all
to God, yet the associations of life beget the idea and opinion of *self*, refer actions to this self, and connect a variety
of applauses and complacencies with those actions; and
therefore, that, as the asserters of philosophical free-will are
not necessarily proud, so the asserters of the doctrine of
mechanism are not necessarily humble." Now what can

be inferred from this concession, but that though the doctrine of necessity *tends* to cure pride and conceit, &c. the
influences to which we are exposed in life counteract this
tendency in a great measure? This, I will venture to say,
is all the *fair* inference that can be drawn from it.

Now what is the inference that you have drawn from it?
I think you will hardly believe that you could have written
any thing so very inconclusive and injurious. For you say,
that "in this the good Doctor, in a fit of holy zeal, was
determined, by one dash of his pen, totally to annihilate all
the boasted excellencies and superior advantages of mechanism. Therefore," you say, "has the doctrine of mechanism,
from the Doctor's own confession, a general tendency to cause
and support the vices of pride, vanity, self-conceit, and
contempt of our fellow-creatures. And I wish to God,"
you add, "these were the only evils which that doctrine is
calculated to generate, and immoveably to rivet in the
human breast—consequences so deleterious—*la tête me
tourne*." P. 193.

I do not, Sir, even in this, charge you, as you do me,
with a *wilful perversion* of the author's meaning. But it is
certainly a very unfortunate oversight, and of a very *calum-
niating and injurious tendency*, for which you will certainly
ask the Doctor and the public pardon. An exact parallel to
this conduct of yours, would be that of a physician; whose
prescription did *not quite cure* a disorder, by reason of the
patient's way of life necessarily promoting it, being charged
with *acknowledging*, that he administered medicines which
tended to aggravate the disease. Dr. Hartley does not say
that the *belief of the doctrine of mechanism*, but that the
associations of life did the mischief, notwithstanding the
good tendency of that doctrine.

Indeed, Sir, with respect to the unjust imputation of bad
designs in your antagonists, you are, whether knowingly or
unknowingly, a very dangerous writer, and such as the
public ought to be cautioned against ; for you have gone far
beyond the bounds, I do not say, of *decorum* only, but of
truth, and even of probability. You hint that Dr. Hartley
" wrote, and wrote so much about a thing, with a design of
puzzling his readers." P. 110. Now, that you should have
read Dr. Hartley's work, as you say, *four times over*, and
retain any such impression as this, astonishes me, but fully
convinces me that it must have been with a prejudice
which would effectually prevent your understanding him at
all. It is, in several respects, evident, that, as yet, you

are very little acquainted with his *theory;* though you tell us that you can say "without vanity, you understand him thoroughly," (p. 10,) and I am now satisfied that you have been as little able to distinguish, or to catch his *spirit.* Of one of my own paragraphs, you say, that it is *replete* with *falsehood and wilful misrepresentation.* I hope you will blush when you reflect a moment upon things so very gross as these.

Gross Misrepresentation of what I have said concerning a FUTURE LIFE, &c.

But I proceed to your account of one of my arguments, of which you seem to have understood as little as of the above-mentioned of Dr. Hartley. I had said what I believe to be very true, that "the doctrine of the immateriality of the soul has no countenance in the Scriptures," and you say, that "if so, the future existence of man must be given up, even on the part of revelation." But, upon the least reflection, you must see that, as a materialist and a Christian, I believe *the resurrection of the body,* that is of *the man;* and that upon this foundation only, in opposition to the opinion which places it on the *natural immortality of the soul,* I rest my belief of a future life.

The paragraph in which you make this strange construction of my meaning, is, in several respects, so curious, that I shall quote the whole of it, and it will serve to give my reader a pretty just specimen of your manner of treating me, and the subjects of this controversy.

"You declare that the doctrine of natural immortality has no countenance from the Scriptures. I am not in the least disposed to pervert your meaning. I am sensible of the enormity of the crime; but I should be exceedingly glad to know whether these words have any meaning at all. For if you mean to say that the doctrine of natural immortality is not itself, as such, contained in the Scriptures, you are, to be sure, in the right, because that doctrine, as the pure result of reason, most evidently is not a revealed truth. But if, as the words themselves express it, this doctrine has really no countenance from the Scriptures, then is the future existence of man not only false in philosophy, as you insist, but likewise in its theological acceptation. What then becomes of that part of the scheme of revelation on which you rest all your hopes of immortality? But such slips of the pen (as has already been urged in justification

of a similar oversight) are perhaps venial, and easily excuse-
able in the rapidity of composition, particularly of so hasty
a composer as Dr. Priestley." P. 221.

Pray, Sir, who is it that has written *hastily*, and needs
an apology in this case? I leave it to yourself to judge ;.
and I hope you will be duly sensible, as you say you are,
of the *enormity of the crime* of perverting my meaning.
Whatever the enormity be, you are certainly guilty of it.

However, you have not done with this subject, on which
you fancy you have so much the advantage of me, and,
poor as is the handle it gives you for cavilling, you are
willing to make a little more of it. You say, that "grant-
ing the notion of the immortality of the soul was imported
into Christianity from the heathen philosophy, how could
it possibly have contributed to deprave that religious system?
If the revealed tenet itself of immortality does not necessarily tend to corrupt the heart, or the christian institution,
can it by any means happen, that the same belief, when
supposed to spring from a second source, should produce
such pernicious effects? I blush, Sir, to suppose you capable of such flimsy reasoning. But the fact stands recorded
against you, and your philosophy must bear you through as
well as it may. It may perhaps be glorious to dissent
from the crowd ; but it is not, I am sure, rational, when
more plausible reasons for such conduct cannot be adduced."
P. 224.

Here again, notwithstanding your insulting me in this
manner, you appear to know so very little of the argument
you have undertaken to discuss, as to take it for granted,
that there can be no foundation for the belief of any future
life, but upon that of the *natural immortality of the human
soul,* as if you had never heard of the scripture doctrine of
the resurrection of the dead.

I shall now recite the whole of the paragraph on which
your most uncharitable censure of me, above-mentioned, is
founded, with another set of your remarks upon it, no less
extraordinary than those quoted above.

"The opinion of the natural immortality of the soul had
its origin in the heathen philosophy ; and having, with
other pagan notions, insinuated itself into Christianity,
which has been miserably depraved by this means, has been
the great support of the popish doctrines of *purgatory,* and
the *worship of the dead.*"

This paragraph I maintain to be, in its utmost extent,
strictly true, and I have little doubt but that the truth of it

will be sufficiently evident from what I have advanced in the *Disquisitions on Matter and Spirit,* and especially in the *Sequel* to them.   But supposing it had not been strictly true, it is not surely so *palpably untrue,* as that the misrepresentation must necessarily be wilful.   You say, however, on this occasion, " That a writer who plumes himself on the character of singular candour and sincerity, could have written a paragraph so replete with falsehood and wilful misrepresentation, is not, at least, a common phenomenon in the history of the human mind."

To the latter part of the paragraph, viz. that " the notion of the natural immortality of the soul has been the great support of the popish doctrines of *purgatory,* and the *worship of the dead,*" you say, " therefore, most certainly, it came from the devil, or what is worse, was invented by one of the antichrists of papal Rome.

" By purgatory (for I also understand something of the popish scheme of faith) is meant a place of expiatory punishment.   It is grounded on the belief of the soul's immortality, joined to a notion that nothing undefiled can enter into heaven.   But why should you fancy that this doctrine rests *solely* on the opinion of natural immortality, when a more adequate basis may be discovered, to wit, an express revelation, which both you and the Papists (what a monstrous coalition !) maintain, is ludicrous enough ?   Besides, what possible support can that romish tenet derive from the pagan sentiment in question ?   Just with equal propriety might you assert that the doctrines of hell and heaven (only that they are not exclusively popish) are sprung from, or at least founded on, the same opinion.

" *En passant,* Doctor, give me leave to ask what objection can you consistently have to the doctrine of *purgatory,* you who, I suppose with Dr. Hartley and others, have adopted the notion of a universal restoration, to take place some time or other ?   That notion annihilates the belief of eternal punishment, and consequently establishes a purgatory upon a more extensive and extraordinary plan, indeed, than is that of Rome ; but still a purgatory it most certainly is. And if you will insist that the popish tenet rests on the sentiment of natural immortality, by what finesse of logic will you be able to prove that your own purgatory is not derived, or upheld, by the same opinion ?

" What you would mean to say by the worship of the dead, another popish doctrine you assert supported by the same opinion, is, to me, quite a mystery.   I have been a

good deal connected with Roman Catholics, both at home
and abroad, but I never understood that worshiping the
dead was a part of their religion.

." What opinion, think you, will your foreign friends
Father Beccari,* and others, form of your candour and simplicity of heart, when they shall read this curious note?
But I beg your pardon, Sir.   Your friends on the other side
of the water are, I suppose, mostly of the infidel cast.
You would not, I dare say, be connected with *bigots* of any
nation.   Seriously to meet with such stale and childish
reflections, in a work, as you tell us, addressed to *philosophers*, gives me a very poor opinion of your ingenuousness,
and liberal turn of mind.   And with what face can you
continue to brand others with the odious appellation of
bigots, and of enemies to free inquiry, whilst you still retain
rankling within your own breast those same ridiculous
prejudices against the Roman, and perhaps other churches,
which you first imbibed within the walls of your nursery?"
P. 225, &c.

On these extraordinary paragraphs of yours I shall make
a few remarks.

    1.   I have no where said that the doctrine of purgatory
rests *solely* on that of the natural immortality of the
soul, but only that the latter is the *great support* of the
former.

    2.   You say that, with equal propriety, I might say
that the doctrine of *heaven* and *hell* is founded on the same
opinion; forgetting that there is no *unembodied spirit* in my
heaven or hell.

    3.   My own *purgatory*, as you are pleased to call it,
(and to which I have no objection), being the temporary
punishment of the wicked, also affects the *body* which rises
from the tomb, and not the *separate soul;* so that it cannot
require much *finesse of logic*, to prove that it does not
rest on the same foundation with the popish doctrine of
purgatory.

    4.   I call the popish custom of praying to St. Peter,
St. Paul, &c., a *worshipping of the dead*, because these
saints are *in a state of death*, as the Papists themselves will
not deny; for if they be not dead, they *never did die at all*,
there not having been, that we know of, any resurrection of
the dead since their decease.   Besides, it would justify me if
I saw them worshiping persons whom *I believed* to be dead.

---

* Of Bologna, quoted by Dr. P. in *Hist. of Vision*, &c.

5. As the paragraph quoted above could hardly be written by any other than a Papist, I will take this opportunity of informing you and others, that if by my *friends* you mean persons connected with me by common pursuits and correspondence, I have among them both infidels and bigots; but that I never trouble myself about any man's faith or pursuits in some respects, if he be a man to my liking in others. Nor do I know that any of my friends in one respect complain of me for troubling them with my creed or my schemes in others. At the same time, my friendships, in some respects, have not biassed my judgment in others. With an unbelieving philosopher, I am a philosopher, but not the less a Christian, if any circumstances should bring the subject of religion in view; though it is a thing that, zealous as I am in that respect, I never obtrude upon any man. And though you treat me as a *bigot*, I do not, like those of your persuasion, confine the favour of God, here or hereafter, to my own sect, or even to the class of Christians; and I consider the immoral Christian, of every persuasion, and especially of my own, as the most criminal of mankind. Many of my philosophical acquaintance treat with a good-natured ridicule my profession of Christianity, and I am ready either to argue the case with them seriously, or to smile in my turn at their ridiculing me; knowing, that in general it is not accompanied with that attention to the subject, and consequently with that knowledge of it, which I at least *pretend* to.

I am even not without friends among zealous Catholics, little as you seem to suspect it; and I know how to value individuals of that or any communion, at the same time that I seriously consider the Pope as *the man of sin* and the *antichrist* foretold in the Scripture, and the popish religion, as distinguished from Protestantism, as a mass of the most horrid corruptions of Christianity. And if you will wait for my *History of the Corruptions of Christianity*, you will see that charge, narrow and bigotted as you will think me, proved in its utmost extent; though I do not say that my reasons will be such as will make any change in your religious creed. The force of prejudice, imbibed as you say *in the nursery*, even in virtuous and ingenuous minds, is often greater than that of any argument.

The article of religion, however, excepted, I really flatter myself that I shall be able to make some impression upon you, and the remarks and observations advanced in this letter I propose by way of an *experiment* of the kind; though

I own I am sometimes ready to despair of my undertaking, when I consider how very fully you seem to be *persuaded in your own mind.* The language in which you have, upon some occasions, expressed this fulness of persuasion, is so peculiarly strong, that I cannot help smiling when I consider on how very weak a foundation this confidence stands, and how very soon I am willing to hope it will fall to the ground.

You say, " with respect to the present debate I am bold to declare that if I am not, on the right side, I will never sacrifice one single moment of my future life to the disco-very of truth." P. 4.

Concerning one argument to prove, against Dr. Hartley, that the mechanical system cannot pre-suppose free-will, in the popular and practical sense, you say, " If this reasoning be not decisive against Dr. Hartley, I am willing to give up all pretensions to the least atom of common sense, and fairly submit to be classed in the same rank of being with the pen I write with." P. 184.

This language, I would observe by the way, very much resembles that of Mr. Venn,[*] in the first controversy in which I was ever engaged. He said he would *burn his Bible* if his conclusions from it were not just. But as I admo-nished him, that his resolution was a very rash one, as he had much to learn from his Bible yet, so though you should be convinced that you have hitherto been engaged in a fruitless pursuit of truth, I would not have you, out of despair, give up the search. If you be not too old, you may recover the time you have lost on the false scent, and by double diligence come up with the foremost, after you have got into the right track.

At present, however, which is curious enough, you express the same persuasion concerning me that I do concerning you. For you say, " I dare defy the most virulent and subtle ad-versary to produce one single absurdity, through the whole system of *immaterialism*, which, with his hand on his breast, the Rev. Dr. Priestley will declare to be such." P. 82.

Now, in my *Disquisitions* I have shewn, as you will see, that the system of immaterialism is *replete with absurdity;* and I do assure you that I can very safely lay my hand on my breast, and declare that I really believe the whole charge to be well founded. In return, I challenge you to prove a single absurdity in the system of *materialism.* I have dis-tinctly replied to all the objections you have advanced

* Who wrote against the "Discourse on the Lord's Supper." 1769. See *Memoirs.*

against it, whether they be peculiar to yourself, or not. Do you shew the futility of these replies, if you can.

I shall now close this letter, after informing you, that though my animadversions on your letters do not make more than about ten distinct articles, I could easily have extended them to three or four times that number For the things I have dwelt upon afford but a sample of the manner in which the whole book is written, with respect both to strength of argument and manner of writing.

I must not, however, quite shut up this letter till I have informed you, how very rash you have been to conclude that, because I did not publicly disown a particular Essay published in the *London Review,** you are authorized, as you say, to deem it mine, or, which *nearly amounts to the same*, that it *came forth under my tutelage* and *kind protection*. P. 7. You repeat the same on several other occasions. P. 40, &c. Now I do not yet know any thing more of the author of that piece than I suppose you do. Even the sentiments of it are, in many respects, not mine, as you may find by my *Disquisitions;* nor do I consider the writer of it as very much my friend. Be this as it will, you certainly had no right to consider any thing as being *mine*, that does not *bear my name*. Besides, can I be supposed either to read every anonymous publication, especially in *periodical works*, of which this country affords so great a number, or know what things are ascribed to me ? I assure you, I never heard of this in particular being by any body supposed to be mine, till I saw the charge in your printed letters.

Let this one *unquestionably false charge* teach you more caution for the future, and let it likewise impress your mind with the idea of its being possible for you to have been as much mistaken in other particulars as you have been in this.

I might have enlarged on your accounts of the advertisement signed *J. Seton*, and of the defence I was compelled to make of myself in the pamphlet entitled *Philosophical Empiricism,†* both of which are gross misrepresentations of

---

* " A Letter to the London Reviewers, occasioned by their insertion of Mr. Seton's Letter to Dr Priestley, on the Materiality of the Soul, in their Review for June last." L. R. Sep. 1775, II. pp. 177—188. This *Letter* appears to have been written by Dr. Kenrick, the Editor of the Review. See my Author's next article. Mr. Seton's Letter to Dr. P. was accompanied with one to the Reviewers, who, in noticing a *foreign* article, had quoted with approbation the passage on the *uniform composition* of man, in *Introd. Essays* (Vol. III. p. 184). See *London Review*, I. pp. 469, 470, 525—531.

† Published 1775 See Vol. III. p. 207.

the facts, and to appearance malevolent; but I am really weary of animadverting upon such things. I leave them to the judgment of the public, and wishing you both more discernment and more candour.

I am, Sir,

Your very humble Servant,

Calne, July, 1777.   ' J. PRIESTLEY.

To Dr. Kenrick.*

Sir,

You and I differ so very little with respect to any thing of importance in my *Disquisitions,* &c. that notwithstanding the obligation I have laid myself under, I should hardly have thought it necessary to address you on the subject; and I freely acknowledge, that it is rather your importunity than any thing else, that has induced me to do it.' .

We equally maintain that matter is not that impenetrable stuff that it has been imagined to be, that man is an homogeneous being, the sentient principle not residing in a substance distinct from the body, but being the result of organization; and, as far as I can perceive, you likewise agree with me in holding the doctrine of philosophical necessity.

Of what then is it that you complain? It seems to be, principally, that I do not acknowledge to have learned my doctrine in your school, and that the manner in which I explain it is not perfectly consistent, or just. You say, *(Review* for 1777,) " I cannot so easily absolve you from the censure of unpardonable neglect, in being ignorant of what has so recently and repeatedly been advanced on the fundamental subject of your *Disquisitions on Matter and Spirit.* Twenty years are now nearly elapsed since I first took up the former subject, on occasion of the late Cadwallader Colden's treatise of the *Principles of Action in Matter,* a subject on which I have frequently descanted, in various publications, as occasion offered." VI. p. 484. In the same page you say, that this *neglect* of mine is not so " much *real* as *affected.*"

Now, Sir, whatever be the degree of *blame* that I have justly brought upon myself, I do assure you that my ignorance of your having maintained what I contend for, is

---

* Editor of the *London Review,* in which he had written six letters to Dr. Priestley, chiefly on his notions of *matter.* A seventh was added in reply to this letter. See L. R. VI. p. 481, VII. pp. 58, 81, 161, 342, VIII. pp. 298, 433. Dr. Kenrick died in 1779.

not affected, but *real;* and indeed my not having learned *more* of you, and my not holding your doctrine with perfect consistency, may be allowed to weigh something in answer to a charge of *plagiarism.* Besides, whatever injury I have done you, I reap no advantage from it; because I do not advance the doctrine as my own discovery, but profess to have learned the system from F. Boscovich and Mr. Michell.*

I am but an occasional reader of *Reviews,* and I have not the least recollection either of Mr. Colden's Treatise, or of any thing that was ever said about it; and yet I am far from thinking disrespectfully either of *anonymous,* or of *periodical* publications, of which, without the least reason, you fre- quently charge me: but certainly there is less chance of an anonymous publication being generally known, and espe- cially of its being ascribed to its right author.

You say, (p. 481,) that you find I do not think you much my *friend,* because I said so of the author of the *Essay* in your Review for September 1775, (II. p. 177); but I had not the most distant suspicion of your being the writer of that Essay. It is there called *a Letter to the Reviewers,* and was announced by yourself, as a piece supposed to be writ- ten either by *myself,* or *some of my able friends;* and, in con- sequence, probably, of that manner of announcing it, it has, with many persons, passed for mine. You must not blame me for not knowing it to be yours, when yourself announced it as mine.

As you seem not to have any recollection of this circum- stance, which has led myself and others into a mistake, I shall take the liberty to recite the whole paragraph, which is in a note of your Review for August 1775. " For the reasons alleged in our account of Dr. Priestley's Essays, we beg to be excused for the present from entering into this in- teresting dispute, and that still the more earnestly, as we have had sent us a long and laboured defence of the passage that appeared so exceptionable to Mr. Seton, intended to have been printed in a pamphlet by itself, had not the author (either the Dr. himself, or some able friend) justly conceived so good an opinion of our candour, as to think we should afford a place for it in our Review, which we purpose to do in our next number." P. 175. Accordingly, in the very next number appeared this Essay, which you now call your own.

* See Vol. III. pp. 192, 231—233.

There are several other things in your letters to me that are almost as unaccountable as this. I am very far from having a mean opinion of your understanding, and men of sense are generally candid; at least they are able to perceive the real meaning of a writer, who wishes to be understood, and they are above little cavils. And yet, you ascribe to me what I am professedly refuting, and only suppose for the sake of that refutation, viz. the solidity of the atoms, or the ultimate constituent parts of bodies. VII. p. 64. You write variously, and perhaps not very consistently with respect to me; but, in general, you seem to think that I write with tolerable *perspicuity*, as well as readiness; you should therefore have reconsidered the passages which you except against. I see little, if any thing, that I can amend in them; and yet you say that " with the best disposition in the world to comprehend me, you cannot possibly conceive what I am about."

Your cavil (p. 65), appears to me to be equally ill-founded: for by the *smallest parts* of bodies, I evidently mean those that are *supposed to be* the smallest, or the solid indiscerptible atoms of other philosophers; which I maintain to be resolvable into still smaller parts. I do not wonder to find this wretched cavil in such a writer as Mr. Whitehead, but it is altogether unworthy of a person who has any degree of reputation, as a writer, or a man of sense and candour.

You ridicule what you call my *pompous list* of authors, prefixed to the *Disquisitions*, when I barely mention those of which there are *different editions*, that, as I quote the *pages*, those who had different editions of the same book might be apprised of it. What could the most modest writer, yourself for instance, who wished to be understood, do less? Had I meant to swell the list, I should have inserted in it *all* that I have quoted; which, however, is a very common practice, and not at all exceptionable. On many occasions you charge me with *vanity* and *conceit;* and once, in imitation, I suppose, of the style of Dr. Johnson,* you term it *an exuberance of self-exaltation:* but this charge is founded upon nothing but the most forced and uncandid construction of my expressions. This I consider as an unworthy artifice. Had I affected an unusual degree of *modesty*, inconsistent with writing so much as I do, (as it certainly implies that I think myself capable of instructing, at least, some part of mankind,) there would have been more reason for your conduct.

---

* Probably a reference to Dr. K.'s ridicule of Johnson's style, in *Lexiphanes.*

As to the work which you promise the public, I shall expect it with some impatience, and shall certainly read it with the greatest attention ; and as you say that " the *theory of physics*, or the systematical principles of natural philosophy, the science which Lord Bacon represents as the basis and foundation of all human knowledge, is the department of your peculiar profession," I do hope that you will throw some light upon it, and I have every reason to wish you success. If you can prove, as you say, that *all matter is possessed of some degree of perception*, you will effectually remove the only difficulty under which my scheme labours ; which is *how* a sentient principle is the result of organization. The *fact* I think indisputable, and must be admitted on the received rules of philosophizing ; but that it *must be so*, from the nature of things, I own I do not yet see, any more than I am yet satisfied that " the form and magnitude of bodies are to be considered as generated by motion," or that " every natural phenomenon, or distinct object of sense, is a compound of active and passive physical powers," notwithstanding the very ingenious observations that you have advanced with respect to them.

You frequently hint that, the reason why I have generally appeared to advantage in controversy, is, that I have always pitched upon *weak antagonists.* I can only say, that, if this has been the case, it has been because I have not had the good fortune to meet with any better ; and in general they have not been weak either in their own eyes, or in those of the public. This character, however, can by no means apply to Dr. Brown, Dr. Balguy, Dr. Blackstone,* Dr. Reid, or Dr. Beattie, whatever you may say of Dr. Oswald, on whose work you will find the highest encomiums in the reviews of the day ; and it was in fact, held in very great and general admiration.

You will also find the same to be, in a great measure, true of the *Letters on Materialism.* Besides, the stating of *objections actually made*, and answering them, has a much better effect than proposing them in other words ; as it may be suspected, that, by this means, the answerer gives himself an unfair advantage ; and when I replied to him, no other answer had appeared. For as to your *Mr. Seton*, (p. 137,) who, it seems, notwithstanding the incredulity of some, did really

* The first of these writers Dr. Priestley had opposed on the subject of *Public Education*, the second, of *Church Power*, and the third, of *Nonconformity*, as will appear in the course of this edition.

live, and is now actually *dead*, I could not, though I endeavoured to do it, persuade myself to take any notice of him ; he appeared to know so very little of the very rudiments of theological knowledge.   Many other opponents I have neglected to notice because I thought them insignificant, though they are not without their admirers, and boast, as you do, that I make no reply, because I am not able to do it.   As to yourself, pretend what you will, I cannot consider you in the light of an adversary.

You ask me repeatedly, why, since I deny all solidity or impenetrability, I should choose to make use of so obnoxious a term as *matter*, when the less exceptionable one of *spirit* would answer my purpose full as well.   I answer, that the cause of truth is best answered by calling every thing by its *usual name*, and I think it a mean subterfuge to impose upon mankind by the use of words.

Man, I believe, was wholly made of *the dust of the ground*, or of the same substance with the earth itself.   Now, by what term has the earth, and all the substances that belong to it, been distinguished, but that of *matter?*   I suppose the sentient principle in man to be the brain itself, and not any *invisible substance* residing in the brain, and capable of subsisting when the brain is destroyed.   Now, of what has the brain been always said to consist, but *matter;* another species indeed from that of the dust of the ground, but still comprised under the same common appellation of matter ?   In what other manner than that which I have chosen, is it possible to rectify the mistakes of men ?   To call matter by the name of *spirit*, might tend to give them an idea that my opinions were, in fact, the same with theirs, though expressed in different words ;   and by this means, I might screen myself from their censure ; but I should only *deceive*, and should not *instruct* them at all.

In this manner, too many christian preachers and writers, adopting the phraseology of the Athanasian system, pass for orthodox, without, as they think, any violation of truth. But what accrues from this conduct?   No advantage to the cause of *truth*, nothing but the mere *safety of the preacher or writer*.

This, Sir, is not my object.   I have hitherto pursued a different plan, and have seen no reason to repent of it. Upon this general principle, I have chosen to say that *man is wholly material*, rather than *wholly spiritual*, though both the terms were in my option.

You must give me leave to close this letter with some

notice of a passage of yours to me, which is in the same strain with many others, and of which we have but too many examples in such writers as Voltaire and Mr. Hume. You say, " As to your concern for the conversion of infidels, I look upon it as the cant of a philosophical crusader, and am sorry that I cannot coincide with you in your projected conciliation of the *rational truths* of philosophy, with the *mysterious truths* of Christianity. I am apprehensive that it is impossible, without endangering the cause of both, to bring them into too close a contact." VI. p. 489. In a note, you add, " It is a moot point with me, whether the really thinking and intelligent philosophers, whom Dr. Priestley wishes to convert, are greater infidels, in their present state of unbelief, than they would be, if converted by him into rational Christians." Ibid.

Now I must take it for granted, that a man of much less discernment than you, cannot but be sensible, that no proposition can be *true* and *false* at the same time, or true with respect to philosophy, and false with respect to theology, or *vice versa;* so that if what is called a *mystery in Christianity*, be really a *falsehood in philosophy*, i. e. reducible to a contradiction, the belief of it must be abandoned altogether, at any hazard; and the scheme of religion that necessarily supposes it to be true must be confessed to be ill-founded, and an imposition on mankind.

If, for example, *bread and wine*, philosophically, i. e. strictly and justly considered, cannot be *flesh and blood*, the popish doctrine of *transubstantiation* cannot be true. So also, if *one* cannot be *three*, or *three one*, mathematically considered, neither can the Athanasian doctrine of the *Trinity* be true. It certainly, therefore, behoves every rational Christian to prove the consistency of the articles of his faith with true philosophy and the nature of things. This is the only method of effectually silencing such unbelievers as, with the low view of imposing on the weakest Christians, pretend to believe *Christianity*, at the same time that they maintain it is *not founded on argument ;* [*] thinking to lose no character with men of sense, like themselves, who will easily perceive the design with which such absurd professions are made, and will be ready to join in the laugh at the credulity of those who are taken with them. If I were really an unbeliever, I think I should not scruple to avow it, rather

---

[*] Probably referring to a work with that title, written by *Dodwell,* son of the celebrated clergyman. See Biog. Brit. V. p. 327.

than debase my mind by such paltry evasions.   But it must
be owned,. that an unbeliever has not the same cause for *a
strict attachment to truth,* that a Christian has.

          I am, Sir,

               Your very humble Servant,

                       J. PRIESTLEY.

Calne, June, 1778.

               To MR. WHITEHEAD.*

SIR,

AN attack from a person of your religious persuasion is a
thing that is new to me ; and as I have frequently mentioned
your people with respect, and have always had very agreeable connexions with individuals of your body, it would
have been a real satisfaction to me to have found that, even
in their *opposition* to me, they were respectable ; and therefore to have had it in my power to speak as handsomely of you
all, as I have hitherto done.   However, though an individual has shewn that want of civility and candour, which I
had thought inseparable' from all Quakers, and, also too
little acquaintance with his subject, I shall by no means
impute these faults to the whole body to which you belong,
many of whom I know to be equally distinguished for their
candour and knowledge.†

You know, Sir, I presume, that I profess to believe in a
God, a *providence,* and a *future state,* in the *divine mission of
Christ,* and the *authority of the Scriptures.*   I have written
not a little in the direct defence of these principles, and I
hope my general character and conduct does not give the lie
to my profession.   Why then should you suppose me not
to be *sincere,* and to be *secretly undermining* these great
principles of religion ?   Might not I, if I were so disposed,
retort the same surmises and calumnies respecting you ?
You are certainly at liberty to urge me with what you
apprehend to be the real consequences of my doctrine, but
this you might do without intimating, as you frequently do,
that I was *apprised* of the immoral and dangerous conse-

---

* See " Materialism philosophically examined, or the Immateriality of the Soul
asserted and proved, on Philosophical Principles; in Answer to Dr. Priestley's Disquisitions on Matter and Spirit. By John Whitehead, Author of an Essay on
Liberty and Necessity." 1778. When young, he had been a preacher among the
Methodists, and was the master of a Quakers' school at Wandsworth. He afterwards became a physician, and rejoined the connexion of *John Wesley,* whose life
he wrote. Dr. Whitehead died in 1804.   See Gent. Mag. LXXIV. p. 283.

† See the Author's *Memoirs,* on the kindness of " Mr. S. Alexander," of Need-
ham, to whose library he " had the freest access," when he himself possessed very
few books.

quences of my principles, and wished to propagate them *on that account.*

"Materialism," you say, "must terminate in Atheism;" (p. 163,) and "the doctrine of materialism must be attended with the most destructive and fatal consequences. It supposes that this life is our only place of existence, and by this means takes away all confidence in God, all hope of future rewards and fear of punishment. It tears up all religion by the very roots, and renders all our moral powers and faculties wholly useless, or supposes them to be mere creatures of education and human policy. In short, its language is, *let us eat and drink, for to-morrow we die.*" P. 90. You are pleased to add, "I do not say that Dr. Priestley will *directly* defend these principles, or that he *altogether* believes them to be the consequences of his doctrine." This, however, is an insinuation, that, though not *altogether*, I do *in part* believe them to be the consequences of my doctrine; and other passages in your work sufficiently shew, that you think me capable of advancing and supporting these principles, even though I should be altogether persuaded of their horrid consequences.

"It must be owned," you say, "that our author shews no great delicacy respecting the character of the sacred penmen. He very freely, though indirectly, bespatters them with dirt; from whence one might naturally suspect, that he owes them no very good will." P. 108. "Professions of this kind," you say, "from one who professes to believe the gospel, looks so much like a *feigned friendship*, in order to deliver it more securely into the hands of the Deists, that it will not fail to recall to memory the treatment of our Lord by one of his professed disciples, to which, with respect to the gospel revelation, it bears a striking resemblance." P. 110. "There," you say, "is an end of all scripture authority at once, which perhaps would not be very disagreeable to this writer." P. 112. Lastly, you scruple not to say, "I should not wonder to hear this learned gentleman, armed cap-a-pee, with logic and philosophy, represent his Lord and Saviour as a greater deceiver than Mahomet. To such miserable and profane shifts, may rash reasoning bring an unguarded man." P. 106.

For the honour of the christian name, and of the particular profession to which you belong, I hope that, on reflection, yourself, or at least your friends, will blush for these things. In the preceding quotation, I hope, Sir, you will be thought to have given a very unfair account of my

moral principles and *views;* let us now see whether you be
any better acquainted with the *professed design* of my work,
and the *nature of the argument.*

" The great object in view," you say, " it seems, in con-
triving and modelling these inquiries into matter and spirit,
was to lay a foundation for the better support of *Arianism.*"
P. 171. Now, Sir, so much are you mistaken, that the
great object in view was the very reverse of what you suppose, viz. the radical overturning of the system of Arianism,
by proving the absurdity, and explaining the origin of the
doctrines of a *soul,* and of *pre-existence,* which are necessarily
supposed in the Arian system; and a very great part of my
work is, not indirectly, but *openly,* and both *really,* and *by
name,* an attack upon Arianism, and both what is called
the *high* and the *low Arian hypothesis,* which I consider
separately.

Let us now see the light in which my account of *the
opinions of the christian fathers,* has happened to strike you;
and in this you are no less unfortunate. " The thing he
proposes to prove," you say, " is that the christian fathers
believed that the soul can have no existence separate from
the body, that thought and consciousness may be the result
of an organized system of matter." P. 140. " Consequently," you say, " our author's grand boast, that the
apostles and primitive fathers thought with him, that the
soul is material and mortal, vanishes into air; where, perhaps, this experimental philosopher may be able to make
more of it than we can do in these lower regions." P. 149.

Again, after reciting the opinion of Cl. Mamertus, who
says of the soul, that it is neither *extended* nor *in place,* you
say, " These seem to me most extraordinary assertions, to
prove that the soul is material and dies with the body. It
requires more skill in logic than I am master of, to find this
conclusion in either of the premises." P. 148.

A very extraordinary conclusion indeed; but, if that had
been my idea, it would not have been more extraordinary
than your mistake of the whole drift of my argument in this
business. I had asserted that the idea of *refined spiritua-
lity,* maintained, I find, by yourself, was unknown to all
antiquity; and therefore I have shewn, that though, according to the notion of the heathen philosophers, the soul was
considered as a substance distinct from the body, being a
detached part of the great soul of the universe, it had the
property of *extension,* and was, in reality, what we should
now call a *more refined kind of matter;* and that true *spiritu-*

alism was introduced gradually; but, if any more distinct æra can be fixed on, it was that of this very Mamertus.

I farther prove, that, according to the true system of re-velation, though the sentient and thinking principle may be spoken of as distinct from the other functions of the man, it was always supposed to reside in some part of his body, and to be inseparable from it. For the sacred writers never speak of the soul as in one place, and the body in another; and it was not till the introduction of the heathen philoso-phy into Christianity, that it was imagined that the soul retained its perceptivity and activity while the body was in the grave. Of this, I presume, I have given sufficient proof.

You are pleased, indeed, to allege, as a proof that the early Christians thought differently, a passage in the epistle of Polycarp, who says that " Paul, and the rest of the apos-tles, are in the place appointed for them, παρα τω Κυριω, with the Lord." P. 144. But if you had attended to the Greek, you would have perceived that this is not the *necessary* sense of the passage, and archbishop Wake renders it " are gone to the place that was due to them, from the Lord."* Indeed, had you been sufficiently conversant with *ecclesiastical his-tory*, you would have known, that it was not till many cen-turies after the time of Polycarp, that any Christian thought that the separate soul, whether sentient or not, was in any other place than that which is distinguished by the term *hades*. It was universally thought that good men were not *with God and Christ* till after the resurrection,† which is clearly the scripture doctrine.

Our Lord says, John xiv. 3, " I will come again, and receive you unto myself, that where I am, ye may be also." Here is a plain limitation of the time when the disciples of our Lord, and even the apostles themselves, were to be ad-mitted to his presence, and live with him, viz. at his return to raise the dead, and not before.

What you say on the subject of the state of the soul between death and the resurrection, is too trifling to deserve a particular notice. As you seem not to have given sufficient attention to this subject, I would take the liberty to recom-mend to your careful perusal, what the excellent Bishop of Carlisle has written on it; archdeacon Blackburne's *Histo-rical View of this Controversy;* the Dissertation prefixed to *Alexander's Commentary on* 1 *Cor.* xv.; and a summary of

---

* No. ix. " Genuine Epistles of the Apostolical Fathers." Ed. 4, 1737, p. 57.
† See Vol. III p. 374, &c.

the principal arguments in the third part of my *Institutes of Natural and Revealed Religion.* (Vol. III. pp. 3)4—362.)

It is upon this subject that you note, with great triumph, that I have quoted as one, two similar passages in the book of *Revelation.* Another person would have supposed this to have happened through *inadvertency*, and not, as you will have it, *with design.* It must have been infatuation to have done this in a work so inviting of criticism as mine is. A new edition of the work will shew you that my argument loses nothing by the rectification of that mistake.

I shall mention one more mistake of my meaning, though in a thing of no great consequence. " It is a great mistake," you say. " to suppose, with Dr. Priestley and some other philosophers, that there is some unknown substance in material nature, distinct from the properties of solidity and extension." P. 10. Now what I have said, and repeated many times, is, that when all the properties of substance are taken away, the substance itself is gone ; and that the terms *substance, essence,* &c. &c. are merely a convenience in speech.

You triumph exceedingly in my speaking of the *smallest particles of matter* being resolved into others still *smaller.* For an explanation of this, I refer you to my letter to Dr. Kenrick, (p. 140.)

Your strictures on the subject of *personal identity* I freely leave to have their full effect on the minds of our readers, without any apprehension of the consequence.

Before I close this letter, I shall briefly mention a few particulars, which shew that you are not sufficiently acquainted with the *state of opinions* for a controversial writer on such subjects as those of the *Disquisitions.*

" Nor do I presume," you say, " that any philosopher will contend for an earlier and earlier existence of this world, and the creatures in it, *ad infinitum.*" P. 25. Now, Sir, many philosophers and divines maintain the very doctrine that you think not to exist. It was the opinion of the Platonists, it is asserted by Dr. Hartley, it is what I have given in my *Institutes,* and I believe it is that of Dr. Price, who is far from thinking with me on the subject of the *Disquisitions.*

" Our learned author," you say, " indeed, affects to disbelieve the continual flux of the particles of the human body; but this I presume no one will seriously deny, who has a competent knowledge of its structure and œconomy." P. 81.

Now many persons, Sir, and even Dr. Watts, whom you quote with so much respect, seriously believed that there are parts of the body, some *stamina*, that never change.*

There is another thing that you take for granted, in which I believe you are quite singular, and it is, indeed, sufficiently curious. You say, that " where body is, space is necessarily excluded," (p. 167); and from this extraordinary supposition you draw many curious inferences, in your reasoning about the nature of spirit, and of the Deity. Now I have heard of space being *occupied*, but never of its being *excluded* before.

I must not quite conclude without acknowledging myself obliged to you for furnishing me with a proof, which you will find, by Dr. Price's remarks, was in some measure wanting, of its being the *real opinion* of any person, that *spirit bears no relation to space*. You do it in the amplest manner, and build upon it your argument against the materiality of the human soul. According to you, Dr. Clarke, Dr. Price and others, who maintain the *locality*, and consequently the *extension* of spirit, are as much materialists as myself. I leave them and you to dispute that point; and you may imagine I shall not feel unpleasantly in the situation of a *spectator*. It will give me some respite, and I shall expect to derive some advantage from the issue of the contest, in whose favour soever it may be.

" No corporeal substance whatever," you say, " can possibly be the seat of sensation ; for all of them have extension, and must be of some figure or form." P. 63. " On the same principles we may explain the omnipresence of God, not by extension through all bodies, as this writer seems to believe, which is an idea so gross that it deserves a name which, for the sake of the author, I shall not bestow upon it." P. 128.

Now, as you have not scrupled to make use of the terms *materialist* and *atheist* in this controversy, I have really a good deal of curiosity to know what dread name it is, that, *out of regard to me*, you suppress the mention of. If it be too dreadful for the *public ear*, could you not favour me with the intimation of it in a private letter? I shall communicate it to my friend Dr. Price, whom it concerns as much as it does myself. Dr. Clarke, you will also find, and, in the opinion of Dr. Price, all the most distinguished immaterialists, will fall under this dread censure. But, being so many

---

* See his *Philosophical Essays*, No. viii. *ad fin.* Works, VI. pp. 558, 559.

of us, materialists and immaterialists, we shall bear it the better; for bodies, and large companies of men, we know, are not easily affected either by *shame* or *fear.*

I am, Sir,

Your very humble Servant,

Calne, June, 1778.   J. PRIESTLEY.

To Dr. Horsley.

Dear Sir,

I think myself particularly happy that a person of. your abilities, and mathematical and philosophical knowledge, has vouchsafed to allude to my. work, though only in a *sermon,** as it gives me an opportunity of explaining myself more fully with respect to the state of the question concerning *liberty* and *necessity,* and likewise of shewing that the *sect* of necessarians, though almost *every where spoken against,* is more numerous and respectable than is generally imagined; for that you, Sir, belong to it as much as I do; with this only difference, that you choose to make use of one set of phrases, and I of another.

It is impossible for me to express in stronger terms than you do, the absolute certainty of every determination of the will of man, as depending upon the circumstances he is in, and the motives presented to him. " A moral motive and a mechanical force," you say, " are equally certain causes, each of its proper effect. A moral motive," you say, " is what is more significantly called the final cause, and can have no influence but with a being that proposes to itself an end, chooses means, and thus puts itself in action. It is true that while this is my end, and while I conceive these to be the means, a definite action will as certainly follow that definite choice and judgment of my mind, provided I be free from all external restraint and impediment, as a determinate motion will be excited in a body by a force applied in a given direction. There is, in both cases, an equal certainty of the effect." P. 10.

Having granted this, it is not possible that you and I can have any difference that is not merely *verbal.* Our *ideas* are precisely the same; nor have I indeed any objection to your *language,* in any sense in which it can be consistent with the above assertions,

* " Providence and Free Agency. A Sermon preached in the Cathedral Church of St. Paul, April 17, 1778. By Samuel Horsley, LL.D." 4to.

You are too good a mathematician to require being told, that, if every determination of the mind of man certainly depends upon preceding causes, whether the causes be moral or physical, it is not possible that any determination, or consequently that any event, in which men are concerned, coul. have been otherwise than it *has been*, *is*, or *is to be;* or that the Divine Being, who, as you justly say, " knows things by their causes, as being himself the first cause. the source of power and activity to all other causes," should not have *intended* every thing to be just as it is. On this ground only can you affirm, as you do, that " to him every thing that shall ever be is at all times infinitely more certain; than any thing, either past or present, can be to any man," &c. This, I say; you need not be told. It is an immediate and necessary inference from your own principle. Indeed; it is little more than repeating the same thing in other words.

You even apply these principles to a case of the greatest virtue that was ever exerted by man, viz. the voluntary sufferings and death of Christ; and likewise to a case of the greatest wickedness, viz. that of his enemies in voluntarily inflicting those sufferings upon him. No person can express this with more perspicuity or energy than you have done.

" Now therefore," you say; " he begins to shew them (his disciples) that he *must* go to Jerusalem, and, after much malicious persecution from the leaders of the Jewish people, he *must* be killed. The form of expression here is very remarkable in the original, and it is well preserved in our English translation. He *must* go, he *must* suffer; he *must* be killed, he *must* be raised again on the third day. All these things were fixed and determined—must inevitably be—nothing could prevent them—and yet the greater part of them were of a kind that might *seem* to depend entirely upon man's free-agency. To go, or not to go to Jerusalem, was in his own power, and the persecution he met with there, arising from the folly and the malice of ignorant and wicked men, surely depended upon the human will ; yet, by the form of the sentence, these things are included under the same *necessity of event* as that which was evidently an immediate effect of divine power, without the concurrence of any other cause, the resurrection of Jesus from the dead. The words which in the original express the *going*, the *suffering*, the *being killed*, the *being raised again*, are equally subject to the verb which answers to the word *must*, of our language, and in its proper meaning predicates *necessity*. As he *must* be raised on the third day, so he *must* go; he *must* suffer, he *must* be killed. 'Every one of these events, his going to Jerusalem, his suffering, and his death there, and that these sufferings and that death should be brought about by the malice of the elders and chief priests and scribes; every one of these things is plainly announced, as no less unalterably fixed, than the resurrection of our Saviour, or the time of his resurrection, that it was to happen on the third day." P. 9.

If then the virtuous determinations of Christ, and the wicked determinations of his enemies, were equally neces-sary (for I have no other idea to the word *must be*, and indeed you yourself use them as synonymous), every other act of virtue, or act of vice, is equally necessary, or *must be*, and nothing but a miracle, or an arbitrary infringement of the laws of nature, can prevent its taking place. Though you do not choose to call this a *physical*, but a *moral* necessity, you allow it to be a *real* necessity, arising from the operation of the established laws of nature, implying an impossibility of the thing being otherwise than it is, which is all that I wish you to grant.

For any man to have acted differently from what he did, in any given case, he must have been differently disposed at the time, or must have had different views of things present to his mind; neither of which, properly speaking, depends upon himself. For though it does so *immediately*, it does not do so *ultimately;* for since every particular determina-tion depends upon his immediately preceding circumstances, it necessarily follows that the whole chain of his determina-tions and actions depends upon his *original make,* and *ori-ginal circumstances.* And who is our maker but God; or who is it that disposes of us but the same God?

You could not, dear Sir, have written what you have done, if you had not felt, and enjoyed this most important truth. Let us do it freely and without reserve, let us not scruple to express it in its proper language, and let us openly acknow-ledge, and cheerfully embrace, all the fair consequences of it. I need not with you, Sir, make any encomium on our common principles. The doctrine of necessity (moral neces-sity, if you choose to call it so) contains, or implies, all that the heart of man can wish. It leads us to consider our-selves, and every thing else as at the uncontrouled disposal of the greatest and best of Beings; that, strictly speaking, nothing does, or can go wrong; that all *retrograde motions,* in the moral as well as in the natural world, are only *ap-parent,* not *real.* Being under this infallible guidance, our final destination is certain and glorious.   In the language of Pope,

> All nature is but art, unknown to thee;
> All chance, direction, which thou canst not see;
> All discord, harmony, not understood ;
> All partial evil, universal good ,
> And, spite of pride, in erring reason's spite,
> One truth is clear, *whatever is, is right.*

Let us now consider why it is that you object to the term *physical*, as applied to the causes of human actions.   For I am ready to disuse it, if it imply any thing more than we both agree in maintaining.   The word itself is derived from φυσις, *nature*, and therefore literally rendered, signifies *agreeable to nature*, or the *laws of nature*.   A physical cause, therefore, is simply that which, according to the established laws of nature, will produce a given effect ; and of course respects the laws to which the mind is subject, as well as those by which the external world is governed, both being equally within the compass of *nature*.   I therefore apply it to both cases indiscriminately.

If you say the *operations*, and therefore the *laws*, are of a very different nature, I readily acknowledge it.   For, with respect to this, it is impossible that we can really differ. The compass of nature is great, and comprises very various things.   *Chemistry*, for instance, and common *mechanics* are very different things ;   and accordingly we have different *kinds of laws* or *rules*, by which to express and explain, their operations ;   but still they are equally branches of *physics*.   So also though the *phenomena*, and consequently the *laws of the mind*, are different from those of the *body*, that is no sufficient reason why we should not comprise them under the same general term of *physics*.   However, if you dislike the word, in the extensive application in which I use it, I am very well content to use it in your more restrained sense, and will call the things that influence the mind *moral*, and not physical causes.   Only allow that there *are* laws and causes, by which the mind is truly and properly *influenced*, producing certain definite effects in definite circumstances, and I shall not quarrel with you for the sake of a term.

You say, that I confound moral and physical necessity, or, to use your own words, that " when I represent the influence of moral motives, as arising from a physical necessity, the very same with that which excites and governs the motions of the inanimate creation, I confound nature's distinctions, and contradict the very principles I would seem to have established; and that the source of the mistake is, that I imagine a similitude between things which admit of no comparison." P. 10.

Now, Sir, I will allow as much difference as you *can* suppose between moral and physical causes. Inanimate matter, as the pen that I write with, is not capable of being influenced by *motives*, nor is the *hand* that holds the pen, but the *mind* that directs both. I think I distinguish these things better by the terms *voluntary* and *involuntary*; but these are mere *words*, and I make no comparison between them, or between moral and physical causes, but in that very respect in which you yourself acknowledge that they agree, i. e. the *certainty* with which they produce their respective effects. And this is the proper foundation of all the *necessity* that I ascribe to human actions. My conclusion, that men could not, in any given case, act otherwise than they do, is not at all affected by the *terms* by which we distinguish the laws and causes that respect the mind, from those which respect the external world. That there are *any laws*, and that there are *any causes* to which the mind is subject, is all that my argument requires. Give me the thing, and I will readily give you the name.

Again, you distinguish between *efficient* and *final* causes; and say that, by means of the latter, a person *puts himself in motion*. But still, if it be true, as you allow, that, notwithstanding this, a definite act will certainly follow a definite choice and judgment of the mind, there is, in no case, any more than *one way* in which the mind can put itself in motion, or only one direction that it can take, which is all the necessity that I contend for. I choose to say that *motives determine the mind*, whereas you say that the *mind determines itself according to the motives;* but, in both cases, the determination itself is the very same, and we both agree that it *could not have been different*. Our difference, therefore, is merely verbal, and cannot possibly be any thing more.

Turn over this subject, Sir, in your own mind as you please, you will find that one who controverts the doctrine of necessity, has the choice of no more than *two things*. He must either say that, in a given situation of mind, with respect to disposition and motives, the determination is *definite*, i. e. agreeable to some general rule, or that it is *indefinite*, i. e. subject to no rule at all. If the former be admitted, which is what you allow, you are, to all intents and purposes, a necessarian. You may (unknown to yourself) conceal your principles under the cover of some specious and ambiguous phraseology, but you certainly maintain the *thing*. If, on the other hand, you say, that the determination is *indefinite*, you are very sensible that you suppose *an effect without a cause*, which is impossible. This side of the dilemma, therefore, you carefully avoid. In short, Sir, there is no choice in the case, but of the doctrine of necessity (disguised, perhaps, under some other name) or absolute nonsense. There is no possibility of finding any medium.

> " *Incidit in Scyllam qui vult vitare Charybdim.*"

You are pleased, Sir, to call philosophical necessity the doctrine of the *subtle moderns*, and that of predestination that of their *more simple ancestors*, saying, that we subtle moderns are *deeply versed in physics, and maintain the regular operation of second causes;* and you candidly acknowledge, that we are both actuated by the *same humble spirit of resigned devotion.* This, Sir, is frank and generous, and I hope true. I only object to your characterizing us necessarians as *subtle*, when, in reality, Sir, our doctrine is the plainest thing in the world, and it requires no small degree of subtlety to believe any thing else.

What are your distinctions between things *moral* and *physical, efficient* and *final, certain* and *necessary*, those relating to *self-determination* or *self-motion*, &c. &c &c. but *subtleties*, to which we have no recourse? We are content to call all things by their common names. With us laws are laws, and causes causes If the laws are invariable, and the causes certain in their operation (and without this they are, in reality, *no laws*, and *no causes* at all), we say that all that follows is *necessary*, or what *could not but be*. What is there, Sir, of *subtlety* in all this?

As you are a man of undoubted sense and candour, and particularly well versed in mathematical and philosophical knowledge, I doubt not you will carefully attend to these few plain considerations; and I am confident that, with the honest mind that I believe you to be possessed of, you will henceforth avow yourself to be what, without hitherto knowing it, you really are, a believer in " the great and glorious, though unpopular doctrine of *philosophical necessity.*"

I am,

With the greatest respect,

Dear Sir,

Yours, very sincerely,

J. PRIESTLEY.

Calne, June, 1778.

P.S. I shall take it as a particular favour, if you will oblige me and the public with your *second thoughts* on this subject. I have had, and expect, so many weak and hasty answers, that, I own, I am eager to lay hold of a man who is equal to the discussion of the subject, and especially one who is, at the same time, truly liberal and candid. The doctrine of necessity is very far from being well understood by the generality of scholars, and it is certainly of great consequence to have their attention drawn to it. I shall be happy, likewise, to walk with you over *all* the ground marked out in the *Disquisitions*, with respect to which I perceive that you hold a system very different from mine.

APPENDIX,

CONTAINING

𝕬 fart𝔥er 𝕮onsi𝔡eration of t𝔥e 𝕺bjection

TO THE

DOCTRINE OF NECESSITY,

AS FAVOURING INDOLENCE AND VICE.

———◆—◆———

NOTWITHSTANDING all that I have advanced in answer to the objection that has been made to the doctrine of necessity, as *leading to indolence, indifference,* and even *vice,* some persons, I find, wish I had been still more particular; the popular cry against it still being, " Why should I exert myself, if my fate be determined? What *must be, must be,* and cannot be prevented." I do not know that I can urge any thing more satisfactory than I have already done in answer to this objection, and which I think abundantly sufficient for the purpose; but I will try another view of the subject.

On the principle of the doctrine of necessity, man is a machine, moved by motives, as ships are by the winds. That *within himself,* by which he is subject to be acted upon, are his *appetites* and *passions,* which resemble the *sails* of the ship. If these be raised, and the wind blow, the ship moves of course. Thus, also, man being furnished by nature with appetites and passions, if the objects that are adapted to gratify them come in view, his *desires* are necessarily excited, and he is prompted to exert himself, in order to attain them. In this manner, it will not be denied, mankind in general are *put in motion,* as we may say, and thus is the business of the world carried on.

Now, by becoming *necessarians* we do not cease to be *men.* We still retain every natural spring or principle of action, and occasions of calling them forth occur to us as much as-to others. All the difference that can take place in consequence of becoming necessarians is, that we are thereby *apprised* of this mechanical structure of our minds. But it is impossible that this circumstance should make us abate our endeavours to gain any favourite object, unless either the object should become less a favourite one with us, or we should see that our endeavours were less necessary to gain it. But neither of these things takes place.

It cannot be denied but that, feeling as men, our *objects* are the same with those of other men, and a necessarian is so far from thinking that his *endeavours* are less strictly connected with his. *end,* that he sees them to be more so; every thing in nature being, in his persuasion, an indissolubly connected chain of *causes and effects;* so that if any one link, his own endeavours among the rest, be interrupted, his object is unattainable. It may, therefore, be expected, that a necessarian, having any favourite object in view, will be more attentive to the means that he believes to be absolutely requisite to gain his end, than other men will be. And this is certainly the case, as far as a man is 'a *practical necessarian,* or reduces to practice the knowledge he has of the mechanical structure of his own mind, and of every thing else in nature.

It is said the *final issue* of his endeavours is *fixed.* But it is only fixed *as connected with his endeavours*; and he has no means of *knowing* how it is fixed, but by its *supposed* connexion with his endeavours; so that the moment he begins to slacken his endeavours, he necessarily begins to think that the end is not fixed as he wished it to be; he himself putting an effectual bar to its taking place. He, therefore, will not slacken his endeavours, unless he either ceases to desire the end; or begins to believe that his endeavours are not necessary to gain it; which is the case with the Calvinists. This, at least, would be the case with them, if other principles, more consonant to nature, did not intervene, and check the natural operation of their religious tenets. But if Calvinists are seldom able to act up to their principles, which really favour indolence; on what grounds can it be apprehended that necessarians should give way to indolence, when their principles lead them from it?

If it was possible for a necessarian to consider his fate as depending on the cast of a die; or any thing else equally *independent of himself,* and unconnected with his efforts, he might feel himself disposed to sit with folded hands, in patient or anxious expectation of the event. But surely when his own opinion of his situation is so very different, it must be impossible that he should *feel* as if it was the same. An objection which goes upon the idea of things so very different, and *apprehended* to be so very different, having the same effect on any human mind, necessarian or not necessarian, cannot be well founded.

If it be said that the supposition of *certainty in the event,* universally considered, will preclude all endeavours, it will affect all mankind, necessarians and those who are not necessarians, without distinction ; because, admitting the *divine prescience,* every thing future is absolutely certain in the eye of God. Or, without any respect to prescience, as *time* and the *course of nature* are continually going on, every thing must have some termination or other ; and this, whether known to any being or not, may be considered as *certain in itself.* But it is not a fact, that any person's endeavours are at all affected by such views and speculations as these ; because while the thing is *depending,* and the event is *unknown to ourselves,* the expectation of it cannot affect us one way more than another. If it could have any operation, it would be that of equal weights in opposite scales, and therefore could not incline us either *to* or *from* any pursuit. In this situation, therefore, we are actuated by our natural desires, just as if no such certainty as this had any existence. A thing altogether *unknown* cannot possibly have influence ; because it is the *knowledge* of it that gives it all the influence it can have. It is impossible, therefore, in any case, that a regard to what will be future should affect our conduct, unless we knew what the future event will be ; and therefore this knowledge is wisely concealed from us.

Let me exemplify this reasoning by my own pursuits. I may be supposed to wish to ascertain some particular fact in natural philosophy ; this wish, arising from my constitution and the usual objects of my attention. In speculating on the subject, it occurs to me, that, by a very easy and simple experiment, I cannot fail to ascertain the fact in question. So far, all my readers will say, the process is mechanical and necessary ; for *volition* and *action* are not concerned. But some, pretending to feel for me, will say I may stop here, and never proceed to make the experiment, because it is in itself certain either that I shall ascertain this fact, or that I shall not do it. If I *shall not,* nothing that I can do will answer; and if I absolutely *shall*, nothing that I can neglect to do will prevent it.

He must, I think, be a very poor logician, who does not perceive a flaw in this chain of reasoning. In the first place, I do not know which of the two possible events is that which *will be future*, and therefore I cannot be affected as I should be if I did know which of them it was. If this consideration could have any weight, it would incline me to *act*, and *not to act* with equal force, and thererore leave me as much at liberty as if it had never interfered at all. In the second place, I do perfectly well know, that unless I make the experiment I never can make the discovery; and this circumstance alone would be a proof that I should not make it. But, on the contrary, if I make the experiment, which depends upon myself, I cannot fail to obtain the knowledge I want.

With this state of mind, which necessarily arises from my situation, let any person say, whether it be possible for me to stop without making the experiment, unless the object of it should suddenly become indifferent to me, any more than I could stop in any other part of the process, in which *direct volitions* were not at all concerned. Having, therefore, all the necessary materials, and a proper apparatus at hand, necessarian as I am, I shall certainly take the first opportunity of doing what I had projected; the connexion between the *desire* and the *action* not being at all broken by any consideration of an unknown future event.

This also must be the case with respect to any other event that depends upon my endeavours or volitions. If I see my child struggling for life in the water, it is impossible I should refrain from endeavouring to save him, unless the life of my child should suddenly become indifferent to me, or I should perceive that all my endeavours could avail nothing to relieve him. I cannot conceive how any speculations about the event being *previously certain*, one way or the other should influence my conduct, so long as that certainty is unknown to me. Let a person consider this case in every possible light, and he must be satisfied, that there must be some fallacy or other in any chain of reasoning, in consequence of which it may be pretended that a father should be restrained from endeavouring to save the life of his child.

The like may be observed with respect to the education of my child. It is certainly known to God, and therefore a thing certain in itself, that he will be either virtuous or vicious, a credit or a disgrace to me. But can the knowledge of this make me indifferent about his education, so long as I believe that my instructions have a necessary connexion with his future conduct? This, though certain in itself, is altogether uncertain with respect to me; but I know that if I conduct myself right, I shall most probably determine the event in my favour.

It may be said that, whatever becomes of myself, my schemes, or my children, the *final issue* is sure to be *right in itself;* being agreeable to the divine plan, which it is not in my power to defeat. Whether, therefore, this plan requires that myself, or my children, be happy or miserable, I ought to acquiesce in it; leaving all concern about that to him who is the best judge concerning it, and who has the appointment of it.

But so long as it is *unknown to me* whether the general plan of Providence requires my happiness or my misery, it can operate no more than the idea of *future certainty* in general; and therefore could not incline me either to negligence or to vigilance with respect to my conduct. For, if my negligence may favour the divine plan, it may also be inconsistent with it. In this case, therefore, my regard for myself and my children must operate uncontrouled, just as if no idea whatever about the divine plan had interfered. Besides, the general scheme of Providence being manifestly in favour of virtue and happiness, the antecedent presumption is, that it requires my virtue and happiness, and also that of my children, rather than our misery, though this catastrophe *may* be consistent with it.

There is, moreover, a fallacy in the general expression, that it is *not in our power* to obstruct the divine purposes. That no man, by setting himself against God, can succeed, so as to carry his own schemes against those of his Maker, is true; and a great and comfortable truth it is. But to say that human endeavours and exertions are not *necessary* to the divine purposes, is to say that the Divine Being never employs the volitions and exertions of men to gain his purposes, which is far from being true. And if these be necessary means to gain his ends, those ends certainly could not be gained, at least so well gained, without them; and therefore there is likewise a sense in which, though it may be strictly true, that it is not in the power of man to *obstruct* the designs of God, yet that it is in the power of man to *promote* the designs of God; and the reflection that we are doing so is a great satisfaction to a virtuous mind, when we are acting such a part, as, from the general plan of Providence, we have reason to conclude that we are favouring it, not indirectly, as we may be doing by our vice and misery, but directly and properly, by our virtue and happiness.

Having heard this objection to the doctrine of necessity frequently urged, and by persons whose judgment I respect, I have given all the attention to it that I possibly can, and I am satisfied that it turns upon a fallacy exactly similar to that by which it is pretended, that the *will itself* is the cause of its own determinations. In this case the will itself cannot be the cause of any one particular determination in preference to another, any more than the motion of the air can be an adequate and proper cause of the wind blowing from the North rather than from the South; because the will itself, independent of *motives*, bears an equal relation to all particular determinations, just as the motion of the air is equally concerned in all particular winds. In like manner, no respect to any thing *future*, to any thing as *right in the plan of Providence*, &c. &c. can possibly influence the mind to indolence or exertion, or to one mode of exertion in preference to another, so long as it is *unknown to us* what is to be future, or what is the plan of Providence, &c., because while it is unknown, it bears an equal relation to indolence or exertion, and to all modes of exertion without distinction. In all cases, therefore, the mind will be decided by other considerations, and such as are common to necessarians and to all mankind.

I have also frequently endeavoured to scrutinize my own feelings with respect to this objection, with the greatest rigour. But though I believe the doctrine as firmly as perhaps any person ever did, without starting at any of the consequences of it, and in the course of writing so much about it, have given as much attention to it as perhaps any other person ever did, I cannot perceive the least tendency that it has to abate my ardour in any pursuit.

Before the various controversies in which I have been engaged on this subject, it may be supposed that these principles, not having been particularly attended to, might have no particular influence; but since I have given so much attention to them, I am conscious that my activity is in no respect abated. On the contrary, I rather flatter myself that my views of the great system to which I belong being thereby more just and enlarged, I feel a growing satisfaction in my contemplation of it; just and proper objects of pursuit are at least not less frequently occurring to me, and I feel perhaps an increasing ardour in the prosecution of them. Feeling this in myself, I cannot help concluding that other persons must feel the same; and therefore I am so far from apprehending any ill consequences from the doctrine, that I sincerely rejoice in finding so many proselytes continually making to it.

No person will be afraid of the doctrine of necessity but he who mistakes its nature and tendency, and therefore will not be a necessarian, and consequently will not be influenced by it at all; and the moment that any person becomes a necessarian, all these fears will vanish. A man of a bad disposition and bad views, may *pretend* to avail himself of *any* principles, in excuse of his conduct; but with respect to the doctrine of necessity, it can be nothing more than a pretence, the thing itself having no such aspect. On the contrary, it will tend, as far as it is understood, to correct and enlarge a man's views of things, and consequently will tend to better his disposition, and to correct his conduct, as I think I have sufficiently shewn in the course of this treatise, and of my several defences of it.

I am very sensible that I have advanced nothing materially new in this *Appendix;* but I have acquitted myself in the best manner that I can with respect to a doctrine which I value, by endeavouring to remove an impediment, which, without feeling myself, I find to be an obstruction to the hearty reception of it with others.

For the benefit of many persons who are altogether unprepared for the discussion of this subject, I shall conclude all that I shall probably ever write about it, with repeating what I observed at the very entrance on it, viz. in the Preface to my *Examination of the Writings of Drs. Reid, Beattie and Oswald*, and which has been fully verified in the course of this controversy.

" As to the doctrine of *necessity*,—it may possibly save some persons (who will think that I would not speak at random) not a little trouble, if I here give it as my opinion, that unless they apply themselves to the study of this question pretty early in life, and in a regular study of Pneumatology and Ethics, they will never truly understand the subject, but will always be liable to be imposed upon, staggered, confounded and terrified, by the representations of the generality of writers.—The common Arminian doctrine of *free-will*, in the only sense of the words in which mankind generally use them, viz. *the power of doing what we please*, or *will*, is the doctrine of the Scriptures, and is what the philosophical doctrine of necessity supposes ; and farther than this no man does, or need to look, in the common conduct of life or of religion.*

* See Vol. III. pp. 7, 8. Yet there have been Christians who, without pursuing the studies here described, have considered the representations of *God* and *man*, in the Scriptures, till they have attained as firm a conviction of the truth and practical tendency of the doctrine of *Necessity* as my author himself. He, I am persuaded, might have found an increasing number of such *Necessarians*, and no man would have rejoiced more in the discovery.

LETTERS

TO THE

Rev. Mr. John Palmer and Jacob Bryant, Esq.

IN DEFENCE

OF THE

ILLUSTRATIONS

OF

PHILOSOPHICAL NECESSITY.

[1779 *and* 1780.]

LETTER

TO THE

REV. MR. JOHN PALMER.

Respecting Man, whatever wrong we call
May, *must be right*, as relative to all

POPE.

DEAR SIR,

NOTWITHSTANDING my unwillingness to engage any
farther in metaphysical controversy, there are some circumstances attending your *Observations on my Treatise on
Philosophical Necessity,** that make me in this case less
averse to it. You are an old acquaintance, whom I respect,
and whom I believe to be actuated by the best views ; you
are thought to be a master of this subject, and have certainly
given very particular attention to it ; thinking, as I myself do,
that it is of the greatest importance, and now, in a work of
considerable extent, you confine your observations to it.

Your publication has also been a work of great expectation among our common friends, who were apprised of your
intentions. By your own account, in your Preface, it must
have been composed more than a year ago.† In this time
it has been submitted to the perusal of persons of great
learning and worth, who, I am informed, think highly of it,
and have recommended the publication, not only as excel-

---

* "Observations in Defence of the Liberty of Man, as a moral Agent; in Answer
to Dr. Priestley's Illustrations of Philosophical Necessity. By John Palmer, Minister
of New Broad Street." 1779. Mr. Palmer also published a pamphlet entitled "Free
Thoughts on a Dissenter's Conformity to Religious Tests," in which he ably advo-
cated Religious Liberty. He had been the friend of Dr. Priestley's early associate,
Mr. Alexander, whose *Paraphrase* he edited in 1766. See Biog. Brit. II. p 207.
Mr. Palmer has been deceased several years.

† "The following Observations were nearly finished before the publication of the
correspondence between Dr. Price and Dr. Priestley; though I have since given
that performance a very careful perusal, and cannot but recommend it to the attention of those, who have leisure and inclination for such studies, both in the view of
it as a work, which manifests distinguished ability, in the defence of each side of the
question, respecting the two important subjects of Materialism and Necessity, and
as exhibiting a specimen of controversial writing, the direct reverse to what we
commonly see, but much to be admired, and most worthy of imitation, for the
liberality with which it is conducted." *Observ.* Pref. p 6.

lent in itself, but as very proper to follow that of Dr. Price, who was thought by them to have been too tender of me, in our amicable discussion, and to have made some imprudent concessions. Your work, it is thought, will supply the deficiency in his.

You had the generosity to propose submitting your work to my own private perusal, and though for reasons of delicacy and propriety I. thought proper to decline it, I encouraged you in your design of publication. Also, though I did not, I believe, make you any particular promise, you will probably expect that, all things considered, I shall give you an answer. I therefore do it, and with the same freedom with which you yourself have written. But I shall confine myself chiefly to the discussion of those points on which the real *merits of the question* turn, without replying at large to what you have advanced with respect to the *consequences* of the doctrine. Indeed, if the doctrine itself be true, we must take all the genuine consequences, whether we relish them or not. I proceed, therefore, to a state of the controversy between us, and the consideration of the nature and weight of what you urge with respect to it.

The principal argument for the doctrine of Necessity is briefly this: if, in two precisely equal situations of mind, with respect both to disposition and motives, two different determinations of the will be possible, one of them must be an effect without a cause. Consequently, only one of them is possible.

Now, all that the ingenuity of man can reply to this is, either that, though the determination be uncertain, or contingent (depending neither upon the previous disposition of mind nor the motives presented to it), it will still, on some account or other, not properly be *an effect without a cause.* For that there can be any effect without a cause, no advocate for the doctrine of liberty has, I believe, ever asserted. Or, in the next place, it may be said, that the above is not a fair stating of the question in debate; for that the determinations may be invariably the same in the same circumstances, being agreeable to some constant law or rule, and yet, not being *necessarily* so, the necessarian, in fact, gains no advantage by the concession.

You, Sir, have combated the necessarians on both these grounds, maintaining that whatever be the state of mind, or the motives present to it, it has within itself a power of determining without any regard to them, the *self-determining power* being itself the proper *cause* of the determination. You likewise assert that, though there should be the greatest *certainty* in all the determinations of the will, yet, because it is not a *physical*, but only a *moral certainty*, it is not a proper *necessity*. I shall consider distinctly what you have advanced on both these views of the subject, in the order in which I have mentioned them.

SECTION I.

Of the Argument for the Doctrine of Necessity from the Consideration of the Nature of Cause and Effect.

" In the very same circumstances," you say, " in which" the mind's " choice or determination was directed to one object of pursuit, it might have brought itself to will, or determine on, the pursuit of a different and contrary one. In other words, the mind is free to deliberate upon, and, in consequence of this, to choose and determine the motives of its conduct." P. 17.

This state of the case, I would observe in the first place, evidently implies that the mind cannot determine itself without some motive; but you think that, because it is capable of *deliberating* upon motives, it can choose what motive it will be determined by. But if the mind cannot finally determine without a motive, neither, surely, can it *deliberate*, that is, *determine to deliberate*, without a motive : because the volition to deliberate cannot be of a different nature from the volition that is consequent to the deliberation. A volition, or a decision of the mind, by whatever name it be denominated, or whatever be its nature, must be one and the same thing. It must, in all cases, be subject to the same rule, if it be subject to rule, or else be equally subject to no rule at all. You had better, therefore, say at once, that every determination of the mind, even the final one, may proceed on no motive at all. And your next retreat will equally serve you here ; for you still maintain that, though there be nothing, either in the disposition of mind or the motives present to it, that was at all the cause of the determination, it will not be an effect without a cause, because the self-determining power is, itself, a proper and adequate cause.

" There remains a proper cause," you say, " a sufficient and adequate cause for every volition or determination which is formed. This cause is that self-determining power, which is essential to agency, and in the exercise of which motion begins." P. 24. Again, " One principle of freedom in the human mind, of which mankind are universally conscious, will sufficiently account for all their actions; and to seek after other causes, must, therefore, in his own way of reasoning, be wholly unnecessary." P. 36.

Now, to every thing that can be advanced to this purpose, I think I have given a satisfactory reply in the *Additional Illustrations*, printed in Vol. III. pp. 466—470, in which I shew that the self-determining power, bearing an equal relation to any two different decisions, cannot be said to be a proper and adequate cause with respect to them both. But this Section, I suppose, you must have overlooked, otherwise you could not but have thought it peculiarly necessary to reply to my observations on that subject, which so very materially affect your argument. I must, therefore, take the liberty to request that you would consider it, and reply to it.

To argue as you do here, in any other case, would be thought very extraordinary. If I ask the cause of what is called the *wind*, it is a sufficient answer to say, in the first instance, that it is caused by the motion of the air, and this by its partial rarefaction, &c. &c. &c.; but if I ask why it blows *north* rather than *south*, will it be sufficient to say that *this* is caused by the motion of the air? The motion of the air being equally concerned in north and south winds, can never be deemed an adequate cause of one of them in preference to the other.

In like manner, the self-determining power, allowing that man has such a thing, and that it may be the cause of determining in general, can never be deemed a sufficient cause of any one particular determination, in preference to another. Supposing, therefore, two determinations to be possible, and there be nothing but the mere self-determining power to decide between them, the disposition of mind and motives being all exactly equal, one of them must want a proper cause, just as much as the north or the south wind would be without a proper cause, if nothing could be assigned but the motion of the air in general, without something to determine why it should move this way rather than that.

Besides, abstractedly and strictly speaking, no *mere power* can ever be said to be an adequate cause of its own acts. It is true that no effect can be produced without a power capable of producing it; but power, universally, requires both *objects* and proper *circumstances*. What, for instance, can

be done with a *power of burning*, without something to
burn, and this being placed within its sphere of action?
What is a *power of thinking*, or *judging*, without ideas, or
objects, to think and form a judgment upon? What, therefore, can be done with a power of *willing*, without something to call it forth? And it is impossible to state any case
in which it can be *called forth*, without implying such *circumstances*, as will come under the description of *motives*, or
reasons for its being exerted one way rather than another,
exactly similar to any other power, that is, *power universally
and abstractedly considered*, corporeal or intellectual, &c.

SECTION II.

*How far the Arguments for the Doctrine of Necessity are
affected by the Consideration of the Soul being material
or immaterial.*

But you have another resource besides that which I have
considered in the preceding Section ; which is, that though
it be true that, supposing the soul to be *material*, and subject
to physical laws, every determination requires a foreign
cause, yet if the soul be *immaterial*, no such cause is
necessary. It may then determine itself in whatever manner it pleases.

" The whole of it," (viz. the Section concerning the argument from cause and effect,) you say, " supposes a similarity
in the constituent principles of matter and spirit ; for by
those only, who confess that similarity, will it be acknowledged that the same general maxims will apply, both to
effects mechanically produced, and those which depend
upon will and choice." P. 20. Again, you say, " To a
principle of thought conceived to be material, a change of
circumstances may be essential to a difference of volition ;
but when the mind is considered as being in its own nature
immaterial, and therefore not subject to the laws of matter,
but as endued with a self-determining power, a variety of
volition or determination in the same situation or circumstances may surely be admitted as possible, without any
contradiction, or seeming difficulty at all." P. 22.
Now I really cannot conceive that the contradiction is at
all the less glaring, or the difficulty more surmountable, on
the hypothesis of the mind being immaterial. It does,
indeed, follow that the mind, being immaterial, is not subject to the laws of matter ; but it does not, therefore, follow

that it is subject to *no laws at all*, and consequently has a self-determining power, independent of all laws, or rule of its determinations.   In fact, there is the very same reason to conclude that the mind is subject to laws as the body. *Perception, judgment*, and the *passions*, you allow to be so ; why then should the *will* be exempt from all law ? Do not perception, judgment, and the passions, belong to the mind, just as much as the will ? Yet, notwithstanding this, it is only in certain cases that the powers of perception, judgment, or the passions, can be exerted. Admitting the mind, therefore, to be immaterial, it may only be in certain cases that a determination of the will can take place. You must find some other substance to which the will is to be ascribed, entirely different from that in which perception and judgment inhere, before you can conclude that its affections and acts are not invariable, and even necessary.

Besides, according to all *appearances*, from which alone we can be authorized to conclude any thing, the decisions of the will as invariably follow the disposition of mind, and the motives, as the perception follows the presentation of a proper object, or the judgment follows the perceived agreement or disagreement of two ideas. This, at least, is asserted by necessarians, and it does not depend upon the mind being material or immaterial whether the observation be just or not. If it be invalidated, it must be on some other ground than this. I am willing, however, to follow you through all that you allege in support of this argument.

Moral necessity, you say, " arises from the influence of reasons and motives ; which, as they are not physical beings or substances, cannot possibly act as one physical being or substance does upon another." P. 45.   Again, " where there is the greatest certainty, or necessity of the *moral* kind, there is always a possibility of a different choice." P. 82.   And, " In the strict philosophical sense, nothing can be necessary, which is not physically so; or which it would not be a contradiction to the nature of things to suppose not to be, or to be otherwise than it is. Now this kind of necessity we clearly perceive in the case of one body acting upon another, and giving motion to it.—But do arguments and motives bear the same physical relation to the determinations of the mind?" , P. 46.

I own I am rather surprised at the confidence with which you urge this argument, when it is maintained, and insisted on by necessarians, that arguments and motives *do* bear as *strict* a relation (call it physical or moral, or by whatever name you please) to determinations of the mind, as any other causes in nature to their proper effects; because, according to manifest appearances, the determinations of the will do, in fact, as certainly follow the apprehension of arguments and motives, as any one thing is ever observed to follow another in the whole course of nature; and it is just as much a contradiction to suppose the contrary in the one case as in the other, that is, a contradiction to the known and observed laws of nature; so that they must have been otherwise than they are now established, if any thing else should follow in those cases. No other kind of contradiction would follow in any case.

You say, however, p. 43, " Physical necessity is a necessity arising out of the nature of things, and immediately depending upon it; so that while things remain to be what they are, it would be a contradiction to suppose, that the consequences flowing from this kind of necessity can be different from those 'which do actually result from it. To say that any thing is necessary, in this sense, is the same as saying that it is a natural impossibility for it not to be, or to be different from what it is." P. 43. And you say, " The fall of a stone is the necessary effect of that law of gravity which is impressed upon it." P. 44.

Now I do maintain, and all appearances will justify me in it, that a determination of the mind according to motives is, using your own words, that which arises from the very nature of the mind, and immediately dependent upon it; so that the mind remaining what it is, and motives what they are, it would be a contradiction to suppose that they should be different from what they are in the same circumstances. The parallel between material and immaterial natures is here most strict, and the inference the very same in the one case as in the other. If the fall of a stone be the necessary effect of gravity impressed upon it, or upon *body*, in the very *same sense* (because for the very *same reason*) the determination of the will is the necessary effect of the laws impressed upon it, or upon *mind*. This conclusion is as much grounded on facts and appearances as the other.

Nay, beginning with *mind*, I might, according to your mode of reasoning, say first, that according to all appearances, the mind is necessarily determined by motives, for every thing we see in human nature confirms it. Mind is, therefore, subject to fixed laws, but matter is a thing totally different from mind. It cannot, therefore (whatever appearances may be) resemble mind in this, or any other respect, and consequently must be free from all fixed laws whatever. Thus might your own arguments be retorted upon you, and bring you to an evident absurdity ; but, in my opinion, not a greater absurdity, or more contrary to fact, than that the mind is free from all fixed laws, and endued with a power of self-determination. .

I wish, however, you would explain in what sense it would be a *contradiction* for a stone not to fall to the ground. It is only from the observation of the *fact* that we find it does tend to the ground. *A priori*, it would have been just as probable that it might have tended to recede from the ground, and to rise upwards. Where also would be the contradiction, in any proper sense of the word, if acids did not unite with alkalies, or if water should take fire and burn, like spirit of wine? No person, I presume, is sufficiently acquainted with the nature of things, to pronounce, that there would be any thing that could be called a *contradiction* in results the very opposite of what we see do take place.

That which approaches the nearest to a properly necessary effect, is *the receding of bodies after impulse*, which you also maintain. But, though you say you *clearly perceive* this necessity, even this is a case in which, I will take upon me to say, you cannot *demonstrate* the consequence to be necessary. For, as I presume I have shewn at large, there is not *actual contact* in *all* cases of seeming impulse, and, therefore, the receding of one body from another, in those circumstances, is owing to a real *repulsion*, which we can no more resolve into a *mechanical effect*, than we can those of *gravity*, because they both take place at a distance from the bodies concerned.

Now, as it is simply in consequence of the observed *uniformity of the fact*, that I conclude a stone will fall to the ground, it is equally in consequence of the observed uniformity of the fact, that I conclude the determination of the mind will follow the motive. An inference from observation is surely as decisive in one case as in the other ; and this is clearly independent of all consideration of the mind being material or immaterial.

SECTION III.

Of Certainty and Necessity.

You seem sometimes willing to allow that the determination of the will may be *certain*, that is, a definite thing in definite circumstances, and yet you maintain that it is not *necessary;* so that the arguments in favour of liberty are not affected by the concession.

" The argument itself," you say, " may be resolved into this short question, Whether certainty implies necessity? Or, whether that which is morally certain, is, therefore, physically necessary?" P. 74. And, as to *motives*, that " it is not their influence, but their necessitating influence, which is denied." P. 23.

Now, this is a case that I had considered so fully in my late *Treatise*, in my *Correspondence with Dr. Price*, and in my *Letters to Dr. Horsley and Mr. Berington*, that I did not think I should have heard any more of it; and yet it seems you have read part, at least, of what I have advanced on that subject; for you say, " The best reason which I can collect from all the Doctor has advanced on this subject, in favour of such a physical connexion respecting the operations of the mind, is the universality or certainty of the effects, that is, of the determination which takes place in any given circumstances. But though it be allowed that any particular effect would ever so certainly follow on a state of mind, and a situation of external objects corresponding with it, this will not prove the effect to be necessary. Certainty, that is, a moral certainty," and a " physical necessity, or a necessity arising out of the nature of things, do and cannot but imply in them very different ideas; nor is the latter by any means the consequence of the former." P. 40.

You have, indeed, been able to collect, which was not difficult, (for I had occasion to repeat it several times,) that, in favour of the *necessary* determination of the mind accord-according to motives, I have urged the *certainty* and *universality* of such a determination; but I wonder you should not likewise have observed, that, in farther support of this, I added, that *certainty or universality is the only possible ground of concluding that there is a necessity in any case whatever;* and to this, which you have not so much as noticed, you ought principally to have replied.

Please, Sir, to reflect a moment, and tell me distinctly, why you believe that there is a necessity that a stone must fall to the ground? Can it be any thing else than its having been observed that it *constantly* and *universally* does so? If, therefore, the determination follows the motives as certainly as a stone falls to the ground, there must be the very same reason to conclude, that, whether we see *why* it is so or not, (which, indeed, we do not in the case of the falling of the stone,) there is a *necessity* for its doing so. The difference cannot be in the *reality,* but only in the *kind* of necessity. The necessity must be the same, or equally strict and absolute, in both, let the *causes* of the necessity in the two be ever so different.

As I have told Dr. Horsley, but which you seem not to have attended to, " I will allow as much difference as you can between moral and physical causes. Inanimate matter, or *the pen* that I write with, is not capable of being influenced by motives, nor is the hand that directs the pen, but the mind that directs both. I think I distinguish these things better by the terms voluntary and involuntary, but these are mere words, and I make no comparison between them, or between moral and physical causes, but in that very respect in which you yourself acknowledge that they agree, i. e. the certainty with which they produce their respective effects. And this is the proper foundation of all the necessity that I ascribe to human actions. My conclusion, that men could not, in any given case, act otherwise than they do, is not at all affected by the *terms* by which we distinguish the laws and causes that respect the mind from those which respect the external world. That there are *any laws,* and that there are *any causes,* to which the mind is subject, is all that my argument requires. Give me the thing, and I will readily give you the name." (See p. 154).

" If" (as I observed to Mr. Berington) " the mind be, in fact, constantly determined by motives, I desire you would say candidly why you object to the mere term *necessity,* by which nothing is ever meant but the *cause of constancy.* It is only because I see a stone fall to the ground constantly, that I infer it does so necessarily, or according to some fixed law of nature. And, please to say, whether you think it could happen, that the mind should be constantly determined by motives, if there was not a fixed law of nature from which that constant determination results?" (See p. 124).

These passages, I presume, you have overlooked. You certainly have not noticed them, or given due attention to them.

You must give me leave to observe, on this subject of *moral certainty*, that you seem sometimes to have deceived yourself, by an ambiguous use of that term. Because we are apt to be deceived in our judgments concerning the sentiments and conduct of men, so that the greatest certainty we can attain to with respect to them is frequently imperfect, we distinguish it from *absolute certainty*, by calling it *moral*, and then apply the same term to other things, calling that a *moral certainty* which is only a great *probability*. Thus, in the doctrine of chances, if there be a thousand to one in my favour, I say there is a moral certainty that I shall succeed. But it does not follow that, because the term *moral certainty* has by this means come to mean the same thing with *a high degree of probability*, nothing relating to the *mind* can have any thing more than a moral certainty, that is, a *probability*, attending it. Many propositions relating to the mind are as absolutely certain as any relating to the body. That the will constantly and invariably decides according to motives, must not, therefore, be concluded to have nothing more than a moral certainty attending it, merely because it is a truth relating to the *mind*, or to *morals*. It may be as absolutely certain as any truth in natural philosophy. It is the evidence of the *fact* that should be considered, and not the mere nominal distinctions of things.

For the farther illustration of this subject, I hope to satisfy you, that even all that you describe as most horrid and frightful in the doctrine of *necessity*, follows as evidently from your doctrine of *certainty*, provided it be a *real* certainty, though not such as you would choose to call a *physical* one; and, therefore, that it can be nothing more than the mere *name* that you object to.

We will suppose that a child of yours has committed an offence, to which his mind was *certainly*, though *not necessarily*, determined by motives. He was not made, we will say, in such a manner as that motives had a *necessary* effect upon his mind, and *physically* or *mechanically* determined his actions, but only that his mind would in all cases *determine itself* according to the same motives. You hear of the offence, and prepare for instant correction, not, however, on the idea that punishment is justifiable whenever it will reform the offender, or prevent the offences of others, but simply on your own idea, of its having been in the power of the moral agent to act otherwise than he had done.

Your son, aware of your principles, says, Dear father, you ought not to be angry with me, or punish me, when you knew that I could not help doing as I have done. You placed the apples within my reach, and knew that my fondness for them was irresistible. No, you reply, that is not a just state of the case, you were not under any *necessity* to take them, you were only so constituted as that you *certainly* would take them. But, says your son, what am I the better for this freedom from necessity? I wish I had been *necessarily* determined, for then you would not punish me; whereas now that I only *certainly* determine myself, I find that I offend just as much, and you always correct me for it.

A man must be peculiarly constituted, if, upon this poor distinction, he could satisfy himself with punishing his son in the one case, and not in the other. The offence he clearly foresaw would take place: for by the hypothesis, it was acknowledged to be *certain*, arising from his disposition and motives; and yet merely because he will not term it *necessary*, he thinks him a proper object of punishment. Besides, please to consider whether, if the child never *did* refrain from the offence in those circumstances, there be any reason to think that he properly *could* have refrained. We judge of all *powers* only by their *effects;* and in all philosophy we conclude, that if any thing never *has* happened, and never *will* happen, there is a sufficient cause, though it may be unknown to us, why it never *could* happen. This is our only ground of concluding concerning what is possible or impossible in any case.

SECTION IV.

Of the Argument for the Doctrine of Necessity, from the Consideration of Divine Prescience.

IF there be any proposition strictly *demonstrable*, it is, as it appears to me, that *a contingent event is no object of prescience*, or that a thing which, in its own nature, *may*, or *may not* be, cannot be certainly known to be future; for then it might be certainly known to be what it confessedly *may not be*. If, therefore, the mind of man be so constituted, as that any particular determination of his will may or may not take place, notwithstanding his previous circumstances, the Divine Being himself cannot tell whether that determination will take place or not. The thing itself is not subject to his controul, nor can be the object of his fore-knowledge.

To say, as you quote from some other person, p. 33, but without any declared approbation, that " fore-knowledge, if it does imply *certainty*, does yet by no means imply *necessity*, and that no other certainty is implied in it than such a certainty as would be equally in the things, though there were no fore-knowledge of them," is too trifling to deserve the least attention. You, therefore, in fact, give it up, and as, according to your system, the Divine Being cannot have this fore-knowledge, you take a good deal of pains to shew that he may do very well without it.

" Prescience," you say, " is by no means essential to the government of free beings.—And a government of this nature, though prescience should be deemed inadmissible, as a contrariety to contingency in the event, may, notwithstanding, be as complete in its designs and operations, as the utmost possible extent of knowledge, that is, the most perfect knowledge, united with almighty power, can make it." Pp. 31, 32. This, however, in these circumstances, may be very incomplete and inadequate for its purpose. You add, " it cannot be impossible to almighty power, when the-characters of men are known, because really existing, to bring about by means which, previous to their operation, we cannot foresee, those events which he judges fit and proper for the maintenance and promotion of the well-being of his rational creation. And, after all, whatever present irregularities may be permitted to take place in the allotments of Providence to the sons of men, the grand and ultimate part of the plan of God's moral government, in the exact and equal distribution of rewards and punishments in a future scene of existence,—stands on the same firm and immoveable grounds, whether the contingent actions of men be foreseen or not." Pp. 30, 31.

This, and what you farther advance on the same subject, I really am not able to read without pain and concern. You say, " that the prophecies of scriptures do imply divine prescience, in certain instances, must be allowed." P. 32. Now, unable as you evidently are to defend the very *possibility* of this prescience, this concession is rather extraordinary. To be truly consistent, and, at the same time, a believer in revelation, you ought to assert, how embarrassed soever you might be in making out the proof of it, that there is no real fore-knowledge where a direct interference is not to be understood.

To lessen this difficulty, you say that, by denying that prescience to God, which is inconsistent with " the idea of liberty or agency in man,—we only deny that to belong to the supreme mind, which is, in truth, no perfection at all. For, if it be really impossible that even infinite knowledge should extend to actions or events in their own nature contingent, that is, where proper liberty or agency is supposed, we no more derogate from the perfection of the divine knowledge, by maintaining that God cannot know such actions or events, than we diminish his power by asserting that it cannot work contradictions, or what is really no object of power at all.   Equally must it consist with the omniscience of the Divine Being, to say he cannot know that which is impossible to be known, as it does with his omnipotence to assert that he cannot do that which is impossible to be done." Pp. 27, 28.

I should think, however, that it must be a matter of deep regret to the human race, that the object of our supreme veneration and worship, on whom we constantly depend for *life, breath and all things*, should want such an attribute as that of *prescience*, though it should be impossible that he could be possessed of it.   It would certainly be more satisfactory to us to be dependent upon a Being who had planned and provided for the whole course of our existence, before we came into being, than on one who could not tell what turn things would take with respect to us the next moment of our lives, and who must, therefore, either interpose by a proper miracle when we fall into any unforeseen misfortune, or leave us to struggle with it and be overwhelmed by it.

It is certainly no reflection upon me that I cannot see into the table I write on, and discover the internal texture of it; but I know that, as a philosopher, it would be a great perfection and advantage to me if I occasionally could.   I cannot help thinking that, with less ingenuity than you have employed to shew how the Divine Being might do without prescience, that is, without *omniscience*, you might prove that a power much short of *omnipotence*, and a degree of goodness much less than infinite, might suffice for him ; and you might say it would be no reflection upon him at all to be less the object of love and reverence than we now conceive him to be.   It can be no *detraction*, you might say, from any being, or *degradation*, to deny him what he never could have.

I rejoice that my opinions, whether true or false, oblige me to think with more reverence of the Supreme Being. It gives me a higher idea of my own dignity and importance, from a sense of my relation to him, and dependence upon him. You say, however, that " the only character which the necessarian tenet, if considered in its due extent, will admit of, as belonging to the uncreated mind, is a mixed one, in which, if I may so speak, *matchless virtues* and *matchless vices* are blended together." P. 216. And again, " he cannot but appear to be (horrid thought!) the most sinful of all beings." P. 188. *Horrid thought* indeed! But remember, it is not the necessarian who has himself this idea of the object of his worship. This is only what *you* think for him; whereas it is yourself that deprive the Divine Being of his prescience; which makes no small difference in the case. It is of little consequence to me what *you* think of the God that I worship, though it hurts me to hear him reproached in this manner. It is as little to you what *I* think of him whom you, or any other person, professes to worship; but what *we ourselves* think of him is a very serious business.

Being aware of the impossibility of carrying on a scheme of perfect moral government on your principles, without having recourse to a future state, you, however, make yourself easy about any irregularities that cannot be remedied here, on the idea that every thing that unavoidably goes wrong in this life will be set to rights in another. But will not the same irregularities unavoidably arise from the same cause, the same self-determining power, in a future life as well as in this? You will hardly suppose that men will ever be deprived of a privilege which, in your estimation, is of so much importance to them. The nature of *man* will not be fundamentally changed, nor the nature of his *will;* and if this faculty retain the same character, it must be as much as ever perfectly uncontroulled either by the influence of motives or by the Deity himself. It will still, then, for reasons of its own, or for no reason at all, pay just as much or as little regard to every thing *foreign to itself* as it pleases. Even *habits*, which may be acquired in this life, operate only as motives, or biases, inclining the mind to this or that choice, and nothing coming under that description has any decisive influence.

Here is, therefore, from the unalterable nature of things, an everlasting source of irregularity, which must always be suffered for the present, and which can only be remedied in some future state. Thus periods of *disorder*, and periods of *rectification*, must succeed one another to all eternity. What a prospect does this view of things place before us! .

. You ask me, p. 33, " how far it would have been agreeable to *my* ideas of civility and candour, had any writer on the side of liberty, under the warm impressions of an honest zeal against the manifest tendency of my *Illustrations of Philosophical Necessity*, adopted the same satirical strain" that I myself, in a *quotation* you make from my treatise, used " in reference to Dr. Beattie," pp. 33, 34, and then you proceed to parody my own words, inserting my entire paragraph in a note.

" Thus," you say, " our author, in the blind rage of disputation, hesitates not to deprive the ever-blessed God of the possibility of creating, what in revelation is represented as the noblest of his works, a being formed in his own likeness, that is *intelligent* and *free;* subverting that great principle of liberty, than which nothing can be more essential to every just idea of a moral government; which yet we are every where throughout the books of Scripture taught, that the Deity constantly exercises over mankind. This he has done rather than relinquish his fond attachment to the doctrines of Materialism and Necessity; doctrines which seem to draw after them an universal fatalism, through the whole extent of nature, and which, if really true, it must be unspeakably injurious both to the virtue and happiness of the generality of mankind to make public." Pp. 34, 35.

I thank you, Sir, for the opportunity you have given me of trying how I should feel on this occasion. For, otherwise, we are so apt to overlook beams in our own eyes, while we can discover motes in the eyes of others, that I might not have attended to it; and I will tell you frankly how it is with me. Had I thought the reflection *just*, I should have felt it; though seeing it to proceed from an *honest zeal*, should not have thought it contrary to any thing that ought to be termed *civility* or *candour*. But because I consider it as altogether founded on a mistake, I think it injurious to me, and unworthy of you.

I really suspect that neither you nor Dr. Beattie have sufficiently *attended to* the proofs of the divine prescience, either from reason or revelation. For they appear to me really stronger, and more strictly conclusive, than the arguments we have for his omnipotence or his infinite goodness; and the Divine Being himself proposes this as the very test and touchstone of *divinity itself*, so that a being not possessed of it is not, in a strict and proper sense, entitled to the appellation of *God*. Thus saith the Lord, Isa. xli. 22, 23, concerning idols, " Let them—shew us what shall happen. Let them shew the former things what they be,—or declare us things to come." Let them " shew the things that are to come hereafter, that we may know that ye are gods."

This, I own, is *preaching* to one whose office it is to preach to others ; but I must preach on, and observe, that if you will only attend to the amazing variety and extent of the scripture prophecies, comprising the fate of all the great empires in the world, the very *minutiæ* of the Jewish history, and all that is to befall the christian church to the very end of the world, you cannot entertain a doubt, but that every thought in the mind of every man (astonishing as the idea is) *must* have been distinctly perceived by the Supreme Ruler of all things from the beginning of the world.

• You say, " the prophecies of Scripture imply prescience *in certain instances.*" This is greatly narrowing the matter, and giving an idea of it far below the truth. They not only *imply*, but directly *assert* it in *numberless instances ;* and it is implied, I may say, in an infinity of instances. Consider only, for I think it very possible that you may never have attended to it at all (as your principles will naturally incline you to look another way), consider, I say, how many millions of human volitions must have taken place from the beginning of the world, that really (directly or indirectly) contributed to the *death of Christ*, in the *very peculiar circumstances* in which it was actually foretold ; volitions which, according to all appearance (from which alone we are authorized to form any conclusion) were perfectly natural, and uncontroulled by supernatural influence ; and you cannot think it extravagant to say, that all the volitions of the minds of all men must have been known to him that could foretell that one event, *in its proper circumstances.* Not only must he have foreseen the tempers and dispositions of the rulers and common people of the Jews, the peculiar character of Pilate, Herod, and of every man immediately concerned in the transaction, and the peculiar manners and customs of the Romans, but all that had *preceded*, to give the Romans their power, and form their manners and customs, as well as those of the Jews and other nations. Think but a few minutes on the subject, and it will swell far beyond your power of conception, and overwhelm you with conviction. It impresses my mind in such a manner, that, I own, I cannot help being extremely shocked at the seeming *levity* with which you treat this most serious of all subjects.

Such is the evidence of the divine prescience, from the consideration of the scripture prophecies, that, if they be duly considered, I do not think it in the power of the human mind to resist it; and without regard to any *consequences*, that metaphysical system which implies it, and is implied by it, *must be true.* And when the whole scheme is seen in its true colour and form, nothing can appear more admirable and glorious, more honourable to God, or more happy for man. But I will not enlarge on the subject, though I can hardly forbear doing it.

Compared with this, how exceedingly low and poor must be their idea of the moral government of God, who hold him to have no fore-knowledge of the actions of men; and with what little satisfaction can they contemplate it! Only consider on that hypothesis, the millions, and millions of millions of volitions that take place every moment, on the face of this earth only, which the Divine Being, having no proper foresight of, cannot possibly controul. For the mind of man is held to be as absolute, and uncontroulled, within its proper sphere, as the Divine Being is in his. The unknown effects of all these volitions he must always be anxiously watching, in order to remedy the inconveniencies that may arise from them as soon as possible; and he must have a distinct expedient provided for every contingency. What regularity or harmony can there be on such a scheme as this? What strange uncertainty, confusion and perplexity, must reign every where! I am unable to proceed any farther with the shocking picture. I thank God that such is not my idea of the government under which I really live.

To give our common readers an opportunity of judging of the paragraph which you think so obnoxious, and which you have taken care to bring into their view more than once, I shall myself recite the whole, with some things that precede and follow it.

" Among other things, our author gently touches upon the objection to the contingency of human actions from the doctrine of the divine prescience. In answer to which, or rather in descanting upon which (thinking, I suppose, to choose the less of two evils), he seems to make no great difficulty of rejecting that most essential prerogative of the divine nature, though nothing can be more fully ascertained by independent evidence from revelation, rather than give up his darling hypothesis of human liberty; satisfying himself with observing, that *it implies no reflection on the divine power that it cannot perform impossibilities.* In the very same manner he might make himself perfectly easy if his hypothesis should compel him to deny any other of the attributes of God, or even his very being; for what reflection is it upon any person, or thing, that things impossible cannot be? Thus our author, in the blind rage of disputation, hesitates not to deprive the ever-blessed God of that very attribute, by which, in the books of Scripture, he expressly distinguishes himself from all false gods, and than which nothing can be more essentially necessary to the government of the universe, rather than relinquish his fond claim to the fancied privilege of *self-determination;* a claim which appears to me to be just as absurd as that of *self-existence,* and which could not possibly do him any good if he had it.

" Terrified, however, as I am willing to suppose (though he does not express any such thing)—at this consequence of his system, he thinks, with those who maintain the doctrine of a *trinity* of persons in the unity of the divine essence, and with those who assert the doctrine of *transubstantiation,* to shelter himself in the obscurity of his subject; saying, that *we cannot comprehend the manner in which the Divine Being operates.* But this refuge is equally untenable in all the cases, because the things themselves are, in their own nature, impossible, and imply a contradiction. I might just as well say that, though to us, whose understandings are so limited, *two* and *two* appear to make no more than *four,* yet in the divine mind, the comprehension of which is infinite, into which, however, we cannot look, and concerning which it is impossible, and even dangerous, to form conjectures, they may make *five.*"

" Were I possessed of Dr. Beattie's talent of declamation, and had as little scruple to make use of it, what might I not say of the absurdity of this way of talking, and of the horrible immoral consequences of denying the fore-knowledge of God? I should soon make our author, and all his adherents, as black as Atheists. The very admission of so untractable a principle as *contingency* into the universe, would be no better than admitting the Manichæan doctrine of *an independent evil principle.* Nay, it would be really of worse consequence, for the one might be controulled, but the other could not. But, I thank God, my principles are more generous, and I am as far from ascribing to Dr. Beattie all the real consequences of his doctrine, (which, if he could see with my eyes, I believe he would reprobate as heartily as I do myself,) as I am from admitting his injurious imputations with respect to mine." (Vol. III. pp. 90—92.)

I do assure you, Sir, I see nothing to retract in all this, though it is in the first of my works in which I mentioned the subject of *Necessity;* and I do not at all envy you the discovery, that, for the purposes of the moral government of God, *fore-knowledge* is a superfluous attribute.

SECTION V.

Of the MORAL TENDENCY *of the Doctrine of Necessity.*

IT is on the subject of the *moral tendency* of the doctrine of necessity, that you imagine your arguments the strongest, and that you declaim with the greatest warmth and confidence. To all this, however, I think it unnecessary for me to reply. For, notwithstanding all you have written on this favourite theme, I am perfectly satisfied with what I have already advanced, and think it altogether unaffected by your reply. Besides, it behoves you, in the first place, to prove the doctrine to be false. For if it be true, the consequences will follow, and you as well as myself, must make the best we can of them. And I beseech you, for your own sake, that you would not represent them as so very frightful, lest, after all, *they should prove true.*

In the mean time, have some little tenderness for *me*, and consider with what sentiments, one who firmly believes the doctrine of necessity to be true, and at the same time to abound with the most glorious consequences, who imagines he feels it favourable to true elevation of mind, leading, in an eminent manner, to piety, benevolence, and self-government, must peruse the account you have been pleased to draw of his principles. The following are but a few of the features:

" I cannot but think," you say, " that the doctrine of necessity looks very much like a refinement on the old Manichæan notion—of two independent principles of good and evil, which, in this system, are blended in one." P. 242. " I cannot but think," you say, " such sentiments as dangerous in their tendency, as they are false and absurd in themselves. They seem very materially, though undesignedly, to affect the moral character of the Deity, and to be big with consequences the most fatal to the virtue and happiness of mankind." P. 183. " I cannot but look upon the promulgation of the scheme of necessity, as highly exceptionable, because it is likely to do unspeakable mischief." P. 175. " In these most exceptionable and dangerous principles of Calvinism, the doctrine of necessity,—is, when examined to the bottom, really the very same." P. 238. And in your preface, p. 4, you say, " nor can i help expressing very strong apprehensions of the dangerous tendency of the necessarian tenet as a practical principle ; for—that the generality of mankind would—think themselves fully warranted in concluding, that they could not, on any account, deserve punishment, and had therefore nothing to fear." Pp. iv. v.

Before you had concluded, as you have done, that the publication of the doctrine of necessity *must* do such unspeakable mischief to *the generality of mankind*, you would have done well, I think, to have considered the state of the *fact*. Cast your eye over those of your acquaintance, and whom you know to be necessarians, especially those who have been so in early life, and who are the most attached to the doctrine. They are numerous enough to enable you to form some judgment of the practical tendency of their principles. Are their minds more depraved, their objects of pursuit less noble, or their exertions less strenuous, than you have reason to think they would have been if they had not been necessarians?

Had I not been engaged in this controversy, you would probably have thought my own evidence as unexceptionable as that of any other person. But on this I lay no stress, though the compliments you pay me would give me some advantage in this case. If you say that *principles in general* have but an inconsiderable influence on practice, why should you suffer your fears to get the better of your reason in this particular case, and why should you urge what is, in fact, no proper argument at all, with more force, than every other consideration, respecting the real merits of the question?

However, light as I should be disposed to make of your accusation, I shall now treat it with the gravity that yourself will think it entitled to; and I think I may undertake to satisfy you, from your own mode of arguing, that there is no evil whatever to be apprehended from the doctrine of necessity, but, on the contrary, the greatest good, and that you evidently argue on principles inconsistent with each other when you throw so much odium on the scheme.

In the first place, you say, that on the scheme of necessity " all is resolved into a divine constitution, which is unalterably fixed. If any, therefore, are to succeed better, or be happier, in any part of their existence, than others, their superior prosperity and happiness will be infallibly secured to them ; and though there is a certain disposition of mind, and course of action, which are inseparably connected with their success and happiness, as means to bring about those events, yet the means as well as the end are alike necessary ; and having no power to make either the one or the other at all different from what they are, or are to be, their lot, through the whole of their being, is by them absolutely unalterable. What, again, I say, can have a stronger tendency to relax the mind, and sink it into a state of indolence and inactivity ?"   P. 149.

Here then you reduce the necessarian to a state of absolute *inactivity*, that is, indisposed to *any pursuits*, virtuous or vicious. For your argument, if it goes to any thing, goes to both alike.

But, on the other hand, you constantly suppose, so that I have no occasion to quote particular passages, that the necessarian will, of course, give himself up to the gratification of all his passions, and pursue without restraint whatever he apprehends to be his interest,or happiness.

Here then, notwithstanding the natural *indolence* of the necessarian, you are able, when your argument requires it, to find a considerable source of *activity* in him ; because you have discovered, that, like other men, he has *passions*, and a *regard to his interest and happiness*.

But, surely, it is not difficult to conceive, that this activity, from whatever source it arises, may take a good as well as a bad turn, and lead to virtue or vice, according as it is directed. If the gratification of our lower appetites leads to evil, the gratification of the higher ones, as benevolence, &c. (of which, I hope, you will admit that a necessarian, being a man in other respects, may be possessed,) must lead to good ; and that, if false notions of interest and happiness instigate a man to vice, just notions of his interest and happiness must lead to virtue. In fact, therefore, upon your own principles, nothing is requisite to convert even a necessarian from vice to virtue, but the better informing his understanding and judgment, which you expressly allow to be mechanical things, being always determined by a view of the objects presented to them, and to have nothing of self-determination belonging to them.

This, if there be any force in your own reasoning, must be a sufficient answer to every thing that you so pathetically and repeatedly urge concerning the mischiefs to be dreaded

from the doctrine of necessity. · It would be very disagreeable to me to go over all that you say on this subject,
and, therefore, I am glad to find that I have no occasion
to do it.

I am sorry to find that, in pursuing your supposed advantage so inconsiderately as you do, you, in fact, plead the
cause of vice, and represent it as triumphing over every
consideration drawn from the present or a future state.
" How is a vicious man," you say, " who finds that the
present natural good of *pleasure* or *profit* results.from the
gratification of his appetites, and from defrauding or over-
reaching his neighbour, to be persuaded to think that vice
is productive of evil to him here? On the supposition
that there is no moral difference in things, all moral
arguments against the course of conduct to which his appetites or inclinations prompt him, immediately vanish. As
long, therefore, as he can make his present conduct consistent with what is his natural good, or which he looks
upon to be so, that is, with sensitive pleasure, or his worldly
advantage, all is right and well, so far as regards the
present scene of things." P. 185.

Now I am really surprised that you, who have been so
long a preacher, could not, on this occasion, recollect any
thing in answer to such a libertine as this, without having
recourse to arguments drawn from a future state, and even
independent of moral considerations, of which it is but too
apparent that mere sensualists and worldly-minded persons make little account. Do no evils arise to the bodily
constitution, to the mental faculties, or to society, from
habitual excess in eating or drinking, or from the irregular
indulgence of other natural appetites? And short of
excess we are within the bounds of virtue ; for in fact,
nothing is ever properly termed excess, but what does terminate (and it is so called because it terminates) in pain and
misery. Is it not possible that a man may both shorten
his life, and make his short life miserable, by his vices?
Only re-peruse your own excellent sermon, entitled, *The
Insanity of the Sensualist*, written long before this controversy, and you will find many valuable observations to
this purpose.

Supposing conscience entirely out of the question, are
injustice and oppression always successful, and are there
not many proverbs founded on general experience, teaching
even the vulgar, in a variety of expression, that, somehow
or other, ill-gotten wealth does not contribute to happiness?

Or, exclusive of the natural course of things, are there no no such things as laws and magistrates in human society? Are there no gallows, gibbets, or wheels, to which flagrant wickedness may bring a man? Now may not a necessarian see the necessary connexion of these *natural evils* with a course of vicious indulgence, as well as any other person; and, fully apprehending this, can he pursue the one with. out choosing his own destruction, of which I fancy you will allow that he is just as incapable as any person whatever.

Besides, it is very unfair to say that because a necessarian considers those things which are generally termed *moral*, as coming ultimately under the same description with things *natural*, that, therefore, he believes there are no such things at all. You well know that he does not consider these things as at all the less *real*, though, as a philosopher, he chooses to give them another name. A sense of right and wrong, the stings of conscience, &c.,) which, however, will not, in general, be so much felt, by those who believe no future state) are things that actually exist, by whatever names they be signified, and will be felt in a greater or less degree by the most hardened transgressor.

Dr. Hartley and myself (Vol. III. p. 518), have endea. voured to shew that the peculiar feeling of *remorse*, arising from ascribing our actions to ourselves, can never vanish, or cease to influence us, till we arrive at such a comprehension of mind, as will enable us habitually to ascribe every thing to God, and that when we are arrived at this state, we shall live in communion with God, and shall stand in no need of such a motive to virtue. Before this period, let a man be speculatively a necessarian, or whatever he will, and let him pretend what he pleases, it will be *naturally impossible* for him not to feel all the pungency of remorse, whenever even yourself would say that he ought to feel it. You must invalidate our reasoning on this subject, from the consideration of the nature of the human mind, before you can make it appear that a necessarian, *as such*, will be a bad man. But as you lay so very much stress on this subject of remorse of conscience, I will discuss the matter a little farther with you.

You say that remorse of conscience implies that a man thinks he could have acted otherwise than he did. I have no objection to admit this, at the same time, that I say he deceives himself in that supposition. I believe, however, there are few persons, even those who blame themselves with the greatest pungency, but, if they will reflect, will acknowledge, that in so supposing, they leave out the consideration of the situation they were in at the time of the transaction, and that with the same disposition of mind that they had then, and the same motives, they should certainly have acted the same part over again ; but that having, since that time, acquired a different disposition, and different views of things, they unawares carry them back, and consider how they would have acted with their present acquired dispositions, However, their disposition being really altered by what has occurred to them since, they would not *now* act the same part over again, and therefore, all the proper ends of remorse are sufficiently answered.

If you say that the peculiar feeling of remorse is founded on a mistake, I answer, so are the peculiar feelings of anger in most cases, and likewise the peculiar feelings of all our passions ; and that a philosopher, who should have strength of mind to consider his situation, would do the same things coolly and effectually without that *stimulus,* that the vulgar do with it.   He would punish an offender without anger, and he would reform his own conduct without remorse.   But neither you nor myself, necessarian as I am, can pretend to this degree of perfection.   It is acquired by experience ; and the firmest belief of the doctrine of necessity can only accelerate our progress towards it to a certain degree.   All this I have endeavoured to explain in my *Additional Illustrations,* (Vol. III. p. 516,) but you have not noticed it.

What you say of the little influence of the motives to virtue which the necessarian can draw from the consideration of a *future life,* by no means concerns the necessarian as such.   " In relation to futurity," you say, " it is naturally to be supposed, that a man of this disposition, (i. e. a vicious necessarian) will not concern himself about it, or if he does, his necessarian principle, by holding up to his view his future moral good or happiness, as secured to him by his omnipotent Creator, will lead him hastily to pass over all the intermediate sufferings with which he is threatened, how long or severe soever, considering them only as natural evils, which he can no more avoid than the course of action which is connected with him." Pp. 185, 186.

You know very well that they are not necessarians only who believe, that all the sufferings of a future life are corrective, and will terminate in the reformation of those who are exposed to them.   And a man must not be a necessarian, but the reverse of one, and the reverse of every thing that *man* is, before he can be made to slight the consideration either of present or future evils, especially long and severe ones, provided he really believes them, and gives proper attention to them. But with this *belief* and *attention* they cannot but influence any man who regards his own happiness, and who believes the inseparable connexion between virtue and happiness (which no man believes more firmly than the necessarian) to have recourse to a life of virtue, as the only road to happiness, here or hereafter. And having, from whatever motive, begun to tread this path, he will persist in it from a variety of other and better principles.

That you should prefer the Calvinistic doctrine of *eternal punishments*, horrible as you say it is, to that of *universal restoration* to virtue and happiness, could surely be dictated by nothing but your abhorrence of the doctrine of necessity in general, to which it is usually, but not necessarily, an appendage. " I cannot but be of opinion," you say, " that the persuasion of the final restoration of all the wicked to virtue and happiness, which it (the doctrine of necessity) supports, will, in its natural operation, have a very pernicious influence on the unsettled minds of the generality of mankind : while the doctrine of eternal remediless torments for the non-elect, taught by Calvinism, horrible as it is in itself, may, in the way of restraint, have a considerable effect, and in some instances may probably produce an external reformation of life." P. 239.

You may just as well say, that a civil magistrate who punishes without reason, mercy, or bounds, will be more respected than an equitable judge, who exacts an adequate punishment for every offence. Besides, the doctrine of eternal punishments for the offences of a short life is so very absurd, that it must ever be attended with a secret incredulity. At least, a man, though wicked, yet thinking he does not deserve the everlasting pains of hell, will not believe that he shall be sent thither, and therefore will indulge a notion that he shall go to heaven, and escape punishment altogether. But I need not argue this point, as it does not belong to me, as a necessarian, to do it. I have already argued it in my *Institutes of Natural and Revealed Religion.**

* See Vol. II. pp. 61—64, 294, 351—353; also Vol. III. pp. 514, 515.

SECTION VI.

What makes Actions a MAN'S OWN, *and* DEPENDING ON
HIMSELF.

To what I have already advanced in reply to your remarks
on the moral influence of the doctrine of necessity, and the
comparison of it with the Calvinistic doctrine of predestination, I shall add, in a separate Section, some considerations
on men's actions as *depending on themselves,* and being *their
own,* on which you lay so much stress, and which runs
through your whole book. Now I am confident that, in
what you say on this subject, you deceive yourself by the
use of words, or you could not draw the consequences that
you do from what you suppose to be my doctrine on this
subject.

Strictly and philosophically speaking, my success in any
thing I wish to accomplish, depends upon myself, if my
own exertions and actions are necessary links in that chain
of events by which alone it can be brought about. And,
certainly, if I do know this, and the object or end be desirable to me, this desire (if it be of sufficient strength) cannot
but produce the exertion that is necessary to gain my end.
This reasoning appears to me extremely easy, and perfectly
conclusive, and yet, though I have repeated it several times,
and have placed it in a variety of lights, you do not seem to
have considered it. I shall, therefore, give another instance,
and add some farther illustrations.

Can I have a sufficiently strong wish to answer your
book, and not of course read it, mark proper extracts from
it, arrange them, write my remarks upon them, then trans-
cribe them for the press, and put them into the hands of a
bookseller or printer, &c. when I know, that if all this be
not done, the book will never be answered? Surely my firm
belief that all these things are necessarily connected, must
convince me of the necessity of setting about the work, if I
wish to do it all; and my *wish* to have it done is here to be
supposed, as having arisen from a variety of previous circumstances.

If, therefore, I shall certainly find myself disposed to act
just as I now do, believing my actions to be necessary, your
objection to my doctrine on this account cannot have a
sufficient foundation. You say, that if the thing *must be,*
it *must be;* if your book *is to be* answered by me, it *will be*

answered by me; and that I may, therefore, make myself
easy about it, and do nothing. I answer, that so I should,
either if I had no desire to have it done, which happens not
to be the case, or if I thought that no exertions of mine
were necessary to gain my end, which is not the case neither.
On this consideration depends the capital distinction that I
make between the doctrines of philosophical necessity and
calvinistic predestination.

The Calvinists make the work of conversion to be wholly
of God's free and sovereign grace, independent of every
thing in the person thus regenerated or renovated, and to
which he cannot in the least contribute. In this work, they
say, God is the sole agent, and men altogether passive; that
both to *will* and to *do* is of God's pleasure; and so much so,
that without his immediate agency, to which nothing on the
part of man can contribute, let a man exert himself ever so
much, in the use of all possible means, yet all his volitions
and all his actions would be only sinful, and deserving of the
wrath and curse of God to all eternity.

In this case I do not see what a man can have to do,
because his doing, or his not doing, is equally unconnected
with the end he has in view. But this is the very reverse
of the doctrine of philosophical necessity, which supposes
a necessary connexion between our endeavours and our
success; so that if only the *desire of success*, the first link in
this chain, be sufficiently strong, all the rest will follow of
course, and the end will be certainly accomplished.

According to the Calvinists, there may be the most
earnest desire, without a man's being at all the nearer to his
end, because the *desire* and the *end* have no necessary connexion, by means of intermediate links, as we may say, in
the chain that joins them.

It is on this ground that Dr. Hartley justly supposes that
the doctrine of necessity has a tendency to make men exert
themselves, which he makes the fifth advantage attending
the scheme. " It has a tendency," he says, p. 344, of my
edition, " to make us labour more earnestly with ourselves
and others, particularly children, from the greater certainty
attending all endeavours that operate in a mechanical way."
(Ed. 1791, I. p. 510.)

Another of your arguments relating to this subject, I
really cannot treat with so much seriousness as you will
probably expect. I shall not, however, dwell long upon it,
and with this I shall close the Section.

I had observed, that a volition may be termed *mine*, if it

takes place in my mind. Animadverting on this, you say, " Can that be truly said to be my volition, my act, which is produced by something over which I had no power? On that ground every thing that takes place in my body, as well as my mind, may with equal propriety be called my act or volition ; and so the circulation of the blood, and the pulsation of the heart,—may with equal reason be called my volitions." Pp. 80, 81.

Now, Sir, is not *judgment* always called an *act of the mind*, as well as volition ? But has any man power over this ? Is not this necessarily determined by the view of arguments, &c. ? You will not deny it. Does it not therefore follow, on your own principles, that whatever passes in your body, as well as in your mind, may with equal propriety be called an act of your judgment ; and so the circulation of your blood, and the pulsation of your heart, may with equal reason be called your *judgment ?* But the very same things were before proved to be *volitions*. *Ergo, judgments* and *volitions* are the same things. By the same mode of reasoning, it would be easy to prove your head to be your feet, and your feet your head, and both of them to be the same with your understanding, or any thing else belonging to you.

SECTION VII.

Of the proper Object of this Controversy, and a summary View of the principal Sources of Mistake with respect to it.

As I take it for granted you would not have engaged in this controversy, especially after a person for whom you profess so great an esteem as Dr. Price, without thinking you felt yourself fully equal to it, and without being determined to see it fairly out, I shall take the liberty, which I hope you will also do with respect to me, (that we may save ourselves as much trouble as possible) to point out what I think will be of use to us in conducting it. And in doing this, I shall purposely go over some of the ground I have already trod, but in a different direction, hoping that different views of the same objects may be both pleasing and useful.

In general, I think, we shall do well to consider things as much as possible *without the use of words*, at least such words as are, on either side, charged with being the causes of mistake. I shall treat of the principal of them separately.

1. *Of the Term* AGENT.

In the farther prosecution of this debate, do not begin, as you have done now, with assuming that man, in consequence of having a power of choice, is an *agent*, and that being an agent, he cannot be a mere passive being, acted upon by motives, &c., but must be possessed of a power of proper self-determination. In fact, this is no better than taking for granted the very thing in dispute, and therefore you might as well, with Dr. Beattie, disclaim all *reasoning* on the subject, and assert your liberty, on the footing of *common sense*, or *instinct* only.

The only unexceptionable method is, to attend to the real *phenomena of human nature*, and to consider the known actions of men in known situations, in order to determine whether our volitions, which precede all our actions, and direct them, be not always *definite in definite circumstances*. If you admit this, and I think it almost impossible not to admit it, you admit all that I contend for; because it will then follow, that from a man's birth to his death, there is an unalterable chain of *situations* and *volitions*, invariably depending on one another. Your saying that, if this be the case, man is no *agent*, will avail nothing; for if that word imply more than the actual phenomena will authorize, the agency of man, in that sense of the word, flattering as it may sound, must be given up.

Dr. Price does, in fact, allow that men's volitions are definite in definite circumstances, for he says it is the greatest absurdity to suppose that men ever act either without or against motives, but that the self-determining power is wanted only when the motives are equal; which, considering how very seldom this can be supposed to be the case, reduces this boasted liberty of man, in my opinion, to a very small matter, hardly worth contending for.

In this you differ from him: for you carefully avoid making that concession, and always, at least generally, suppose the mind capable of acting contrary to any motive whatever. But then you will do well to consider whether, consistently with the phenomena, Dr. Price could avoid making that concession, alarming as you may think it; and whether it be probable that, in fact, men ever do act either without, or contrary to motives. And if he never *does*, you will not easily prove that he *can*.

If man be an agent, in your sense of the word, that is, if

his will be properly *self-determined*, you must shew that nothing foreign to the will itself, nothing that can come under the description of *motive*, or the circumstances in which the mind is, regularly precedes the determination. For if any such foreign circumstances, any thing that is not *mere will*, does constantly precede every determination, we are certainly authorized, by the established rules of philosophizing, to consider these circumstances as the proper causes of the determination, and may, therefore, say that the will is influenced or acted upon by them. and so, going backwards in the same train, we shall conclude that there can be no more than one proper agent in the universe.

2. *Of Responsibility.*

Let us likewise consider the nature and use of *moral government*, as much as possible, without the use of such words as *responsibility, praise, blame,* &c. and only consider how a wise governor would treat beings whose wills should be invariably influenced by motives ; and if the proper ends of government would, in fact, be answered by annexing happiness to such actions as we call virtuous, and misery to such as we call vicious, (so that every thing we now see or expect would be done,) it will follow, that, for any thing that appears to the contrary, we *may* be so constituted. If the word *responsibility*, as you arbitrarily define it, will not apply to such a system, it ought to be discarded from the language of philosophers.

Take the same course with the words *merit* and *demerit, virtue* and *vice,* &c. and on this subject attend particularly to what Dr. Hartley, in a very short compass, most excellently observes : " It may be said," says he, p. 343, " that the denial of free will destroys the distinction between virtue and vice. I answer, that this is according as these words are defined. If free will be included in the definition of virtue, then there can be no virtue without free will. But if virtue be defined *obedience to the will of God, a course of action proceeding from the love of God,* or *from benevolence,* &c., free will is not at all necessary ; since these affections and actions may be brought about mechanically.

" A solution analogous to this may be given to the objection taken from the notions of merit and demerit. Let the words be defined, and they will either include free will, or, not including it, will not require it ; so that the proposition, *merit implies free will,* will either be identical or false." (Ed. 1791, I. p. 509.)

In all that you have said on the subject of responsibility, you take your own principles for granted, and then it can be no wonder that all your conclusions follow. You make it essential to responsibility, that man has a power, independent of his disposition of mind at the particular time, and of all motives, of acting otherwise than he did, and you take not the least notice of what I have advanced on that subject in the *Correspondence with Dr. Price,* p. 74, &c., where I shew that, notwithstanding it be not in the power of moral agents to act otherwise than they do, yet that a moral governor, who consults the good of his subjects, (whose minds and whose conduct he knows to be influenced by motives,) must treat them in the very same manner that you yourself acknowledge he ought to do. He will apply suffering with propriety, and with good effect, in any case in which the apprehension of it will so impress the minds of his subjects, offenders and others, as to influence their wills to right conduct. So that, as I have observed, p. 74, " though the vulgar and philosophers use different language, they would see reason to *act* in the same manner. The *governors* will rule voluntary agents by means of rewards and punishments ; and the *governed*, being voluntary agents, will be influenced by the apprehension of them. It is consequently a matter of indifference in whatever language we describe actions and characters." This you should have particularly considered and have replied to. You must not tell me what the word *responsibility* requires ; but you must shew that, supposing men to be what I suppose them, the Supreme Ruler ought to have treated them otherwise than he actually has done. If not, every fact exactly corresponds with my hypothesis, and then on what can your objection be founded, except on something that is merely verbal ?

3. *Of the Prejudice arising from the Terms* MACHINE *and* NECESSITY.

You mislead and deceive yourself, I am persuaded, not a little, by the frequent use of the opprobrious term *machine,* saying, in the first place, that because a man wills *necessarily*, that is, definitely in definite circumstances, he wills *mechanically;* and then, having made a man into a *machine,* you, unknown to yourself, connect with it every thing opprobrious and degrading belonging to a common clock, or a fulling-mill.

But you might easily correct this by only considering what you yourself allow to be necessary relating to the mind of man, viz. *perception* and *judgment.* Is there not something inconceivably more excellent in these powers than in those of common machines, or mills, and even something that bears no resemblance to any thing belonging to them, though they all agree in this one circumstance, that their respective affections are necessary ? Now suffer your mind to be sufficiently impressed with the wonderful nature and excellence of the powers of *perception* and *judgment,* and you cannot think the *will* at all degraded by being put on a level with them, even in the same respect in which they all agree with any common machine, or a mill, viz. that all its affections are definite in definite circumstances, though this property be best expressed by the term *necessary.*

If you suffer your mind to be affected by such prejudices as these, you may decline applying the term *substance* to the mind, because it is likewise applied to wood and stone, and oblige yourself to invent some other term by which to distinguish it from them.

With respect to the Divine Being, you will not scruple to say, that his actions are always definite in definite circumstances, and if you decline applying the term *necessary* to them, it is only because you conceive that it implies something more than *definite in definite circumstances:* whereas the two phrases are perfectly synonymous, and it is nothing but the word that you can dislike. The *reasons* why we say that any affection or action is necessary, and why it is definite in definite circumstances, are the very same, and cannot be distinguished in the mind. It is the *constant observation of its taking place in those circumstances.*

It is because we see that a clock always strikes when the hands are in certain positions, that we conclude it always *will* do so, and, therefore, *necessarily must* do so, or that (whether it be known or unknown to us) there is a *cause* why it cannot be otherwise. Now, can you help applying this mode of reasoning, and, consequently, this phraseology, to the mind, and even the Divine Mind, and, at the same time, be free from weak and unworthy prejudices? For, if the will cannot act but when motives are present to it, and if it always determines definitely in definite circumstances, with respect to motives, you cannot but conclude that there is a sufficient reason, known or unknown to you, why it *must* be so, and you can have no reason to suppose that it ever can be otherwise. And, in this case, whether you scruple to say, that such a determination can be called *action*, or be said to be *necessary*, your ideas of the things are the same. If any thing always *will* be so, there can be no good reason why we should scruple to say that it *must*, and *must necessarily* be so.

The Divine Being, you will allow, notwithstanding the incomprehensibility of his nature, always acts definitely in definite circumstances. It would be a weakness and imperfection to do otherwise. In fact, it is no more a degradation of him to say that he acts *necessarily*, than that his essence may be termed *substance*, or *being*, in common with that of the human mind, or even that of wood and stone.

You will say, and justly enough, that this observation applies to the Divine Being only as *actually existing* and *operating ;* and that originally, and before the creation, when there were no external circumstances by which his actions could be determined, his volitions must have been, in the proper and strict philosophical sense of the word, *free*. But then there never can have been a time, to which that observation applies, because there never can have been any time in which the Deity did not *exist*, and consequently *act*. For, supposing him not to have been employed in creation, &c. (which, however, I think we can hardly avoid supposing), he must at least have *thought*, and *thinking*, you will not deny to be the acting of the mind. The origin of action, therefore, in your sense of the word, that is, the origin of self-determination, is the same as the origin of the Deity, concerning which we know nothing at all.

Besides, how can you, or any of Dr. Clarke's admirers, think it any degradation to the Deity, that he should *act* necessarily, when you allow that he *exists* necessarily? Is not the term just as opprobrious in the one case as in the other? Nay, might it not rather be supposed, by analogy, that the actions of the Being whose existence is necessary, must be necessary too? With respect to your notion of dignity and honour, I would ask, Is not the *existence* of any being or thing, of as much importance to him, as his *acting ?* Is not then his being subject to necessity as great a reflection upon him in the former case as in the latter? In short, every thing that you consider as *degrading* and *vilifying* in

man, on account of his being subject to necessity, in his
existence or actions, might, if I were disposed to retort so
trifling and mistaken a consideration, be applied to the
Divine Being himself.   What I now observe is only to
take off the force of your prejudice against the doctrine
of necessity, on account of its exhibiting man, as you suppose, in a degrading and unimportant light.

THE CONCLUSION.

DEAR SIR,

I HAVE now gone over all the topics that I think of
much importance to discuss with you.   I might have taken
a much larger compass; but I was unwilling to take in
more objects than such as I thought I might possibly throw
some new light upon.   As to what you say concerning the
doctrine of the Scriptures, and several other articles, I leave
the field open to you, being fully satisfied with what I
have already advanced, and having nothing material to add
to it.

You will probably think there is an appearance of *arrogance* in the tone of this letter.   But in this, I think, you
will do me injustice; my manner of writing being nothing
more than what necessarily arises from the fulness of my
persuasion concerning the truth and importance of the doctrine I contend for; and this, I think, is not greater than
your own.   But in this I must appeal to indifferent persons,
if any such there be, who will give themselves the trouble
to read what we have written.

We all see *some things* in so clear and strong a light, that,
without having any high opinion of our own understandings,
we think we may challenge all the world upon them.   Such
all persons will think to be most of the propositions of
Euclid, and such, I dare say, with you are many tenets in
theology.   You would not hesitate, I presume, to maintain
that *bread and wine* cannot be *flesh and blood*, against even
a Bossuet, or a Thomas Aquinas, than whom, it is probable,
the world never produced a greater man; and that *three
persons*, each possessed of all the attributes of God, must
make more in number than *one God*, against all the divines
that the three churches of Rome, England and Scotland,
could name to hold the disputation with you.   And, though
it should be deemed, as by them it certainly would be, the
height of arrogance in you to hold out this challenge, it

would not give you any disturbance ; nor, in fact, would you think very highly of yourself, though you should gain a decided victory in such a contest.

Now this happens to be my case with respect to the doctrine of necessity. I really think it the clearest of all questions, the truth of it being as indubitable as that the three angles of a right-lined triangle are equal to two right angles, or that *two* and *two* make *four*, and, therefore, I have no feeling either of *fear* or *arrogance*, in challenging the whole world in the defence of it. This argument I compare to such ground as one man may defend against an army. It is, therefore, absolutely indifferent to me by *whom*, or by *how many*, I be assailed. You would, probably, say the same with respect to the doctrine of Liberty, at least the style in which your book is written seems to speak as much ; and yet I by no means think you deficient in modesty, any more than I do in understanding and ability. I only wish, therefore, that, notwithstanding the confidence with which I have written, you would put the same candid construction on my conduct, that I do on yours.

I make allowance for our difference of opinion, on account of the different lights in which we happen to see things, or in which they have been represented to us ; nor do I at all expect that any thing I have now advanced, or am capable of advancing, will make the least change in your view of things. A change in things of so much moment, which would draw after it a thousand other changes, is not to be expected either in you or myself, who are both of us turned forty, and who were, I suppose, metaphysicians before twenty. Judging of ourselves by other men, we must conclude that our present *general system of opinions*, whether right or wrong, is that which we shall carry to our graves. Those who are younger than we are, and whose principles are not yet formed, are alone capable of judging between us, and of forming their opinions accordingly ; and in that respect they may derive an advantage from these publications that we cannot derive from them ourselves.

We see every day such instances of *confirmed judgments* in things of the greatest, as well as of the least moment, as ought to make the most confident of us to pause, though every man is necessarily determined by his own view of the evidence that is before him. I am well aware that, let me place the evidence for the doctrine of necessity in the strongest and clearest light that I possibly can, arguing either from the nature of the will, observations on human life, or the consideration of the divine prescience ; let me describe the doctrine of imaginary liberty as a thing ever so absurd, and impossible in itself, as totally foreign to, and inconsistent with all principles of just and moral government, and supplying no foundation whatever for praise or blame, reward or punishment, the generality of my readers will never get beyond the very threshold of the business. They will still say, " Are we not conscious of our freedom, cannot we do whatever we please, sit still, walk about, converse, or write, just as we are disposed?" And they will fancy that all my reasoning, plausible as it may seem, cannot, in fact, deserve any attention ; and even though they should be silenced by it, they will not be the nearer to being convinced.

But just so we see it to be in politics. Let such writers as Dr. Price explain ever so clearly the injustice of taxing any people without their consent, shewing that the same power that can compel the payment of one penny, may compel the payment of the last penny they have, and that a foreign people or nation, easing themselves by laying the burthen upon others, will be disposed to proceed as far as possible in this way ; still he will never satisfy many persons of landed property in this country, who will answer all he can say by one short argument, the force of which they feel and comprehend, saying, " What, shall we pay taxes, and the Americans none ?" The Doctor may repeat his arguments, and exhibit them in every possible light, he will get no sufficient attention to them from a person whose whole mind is occupied with the *single idea* of his paying taxes, and the Americans paying none.

Notwithstanding, therefore, all that I shall ever be able to write in favour of the doctrine of necessity, your supposed *consciousness of liberty*, and other popular arguments, (though when analyzed, they really make against your hypothesis,) will always secure you *nine* out of *ten* of the generality of our readers. All that I can do must be to make the most of my *tenth man ;* and, if I possibly can, fancy his suffrage equivalent to that of your nine. And to allay your fears of another kind, be assured that this tenth man will generally be of so *quiet* and *speculative* a turn, that you need be under no apprehension of his engaging in riots or rebellions. He will neither murder you in your bed, nor subvert the state.

I think, therefore, now that I have advanced, I verily believe, all that I can, in support of my opinion, I ought to acquiesce in the success of my labours, be it more or less. I see nothing *new* in any thing that you have advanced, and you will see nothing new, at least more forcible, in this reply. I do not, however, make any fixed resolutions. If you make a *rejoinder*, as I think you *ought*, and will be advised to do, I, true to my principles as a necessarian, *shall act as circumstances shall determine me.*

I am,

With much respect,

Dear Sir,

Yours sincerely,

J. PRIESTLEY.

Calnè, August, 1779.

A SECOND

LETTER

TO THE

Rev. Mr. JOHN PALMER.

———

I love to pour out all myself, as plain
As downright Shippen, or as old Montaigne.

POPE.

———

DEAR SIR,

YOU, as I foretold, have thought proper to reply to my letter,* and, as I suspected, *circumstances have determined me* to write you a *second letter;* and my motives have, I suppose, been the same with those that determined you to reply to the first. For I by no means think your reply to be satisfactory, and I am willing to try whether I cannot convince you, or at least our readers, that this opinion is well founded.

Your treatise, I perceive, is deemed to contain the strength of the cause you have espoused; and I think I should do wrong to shrink from the discussion, while I have any hope of prevailing upon a person so fully equal to it, to canvass it with me, and while I think there is any reasonable prospect that, by continuing a friendly controversy, any of the difficulties attending the subject may be cleared up. The question before us is truly momentous; the arguments that decide in my favour I think to be very plain; your objections appear to me to admit of sufficiently easy answers; and, in my opinion, it is nothing but imaginary consequences, or such as are grossly misunderstood, at which the mind of any man can revolt.

You, who know me pretty well, will not say that I would slur over a difficulty by which I was really pressed; and *arrogant* as you may suppose me to be, you will think me

———

* In an " Appendix to the Observations, occasioned by Dr. Priestley's Letter to the Author." 1780.

sincere, and that my confidence is derived from a full persuasion, well or ill founded, on a subject which I have long
considered, and with respect to which I have formed so
deliberate and decided a judgment.

I shall divide my present letter, as I did my former, into
distinct heads, and shall discuss them in what appears to
me to be their most natural order.   I wish you had divided
your *Appendix* in the same manner, as it contributes much
to perspicuity, and relieves the attention of the reader.

SECTION I.

Of the stating of the Question.

You complain of me for having *misrepresented your meaning*, when what you assert on the occasion, in my opinion,
confirms my representation.   I said that you supposed the
mind capable of determining *contrary to any motive whatever*,
or, as I afterwards express it, either *without, or contrary to
motives*.   You reply, " I never said, or supposed, that a
rational being can act without any motive, good or bad ; but
the most that I ever said was, that, in the very same circumstances, in which the choice or determination of the mind
was directed to one object of pursuit, it might have brought
itself to will or determine on the pursuit of a different and
contrary one."   P. 24.

Now where is the real difference between my stating of
the case and yours ?   You say you make choice of one object
of pursuit, for which, by your present confession, you must
have had *some motive*, and yet might have taken a different
and contrary one.   But how could you do this, without acting against the motives which led you to prefer the other ?
If you admit that we never act but with the *strongest* motives,
as well as never without *some* motive, (and one of these seems
to be the necessary consequence of the other,) you must, in
this case, have acted against the strongest motive.   And, if
for this possible determination there was no *motive at all*,
(and if it was overbalanced by other motives, it was, in fact,
no motive at all,) you must have acted *without* any motive for
what you did, as well as *against* motives to the contrary.

Besides, what is the boasted power of *self-determination*,
if the mind cannot actually determine itself *without* any
motive at all, or *contrary* to any motives, at pleasure ?   If
this be not the case, it is very improperly called *self-determination*.

SECTION II.

Of CERTAINTY, *or* UNIVERSALITY, *as the Ground of concluding that any Thing is* NECESSARY.

IN order to shew that the distinction between *certainty* and *necessity*, on which you and others lay so much stress, is nothing to your purpose, I observed that all that we mean by *necessity*, in any case, is *the cause of certainty*, or of universality, and that this is applicable to things *corporeal* or *mental*, without distinction ; that the reason, and the only reason, why we say a stone falls to the ground, *neces-sarily*, is, that it *constantly* and *universally* does so; and therefore that, if the determination of the mind be always according to motives, the difference as I said, p. 176, "cannot be in the *reality*, but only in the *kind* of necessity. The necessity must be—equally strict and absolute in both cases, let the *causes* of the necessity be ever so different."

This argument I said you had not given sufficient atten-tion to. But you now tell me, you are " so far from overlooking it, that *you* regarded it as the basis on which *my* argument for the necessary determination of the mind rested," (p. 7,) but that you considered, that what you had " insisted on to establish the distinction between phy-sical and moral necessity, as really replying to this very argument," p. 8, and you refer me to p. 49, &c. of your treatise.

Now I have carefully read over those pages, but I am very far from finding in them any thing to justify your refer-ence. Because, admitting the distinction you contend for between *physical* and *moral* necessity, still it is a *necessity;* and if necessity have any meaning at all, it is that, while the laws of nature are what they are, the event denominated necessary *could not have been otherwise.* ·

You say, " If we multiply ever so many other causes, or circumstances, concurring with and leading to the choice that is made, it is plain they can only operate as *moral*, not as *physical* causes." *Obs.* p. 50. But to what purpose is the distinction of physical and moral, if they be *real* causes, when all real causes must, in given circumstances, produce real and constant effects ?

" They will be," you say, " *occasions,* or *grounds,* of de-

termination, but they do not *form*, or *necessitate* the determination." Ibid.   I will allow your language ; but if, in
fact, the mind never *does* determine otherwise than according to these same *motives*, *occasions*, or *grounds*, there is
nothing in any received mode of reasoning that will justify
you in saying, that the mind, even *could*, in those circumstances, have determined otherwise, or that, according to the
present laws of nature respecting the mind, the determination was not, in the strictest sense of the word, *necessary*.
For there cannot be any evidence of the existence of a
power independent of its known *effects*.

In what manner do we prove the existence of *all powers*
but by their actual *operation ?*   Give me, in the whole compass of nature, any other case similar to this of your *self-
determining power*, that is, a case in which we admit a *real
power* without having ever seen its *effects*.   All our rules of
reasoning in philosophy would be violated by such a proceeding.   *Effects* are the only evidences of *powers*, or *causes ;*
and the immediate consequence of this is, that if no event
ever *does* take place, we can have no reason to believe that
it *can* take place.   This is as easily applicable to the case
before us as any whatever.   Produce a case in which the
mind indisputably *determines itself* without any motive
whatever, and then, *but then only*, shall I admit that motives have no necessary influence over its determination.

I must still maintain, therefore, that you have given no
answer at all to my argument for the doctrine of necessity,
as inferred from the consideration of *constancy* and *universality*.

There is, I repeat it, just the same propriety in calling the
determinations of the mind, as there is in calling the falling
of a stone, *necessary*.   It is not the *same law*, or power, in
nature, that causes both, and therefore they may be distinguished by what names you please ; but they equally
ensure the event; and the course of nature must be changed
before the results, in either case, can be otherwise than they
are observed to be.

SECTION III.

Of the Consequence of admitting the CERTAINTY *of
Determination.*

WHAT you reply to my observations concerning *certainty*,
and the several distinctions of it, is so manifestly unsatis-

factory, that I must beg leave to recall your attention to the argument. I asserted that if the determination of the mind be, in any proper sense of the word, *certain*, all the same consequences, even the very frightful ones that you describe, will follow, just as on the supposition of its being *necessary;* for that, in this case, the two words cannot but mean the very same thing.

You now acknowledge, that " *Certainty is a real certainty,* though it be only a *moral* one ; and yet it is not a *physical* one." P. 9. And, that "certainty is as different as the different causes or occasions of it." P. 8. Now I really cannot see what these differences (which I will admit to be as many as you please) can signify; if, as you allow, the result is invariably the same. This is certainly a case to which you cannot have given sufficient attention, or you could not treat it so lightly as you do. I shall therefore *open* and *expand* it a little for you, to give you an opportunity of seeing more distinctly what it is that you *do* admit, when you allow, under whatever distinction you please, that the determination of the mind is *certain*, or, in other words, *definite in definite circumstances.*

Every man, you must allow, is born with a certain constitution of body and mind entirely independent of his own choice. The circumstances in which he is born, with respect to country, parents, education and advantages, or disadvantages, of all kinds, are likewise altogether independent of himself. It is no matter when you say that *his first proper volition* takes place; for you must admit it is, in *certain definite circumstances*, independent of himself. His determination, therefore, being by the hypothesis, *certain*, or *definite* in those circumstances, whatever it be, it brings him into other, but definite, circumstances ; whether foreseen or unforeseen by himself depends upon his judgment or sagacity. In these new circumstances, he makes another *definite choice*, or determination, concerning the *new objects* that are now before him ; and this new determination brings him into other new circumstances. And thus, his, whole life passes in a constant succession of *circumstances* and *determinations*, all inseparably connected, till you come to the last determination of all, immediately preceding the extinction of all his powers by death.

Now it is obvious to ask, if all this be really *certain*, one thing strictly depending upon another, so that there is never known to be any variation from it, in what does it, or *can*

it, differ from what is contended for by the necessarian? If
I know my own principles, it is all that I want, call it by
what name you please.   You happen to like the word *certain*, whereas I prefer the word *necessary;* but our ideas *must*
be the very same.   We both chalk out a *definite path* for
every man to walk in, from the commencement of his life to
the termination of it.   The path is the same, drawn by the
same line, and by the same rule : it is a path that you admit
no man ever gets out of; and this, I do assure you, is all that
I mean, if I know my own meaning, when I say he never *can*
get out of it: for the laws of his nature must be changed,
so that his determinations must (contrary to the present
hypothesis) not be definite in definite circumstances, before
he *can* get out of it, from his birth to his death.

But you say, " where moral certainty only, takes place,
the power of agency still remains ; whereas by that which is
physical it is entirely destroyed." P. 9.   But if you reflect
a moment, you will perceive, that this is inconsistent with
what you just before granted.   Because if, in any case, the
determination *might have been* otherwise than it is, it would
not have been *certain*, but *contingent*. *Certainty* undoubtedly
excludes all *possible variety*, for that implies *uncertainty*.
Besides, as I observed before, and I cannot repeat it too
often, till I ensure your attention to it, what *proof* or *evidence*
can you produce of the reality or existence of any *power,*
that is never exerted ?   If, therefore, you allow that all
determinations whatever are certain, being directed by
motives, what evidence can there be of a power to act contrary to motives ?

How unreasonable then is it to reply, as you do to your
child, " Do not you, my son, see a vast difference between
determining yourself, call it *certainly*, if you please, and
being *necessarily* determined by something else ?" P. 13.
Because knowing the *absolute certainty* (though not necessity)
of his determination, in the circumstances in which you
placed him, you should not have placed him in them, unless
you really *chose* that he should make the determination that
you knew he *certainly would* make; and therefore, on your
own maxims, you would do wrong to *blame* or *punish* him.

You ask him (p. 14) whether he was not conscious he had
a power of refusing the apples ; whereas, by your own concession, that power could not possibly be *exerted,* so as to be
of any *use* to him, but on the supposition of what you previously knew did not exist, viz. *a different disposition of*

mind, in consequence of which his love of apples would have been less, or his fear of punishment greater, than you *knew* it to be.

SECTION IV.

Of the supposed Consciousness of Liberty.

I desired you to attend to the *phenomena of human nature*, to consider whether it be not a *fact*, that human volitions depend upon the previous disposition of their minds and the circumstances in which they are placed, in order to determine whether their volitions are not invariably *according to those circumstances;* and therefore whether, in propriety of language, it should not be said that they are always, and necessarily, determined by those circumstances or motives. You reply, " If the *phenomena of human nature* are to determine the question, we must certainly include the *whole* of the phenomena ; one of which is, that let actions be ever so *definite in definite circumstances,* they are still conscious of having it in their power to determine otherwise than they actually did." P. 22. Now I am surprised that you should not have been aware, that this is directly inconsistent with your own supposition, viz. the determination being *definite;* for if it might have been *otherwise*, it would have been *indefinite.* No man can be conscious of an *impossibility.* If, therefore, the real phenomena, exclusive of all pretended consciousness, are in favour of our volitions being definite, all *possibility* of their being indefinite is necessarily excluded ; so that they could not have been different from what they actually are, in any given circumstances.

Besides, reflect a little what is it of which we *can* be conscious ; for consciousness has its limits as well as other things. It is not that, with the same disposition of mind and in the same circumstances, the determination might have been different. This is a manifest fallacy. All that, in the nature of things, we *can* be conscious of is, that had we been differently disposed, we might have acted differently ; that nothing but our own *will* or pleasure prevented our acting differently ; which you know is not at all contrary to any thing contended for by necessarians. Consider particularly my *Additional Illustrations*, Vol. III. p. 294, &c.

SECTION V.

Of the Difference between the WILL *and the* JUDGMENT.

IN the passage to which you have now referred me, in your former treatise, you lay great stress on the essential difference between the nature of the *will*, and that of the *judgment*. " The will," you say, " implies in its very nature, a freedom from all controulling, necessitating influence. It is a power of *self-determination* belonging to an agent, the physical independency of which, on any thing foreign to itself, makes it to be what it is, or constitutes its very essence." *Obs.* p. 51. " The different mode of operation belonging to the will, as distinct from the other faculties of the mind, arises out of its different nature. The will is an independent, active principle or faculty. The other faculties are dependent, and merely passive," &c. *Obs.* p. 52.

Now I rather wonder that, in all this loftiness of language, you should not have perceived, that you are taking for granted the very thing in dispute. If we judge of the *powers* and faculties of man by his *actions* (and *what can we reason but from what we know?*) we must conclude that he is *not* possessed of any such faculty as you describe. On the contrary, we see all men, without exception, driven to and fro, just as their circumstances and motives impel them, without ever once exerting (as far as appears) a single act of proper *self-determination.* In all cases of sufficient magnitude, and in which there is sufficient opportunity given us to examine them, we see very plainly, that men are actuated by very *determinate motives;* and we are here, as in other similar cases, authorized to judge of obscure cases by those which are more distinct and evident, of the same kind.

Besides, so far am I from perceiving any such essential *difference* as you describe between the *will* and the *judgment,* that I perceive a remarkable *resemblance* between them, and in that very respect in which you state them to differ the most. Does the judgment decide according to the appearance of objects ? So does the will ; and if we consult fact, in no other way ; insomuch that the *will itself,* exclusive of the *actions* or *motions,* that follow the will, may not be improperly called a *particular judgment,* deciding on the *preferableness* of objects, according to their appearances, which are often very deceitful. For, judging by whatever *rule* you please, whatever object, at the moment of determination appears *preferable*, that we always choose. If, therefore, as I have said before, there be a power of self-determination in the will, I should expect to find the same in the judgment also, and if you will distinguish them, in the judgment preferably to the will ; if that may be called *judgment* which *decides*, though concerning the *preferableness* of objects. And there is no reason why this should not be the province of judgment, properly so called, as well as that of deciding concerning the *truth* of objects.

You object to the conclusiveness of my reasoning, p. 195, to prove that from one of your arguments it would follow that *judgment* and *volition* were the same thing, and the same with the *circulation of the blood*, &c. supposing that it goes on the idea of judgment being an *act* of the mind, only in the popular sense of the word. Now I will shew you that my inference was truly drawn, independent of any such definition of the word, as will appear by leaving out the word *act* altogether. You will then say, " Can that be truly said to be my *volition*, which is produced by *something over which I had no power ?* On that ground, every thing that takes place in my *body*, as well as my *mind*, may, with equal propriety, be called my volition ; and so the *circulation of the blood*, and the *pulsation of the heart*, may, with equal reason, be called my volitions." Pp. 80, 81.

The medium of your proof, or the *middle term* in your syllogism, is not *an act*, but *something over which we have no power*. But, though the *circulation of the blood*, &c. should, upon the doctrine of necessity, agree with *volition*, in being *a thing over which we have no power*, it does not, in that respect, agree with *volition only*, but with *judgment* also, and every other affection of the mind.

I may, perhaps, make the inconclusiveness of your argument more apparent, by reducing it to the form of a *syllogism*, and framing another exactly similar to it. Your argument will then stand as follows : " According to the necessarians,

" Volition is a thing over which a man has no power.

" But the pulsation of the heart is a thing over which a man has no power.

" *Ergo*, The pulsation of the heart is a volition."

A syllogism exactly parallel to this of yours is the following :

A goose is an animal that has two feet.

But a man is an animal that has two feet.

Ergo, A man is a goose.

I am sorry to have occasion to recall to your attention the first principles of logic, but it is plain you had overlooked them, when you thought you had reduced the necessarian to acknowledge that, on his principles, the *circulation of the blood*, and the *pulsation of the heart*, must be termed *volitions.* You meant to turn our principles into ridicule, and must take the consequence if the ridicule rebound upon yourself. You certainly had the merit of attempting something *new* in this, but there is always some *hazard* in attempting novelties.

SECTION VI.

Of the Argument from the supposed CONSEQUENCES *of the Doctrine of Necessity.*

To my objection to your reasoning from the *consequences* of the doctrine of necessity, you reply, there are consequences that "seem greatly to outweigh all speculative reasonings of every sort which can be thought of, and incontestably to prove that the doctrine which such consequences attend is not and cannot be true." P. 5. You add, that Dr. Watts recommends the mode of arguing from consequences, and that I myself have adopted it.

Now this, Sir, you do without making proper *distinctions*, which Dr. Watts, in the very passage which you have quoted, might have taught you to make. He says, that "It is a useful way of arguing, to refute a false proposition by shewing what evident *falsehood* or *absurdity* will follow from it;" which is the very thing that I did, when I shewed that, in consequence of admitting your doctrine of liberty, you must suppose that *effects* take place without *adequate causes*, and that the Divine Being could have no prescience of human actions, which the Scriptures every where suppose. On the other hand, the consequences that you draw from the doctrine of necessity only relate to things that you *dislike* and *abhor*, and which have nothing to do with *truth*.

Shew me that any *falsehood* or *absurdity*, as Dr. Watts says, follows from the doctrine of necessity, and I shall not then say, that we must *acquiesce* in it, and *make the best we can* of it. For it is absolutely impossible to acquiesce in an acknowledged falsehood, as we may in a thing that we merely cannot *relish*. With respect to all things that merely excite *disgust*, besides that it may be conceived that the disgust may be *ill founded* (and in this case it appears to me to be manifestly so), it is well known that there are many *truths*, and valuable ones too, that are *ungrateful*, especially at the first proposal.

Now I challenge you to shew that any proper *falsehood* or *absurdity*, will follow from the principles of necessity, a thing that I *do* pretend to with respect to the doctrine of liberty. And do not any more say, as you do now, that " it is only in the same way of reasoning" with that which I have used, that you " have endeavoured to support the doctrine of liberty." P. 6. By this time, I hope, you see there is a great difference between the two cases.

SECTION VII.

Of the MORAL INFLUENCE *of the Doctrine of Necessity.*

You complain, but very unjustly, of my mode of reasoning, when I endeavour to undermine all that you have urged on the subject of the *dangerous consequences* of the doctrine of necessity. Your meaning, you say, was, that " it tended to indispose " a person "for virtuous activity and self-command," but that you suppose the necessarian " to be active enough in gratifying his irregular and vicious inclinations." Pp. 17, 18. Now I had no doubt of your *willingness* to make a distinction in this case, that is, to make the necessarian *indolent to good*, and at the same time *active to evil;* but nature, not being of the party, makes no such distinction, so that the case you suppose is an impossibility.

If the belief of the doctrine of necessity has any operation at all, either to *activity* or *inactivity*, it must respect all *ends* or *objects, as such,* and without distinction, whatever they be, and can never operate one way if a man's inclinations be virtuous and another way if they be vicious. If on the one hand, I believe that my object will be accomplished, and my belief lead me to *overlook all means*, and therefore I give myself no trouble about it; or if, on the other, my belief of the necessary connexion of means and ends be such as that my exertions are redoubled; still these different consequences respect *all objects alike,* and can never operate to the disadvantage of virtue, but on the supposition that all necessarians, *as such,* either are more indifferent to their own happiness than other men, or have less knowledge of the necessary connexion between virtue and happiness.

If this was the case, surely you might, considering the

length of time that has elapsed since the doctrine of necessity was first proposed by Mr. Hobbes, and even since it has been fully established, as I may say, by Dr. Hartley, (and before my recollection or yours, it had numerous advocates among men of letters,) have been able to collect something like *positive evidence;* and you certainly should not have raised all this outcry without some better foundation than your own suspicious *imagination.*

SECTION VIII.

Miscellaneous Observations.

You eagerly catch at a casual, and, as you think, an improper expression of mine, p. 200, when I said that " the origin of action, or of self-determination, is the same as the origin of the Deity, concerning which we know nothing at all,"* as if I really supposed the Deity to have had an origin, or a beginning. Whereas, besides that you well know that I suppose, just as much as yourself, that the Deity is properly *uncaused,* and consequently had *no origin,* and therefore that it *could* be no more than an inadvertent expression that you had got hold of, I have, in fact, said the same thing in this very place, viz. that proper action, or self-determination, can have no beginning, because it must have commenced with the Deity, who had none. ' This triumph of yours, of which you seem willing to make so much, is, indeed, premature.

If, in maintaining an opinion common to myself and Dr. Price, I should have said, that " the commencement of the creation was the same with that of the Deity himself," would not the obvious construction have been, not that they both had a beginning, but that *neither* of them had any? In this case, also, I am just as far from intimating, in the most distant manner, that it was even *possible* for the Deity to have had any *origin.* I must say that this construction of my words is very extraordinary.

You charge me (p. 23) with having mistated Dr. Price's opinion on the subject of liberty, as well as your own ; but, though I am not sensible of having made any mistake in this respect, it is not a point that I choose to discuss with

---

* " It is common with philosophers to speak of the origin of created beings; but to speak of *the origin of the Deity,* that is, of an eternal, uncreated Being, seems to be a new mode of expression, and peculiar to the Doctor." *Appendix,* 28.

you. It is sufficient for my present purpose, if I truly state, and fully refute, *your* opinion on the subject.

Here you must give me leave to observe, that it was very improper, on several accounts, to add the name of Dr. Price to those of Locke, Wollaston, Clarke and Foster, as authorities in favour of the doctrine of liberty, for whom I ought to have had a *greater reverence.** I also could muster up a list of very respectable authorities, such as Collins, Leibnitz, Hutcheson, Edwards, Hartley, &c.; but, for obvious reasons, I should have chosen to have confined it to the *dead*, and should have omitted the *living*, especially the man with whom my antagonist had a public and truly amicable controversy on the subject. Dr. Price, however, I am well persuaded, believes that my respect for him is not less than yours, notwithstanding I may imagine that his eye, though much stronger than mine, is not able to see through some little *cloud* that happens to hang between it and this particular subject.

Were I to set about it, I should not doubt but that, though I cannot say *nos turba sumus*, I could draw out a very decent list of *living authorites*, in favour of the doctrine of necessity, consisting of persons whose *ability*, *virtue*, and I will add *activity* too, you would not question. And were we to leave out those who would not pretend to have properly *studied* the subject, and therefore could not be said to give a vote, except by *proxy*, my list, among men of letters, might perhaps be not only as *respectable*, but even as *numerous* as yours. But this is a question that is not to be decided by *vote* or *authority*, but by *argument;* and it is on this ground that we are now engaged.

SECTION IX.

QUERIES *addressed to* MR. PALMER.

THUS, Sir, I have distinctly replied to every thing that I imagine yourself can think *material* in your *Appendix*, in which you say " those parts of the Letter which were deemed most material are noticed." *Adv.* Now, as you would not have *voluntarily* undertaken the discussion of this argument

---

* " Whatever the Doctor might say, or insinuate, of some of the defenders of liberty, whom he thought by no means equal to the task they had undertaken ; let him not deem me arrogant in asking, whether it might not have been expected, that the reverence due to such authors as a Locke, Wollaston, Clarke, Foster, and Price, should have put some restraint on his pen ?" *Appendix*, p. 31.

with me, without having well weighed your force in it, being determined to bring it to something more like a proper *close;* I hope that, notwithstanding you say you shall now " decline the controversy," you will, on more mature consideration, *resume* it, and give me, as the Spectator pleasantly says, *more last words of Richard Baxter.* I shall therefore tell you what I think you have omitted, and what it behoved you more particularly to have replied to in my *Letter.* And, farther, to make the *continuation* of the correspondence more easy to you, I shall state those matters in distinct *queries,* to which, if you please, you may reply in order.

. 1. You had said that a determination of the mind is not *an effect without a cause,* though it be not produced by any motive, because the *self-determining power itself* is the cause. I replied, that, allowing this supposed power to be the cause of *choice in general,* it can no more be considered as the cause of any *particular choice,* than the *motion of the air* in general can be said to be the cause of any particular *wind;* because all winds are equally motions of the air, and therefore, that there must be some *farther cause* of any particular wind. I desire you to point out the insufficiency of this answer. This it the more behoves you to do, because it respects not the *outworks,* but the very *inmost retreat* of your doctrine of liberty. If you cannot defend yourself against this attack, you must surrender at discretion. Necessity, with all its *horrid consequences,* will enter in at the breach ; and you know that necessarians, though slothful to good, are active enough in mischief, and give no quarter.

That you should say you had not passed over any thing of *the argumentative kind* in my *Letter, which seemed to require a reply,* and yet have overlooked this most material article, as well as many others, surprises me not a little.

On this subject, I also beg you would not fail to give particular attention to my *Additional Illustrations* (Vol. III. p. 467), in which, I think, I have proved decisively, that the *mind itself* can never be considered as a proper and sufficient cause of *particular determinations.*

It was unfortunate for these *Illustrations,* that they did not appear till after the greatest part of your first treatise was written, and yet so long before your *Appendix,* that I suppose they were forgotten. Though, as you had seen them before you wrote the *Preface,* and consequently some time before the publication of your first piece, you had a good opportunity of animadverting upon them, and might be expected to do it in a case that so materially affected your main argument.

You now say, in general, that " now I have read them, they appear as little satisfactory as the former; and that to all which Dr. Priestley has advanced, on this part of the argument, in the correspondence, Dr. Price appears to have given a very clear and sufficient reply." P. 3. But this particular article, not being a proper part of the correspondence, you will find, that Dr. Price has not replied to it at all, and therefore your answer to it is not precluded. I particularly entreat you to refute what is there advanced. Point out to me any thing in *your work*, which you think I have not sufficiently considered, and I promise to be as particular in my discussion of it as you please.

2. I endeavoured to shew, in my second Section, that the argument from the consideration of cause and effect does not, as you say, go on the supposition of *a similarity of the constituent principles of matter and spirit*, but only on the determination of the mind being subject to *any laws at all;* and therefore that the cause of liberty can derive no advantage from the commonly received principles of the *immateriality of the human soul.* You should have said, whether my reply was satisfactory to you, or not. But perhaps I am to interpret your *silence* on any subject to be an *acquiescence* in what I observed concerning it, and not as an article that you thought too obviously inconclusive to demand any reply.

3. Please to produce some direct proof of the existence of the *self-determining power* you boast so much of. I mean a proof from *fact,* and not from a merely imagined *feeling,* or *consciousness* of it, which one person may assert, and another, who is certainly constituted in the same manner, may deny. What I assert is, that all we *can feel,* or be *conscious of,* in the case, is, that our actions, corporeal or mental, depend upon our *will,* or *pleasure;* but to say that our wills are not always influenced by *motives,* is so far from being *agreeable,* that it is directly *contrary* to all experience in ourselves, and all observation of others.

4. You have said nothing to explain, or soften your denial of the doctrine of *divine prescience,* which, as a *Christian,* and a *christian minister,* it greatly behoves you to do. You pretend to be shocked at the consequences of the doctrine of necessity, which exist only in your own imagination; but here is a consequence of your doctrine of liberty, directly repugnant to the whole tenor of revelation, as it has been understood by all who have ever pretended to any faith in it,

though they have differed ever so much in other things.. It will be well worth your while to make *another appendix* to your hook, if it were only to give some little *plausibility* to this business, and either to shew, if you can; that the divine prescience is not a doctrine of the Scriptures, or that the sacred writers were mistaken with respect to it. Besides, it is incumbent upon you to shew, independent of your profession as a Christian, how, on your own principles, any such *government of the world* as we see to take place could exist. To say, as you do, that God, notwithstanding his want of prescience, may yet govern free beings in the best manner that free beings *can* be governed, will avail you nothing; because I maintain, that if liberty be what you define it to be, a power of *proper self-determination*, such beings *cannot be governed at all.* I have shewn that it is impossible they should ever be proper subjects of moral government. The Divine Being cannot controul their actions; the influence of all motives (the only instruments of moral government) will be altogether uncertain; he can form no judgment of their effect; and in consequence, all must be anarchy and confusion.

But I would rather advise you to *retract* what you have too hastily advanced. If possible, think of some method of reconciling *prescience* with *liberty ;* and by no means purchase your liberty at so very great a price. At least, be *very sure*, in the first place, that it is worth so much.

If, as I suppose will be the case, you should not be able to reconcile *prescience* with your more favourite doctrine of *free will*, be advised by me, rather than give up the former so lightly as you do, to keep it *at all events ;* even though, in order to do it, you should be obliged to rank it (as many truly pious Christians do the doctrines of *transubstantiation* and the *Trinity*) among the *mysteries of faith*, things to be held sacred, and not to be submitted to rational inquiry. On no account would I abandon such a doctrine as that of *divine prescience*, while I retained the least respect for revelation, or wished to look with any satisfaction on the moral government under which I live.

Lest you should think all this to be nothing more than affected seriousness, and the language of a mere controversialist, pushing his adversary on a precipice, I shall quote what a brother of yours, in this very controversy with me, observes; and it is no less a person than the celebrated Mr. Bryant. And when he (after Dr. Price and yourself) shall have advanced all that he is able, I should think the public will be satisfied that the most ample justice must have been done to that side of the question. Speaking of those who scruple not to give up the doctrine of *divine prescience*, rather than abandon that of *liberty*, he says, in his *address to me*, "·They must then give up the *Scriptures* at the same time, and with the Scriptures their *religion* and *faith*. For, in the sacred writings, the foreknowledge of the Deity, is not only inculcated as a *doctrine*, but proved by a variety of *events*." P. 36. ·If, Sir, the earnest language of what you may suppose (though very unjustly) to be *enmity*, fail to move you, let that of *friendship* prevail.

· If, after this repeated warning, you should persist in treating the doctrine of divine prescience, as a thing of so little consequence, the most truly *candid* thing I can say is what you have quoted, and endeavoured to expose, (p. 182,) as the extreme of *uncharitableness*, when first advanced in my controversy with Dr. Beattie, on the same occasion. But because you may think the figurative expression too strong (though in fact, the stronger it is the better apology it makes) I shall say the same thing in other words : "It is what the heat of disputation has betrayed you into. You are blind to the consequences, and therefore *you know not what you do.*"

· 5. I particularly desire you would once more go over with me the subject of the *practical influence* of the doctrine of necessity. This is far from being, in my opinion, the *dark* side of my argument. I love and rejoice in this view of it; confident, and I hope I may add *feeling*, that, when rightly understood, it is highly favourable to every thing that is great and good in man. Tell me whether the belief of the certainty of the end, *without* any idea of the necessary connexion of the means by which it is brought about, (which is the doctrine of *Calvinism*) does not work one way, and the belief of the certainty of the end, only *as a consequence* of its necessary connexion with the previous means (which is the .doctrine of. *philosophical necessity*), does not work another way. , Re-peruse my account of their different influences, and shew, from a juster view of the principles of human nature, that, with those apprehensions, men must feel and act differently from what I have supposed they naturally would do. ·

·· 6. I likewise desire you would particularly attend to what I have, observed in my seventh Section, with respect to the use of the term *agency* and *responsibility ;* because, if what I have there observed be just, you, and other defenders of the doctrine of liberty, can derive no advantage whatever from any argument in which it is taken for granted, that man, in your sense of the terms, is an *agent,* and a *responsible* being; as I shew, that the state of moral government in which we are, is perfectly consistent with, nay, pre-supposes the doctrine of necessity; that, for this purpose, it is sufficient that man be, in the popular sense of the word only, and not in a sense that pre-supposes the doctrine of liberty, an *agent,* and *responsible.* Nay, I beg you would shew how man, constituted as you suppose him to be, can be a subject of moral government at all.

7. As you lay great stress on the feeling of *remorse,* I beg you would consider and reply to what I have urged on that subject, in my letter to you, (p. 191,) and my *Additional Illustrations;* (Vol. III. p. 516). If my state of the fact be just, no argument from that topic can avail you any thing; every just view of that subject being extremely favourable, rather than unfavourable to the doctrine of necessity.

Please to observe that all these queries relate to matters strictly *argumentative,* or that must be allowed to have weight in forming our judgment on the subject in debate; and do not pass them over a second time, as if they were things of *another nature,* and such as you are under no obligation to notice. Say, if you please, and *prove* it, if you can, that what I have advanced, with respect to them, is *inconclusive;* but do not pass them over in silence, as if they were not of an *argumentative* nature, or indeed, not very *materially* so.

THE CONCLUSION.

DEAR SIR,

I DO not know that it is necessary for me to call your attention particularly to any other points in contest between us; but I earnestly beg your explicit reply to these few. Many controversies have terminated without effect, and without any advantage to the cause of truth, merely because the parties have not come to a fair *issue,* but have left their readers wishing to know what the one or the other of them would have replied to this or that argument, or to this or that state or view of it. I wish to carry this controversy to its *proper conclusion.* For my part, I will readily answer any question you shall think proper to propose to me, and shall do it without the least reserve or evasion. You *believe* that I would. I only beg that you would, in like manner, reply to me. More, I think, is to be done by distinct *interroga-*

tories, and categorical *answers*, than in any other manner. Let us, however, try this method. A very few more short pieces, which, with what we have already published, would not make too bulky *a single volume*, for each of us, might, I think, exhaust all that we can now have to say that is mate-rial. Why then, when the trouble will be so little, and the advantage may be so great, should you decline this business prematurely? You have certainly as much *leisure* for the discussion as I have; and as it was you that called me out, and not I that called upon you, I should imagine you have not less *zeal* in the cause than myself.

You cannot apprehend from me any thing offensive to you in my manner of writing, any more than I can with respect to you; nor shall I take offence at *little things*. You may make what reflections you please on my *temper* or *manner*, and there are points enow to hit in both, if you be so disposed. You have my leave beforehand to say that I am *insolent* in one place, and *arrogant* in another; and you may parody my most obnoxious paragraphs, whether *in* the work you are answering, or *out of it*, if it will serve to amuse yourself or your readers. If there be more of plea-santry than ill-nature in your strictures, I will cheerfully bear it all, and with Themistocles to Pausanias, say, *strike me*, and as often as you please, *but hear me*, and answer me.

Whatever I *have been*, or may be to *others*, *you* shall have nothing to complain of with respect to *yourself personally;* and I am so happy to find myself engaged with a person of undoubted judgment in the controversy, that, I own, I am very unwilling to part with you so soon. I shall be like Horace's friend, and you must have recourse to as many shifts to get quit of me.

Hoping, therefore, to have the satisfaction of hearing from you again on the subject,* and wishing your reply may be as speedy as will be consistent with its being *well weighed,*

I am,

Dear Sir,

Your very humble servant,

J. PRIESTLEY.

Calne, April, 1780.

* This satisfaction was never received, though Mr. Palmer survived the contro-versy ten years. He died 1790, aged 60. See a Memoir by Dr. Toulmin, *M. Mag.* 1797.

A
LETTER

, TO

JACOB BRYANT,* Esq.

IN DEFENCE OF

PHILOSOPHICAL NECESSITY.

Drink deep, or taste not.

POPE.

A PREFATORY LETTER.

SIR,

IT is with real pain that I put into your hands the following letter, written in such a manner as may perhaps give *you* pain, and it would have given me real pleasure to have addressed you with that *respect* to which your character has hitherto entitled you. But in this case you left me no choice. Such an *Address*† as yours could not be answered, with propriety, in any other manner than that in which I have treated it. It is only *measure for measure*, and, indeed, far short of that. For all that I censure in you is your challenging me, in so high a tone of authority, on a subject of which you are perfectly ignorant. I no where tax you with *hypocrisy, impiety*, or *infidelity;* though I could have found just as much pretence for those charges with respect to you, as you have with respect to me.

It might, I often think, have a good effect to temper the acrimony of controversial writing, to consider ourselves as addressing our antagonists *in person*, as we should not then be so apt to neglect the forms of *civility*, that we hold ourselves obliged to observe in a personal interview. Had

---

* This classical scholar and learned writer is now chiefly known by his "Analysis of ancient Mythology." He died in 1804, aged 88.

† "An Address to Dr. Priestley upon his *Doctrine of Philosophical Necessity Illustrated*. By Jacob Bryant, Esq. 1780."

you, Sir, been introduced to me on purpose to *talk* with me
on the subject of necessity, or had we met accidentally, and
entered upon it, you would have felt, I am confident, an
insurmountable aversion to pronouncing to my face what
you have addressed to me in print. It would have appeared
to yourself unpardonable- rudeness. What you now term
arrogance, insincerity, &c. you would have softened down to
a *mistake, misapprehension, oversight,* or some other thing of
the same venial nature.

We are all too apt to lose sight of the *persons* of our
opponents, and with that, to forget our good manners; and
indeed custom has, in a manner, justified a good deal of
asperity in controversial writings of all kinds, so that the
world in general is not so much offended at it as they would
be at any rudeness in conversation. And with respect to
the proper *use* of controversial writing, I do not know but
that this may have been the best upon the whole; as, by
this means, men have been roused to exert themselves to
the utmost in the defence of their several opinions, so that
the subject in debate has been more thoroughly investigated,
for the benefit of the cool bystander.

But with respect to the writers themselves, if my experience may be thought to qualify me to judge in the case, the
preference is unspeakably in favour of an *amicable discussion*
of any important question. The controversy that I look
back upon with the most satisfaction is that with Dr. Price,
which you, Sir, do not seem to have thought it worth your
while to look into. And, though I have been more than
once urged to write in the style of my letter to you, and, as
I have imagined, with some success, a triumph so gained
has never given me more than a momentary exultation. It
is a feeling too nearly resembling those emotions which a
Christian ought to repress rather than encourage.

I wonder particularly, Sir, that you should not have
thought proper before you engaged in this controversy, to
peruse the performances of those who had preceded you in
it. For you seem to be quite ignorant of what has been
advanced by Dr. Price, or Mr. Palmer, from both of which
you might have acquired a better knowledge of the subject,
and not have entered the lists so unprepared as you have
done.

I cannot account for this neglect, but from the contempt
in which you seem to hold *Dissenters* in general, a prejudice
very unworthy of a liberal scholar, and a prejudice by which
you are a considerable loser. For though we are excluded

from your universities, evidently with a design to keep us in ignorance, our common Creator, who is *no respecter of persons*, distributes *his* gifts with an impartial hand; and by making the most of such faculties, and opportunities, as he has been pleased to give us, and which he does not permit you to deprive us of, we are enabled both to *study* and to *write*, and even things not unworthy the notice of Mr. Bryant.

We, Sir, ill-educated, and, as you seem to think, narrow-minded Dissenters, being excluded from what you consider as the only fountains of knowledge,* are perhaps, on that very account, less confined in our reading and study, and, in consequence, more liberal. We are glad to pick up the crumbs that fall from your table, or from any table. I have read with much pleasure, and some instruction, every thing that bears the name of Mr. Bryant. I have even wished for an opportunity of being introduced to his acquaintance, and I am truly sorry that this *Address* of yours to me, and the manner in which I have been obliged to reply to it, will make it rather too unpleasant a thing to both of us.

Notwithstanding this, which is a subject of real regret to me, I am with sincere admiration of your learning, and esteem for your character,

Sir,

Your very humble servant,

J. PRIESTLEY.

London, 28th April, 1780.

—◆—

To JACOB BRYANT, Esq.

SIR,

I cannot do less than take some public notice of an *Address* to me from a person so distinguished in the republic of letters as Mr. Bryant; and had your letter been uniformly respectful, I should have thought myself honoured by it, though you had differed from me ever so much in opinion, and had even expressed ever so much abhorrence of the doctrine I have maintained. But when you compliment me in some places, and load me with abuse in others,

---

* I know not to what work of his opponent my Author refers, as I cannot find any such sentiments in the *Address*.

taxing me with *self-sufficiency, arrogance, insincerity, impiety*
and *infidelity*, and treat me with ridicule and sarcasm
throughout, I think that, on the balance, but little remains
due to you on that score; though, perhaps, any kind of
notice from Mr. Bryant must be *some* honour.

It is, however, I assure you, Sir, your *name* only, together
with the solicitations of some friends, that induces me to
take any notice of your *Address;* and had not a letter to me
from yourself accompanied the pamphlet, which is anonymous,* I really believe I should not even have read more
than a page or two in the whole work.

So gross, Sir, and so uniform has been your misconception of the whole subject, in all its parts, and so strange has
been your misapprehension of my meaning throughout, that
I think myself justified in saying, that I have not found one
pertinent observation in the whole piece.   Your style is
also affectedly rhetorical, and on that account exceedingly
improper for controversy.

Had there not been an air of seriousness in some parts of
your work (though rhetorical declamation is not the natural
expression of seriousness), and had you not begun with
assuring me, that the doctrine of necessity was " a subject
which you had much considered, and that you had even
long since, for your private satisfaction, written down your
thoughts upon it," and also said, that " when you took my
treatise in hand, you formed a resolution not to be too hasty
in your conclusions, but to read it over with that attention
and care which every thing deserves that proceeds from a
person so justly celebrated," you are pleased to say, " as
Dr. Priestley ;" I should have been apt to imagine, that the
pamphlet had been a mere *jeu d'esprit*, written by way of
an experiment, to try how much absurdity might be passed
upon the public under the sanction of such a name as yours.

Finding the work to be really *your own*, that hypothesis
must be set aside ; and I am obliged to have recourse to
some other.   But the fact is so extremely strange, that I do
not know whether any thing that has occurred to me will
throw any light upon it.   Two of my conjectures are all
that I shall mention.   The first is, that though you say you
formed a resolution not to be too hasty in your conclusions,
you did not really *execute* it.   The other is, that you have
been so bewildered in this business, that you have neither
been able to preserve your temper nor retain the perfect use

---

* This must refer only to the copies first distributed.   See p. 224.   *Note* †.

of your faculties. For you say, " Your arguments—confound, rather than convince ; so that believe me, good Sir, I scarcely know where I am, or upon what ground I stand." P. 13.

Upon the whole, this solution, suggested by yourself, appears the most probable. Indeed, Sir, in this region of *metaphysics* you have quite lost yourself. You do not know where you are, or on what ground you stand, as I have little doubt of fully satisfying all competent judges of the subject, and perhaps even yourself; though, considering your age, and your long study of this subject, I cannot promise myself much success, in my attempts to disentangle and new-arrange your ideas.

As to myself, I may, to be sure, be mistaken, but I think that, with respect to this subject, and your address to me relating to it, I *do* know perfectly well where I am, and on what ground I stand. My only difficulty is how to place in the clearest light a variety of fallacies and mistakes, that are sufficiently manifest in every light. It is this *choice* that breeds all my *care*. This, Sir, though you may think it said lightly, I should not advance at random. My letter to you, as well as yours to me, will be open to the public ; and my reputation (which I must suppose to be as great as you represent it) is at stake.

SECTION I.

Observations relating chiefly to CANDOUR.

IN the whole of this business, I shall, if possible, take away every pretence for *one* part of your charge against me. You say that " I write with so much reserve, and my words are so guarded, that you are not always sure that you arrive at my true meaning." P. 119. You also say, that " I soften and extenuate *things* by means of ambiguous terms, of which I afterwards take an undue advantage, and that I speak in general, where I should be particular, and in particular, when I should be general." P. 54.

Now, whatever other faults I may be chargeable with, I had flattered myself that I was innocent of *this*, and, that I had been generally *thought* to be so. If not, I have taken a good deal of pains to little purpose. I had thought that, of all writers, I had always written with the least reserve, and that it had been hardly possible to mistake my meaning. I have been commended even by several of my antagonists for my *fairness* in this respect. Dr. Price says, in our *Correspondence*, p. 97, that " I cannot be sufficiently admired for my fairness in the pursuit of truth," and that I " follow it into all its consequences, without attempting to evade or palliate them."

As I really do not know how to write with more plainness than I have hitherto done, I am afraid that, do what I will, I shall not, after all, be able to make myself understood by *you*. But if I be understood by *others* I must be content ; and of this I do not much despair.

As to the want of *sincerity* with which you repeatedly charge me, it is an affair between God and my own conscience. Many circumstances, however, on which we form judgments in such cases, are before the world ; and some persons may judge that if I had been possessed of much of the commodity called *hypocrisy*, as it is a very *marketable* one, I might have made something more of it, and have kept myself out of some difficulties by the help of it.

It is possible, however, that, in reality, you may not be quite so uncharitable to me as I first imagined ; since in one of the places, in which you suggest this charge, you seem to use the term in a sense somewhat different from that in which it is commonly used. For you speak of it as of a thing of which I may not be conscious myself. " I should be afraid," you say, " that you have, in this instance, forgot yourself, and not acted with that sincerity which the world may have expected from you.—I fear this declaration will not be to your advantage in the opinion of your adversary. He will think it affects either your head, or your heart." P. 49.

Now, Sir, I must inform you, since you seem to be ignorant of it, that though a man's *memory* may fail him, and he may forget a thing of which he had been informed, and might have been expected to remember, it is not, in the nature of things, that this should ever be the case with respect to *conscience* and *sincerity*. If I tell a *lie*, I must know it at the time ; because the very definition of a lie implies that it *is* known at the time. A lie is not a mere *falsehood,* or untruth, but an *untruth known to be so.* This, however, is exactly of a piece with every other definition, or distinction, on which any thing has depended in the whole of your book.

Another charge of *forgetfulness* is rather better stated than this, though the argument in which it is introduced is not more solid than the rest. You say, " How comes it that you sometimes forget your necessarian charity, and so cruelly fall foul of Dr. Beattie, and not only of Dr. Beattie, and his *instinctive common sense*, but of some others who differ from you in opinion, and whom you treat with not a little roughness? Perhaps, as a necessarian, you do not abuse them for their failings *in the ultimate sense of the word*, but *in the common sense of it*, which may afford them some consolation, if they understand your meaning." P. 78. And, indeed, Sir, they must have gone a little deeper into this business than you seem to have done, if they do understand this distinction.

After a good deal of *sarcastic humour*, terminating with your supposing that I must " be looked upon as the chief pillar" of the necessarian cause, you say, " If the 'virtues above-mentioned" (those which I have ascribed to the influence of the doctrine of necessity), "do naturally arise from your system, we may suppose them to be eminently in you. But herein, I think that I perceive some little failure. If anger and resentment are incompatible with necessity; if, when devoted to that system, you cannot *hate a man*, and are really gifted with that infinitely refined tenderness and compassion for others, which you have mentioned, how comes it that there is not a greater show of it; for you are sensible that *the tree is known by its fruits?*" P. 78.

But pray, Sir, do not you profess the christian religion, and to be a member of the established church of England, and yet declare every day, that you " do things that you ought not to do," that is, things inconsistent with Christianity? You also pretend to *reason*, but is every thing you say or write *rational?* If you do think so, you are greatly mistaken; and yet I would not thence infer that you are not a man, or a worthy man. Now I do not pretend to perfection, or a perfect correspondence between my principles and my conduct, any more than you do. I have several times disclaimed it, and in this very respect, as, with a proper share of candour, you should have quoted.

Besides, how do you know but that, notwithstanding all the crimes you charge me with, I am not a much better man than I should have been with other principles; and that, bad as the case is, it is not much better both for Dr. Beattie and yourself, that I am even a necessarian?

But indeed, good Sir, (to return your own mode of complimenting) you greatly overcharge this part of your picture. I do not *hate* Dr. Beattie. I appeal to impartial readers, whether my address to him be not on the whole, expressive of respect. I am sure I did not intend it to be otherwise; and the only harsh expression I have used with respect to him, is that which constitutes the best apology that I could suggest, for the readiness he seemed to express to give up the doctrine of divine prescience rather than that of philo- sophical liberty, concerning which you yourself say, that " a man must then give up the *Scriptures*, and, with them, his *religion* and his *faith*." Is not this much harsher than any thing that I have said on the same subject? If Dr. Beattie be offended with *me*, he must be much more, Sir, with you.

I am very far from charging Dr. Beattie, as you repeatedly charge me, with *insincerity* or *impiety;* and I appeal to our common readers, if his arrogance, I mean as a *writer*, (for I have not the pleasure that you have, of being acquainted with him personally,) be not much greater than mine. He even thought it necessary to make a laboured apology for it. If there be any thing too strongly expressed in that per- formance, it is in my examination of Dr. Reid's Treatise. For as to Dr. Oswald, I still say of *his* work, that could I have expressed even more indignation and contempt, I should have done it, and have thought it justifiable. And yet I am far from charging him with *insincerity*.

It is something too curious to be suffered to pass un- noticed, that, after quoting at full length two paragraphs of mine, which you censure as peculiarly obnoxious, making the amount of them to be equivalent to making Dr. Beattie " an Atheist," and to " deny his Creator," you add, " But let us stop here ; and it were well if we could draw a veil over what has preceded, that it might be had no more in remembrance." P. 38. I suppose, therefore, that by this you mean *to draw a veil over* my infirmities. But pray then, Sir, what would you have done if you had meant to *expose* them? If this be to consign them to oblivion, what would you have done to perpetuate the remembrance of them? For, certainly, there must be some difference, though I am not able to find it.

In this, your favourite chapter of *abuse*, which occupies a great proportion of your pamphlet, you, on one occasion, take a method, which, for *absurdity* or *assurance* (of which you may take your choice) has, I think, never yet been equalled, if attempted, by any controversial writer. It is when you declaim at large on the supposition that I myself confess the necessarians to be guilty of the very faults that I ascribe to the Calvinists, as distinguished from the necessarians. Now to allege that, in *your* opinion, there is no difference between them, is no apology for you; because your argument, or ridicule, whatever you call it, goes upon the idea of that being *my own* opinion.

Among other things I have charged some Calvinists with *malignity of heart.* You answer, " But if your system, as you say, is superior to all others, and is productive of nothing but peace, charity and benevolence, attended with all the gentle affections of tenderness and compassion, whence proceeds such malignity and ill-will, with all the bitterness of gall ? How came the elect, whom we should have thought exempt from these inferior qualities, to abound with them more than others ?" Pp. 80, 81.

I had charged the system of Calvinism with a tendency to *gloom* and *melancholy*, and had represented Calvinists as " in a state of *doubt* with respect to the evidence of their conversion, and what they call the work of grace in their hearts," &c. You immediately reply, " At this rate, I do not see any the least advantage that a necessarian has in proof of his orthodoxy. There is nothing that can persuade us of the superior excellence of his system. He is described as in a state of uncertainty, if not of infatuation; and his principles are said to lead to gloom and melancholy," &c. P. 82. You, Sir, on a former occasion, expressed a doubt whether my *head* or my *heart* was in fault. Pray where is the fault in this case ? Wherever it lies, it is a very gross one.

On this subject, I must, likewise, mention your truly pitiable ignorance of what relates to religion, and the obvious distinctions of it in this country. When you charge me with abusing the Calvinists, you consider me as speaking ill of a *community* to which I once belonged, and " a community which has produced some excellent men, particularly a Leland and a Foster." P. 81. Now, Sir, I must inform you (happening to be a little better informed myself) that the Calvinists are no community at all, in this country, except your own church, the tenets of which are strictly Calvinistical, be that community; and of this community Leland and Foster certainly were not.

Calvinism, Sir, is a denomination that respects *opinions* only, and not *societies* or *communities*. But, still, if you had known any thing of Leland or Foster, you must have known that they were the farthest in the world from being in opinion Calvinists, all of whom, though you say, p. 79, only *many of them*, are rigid predestinarians. On the contrary, they were men particularly obnoxious to the Calvinists, the latter of them especially.*

If by Calvinists you mean the *Independents*, which is now a common use of the term, it makes no better for you; for Leland was a Presbyterian, and Foster a Baptist.

If by Calvinists you mean *Dissenters* in general, which I suspect from your saying that many of them are rigid pre-destinarians, how have I quitted them, as you say I have done? I assure you, Sir, I am no member of the church of England, any more than I am of the church of Rome. Great as my crimes are, not being any son of hers, I have not disgraced that venerable matron. In every possible sense of the word, therefore, what you say of Calvinists is absurd and contrary to fact. Such extreme ignorance of *things at home* is altogether inexcusable in any writer.

Call the subject of this Section, if you please, *prefatory matter*; it was no more than necessary to prepare the reader for the still grosser blunders, if possible, that you have made respecting the main argument.

SECTION II.

Of what relates to the proper ARGUMENT *for the Doctrine of Necessity.*

I HAD thought that, if it had been possible, by the use of language, to explain wherein *necessary determination*, as opposed to proper *self-determination* consists, so that no person could have mistaken it, it had been done by myself. It is not that a man has no *will* at all, or that he cannot *do* whatever he wills or pleases; but that his voli-tions are *definite in definite circumstances*. Therefore, though a man exerts a real and proper volition, it is so circumscribed by the circumstances, or motives, under which it is made, that it *cannot be otherwise than it is*. Now this, Sir, you appear never to have rightly apprehended; and there would be no end of quoting all you say that might be produced in proof of what I have now advanced.

The very first passage that occurs on the subject, shews it sufficiently. "Upon the most diligent inquiry," you say, "I am persuaded that mankind have a self-deter-

---

* This account is incorrect as to Dr. Leland. He does not appear to have been "obnoxious to the Calvinists," but rather approved by them, and I am not aware that he ever controverted their opinions.

mining power, that, *upon mature deliberation and just reasoning*, they can make a free and proper election, and can not only choose, but reject, as shall seem best to their judgment." P. 2. But pray, good Sir, did any necessarian ever deny this? · If he did, he must have been such a defender of *necessity* as you are of *liberty*. A necessarian is so far from denying this, that his principles absolutely require it. For, according to them, something that may be called *judgment* necessarily precedes volition, and the volition is always directed by that judgment, being determined by what to it appears preferable at the time.

" Who," you say, " ever asserted that the mind was never under any influence, and that the will was not determined by motives ?" P. 39. What could any necessarian say more to his own purpose? For my own part, I cannot express my own principles in more proper, or more decisive language.

But you add, " the great question is, whether these motives are coercive, whether this influence be irresistible ; so that the mind has no power of election, and cannot by any means reject.—You will tell me that this is owing to a stronger motive, which overcomes the weaker. This I shall not controvert." Pp. 40, 41. Then, let me tell you, Sir, there is nothing in the whole business that you *can* controvert that will be to any purpose.

But I must take in what you subjoin. " All I know is, that whatever influences there may be, we are blessed with reason to consider and to judge, and with a power to reject or to choose." But, Sir, does any necessarian deny that man is endued with reason ? So far is he from denying that *consideration* and *judgment* precede volition and direct it, that this is the very circumstance that his scheme requires in order to exclude *self-determination*, which it effectually does. Indeed, Sir, here you are got upon clear *necessarian ground*, though, being unfortunately bewildered, as you truly say of yourself, *you know not where you are.*

Very far, Sir, are you from advancing any thing that I can condemn when you say, " Contrary to your notion, a thing which at any time happened might have happened otherwise, *if we had chosen it.*" P. 131. Now this, also, is so far from being contrary to my notion, as you call it, that it is perfectly agreeable to my notion. For it implies that to have happened otherwise, a different choice must have been made ; and you are as far as I can be from supposing that choice is not determined by motives.

In p. 27, you describe a particular mental process, and then add, " You will say, as usual, that there must be a motive for this.   We will grant that there may be, for instance, a prospect of future good or immediate satisfaction.   But this motive often arises at my will, and proceeds from my own bosom."   But if so, then, according to your own supposition, whence arises that will which called up the motive, but from some antecedent motive ?   For certainly the volition that calls up the motive is as much a volition as that which is finally produced by the motive. Will cannot be one thing, and have one set of properties, in one case, and be quite another thing, and have another set of properties, in another case.

What, Sir, but a mistake of the very ground of this controversy could make you say, " What is *involuntary* but another word for *necessary?*" p. 16, whereas, I had said that *voluntary* is properly opposed to *involuntary*, and *contingent* to *necessary;* and this is what the first metaphysical writer you shall look into will tell you.   Consequently, if a volition be so determined by the circumstances in which it is made, as to be strictly *definite*, it could not have been otherwise than what it is.   It is, therefore, *necessary.*   For it is upon this ground, and this only, that we denominate even the falling of a stone, or any thing else in the physical world, necessary.   A thing is always said to be *necessary*, if, *ceteris manentibus*, it could not have been otherwise than it is, and *contingent*, if, *ceteris manentibus*, it might have been otherwise.

Hence, Sir, the *contradictions* with which you are perpetually, but ignorantly, charging me, as in pp. 13, 14 : " I have been one while told that a man has a power of doing whatever he pleases, uncontroulled by any foreign principle or power.   You, in a few pages after, assure me, that the mind and will is always determined by a cause foreign to itself."   Indeed, Sir, this is no contradiction at all, because foreign to the *will* is one thing, and foreign to the *mind* another.   Also, in direct contradiction to yourself, you speak of an *irresistible motive*, p. 96, as taking away all mental determination; though, in the passages lately quoted, you yourself suppose motives necessary to volition.   Nothing sure can be at the same time necessary to volition, and yet necessarily take away all volition.   This, Sir, is too palpable.   Though the motive be *irresistible*, if it be a *motive*, it can influence nothing but the will, and therefore, what it produces cannot be any thing but a volition.

In the same place you give such an account of the principles of the necessarians, as I really cannot tell what to make of. " Does it not seem in vain," you say, " to give a power of choosing, and at the same time to abridge us of all choice; to allow us a will, but to take away the power of volition, which, according to you, Sir, is ever to be directed by a foreign influence, an influence not arising from our own judgment, but from an absolute decree, an irresistible motive," &c. ? P. 96.

But if, as you yourself allow, choice be always determined by motives, can a choice so made be called no choice, or is a choice determined by motives a thing that does not arise *from within ourselves?* Is an irresistible motive and an absolute decree, the same thing? Are they equally foreign influences; when a mere *decree* is, in its own nature, so very foreign to us, that it is not possible that it should, of itself, affect the will at all; and a *motive* you allow to be *within us,* and always to influence us. This account, Sir, is so very full of contradiction and embarrassment, that I can hardly persuade myself but that there must be something misprinted in the paragraph. So very incoherent a sentence I think I never met with before.

I must also notice another curious contradiction, which you fancy you have discovered in what I have observed on this subject. " You assert," you say, " that the *mind,* with all its powers, and particularly the *will,* is never determined without some real or apparent cause foreign to itself. —It seems impossible to make what you say here consistent with that which you maintained above. In this place the will, and the mind in general, must be determined by a foreign cause. If we look but six pages backward, we find just the contrary asserted, viz. that men are quite free to do whatever they will or please, both with respect to the operations of their own minds and the motions of their bodies, uncontrolled by any foreign principle or cause. This seems to be an absolute contradiction." Pp. 8, 9.

Now, Sir, all this that you have quoted would have appeared perfectly easy and consistent if you had only known the very first principles of the doctrine of the human mind, as laid down by Mr. Locke and others, or had only considered, that the will is only *one* faculty of the mind, so that, as I have just observed, what is foreign to the *will,* may not be foreign to the *mind* or the *man*. *Judgment* is not the *will*, nor are *motives* the will; but yet they are not things *foreign to the mind*, since they necessarily belong to it, and exist in it. Long, Sir, as you say you have studied this subject, you must study it again, and under some new master, and one who shall have the art of making things very plain indeed.

I cannot resist the temptation of quoting another extraordinary mistake of yours, though I must own that the time employed in transcribing so long an extract might have been better employed. " When this has been thus settled," you say, " you seem somehow to compromise matters, and, after all, to allow to the mind some power of judging for itself, the result of which you term a *definite choice*, and a *definite voluntary determination*. By this, if I apprehend you right, is meant that a man has a *partial* and *limited* power of election. But in another part of the work you assert, that in the scheme of liberty and necessity there is no medium. How then can we admit of this *compromise*, and by what means can these different assertions be rendered consistent? After all that you have been so good as to explain, I am still left to ask whether I am free, or not free? For, as to this *qualifying medium*, I know not what to make of it, as you do not sufficiently either define or prove it; and, at the same time, it seems to militate against your own avowed principles. I therefore again request to know, in respect to my thoughts and actions, whether I am *voluntarily* or *necessarily* determined?" Pp. 14, 15.

Now, if you had taken the trouble to look into any common *English dictionary*, you would have saved yourself the trouble of this remark, and me the trouble of copying it. For you would have found that the word *definite* means *strict* and *invariable;* and, therefore, a *definite choice* is far from being any medium between liberty and necessity, but a proper *necessary choice*, or a choice that, constituted as man is, he could not but have made in any given circumstances.

Every thing, Sir, begets its like, and one mistake introduces another. Or else they naturally follow one another, to steal your own quotation, *velut unda supervenit unda*. " I cannot," you say, " conceive how your discipline and influence can have a certain and necessary effect, when other influences may counteract your views, and when your object may be frustrated." P. 60. If, dear Sir, this case be too hard for you, I will put another exactly similar to it, that you may perhaps understand better. Cannot you then conceive that a weight of *one pound* in the scale A, has a certain and necessary effect, though it be overbalanced by a weight of *three pounds* in the opposite scale B ? Is it not of so much consequence, that if *two* more pounds be added to it, it will completely balance the weight in B ; whereas, without this one pound, *three* would be necessary for the same purpose. Make the experiment, if you please, and you will certainly find it to be so.

The next mistake on which I shall animadvert is no less extraordinary. When I spoke of the *indissoluble chain of causes*, determining a man's volitions and actions, from his birth to his death, what ground you then stood upon, or whether you stood upon any ground at all, I cannot tell (and perhaps you will be as much at a loss to recollect yourself) ; but certainly, you so far lost hold of this same chain, that you forgot what the links were made of. To drop this figure : you imagine that the whole of this chain consisted of *volitions*, that the thing represented by it was a mere *mental process*, and required uninterrupted thinking, from a man's birth to his death. But you must, and you shall be heard at length on this curious subject. We must see with what wonderful dexterity you handle this chain.

" Let us still farther consider," you say, " this series of events, this indissoluble chain of causes upon which your system is founded.—The chain of causes is never interrupted.—Motive arises from motive, and one idea produces another, and this inevitably.—But, may I ask, Sir, if you have ever considered the case of *sleep?* What connexion has the last idea of a man, when he sinks at night into oblivion, with the first thought which occurs to him upon his awaking in the morning? We have reason to think there is scarcely a revolution of four-and-twenty hours but this indissoluble chain is interrupted.——

" You will perhaps say that men think in their sleep, as is evident from their dreams. But do all men dream ? Or, if they do, what ensues, but a train of irregular and incoherent ideas, which are unconnected with one another, and quite independent of all foreign and remote influence? But, setting these things aside, have you considered the state of persons who suffer a deliquium—of people drowned, &c.? In these instances, the connexion spoken of must have been entirely broken off. If, then, the mind has no internal power of its own, by what means does it renew its train of thoughts, and how is it able to think again at all? The last idea when it sunk into forgetfulness, and the first which occurred when it *languished into day*, cannot possibly have had any relation to each other. There has been a manifest breach in the chain, and the primary influence, if it existed, must have been in like manner interrupted. From whence then does the mind recover itself, and what impression is it which sets the train of ideas in motion, &c.? Is the influence from within or from without? It cannot be any external impulse. For in these circumstances no immediate operation of the senses can make a person recur to events long past. The immediate impulse of the senses, and the surrounding objects, cannot bring this about. And as to *original influence* of which you treat, and the *chain of causes*, there has been a stop put to the whole, and the connexion no longer subsists. This power of recollection must therefore be from within, and is undoubtedly owing to a peculiar energy of the mind, a power of *self-exertion*, by which it is enabled to call up and arrange its ideas at pleasure, and to determine upon them as shall seem best. And in consequence of this we may conclude, that the will is not under any arbitrary and blind influence, nor directed by necessity." Pp. 22—24.

I think, Sir, I have given you sufficient time to manage this *chain*, but I perceive you have quite lost your hold. However, as I have kept mine, I may perhaps assist you to lay hold of it once more,

Know then, that there is in the human mind a power, or faculty, which Mr. Locke calls *the principle of association*, by means of which one idea recalls another formerly connected with it, and that, at all times, external objects have a power of exciting some ideas in us.—Please, Sir, to read what I have now said over again. And when you are quite sure that you understand thus much, consider farther whether it be not possible, that, after the soundest sleep, or deliquium (the senses and brain not being materially injured, and the ideas formerly impressed upon it not being entirely cancelled), some object casually present, to the eye for instance, may affect the retina, and consequently an idea be conveyed to the sensorium. That idea, having had old connexions with others, may call up its friends, and these in like manner, their several friends and acquaintance, till the whole crowd of former ideas occupies the mind, and the business of combination and arrangement, &c. &c., as described by Mr. Locke, goes on as usual. In the next article you are utterly bewildered and lost in your own eloquence.

" From these principles which you lay down," you say, " that all, in the same situation, would, after any interval, act precisely as they have done, it follows that if the world were renewed, all the same occurrences would necessarily happen again. If, after ever so many myriads of ages, a man were formed in the same manner, and in the same circumstances, as the person from whom we are all descended, he would act exactly as Adam is presumed to have acted ; he would have the same posterity, they would travel over the same ground, find out the same arts, at the same periods, and perform, without the least deviation, all and every of those things which have been already performed. Every step they should take would be found the same, every look, every turn, every involuntary gesture would be repeated. The winds would blow with the same variation, the rain must fall to a drop—as it had done before. The very dust and the smallest motes, which float in any medium, would be, in number and quality, the same. For, according to your principles, the same original impulse must be attended with the like consequences. And if we allow a failure in the smallest degree, there must be ultimately an unavoidable difference through the whole arrangement. But such difference is inconsistent with that primary influence, and that necessity which you maintain. There must, therefore, be a perfect similarity throughout. These are the necessary consequences from your principles, but I believe nobody will be persuaded that this would ever obtain. Let any person, after he has signed his name, try to write it three or four times precisely in the same manner, and see whether it perfectly accords. If he cannot do it when he undertakes it with premeditation, he will hardly bring it to perfection when he acts without design. Or let him walk a hundred yards, and then try to pace the same ground at the like intervals, and in the same time. If he could not perform it immediately, he would not effect it at the distance of three days, or thirty days, much less after an interval of ages." Pp. 19—21.

I have made this long quotation to give my reader a just idea of your great powers in the *rhetorical way*, in order to make him some amends for his disappointment with respect to excellence of any other kind. What you want in *ideas* you make up in *words*, and though you have not *precision;* you excel in *amplification*. Now I do not pretend to any excellence of *this* kind. Every man, and every animal, has his own weapons. The bull has his horns, and the horse his heels. You have oratory, I have logic. So conspicuous in you, Sir, are the powers of *imagination*, that they go hand in hand with your *learning*, in the most elaborate of your works.

Whether you will think the return adequate or not, you must be content with a *logical distinction*, in return for the entertainment you have afforded me ; and my distinction is a very plain one. It is between the power of *man* and that of *God*, which, great as it is, you had quite overlooked upon this occasion ; though, when it serves your purpose, you can declaim on this topic as copiously as upon any other, and of this I shall produce a specimen in its proper place.

It is true, as you say, that no man can do any very complex thing twice over exactly in the same manner ; but it is because it is not possible for him to place himself, body and mind, in a situation sufficiently exact for the purpose. But to convince you how little your mode of reasoning affects a necessarian, I must give you a case similar to it, and one that you may better comprehend.

Fill a bag with billiard balls, and then shake them out on the table. Every ball will, at length, settle in a definite place, (please here to recollect the definition of the word *definite*, or my instance will be nothing to the purpose,) and were it possible to place them all exactly as they were before, and to pour them out exactly in the same manner, they would certainly settle in the same places that they occupied before. You cannot doubt of this, because nothing is concerned besides physical and mechanical laws, all of which you allow to operate necessarily ; and you would laugh at any man who should deny the necessary influence of those laws, merely because neither he nor you, if you were to make the trial, could so place the balls in the bag, and so shake them out, as that they should actually settle in the same places twice together. And, to adopt one of your own modes of polite address, believe me, Sir, the brain of a man is a much more complex thing than a bag of billiard balls. Here then, Sir, is my logical *distinction* and *example*, in return for your rhetorical declamation.

As I hope I have given you some pleasure in submitting to the perusal of my readers so very long an extract from your work as the preceding, and I am desirous of gratifying you as far as I can, I shall proceed to make another long extract of a similar kind, and not less excellent. " You, indeed, tell me, Sir, that every thought is predetermined, and in every act of volition I am forcibly impelled, so that I

could not, in any instance, have made my election otherwise than I have done. Every movement of the mind, you
say, arises from a *pressing uneasiness.*" By the way this is
not what I say, but what Mr. Locke says. " This theory
may appear specious, but it seems to run counter to all experience ; and the contrary, if I mistake not, is self-evident.
I sit at this instant at my ease, in a calm and dispassionate
state of mind, as you are pleased, Sir, to recommend. I
perceive myself at full liberty, and know not of any external
impulse to determine me either in my thoughts or actions.
I purpose to move, but antecedently examine whether I am
under any bias, or necessity, or directed by any foreign
power. I find none. In the vast series of causes, so often
mentioned, I do not perceive one that will have any share
in the effect which I am about to produce. The whole
originates in myself, whether I move my body, or my arm,
or am content with extending a finger. The like appears in
respect to my thoughts. I am here equally free, and among
the various objects which are ready at my call, I arbitrarily
choose those to which my fancy leads me. You tell me
every thought is an effect, and that it is connected with a
prior idea, by which it was produced. I cannot see any
such uniform affinity or correspondence ; and to give a proof
of my liberty and independence, I will for once expatiate
freely, and produce a series of unconnected ideas from my
own imagination. I accordingly, without any pressing
uneasiness, think of a tree, of time, of the ocean, of darkness
of a cone, of truth, of a tower, of probability, of Thersites,
of love, of Epidaurus, of Socrates, of a mite, of casuistry, of
the Iliad, of Otaheite, of Tenterden steeple, of a mole, of a
mouse-trap. In doing this I did not find that I was restrained by any law of nature, or impelled by any foreign
power. Nor can I at last perceive that these desultory
thoughts have the least connexion with one another, much
less with any prior ideas. You assure me that they must
unavoidably have a reference, and that they are dependent
upon others which have preceded. In short, according to
your principles, they arose so necessarily in my mind, that
five days hence, or five years hence, in the same circumstances, and with the same disposition, I should infallibly
make the very same choice. But this seems contrary to
experience : for though I am as precisely in the same circumstances as we can suppose any man to be, and likewise
in the same disposition of mind ; yet, after an interval of a
very few minutes, I am not able to go over a fourth part of

this series. And however cogent the necessity may be, I can recollect very little more than the mole and the mouse-trap." Pp. 25—27.

You think, Sir, that the curious assortment of ideas you have presented us with had no connexion, mediate, you must mean, or immediate. But odd as you, who appear to know so little of the human mind, may think it, I have no doubt but they really had. Are you sure that you have omitted no other ideas, that might connect those that you have produced? Or, which you may better recollect, did you at first set them down exactly in the order in which they now stand? Were not the words *love* and a *tower* a little nearer together, and did not the story of Hero and Leander occur to you; and are you quite sure that nothing squeezed in between the *mole* and the *mouse-trap?*

You say you place yourself as precisely in the same circumstances as we can suppose any man to be, and likewise in the same disposition of mind. But, Sir, what you may *suppose* to be the same, may not be *precisely so*, and a very slight alteration in the disposition of your mind, perhaps the position of your body, may put the *mole* in the place of the *mouse-trap*, or, vice versa.

That you have never read Mr. Hobbes, I take for granted. Indeed if you had, you would have known a little more of the subject of which you treat than you now do. Somewhere in his writings, but I do not now recollect the place, you would have found a pertinent observation to the present purpose, and a proper example. Some gentlemen were talking of the *civil wars* in England, when one of them suddenly asked what was the value of a *Jewish shekel*. To appearance, these had as little connexion as any two in your group. But this gentleman was more ingenuous, or more fortunate than you; for being interrogated while the whole train was fresh in his memory, he said the *civil war* brought to his mind the *death of king Charles*, the death of Charles *that of our Saviour*, and this made him think of the *thirty pieces of silver*, which he supposed were *shekels*, for which Judas betrayed him. Now all this process might take place in less time than would be sufficient to write down any of the two words in your collection.* But you

---

* The passage to which my author must here refer is the following, and it will be seen that he has inadvertently attributed to a confession of the *Querist*, the happy conjecture of *Hobbes*. "In a discourse of our present civil war, what could seem more impertinent than to ask (as one did) what was the value of a Roman penny? Yet the coherence to me was manifest enough. For the thoughts of the war introduced

seem to have no idea of the rapidity of thought, or how slight circumstances are sufficient, by the law of association, to introduce any particular idea. And yet the connexion of the several parts of your ingenious system of mythology is often extremely delicate.

When I look over the several articles of this.Section, and see that you speak of necessity as something that *excludes will,* calling it a *foreign influence, arbitrary decree, chain of causes,* &c. &c., I cannot help thinking but that, as all our ideas of things *mental* are derived from things *corporeal,* your idea of necessity is that of a great iron chain, fastened round a man's body, which he cannot get rid of, and, by which he is dragged *nolens, volens.* But, dear Sir, do not fright yourself in this manner. *Necessity,* Sir, *philosophical necessity,* is a more gentle thing than this iron chain that haunts your imagination ; and though you are led by it, you at the same time go just where you please ; and whenever you become a necessarian, you will be in the case of the man who found that he had been speaking *prose* all his life, though without knowing it.

SECTION III.

Of the Divine Prescience.

I AM at length come to the topic on which you write with the greatest pomp and power ; and here being, as I suppose you thought, a *nodus deo vindice dignus,* you introduce the Divine Being himself as imposing everlasting silence upon me, and you pour out such a torrent of scripture quotations, that if the *application* was at all pertinent, I should have no power of reply. But this being wanting, your argument is *brutum fulmen.* As I perceive you have not yet understood my argument on this subject, I shall repeat it more particularly ; and I think it is capable of being made so plain that it shall be impossible either to misunderstand or refute it. I state it as follows :

Nothing can be *seen to be* what it is not, because it would then *be* what it is not. The Deity himself cannot see *black* to be *white,* or *white black ;* because black is not white, nor.

---

the thought of the delivering up the king to his enemies. The thought of that brought in the thought of the delivering up of Christ; and that again the thought of the thirty pence, which was the price of that treason, and thence easily followed that malicious question; and all this in a moment of time, for thought is quick. *Leviathan,* Pt. I. Ch. iii. fol. 1651, p. 9.

is white black.· If *sight*, or *perception*, or *knowledge in general*, cannot change the antecedent nature of objects, neither can the *divine* perception or knowledge.   Otherwise the Deity might see *two* to be *three*, or *three* to be *two*. And surely, Sir, with your leave, there cannot be any presumption, or impiety, in saying this.

If this be just, it must be true, and no presumption, to assert, that the Deity himself cannot *see* that to be *certain*, which is *in itself contingent*, or that to be contingent, which is absolutely certain.   Now, Sir, what is meant by any thing being *contingent* but that it either *may* or *may not* be? But for a thing to be *seen* as certain, it must *in itself* be certain ; and therefore the *possibility* of its *not being*, must be excluded.   Consequently, any event being foreseen *certainly to be*, is incompatible with its being even *possible* not to be. Nothing, therefore, of which it can be truly said that it either *may or may not be* (which you maintain is the case with every determination of the mind of man), can be an object of foreknowledge, even to the Deity himself.   To maintain the contrary is, in fact, the same thing as saying that the same event is both *contingent in itself*, and yet *certain to God;* or that though, in reality, it may or may not be, yet, contrary to the nature and truth of things, he knows that it certainly will be.   I therefore say that if a man be possessed of a power of proper self-determination, which implies that the Deity himself cannot controul it, the Deity himself cannot foresee what the actual determination will be.   Surely, Sir, there cannot be any argument more conclusive than this.   You, however, reply as follows :

" Surely, Sir," you say, " this is very bold, even to a degree of rashness, and at the same time your mode of reasoning seems to my judgment totally inconclusive.   It, I think, may be obviated by a thousand circumstances in common life."   Pp. 28, 29.   Let us hear one of them.

" A child," you say, " may determine to take a walk in a garden, and I may have a power to controul his purpose." P. 29.   Indeed, Sir, I cannot go any farther with you in this case, because I want a case in which there is a power of determination that I *cannot* controul.   What is your next instance out of the thousand that you say you could produce ?

" I sow a field," you say, " with wheat, and, if I please, I could make an alteration, by plowing it up, and sowing it with rye or barley.   But I cannot see how the mere power of varying my purpose can ruin that purpose."   P. 29.   But pray, Sir, what has this to do with *prescience ?* Some of the remaining nine hundred and ninety-eight cases must be produced, but all the thousand will avail nothing, unless they be very different from these ; and certainly you would not have given a specimen of the *worst* in the thousand.

But you add, and insist upon being heard, " You make no distinction between what the Deity can do, and what he really does ; and you argue as if power and performance were the same thing." P. 29. But, surely, Sir, before any act of man can be *foreseen*, it must be rendered *certain*, and there is no method of making it certain, but by controulling that power which would make it uncertain. Consequently the foreknowledge of God must be perpetually at variance with the self-determining power of man.

But I must, it seems, hear you farther, and I am willing to exercise as much patience as possible. " You proceed to enforce your argument by the authority of Mr. Hobbes, by whom you think the affair has been satisfactorily stated. *Denying necessity*, says this writer, Works, p. 485, *destroys both the decrees and prescience of Almighty God. For whatever God has purposed to bring to pass by man, as an instrument, or foresees shall come to pass, a man, if he has liberty, might frustrate, and make not come to pass ; and God should either not foreknow it and not decree it, or he shall foreknow such things shall be as shall never be, and decree what shall never come to pass.* What a rash, contemptible and short-sighted reptile is man ! Who would think that this insect of a day would presume to limit omniscience and controul the powers of the Almighty ! Bold and inconsiderate, to form a judgment of the divine energy by his own scanty faculties, and endeavour to reduce his Creator to the standard of man ! Besides, what a round of absurdity is there in this weak and impious supposition ? One would imagine that none but an idiot could have stated such a case ; wherein things are supposed to be foreknown which shall never be, and things decreed in consequence of foreknowledge which shall never come to pass ; in short, when it is said that what God foresees is not foreseen, for it may be frustrated by man and rendered ineffectual. This, Sir, is the argument which you think is clearly stated." P. 30.

I hope, Sir, you are now satisfied, and will not complain of my not giving you sufficient attention. I did not even stop you when you called Mr. Hobbes, and consequently myself, who quoted the passages from him with approbation, *weak, impious, and an idiot.*

Mr. Hobbes's argument is a very p a n one, and the man-ner in which it is expressed is sufficiently clear to every candid and intelligent reader. For the sake, however, of very dull, or very captious readers (for whom it is hardly worth while to write at all), it might perhaps have been better expressed as follows: Whatever God purposes to accomplish by means of men, they, if they be possessed of a self-determining power, may frustrate. In which case, God must either never foretell any thing, or declare that a thing shall come to pass, which, for any thing that he can tell, may never come to pass at all.

, Now, Sir, how does your fine flourish about the *power of God* and the *weakness of man*, at all apply to such an argu-ment as this? What *round of absurdity* (or square of absur-dity) what *weakness*, or *idiocy*, or *impiety*, is there in this? There are, Sir, as genuine marks of a reverence for God in the writings of Mr. Hobbes as in any of yours ; and it little becomes you to charge so superior a genius, so wonderfully acute a writer, and so excellent a scholar as he was, one of the first characters of his age in those respects, with *weakness* or *idiocy*, whatever right you may have to involve *me* in the same charge with him. Besides, if you mean to enter upon the stage of controversial writing, and wish that such oppro-brious epithets as these should have any effect, you should be more sparing of them, and at least not produce them but where there was more of the face of probability in the appli-cation of them. Should such an use of these terms, by your example, become general, we shall be obliged to change their signification in all English dictionaries.

I have another fault to find with your argument, which is, that you make that to be assumed by Mr. Hobbes, which he expressly charges upon his adversary. But this is a practised feint with you, and an improvement of your own in the art of controversy.

In the next place, you describe at large the manner in which man gains his knowledge. " But, my good Sir," you say, " can you possibly think that the knowledge of the Almighty is obtained in this servile and precarious manner, and that his wisdom proceeds after the human mode of reasoning? You may as well—ascribe to him the eyes of a man to get intelligence, and human limbs to per-form his high operations." P 31.

Now, to return your compliment, my good Sir, you make this slight mistake ; the question is not at all concerning the *manner* of obtaining knowledge, but concerning *the thing to be known.* I may go laboriously to work, in order to prove that the three internal angles of a right-lined triangle are equal to two right angles, and the Deity may know this in any other manner that you can, or cannot conceive, but he cannot see them to be equal to *three* or *four* right angles. So, also, if a thing be in itself contingent, he cannot see it to be certain, let his *manner* of knowing be what it will.

I perceive, however, you will not be satisfied unless I hear you farther in the tone of *authority*, now that *argument* fails you " Now, Sir," you say, " I should be very unwilling to be guilty of any disrespect towards you, and to make use of any harsh expression ; but surely you are highly presumptuous, not to say *self-sufficient.*" P. 32. By the way, in what respect is *self-sufficiency* more reprehensible than *presumption ?* " How can you, limited as you are in your faculties,—pretend to determine about divine intelligence ?—You tell me that you believe the Scriptures, and I presume that you are sincere.". For this I am obliged to you, Sir, as it is more than you always allow me. " Do you not then know that ' the wisdom of man is foolishness with God,' Cor. iii. 19 ; that, ' his ways are higher than our ways, and his thoughts than our thoughts' ? Isa. lv. 9. ' To whom then will you liken me, and shall I be equal, saith the holy one ?' Isa. xl. 25. ' Hast thou not known, hast thou not heard, that the everlasting Lord, the Creator of the ends of the earth, fainteth not, neither is weary : there is no searching of his understanding ?' Isa. xl. 28. ' Thy righteousness,' says the Psalmist, ' standeth like the great mountains, thy judgments are like the great deep.' Ps. xxxvi. 6. ' Who hath directed the spirit of the Lord, who instructed and taught him in the path of judgment, and shewed him the way of understanding ?' Isa. xl. 13, 14. This last, Sir, I am sorry to say, is the part which you have taken, by pretending to prescribe to the Deity. You have joined yourself with those who say, ' How doth God know, and is there wisdom in the Most High ?' Ps. lxxiii. 11. ' And thou sayest, how doth God know, can he judge through the dark cloud ?' Job xxii. 13. In what manner does the same sacred writer finally determine this point ? Attend, Sir, for he settles the whole in these few but important words : ' He beholdeth all high things, He is a king over all the children of pride.' Job xli. 34. From the quotations above given we may learn to humble ourselves when we speak of our Creator, and to mention his divine attributes with reverence." Pp. 32—34.

Well, Sir, I have now heard you fairly out, and have had the patience to hear myself ranked with *Atheists*, and per. sons utterly *profligate and abandoned.;* for such only the passages you have quoted from the Psalms and the book of Job respect.   But I want to know what is all this to your purpose?   Had you been a divine I should have concluded that it had been an extract from some *practical sermon*, and that your amanuensis had, by mistake, got hold of this, instead of something else that you had given him to trans. cribe for this place.

If, in this place, your amanuensis has deceived you, I suspect, that in the next your printer has omitted the word *not*.   You say, the " interfering of the Deity is quite op. posite to the doctrine of absolute decrees."   P. 116. Whereas, I think it favourable to that doctrine, and, in fact, they have always been held together.   Who, Sir, believe more concerning frequent interpositions of the Deity than the Calvinists, the great advocates for absolute decrees? But as you appear not to know who the Calvinists are, you are probably unacquainted with this circumstance.

SECTION IV.

Of the Charge of INFIDELITY, *and the Conclusion.*

How you should have taken it into your head that I am an unbeliever in revelation, is to me altogether unaccount. able.   If you had known any thing of me, either from my writings, or by character, you must have known that I am, by profession, a *Dissenting minister;* that till lately I was a stated preacher, and now am an occasional, and pretty frequent one.   Doing this, as I now must do, from *choice*, certainly affords very little presumption for your charge, unless you imagine (which, with your extreme ignorance of every thing relating to Dissenters, you very possibly may) that *all Dissenters* are unbelievers, and that your church of England has the sole right and property of all the Christia. nity there is in the world.

If you look over the catalogue of my publications, you will find that the greatest part of them are on theological subjects.   The second volume of my *Institutes* is a regular defence of the system of revelation, and most of my philo. sophical writings bear sufficient marks of a respect for religion and Christianity.

To imagine, after this, that I am an unbeliever in Christianity, is not easily accounted for, in a *man of letters*, who might be expected to be free from the prejudices of the vulgar, who, in all ages and nations, have ranked those whose opinions have been considerably different from their own, with Atheists or unbelievers. You, Sir, I must suppose had no other information than this, and then (not to offend your ears with the sound of too vulgar a proverb) taking this notion, that I am an unbeliever, for granted, you fancied you found traces of it in this treatise of *Necessity*, the only work of mine, I presume, that you ever looked into.

I shall only animadvert on a few of the passages in which this charge of infidelity is insinuated or expressed. The first is so little to your, or to *any* purpose, that I own I can make nothing of it, and quote it only that persons of more sagacity than myself may try what they can do with it. " When you have mentioned the providence of God in one part, you seem to set it aside in the next. In this you go great lengths. The interposition of the Deity, mentioned in the Old and New Testament, is not by you uniformly allowed. You aver boldly that many particular events, said expressly to have been appointed by God, were not appointed by him, and even the persons who have been represented as inspired by God, were not under any divine influence; and you add, in confirmation of what you have said, that in the instances, whatever they may be, to which you allude, there appears, from the circumstances of the history, to have been no proper interposition of the Divine Being, no real miracle, but every thing took place according to the common established course of nature. As this is somewhat extraordinary, it is a pity that you did not illustrate what you maintain by some examples. What you may mean by there being no proper interposition I know not. We have before us an alternative which admits of no medium. The Deity either does interpose, or he does not. Therefore, if you are true to your principles, you should speak out, and maintain, without equivocation, that God does not at all interfere in the world; in other words, that there is no providence." Pp. 117, 118.

I ask pardon, Sir, I do think I now understand something of what you are about. But I perceive you are not at all apprised of what *I* was about. I had said, that many things were foretold which depended upon the volitions of men, which volitions were produced exactly as other volitions are, without any particular interference of the Deity to controul them. But though I was expressly referring to the Jews and Romans, by whom our Saviour was crucified, and who you yourself will hardly say were *miraculously inspired* with their determination for that purpose, you seem to have imagined that I was treating concerning the providence of God in general, or of miraculous interpositions. To make out of this that I am an unbeliever in all revelations, discovers such a perverseness of understanding, as I have not yet seen in any writer. Sir, you will find much better proof of my being an unbeliever, in my *History of Electricity*, or on the very face of my *Chart of Biography;* and I rather wonder you should not have quoted both those works for that purpose. It must certainly have been because you were not acquainted with them. I shall not presume to follow you in what you here add concerning the *influence of God* and the *Holy Spirit*, as you and I, I perceive, have very different ideas of what is meant by the Holy Spirit in the Scriptures.

Indeed, Sir, this article is of a much more serious nature than any that I have animadverted upon hitherto. With respect to other things, I have chiefly indulged myself in laughing at your *ignorance* and *conceit;* but this charge of infidelity, is a most gross and groundless *calumny*, for which you are accountable to a higher tribunal than that of the public, to which we now appeal.

In what I am now going to quote, you charge me, Sir, with *vilifying and debasing the apostles*, and more than insinuate that I am an unbeliever in their divine mission; and all this merely for having advanced that they were not strictly speaking necessarians or philosophers. The only extenuation of your guilt is your extreme ignorance of the subject on which your presumption has led you to write; on which account, the malignant paragraph I am about to quote affords abundant matter for its own refutation.

" Though you speak with your usual caution and reserve," you say, " yet you afford us too plainly an indication of your real opinion of those writers, to whom you pretended that you had been so much beholden. Your words are very remarkable.' *Not that I think the sacred writers were, strictly speaking, necessarians, for they were not philosophers; but their habitual devotion naturally led them to refer all things to God, without reflecting on the rigorous meaning of their language; and very probably had they been interrogated on the subject, they would have appeared not to be apprised of the proper extent of the necessarian scheme, and would have answered in a manner unfavourable to it.* [Vol. III. p. 520.] Who must not after this, pity the fate of the poor apostles and evangelists? Alas, Sir, how very low they must be in your estimation. They, who for ages were thought to have been inspired, and to have been peculiarly directed by the spirit of truth, are at last supposed not to understand their own meaning." P. 121.

Here, Sir, you are once more making use of your own *original artifice*, and indeed we are all too apt to make the most of any little discovery of our own. When I expressly say the sacred writers were *not necessarians*, and did not even understand the system, could I possibly suppose that they meant to establish it?

" They were not, you say, strictly speaking, *necessarians*. No, in good truth, Sir, nor were they in any respect of that denomination. They were not, you say, *philosophers.* It is true, Sir, they might not understand the doctrine of fixed air, nor had they ever made any discoveries in electricity. To the squaring of the circle they were probably utter strangers. Yet, believe me, Sir, they were great philosophers. And however you may rank yourself above them, they were far your superiors in true knowledge." Pp. 121, 122. But, Sir, do you suppose the apostles knew so much of the *heathen mythology* as you do? : If not, do not you, in that respect, rank yourself above them?

" They were blessed above others," you say, " with rational philosophy, and likewise with a philosophy to which reason could not possibly arrive, and which could only be obtained from the fountain of all wisdom. This they had in full plenitude; and the whole of our religion, and our happiness in consequence of it, depends upon the testimony of these apostles, whom you thus vilify and debase. Such were these lights of the world, these preachers of divine truth, who, it seems, if they had been interrogated by Dr. Priestley, would not have been able to have given him a proper answer." P. 122. A proper answer to *what*, Sir; to a thing which it no more behoved them to know, than to understand heathen mythology or fixed air?

This business, Sir, is of a nature too serious to be treated with ridicule. If we must give an account of every *idle* word at the day of judgment, what apology can be made for such shocking calumny as this? You charge me, Sir, with not being a believer in revelation: what proof have *you* given.

the public that you are one? If you look into my *writings*, you will find ten times as much evidence of *my* being a Christian; and yet I entertain no doubt of your being a believer in Christianity, or that your general conduct is not governed by it, though you have so grossly violated its precepts in this particular case; for which, if you *really* be a Christian, in the only important sense of the word, you will ask pardon of God, if not of myself, and of the public also.

As to the *history* of the doctrine of necessity, till you know what *the thing itself* is, it is impossible you should make any thing of the investigation. As far as I yet see, Mr. Hobbes was the first who properly understood and explained the doctrine. And though you rank me, p. 131, with what you call the *inglorious triumvirate of Collins, Hume and Hobbes,* saying, p. 132, that *the world would have been glad to have found me in other company,* I can only say that, if I be in company with *truth* and *good sense,* I always think myself in *good* company, whoever else be of the same party.* It was disingenuous in you, Sir, not to mention the name of Hartley on this occasion, when I have made much more use of it, as an authority, than of any other. It looks as if you wished to conceal any credit I might derive from the respect I bear to so excellent a man, and so good a Christian. Had you been so disposed, you might have grouped me with a triumvirate of *christian necessarians,* for Leibnitz, Hutcheson and Hartley were such.

I shall now, Sir, close this letter, which I do without noticing many things that are extremely inconclusive and weak in your *Address* to me. Had I thought you at all qualified to discuss this question, I should have proposed a few *queries* to your consideration, as I have done to others with whom I have discussed it; and, I believe I shall now take my final leave of you.

The very poor figure you have made in this business (so little *judgment,* accompanying a boundless *imagination,*) makes me suspect more than I ever did before, that there

---

* Similar was the reply of *Lowth* to *Warburton,* when that acute and insolent polemic had connected his name, for an obvious purpose, with that of the philosopher of Malmesbury. " For my part, my Lord, I have no sort of objection to Mr. Hobbes's company, provided he behave decently and properly, and talk like a learned and a sensible man; and I had as lief say a thing after him as after another, provided the thing be true. And really Hobbes was a man of great learning and abilities." *A Letter,* &c., *by a late Professor in the University of Oxford.* Ed. 4. 1766, p. 21.

may be something amiss with your *System of Mythology.* The building you have reared has a fair front, the decorations are fine, and many of the rooms, I doubt not, are well proportioned; but I suspect the *foundation;* and it is very possible that, in some of my rambles, which are pretty various and excursive, I may take a walk that way, in order to take a nearer view of it.

In the mean time, I am,

Sir,

Your very humble servant,

J. PRIESTLEY.

London, April 17th, 1780.*

---

* In a summary review of " Domestic Literature" for this year, 1780, Dr. Priestley and Mr. Palmer are described as "antagonists well matched," and Mr. Bryant, with " great abilities in his own walk of learning," as " drawn into a controversy in which he could not shew himself to the best advantage." The reviewer then notices " an ingenious advocate for Dr. Priestley's system, in a pamphlet," which I have not met with. It is attributed to " some gentlemen of the medical profession." See *New Ann. Reg,* I. p. 205.

A

Philosophical Enquiry

CONCERNING

HUMAN LIBERTY:

[1715]

By ANTHONY COLLINS, Esq.

―――――

REPUBLISHED,

WITH A PREFACE,

[1790.]

A PREFACE,

BY THE EDITOR.

....

THE subject of *philosophical liberty and necessity* having engaged much of the public attention, many persons have wished to see this treatise of Mr. Collins's; but the copies being now become very scarce, few have been able, to procure it. On this account, at the request of several persons, I have been induced to republish it, making use of the *third edition*, printed in 1735, which, as far as I know, was the last.

The great merit of this piece consists in its conciseness, its clearness, and its being the first regular treatise on the subject. Mr. Hobbes, I am still of opinion, was the first who, in this or any other country, rightly understood, and clearly stated, the argument; but he wrote nothing, *systematical,* and consequently nothing that could be of much use to a student. For this purpose, this treatise of Collins's is excellent, there being few topics in the whole compass of the argument which he has not touched upon; and, being *methodical,* it is valuable as an *elementary treatise.*

My own work I have called *An Illustration of the Doctrine of Necessity*, having contented myself with explaining such of the arguments as appeared to me to have been misunderstood, though I was led, before I had done, to treat more or less largely of almost every thing that had been advanced relating to it; and I flatter myself that I have thrown some new light upon it. Dr. Hartley's sections on *the mechanism of the mind* * are indeed most excellent for their conciseness and clearness, beyond any thing in our language, or, I believe, in any other; but they are too short for the purpose of the young metaphysician. *Edwards's Treatise on Free-Will,*† though a most masterly performance, is in the extreme of diffuseness; and in many cases an argument is better understood by being expressed in few words.

---

* *Observations,* Pt. i. *Conclusion,* and Pt. ii. Prop. xiv.—xvi.
† See an account of this work and the author, Vol. III. pp. 8, 9.

The article with respect to which this treatise of Collins, and indeed every thing else that I have yet seen on the subject, except Dr. Hartley's, is most defective, is that which relates to moral sentiment, the foundation of praise or blame, and the nature of *accountableness*, which I have therefore more particularly considered in my *Illustration* of the doctrine, in my *Correspondence with Dr. Price*, and my *Letters to Mr. Palmer*, to which I have nothing to add.

The only seeming advantage of those who oppose the doctrine of necessity, arises from the consideration of the introduction of moral evil, and the connexion that it has with suffering. But if the doctrine of *prescience* be allowed, (which every believer in revelation *must* do, and without which there could be no proper government of the world at all,) whatever be the consequence of *appointment*, will also be the consequence of *permission*. If good would not ultimately arise from any kind or degree of evil, natural or moral, a good Being would not permit it; and if good would necessarily arise from it, he would be justified in appointing it, being the proper and necessary means to a valuable end.

It is likewise said, and with great plausibility, that there is no foundation for *praise or blame, merit or demerit*, upon the doctrine of necessity. But if the proper definition of philosophical liberty be attended to, even the common idea of praise or blame will be perceived to be as incompatible with *it*, as with the doctrine of *necessity*. For with what reason would any person be praised or blamed for an action which arose from no proper motive, but an arbitrary determination of the will, independent of *motive*, and consequently of *fixed principle?* And if, without attending to the popular idea of praise or blame, merit or demerit, we only consider the effect of annexing pleasing consequences to what we call *virtue*, and unpleasing ones to what we term *vice*, we shall see that such a system of government, with respect to beings influenced by motives, will actually tend to produce virtue, by supplying sufficient motives to the practice of it. And what else is the object and end of any wise and righteous government, the virtue of intelligent and social creatures being necessarily connected with their happiness?

If persons have strength of mind not to be frightened by *names*, and be capable of attending to *things* only, the strongest objections to the doctrine of necessity will not affect them. If they be unequal to this, they had better desist from the consideration of the subject, and content themselves with popular ideas and popular language. Only let them cease to censure what they do not understand, and what they see does no real harm.

These remarks I have thought proper to prefix to this treatise, because the subject of them is of particular importance, being the foundation of much popular declamation against the doctrine of necessity, and such as is acknowledged not to be easily answered to the satisfaction of a common reader ; and because it has not been sufficiently considered by Mr. Collins, Mr. Hume and other unbelievers seem willing to abandon the doctrine, without concern, to any immoral consequences that licentious persons may be disposed to draw from it; and christian metaphysicians have sometimes appeared to have been afraid of this objection to their doctrine, and willing to evade the force of it. This, however, has not been objected to *my* writings on the subject. I have acknowledged every consequence in its fullest extent, and in the strongest terms ; and yet I flatter myself that the doctrine, with all its consequences, has appeared to be highly favourable to virtue, in minds properly enlarged ; and weak minds, disposed to licentiousness, do not stand in need of the doctrine of philosophical necessity to reconcile to themselves any gratifications to which they are on other accounts strongly impelled.

When young necessarians, who wish to prolong their lives, shall neglect the necessary means of preserving them, by taking wholesome food or poison promiscuously; or when they shall carelessly throw themselves down precipices, or walk indifferently where there is danger and where there is none, I shall then acknowledge that the doctrine of necessity, simply considered, has, indeed, dangerous consequences. But if necessarians, whether virtuously or viciously disposed, take the same care of themselves in these respects as other people do, I shall say that, if they do not pay the same rational attention to their conduct in a moral respect, so as to guard against inconveniencies equally foreseen, whatever else be the cause, their inattention and misconduct did not arise from their being believers in the doctrine of necessity.

I would farther observe, that Mr. Collins takes it for granted (which I believe was true in his time) that the advocates for philosophical liberty admitted that all brutes were mere machines, necessarily impelled by their appetites and passions. But, for some time past, these writers have been compelled, by the similarity of the two cases, to admit that brutes have the same power of choice with men, and that if *choice*, as such, be free from necessity in men, it is no less so in brutes. For the same reason they have also been compelled to acknowledge, that if men be animated by an immaterial and naturally immortal principle, called a *soul*, brutes also have such souls; and therefore, if they do not survive death, it must be owing to an express volition on the part of the Deity to *annihilate* their immortal souls.

Mr. Collins also supposes that the *fate* of the ancient philosophers, and the *predestination* of mahometan and christian divines, was the same thing with the modern doctrine of *philosophical necessity;* whereas they were things of a very different nature, as I have observed in my writings on the subject. Till of late the necessary connexion of events and their causes, when those causes were the voluntary actions of men, was not sufficiently attended to. The fatalist and the predestinarian both admitted freedom of choice in common things, but they imagined that, with respect to those particular events which were *destined* to take place, human volitions would either be supernaturally over-ruled, or that the events would take place in some other manner, independently of their volitions.

It has been unfortunate for the doctrine of necessity, that some of its first and ablest defenders were either unbelievers in Christianity, or at least generally considered as such. This was the case with Mr. Hobbes in an early period of the business, of Mr. Hume in a later, and also of Mr. Collins, who came between them. Mr. Collins was the friend and correspondent of Mr. Locke,* who had a high opinion of him. He was a man of irreproachable morals, and a most excellent magistrate; but he saw in a strong light the absurdity of the established system,† and the freedom of his publications having given much offence to the clergy, he was irritated by their opposition to him; and from this cause it is very possible he might be instigated to throw as many difficulties in their way as he could, whether he was an unbeliever or not.‡

---

* His Letters to Mr. Collins, 32 in number, were first published in Locke's *Pieces*, 1720. Mr. L. evidently considers his correspondent as a Christian and a serious inquirer into the sense of Scripture. He was then a young man, and had published nothing besides a tract on Nonconformity.

† See his View of the *Orthodox* Faith, Vol. II. p. 102, note § *ad fin.*

‡ See *Bibliothèque Raisonnée*, Tom. IV. P i. p. 233, quoted in Collins's Life, *Biog. Brit.* IV. p. 26, and the extracts from Hollis's *Memoirs*, &c. p. 27. Collins, like Hobbes, was unfairly treated by the censors of supposed *deistical writers.* For instance, he had mentioned, after *Victor*, " the holy gospels as written *Idiotis Evangelistis*," leaving the last words untranslated. Yet *Bentley*, referring to the page, makes him describe " the holy gospels, as written by Idiot Evangelists," and, with a sneer at this ignorance of language, severely censures " his scandalous translation."

·" His writings 'on 'the' subject of *prophecy**   have' certainly occasioned more' real difficulty to the friends of revelation than all the other writings of unbelievers at home or abroad; and it is the opinion of many, that they have not yet been properly answered. I do not indeed see how Mr. Collins's writings on this subject can be answered, so long as we retain the idea of the universal infallibility of the apostles, or of Christ himself. But if we admit that they had no particular instruction from above in the *interpretation of Scripture* (which, as they no where *say* that they had, we have no occasion to suppose), and that, with the prejudices common to all Jews of that 'age, they were led' to suppose more passages in their Scriptures to relate to the Messiah than really did so, we may make ourselves perfectly' easy on the subject; because the *testimony* of the apostles to the leading facts in the gospel history, such as the miracles, the death and the resurrection of Christ, on the truth of which alone our belief of Christianity properly rests, stands unimpeached by any instances of their mistakes in point of *judgment*. They were plain, honest men, incapable of im-¹ posing upon the world what they knew to be false, and indeed unable' to do so, if they had been capable of intending it.

' 'In fact, the reception that was given to Christianity' at the first promulgation of it, especially considering how highly interested 'both the friends and the enemies of it were to find· out the truth, is its proper proof. The witnesses of the facts

Compare the *Discourse on Freethinking*, 1713, p. 90, with *Remarks*, No. 83, by *Phileleutherus Lipsiensis*, 1743, Ed. 8, pp. 112, 113.

' 'I am sorry to find Dr. Leland supplying another instance, in his article *Collins*. Having observed, that "the ancient prophets have been the constant object of the sneers and reproaches of these gentlemen," he adds, "And accordingly this writer has told us, that to *obtain the prophetic spirit, they played upon music, and drank wine*." Now the writer who first *told* this, and as to whom Dr. Leland is silent, was the learned clergyman *Dodwell*, in his book against Grotius *de Jure Laic*. The original Latin is given at length, with the name of the author, in the page of the *Discourse* to which Leland refers. Compare the *View*, &c. Ed 2, p. 121, with *Discourse*, &c. 1713, p 153, *Note*. Unless we charge these christian advocates with culpable inattention, these are instances of *pious frauds*, such as Christians should be among the first to disavow and discountenance My author had now become more doubtful as to Mr. Collins's rejection of Christianity, than when he published the *Institutes*. See the page mentioned in the last note.

* The work to which my author refers was published, 1724, *anonymously*, like all Mr. Collins's writings. It has the following title: "A Discourse of the Grounds and Reasons of the Christian Religion; in two parts the first containing some Considerations on the Quotations made from the Old in the New Testament, and particularly on the Prophecies cited from the former and said to be fulfilled in the latter· the seond containing an Examination of the Scheme advanced by Mr. Whiston in his *Essay towards restoring the true Text of the Old Testament, and for vindicating the Citations thence made in the New Testament*. To which is prefixed, an Apology for Free Debate and Liberty of Writing." 1724.'

were not the apostles only, the evangelists, and other writers, whose works are now come down to us, but *the age* itself. In like manner, it is not on the authority of Rapin only, or that of all the other English historians of his time, put together, that we believe the history of the *Revolution* under King William: but because we perceive, by the reception which their writings met with, that it was the belief of the age, which would have rejected their histories if they had not been narratives of well-known facts; and, also because all other subsequent events, and those of our own times, imply the truth of it.

But though the primitive Christians were honest men, who received and propagated what they apprehended to be true, yet, where *judgment*, and not simple *testimony, to facts*, was required, they might be mistaken themselves, and lead others into mistakes. On this subject, I have written more largely in the *Theological Repository, Vol. IV.* &c. under the signature of *Pamphilus*; but I thought it not amiss to observe thus much in this place, on the republication of this piece of Mr. Collins's.

Whatever Mr. Collins was himself, and whatever be the merits of his writings against revealed religion, this tract of his on the subject of *philosophical necessity*, and the doctrine itself, ought not to suffer in consequence of it. Let every tenet be tried by its own proper evidence, and stand clear of any odium that may be thrown upon it from the characters of those that have maintained it. Unfortunately, this has been more particularly the case with the doctrines of *materialism* and *necessity*. Because both materialists and necessarians were some time ago generally unbelievers, it has been taken for granted that *all* necessarians, and especially all materialists, must be deists, if not atheists. It has, however, sufficiently appeared, from the writings of Dr. Hartley, Dr. Edwards and many others, that all *necessarians* are not unbelievers; and, the same is, I hope, now the case, with respect to *materialists*, who, as I have shewn at large, are the only consistent believers in revelation; the doctrine of a *separate soul* having been introduced from the heathen philosophy, and being irreconcileable with the scripture account of a future state, viz. that of the *resurrection of the dead* at a future period; and not the continued existence of an immaterial soul, incapable of dying at all.

The time I hope is approaching, when Christians in general will be better able to distinguish their friends from their enemies, and the genuine doctrines of their religion from the corruptions of it. And this period will be much accelerated by the friends of truth and genuine Christianity not being afraid of lying under the imputation of being its enemies for a time. They must openly avow their principles, under the most obnoxious appellations, and with all their consequences ; and in time it will be evident, even to the most uninstructed and prejudiced, that men professing Christianity, who devote themselves to the study of it, and whose lives are no reproach to it, are not to be rejected from the class of Christians. By this means the attention of the inquiring part of the world will be attracted to their sentiments. This will occasion *examination*, and the result of examination will be *conviction* with respect to whatever is *truth*. After this we shall no more hear of Socinians, Necessarians and Materialists being of course *no Christians*. On the contrary, they will be found to be the only enlightened and consistent Christians, and the only ones qualified to answer the objections of unbelievers. It is their Christianity only that is *founded upon a rock*, and to their firm and judicious labours in its support will be owing its universal prevalence in the world.

N. B. There are two translations of Mr. Collins's work into French.* A new edition of the second of them was given to me when I was at Paris, printed in the year 1756. The translator has added many *notes*, which I should have translated, if they had appeared to me to be of much importance in this country.

---

* "The Inquiry was translated into French by the Rev. Mr. D****, and printed in the first volume of *Recueil de diverses Pièces*, &c. published by M. Des Maizeaux, Amst. 1720, 2 vols. 12mo:". Biog. Brit. IV. p. 24. Of the original *the second edition corrected* was published, *London*, 1717; the last, I apprehend, before the death of Mr. Collins in 1729. From this I have, in a few instances, corrected my author's edition.

THE

AUTHOR'S PREFACE.

Too much care cannot be taken to prevent being misunderstood and prejudged, in handling questions of such nice speculation as those of *Liberty* and *Necessity;* and therefore, though I might in justice expect to be read before any judgment be passed on me, I think it proper to premise the following observations:

1. First, though I deny *liberty* in a certain meaning of that word; yet I contend for *liberty*, as it signifies *a power in man to do as he wills or pleases*, which is the notion of *liberty* maintained by Aristotle, Cicero, Mr. Locke, and several other philosophers, ancient and modern; and indeed, after a careful examination of the best authors who have treated of *liberty*, I may affirm, that however opposite they appear in words to one another, and how much soever some of them seem to maintain another notion of *liberty*, yet at the bottom there is an almost universal agreement in the notion defended by me, and all that they say, when examined, will be found to amount to no more.

2. Secondly, when I affirm *necessity*, I contend only for what is called *moral necessity*, meaning thereby, *that man, who is an intelligent and sensible being, is determined by his reason and his senses;* and I deny man to be subject to such necessity as is in clocks, watches and such other beings, which, for want of *sensation* and *intelligence*, are subject to an *absolute, physical,* or *mechanical necessity*. And here also I have the concurrence of almost all the greatest asserters of *liberty*, who either expressly maintain *moral necessity*, or the thing signified by those words.

3. Thirdly, I have undertaken to shew, that the notions I advance are so far from being inconsistent with, that they are the sole foundations of morality and laws, and of rewards and punishments, in society; and that the notions I explode are subversive of them. This I judged necessary to make out, in treating a subject that has a relation to morality, because nothing can be true which subverts those things; and

all discourse must be defective, wherein the reader perceives any disagreement to *moral truth;* which is as evident as any speculative *truth*, and much more necessary to be rendered clear to the reader's mind than *truth* in all other sciences.

4. Fourthly, I have entitled my discourse, *A Philosophical Inquiry, &c.* because I propose only to prove my point by experience and by reason, omitting all considerations strictly *theological.* By this method I have reduced the matter to a short compass; and hope I shall give no less satisfaction, than if I had considered it also *theologically;* for all but enthusiasts must think *true theology* consistent with reason and with experience.

5. Fifthly, if any should ask, *of what use* such a discourse is, I might offer to their consideration, first, the *usefulness* of truth in general: and secondly, the *usefulness* of the truths I maintain, towards establishing laws and morality, rewards and punishments, in society; but shall content myself with observing, that it may be *of use* to all those who desire to know the truth in the questions I handle, and that think examination the proper means to arrive at that knowledge. As for those who either make no inquiries at all, and concern not themselves about any speculations; or who take up with speculations, without any examination; or who read only books to confirm themselves in the speculations they have received; I allow my book to be of *no use* to them, but yet think they may allow others to enjoy a taste different from their own.

A

Philosophical Inquiry

CONCERNING

HUMAN LIBERTY.

―――◆―――

To LUCIUS.

" I HERE send you, in writing, my thoughts concerning
LIBERTY and NECESSITY, which you have so often desired
of me : and in drawing them up, have had regard to your
penetration, by being as short as is consistent with being
understood, and to your love of truth; by saying nothing,
but what I think true, and also all the truth that I apprehend
relates to the subject, with the sincerity belonging to the
conversation of friends. If you think me either too short in
any respect, or to have omitted the consideration of any
objection, by its not occurring to me, or that you think of
importance to be considered, be pleased to acquaint me
therewith, and I will give you all the satisfaction I can."

INTRODUCTION.

It is a common observation, even among the learned, that
there are certain matters of speculation, about which it is
impossible, from the nature of the subjects themselves, to
speak clearly and distinctly. Upon which account, men are
very indulgent to, and pardon the unintelligible discourses of
theologers and philosophers, which treat of the sublime
points in theology and philosophy. And there is no question in the whole compass of speculation, of which men
have written more obscurely, and of which it is thought
more impossible to discourse clearly, and concerning which
men more expect, and pardon obscure discourse, than upon
the subjects of *Liberty* and *Necessity*. But this common
observation is both a common and a learned error. For
whoever employs his thoughts either about God, or the
Trinity in Unity, or any other profound subject, ought to

have some ideas, to be the objects of his thoughts, in the same manner as he, has in thinking on the most common subjects : for where ideas fail us in any matter, our thoughts must also fail us. And it is plain, whenever we have ideas, we are able to communicate them to others by words :* for words being arbitrary marks of our ideas, we can never want them to signify our ideas, as long as we have so many in use among us, and a power to make as many more as we have occasion for. Since then we can think of no thing farther than we have ideas, and can signify all the ideas we have by words to one another, why should we not be able to put one idea into a proposition as well as another ? Why not to compare ideas together about one subject as well as another ? And why not to range one sort of propositions into order and method, as well as another ? When we use the term God, the idea signified thereby ought to be as distinct and determinate in us, as the idea of a triangle or a square is, when we discourse of either of them ; otherwise, the term God, is an empty sound. What hinders us then from putting the idea signified by the term God, into a proposition, any more than the idea of a triangle or a square ? And why cannot we compare that idea with another idea, as well as any two other ideas together ; since comparison of ideas consists in observing wherein ideas differ, and wherein they agree : to which nothing is requisite in any ideas, but their being distinct and determinate in our minds ? And since we ought to have a distinct and determinate idea to the term God, whenever we use it, and as distinct and determinate as that of a triangle or a square ; since we can put it into a proposition ; since we can compare it with other ideas on account of its distinctness and determinateness ; why should we not be able to range our thoughts about God in as clear a method, and with as great perspicuity, as about figure and quantity ?

I would not hereby be thought to suppose, that the idea of God is an adequate idea, and exhausts the subject it refers to, like the idea of a triangle or a square ; or that it is as easy to form in our minds, as the idea of a triangle or a square ; or that it does not require a great comprehension of mind, to bring together the various ideas that relate to God, and so compare them together ; or that there are not several propositions concerning him, that are doubtful, and of which

* I do not mean, unknown, simple ideas. These can, at first only, be made known by application of the object to the faculty ; but when they have been once perceived, and a common name agreed upon to signify them, they can be communicated by words. (C.)

we can arrive at no certainty; or that there are not many propositions concerning him subject to very great difficulties
or objections. All these I grant: but say, they are no
reasons to justify obscurity. For, first, an inadequate idea
is no less distinct, as such, than an adequate idea, and no less
true, as far as it goes; and therefore may be discoursed of
with equal clearness and truth. Secondly, though the idea
of God be not so easy to form in our minds as the idea of a
triangle or a square, and it requires a great comprehension of
mind to bring together the various ideas that relate to him,
and compare them together; yet these are only reasons for
using a greater application, or for not writing at all. Thirdly,
if a writer has, in relation to his subject, any doubts or
objections in his mind, which he cannot resolve to his own
satisfaction, he may express those conceptions or thoughts no
less clearly than any other conceptions or thoughts. He
should only take care not to exceed the bounds of those
conceptions, nor endeavour to make his reader understand
what he does not understand himself: for when he exceeds
those bounds, his discourse must be dark, and his pains useless. To express what a man conceives, is the end of writing;
and every reader ought to be satisfied when he sees an author
speak of a subject according to the light he has about it, so
far as to think him a clear writer.

When, therefore, any writer speaks obscurely, either about
God, or any other idea of his mind, the defect is in him.
For why did he write before he had a meaning; or before he
was able to express to others what he meant? Is it not
unpardonable for a man to cant who pretends to teach?

These general reflections may be confirmed by matter of
fact, from the writings of the most celebrated dogmatical
authors.

When such great men as *Gassendus, Cartesius, Cudworth,
Locke, Bayle, Sir Isaac Newton,* and *M. de Fontenelle* treat
of the most profound questions in metaphysics, mathematics,
and other parts of philosophy, they, by handling them as far
as their clear and distinct ideas reached, have written with
no less perspicuity to their proper readers than other authors
have done about historical matters, and upon the plainest
and most common subjects.

On the other side, when authors, who in other respects are
equal to the foregoing, treat of any subjects farther than they
have clear and distinct ideas; they do, and cannot but
write to as little purpose, and take as absurd pains as the
most ignorant authors do who treat of any subject under a total

ignorance or a confused knowledge of it. There are so many examples of these latter occurring to every reader, and there are such frequent complaints of men's venturing beyond their ability in several questions, that I need not name particular authors, and may fairly avoid the odium of censuring any one. But having met with a passage concerning the ingenious Father *Malebranche*, in the *Letters* of *Mr. Bayle*, who was an able judge, a friend to him, and a defender of him in other respects, I hope I may, without being liable to exception, produce Father *Malebranche* as an example. He has in several books, treated of and vindicated the opinion of *seeing all things in God;* and yet so acute a person as *Mr. Bayle*, after having read them all, declares, that he *less comprehends his notion from his last book than ever.** Which plainly shews a great defect in *F. Malebranche* to write upon a subject he understood not, and therefore could not make others understand.

You see I bespeak no favour in the question before me, and take the whole fault to myself if I do not write clearly to you on it, and prove what I propose.

And that I may inform you in what I think clear to myself, I will begin with explaining the sense of the question.

The Question stated.

Man is a *necessary agent*, if all his actions are so determined by the causes preceding each action, that not one past action could possibly not have come to pass, or have been otherwise than it hath been ; nor one future action can possibly not come to pass, or be otherwise than it shall be. He is a *free agent*, if he is able, at any time under the circumstances and causes he then is, to do different things : or, in other words, if he is not unavoidably determined in every point of time by the circumstances he is in, and the causes he is under, to do that one thing he does, and not possibly to do any other.

First Argument, wherein our Experience is considered.

I. This being a question of fact, concerning what we

---

* " J'ai parcouru le nouveau livre du Père Malebranché contre M. Arnauld & j'y ai moins compris que jamais sa pretension, que les idées, par lesquelles, nous connoissons les objets, sont en Dieu, & non dans notre ame. Il y a là du malentendu: ce sont, ce me semble, des equivoques perpetuelles." *Letter of the 16th of October*, 1705, *to M. Des Maizeaux.* (C.) See Vol. III. p. 48.

ourselves do, we will first consider our own experience, which if we can know, as sure we may, will certainly determine this matter. And because experience is urged with great triumph, by the patrons of *liberty*, we will begin with a few general reflections concerning the argument of experience, and then we will proceed to our experience itself.

General Reflections on the Argument of Experience.

1. The vulgar, who are bred up to believe *liberty* or *freedom*, think themselves secure of success, constantly appealing to *experience* for a proof of their freedom, and being persuaded that they feel themselves free on a thousand occasions. And the source of their mistake seems to be as follows: they either attend not to, or see not the causes of their actions, especially in matters of little moment, and thence conclude they are free, or not moved by causes to do what they do.

They also frequently do actions whereof they repent : and because, in the repenting humour, they find no present motive to do those actions, they conclude that they might not have done them at the time they did them, and that they were *free* from necessity (as they were from outward impediments) in the doing them.

They also find that they can do as they will, and forbear as they will, without any external impediment to hinder them from doing as they will ; let them will either doing or forbearing. They likewise see that they often change their minds ; that they can and do choose differently every successive moment; and that they frequently deliberate, and thereby are sometimes at a near balance, and in a state of indifference with respect to judging about some propositions, and willing or choosing with respect to some objects. And experiencing these things, they mistake them for the exercise of *freedom*, or *liberty* from *necessity*. For ask them, whether they think themselves *free?* and they will immediately answer, *Yes :* and say some one or other of these foregoing things, and particularly think they prove themselves *free*, when they affirm, *they can do as they will*.

Nay, celebrated philosophers and theologers, both ancient and modern, who have meditated much on this matter, talk after the same manner, giving definitions of *liberty*, that are consistent with *fate* or *necessity ;* though, at the same time, they would be thought to exempt some of the actions of man from the power of *fate*, or to assert *liberty* from *necessity*. *Cicero* defines *liberty* to be, " a power to do as we will."[*] And therein several moderns follow him. One defines *liberty* to be, " a power to act or not to act, as we will."[†] Another defines it in more words thus: " a power to do what we will, and because we will; so that if we did not will it, we should not do it; we should even do the contrary if we willed it."[‡] And another, " a power in any agent, to do or forbear any particular action, according to the determination or thought of the mind, whereby either of them is preferred to the other."[§] On all which definitions, if the reader will be pleased to reflect, he will see them to be only definitions of *liberty*, or *freedom* from *outward impediments of action*, and not a *freedom* or *liberty* from *necessity*; as I also will shew them to be, in the sequel of this discourse, wherein I shall contend equally with them for such a power as they describe, though I affirm, that there is no *liberty* from *necessity*.

Alexander the *Aphrodisæan*,[||] (a most acute philosopher of the second century, and the earliest commentator now extant upon *Aristotle*, and esteemed his best *defender* and *interpreter*) defines *liberty* to be "a power to choose what to do, after deliberation and consultation, and to choose and to do what is most eligible to our reason; whereas otherwise we should follow our fancy."[¶] Now a choice after deliberation, is a no less necessary choice, than a choice by fancy. For though a choice by fancy, or without deliberation, may be one way, and a choice with deliberation may be another way, or different; yet each choice being founded on what is judged best, the one for one reason, and the other for another, is equally necessary; and good or bad reasons, hasty or deliberate thoughts, fancy or deliberation, make no difference.

In the same manner, *Bishop Bramhall*, who has written several books for *liberty*, and pretends to assert the liberty taught by *Aristotle*, defines *liberty* thus: He says, " That act which makes a man's actions to be truly free, is *election*;

[*] Opera, p. 3968. Ed. Gron. (C.)

[†] Placette, Eclaircis. sur la Liberté, p. 2. (C.) *Jean de la Placette*, a Protestant minister, was a native of Bearn. He died at Utrecht, 1718, aged 80. See Nouv. Dict. 1772, IV. p. 1079.

[‡] Jacquelot, sur l'Exist. de Dieu, p. 381. (C.) *Isaac Jacquelot*, a French Protestant minister, died at Berlin, 1708, aged 61. *Ibid*, III. p. 419.

[§] Locke's Essay of Human Understanding, Book II. C. xxi. § 8. (C.)

[||] Fabricii Bibl. Gr. Vol. IV. 68. Vossius de Sect. Phil. C. 18. (C.)

[¶] De Fato. p. m. 57. (C.)

which is the deliberate choosing or refusing of this or that means, or the acceptation of one means before another, where divers are represented by the understanding."* And that this definition places *liberty* wholly *in choosing* the seeming best *means,*† and not in choosing the seeming worst means, equally with the best, will appear from the following passages. He says, " actions done in sudden and violent passions, are not free; because there is no deliberation nor election.‡ To say the will is determined by motives, that is, by reasons or discourses, is as much as to say that the agent is determined by himself, or is *free.* Because motives determine not naturally, but morally; which kind of determination is consistent with true liberty.—Admitting that the will follows necessarily the last dictate of the understanding, this is not destructive of the liberty of the will; this is only an hypothetical necessity."§ So that *liberty*, with him, consists in choosing, or refusing necessarily after deliberation; which choosing or refusing is morally and hypothetically determined, or necessary by virtue of the said deliberation.

Lastly, A great *Arminian* theologer, who has writ a course of *philosophy*, and entered into several controversies on the subject of *liberty*, makes *liberty* to consist in " an indifferency of mind while a thing is under deliberation. For," says he, " while the mind deliberates, it is free till the moment of action; because nothing determines it necessarily to act, or not to act."‖ Whereas, when the mind balances or compares ideas or motives together, it is then no less *necessarily* determined to a state of *indifferency* by the appearances of those ideas and motives, than it is *necessarily* determined *in the* very *moment of action*. Were a man to be at liberty in this state of *indifferency*, he ought to have it in his power to be *not indifferent*, at the same time that he is *indifferent*.

If *experience*, therefore, proves the *liberty* contended for by the foregoing asserters of *liberty*, it proves men to have *no liberty from necessity*.

2. As the foregoing asserters of liberty, give us definitions of *liberty*, as grounded on experience, which are consistent with *necessity*; so some of the greatest patrons of liberty, do by their concessions in this matter, sufficiently destroy all argument from *experience*.

Erasmus, in his treatise for *Free-will*, against *Luther*, says,

---

* Bp. Bramhall's Works, p. 735. (C.)   † Ibid. p. 697. (C.)
‡ Ibid. p. 702. (C.)   § Ibid. p. 707. (C.)
‖ Le Clerc, Bibl. Chois. Tom. xii. pp. 103, 104. (C.)

That "among the difficulties which have exercised the theologers and philosophers of all ages, there is none greater than the question of free-will."* And *Mr. Le Clerc*, speaking of this book of *Erasmus*, says, That " the question of free-will was too subtile for *Erasmus*, who was no philosopher; which makes him often contradict himself."†

The late *Bishop of Sarum*, though he contends, *Every man experiences liberty*, yet owns, that *great difficulties* attend the subject *on all hands*, and that therefore *he pretends not to explain or answer them.*‡

The famous *Bernard Ochin*, a great *Italian* wit, has written a most subtile and ingenious book, entitled, *Labyrinths concerning Free-will and Predestination*, § &c. wherein he shews, that they who assert that man acts freely, are involved in four great difficulties, and that those who assert that man acts necessarily, fall into four ' other difficulties. So that he forms eight *labyrinths*, four against *liberty* and four against *necessity*. He turns himself all manner of ways to get clear of them; but not being able to find any solution, he constantly concludes with a prayer to God to deliver him from these abysses. Indeed, in the progress of his work, he endeavours to furnish means to get out of this prison : but he concludes that the only way is to say, with *Socrates*, *Hoc unum scio quod nihil scio*. " We ought," says he, " to rest contented, and conclude, that God requires neither the affirmative nor negative of us." This is the title of his last chapter, *Qua via ex omnibus supradictis labyrinthis cito exiri possit, quæ doctæ ignorantiæ via vocatur.*

A famous author, who appeals to *common experience*, for a proof of *liberty*, confesses that " the question of liberty is the most obscure and difficult question in all *philosophy:*" that " the learned are fuller of contradictions to themselves, and to one another, on this, than on any other subject:|| and that he writes " against the common notion of liberty," and endeavours to establish *another notion*, which he allows to be *intricate*.

But how can all this happen in a plain matter of fact, supposed to be experienced by every body? What difficulty can there be in stating a plain matter of fact, and describing what every body feels? What need of so much *philosophy?*

* Opera, Tom. IX. p. 1215. (*C.*) † Bibl. Chois. Tom. XII. p. 51. (*C.*)
‡ Expos p. 117. (*C.*) *Burnet* on Article x. *ad init.*
§ " Labyrinthi de Prædestinatione et libero Arbitrio." *Basil,* 8vo. *Ochinus* died in 1564, aged 77. He is classed by *Sandius* among the Antitrinitarians. See *Bib. Anti-Trin.* 1684, pp. 2—6.
|| King de Orig. Mali. pp. 91—127. (*C.*) By *Law*, Ch. v. S. i. Ed. 5, pp 182, &c.

And why so many contradictions on the subject ? And how can all men experience *liberty*, when it is allowed, that the *common notion* of liberty *is false*, or not experienced ; and *a new notion of liberty*, not thought on before (or thought on but by few) is set up as matter of experience ? This could not happen, if matter of fact was clear for liberty.

3. Other asserters of *liberty* seem driven into it on account of supposed inconveniencies attending the doctrine of *necessity*. The great *Episcopius*, in his *Treatise of Free-will*, acknowledges, in effect, that the asserters of *necessity* have seeming experience on their side, and are thereby very numerous. " They," as he observes, " allege one thing of moment, in which they triumph," viz. " that the will is determined by the understanding : and, assert, that unless it were so, the will would be a blind faculty, and might make evil, as evil, its object ; and reject what is pleasant and agreeable : and by consequence, that all persuasions, promises, reasonings and threats, would be as useless to a man, as to a stock or a stone. This," he allows to be very " plausible," and to " have the appearance of probability ;" to be " the common sentiment of the schools ;" to be " the rock on which the ablest defenders of liberty have split, without being able to answer it ;" and to be " the reason" or argument (or rather the matter of experience) " which has made men in all ages, and not a few in this age, fall into the opinion of the fatal necessity of all things." But " because it makes all our actions necessary, and thereby," in his opinion, " subverts all religion, laws, rewards and punishments ;" he concludes it " to be most certainly false :" and " religion makes" him " quit this common and plausible opinion."[*] Thus also many other strenuous asserters of *liberty*, as well as himself, are driven by these supposed difficulties, to deny *manifest experience*. I say, *manifest experience*, for are we not manifestly determined by pleasure, or pain, and by what seems reasonable or unreasonable, to us, to judge, or will, or act ? Whereas, could they see that there are no grounds for laws and morality, rewards and punishments, but by supposing the doctrine of *necessity*, and that there is no foundation for laws and morality, rewards and punishments, upon the supposition of man's being a free-agent, (as shall evidently and demonstratively appear,) they would readily allow experience to be against *free-will*, and deny *liberty*, when they should see there was no need to assert it,

---

[*] Opera, Vol. I. pp. 198—200. (C.)

in order to maintain those necessary things. And, as a farther evidence thereof, let any man peruse the discourses written by the ablest authors for liberty, and he will see (as they confess of one another) that they frequently contradict themselves, write obscurely, and know not where to place *liberty;* at least he will see that he is able to make nothing of their discourses, no more than *Mr. Locke* * was of this treatise of *Episcopius,* who, in all his other writings, shews himself to be a clear, strong and argumentative writer.

4. There are others, and those contenders for *liberty,* as well as deniers of it, who report the persuasions of men, as to the matter of fact, very differently, and also judge very differently themselves about the fact, from what is vulgarly believed among those who maintain *free-will.*

An ancient author speaks thus : " Fate," says he, " is sufficiently proved from the general received opinion and persuasion of men thereof. For, in certain things, when men all agree, except a few, who dissent from them on account of maintaining some doctrines before taken up, they cannot be mistaken. Wherefore, *Anaxagoras,* the *Clazomenian,* though no contemptible naturalist, ought not to be judged to deserve any regard, when opposing the common persuasion of all men, he asserts, ' That nothing is done by fate, but that it is an empty name.' "† And according to all authors, recording the opinions of men in this matter, the belief of *fate,* as to all events, has continued to be the *most common persuasion* both of philosophers and people, as it is at this day the persuasion of much the greatest part of mankind, according to the relations of voyagers. And though it has not equally prevailed among Christians, as it has and does, among all other religious parties, yet it is certain the fatalists have been and are very numerous among Christians ; and the free-will theologers themselves allow, " that some Christians are as great fatalists as any of the ancient philosophers were."‡

The acute and penetrating *Mr. Bayle,* reports the fact as very differently understood by those who have thoroughly examined and considered the various actions of man, from what is vulgarly supposed in this matter. Says he, " They who examine not to the bottom what passes within them, easily persuade themselves that they are free: but they

* Letters, p. 521. (*C.*) *Philippo à Limborch,* 19 Nov. 1701, Works, Ed. 4. III. p. 681.

† Alexander de Fato, p. 10. (*C.*)

‡ Reeves's Apol. Vol. I. p. 150. Sherlock of Prov. p. 66. (*C.*)

who have considered with care the foundation and circumstances of their actions, doubt of their freedom, and are even
persuaded, that their reason and understandings are slaves
that cannot resist the force which carries them along."* He
says also, in a familiar letter, that " The best proofs alleged
for *liberty* are, that without it man could not sin ; and that
God would be the author of evil, as well as good
thoughts."†

And the celebrated *Mr. Leibnitz*, that universal genius,
on occasion of *Archbishop King's Appeal to Experience*, (in
behalf of his notion of *liberty*, viz. " A faculty, which being
indifferent to objects, and over-ruling our passions, appetites, sensations and reason, chooses arbitrarily among
objects, and renders the object chosen agreeable, only
because it has chosen it,")‡ denies that we experience such,
or any other *liberty*, but contends that we rather experience
a determination in all our actions.   Says he, " We experience something in us which inclines us to a choice ; and
if it happens that we cannot give a reason of all our inclinations, a little attention will shew us, that the constitution
of our bodies, the bodies encompassing us, the present, or
preceding state of our minds, and several little matters comprehended under these great causes, may contribute to make
us choose certain objects, without having recourse to a
pure indifference, or to I know not what power of the
soul, which does upon objects, what they say colours do
upon the camelion." In fine, he is so far from thinking
that there is the least foundation, from *experience*, for the
said notion of *liberty*, that he treats it as a *chimera*, and
compares it " to the magical power of the fairies to trans-
form things."§

Lastly, The journalists of *Paris* are very far from thinking
Archbishop King's notion of liberty to be matter of experience, when they say, that *Dr King*, " not satisfied with
any of the former notions of liberty, proposes a new notion,
and carries indifference so far, as to maintain that pleasure
is not the motive, but the effect of the choice of the will ;"
placet res quia eligitur, non eligitur quia placet. " This
opinion," add they, " makes him frequently contradict himself."‖

* *Dictionaire*, p. 1497. Ed. 2   (*C.*)
† Letter of the 13th of December, 1696, to the Abbot du Bos, (*C.*)
‡ De Orig. Mah. C. v.   (*C.*) Law's *Trans.* pp. 267, &c.
§ Remarques sur le Liv. de l'Orig. du Mal. pp. 76, 84. (*C.*)
‖ Journal des Savans of the 16th of March, 1705. (*C.*)

So that upon the whole, the affair of experience, with relation to *liberty*, stands thus : some give the name *liberty* to actions, which, when described, are plainly actions that are necessary ; others, though appealing to vulgar experience, yet, inconsistently therewith, contradict the vulgar experience, by owning it to be an *intricate matter*, and treating it after an intricate manner : others are driven into the defence of *liberty*, by difficulties imagined to flow from the doctrine of *necessity*, combating what they allow to be matter of seeming experience : others, and those the most discerning, either think liberty cannot be proved by experience, or think men may see by experience that they are *necessary agents;* and the bulk of mankind have always been persuaded that they are necessary agents.

Our Experience itself considered.

Having thus paved the way, by shewing that liberty is not a plain matter of experience, by arguments drawn from the asserters of liberty themselves, and by consequence subverted the argument from experience for liberty ; we will now run over the various actions of men which can be conceived to concern this subject, and examine, whether we can know from experience, that man is a free, or a necessary agent. I think those actions may be reduced to these four : 1. Perception of ideas. 2. Judging of propositions. 3. Willing. 4. Doing as we will.

1. *Perception of Ideas.* Of this there can be no dispute, but it is a necessary action of man, since it is not even a voluntary action. The ideas, both of sensation and reflection, offer themselves to us whether we will or no, and we cannot reject them. We must be conscious that we think when we do think ; and thereby we necessarily have the ideas of reflection. We must also use our senses when awake, and thereby necessarily receive the ideas of sensation. And as we necessarily receive ideas, so each idea is necessarily what it is in our mind : for it is not possible to make any thing different from itself. This first necessary action, the reader will see, is the foundation and cause of all the other intelligent actions of man, and makes them also necessary. For, as a judicious author, and nice observer of the inward actions of man, says truly, " Temples have their sacred images, and we see what influence they have always had over a great part of mankind. But, in truth,

the ideas and images in men's minds, are the *invisible powers* that constantly govern them, and to these they universally pay a ready submission."*

2. The second action of man is *judging of propositions.* All propositions must appear to me either self-evident, or evident from proof, or probable, or improbable, or doubtful, or false. Now these various appearances of propositions to me, being founded on my capacity, and the degree of light propositions stand in to me, I can no more change those appearances in me, than I can change the idea of *red* raised in me. Nor can I judge contrary to those appearances ; for what is judging of propositions, but judging that propositions do appear as they do appear? Which I cannot avoid doing, without lying to myself: which is impossible. If any man thinks he can judge a proposition, appearing to him evident, to be not evident, or a probable proposition to be more or less probable than it appears by the proofs to be; he knows not what he says, as he may see if he will define his words. The necessity of being determined by appearances, was maintained by all the old philosophers, even by the *academics* or *sceptics.* *Cicero* says, " You must take from a man his senses, if you take from him the power of assenting, for it is as necessary the mind should yield to what is clear, as that a scale, hanging on a balance, should sink with a weight laid on it. For as all living creatures cannot but desire what is agreeable to their natures, so they cannot but assent to what is clear. Wherefore, if those things whereof we dispute are true, it is to no purpose to speak of assent. For he who apprehends, or perceives any thing, assents immediately. Again, assent not only precedes the practice of vice, but of virtue, the steady performance whereof, and adherence to which, depend on what a man has assented to and approved. And it is necessary that something should appear to us before we act, and that we should assent to that appearance. Wherefore he who takes away appearances and assent from man, destroys all action in him."† The force of this reasoning manifestly extends to all the various judgments men make upon the appearances of things. And *Cicero,* as an academic or sceptic, must be supposed to extend *necessity* to every kind of *judgment* or *assent* of man upon the *appearances* (or as the *Greeks* call them, Φαινομένα, and himself the *Visa*) of things. *Sextus Empiricus* says,

---

Locke's Posth. Works, pp. 1, 2. (*C.*)   *Conduct,* &c. Works, III. p. 385.
† Academ. Quest. Lib, ii. (*C.*)

" They who say the sceptics take away appearances, have not conversed with them, and do not understand them. For we destroy not the passions, to which our senses find them-selves exposed whether we will or no, and which force us to submit to appearances. For when it is asked us, *whether objects are such as they appear ?* we deny not their appear-ances, nor doubt of them, but only question whether the external objects are like the appearances."*

3. *Willing* is the third action of man, which I propose to consider. It is matter of daily experience, that we begin or forbear, continue or end several actions barely by a thought, or preference of the mind ; ordering the doing or not doing, the continuing or ending such or such actions. Thus, before we think or deliberate on any subject, as before we get on horseback, we do prefer those things to any thing else in competition with them. In like manner, if we forbear these actions, when any of them are offered to our thoughts ; or if we continue to proceed in any one of these actions once begun ; or if at any time we make an end of prosecuting them ; we do forbear, or continue, or end them on our preference of the forbearance to the doing them, of the continuing them to the ending them, and of the ending to the continuing them. This power of the man thus to order the beginning or forbearance, the continuance or ending of any action, is called *the will*, and the actual exercise thereof, *willing*.

There are two questions usually put about this matter : *first,* Whether we are at liberty to will or not to will ; *secondly,* Whether we are at liberty to will one or the other of two or more objects.

1. As to the first, *whether we are at liberty to will or not to will,* it is manifest we have not that liberty. For let an action, in a man's power, be proposed to him as pre-sently to be done, as for example, *to walk,* the will to walk or not to walk exists immediately. And when an action, in a man's power, is proposed to him to be done to-mor-row, as *to walk to-morrow,* he is no less obliged to have some immediate will. He must either have a will to defer willing about the matter proposed, or must will immediately in relation to the thing proposed ; and one or the other of those wills must exist immediately, no less than the will to walk or not to walk in the former case. Where-fore, in every proposal of something to be done which is in a man's power to do, he cannot but have some immediate will.

* Pyrrhon. Hypot. Lib. ii. C. x. (*C.*)

Hence appears the mistake of those who *think* men at *liberty to will, or not to will, because,* say they, *they can suspend willing,** in relation to actions to be done to-morrow ; wherein they plainly confound themselves with words. For when it is said, man is necessarily determined to will, it is not thereby understood, that he is determined to will or choose one out of two objects immediately in every case proposed to him, (or to choose at all in some cases, as whether he *will* travel into *France* or *Holland,*) but that on every proposal he must necessarily have *some will.* And he is not less determined to will, because he does often suspend willing or choosing in certain cases : for *suspending to will,* is itself an *act of willing ;* it is willing to *defer willing* about the matter proposed. In fine, though great stress is laid on the case of *suspending the will* to prove *liberty,* yet there is no difference between that and the most common cases of willing and choosing upon the manifest excellency of one object before another. For, as when a man wills or chooses living in *England* before going out of it, (in which will he is manifestly determined by the satisfaction he has in living in *England,*) he rejects the will to go out of *England ;* so a man, who suspends a will about any matter, wills doing nothing in it at present, or rejects for a time willing about it ; which circumstances, of wholly rejecting and rejecting for a time, make no variation that affects the question. So that willing or choosing *suspension,* is like all other choices or wills that we have.

2. Secondly, Let us now see, *whether we are at liberty to will or choose one or the other of two or more objects.* Now, as to this, we will, *first,* consider, whether we are at liberty to will one of two or more objects wherein we discern any difference : that is, where one, upon the whole, seems more excellent than another, or where one upon the whole seems less hurtful than another. And this will not admit of much dispute, if we consider what willing is. Willing or preferring is the same with respect to good and evil, that judging is with respect to truth or falsehood. It is judging that one thing is, upon the whole, better than another, or not so bad as another. Wherefore, as we judge of truth or falsehood, according to appearances, so we must will or prefer, as things seem to us, unless we can lie to ourselves, and think that to be worst which we think best.

---

* Locke's Essay of Hum. Und. Lib. ii. Ch. xxi. (*C.*)

An ingenious author expresses this matter well, when he says, " Whether a man be at liberty to will which of the two he pleases, motion or rest ?   This question carries the absurdity of it so manifestly in itself, that one might thereby sufficiently be convinced, that liberty concerns not the will. For, to ask whether a man be at liberty to will either motion or rest, speaking or silence, which he pleases, is to ask whether a man can will what he wills, or be pleased with what he is pleased with.   A question which, I think, needs no answer."*

To suppose a sensible being, capable of willing or pre- ferring (call it as you please), misery, and refusing good, is to deny it to be really sensible ; for every man, while he has his senses, aims at pleasure and happiness, and avoids pain and misery ; and this, in willing actions, which are supposed to be attended with the most terrible conse- quences.   And, therefore, the ingenious *Mr. Norris* very justly observes, that " all who commit sin, think it at the instant of commission, all things considered, a *lesser evil;* otherwise it is impossible they should commit it :" and he instances in *St. Peter's* denial of his master, who, he says, " judged that part *most eligible* which he chose ; that is, he judged the sin of denying his master, at that present junc- ture, to be a *less evil*, than the *danger* of not denying him, and so chose it.   Otherwise, if he had then actually thought it a *greater evil*, all *that* whereby it *exceeded* the other, he would have chosen *gratis* and consequently have willed *evil* as *evil* ;"† which is impossible.   And another acute philosopher observes, that " there are in France many new converts, who go to mass with great reluctance. They know they mortally offend God, but as each offence would cost them (suppose) two pistoles, and having reckoned, the charge, and finding that this fine, paid as often as there are festivals and sundays, would reduce them and their families to beg their bread, they conclude that it is better to offend God than beg "‡

In fine, though there is hardly any thing so absurd, but some ancient philosopher or other may be cited for it, yet, according to *Plato*, " none of them were so absurd as to say that men did evil voluntarily ;" and he asserts, that " it is contrary to the nature of man to follow evil, as evil, and not pursue good ; and that when a man is compelled to

* Locke's Essay of Hum. Und. Lib. ii. Ch. xxi. S. xxv.   (*C.*)
† Theory of Love, p. 199.   (*C.*)   Letter to Dr. More, Ed. ii. pp. 168, 169. .
‡ *Bayle*, Reponse aux Ques. &c. Tom. III. p. 756.   (*C.*)

choose between two evils, you will never find a man who chooses the greatest, if it is in his power to choose the less;" and that " this is a truth manifest to all."* And even the greatest modern advocates for *liberty* allow, that " whatever the will chooseth, it chooseth under the notion of good ; and that the object of the will is good in general, which is the end of all human actions."†

This I take to be sufficient to shew that man is not at liberty to will one or the other of two or more objects, between which (all things considered) he perceives a difference ; and to account truly for all the choices of that kind which can be assigned.

But, secondly, some of the patrons of liberty contend that we are free in our choice among things indifferent, or alike, as in choosing one out of two or more eggs ; and that, in such cases, the man having no motives from the objects, is not necessitated to choose one rather than the other, because there is no perceivable difference between them, but chooses one by a mere act of willing, without any cause but his own free act.

To which I answer. First, by asking whether this, and other instances like this, are the only instances wherein man is free to will or choose among objects ? If they are the only instances wherein man is free to will or choose among objects, then we are advanced a great way in the question ; because there are few (if any) objects of the will that are perfectly alike ; and because necessity is hereby allowed to take place in all cases where there is a perceivable differ- ence in things, and consequently, in all moral and religious cases, for the sake whereof such endeavours have been used to maintain so absurd and inconsistent a thing as *liberty*, or *freedom* from *necessity*. So that liberty is almost, if not quite, reduced to nothing, and destroyed, as to the grand end in as- serting it. If those are not the only instances wherein man is free to will or choose among objects, but man is free to will in other cases, these other cases should be assigned, and not such cases as are of no consequence, and which by the great likeness of the objects to one another, and for other reasons make the cause of the determination of man's will less easy to be known, and consequently serve to no other purpose but to darken the question, which may be better determined by considering, *whether man be free to will or no* in more important instances.

* Opera, Edit. Serran. Vol. I. pp. 345, 346. (*C.*) .
† Bramhall's Works, pp. 656, 658. (*C.*)

Secondly, I answer, that whenever a choice is made, there can be no equality of circumstances preceding the choice.   For in the case of choosing one out of two or more eggs, between which there is no perceivable difference, there is not, nor can there be, a true equality of circumstances and causes preceding the act of choosing one of the said eggs.   It is not enough to render *things* equal to the will, that they are equal or alike in themselves.   All the various modifications of the man, his opinions, prejudices, temper, habit and circumstances, are to be taken in, and considered as causes of *election* no less than the objects without us among which we choose; and these will ever incline or determine our wills, and make the choice we do make, preferable to us, though the external objects of our choice are ever so much alike to each other.   And, for example, in the case of choosing one out of two eggs that are alike, there is, first, in the person choosing, a will to eat or use an egg.

There is, secondly, a will to take but one, or one first.

Thirdly, consequent to these two wills, follow, in the same instant, choosing and taking *one;* which *one* is chosen and taken most commonly, according as the parts of our bodies have been formed long since by our wills,. or by other causes, to an habitual practice, or as those parts are determined by some particular circumstances at that time. And we may know by reflection on our actions, that several of our choices have been determined to one, among several objects, by these last means, when no cause has arisen from the mere consideration of the objects themselves.   For we know by experience, that we either use all the parts of our bodies by habit, or according to some particular cause determining their use at that time.

Fourthly, There are in all trains of causes that precede their effects, and especially effects which nearly resemble each other, certain differences undiscernible on account of their minuteness, and also on account of our not accustoming ourselves to attend to them, which yet, in concurrence with other causes, as necessarily produce their effect, as the last feather laid on, breaks the horse's back; and as a grain necessarily turns the balance between any weights, though the eye cannot discover which is the greatest weight or bulk by so small a difference.   And I add, that as we know, without such discovery by the eye, that if one scale rises and the other falls, there is a greater weight in one scale than the other, and also know, that the least additional weight is sufficient to determine the scales ; so likewise we may know that the least circumstance, in the extensive chain of causes that precede every effect, is sufficient to produce an effect; and also know, that there must be causes of our choice (though we do not, or cannot discern those causes) by knowing, *that every thing that has a beginning must have a cause.* By which last principle we are as necessarily led to conceive a cause of action in man, where we see not the particular cause itself, as we are to conceive that a greater weight determines a scale, though our eyes discover no difference between the two weights.

But let us put a case of true equality or indifference, and what I have asserted will more manifestly appear true. Let two eggs appear perfectly alike to a man, and let him have no will to eat or use eggs, (for so the case ought to be put to render things perfectly indifferent to him, because, if once a *will* to eat eggs be supposed, that *will* must necessarily introduce a train of causes which will ever destroy an equality of circumstances, in relation to the things which are the objects of our choice. There will soon follow a second will to eat one first. And these *two wills* must put the man upon action, and the usage of the parts of his body to obtain his end ; which parts are determined in their motions, either by some habitual practice, or by some particular circumstance at that time, and cause the man to choose and take one of them first rather than the other.) The case of equality being thus rightly stated, I say, it is manifest no choice would or could be made ; and the man is visibly prevented in the beginning from making a choice. For every man experiences, that before he can make a choice among eggs, he must have a will to eat or use an egg, otherwise he must let them alone. And he also experiences, in relation to all things which are the objects of his choice, that he must have a precedent will to choose, otherwise he will make no choice. No man marries one woman preferable to another, or travels into *France* rather than into another country, or writes a book on one subject rather than another, but he must first have a precedent will to marry, travel and write.

It is therefore contrary to experience, to suppose any choice can be made under an equality of circumstances: and, by consequence, it is matter of experience, that man is ever determined in his willing or acts of volition and choice.

Doing as we will.

4. Fourthly, I shall now consider the actions of man consequent to *willing*, and see whether he be *free* in any of those actions. And here also we experience perfect neces-sity. If we will thinking, or deliberating on a subject, or will reading, or walking, or riding, we find we must do those actions, unless some external impediment, as an apoplexy, or some intervening cause, hinders us; and then we are as much necessitated to let an action alone, as we were to act according to our will, had no such external impedi-ment to action happened. If also we change our wills after we have begun any of these actions, we find we neces-sarily leave off these actions and follow the *new will*, or choice. And this was *Aristotle's* sense of such actions of man. " As," says he, " in arguing, we necessarily assent to the inference or conclusion drawn from pre-mises, so if that arguing relate to practice, we necessa-rily act upon such inference or conclusion. As, for example, when we argue thus, *whatever is sweet is to be tasted, this is sweet*, he who infers, *therefore this ought to be tasted*, necessarily tastes that sweet thing if there be no obstacle to hinder him."*

For a conclusion of this argument from experience, let us compare the actions of inferior, intelligent and sensible agents, and those of men, together. It is allowed that beasts are necessary agents, and yet there is no perceivable difference between their actions and the actions of men, from whence they should be deemed *necessary*, and men, *free* agents. *Sheep*, for example, are supposed to be *necessary agents*, when they stand still, lie down, go slow or fast, turn to the right or left, skip, as they are differently affected in their minds; when they are doubtful or deli-berate which way to take, when they eat and drink out of hunger and thirst; when they eat or drink, more or less, according to their humour, or as they like the water or the pasture; when they choose the sweetest and best pasture; when they choose among pastures that are indif-ferent or alike; when they copulate; when they are fickle or stedfast in their amours; when they take more or less care of their young; when they act in virtue of vain fears; when they apprehend danger, and fly from it, and sometimes

* Ethica, Lib. vii. C. v. ap. Opera Edit. Par. Vol. II. pp. 88, &c. (*C.*)

defend themselves ; when they quarrel among themselves about love or other matters, and terminate those quarrels by fighting ; when they follow those leaders among themselves that presume to go first ; and when they are either obedient to the shepherd and his dog, or refractory.   And why should man be deemed *free* in the performance of the same or the like actions ? He has indeed more knowledge than sheep. He takes in more things as matter of pleasure than they do, being sometimes moved with notions of honour and virtue, as well as with those pleasures he has in common with them.   He is also more moved by absent things, and things future, than they are.   He is also subject to more vain fears, more mistakes and wrong actions, and infinitely more absurdities in notions.   He has also more power and strength, as well as more art and cunning, and is capable of doing more good and more mischief to his fellow men, then they are to one another.   But these 'larger powers and larger weaknesses, which are of the same kind with the powers and weaknesses of sheep, cannot contain liberty in them, and plainly make no perceivable difference between them and men, as to the general causes of action, in finite, intelligent and sensible beings, no more than the different degrees of these powers and weaknesses among the various kinds of beasts, birds, fishes and reptiles do among them. Wherefore I need not run through the actions of *foxes*, or any of the most subtile animals, nor the actions of *children*, which are allowed by the advocates of *liberty*, to be all necessary.*   I shall only ask these questions concerning the last.   To what age do children continue necessary agents, and when do they become *free ?* What different experience have they when they are supposed to be free agents, from what they had while necessary agents ?   And what different actions do they do, from whence it appears, that they are *necessary* agents to a certain age, and *free* agents afterwards ?

Second Argument taken from the Impossibility of Liberty.

II. A second reason to prove man a necessary agent is, because all his actions have a beginning. For whatever has a beginning must have a cause, and every cause is a necessary cause.

If any thing can have a beginning which has no cause,

* Bramhall's Works, pp. 656, 662.   (C.)

then nothing can produce something. And if nothing can produce something, then the world might have had a beginning without a cause; which is not only an absurdity commonly charged on atheists, but is a real absurdity in itself.

Besides, if a cause be not a necessary cause, it is no cause at all. For if causes are not necessary causes, then causes are not suited to, or are indifferent to effects; and the *Epicurean system* of chance is rendered possible : and this orderly world might have been produced by a disorderly or fortuitous concourse of atoms, or, which is all one, by no cause at all. For in arguing against the Epicurean system of chance, do we not say (and that justly) that it is impossible for chance ever to have produced an orderly system of things, as not being a cause suited to the effect; and that an orderly system of things which had a beginning, must have had an intelligent agent for its cause, as being the only proper cause to that effect? All which implies, that causes are suited, or have relation to, some particular effects, and not to others. And if they be suited to some particular effect, and not to others, they can be no causes at all to those others. And therefore a cause not suited to the effect, and no cause, are the same thing. And if a cause not suited to the effect, is no cause, then a cause suited to the effect is a necessary cause: for if it does not produce the effect, it is not suited to it, or is no cause at all of it.

Liberty therefore, or a power to act or not to act, to do this or another thing, under the same causes, is an *impossibility*, and *atheistical*.

And as *liberty* stands, and can only be grounded on the absurd principles of *Epicurean atheism;* so the *Epicurean atheists,* who were the most popular and most numerous sect of the *atheists* of antiquity, were the great asserters of *liberty;* [*] as, on the other side, the *Stoics,* who were the most popular and most numerous sect among the religionaries of antiquity, were the great asserters of fate and necessity.[†] The case was also the same among the *Jews,* as among the heathen : the *Jews,* I say, who, besides the light of nature, had many books of Revelation (some whereof are now lost), and who had intimate and personal conversation with God himself. They were principally divided into three sects; the *Sadducees,* the *Pharisees* and the *Essenes.*[‡] The Sadducees, who were esteemed an irreligious and atheistical sect,

---

[*] Lucretius, Lib. ii. v. 250, &c. Euseb. Prep: Ev. Lib. vi. C. vii. (*C.*)
[†] Cicero de Nat. Deor. Lib. i. (*C.*) S. xx; *ad fin.*
[‡] Josephus Antiq. Lib. xviii. C. i. S. iii. iv. v. (*C.*)

maintained the *liberty of man.* But the *Pharisees,* who were a religious sect, *ascribed all things to fate,* or to *God's appointment,* and it was * *the first article of their creed, that fate and God do all;* and consequently they could not assert a *true liberty,* when they asserted a *liberty* together with this *fatality* and *necessity* of all things. And the *Essenes,* who were the *most religious sect* among the *Jews,* and fell not under the censure of our Saviour for their hypocrisy as the *Pharisees* did, were asserters of *absolute fate* and *necessity.* St. *Paul,* who was a *Pharisee, and the son of a Pharisee,*† is supposed by the learned *Dodwell* " to have received his doctrine of fate from the masters of that sect, as they received it from the Stoics." And he observes further, that " the Stoic philosophy is necessary for the explication of christian theology; that there are examples in the Holy Scriptures of the Holy Ghost's speaking according to the opinions of the Stoics;" and that in particular " the apostle *St. Paul,* in what he has disputed concerning Predestination and Reprobation, is to be expounded according to the Stoics' opinion concerning fate."‡ So that *liberty* is both the real foundation of popular Atheism, and has been the professed principle of the Atheists themselves; as, on the other side, *fate,* or the *necessity of events,* has been esteemed a religious opinion, and been the professed principle of the religious, both among Heathens and Jews, and also of that great convert to Christianity, and great converter of others, *St. Paul.*

Third Argument, taken from the Imperfection of Liberty.

III. Thirdly, *Liberty* is contended for by the patrons thereof as a great *perfection.* In order, therefore, to disprove all pretences for it, I will now shew that, according to all the various descriptions given of it by theologers and philosophers, it would often be an *imperfection,* but never a *perfection,* as I have in the last article shewed it to be *impossible* and *atheistical.*

1. If *liberty* be defined, *a power to pass different judgments* at the same instant of time *upon the same individual propositions that are not evident*§ (we being, as it is owned, *necessarily determined* to pass but *one judgment on evident propositions*), it will follow, that men will be so far irrational, and by consequence *imperfect* agents, as they have that *freedom of judgment.* For, since they would be irrational agents, if

* De Bello Jud. Lib. ii. C. viii. S. xiv. *(C.)* † Acts xxii. 6. *(C.)*!
‡ Proleg. ad Stearn. de Obstin. Sect. xl. and xli. *(C.)*
§ Le Clerc. Bibl. Chois. Tom. XII. pp. 88, 89. *(C.)*

they were capable of judging evident propositions not to be evident; they must be also deemed irrational agents, if they are capable of judging the self-same probable or improbable propositions not to be probable or improbable. The appearances of all propositions to us, whether evident, probable or improbable, are the sole rational grounds of our judgments in relation to them: and the appearances of probable or improbable propositions are no less necessary in us, from the respective reasons by which they appear probable or improbable, than are the appearances of evident propositions from the reasons by which they appear evident. Wherefore if it be rational, and a perfection, to be determined by an evident appearance, it is no less so to be determined by a probable or improbable appearance, and consequently an imperfection not to be so determined.

It is not only an absurdity, and by consequence an *imperfection*, not to be equally and necessarily determined in our respective judgments, by probable and improbable, as well as by evident appearances, which I have just now proved; but even not to be necessarily determined by probable appearances, would be a *greater imperfection*, than not to be necessarily determined by evident appearances: because almost all our actions are founded on the probable appearances of things, and few on the evident appearance of things. And therefore, if we could judge that what appears probable is not probable, but improbable or false, we should be without the best rule of action and assent we can have.

2. Were *liberty* defined *a power to overcome our reason by the force of choice*, as a celebrated author may be supposed to mean, when he says, " the will seems to have so great a power over the understanding, that the understanding, being over-ruled by the election of the will, not only takes what is good to be evil, but is also compelled to admit what is false to be true;"* man would, with the exercise of such *a power*, be the most irrational and inconsistent being, and, by consequence, the most *imperfect* understanding being, which can be conceived. For what can be more irrational and inconsistent, than to be able to refuse our assent to what is evidently true to us, and to assent to what we see to be evidently false, and thereby inwardly give the lie to the understanding?

3. Were *liberty* defined *a power to will evil* (knowing it to be evil) *as well as good;*† that would be an imperfection in man, considered as a sensible being, if it be an imperfection

---

* King de Orig. Mali, p. 131. (*C.*) C. v. S. i. Sub. 5, XII. *Law*, p 282.
† Cheyne's Phil. Prin. Ch. ni. S. xiii. (*C.*)

in such a being to be miserable. For *willing evil* is choosing to be miserable, and bringing, knowingly, destruction on ourselves. Men are already sufficiently unhappy by their several judgments, and by their several volitions, founded on the wrong use of their faculties, and on the mistaken appearances of things. But what miserable beings would they be, if, instead of choosing evil under the appearance of good (which is the only case wherein men now choose evil), they were indifferent to good and evil, and had the power to choose *evil as evil*, and did actually choose *evil as evil* in virtue of that power? They would, in such a state, or with such a liberty, be like infants that cannot walk, left to go alone, with liberty to fall ; or like children, with knives in their hands ; or, lastly, like young rope-dancers, left to themselves, on their first essays upon the rope, without any one to catch them if they fall. And this miserable state following from the supposition of *liberty*, is so visible to some of the greatest advocates thereof,* that they acknowledge that " created beings, when in a state of happiness, cease to have liberty, (that is, cease to have liberty to choose evil,) being inviolably attached to their duty by the actual enjoyment of their felicity."†

4. Were *liberty* defined, as it is by some, *a power to will or choose at the same time any one out of two or more indifferent things*, that would be no perfection. For those things called here *indifferent*, or alike, may be considered either as really different from each other, and that only seem indifferent or alike to us through our want of discernment, or as exactly like each other. Now the more *liberty* we have in the first kind, that is, the more instances there are of things which seem alike to us, and are not alike, the more mistakes and wrong choices we must run into: for if we had just notions, we should know those things were not indifferent or alike. This *liberty* therefore would be founded on a direct imperfection of our faculties. And as to a *power of choosing* differently at the same time among *things really indifferent*, what benefit, what perfection, would such a power of choosing be, when the things that are the sole objects of our *free choice* are all alike?

5. Lastly, a celebrated author seems to understand by liberty, " a faculty which, being indifferent to objects, and over-ruling our passions, appetites, sensations and reason, chooses arbitrarily among objects, and renders the object chosen agreeable, only because it has chosen it."‡

---

* Bibl. Choisie, Tom. XII. p. 95. *(C.)*   † Bramhall's Works, p. 655. *(C.)*
‡ King de Orig. Mali, C. v. *(C.)* S. i. Sub. 5, I. *Law*, p. 266.

My design here is to consider this definition with the same view that I have considered the several foregoing definitions, viz. to shew that *liberty, inconsistent with necessity*, however described or defined, is an *imperfection*. Referring, therefore, my reader, for a confutation of this *new* notion of *liberty*, to the other parts of my book, wherein I have already proved that the existence of such an *arbitrary faculty* is contrary to experience, and impossible; that our *passions, appetites, sensations* and *reason* determine us in our several choices; and that we choose objects because they please us, and not, as the author pretends, that *objects please us only because we choose them;* I proceed to shew the *imperfection* of this last kind of *liberty*.

1. First, the pleasure or happiness accruing from the *liberty* here asserted, is less than accrues from the *hypothesis* of *necessity*.

All the pleasure and happiness said to attend this pretended *liberty* consists *wholly* in *creating* pleasure and happiness by *choosing objects*.*

Now man, considered as an intelligent necessary agent, would no less *create* this pleasure and happiness to himself by *choosing objects*, than a being endued with the said *faculty;* if it be true, in fact, that *things please us, because we choose them*.

But man, as an intelligent necessary agent, has these further pleasures and advantages. He, by not being indifferent to objects, is moved by the goodness and agreeableness of them, as they appear to him, and as he knows them by reflection and experience. It is not in his power to be indifferent to what causes pleasure or pain. He cannot resist the pleasure arising from the use of his passions, appetites, senses and reason; and if he suspends his choice of an object that is presented to him by any of these powers as agreeable, it is because he doubts, or examines, whether upon the whole the object would make him happy; and because he would gratify all these powers in the best manner he is able, or at least such of these powers as he conceives tend most to his happiness. If he makes a choice which proves disagreeable, he gets thereby an experience, which may qualify him to choose the next time with more satisfaction to himself. And thus wrong choices may turn to his advantage for the future. So that, at all times, and under all circumstances, he is pursuing and enjoying the greatest happiness which his condition will allow.

* Bramhall's Works, pp. 107, 108. (*C*.)

It may not be improper to observe, that some of the pleasures he receives from objects are so far from being the effect
of *choice*, that they are not the effect of the least premeditation, or any act of his own ; as in finding a treasure on the
road, or in receiving a legacy from a person unknown to
him.

2. Secondly, this *arbitrary faculty** would subject a man
to more *wrong choices* than if he was determined in his
choice.

A man determined in his choice by the appearing nature
of things, and the usage of his intellectual powers, never
makes a wrong choice, but by mistaking the true relation of
things to him.   But a being, indifferent to *all objects,*† and
swayed by no motives in his choice of objects, chooses at a
venture; and only makes a right choice, when it happens
(as the author justly expresses his notion) " that he chooses
an object, which he can by his *creating* power render so
agreeable, as that it may be called a *rightly-chosen object.*" ‡
Nor can this faculty be improved by any experience, but
must ever continue to choose at a venture, or as *it happens.*
For if this *faculty* improves by experience, and will have
regard to the agreeableness or disagreeableness of objects in
themselves, it is no longer the *faculty* contended for, but a
faculty moved and affected by the nature of things.

So that man, with a *faculty* of choice indifferent to all
objects, must make more *wrong choices* than man considered
as a necessary being, in the same proportion as *acting as it
happens* is a worse direction to choose right than the use of
our senses, experience and reason.

3. Thirdly, the existence of such an *arbitrary faculty*, to
choose without regard to the qualities of objects, would destroy the use of our senses, appetites, passions and reason ;
which have been given us to direct us in our inquiries after
truth, in our pursuit after happiness, and to preserve our
beings.   For, if we had *a faculty* which chose without
regard to the notices and advertisements of these powers,
and by its choice over-ruled them, we should then be endued
with *a faculty* to defeat the end and uses of these powers.

The Perfection of Necessity.

But the *imperfection* of liberty inconsistent with necessity,
will yet more appear by considering the great *perfection* of
being necessarily determined.

---

* Bramhall's Works, pp. 147—150. (*C.*)　　　† Ibid. pp. 106, 111. (*C.*)
‡ Ibid. pp. 106, 107, 113, 139, 141, 147. (*C.*)

Can any thing be perfect that is not necessarily perfect?
For whatever is not necessarily perfect may be imperfect,
and is by consequence imperfect.

Is it not a perfection in God, necessarily to know all
truth?

Is it not a perfection in him to be necessarily happy?

Is it not also a perfection in him to will and do always
what is best? For if all things are *indifferent* to him, as some
of the advocates of liberty assert, and become *good* only by
his *willing* them,* he cannot have any motive from his own
ideas, or from the nature of things, to *will* one thing rather
than another, and consequently he must *will* without any
reason or cause; which cannot be conceived possible of any
being, and is contrary to this self-evident truth, that *whatever
has a beginning must have a cause.* But if things are not
indifferent to him, he must be necessarily determined by
what is best. Besides, as he is a wise being, he must have
some end and design; and, as he is a good being, things cannot be *indifferent* to him, when the happiness of intelligent
and sensible beings depends on the will he has in the formation of things. With what consistency, therefore, can those
advocates of liberty assert God to be *a holy and good being,*†
who maintain that *all things are indifferent* to him before he
wills any thing; and that he may will and do *all things*
which they themselves esteem wicked and unjust?

I cannot give a better confirmation of this argument, from
the consideration of the attributes of God, than by the
judgment of the late Bishop of Sarum; which has the more
weight, as proceeding from a great asserter of liberty, who,
by the force of truth, is driven to say what he does. He
grants, that *infinite perfection excludes successive thoughts in
God;* and *therefore* that " the essence of God is one perfect
thought, in which he both views and wills all things. And
though his transient acts,—such as creation, providence and
miracles, are done in a succession of time, yet his immanent
acts, his knowledge and his decrees, are one with his essence."
And as he grants this to be a true notion of God, so he allows
that " a vast difficulty arises" from it against the liberty of
God. For, says he, the immanent " acts of God" being
" supposed free, it is not easy to imagine how they should
be one with the divine essence; to which necessary existence does certainly belong." And if the immanent acts of
God " are necessary, then the transient must be so likewise,"

---

* King de Orig. Mali. p. 177. (C.   † Ibid. p. 117. (C.).

as being "the certain effects of his immanent acts:" and "a chain of necessary fate must run through the whole order of things: and God himself then is no free being, but acts by a necessity of nature." And this necessity, to which God is thus subject, "some," adds he, "have thought was no absurdity. God is," according to them, "necessarily just, true and good,—by an intrinsic necessity that arises from his own infinite perfection." And "some have from hence thought, that, since God acts by infinite wisdom and goodness, things could not have been otherwise than they are; for what is infinitely wise or good cannot be altered, or made either better or worse." And he concludes, that he "must leave this difficulty without pretending that we can explain it, or answer the objections that arise against all the several ways by which divines have endeavoured to resolve it."*

Again, are not angels and other heavenly beings esteemed more perfect than men;† because, having a clear insight into the nature of things, they are necessarily determined to judge right in relation to truth and falsehood, and to choose right in relation to good and evil, pleasure and pain; and also to act right in pursuance of their judgment and choice? And therefore would not man be more perfect than he is, if, by having a clear insight into the nature of things, he was necessarily determined to assent to truth only, to choose only such objects as would make him happy, and to act accordingly?

. Further, is not man more perfect, the more capable he is of conviction? And will he not be more capable of conviction, if he be necessarily determined in his assent by what seems a reason to him, and necessarily determined in his several volitions by what seems good to him, than if he was indifferent to propositions, notwithstanding any reason for them, or was indifferent to any objects, notwithstanding they seemed good to him? For otherwise, he could be convinced, upon no principles, and would be the most undisciplinable and untractable of all animals. All advice and all reasonings would be of no use to him. You might offer arguments to him, and lay before him pleasure and pain, and he might stand unmoved like a rock. He might reject what appears true to him, assent to what seems absurd to him, avoid what he sees to be good, and choose what he sees to be evil. Indifference therefore to receive truth, that is, *liberty* to deny it when we see it, and indifference to plea-

---

* Expos. pp. 26, 27. (*C.*) *Burnet* on Art. 1.
† Bramhall's Works, pp. 656 and 695. (*C.*)

sure and pain, that is, *liberty* to refuse the first and choose the last, are direct obstacles to knowledge and happiness. On the contrary, to be necessarily determined by what seems reasonable, and by what seems good, has a direct tendency to promote truth and happiness, and is the proper perfection of an understanding and sensible being. And indeed, it seems strange that men should allow that God and angels act more perfectly because they are determined by reason; and also allow, that clocks, watches, mills and other artificial unintelligent beings are the better, the more they are determined to go right by weight and measure; and yet that they should deem it a perfection in man not to be determined by his reason, but to have liberty to go against it. Would it not be as reasonable to say, it would be a perfection in a clock not to be necessarily determined to go right, but to have its motions depend upon chance?

Again, though man does, through weakness and imperfection, fall into several mistakes, both in judging and willing, in relation to what is true and good, yet he is still less ignorant and less unhappy, by being necessarily determined in judging by what seems reasonable, and in willing by what seems best, than if he was capable of judging contrary to his reason and willing against his senses. For, were it not so, what *seems false* would be as just *a rule of truth*, as what *seems true*, and what *seems evil* as just *a rule of good*, as what *seems good:* which are absurdities too great for any to affirm, especially if we consider, that there is a perfectly wise and good Being, who has given men senses and reason to conduct them.

Lastly, it is a perfection to be necessarily determined in our choices, even in the most indifferent things; because, if in such cases there was not a cause of choice, but a choice could be made without a cause, then all choices might be made without a cause, and we should not be necessarily determined by the greatest evidence to assent to truth, nor by the strongest inclination for happiness to choose pleasure and avoid pain; to all which it is a perfection to be necessarily determined. For if any action whatsoever can be done without a cause, then effects and causes have no necessary relation, and by consequence we should not be necessarily determined in any case at all.

Fourth Argument, taken from the consideration of the Divine Prescience.

IV. A fourth argument to prove man a necessary agent, shall be taken from the consideration of the divine prescience. The divine prescience supposes, that all things future will certainly exist in such time, such order and with such circumstances, and not otherwise. For if any things future were contingent or uncertain, or depended on the liberty of man, that is, might or might not happen, their certain existence could not be the object of the divine prescience; it being a contradiction to know that to be certain, which is not certain; and God himself could only guess at the existence of such things. And if the divine prescience supposes the *certain* existence of all things future, it supposes also the *necessary* existence of all things future; because God can foreknow their certain existence only, either as that existence is the effect of his decree, or as it depends on its own causes. If he foreknows that existence, as it is the effect of his decree, his decree makes that existence necessary; for it implies a contradiction for an all-powerful being to decree any thing which shall not necessarily come to pass. If he foreknows that existence, as it depends on its own causes, that existence is no less necessary; for it no less implies a contradiction, that causes should not produce their effects (causes and effects having a necessary relation to and dependence on each other), than that an event should not come to pass, which is decreed by God.

Cicero has some passages to the purpose of this argument. Says he, " Qui potest provideri quidquam futurum esse quod neque causam habet ullam, neque notam, cur futurum sit ?—Quid est igitur, quod casu fieri aut forte fortuna, putemus ?—Nihil est enim tam contrarium rationi et constantia quam fortuna; ut mihi ne in Deum cadere videatur, ut sciat, quid casu et fortuito futurum fit. Si enim scit, certe illud eveniet. Sin certe eveniet, nulla est fortuna. Est autem fortuna. Rerum igitur fortuitarum nulla est presentio." * Also that illustrious Reformer *Luther*, says, in his *Treatise against Free-will:* " Concessa Dei præscientia et omnipotentia, sequitur naturaliter irrefragabili consequentia, nos per nos ipsos non esse factos, nec vivere, nec agere quicquam, sed per illius omnipotentiam. Cum autem tales nos ille ante præscierit futuros, talesque nunc faciat, moveat, et gubernet; quid potest fingi quæso, quod in nobis liberum sit, aliter et aliter fieri, quam ille præscierit, aut nunc agat? Pugnat itaque ex diametro præscientia et omnipotentia Dei cum nostro libero arbitrio. Aut enim

---

* De Divin. C. ii. · (*C.*)

Deus falletur præsciendo, errabit et agendo (quod est impossibile) aut nos agemus et agemur secundum ipsius præscientiam et actionem."* And our learned *Dr. South* says, " The fore-knowledge of any event--does certainly and necessarily infer, that there must be such an event; for as much as the certainty of the *knowledge* depends upon the certainty of the thing *known*. And in this sense it is, that God's decree and promise give a necessary existence to the thing decreed or promised, that is to say, they infer it by a necessary infallible consequence; so that it was as impossible for Christ not to rise from the dead, as it was for God absolutely to decree and promise a thing, and yet for that thing not come to pass."†

I could also bring in the greatest divines and philosophers, who are asserters of liberty, as confirming this argument;‡ for they acknowledge, that they are unable to reconcile the *divine prescience* and the *liberty* of man together: § which is all I intended to prove by this argument, taken from the consideration of the *divine prescience.* ||

Fifth Argument, taken from the Nature of Rewards and Punishments.

V. A fifth argument to prove man a necessary agent, is as follows: if man was not a necessary agent, determined by pleasure and pain, there would be no foundation for rewards and punishments, which are the *essential supports* of society.¶

For if men were not necessarily determined by pleasure and pain, or if pleasure and pain were no causes to determine men's wills, of what use would be the prospect of rewards to frame a man's will to the observation of the law, or punishments to hinder his transgression thereof? Were pain, as such, eligible, and pleasure, as such, avoidable, rewards and punishments could be no motives to a man to make him do or forbear any action. But if pleasure and pain have a necessary effect on men. and if it be impos-

---

* Cap. 147. (*C.*) *De servo Arbitrio.* See p. 272.
† Sermons, Vol. III. p. 397 (*C.*)
‡ See among others Cartesii Prin. Pars I. Art. 41. Locke's Letters, p. 27. (*C.*)
§ Tillotson's Sermons, Vol. VI p. 157. Stillingfleet of Christ's Satisfaction, p. 355. (*C*)
|| See a passage on the same subject, from an earlier piece, by this author, at the end of *the Inquiry*
¶ Solon rempublicam contineri dicebat duabus rebus, præmio et pœnâ. Cicero Epist. 15, *ad Brutum.* (*C.*)

sible for men not to choose what seems good to them, and not to avoid what seems evil; the necessity of rewards and punishments is then evident, and rewards will be of use to all those who conceive those rewards to be pleasure, and punishments will be of use to all those who conceive them to be pain ; and rewards and punishments will frame those men's wills to observe, and not transgress the laws.

Besides, since there are so many robbers, murderers, whore-masters, and other criminals, who, notwithstanding the punishments threatened, and rewards promised, by laws, prefer breaking the laws as the greater good or lesser evil, and reject conformity to them as the greater evil or lesser good : how many more would there be, and with what disorders would not all societies be filled, if rewards and punishments, considered as pleasure and pain, did not determine some men's wills, but that, instead thereof, all men could prefer, or will, punishment considered as pain, and reject rewards considered as pleasure ? Men would then be under no restraints.

Sixth Argument, taken from the Nature of Morality.

VI. My sixth and last argument to prove man a necessary agent is, if man was not a necessary agent determined by pleasure and pain, he would have no notion of *morality*, or motive to practise it: the distinction between morality and immorality, virtue and vice, would be lost, and man would not be a moral agent.

Morality or virtue consists in such actions as are in their own nature, and, upon the whole, *pleasant;* and immorality or vice consists in such actions as are in their own nature, and upon the whole, *painful.** Wherefore a man must be affected with pleasure and pain, in order to know what morality is, and to distinguish it from immorality. He must also be affected with pleasure and pain, to have a reason to practise morality ; for there can be no motives, but pleasure and pain, to make a man do or forbear any action. And a man must be the more moral, the more he understands or is duly sensible, what actions give pleasure and what pain ; and must be perfectly moral, if necessarily determined by pleasure and pain, rightly understood and apprehended. But if man be *indifferent* to pleasure and pain, or is not duly affected with them, he cannot know what morality is,

---

* Locke's Hum. Und. L. ii. Ch. xx. Serjeant's Solid. Philos. asserted, p. 215. (C.)

nor distinguish it from immorality, nor have any motive to practise morality, and abstain from immorality ; and will be equally indifferent to morality and immorality, or virtue and vice. Man in his present condition is sufficiently immoral by mistaking pain for pleasure, and thereby judging, willing and practising amiss ; but if he was indifferent to pleasure and pain, he would have no rule to go by, and might never judge, will and practise right.

OBJECTIONS ANSWERED.

Though I conceive I have so proposed my arguments, as to have obviated most of the plausible objections usually urged against the doctrine of necessity, yet it may not be improper to give a particular solution to the principal of them.

1. First then, it is objected, that " if men are necessary agents, and do commit necessarily all breaches of the law, it would be unjust to punish them for doing what they cannot avoid doing." *

To which I answer, that the sole end of punishment in society is to prevent, as far as may be, the commission of *certain* crimes ; and that punishments have their designed effect two ways ; first, by restraining or cutting off from society the *vicious* members, and secondly, by correcting men, or terrifying them from the commission of those crimes. Now let punishments be inflicted with either of these views, it will be ·manifest, that no regard is had to any *free-agency* in man, in order to render those punishments just ; but that on the contrary, punishments may be *justly* inflicted on man, though a necessary agent. For, first, if *murderers*, for example, or any such *vicious* members, are cut off from society, merely as they are public nuisances, and unfit to live among men ; it is plain, they are in that case so far from being considered as *free-agents*, that they are cut off from society as a cankered branch is from a tree, or as a mad dog is killed in the streets. And the punishment of such men is *just*, as it takes mischievous members out of society. Also, for the same reason, *furious madmen*, whom all allow to be necessary agents, are in many places of the world, either the objects of judicial punishments, or are allowed to be dispatched by private men. Nay, even *men infected with the plague*, who are not

---

* Auli Gellii noctes Att. L. vi. C. ii. (*C*)

voluntary agents, and are guilty of no crime, are sometimes thought to be justly cut off from society, to prevent contagion from them.

2. Secondly, let punishments be inflicted on some criminals with a view to terrify, it will appear that in inflicting punishments with that view, no regard is had to any *free agency* in man, in order to make those punishments *just.* To render the punishment of such men *just*, it is sufficient that they were *voluntary* agents, or had the will to do the crime for which they suffer; for the law very justly and rightly regardeth only the will, and no other preceding causes of action. For example, suppose the law, on pain of death, forbids theft, and there be a man who, by the strength of temptation, is necessitated to steal, and is thereupon put to death for it, doth not his punishment *deter* others from theft? Is it not a cause that others steal not? Doth it not frame their wills to justice? Whereas, a criminal who is an involuntary agent (as for instance, a man who has killed another in a chance medley, or while in a fever, or the like) cannot serve for an example to *deter* any others from doing the same, he being no more an intelligent agent in doing the crime than a house is, which kills a man by its fall; and by consequence, the punishment of such an involuntary agent would be unjust. When, therefore, a man does a crime *voluntarily*, and his punishment will serve to deter others from doing the same, he *is justly punished for doing what* (through strength of temptation, ill habits, or other causes) *he could not avoid doing.*

' It may not be improper to add this farther consideration from the law of our country. There is one case, wherein our law is so far from requiring that the persons punished should be *free agents*, that it does not consider them as voluntary agents, or even as guilty of the crime for which they suffer, so little is *free agency* requisite to make punishments just. The children of rebel parents suffer in their fortunes for the guilt of their parents; and their punishment is deemed just, because it is supposed to be a means to prevent rebellion in parents.

II. Secondly, it is objected, that " it is useless to threaten punishment, or inflict it on men to prevent crimes, when they are necessarily determined in all their actions."

1. To which I answer first, that *threatening of punishments* is a cause which necessarily determines some men's wills to a conformity to law, and against committing the crimes to which punishments are annexed; and, there-

therefore, is useful to all those whose wills must be determined by it. It is as useful to such men, as the sun is to the ripening the fruits of the earth, or as any other causes are to produce their proper effects; and a man may as well say the sun is useless, if the ripening the fruits of the earth be necessary, as say, there is no need of threatening punishment for the use of those to whom threatening punishment is a necessary cause of forbearing to do a crime. It is also of use to society to *inflict* punishments on men *for doing what they cannot avoid doing*, to the end that necessary causes may exist, to form the wills of those who in virtue of them necessarily observe the laws, and also of use to cut them off as *noxious members* of society.

2. But, secondly, so far is threatening and inflicting punishments from being useless, if men are necessary agents, that it would be useless to *correct* and *deter* (which are the principal effects designed to be obtained by threatening and inflicting punishments), unless men were necessary agents, and were determined by pleasure and pain; because, if men were free, or indifferent to pleasure and pain, pain could be no motive to cause men to observe the law.

3. Thirdly, men have every day examples before them of the usefulness of punishments upon some intelligent or sensible beings, which they all contend are necessary agents. They punish dogs, horses and other animals every day with great success, and make them leave off their vicious habits, and form them thereby according to their wills. These are plain facts, and matters of constant experience, and even confirmed by the evasions of the advocates of liberty, who call *the rewards and punishments* used to brute beasts *analogical;* and say, that " beating them and giving them victuals, have only the shadow of rewards and punishments." * Nor are capital punishments without their use among beasts and birds. *Rorarius* tells us, that " they crucify lions in *Africa* to drive away other lions from their cities and towns; and that, travelling through the country of *Juliers*, he observed they hanged up wolves to secure their flocks." † And in like manner with us, men hang up *crows* and *rooks* to keep birds from their corn, as they hang up murderers in chains to deter other murderers. But I

---

* Bramhall's Works, p. 685.

† Quod bruta Anim. &c. L. ii p. 109. (*C.*) *Rorarius* was Nuncio to the Court of Hungary from Clement VII., who became Pope in 1523. The treatise was entitled " Quod Animalia bruta Ratione utantur melius Homine." 12mo. *Nouv. Dict.* 1772. V. p. 215.

need not go to brutes for examples of the usefulness of punishments on necessary agents. Punishments are not without effect on *some idiots* and *madmen*, by restraining them to a certain degree; and they are the very means by which the minds of *children* are formed by their parents. Nay, punishments have plainly a better effect on *children* than on grown persons, and more easily form them to virtue and discipline, than they change the vicious habits of grown persons, or plant new habits in them. Wherefore the objectors ought to think punishments may be threatened and inflicted on men usefully, though they are necessary agents.

3. Thirdly, it is objected, *if men are necessary agents, it is of no use to represent reasons to them, or to entreat them, or to admonish them, or to blame them, or to praise them.*

To which I answer, that all these, according to me, are necessary causes to determine certain men's wills to do what we desire of them, and are therefore useful, as acting on such necessary agents to whom they are necessary causes of action; but would be of no use, if men had *free will*, or their wills were not moved by them. So that they who make this objection must run into the absurdities of saying, that *that cause is useful, which is no cause of action, and serves not to change the will,* and that *that cause is useless which necessitates the effect.*

Let me add something further in respect of praise. Men have at all times been praised for actions judged by all the world to be necessary. It has been a standing method of commendation among the epic poets, who are the greatest panegyrists of glorious actions, to attribute their hero's valour, and his great actions, to some deity present with him and assisting him. *Homer* gives many of his heroes a god or a goddess to attend them in battle, or be ready to help them in distress. *Virgil* describes *Æneas* as always under the divine direction and assistance. And *Tasso* gives the Christians in their holy war divine assistance.

Orators also, and historians, think necessary actions the proper subjects of praise. *Cicero,* when he maintained that the gods inspired *Milo* with the design and courage to kill *Clodius,** did not intend to lessen the satisfaction or glory of *Milo,* but on the contrary to augment it. But can there be a finer commendation than that given by *Velleius Paterculus* to *Cato,* that he *was good by nature, because he could not be otherwise.* For, that alone is true goodness which flows

---

* Oratio pro Milone. (*C.*)

from disposition, whether that disposition be natural or acquired. Such goodness may be depended on, and will seldom or ever fail. Whereas, goodness founded on any reasonings whatsoever, is a very pecarious thing, as may be seen by the lives of the greatest declaimers against vice, who, though they are constantly acquainting themselves with all the topics that can be drawn from the excellency of goodness or virtue, and the mischiefs of vice; the rewards that attend the one, and the punishments that attend the other; yet are not better than those who are never conversant in such topics. Lastly, the common proverb, *gaudeant bene nati*, is a general commendation of men for what plainly in no sense depends on them.

4. Fourthly, it is objected, that "if all events are necessary, then there is a period fixed to every man's life: and if there is a period fixed to every man's life, then it cannot be shortened by want of care or violence offered, or diseases; nor can it be prolonged by care or physic: and if it cannot be shortened or prolonged by them, then it is useless to avoid, or use any of these things."

In answer to which, I grant, that if the period of human life be fixed (as I contend it is) it cannot but happen at the time fixed, and nothing can fall out to prolong or shorten that period. Neither such want of care, nor such violence offered, nor such diseases can happen, as can cause the period of human life to fall short of that time; nor such care, nor physic be used, as to prolong it beyond that time. But though these cannot so fall out, as to shorten or prolong the period of human life; yet, being necessary causes in the chain of causes to bring human life to the period fixed, or to cause it not to exceed that time, they must as necessarily precede that effect, as other causes do their proper effects; and, consequently, when used or neglected, serve all the ends and purposes that can be hoped for, or feared, from the use of any means, or the neglect of any means whatsoever: for example, let it be fixed and necessary for the river *Nile* annually to overflow, the means to cause it to overflow must no less necessarily precede. And as it would be absurd to argue that, *if the overflowing of the Nile was annually fixed and necessary, it would overflow, though the necessary means to make it overflow did not precede;* so it is no less absurd to argue from the fixed period of human life, against the necessary means to bring it to its fixed period, or to cause it not to exceed that period.

5. Fifthly, it is asked, "How a man can act against his

conscience, and how a man's conscience can accuse him, if he knows he acts necessarily, and also does what he thinks best when he commits any sin."

. I reply, that conscience being a man's own opinion of his actions, with relation to some rule, he may, at the time of doing an action contrary to that rule, know that he breaks that rule, and, consequently, act with reluctance, though not sufficient to hinder the action. But after the action is over, he may not only judge his action to be contrary to that rule; but by the absence of the pleasure of the sin, and by finding himself obnoxious to shame, or by believing himself liable to punishment, he may *really accuse himself;* that is, he may condemn himself for having done it, be sorry he has done it, and wish it undone, because of the consequences that attend it.*

6. Sixthly, it is objected, " that if all events are neces- sary, it was as impossible (for example) for *Julius Cæsar* not to have died in the Senate, as it is impossible for two and two to make six. But who will say the former was as impossible as the latter is, when we can conceive it possible for *Julius Cæsar* to have died any where else as well as in the Senate, and impossible to conceive two and two ever to make six ?"

To which I answer, that I do allow, *that if all events are necessary, it was as impossible for Julius Cæsar not to have died in the Senate, as it is impossible for two and two to make six :* and will add, that it is no more possible to conceive the death of *Julius Cæsar* to have happened any where else but in the Senate, than that two and two should make six. For whoever does conceive his death possible any where else, supposes other circumstances preceding his death than did precede his death. Whereas, let them suppose all the same circumstances to come to pass that did precede his death, and then it will be impossible to conceive (if they think justly) his death could have come to pass any where else, as they conceive it impossible for two and two to make six. I observe also, that to suppose other circumstances of any action possible, than those that do precede it, is to sup- pose a contradiction or impossibility : for, as all actions have their particular circumstances, so every circumstance preced- ing an action, is as impossible not to have come to pass, by virtue of the causes preceding that circumstance, as that two and two shouldmake six.

---

* See *Law* on this passage, in " Origin of Evil," p. 272. *Note.*

The Opinions of the learned concerning Liberty, &c.

Having, as I hope, proved the truth of what I have advanced, and answered the most material objections that can be urged against me ; it will, perhaps, not be improper to give some account of the sentiments of the learned, in relation to my subject, and confirm by *authority* what I have said, for the sake of those with whom *authority* has weight in matters of speculation.

The questions of *liberty*, ·*necessity* and *chance*, have been subjects of dispute among philosophers at all times ; and most of those philosophers have clearly asserted *necessity*, and denied *liberty* and *chance*.

The questions of *liberty* and *necessity*, have also been debated among divines in the several ages of the christian church, under the terms of *free-will* and *predestination;* and the divines who have denied *free-will*, and asserted *predestination*, have enforced the arguments of the philosophers, by the consideration of some doctrines peculiar to the christian religion. And as to *chance, hazard,* or *fortune,* I think divines unanimously agree that those words have no meaning.

Some christian communions have even proceeded so far in relation to these matters, as to condemn in councils and synods, the doctrine of *free-will* as heretical ; and the denial thereof is become a part of the *confessions of faith,* and *articles of religion* of several churches.

From this state of the fact, it is manifest, that whoever embraces the opinion I have maintained, cannot want the *authority* of as many learned and pious men, as in embracing the contrary.

But considering how little men are moved by the *authority* of those who professedly maintain opinions contrary to theirs, though, at the same time, they themselves embrace no opinion but on the *authority* of somebody ; I shall wave all the advantages that I might draw from the authority of such philosophers and divines as are undoubtedly on my side, and for that reason shall not enter into a more particular detail of them ; but shall offer the *authority* of such men who profess to maintain *liberty.* There are indeed very few real adversaries to the opinion I defend among those who pretend to be so ; and upon due inquiry it will be found, that most of those who assert *liberty* in words, deny the thing, when the question is rightly stated. For proof whereof, let any man examine the clearest and acutest authors who have written for *liberty*, or discourse with those who think *liberty* a matter of experience, and he will see, that they allow that the *will follows the judgment of the understanding;* and *that when two objects are presented to a man's choice, one whereof appears better than the other, he cannot choose the worst;* that is, cannot choose *evil* as *evil.* And since they acknowledge these things to be true, they yield up the question of *liberty* to their adversaries, who only contend, that the will or choice is always determined by what seems best. I will give my reader one example thereof in the most acute and ingenious *Dr. Clarke,* whose authority is equal to that of many others put together, and makes it needless to cite others, after him. He asserts, that *the will* is determined by *moral motives,* and calls the *necessity,* by which a man chooses, in virtue of those motives, *moral necessity.* And he explains himself with his usual candour and perspicuity by the following instance : " A man," says he, " entirely free from all pain of body and disorder of mind, judges it unreasonable for him to hurt or destroy himself; and being under no temptation or external violence, he *cannot possibly* act contrary to this judgment; not because he wants a natural or physical power so to do, but because it is absurd and mischievous, and morally impossible for him to choose to do it. Which also is the very same reason, why the most perfect rational creatures, superior to men, cannot do evil ; not because they want a natural power to perform the material action, but because it is morally impossible that, with a perfect knowledge of what is best, and without any temptation to evil, their will should determine itself to choose to act foolishly and unreasonably."*

In this he plainly allows the *necessity* for which I have contended. For he assigns the same causes of human actions that I have done, and extends the *necessity* of human actions as far, when he asserts that a man *cannot,* under those causes, *possibly do the contrary to what he does;* and particularly, that *a man,* under the circumstances of *judging it unreasonable to hurt or destroy himself, and being under no temptation or external violence, cannot possibly act contrary to that judgment.* And as to *a natural* or *physical power* in man *to act contrary to that judgment,* and to *hurt* or *destroy* himself, which is asserted in the foregoing passage, that is so far from

---

* Demonstration of the Being and Attributes of God, Ed. 4, 1716, p. 105. (C.)

being inconsistent with the doctrine of *necessity*, that the said *natural power to do the contrary*, or *to hurt* or *destroy* himself, is a consequence of the doctrine of *necessity*. For, if man is *necessarily* determined by particular *moral causes*, and *cannot then possibly act contrary* to what he does, he must, under opposite *moral causes*, have *a power to do the contrary*. Man, as determined by *moral* causes, *cannot possibly* choose evil as evil, and by consequence chooses *life* before *death*, while he apprehends *life* to be *a good*, and *death* to be *an evil;* as, on the contrary, he chooses *death* before *life*, while he apprehends *death* to be *a good*, and *life* to be *an evil*. And thus *moral* causes, by being different from one another, or differently understood, do determine men differently ; and by consequence suppose *a natural power* to choose and act as differently as those causes differently determine them.

If therefore men will be governed by authority in the questions before us, let them sum up the real asserters of the *liberty* of man, and they will find them not to be very numerous ; but, on the contrary, they will find far the greater part of the pretended asserters of *liberty* to be real asserters of *necessity*.

The Author's Notion of Liberty.

I shall conclude this discourse with observing, that though I have contended, that *liberty from necessity* is contrary to experience ; that it is impossible, and, if possible, that it is an imperfection ; that it is inconsistent with the divine perfections, and that it is subversive of laws and morality ; yet, to prevent all objections to me, founded on the equivocal use of the word *liberty*, which, like all words employed in debates of consequence, has various meanings affixed to it, I think myself obliged to declare my opinion, that I take *man* to have a truly valuable *liberty* of another kind. He has *a power to do as he wills or pleases*. Thus, if he wills or pleases to speak or be silent, to sit or stand, to ride or walk, to go this way or that way, to move fast or slow, or, in fine, if his will changes like a weather-cock, he is able to do as he wills or pleases, unless prevented by some restraint or compulsion, as by being gagged, being under an acute pain, being forced out of his place, being confined, having convulsive motions, having lost the use of his limbs, or such-like causes.

He has also the same power in relation to the actions of his mind, as to those of his body. If he wills or pleases, he can think of this or that subject, stop short or pursue his thoughts, deliberate or defer deliberation, or resume deliberation, as he pleases ; resolve or suspend his resolution as he pleases, and, in fine, can every moment change his object when he pleases, unless prevented by pain, or a fit of an apoplexy, or some such intervening restraint and compulsion.

And is it not a great perfection in man to be able, in relation both to his thoughts and actions, to do as he wills or pleases, in all those cases of pleasure and interest? Nay, can a greater and more beneficial power in man be conceived, than to be able to do as he wills or pleases ? And can any other *liberty* be conceived beneficial to him ? Had he this power or *liberty* in all things, he would be omnipotent!

The seeming Inconsistence of the Divine Prescience with the Liberty of Man.

[From the same Author's " Essay concerning the Use of Reason in Propositions, the Evidence whereof depends upon Human Testimony." 1707]

The irreconcileableness of the divine prescience with the liberty of man, though it has been a problem which has exercised the learned in all ages, yet I take the matter to be so clear, that I cannot forbear thinking, that nothing but the interest of some, or prejudice of others, in behalf of received systems, could make it a question of difficulty. I know very well, that divines put such an idea to the term *liberty,* as is directly inconsistent with the divine prescience ; for they suppose liberty to stand for a power in man to determine himself, and consequently that there are several actions of man absolutely contingent, since they depend, as to their existence, on man, who determines their existence from himself, without regard to any extrinsical causes. Now I readily own it impossible to make the divine prescience consist with such an idea of liberty : for all actions whatever are proved to be certain by the supposition of a divine prescience, (for if they are foreknown they must certainly be,) and by the supposition of man's liberty in this sense are proved to be contingent. Now I cannot put together certain and contingent, or certain and incertain, at the same time. I allow the same action may be certain and relatively contingent (that is, contingent as to us, or of which together with its causes we are ignorant before they happen, however certain in themselves ; and thus we apply the word chance, when we are ignorant of the causes of an action, though properly speaking there is no such thing as chance, because no action is without its causes) ; but the word contingent is here taken absolutely, or else the idea of liberty, as it consists in a power to determine one's self, without regard to any external causes compelling it, is destroyed, and another idea put into its room, inconsistent with the liberty contended for.

Now this idea of liberty is not only inconsistent with the supposition of the divine prescience, but inconsistent with truth : and to make that appear, I shall shew wherein our liberty consists, and then, its consistency with the divine prescience. Every man may observe in himself a power to do or forbear several actions, according to the determination of his mind : if the mind determines the doing of an action, there is in some cases no outward impediment to hinder him from acting according to that determination ; and not only no outward impediment, but the forbearance of the action would have been equally in his power, if the mind had determined a forbearance. As for instance, if a man sits in a room with the door open, he has plainly a power to go out of that room, if he prefers going out to staying in ; he has likewise a power to stay, if he prefers staying to going out : let his mind determine which way it will, he has then a power of acting according to that determination. And this is the greatest freedom or liberty we can conceive to belong to any being ; and by this idea of liberty, or freedom from compulsion, God is plainly the most free being that can be conceived, because the doing or forbearing all actions, according to the determination of his will, are in his power. He can will nothing but what is possible, and there can be no bar or impediment to hinder an omnipotent Being from doing or forbearing things possible in themselves, though man's liberty is restrained to a few actions by the weakness of his powers, very much below the possibility of things. This idea of liberty is far from being inconsistent with the certainty of an action, and consequently with the divine prescience : for here is nothing contingent in the whole chain, but every thing as certain as our knowledge that God foresees every thing, supposes. For there are causes that ever determine the will, as the appearing good or evil consequences ; there are other causes of the appearing good or evil consequences, and causes of those causes, and so on ; and no one action in this long progression of causes, extend it as far as you please, could possibly not happen. For suppose the colour and flavour of a peach makes me will it, while it appears thus agreeable, I must will it. The peach must appear thus agreeable, while my appetite and organs are disposed as they are ; and innumerable causes have preceded to make the peach appear in the manner it does, such as the care of the gardener, &c.   Now my action of taking or forbearing this peach is as certain as is the colour and flavour which makes it agreeable or disagreeable, or as is the determination of my will, according to its appearing agreeableness or disagreeableness (though it was equally in my power to take or forbear it according to the determination of my will ; that is, had my mind determined a forbearance, there was no compulsive external force to oblige me to take it ; or had my mind determined the taking of it, there was no external compulsive force to oblige me to forbear taking it) ; for while I prefer or will taking the peach to letting it alone, I cannot help acting, that preference being the immediate, necessary, impelling cause ; though I could as plainly, and must as necessarily have let it alone, had my mind given a different determination.   So that stop where you will in this train of causes, you will not, nor cannot, have the idea of any thing but what has certain and necessary causes, and consequently what must certainly and necessarily be.   I have used the words certainly and necessarily for the same thing in this case, because I cannot distinguish between *certainly be* and *must be*.   They who object this to me must define, that I may see the difference.   Now if all the liberty we have, consists in a power to do or forbear several actions, according to the determinations of our mind, and that *liberty* is perfectly consistent with that certainty of our actions before they are produced, then our liberty is reconcilable with the divine prescience, since all the difficulty lay in reconciling the certainty of all future actions with our liberty. Nay, I have shewn there can be no liberty but what supposes the certainty and necessity of all events.   True liberty therefore is consistent with necessity, and ought not to be opposed to it, but only to compulsion.   Pp. 45—50.

LETTERS

TO

𝔄 𝔓𝔥𝔦𝔩𝔬𝔰𝔬𝔭𝔥𝔦𝔠𝔞𝔩 𝔘𝔫𝔟𝔢𝔩𝔦𝔢𝔳𝔢𝔯.

————

—————— I cannot go
Where *universal Love* not smiles around;
From seeming *Evil* still educing *Good,*
And *Better* thence again, and *Better* still,
In infinite Progression.——————

THOMSON.

————

TO

WILLIAM TAYLEUR,* Esq.

OF

SHREWSBURY.

———◆———

Dear Sir,

I shall think myself highly honoured, if, in dedicating this work to you, I can perpetuate the memory of our friendship, and at the same time procure for revealed religion the advantage that it may derive from the knowledge of your zealous attachment to it.

We live in an age in which many persons of a philosophical turn of mind, are disposed to reject revelation. This you and I equally lament. But we consider it as a temporary circumstance, since the principles of true philosophy lead to the most satisfactory conclusion in favour of it; and, therefore, we doubt not but that, in due time, the justness of the conclusion will be apparent to all who give sufficient attention to the subject.

It is, we are sensible, either a misunderstanding of the nature and object of revealed religion (arising from the manifold corruptions and abuses of it), or an inattention to the nature of its evidence, that is the cause of the present unbelief. But when these corruptions and abuses shall be clearly traced to their source, and this source shall appear to be something quite foreign to the genuine principles of this religion; and when the evidence of the facts, on which

---

* Whose liberal contributions " to defray the expenses incurred" by the author's " theological inquiries and publications" are acknowledged in his *Memoirs.* Mr. Tayleur, who also largely contributed to the erection of Essex Street Chapel, died 1796, aged 83. See an interesting account of this zealous *Unitarian*, by Rev. T. Belsham, in *Memoirs* of Lindsey, pp. 138—142. This dedication did not appear till the publication of Part II., to which it chiefly refers; but it was then prefixed to the 2d. edition of Part I.

the truth of it depends, shall appear to rest on the very same foundation with all our *faith in history*, nothing will be wanting to the complete satisfaction of the truly philoso-phical and the candid.

In the mean time it is, no doubt, to be lamented, that so many of those persons who are joined with us in the investi-gation of natural phenomena, who, together with ourselves, receive so much pleasure from the discovery of the laws to which they are subject, should be so far disjoined from us, when we begin to look a little farther into the same glorious system ; that they should attend with rapture to the voice of nature, and not raise their thoughts beyond this, to the author of nature. It gives us equal concern, that others should acknowledge the voice of God in his works, and yet turn a deaf ear when the same great Being condescends to display his power, and to signify his will, in a still more direct and emphatical manner, and respecting things of infinitely more moment to us than any thing that can engage our attention here.

We are concerned to perceive that every thing that is the object of our senses, and that relates to this life, should be so highly prized by them ; and yet, that they should shew a perfect indifference, with respect to the continuance of life, in a future and better state, in which we shall have an infi-nitely wider field of inquiry, and which we shall enter upon with the advantage of all the experience that we have acquired in the methods of investigation here.

But this circumstance has arisen from influences which, we trust, are daily diminishing. True philosophy necessa-rily inspires the greatest veneration for the constitution and laws of nature. It, therefore, leads to devotion, and, con-sequently to the practice of all virtue. And when the pious philosopher shall be convinced that there is nothing *irrational* in that religion which alone teaches the great doctrine of *a future life*, he will, at least with that candour, and that cool and dispassionate temper, which accompanies him in all his other inquiries, attend to the evidences of it. And when he shall find that he is so far from being required, on his approaching the province of revelation, to depart from those *rules of philosophizing* which have the sanction of all our experience, that the pursuit of them necessarily carries him into it, (so that he must even cease to be a philosopher, if he refuse to be a Christian,) he will rejoice in the union of two such characters, and will continue his researches with double satisfaction, confident that whatever may be begun and left imperfect here, will be resumed and completed hereafter; that nature, and the author of nature, will be for ever the delightful objects of his veneration, and furnish an inexhaustible source of employment and of happiness.

We are ignorant, indeed, of the particulars of our condition in a future state, (and the wisdom of Divine Providence is conspicuous in this our ignorance,) but we may assure ourselves that, continuing to be a part of the same great system, of which the present state is only the commencement, and under the government of the same great and good Being, we shall be possessed of whatever shall be requisite for our own happiness, and of the means of promoting the happiness of others.

You, Sir, have always been happy in your attachment to mathematical and philosophical studies, but more so in your just preference of theological ones. These employ and brighten the evening of your life, as they did that of the great Newton, whose example, if it were necessary, would alone be a sufficient justification of us, in uniting two pursuits which are too often considered as the reverse of each other. You, therefore, naturally join with me in wishing to recommend to others those studies which give so much satisfaction to ourselves.

Your attachment to the cause of genuine Christianity was conspicuous in your relinquishing a Trinitarian form of worship, and adopting an Unitarian one in your own family, till you had procured it a more public and permanent establishment.* Fortitude in such a cause as this, while the world in general is too ready to acquiesce in every thing that has the countenance of *fashion* and of *power*, is truly worthy of a christian philosopher; and such an example as you have set cannot be too generally known, being so rare, and therefore so much wanted. The great Newton, though an Unitarian, had not the courage to declare himself and act as one.†

Notwithstanding the present general aversion to theological inquiries among persons engaged in philosophical pursuits, we are by no means singular in our respect for

* See *Mem.* of Lindsey, pp. 140, *Note,* and 142.

† Thus in the *Historical Account,* there is an apparent reserve as to his own faith, accompanied with sufficient incidental notices that the writer could not have

them ; and such examples as yours, when sufficiently
known, must contribute to make us still less so. With the
view of accèlerating so desirable an event was this work
composed ; and should it, in the smallest degree, be the
means of accomplishing so great an end, it will give me
more satisfaction than any other of my publications.

With the greatest respect, I am,

Dear Sir,

Your most obliged humble servant,

J. PRIESTLEY.

Birmingham,
February 1, 1787.

been a Trinitarian. As to the forgery of the *heavenly witnesses,* (1 John v. 7,) he
remarks how long " the faith subsisted without this text," and that " it is rather a
danger to religion than an advantage to make it now lean upon a bruised reed,"
without particularizing the *faith* or *religion* he intends. He, however, describes the
baptismal form in *Matthew* as " the place from which they tried, at first to derive
the Trinity," an *insinuation,* as Mr. Matthews observes, " very extraordinary to
come from a writer who was no Socinian." Afterwards it is said of Jerome's professed correction of the Latin version, by inserting the *forged* text, that " he recommends the alteration by its usefulness for establishing the Catholic faith," adding
that it is accounted the main text for the business."
As the writer of the *Historical Account* proceeds, he says that *Basil* " perplexes
himself in citing places which are nothing to the purpose," yet " does not produce
this text of the *three in heaven,* though it be the most obvious and the only proper
passage." As to the adducing this *forged* testimony, he says, that " it is probable—
it began first in Africa, in the disputes with the ignorant Vandals, to get some
credit." On *Erasmus* having printed " The Triple Testimony in Heaven," from an
" English manuscript," he speaks of " his adversaries" as having thus " got the
Trinity into his edition." He had just before remarked, that " it is the temper of the
hot and superstitious part of mankind, in matters of religion, ever to be fond of
mysteries ; and, for that reason, to like best what they understand least." See
Hist. Ac. in the late Mr. Matthews's Recorder, 1803, II. pp. 185, 189, 194, 197,
200, 206, 228, 229. See also, Vol. II. p. 464, and the reference, *Note* *; *Cordial
for Low Spirits,* 1763, I. *Pref.* p. xviii. and a *paper* in the Third volume of that
work ·This question has been very lately revived in " A Letter to the Rev. Dr.
Chalmers, occasioned by his notice of Unitarians in the Appendix to his Sermon,
&c. to which is subjoined a statement of the evidence of Sir Isaac Newton's Unita-
rianism, by Benjamin Mardon, Minister of the Unitarian Church, Glasgow, 1818."
This Letter I have not yet had an opportunity of seeing.

LETTERS

TO A

Philosophical Unbeliever.

PART I.

CONTAINING

An Examination of the principal Objections to the Doctrines of Natural Religion, and especially those contained in the Writings of Mr. Hume.

Scilicet haud satis est rivos spectare fluentes—
Fontem ipsum spectare juvat.

ANTI-LUCRETIUS.

[1780.]

[Re-printed from the Second Edition 1787.]

THE

PREFACE.

It will, I think, be acknowledged by all persons who are capable of reflection, and who *do* reflect, that in the whole compass of speculation, there are no questions more interesting to all men than those which are the subject of these *Letters*, viz. Whether the world we inhabit, and ourselves who inhabit it, had an intelligent and benevolent author, or no proper author at all? Whether our conduct be inspected, and we are under a righteous government, or under no government at all? And, lastly, whether we have something to hope and fear beyond the grave, or are at liberty to adopt the Epicurean maxim, *Let us eat and drink for to-morrow we die?* This may strike us more forcibly if we attend a little to the principles of human nature.

The great superiority of man over brutes consists in the greater *comprehensiveness of his mind*, by means of which he is, as it is commonly expressed, capable of *reflection*, but more accurately speaking, capable of contemplating, and, therefore, of enjoying the *past* and the *future*, as well as the *present.* And what is most extraordinary and interesting to us, this power, as far as appears, has no limits.

In infancy we feel nothing but what affects us for the moment, but *present feelings* bear a less and less proportion to the general mass of sensation, as it may be called, consisting of various elements, the greatest part of which are borrowed from the *past* and the *future;* so that, in our natural progress in intellectual improvement, all temporary affections, whether of a pleasurable or of a painful nature, will come at length to be wholly inconsiderable, and we shall have, in a greater degree than we can at present conceive, an equable enjoyment of the whole of what we *have been* and *have felt,* and also of what we have a confident *expectation of being,* and of feeling in future.

Our progress, however, in this intellectual improvement is capable of being accelerated or retarded, according as we accustom ourselves to reflection or live without it. For certainly, though, while we retain the faculties of memory and reasoning, we cannot whether we choose it or not, wholly exclude reflection on the past or anticipation of the future, (and, therefore, some kind of advance in intellectual improvement is unavoidable to all beings possessed of intellect,) yet it is in our power to exclude what is of great moment, viz. all that is *voluntary* in the business ; so that being in a great measure deaf to what is behind, and blind to what is before, we may give ourselves up to mere sensual gratifications, and, consequently, no question, concerning what is *past* or *future* may interest us. In this state of mind a man may think it absurd to trouble himself either about how he came into the world, or how he is to go out of it.

It would be too hasty, however, to assert, that it can only be in this very lowest state of intellect, a life of mere sensation or very imperfect reflection, that any person can be unconcerned about the belief of a God and the doctrines of natural religion. For a man may get above mere sensual indulgence, and give great scope to his intellectual faculties with respect to some objects, and be wholly inattentive to others. And it is in the power of little things, by wholly occupying the mind, not only to exclude the consideration of greater things, but even the idea of their being greater.

This, indeed, comes within the description of a kind of proper *insanity,* but then it may be justly asserted, that in a greater or less degree, all persons who do not prize every thing according to its real value, and regulate their pursuits accordingly, are insane; though, when the degree is small, it passes unnoticed, and when the consequences are inconsiderable, it is far from being offensive. Nay, in some cases, the world derives great and manifest advantage from a partial disorder, as it may be called, of this kind. For great excellence in particular arts and sciences, is perhaps seldom attained without it. Indeed, it cannot be expected that a man should greatly excel in some things, without neglecting, and consequently, undervaluing others.

We are shocked at a man's insanity only when it makes him inattentive to things that immediately concern him, as to the necessary means of his subsistence or support, so that he must perish without the care of others. But when the interest, though real, is *remote*, a man's inattention to it passes unnoticed. By this means it is that, without being surprised or shocked, we every day see thousands, who profess to believe in a future world, live and die without making any provision for it, though their conduct is much more inexcusable than that of the atheist who, not believing in futurity, minds only what is present.

But though the conduct of the atheist be consistent with itself, it must give concern to those who are not atheists, and who have a just sense of the importance of the belief of a God, of a providence and of a future state, to the present dignity and the future happiness of man

An atheist may be a temperate, good-natured, honest, and in the common, and less extended sense of the word, a *virtuous* man ; because if he be a man of good understanding, of naturally moderate passions, and have been properly educated, the influences to which he will have been exposed may be sufficient to *form* those valuable and amiable habits, and to *fix* him in them. But, notwithstanding this, an atheist has neither the *motive* nor the *means* of being what he might have been if he had not been an atheist.

An atheist cannot have that sense of *personal dignity* and *importance* that a theist has. For he who believes that he was introduced into life without any design, and is soon to be for ever excluded from life, cannot suppose that he has any very important part to act in life : and, therefore, he can have no motive to give much attention to his conduct in it. The past and the future being of less consequence to him, he will naturally endeavour to think about them as little as possible, and make the most of what is before him.

But the necessary consequence of this is the *debasement of his nature,* or a foregoing of the advantages that he might have derived from that power of comprehension, which will have full scope in the theist ; the man who considers him-self as a link in an immensely connected chain of being, as acting a part in a *drama,* which commenced from eternity, and extends to eternity ; who considers that every gratifica-tion and every action, contributes to form a *character,* the importance of which to him is, literally speaking, infinite ; who considers himself as standing in the nearest and most desirable relation to a Being of infinite power, wisdom and goodness ; a Being who gives unremitted attention to him, who plans for him, and conducts him through this life, who does not lose sight of him even in the grave, and who will, in due time, raise him to a life, which, with respect both to gratifications and pursuits, will be of unspeakably more value to him than the present, and whose views, with respect to him and the universe, are boundless.

A man who really believes this, and who gives that *attention* to it which its great importance to him manifestly requires, must be *another kind of being* than an atheist, and certainly a being of unspeakably greater dignity and value. His *feelings* and his *conduct* cannot but be greatly superior.

This, however, from the nature of the thing, must depend upon the *attention* that a theist gives to his principles, and to the situation in which he believes himself to be placed. And therefore, it is very possible that a merely *nominal believer* in a God may be a *practical atheist,* and worse than a mere speculative one, living as *without God in the world,* entirely thoughtless of his being, perfections and providence. But still, nothing but *reflection* is wanting to reclaim such a person, and recover him to a proper dignity of sentiment, and a propriety of conduct ; whereas, an atheist thus sunk has not the same *power of recovery.* He wants both the *disposition* and the necessary *means.* His mind is destitute of the *latent seeds* of future greatness.

If, according to the observation of Lord Bacon, it be *knowledge* that constitutes *power :* if it be our knowledge of the external world that gives us such extensive power over *it,* and adds to our happiness in it, knowledge so materially respecting ourselves, our general situation and conduct, must have great power over *ourselves.* It must, as it were, new make us, and give us sentiments and principles greatly superior to any that we could otherwise be possessed of, and add to our *happiness* as much as it does to our *dignity.*

If, as Mr. Hume observes,* " the *good*, the *great*, the *sublime*, the *ravishing*, be found eminently in the genuine principles of theism," I need not say that there must be something *mean*, *abject* and *debasing*, in the principles of atheism. If, as he also says, (p. 116,) " a people entirely devoid of religion" are sure to be " but few degrees removed from brutes," they must be this, or something worse than this, who, having been acquainted with the principles of religion, have discarded them. The consistency of these sentiments with those advanceed in other parts of Mr. Hume's writings, it is not my business to look to.

I shall think myself happy if, in these *Letters*, I have advanced any thing that may tend either to lessen the number of speculative atheists, or, which is no less wanting, convert nominal believers into practical ones. It is not, in general, *reason* and *argument*, but the pleasures and bustle of the world that prevent both ; and proper moderation in our desires and pursuits, accompanied with serious reflection, would be of the greatest use in both cases. I wish to give occasion, and to furnish the means for this cool recollection of ourselves.

It is the too eager pursuit of pleasure, wealth, ambition, and I may add of the arts, and even of science (theological science itself not wholly excepted) that is our snare. All these may equally *occupy the mind*, to the exclusion of the greater views that open to us as *men* and subjects of moral government, who are but in the infancy of an endless, and, therefore, an infinitely important existence. All these pursuits are equally capable of confining our attention to what is immediately before us, and of hiding from our view whatever in the past or the future, most nearly concerns us to attend to.

The great book of nature is always open before us, and our eyes are always open upon it, but we pass our time in a kind of *reverie*, or absence of thought, inattentive to the most obvious connexions and consequences of things. The same is the case with the book of revelation. But it is the former only that I have a view to in the present publication.

My design, however, is to proceed to consider the speculative difficulties which attend the doctrines of *revelation*, with philosophical and thinking persons in the present age, if the reception of this part shall give me sufficient encouragement to proceed farther. But if I succeed in this

* In his *Dissertation* on the Natural History of Religion, p. 114. (*P.*) 1757.

first part, I shall consider my great object as nearly attained.; there being, as I have reason to think, many more atheists at present than mere unbelievers in revelation, especially out of England; and, for my part, I cannot help considering the difficulties that attend the proof of the Jewish and Christian revelations, as not greater than those which relate to the doctrines of natural religion.

Whenever, therefore, I shall hear of the conversion of a speculative atheist to *serious deism* (an event which has never yet come to my knowledge) I shall have little doubt of his soon becoming a serious Christian. As, on the other hand, the same turn of mind that makes a man an unbeliever in Christianity has, in fact, generally carried men on to a proper atheism. But, in other cases, this progress in speculation requires some degree of *attention* to the subject; for, with a total *listlessness and unconcern*, a man may rest *any where*. He may understand the first book of Euclid, and have no knowledge of the second, and therefore, no opinion about any of the propositions in it.

In both parts of this work it is my wish to speak to *the present state of things*, and to consider the difficulties that really press the most, without discussing every thing belonging to the subject; for which I must refer to more systematic writers, and for a short view of the whole chain of argument, with some original illustrations to my *Institutes of Natural and Revealed Religion*. (Vol. II. pp. 1—25.)

In some respects, I may, perhaps, flatter myself that I write with more advantage than any of those who have preceded me in the same argument, as I shall particularly endeavour to avail myself of the real service that infidelity has been of to Christianity, in freeing it from many things which, I believe, all who have formerly undertaken the defence of it have considered as belonging to it; when they have, in reality, been things quite foreign to it, and in some cases subversive of it. I shall hope, therefore, to exhibit a view of Christianity to which a *philosopher* cannot have so much to object, every thing that I shall contend for, appearing to me perfectly consonant to the principles of sound philosophy; and I shall use no other *modes of reasoning* than those that are universally adopted in similar cases, as I hope to make appear. Whether I succeed to my wish or not, I shall be *ingenuous*, and as impartial as I can. As to any bias that I may lie under, those who know me and my situation, are the best judges; it being impossible I should be aware of this myself. Whatever cause we our-

selves wish well to, we necessarily imagine we have sufficient reason for so wishing.

I am far from meaning to hold myself forth as an oracle
in this business ; but I shall be really obliged to any person who shall propose to me any objection that he really
thinks materially to affect the credibility of the Jewish or
the Christian system : no objection so proposed to me shall
pass unnoticed, whether I be able to give satisfaction with
respect to it or not. If I myself feel the difficulty, I shall
freely acknowledge it, and endeavour to estimate the force
of it.

I, together with the persons to whom I am addressing
myself, am a speculative inhabitant of the earth, actuated
by the same passions, engaged in a variety of the same pursuits, and (as we have not yet made any discovery that will
enable us to cure the disease of *old age*, and to prolong life
ad libitum) I, together with them, am hastening to the
grave ; and, therefore, I am equally interested with them to
find whether any thing awaits us after death, and, if any
thing, what it is. This is, in its own nature, a more important object of inquiry than any thing that we have hitherto
so laboriously investigated. It behoves us, therefore, to be
cool and patient, attentive to every circumstance that can
throw light upon the great question, and to give one another
all the assistance we can with respect to it.

Truth, and the *laws of nature*, are our common object ;
but we are necessarily more *interested* in the investigation,
in proportion to the *magnitude* of the object and the *concern*
we have in it. In these questions, therefore, there is a concurrence of every thing that can render the investigation
interesting to us ; and as there is no interference of *particular interests* in the case, there is all the reason imaginable to
lay aside every prejudice, to unite our labours, and give
one another all the assistance in our power, either by *proposing difficulties* or *solving* them. Assistance, in either of
these forms, I sincerely intreat, and shall be truly thankful
for.

With respect to this publication, concerning *natural religion*, it may not be improper to observe, as I did in my
Institutes of Natural and Revealed Religion, " that, in
giving a delineation of natural religion, I shall deliver what I
suppose *might* have been known concerning God, our duty,
and our future expectations, by the light of nature, and not
what was *actually* known of them by any of the human
race ; for these are very different things. Many things are

in their own nature attainable, which, in fact, are never attained; so that though we find but little of the knowledge of God and of his providence, in many nations, which never enjoyed the light of revelation, it does not follow, that nature did not contain and teach those lessons, and that men had not the means of learning them, provided they had made the most of the light they had, and of the powers that were given them. I shall, therefore, include, under the head of *natural religion*, all that can be *demonstrated* or proved to be true, by natural reason, though it was never, in fact, discovered by it; and even though it be probable, that mankind would never have known it without the assistance of revelation." (Vol. II. p. 2.)

Mr. Hume acknowledges, that the hypothesis, which would most naturally occur to uninstructed mankind to account for appearances in the world, would be that of *a multiplicity of deities;** and of what mankind, who have been, as far as appears, altogether, or nearly self-taught, in this respect, have been capable, in many hundred, and, in some cases, probably, thousands of years, we have evidence enough. The experiment, as we may call it, has been tried both among the civilized and the uncivilized of our race.

Nothing, therefore, that I have advanced in this work, can be at all understood to lessen the great value of revelation, even admitting, what is far from being probable, that, in some very distant age of the world, men might have attained to a full persuasion concerning all the great truths of religion, as the unity of God, the doctrine of a resurrection to immortal life, and a state of future retribution. What the most enlightened of our race had conjectured concerning these things, in fact, led them rather farther from the truth than nearer to it, and never made much impression on the generality of mankind.

Plain as the great argument contained in these *letters* is, viz. that which establishes the belief of *a God* and a *benevolent providence*, I have not been able to reply to the objections that have been started on the subject, in such a manner as that I can promise myself will be perfectly intelligible to *all* my readers. But, in general, those persons who cannot fully comprehend the answers, will not be able to see the force of the objections; and, therefore, if they have no doubts themselves, and have no occasion to make themselves so far masters of the argument as to

---

* Polytheism or idolatry was, and necessarily must have been, the first and most ancient religion of mankind." *Dissert.* S. i. p. 3.

enable them to satisfy the doubts of others, they may very well content themselves with entirely omitting, or giving but little attention to the third, fourth, twelfth, thirteenth and fourteenth letters.

I give this notice, lest persons not used to metaphysical speculations, looking into those particular letters, and finding unexpected difficulties in the subject of them, should hastily conclude, that the whole is a business of *subtle disputation*, with respect to which, they could never hope to attain to any satisfactory determination, and therefore, that they may as well leave it to be discussed by idle and speculative people, without concerning themselves about it. Whereas, nothing can be more momentous in itself or more important to be known and *attended to*, than the general doctrine of these letters ; and it equally concerns the wise and the ignorant, men of speculation or men of business, those who are capable of the greatest refinement, and those who cannot refine at all. For how different soever our turns of thinking, or modes of life, may be, we are all equally subjects of God's moral government, if there be a God and a governor, and equally *heirs of immortality*, if there be any immortality for man.

Some may consider the critical review of Mr. Hume's metaphysical writings, in the last of these letters, as ungenerous, now that he is dead and unable to make any reply. But this circumstance makes no difference in his particular case, as it was a maxim with him (and perhaps one instance of the great *wisdom* that Dr. Smith * ascribes to him) to take no notice of any objections to his writings ; † and he has left behind him a guardian of his reputation, of ability, in my opinion, fully equal to his own, and whose friendship for him cannot be questioned.

* In the conclusion of his letter to Mr. Strahan, annexed to Hume's *Life.*
† See his *Own Life*, 1777, p. 15, and Vol. III. p. 204.

LETTERS

TO A

PHILOSOPHICAL UNBELIEVER.

———◆◆———

LETTER I.

Of the NATURE of EVIDENCE.

DEAR SIR,[*]

I AM sorry to find that, in consequence of the books you have lately read, and of the company you have been obliged to keep, especially on your travels, you have found your mind unhinged with respect to the first principles of religion, natural as well as revealed. You wish me to attempt the solution of the difficulties you have proposed to me on those subjects; and I shall, without much reluctance, undertake to give you all the satisfaction that I am able.

You have not, that I know, any vicious bias to mislead you, by secretly inclining you to disbelieve a system which threatens vice with future punishment. And, though it is always flattering to a person of a speculative turn to be ranked with those whose mode of thinking is the most *fashionable*, being connected with ideas of liberality, courage, manliness, freedom from vulgar prejudices, &c. yet, as you have not particularly distinguished yourself in this line, either by writing, taking the lead in conversation, or in any other way, I flatter myself that your bias of this kind (though it will draw you more strongly than you can be aware of yourself) may not be too strong for rational evidence, or such as the nature of the thing admits of.

[*] It appears from an early part of the author's *Memoirs*, that he was hardly " reconciled to the idea of writing to a fictitious person on this occasion, though," as he justly adds, " nothing can be more innocent, or sometimes more proper." In another part of the *Memoirs*, he says of these *Letters*, " Having conversed so much with unbelievers, at home and abroad, I thought I should be able to combat their prejudices with advantage, and with this view I wrote," &c.

Otherwise, you are not so little read in the world, as not to have perceived, that there are many prejudices which no *evidence* can overcome. No person can possibly be sensible of this in himself, but we all see it in others; and we see that it extends to subjects of all kinds, theology, metaphysics, politics and common life. These prejudices arise from what are commonly called *false views of things*, or improper associations of ideas, which in the extreme become *delirium* or *madness*, and are conspicuous to every person, except to him who actually labours under this disorder of mind.

Now, as the causes of the wrong associations of ideas affect men of letters as well as other persons (though generally in a different way, and perhaps not, upon the whole, in the same degree), they may have the same bias to incredulity in some cases, that others have to credulity; and the same person, who is the most unreasonably incredulous in some things, may be as unreasonably credulous, and even superstitious, in others; so little ought we to take it for granted, that a man who thinks rationally on some subjects will do so uniformly, and may be confided in as a safe guide in all. This, however, is agreeable to other analogies; as, for instance, with respect to courage; for the extreme of bravery in some respects is often found united with the extreme of cowardice in others.

You know a friend of ours, by no means deficient in point of general understanding, who to the fashionable infidelity adds the fashionable follies of the age. Though he believes nothing of *invisible powers* of any kind, he has a predilection for a certain class of numbers in the lottery, and, when he is eagerly engaged in gaming, must throw his dice in particular, and what we think whimsical, circumstances. Now, what is this better than *whistling for a wind* (which, however, we find many sensible sailors continue to practise), the *Roman auguries*, or the weakest of the Popish superstitions?

The fact is, that in some manner, which perhaps neither himself nor any other person can explain, he has connected in his mind the idea of some peculiar circumstances with that of a successful throw, and the idea of other peculiar circumstances with that of an unsuccessful one, just as we happen to connect in our minds the ideas of *darkness* and of *apparitions;* which association, when it is once formed, often affects the mind more or less through life, and long after all belief in apparitions is given up, and even ridiculed.

I might enforce this observation, which is far from being

foreign to our present purpose, by reminding you, that there are both able and upright men on both sides of what we think the clearest of all questions, in morals, theology and politics. How often have you expressed your astonishment, that any person should hold the doctrine that you reprobate concerning the *Middlesex election*, and the *taxation of America*, and yet think himself the friend of liberty, and the enemy of all oppression and tyranny.

Had not mortality come in aid of the demonstrations on which the Newtonian system of the universe is founded, it is not certain that it would even yet have supplanted the Aristotelian, or Cartesian system, ill-founded as they were. But the old and incorrigibly bigoted abettors of former hypotheses leaving the stage, reason had a better chance with the younger, and the less biassed.

When you reflect on these, and many other facts of the same nature, you will not wonder much, that so many sensible men of your acquaintance, and men of an ingenuous and candid disposition in other respects, struck with the glaring absurdities and mischiefs of superstition, should think it wise and right to take refuge in irreligion, and, not seeing where they can consistently stop, even disclaim the belief of a God. Nor do I wonder that, being men of ingenuity, their reasonings on these subjects should have staggered you. All this may be the case, and yet those reasonings be altogether inconclusive.

As you profess you have no objection to my considering you as ignorant as I please in every thing relating to this subject, I shall, in order to lay the surest foundation of a truly rational faith, take the liberty to begin with explaining what appears to me to be the natural ground of *evidence*, or of the *assent* that we give to propositions of all kinds, that we may see afterwards how far it may be applied to the subject of religion.

Now every *proposition*, or every thing to which we give our assent, or dissent, consists ultimately of two terms, one of which is affirmed of the other; as that *twice two is four*, the *three angles of every right-lined triangle are equal to two right angles; man is mortal, air is elastic*, &c. And the ground of our affirming one of these ideas of the other is either that, when they are considered, they appear to be in fact, the same idea, or perfectly to coincide; or else that the one is constantly observed to accompany the other. Thus the reason why I affirm that *twice two is four*, is, that the idea annexed to the term *twice two*, coincides with the

idea annexed to the term *four;* so does the idea of the
quantity annexed to the *three angles of a right-lined triangle*
with that of *two right angles.*   But the reason why I affirm
that *man is mortal* is of a different nature, and is founded
on the observation that all men are found to be so; and I
say that *air is elastic,* because every substance that bears
that denomination is found to restore itself to its former
dimensions, or nearly so, after having been compressed.

Propositions of the former kind, if they be true at all,
are universally and necessarily so, and the evidence for
them is called *demonstration.*   Of this kind are the indisputable propositions in geometry and algebra.   But propositions of the latter kind are always liable to be corrected
and modified by subsequent and more exact observations;
because it is not by comparing our own ideas only that
we come to the knowledge of their truth, and later observations may correct what was defective in former ones.

There are, however, propositions of the former kind,
the proof of which is not strictly demonstrative, because
the evidence of it does not arise from the comparison of
our ideas, but from the testimony of others, the validity of
which rests ultimately on the association of ideas; human
testimony in certain circumstances not having been found
to deceive us.   Of this kind is the proposition *Alexander
conquered Darius.*   For the proof of it is complete, when it
appears that the person distinguished by the name of
Alexander, is the same with him that conquered Darius.
But since the evidence of this can never be made out by
any operations on my own ideas, I have recourse to the
testimony of others; and I believe the proposition to be
true, because I have all the reason I can have, to think
that a history so authenticated as that of Alexander and
Darius may be depended on.

Now, it is not pretended, that the evidence of the propositions in natural or revealed religion is always of the
former of these two kinds, but generally of the latter, or
that which depends on the association of ideas; and in
revealed religion, the evidence chiefly arises from testimony, but such testimony as has never yet been found to
deceive us.   I do not therefore say, that I can properly
demonstrate all the principles of either; but I presume
that, if any person's mind be truly unprejudiced, I shall
be able to lay before him such evidence of both, as will
determine his assent; and, in some of the cases, his *persuasion* shall hardly be distinguishable, with respect to its

strength, from that which arises from a demonstration properly so called, the difference being, as mathematicians say, less than, any assignable quantity. For no person, I presume, has, in fact, any more doubt either of there having been such a person as Alexander, or of his having conquered Darius, than he has of any proposition whatever. And yet sufficient and plenary as this evidence appears to me, it may fall far short of producing conviction in the minds of all ; for, in some cases, we have seen that demonstration itself will not do this.

I am, &c.

LETTER II.

Of the direct Evidence for the Belief of a GOD.

DEAR SIR,

HAVING premised the observations contained in the preceding letter on the nature of evidence, I proceed to observe, that no person can live long in the world without knowing that men make *chairs* and *tables*, build *houses* and write *books*, and that chairs, tables, houses, or books, are not made without men. This constant and indisputable observation lays the foundation for such an association of the ideas of chairs, tables, houses and books, with that of *men* as the makers of them, that whenever we see a chair, a table, a house, or a book, we entertain no doubt but, though we did not see *when* or *how* they were made, and nobody gives us any information on the subject, yet that some man or other *did* make them. No man can ever suppose that a chair, a table, a house, or a book, was either the production of any tree, or came into being of itself. Nothing, in the course of his own experience or that of others, can lead him to imagine any such thing.

He afterwards sees birds build nests, spiders make webs, bees make honeycombs, &c. and accordingly he, as before, associates in his mind the ideas of all these things with that of the animals that made them ; and therefore he concludes, when he sees a *honeycomb*, for instance, that *bees* have been at work upon it.

Finding, however, that some animals can, to a certain degree, imitate the works of others, and man those of most of them, he sees reason to limit his former conclusion, that such a particular animal, and no other, must necessarily have produced them, but (generalizing his ideas, from ob-serving something of the same nature in whatever can pro-duce the same thing, and calling it *similar power*) he says, that some being, of *sufficient powers*, has produced it.

Advancing, as he necessarily must, in the habit of gene-ralizing his ideas, he calls chairs, tables, nests, webs, &c. by the general term *effects*, and men, animals, &c. that produce them, by the term *causes;* and expressing the result of all his observations, he concludes universally, that *all effects have their adequate causes.* For he sees nothing come into being, in any other way.

He likewise sees one plant proceed from another, and one animal from another, by natural vegetation, or genera-tion, and therefore he concludes that every plant and every animal had its proper parent. But the parent plant, or parent animal, does not bear the same relation to its offspring that men do to chairs, books, &c. because they have no *design* in producing them, and no *comprehension* of the nature or use of what they produce. There is, however, some analogy in the two cases ; and therefore the parent plant, or parent animal, is still termed a *cause*, though in a less proper sense of the word. However, admitting these to be called causes, it is still universally true, that *nothing begins to exist without a cause.* To this rule we see no exception whatever, and therefore cannot possibly entertain a doubt with respect to it.

Again, wherever there are *proper causes*, as of *men* with respect to *chairs, books,* &c. we cannot but be sensible that these causes must be capable of comprehending the nature and uses of those productions of which they are the causes, and *so far* as they are the causes of them. A carpenter may know nothing of the texture of the wood on which he works, or the cause of its colour, &c. for with respect to *them* he is no cause ; but being the proper cause of the conversion of the wood into a chair, or table, he (or the person who employed him, or who first constructed these things, &c.) must have had an adequate idea of their nature and uses.

Observations of this kind extending themselves every day, it necessarily becomes a maxim with us, that wherever there is a fitness or correspondence of one thing to another, there must have been a cause capable of comprehending, and of designing that fitness. The first model of a wind-mill could not have been made by an idiot. Of such conclusions as these we have so full a persuasion, from

constant experience and observation, that no man, let him
pretend what he will, can entertain a serious doubt about
the matter. The experience and observations of all men,
without exception, are so much alike, that such associations
of ideas as these must necessarily have been formed in all
their minds, so that there is no possible cause of any difference of opinion on the subject.

Thus far we seem to tread upon firm ground, and every
human being, I doubt not, will go along with me. And if
they go thus far, I do not see how they can help going one
step farther, and acknowledge, that if a *table* or a *chair*
must have had a designing cause capable of comprehending
their nature and uses, the *wood*, or the *tree*, of which the
table was made, and also the *man* that constructed it, must
likewise have had a designing cause, and a cause or author
capable of comprehending all the powers and properties of
which they are possessed, and therefore of an understanding
greatly superior to that of any man, who is very far, indeed,
from comprehending his own frame ; being obliged to study
it, and make discoveries concerning it, by degrees, as he
does with respect to other things most foreign to himself, in
the general system of nature. And of the nature of the
immediate *perceptive power* itself, it is no more possible that
he should have any idea, than that an eye should see itself.

This reasoning, wherever it may lead us, I do not see how
we can possibly refuse to follow, because it is exactly the
same that we set out with, arising from our own *immediate
experience.* No person will say that one table might make
another, or that one man might make another. Nothing
that man does approaches to it. And if no man now living
could do this, neither could any man's father, or most
remote ancestor ; because we see no such difference in any
beings of the same species. Though, therefore, it should
even be allowed, that *the species* had no beginning, it would
not follow that it could be *the cause of itself,* or that it had
no cause; for the idea of a cause of any thing implies not
only something prior to itself, or at least contemporary with
itself, but something capable at least of comprehending
what it produces ; and our going back ever so far in the
generations of men or animals, brings us no nearer to the
least degree of satisfaction on the subject. After thinking
in this train ever so long, we find we might just as well
suppose that any individual man now living was the first,
and without cause, as either any of his ancestors, or *the
species itself.* For, that there is such a contrivance in the

structure of a man's body, and especially something so wonderful in the faculties of his mind, as exceeds the comprehension of *man*, cannot be denied.

For the same reason that the human species must have had a designing cause, all the species of brute animals, and the *world* to which they belong, and with which they make but *one system*, and indeed all the *visible universe* (which, as far as we can judge, bears all the marks of being *one work*) must have had a cause or author, possessed of what we may justly call *infinite power and intelligence*. For, in our endeavours to form an idea of something actually infinite, we shall fall greatly short of an idea of such intelligence as must belong to the author of the system.

It follows, therefore, from the most irresistible evidence, that the world must have had a designing cause, distinct from, and superior to itself. This conclusion follows from the strongest analogies possible. It rests on our own constant experience, and we may just as well say, that a *table* had not a designing cause, or no cause distinct from itself, as that the *world*, or the *universe*, considered as one system, had none. This necessary cause we call *God*, whatever other attributes he be possessed of.

Whatever difficulties we may meet with as we proceed, *so far* we must go, if we advance even the first step; and not to admit the first step, that is, not to admit that such a thing as a *table* had a prior and superior cause, would be universally judged to proceed from some very uncommon disorder in the mental faculties, and to be incompatible with a sound state of mind.

I shall, in my next, proceed to consider the difficulties that have been started on this subject by metaphysical writers; and whether I be able to do it to your satisfaction or not, I will, at least, do it with all possible fairness. In the mean time,

I am, &c.

LETTER III.

OBJECTIONS *considered*.

DEAR SIR,

HITHERTO we have met with nothing that deserves to be called a *difficulty* in the proof of the being of a God; and if nothing more could be advanced on the subject, it would, I think, justify us in refusing to attend to any thing that could be said by way of *objection;* because so far we have what is fully equivalent to a *demonstration* of the existence of a primary, intelligent cause. I shall now, however, proceed to the consideration of the principal difficulties that have been started on the subject.

The first in importance is, that, for the same reason that the universe requires an intelligent cause, that intelligent cause must require a superior intelligent cause, and so on *ad infinitum,* which is manifestly absurd. We may just as well, therefore, it is alleged, acquiesce in saying, in the first instance, that the universe had no cause, as proceed to say that the cause of the universe had none.

I answer, that to acquiesce in saying that the universe had no cause is, for the reasons that have been given already, absolutely *impossible,* whatever be the consequence. If, therefore, there be ever so little less difficulty on the other side of the dilemma, viz. that the cause of the universe had no cause, it is to that that we must incline.

Let us see then whether there be any other supposition, which, though it be a *difficulty,* or *incomprehensible* by us, does not directly contradict our experience, or whether by some independent argument it may not be proved, that, incomprehensible as it is, there *must* have been an *uncaused intelligent Being.*

Both these things have, in fact, been done before; but I shall here repeat them with illustrations, adapted to this particular difficulty, and, in order to this, I shall resume the argument in the following different manner.

Something must have existed from all eternity, for otherwise nothing could have existed at present. This is too evident to need illustration. But this *original being,* as we may call it, could not have been such a thing as a table, an animal, or a man, or any being *incapable of comprehending itself,* for such a one would require a prior, or superior author. The original being, therefore, must have had this prerogative as well as have been necessarily *uncaused.*

It is not improper to call a being, incapable of comprehending itself, *finite,* and a being, originally and necessarily capable of it, *infinite,* for we can have no idea of any bounds to such knowledge or power; and, using the words in this sense, we may, perhaps, be authorized to say, that, though a finite being must have a cause, an infinite one does not require it. Though it is acknowledged, that these conclusions are above our comprehension, they are such as, by the plainest and the most cogent train of reasoning, we have been *compelled* into, and therefore, though, on account of the finiteness of our understanding, it may be said to be *above* our reason to comprehend *how* this original being, and the cause of all other beings, should be himself uncaused, it is a conclusion by no means properly *contrary* to reason. Indeed, what the universally established mode of reasoning, founded on our own immediate experience, obliges us to conclude, can never be said to be contrary to reason, how *incomprehensible* soever it may be by our reason.

That there actually is an *uncaused intelligent Being*, is a necessary conclusion from what does actually exist; for a series of finite causes cannot possibly be carried back *ad infinitum*, each being supposed capable of comprehending its own effects, but not itself. Since, therefore, an universe, bearing innumerable marks of most exquisite design, *does exist*, and it would be absurd to go back through an infinite succession of finite causes, we *must* at last acquiesce in the idea of an uncaused intelligent cause of this universe, and of all the intermediate finite causes, be they ever so many.

On this side there is only a *difficulty of conceiving*, but nothing *contrary to our experience*, and there is plainly no other choice left us. Our experience relates only to such things as are incapable of comprehending themselves, or finite, and therefore require a cause. Consequently, though this experience furnishes a sufficient analogy for judging concerning all other things which have the *same property*, it by no means furnishes any analogy by which to judge concerning what is totally different from any thing to which our experience extends; things not finite, but infinite, not destitute of original self-comprehension, but possessed of it. Here is so great a difference, that, as the one must necessarily be *caused*, the other may be necessarily *uncaused*.

Though nothing can properly help our conception in a case so much above the reach of our faculties, it may not be amiss to have recourse to any thing in the least degree similar, though equally incomprehensible, as it may make it easier to us to acquiesce in our necessary want of comprehension on the subject. Now, in some respects, the idea of *space*, though not intelligent, and therefore incapable of self-comprehension, and no cause of any thing, is similar to that of the intelligent cause of all things, in that it is necessarily *infinite* and *uncaused*. For the ideas of the creation, or of the annihilation of space, are equally inadmissible: Though we may, in our imagination, exclude from existence every thing else, still the idea of *space* will remain. We cannot, even in idea, suppose it not to *have been*, not to be *infinite*, or not to be *uncaused*. Now it may be, in fact, as impossible that an *intelligent infinite Being* should not exist, as that *infinite space* should not exist, though we are necessarily incapable of perceiving that it *must* be so.

If it be said that space is properly nothing at all, I answer, that space has real properties, as cannot be denied, and I know of no other definition of a *substance* than that which has properties. Take away all the properties of *any thing*, and nothing will be left; just so also, and no otherwise, nothing will be left of *space* when the properties of length, breadth and depth, are supposed to be taken away.

Secondly, it may be said, that *a whole* may have properties which the parts have not, as a sound may proceed from the vibration of a string, the component particles of which could not produce any, or as the faculty of thinking may be the result of a certain arrangement of the parts of the brain, which separately have no thought. I answer, that it cannot but be that every *whole* must have some properties which do not belong to the *separate parts*, but still, if all the separate parts require a cause, the whole must; and whatever peculiar powers belong to a whole, as such, they must be such as necessarily result from the arrangement of the parts and the combination of their powers. But no combination or arrangement whatever of *caused beings* can constitute an *uncaused* one. This affects us like a manifest contradiction.

To say, that the whole universe may have no cause, when it is acknowledged that each of its parts, separately taken, must have had one, would be the same thing as saying that *a house* may have had no maker, though the walls, the roof, the windows, the doors, and all the parts of which it consists, must have had one. Such a conclusion, with respect to a house, or the universe, would equally contradict our *constant experience*, and what we may call our *common sense*.

With respect to *thinking*, we only do not see *how* it results from the arrangement of matter, when facts prove that it *does* result from it, the properties of *thinking* and *materiality* being only *different*, not *contrary;* whereas, *caused* and *uncaused* are the direct reverse of each other.

Supposing, however, that intelligence *could* result from the present arrangement of such bodies as the sun, the earth, and the other planets, &c. (which, however, is so unlike the uniform composition of a *brain*, that the argument from analogy entirely fails) so that all that is *intellectual* in the universe should be the necessary result of what is not intellectual in it, and, consequently, there should be what has sometimes been called *a soul of the universe*, the hypothesis is, in fact, that of a deity, though we ourselves should enter into the composition of it, and there would be a real foundation for religion. But our imagination revolts at the idea, and we are compelled, as the easiest solution of the phenomena, to acquiesce in the belief of an intelligent uncaused Being, entirely distinct from the universe of which he is the author.

Thirdly, it will be said, that, as all the intelligence that we are acquainted with resides in the brains of men and animals, the Deity, if he be a being distinct from the universe, and intelligent, must, whatever be his form, have in him something resembling the structure of the brain.

I answer, that the preceding train of reasoning proves the contrary. An uncaused intelligent author of nature, and one that is distinct from it, there must be. This Being, however, is not the object of our senses. Therefore the seat of intelligence, though it be something visible and tangible in us, is not *necessarily* and *universally* so.

Besides, it only follows from the Deity and the human brain being both intelligent, that they must have this in common, and something (if any such thing there be) on which that property depends; but this may not be any thing necessarily connected with what is visible or tangible, or the object of any of our senses. Many things have common properties that are very dissimilar in other respects. If we had known nothing *elastic* besides *steel*, we might have concluded that nothing was elastic but steel, or something equally solid and hard; and yet we find elasticity belong to so rare a substance as *air*, and altogether unlike steel in every other respect. The divine mind, therefore, may be intelligent, in common with the mind of man, and yet not have the visible and tangible properties, or any thing of the *consistence* of the brain.

There are many *powers* in nature, even those by which bodies are acted upon, where nothing is visible; as the power of *gravitation*, and of *repulsion* at a distance from the visible surfaces of bodies. There are even such powers in places occupied by other bodies. Both gravitation and magnetism act through substances interposed between the bodies possessed of them, and those on which they act.

The Divine power, therefore, may penetrate, and fill all space, occupied or unoccupied by other substances, and yet be itself the object of none of our senses. And what do we mean by *substance*, but that in which we suppose powers to reside; so that wherever powers can exist, what we call the substance cannot be excluded, unless we suppose beings to act where they are not.

Fourthly. It was said by the atheists among the ancients, that the universe might have been formed by the *fortuitous concourse of atoms*, which had been in motion from all eternity, and therefore must, they say, have been in all possible situations.

But, besides many other improbabilities, which may make it doubtful whether any person was ever really satisfied with the hypothesis, those who advanced it were not philosophers enough to know what *atoms* are. If we have any ideas to words, atoms must mean *solid particles of matter*, that is, masses of matter; which, however small, are perfectly *compact*, and therefore consist of parts that have strong powers of *attraction*. But what reason have we, from experience, to suppose it possible, that these small masses of matter could have those powers without communication *ab extra?*

In what respects could those atoms differ from pieces of wood, stone, or metal, at present; and is a piece of wood, stone, or metal, capable even of comprehending, much less of communicating its own powers, any more than a magnet? As well, therefore, might a magnet have been originally existent, as any coherent atom, or an atom possessed of the most simple powers whatever. In fact, we may just as well suppose a *man* to have been that originally existent being, as either of them.

Besides, admitting the existence of these original atoms, can we suppose them to have been moved any otherwise than as such bodies are moved at present, that is, by an external force? It is directly repugnant to all our experience to suppose any such thing; and could they be arranged in a manner expressive of the most exquisite design, without a mover possessed of competent intelligence?

Thus far, I flatter myself, I have advanced on sufficiently solid ground, in proving that there must have been an originally intelligent cause of the universe, distinct from the universe itself; or that *there is a God*. In proceeding farther I cannot promise to be always quite so clear, but I will promise to be *ingenuous*, pursuing such analogies as I am able to find, and no farther than they will naturally lead me.

Whether what I have already advanced will appear as satisfactory to you as it does to me, I cannot tell. If your mind be as unbiassed, as I am willing to hope it is, I think it must make some impression; for there is a strong natural evidence in favour of the belief of a God, and only something *incomprehensible* to us, but by no means contrary to evidence or reason, against it. And there is something so pleasing in the idea of a Supreme *Author*, and consequently, as I shall shew, of a Supreme *Governor* of the world, to virtuous and ingenuous minds, infinitely preferable to the idea of *a blind fate* and a *fatherless deserted world*, that if the mind was only *in equilibrio* with respect to the argument, it would, in fact, be determined by this bias. A truly ingenuous mind, therefore, will not only decide in favour of the belief of a God, but will so decide with joy.

I am, &c.

LETTER IV.

Of the necessary Attributes of the original Cause of all Things.

Dear Sir,

In the preceding letters I hope I have removed your greatest difficulties with respect to the belief of an *original intelligent cause of the universe;* having proved that, how incomprehensible soever such a Being may be to us, yet that such a Being must necessarily exist. My argument in short was this: There are in the universe innumerable and most evident marks of *design*, and it is directly contrary to all our observation and experience, to suppose that it should have come into being without a cause adequate to it, with respect both to power and intelligence. A Being, therefore, possessed of such power and intelligence, *must* exist. If this Being, the immediate maker of the universe, has not existed from all eternity, he must have derived his being and powers from one who has; and this *originally existent and intelligent Being*, which the actual existence of the universe compels us to come to at last, is the Being that we call *God*.

It is of no avail to say, that we have no *conception* concerning the original existence of such a Being, for our having *no idea at all* of any thing, implies no impossibility or contradiction whatever. This is mere *ignorance,* and an ignorance which, circumstanced as we are, we can never overcome; and the *actual phenomena* cannot be accounted for without the supposition of such a Being. Incomprehensible as it may be in ever so many respects, it is an hypothesis that is absolutely necessary to account for evident *facts.* We may, therefore, give what scope we will to our astonishment and admiration, yet *believe* (if we be guided by demonstrative evidence) we *must.* And it is a belief mixed with joy as well as with wonder. Let us now consider what may be either necessarily inferred, or is with the greatest probability implied, in the idea of this *original cause of all things.*

The first observation I would make is, that this Being must be what we term *infinite,* that is, since he is intelligent, there can be no bounds to his intelligence, or he must know all that is capable of being known; and since he is powerful (his works corresponding to what we call effects of power), his power must be infinite, or capable of producing whatever is possible in itself.

Since the reason why we cannot help concluding that a man, or any other being that we are acquainted with, could not be this originally existent Being, is the *limitation* of his knowledge and power (not being capable even of comprehending any thing equal to himself), and since this must have been the case with respect to any other being, how great soever, who had not this self-comprehension, the originally existing Being must necessarily have this power. A Being perfectly comprehending himself and every thing else, cannot have knowledge less than what may, in one sense at least, be termed infinite, for it comprehends *every thing* that exists. Admitting this, we cannot suppose that it does not likewise extend to every thing that *necessarily follows* from all that actually exists; and after this, we shall not know how to suppose that he should not be able to know what would be the result of any *possible* existence, for we cannot think this to be more difficult than the former.

Besides, in pursuance, in some measure, of this argument, we cannot help concluding, that a power capable of producing all that actually exists (so immense and wonderful is what is known of the system of the universe!) must be equal to any effect that is *possible in itself.* At least, if this inference be not strictly *necessary,* yet, having been compelled to admit the existence of a power so far exceeding all that we can comprehend, and all that we can imagine, when we even

strain our conceptions to form an idea of infinite, we can
see no reason why it should not be actually and strictly so.

Nay, having arrived at the knowledge of a Being who must
have the power of self-comprehension, and also that of producing all that exists, we seem to require some external
positive *cause of limitation* to his knowledge and power;
which external positive cause we look for in vain. We therefore cannot feel the least reluctance in acquiescing in the
belief that the original author of all things is infinite in
knowledge and power. Having proved him to be capable
of knowing and doing *so much*, we should, from a natural
analogy, even revolt at the idea of his not being able to know
and to do even *more*, if more were possible. This persuasion we arrive at by pursuing the most natural train of reasoning, and the most obvious deductions from the premises
before us; so that any other inferences would be *unnatural*.
We need not scruple, therefore, to consider it as an undoubted
truth, however exceeding our comprehension, and therefore
our power of *proper demonstration*, that God, the originally
existing being, or the first cause of all things, is a being of
strictly infinite power and knowledge.

Secondly. He must be *omnipresent*, or occupy all space,
though this attribute is equally incomprehensible by us with
the infinite extent of his power or knowledge.

That God must be present to all his works is a necessary
conclusion; while we all admit that no power can act but
where it is. Besides, existing, as he does, without any
foreign cause, by what we call (though inaccurately, as all
our language on this subject must be) *a natural necessity*,
there can be no reason why he should exist in one place
and not in another. He must, therefore, exist equally in
all places, even through the boundless extent of infinite
space, an idea just as incomprehensible as his necessary
existence, but not more so. After this, the probability will
be, that his *works*, as well as *himself*, occupy the whole extent of space, infinite as it must necessarily be, and that as
he could have had no beginning, so neither had his works.

Having been obliged to admit so much that is altogether
incomprehensible by us, it is by an easy chain of consequences that we come to these farther conclusions, which
are not more incomprehensible than the former. Nay, if
the universe had bounds, we should, if we reflect on the
subject, be apt to wonder at those bounds, as much as we
should wonder at any limitation to the knowledge of a
Being who has the inconceivable power of self-comprehen-

sion, or at the limitation of his power who has produced the universe.

Again, that a Being, infinitely intelligent and infinitely powerful, should remain inactive a whole eternity, which must have been the case if the creation had any beginning at all, is also an idea that we can never reconcile ourselves to. An eternal creation, being the act of an eternal Being, is not at all more incomprehensible than the eternal existence of that Being himself. Both are incomprehensible, but the one is the most natural consequence of the other. In fact, there is no greater objection to the supposition of the *creation* having been eternal, than to *duration itself* having been eternal; for there cannot be any assignable or imaginable period in duration, in which the creation might not have taken place.*

Thirdly. That this infinite Being, who has existed without change, must continue to exist without change, to eternity, is likewise a conclusion that we cannot help drawing, though, the subject being incomprehensible, we may not be able to complete the demonstration. It is, however, little, if at all, short of the force of a demonstration, that the same *natural necessity* by which he always has existed, must, of course, prevent any change whatever. Besides, if any cause of change had existed, it must have operated in a whole eternity that is already past. We should also naturally conclude that, as no being could *make* himself (since that would imply that he existed and did not exist at the same time), so neither can any being *unmake*, or materially change, at least not *annihilate* himself; and, being omnipotent, no other being, especially none that he himself has produced (and in reality there cannot be any other), can be supposed capable of producing any change in him. Whatever, therefore, the Supreme Being is, and always has been, he ever must be.

Fourthly. There cannot be more than *one* such being as this. Though this proposition may not be strictly demonstrable by us, it is a supposition more natural than any other, and it perfectly harmonizes with what has been strictly proved and deduced already. Nay, there seems to be something hardly distinguishable from a contradiction in the supposition of there being *two infinite beings of the same kind*, since, in idea, they would perfectly *coincide*. We clearly perceive

---

* This opinion of the infinity and eternity of the works of an infinite and eternal Deity, though it seems to me to be the most probable, is by no means a necessary part of the system of natural religion. The belief of the existence of a God, and of a providence, may very well be held without it. (*P.*) See p. 148, and Vol. II. p. 5.

that there cannot be two *infinite spaces;* and since the analogy between this infinite unintelligent being, as we may
call it, and the infinite intelligent one, has been seen to be
pretty remarkable in one instance, it may be equally strict
here; so that, were our faculties equal to the subject, and
had we proper *data,* I think we should expect to perceive,
that there could no more be two infinite, intelligent and omnipresent Beings, than there can be two infinite spaces. ·

Indeed their being *numerically two* would, in some measure, limit one another; so that, by the reasoning we have
hitherto followed, neither of them could be the originally
existent Being. Supposing them to be equally omnipotent,
and that one of them should intend to do, and the other to
undo, the same thing, their power would be equally balanced;
and if their intentions always coincided, and they equally
filled all space, they would be as much, and to all intents
and purposes, *one and the same being,* as the coincidence of
two infinite spaces would make but one infinite space.

I appeal to yourself, whether, after having admitted what
the *actual phenomena* of nature compel us to admit, we could,
without a real difficulty, and a manifest incongruity in our
mode of reasoning, stop in any part of the progress through
which I have now led you, whether every succeeding step
has been a strictly necessary consequence of the preceding
or not. Nay, the inferences have been so natural, that we
cannot help suspecting that it is owing to the imperfection
of our faculties, and our necessarily imperfect knowledge of
the subject, that we do not *see* the inferences to be perfectly
strict and conclusive.

We can hardly doubt but that a Being of infinite knowledge must clearly comprehend them all; that such a Being
must be able to perceive both that, independently of every
thing else actually existing, *he himself* could not but have
existed; that he could not but have had *infinite knowledge
and power;* that he could not have been excluded from any
part of even infinite space ; that he could not but have acted
from all eternity; that he could not be subject to any change;
and that there could not be any other being equal or comparable to himself, or that should not be dependent upon
himself. We do not see the necessary connexion of all these
properties, and therefore we cannot see *how* any other being
can ; but the case is such, that we cannot help suspecting
that it is owing to our imperfection that we are not able
to do it.

If you say that I have bewildered and confounded you

with these speculations, you must, however, acknowledge, that it has been in consequence of following the best lights the subject could afford us; and that to have come to any other conclusions, we must, in all cases, have taken a less probability instead of a greater, and something less instead of something more consonant to what we were, from the first, compelled by the plainest phenomena, to admit.

You will please, however, to observe that, in all this, I do not pretend to prove *a priori* that, without any regard to the supposition of an external world, there must have been what may be called a *self-existent Being;* but only that, having first proved, from the phenomena of nature, that there must have been an eternally existing intelligent Being, we cannot help concluding (at least according to the strongest probabilities) that, in consequence of being *originally existing*, and the intelligent cause of all things, he must be infinitely knowing and powerful, fill infinite space, and have no equal.

I am, &c.

LETTER V.

The Evidence for the GENERAL BENEVOLENCE *of the Deity.*

DEAR SIR,

I FLATTER myself that, in the preceding letters, I have removed, or at least have lessened, your difficulties relating to the arguments for the being and primary attributes of the Deity. It is true that I have led you into the region of *infinites* and *incomprehensibles,* but then *reason* herself conducted us thither, and we did not lose sight of her while we were there. Among infinites there are analogies peculiar to themselves, and those who cannot form an adequate idea of any thing infinite may yet judge of those *analogies,* as well as of those of finites. Infinites frequently occur in geometrical and algebraical investigations, and yet the most clear and undeniable consequences may be drawn from them.

The phenomena of nature prove that there must have been some *originally existent being,* and of such a nature, that it could not derive its existence and powers from any thing prior to it. Consequently, it could not be any thing of a finite nature, such as plants or animals, or any thing that we see here; for these, not being able even to comprehend their own constitution, must necessarily have derived it from some being of superior knowledge and power; and the idea of the degree of knowledge and power requisite to form such a system as this, of which we are a part, cannot be distinguished from that of *infinite*. Indeed, had it been, in any respect, finite, it would only have been in the condition of a plant, or an animal, of a more perfect kind, and therefore, like them, would have required a superior cause. The evident probability therefore is, that the original intelligent cause of all things, and who must necessarily have been *uncaused*, is, in the strictest sense of the word, *infinite* in knowledge and power; as, for reasons that have been given, he must likewise be infinite in duration and extension, or commensurate with all time and all space. And though we are utterly at a loss to conceive *how* so great a being as this should himself require no cause, it is even demonstrable both that such a being *doth* exist, and that he *could not* have any cause, and therefore we *must* acquiesce in our inability of having any ideas on the subject.

This case is, however, evidently different from that of all finite beings, all of which necessarily require a cause; and, though we cannot conceive it, the reason why this great being requires none, may be *his being infinite;* just as space must necessarily have existed, and have been infinite, and without any cause whatever. A difficulty in conceiving *how* a thing can be, is no proof of its impossibility; and indeed there cannot be a clearer instance of it than the present. For nothing can be more evident than that such beings as plants and animals must have had a superior cause; nothing also can be more evident than that they could not have proceeded from each other by succession from all eternity; and therefore nothing can be more evident, than that the primary cause of all these things must himself have existed from all eternity, without any thing prior or superior to him, notwithstanding our utter inability to conceive *how* all this should be.

Since it is evident, from the innumerable marks of design through the whole system of nature, that the author of it is intelligent, and, consequently, had some *end* in view in what he did, let us, in the next place, inquire what this end probably was; and I flatter myself that, instead of meeting with more difficulties in this part of our inquiry, as has often been represented, we shall, in reality, meet with fewer than we have had before; and here analogy, founded on established associations of ideas, is our only guide.

Means and *ends* are perpetually, occurring to our observa-tion. Hence no habit is more fixed than that of distin-guishing them, and of perceiving the relation they bear to each other. We hardly ever see the hand of man without perceiving marks of. design, and they are not less evident in the works of God. That the *eye* was made for seeing, that is, perceiving the form and colour of remote objects, and the *ear* for hearing or perceiving the sounds made by them, is no less evident than that the *pen* and the *ink* with which I write, were made and provided for the purpose of writing.

We are likewise just as able, in many cases, to distinguish a *perfection* from a *defect* in the works of *nature*, as in those of *art.* For the analogy is so great, that we cannot help applying these terms to them, and reasoning in the same manner concerning them. If I go into a mill, and see every wheel in motion, and going with as little friction and noise as possible, I conclude that every thing is as the maker intended it, and that the machine is complete in its kind, answering the end for which it was made. But if I see a pinion break, and the motion of the machine in part ob-structed by it, I immediately conclude that this was not intended by the maker, since it must contribute to unfit the machine for its proper functions.

In like manner, judging of the works of God as I do con-cerning those of man, when I see a plant in its vigour, and an animal of its proper size and form, healthy and strong, I conclude that these are as they were intended to be, and that they are fitted to answer the end of their creation, whatever that was. These, therefore, I attend to, and not to trees that are blighted, or animals that are maimed and diseased, when I wish to form a right judgment of the design of their maker. And, indeed, we do see that, in general, plants and animals are, to a considerable degree, healthy, and that the sickly and diseased among them are exceptions to the general observation.

Now, what is health but a state of *enjoyment* in beings capable of it, and what is *disease* but a diminution of enjoy-ment, if not a state of actual *pain?* Since then the obvious design of the animal economy was *health*, and not *sickness*, is it not evident that the intention of their maker must have been their *happiness*, not their *misery?* I do not know any conclusion more obvious or more satisfactory than this. What the supreme Author of all things may *farther intend* by the happiness of his creatures, whether a gratification to *himself*, or whether it proceeds from a disinterested regard to *them*, I cannot pretend to judge ; but that the happiness of the creation was intended by the author of it, is just as evident as that the design of the millwright was that the wheels of his machine should keep in motion, and not that they should be obstructed.

If, notwithstanding this obvious design, deduced from the consideration of the animal economy, any of them, or all of them, should not be found in a state of actual health and enjoyment, I should rather infer that their author had missed his aim, and was disappointed in what he had in view, than imagine he had not *intended* their health and their happiness : as though I should find that all the mills in my neighbourhood stood still and could not be kept in motion, I should still be satisfied, from their construction, that they were intended to keep in motion, but that the artificer had been disappointed in his object. However, in nature, it is a fact that a state of health, (that is, tolerable though not perfect health,) is general, and a state of sickness comparatively rare. Upon the whole, therefore, the creation is happy though not perfectly so, and the obvious end of 'the creation is, in fact, in a great measure answered.

It is another argument for the benevolence of the Deity, that many, and perhaps all pains and evils, (the causes of pain,) tend to check and exterminate themselves ; whereas, pleasures extend and propagate themselves, and that without limits.

Pain itself is an affection of sentient beings. Now, all sentient beings that we are acquainted with, (in whatever manner that effect is produced,) endeavour to shun pains and procure pleasures, and all the known causes of them. And as our knowledge and power, in this respect, advance with our experience, nothing is wanting to enable us to exterminate all pain and to attain to complete happiness, but a continuance of being.

Mental pains do as certainly tend to check and exterminate themselves as the corporeal ones. For the sensations of shame and remorse always lead us to avoid whatever it be in our conduct that has exposed us to them ; and the satisfaction we feel from having acquitted ourselves with integrity and honour, does likewise encourage us to act the part that will best secure the continuance of that most valuable species of human felicity.

Where volition is not concerned, (though the laws of volition are as much as any thing else in the system of nature, the laws of God,) and mere mechanism takes place, it is acknowledged by physicians, that all diseases are the effort of nature to remove some obstruction, something that impedes the animal functions, and thereby to defer the hour of dissolution, and to recover a state of more perfect health and enjoyment; so that nothing is wanting to the removal of all this class of evils but a perfect *conformation*, and sufficient *strength* of those parts of the animal frame in which the disorder is seated, with sufficient *time* for them to discharge their proper functions. But the intention of nature, that is, of the God of nature, who works by general laws, (in which, of course, there are many exceptions,) is the same, whether the animal survive the struggle, which is generally the case, or whether it sink under it. A hundred diseases terminate favourably for one that is fatal. Every cold is the beginning of a fever, but very seldom proceeds so far as to receive so alarming an appellation.

If we look into the external world, we shall see equal reason to be thankful for cold weather, storms and tempests, with every thing else that we sometimes complain of, as far as we are able to understand their real tendency and ultimate effects. And they are not only less evils in lieu of greater, but also, (like the disorders to which the animal frame is subject,) tend to remove some obstruction, and to diffuse more equally, either the *electric matter* or something else, the equal distribution of which is requisite to the good condition of the world.

If we consider *man* the most important object in this part of the creation, we must consider corporeal pleasures as being of the least consequence to his happiness, because intellectual gratifications are evidently of unspeakably more value to him. Man enjoys the time past and future, as well as the present; and, in general, mankind are tolerably happy in this respect, deriving more pleasure than pain from *reflection*. Man always hopes for the best, and even past labour and pain is generally pleasing in recollection, so that whether he looks backwards or forwards, his views are, upon the whole, pleasing.

If we consider man in a moral respect, we shall find that for one man who really suffers from remorse of conscience, numbers think so well of themselves and of their conduct, that it gives them pleasure to reflect upon it; and, in fact, acts of kindness and benevolence far exceed those of cruelty; and in all respects, *moderation*, (which is the standard of virtue,) is much more common than *excess*; and, indeed, if it was not so, excess would not be so much noticed and .censured as it is. Upon the whole, virtue seems to bear the same proportion to vice, that happiness does to misery, or health to sickness, in the world.

Besides, to judge of the intention of the Creator, we should not only consider the actual state of things, but take in as much as we can of the *tendencies* of things in future. Now, it requires but little judgment to see that the world is in a state of *melioration* in a variety of respects ; and, for the same reason, it will probably continue to improve, and, perhaps, without limits, so that our posterity have a much better prospect before them than we have had.

A great proportion of the misery of man is owing to *ignorance,* and it cannot be denied that the world grows wiser every day. Physicians and surgeons know how much less, men suffer now than they did in similar cases formerly, owing to improvements in the science of medicine and in surgical operations. To read of the methods of the ancients, with respect to the stone in the bladder, is enough to fill one with horror. It was not till the time of Celsus, that the practice of extracting the stone was known ; and, till of late years, in comparison, it was not expected that one in twenty of those who submitted to the operation would recover ; whereas, it is now a tolerably safe operation, and besides, we are not without the hope of discovering methods of dissolving the stone without pain in the bladder. This is only one of many instances of improvements that lessen the sufferings of mankind. This skill is, indeed, in a manner confined to Europeans, but these occupy a considerable part of the globe, and the knowledge of Europeans will, no doubt, gradually extend over the whole world.

Civilization and good government have made great advances in Europe, and by means of this, men live in a state of much greater security and happiness; and even the intercourse between distant places and distant countries is both safe and pleasurable ; whereas, in former times, this intercourse was hardly practicable. Let any person read of the state of Italy, and that of the continent of Europe in general in the times of Petrarch, and he will be satisfied that the present state of things is a paradise in comparison with it.

War is unspeakably less dreadful than formerly, though it is a great evil still ; and as true political knowledge advances, and the advantages of *commerce*, which supposes a peaceable intercourse, are more experienced, it is fairly to be pre-

sumed that wars will not fail to be less frequent, as well as
less sanguinary ; so that societies of men, as well as families
and individuals, will find it to be their common interest to
be good neighbours, and national jealousy will give place to
national generosity.

The progress of knowledge and other causes, have greatly
improved the spirit of the various *religions* that have prevailed
in the world. Those peculiarly horrid modes of religion
which enjoined human sacrifices, as well as many abomi-
nable practices, have been long extinct ; and persecution to
death for conscience' sake, by which the world suffered so
much under the Pagan Roman emperors, and even the philosophical and mild Marcus Aurelius, as well as in the days
of Papal tyranny, and under other ecclesiastical hierarchies,
we have reason to think will hardly ever be revived, the
folly as well as the cruelty of these practices is so generally
acknowledged. In consequence of this greater liberty of
speculating upon all subjects, truth has a much fairer
chance of prevailing in the world, and the knowledge and
general spread of truth cannot fail, to be attended with a
great variety of advantages favourable to the virtue and happiness of mankind.

We have no occasion to consider by what particular
means these advantages have accrued to mankind ; for,
whatever the *secondary causes* may have been, they could
not have operated without the kind provision of the first
and proper cause of all, and therefore they are to be considered as arguments of his benevolence, or of the preference
that he gives to happiness before misery.

Upon the whole, the evidence for the *general benevolence*
of the Deity seems to be abundantly satisfactory, and all
that can be objected on this subject is to the *infinite extent*
of it. And yet it should seem that there can be no bounds
to an affection that has been proved to be *real*. Why the
Divine Being should love his creatures *to a certain degree*
and no more, why he should intend them a certain portion of happiness and not a greater, is a question that cannot easily be answered. The probability that an affection
unquestionably real is actually unbounded, disposes us
to inquire whether, notwithstanding appearances, this may
not be the case here. And, though we cannot prove, the
strict infinity of the divine benevolence, or give so much
evidence for it as we can for that of his power and knowledge, yet the probability will, I think, appear to be in

favour of it, if we sufficiently attend to the considerations that I shall urge in my next.

I am, &c.

—————

LETTER VI.

Arguments for the Infinite Benevolence of the Deity.

DEAR SIR,

HAVING shewn in my last letter, that the Supreme Cause of all things must be possessed of at least *general benevolence*, in this I shall endeavour to shew that, notwithstanding some seemingly contrary appearances, this benevolence *may*, in a sufficiently proper sense, be considered as *infinite*. For this purpose I would wish you to attend to the following considerations.

First. That any *dependent being* should be at all times infinitely happy must necessarily be impossible, for such a being must be infinitely knowing and powerful, that is, in fact, equal to the Divine Being himself. The happiness of every individual must, therefore, necessarily be *limited*, either in *degree* or by a *mixture of unhappiness;* and whether this necessary limitation is best made in one way or the other, can only be determined by the Deity himself. However, the method of limitation by *a mixture of pain*, will not, I dare say, appear uneligible to persons of competent judgment.

It is even a common thing, in human life, to prefer this *variety* rather than an unvaried degree of *moderate enjoyment*. This mode of limitation being supposed preferable, nothing remains to be censured but the *degree* of misery proper or necessary to be mixed with any proportion of happiness, and the *time*, and other *circumstances* of the introduction of this misery. And in this, no person, surely, will pretend to dictate to a Being of infinite wisdom, whose general benevolence is unquestionable. No objection of this kind, therefore, can deserve any reply.

In these respects, however, the probability *a priori*, in general at least, is in favour of what we see actually to take place; so that it is a fair presumption, that, as our experience advances, we shall see more and more reason to be satisfied with the dispensations of Providence: because, in general, we perceive a *gradation*, in every thing from worse to better, which is a circumstance highly favourable to happiness, as it encourages *hope*, which is itself a principal ingredient in human happiness. .

Several improvements in the state of the world in general have been mentioned already, and the like is no less manifest in the case of individuals; the sufferings of our infant state exceeding those that we meet with afterwards, all things considered. Supposing a state of health, and competent subsistence for all, which (being the evident intention of nature) must here be supposed, our enjoyments are continually increasing in real value from infancy to old age. Let a child have the most perfect health, it is impossible to educate him in a proper manner, so as to lay a foundation for his own future happiness, without subjecting him to many disappointments and mortifications, with respect to which, no satisfactory account can be given *him*, so as to make him acquiesce under them. Whereas, besides that the pursuits and enjoyments of manhood are in themselves greatly superior to those of childhood, we acquire by experience such a *comprehension of mind* as enables us to bear without murmuring the evils that fall to our lot; and as this comprehension of mind extends itself every day, supposing what here must also be supposed, (as being within the intention of nature,) a rational and virtuous life, our stock of intellectual enjoyments is augmenting continually, so that the most desirable part of a well-spent life is *old age.* And it is evidently and highly so, provided that, together with health, a man enjoys what is also the intention of nature, the society of a rising and promising family.

The peculiar satisfaction with which a Christian shuts his eyes on the world, will not, perhaps, be thought a proper article in this account; though, whether these hopes be well or ill-founded, they are *actually enjoyed* by great numbers of the human race, and, together with every thing else that actually takes place, must have been intended for us in this life. However, I am well satisfied that a properly natural death, or death occasioned by the mere exhausting (as we may term it) of the vital powers in a sufficient length of time provided no superstitious fears accompany it, is not attended with aversion or pain.

Perhaps no part of the general system will appear at first sight more liable to objection than this circumstance of *death*, and the train of diseases that lead to it. But, by this means, room is made for a *succession of creatures* of each species, so that the *sum of happiness* is, upon the whole, greater. With respect to man, unless the whole plan of his constitution, and all the laws of his nature were changed, it is unspeakably more desirable that there should be a suc. cession, than that the same individuals should continue on the stage always. For a new generation learns wisdom from the follies of the old, which would only have grown more inveterate every year. Thus the whole species advances more quickly to maturity; and to the *species*, the obstinacy, and other infirmities of old age, will probably be ever unknown.

Secondly. Pain itself, and *as such*, is not without its real. use, with respect to true happiness, so that, other circumstances (of which we can be no judges) being supposed right, we have reason to be thankful for the pains and distresses to which we are subject. For pain must not be considered only with respect to the moment of sensation, but also as to its future necessary effects ; and according to the general law of our nature; admirably explained by Dr. Hartley, the impressions of pain remaining in the mind, fall at length within the limits of pleasure, and contribute most of all to the future enjoyment of life : so that, without this resource, life would necessarily grow insipid and tiresome.

However, without recurring to abstruse considerations, it is well known that the recollection of past troubles, after a certain interval, becomes highly pleasurable; and it is a pleasure of a very durable kind. It is so generally known to be so as to furnish an argument for hearing troubles, and making them less felt at the time of their greatest pressure. Thus Æneas, in Virgil, is represented as saying to his companions in distress, *post hæc meminisse juvabit.**

Nothing can be more evident than the use of pain to children. How is it possible to teach them sufficient caution against absolute destruction, by falls, burns, &c. but by the actual feeling of pain from these circumstances? No parent, or any person who has given much attention to children, will say that admonition alone would answer the purpose ; whereas, greater evils are most effectually prevented in the admirable plan of nature, by the actual experience of less evils. What is more pungent than the stings of shame and remorse, in consequence of improprieties in conduct, and of vices? But

---

* Quoted, probably, from memory, instead of *forsan et hæc olim meminisse juvabit.* Æn. i. 203.

could prudence and virtue be effectually, inculcated by
any other means ? No person conversant in the business
of education will venture to say that they could.

As the pains and mortifications of our infant state are
the natural means of lessening, the pains and mortifications of advanced life, so I made it appear to the satisfaction of Dr. Hartley, in the short correspondence I had
with him, that his theory furnishes pretty fair presump-
tions that the pains of this life may suffice for the whole
of our future existence, we having now resources enow
for a perpetual increase in happiness, without any assis-
stance from the sensation of future pain. This speculation
will probably appear before the public in due time, together
with other observations relating to the extension and application of this wonderfully simple theory of the mental
affections.*

These considerations appear to me abundantly sufficient
to convince us that even the unlimited benevolence of the
Author of nature is not affected by the partial evils to
which we are subject. But still it will be said, that a
Being of pure and perfect benevolence might have obviated this inconvenience, by a different original constitution
of nature, in which evils might not have been necessary,
not being of any use to us, as such.

But, I answer, this is more than we can pretend to say is
even *possible*, or within the limits of infinite power itself;
and there is this pretty good reason for presuming that it is
so, which is, that in present circumstances, we always see,
(wherever we can see enough to be in any measure judges,)
that the methods that are taken are the best for us, all other
things connected with them being considered, and the same
disposition in our author to provide the best for us in one
case would lead him to provide the best for us in another ;
so that, if *cæteris manentibus*, every thing is for the best, we
may conclude that the *whole* is for the best ; the disposition
of mind to make this provision being the very same in both
cases.

Supposing it possible, therefore, for the Divine Being
to have created men with all the feelings and ideas that
are acquired in the course of a painful and laborious
life, since it must have been in violation of all *general
laws*, we have reason to conclude that laws, or general
methods of acting, are preferable to no laws at all ; and

---

* See how this design was frustrated. Vol. III. p. 7, Note.

that it is better, upon the whole, that the divine agency should not be so very conspicuous, as it must have been, upon the plan of a constant and momentary interference.

It is plain there could be little room for the exercise of *wisdom* in God or man, if there had been no general laws. For the whole plan of nature, from which we infer design or wisdom, is admirable, chiefly on account of its being a system of wonderfully general and simple laws, so that innumerable ends are gained by the fewest means, and the greatest good produced with the least possible evil. And the wisdom and foresight of man could have had no scope if there had been no invariable plan of nature to be the object of his investigation and study, by which to guide his conduct and direct his expectations.

In comparison with the solid advantages we derive from the exercise of our faculties on this plan of general laws, how trifling are those that would accrue to us from even the frequent interruption, and much more, from the total abrogation of them. What could we gain but that a child falling into the fire should not be burned, or that a man falling from a precipice should not be dashed to pieces ? But all the accidents that happen of this kind, and which our reason is given us to enable us to guard against, are surely not to be bought off at such a price as this. How little do we suffer on the whole by accidents from *fire*, compared with the benefits we derive from it; and how much greater gainers are we still on the balance, by the great *law of gravitation!*

The advantage, if not the necessity of general laws, is best seen in the conduct of a large family, of a school, or of a community, because the good of the whole must be consulted in conjunction with that of each indivi-dual; and we often find it to be wise and right to suffer individuals to bring themselves into difficulties, from which we would gladly relieve them, if we had not respect to others who are equally under our care. How often is a favourite child or pupil punished, or an useful member of society falsely convicted of a crime, suffered to die, rather than violate general rules salutary to the whole! Now, as small societies cannot be governed without general rules and particular inconveniences, it may, for any thing that we know, be naturally impossible to govern the large society of mankind without such general laws, though attended with particular inconveniencies. [11]

If it be said that the Divine Being might *conceal* his violation of the laws of nature for the benefit of individuals, I answer that those individuals would, without a second interference, lose the benefit they would have derived from their sufferings, as such (teaching them caution, &c.) ; and if the Divine Being did this in all cases to prevent all evil, there would be no general laws at all ; and who can direct him when to interfere and when not ? As to very rare cases, it is possible, though I own not probable, because it would imply a want of foresight in the original plan, that the Divine Being does interfere in this invisible manner.

If we consider the human race as the most valuable of the divine productions on the face of the earth, and intellectual happiness as the most valuable part of their happiness ; if the training of men to get elevation of thought, comprehension of mind, virtuous affections and generous actions, be any object with the great Author of all things, (and the good of the whole seems to require that there should be a proportion of such exalted beings,) this world, with all its imperfections, as we think them, is perhaps the best possible school in which they could be thus trained. How could we be taught compassion for others, without suffering ourselves, and where could the rudiments of the heroic virtues of fortitude, patience, clemency, &c. be acquired but in the school of adversity, in struggling with hardships, and contending with oppression, ingratitude, and other vices, moral evils as well as natural ones ?

If we suppose these truly great minds formed here as in a *nursery,* for the purposes of future existence respecting their own happiness or that of others, the consideration will furnish another argument for the present state of things. What evidence there is of this being the case we shall see hereafter.

Upon the whole, it is very possible, notwithstanding some appearances to the contrary, that the affection of the Universal Parent to his offspring may be even *boundless,* or, properly speaking, *infinite,* and also that the actual happiness of the whole creation may be considered as infinite, notwithstanding all the partial evil there is in it. For if good prevail upon the whole, the creation being supposed infinite, happiness will be infinitely extended ; and in the eye of a being of perfect comprehension, such as the Divine Being must be, capable of perceiving the balance of good only, it will be happiness unmixed with misery. Nay, supposing men, (and it is of men only that I am now treating,) to live for ever, if each be happy upon the whole, and especially if the happiness of each be constantly accelerated, each individual may be said to be infinitely happy in the whole of his existence, so that to the divine comprehension, the whole will be happiness *infinito-infinite*. See Dr. Hartley's admirable illustration of this subject, in the second volume of his *Observations on Man*, Prop. iv.

I am, &c.

LETTER VII.

The Evidence of the Moral Government of the World, and the Branches of Natural Religion.

DEAR SIR,

IF you will admit that I have proved to your satisfaction that there is a God, a first cause, possessed of infinite power, wisdom and goodness, or only of such degrees of those attributes as, in a popular sense of the word, may be deemed infinite, that is, far exceeding our comprehension, nothing more will be requisite to prove every moral perfection, and that we are under a proper *moral government*.

Justice, mercy and veracity, with every thing else that is of a *moral nature*, are in fact, and philosophically considered, only modifications of benevolence. For a Being, simply and truly *benevolent*, will necessarily act according to what are called the rules of *justice*, *mercy* and *veracity*, because in no other way can he promote the good of such moral agents as are subject to his government. Even *justice* itself, which seems to be the most opposite to goodness, is such a degree of severity, or pains and penalties so inflicted, as will produce the best effect, with respect both to those who are exposed to them, and to others who are under the same government; or, in other words, that degree of evil which is calculated to produce the greatest degree of good: and if the punishment exceed this measure, if, in any instance, it be an *unnecessary* or *useless suffering*, it is always censured as *cruelty*, and it is not even called justice, but real injustice.

For the same reason, if, in any particular case, the strict execution of the law would do more harm than good, it is universally agreed that the punishment ought to be remitted, and then what we call *mercy* or clemency will take place; but it does not deserve the name of clemency, nor is it worthy of commendation as a virtue, but it is censured as a weakness, or something worse, if it be so circumstanced as to encourage the commission of crimes, and, consequently, make, more suffering necessary in future. In short, a truly good and wise governor frames the whole of his administration with a view to the happiness of his subjects, or he will endeavour to produce the greatest sum of happiness with the least possible mixture of pain or misery.

But you will check me in the course of this argument, and say that if moral government be the necessary result of benevolence, we ought to perceive some traces of this moral government before we can admit the Supreme Being to be benevolent, and that this ought to be the principal argument for his benevolence.

I acknowledge it, but at the same time I must observe that any independent evidence of benevolence, such as I have produced, is a strong proof, *a priori,* that there will be a moral government ; because, as I have just shewn, if benevolence be uniform and consistent, it must produce moral government where moral agents are concerned, so that, having this previous reason to expect a moral government, we ought to suppose that such a government *does* exist, unless there be evident proof of the contrary : because if this proof be indisputable, it must be concluded that the Supreme Being is benevolent, of which we are supposed to have already other independent evidence.

Now, the mere *delay of punishment,* which is all that we can allege against the reality of a present moral government, is no evidence against it, so long as the offender is within the reach of justice, because it may be an instance of the wisdom and just discretion of a governor to give all his subjects a sufficient *trial,* and treat them according to their *general character,* allowing sufficient time in which to form that character, rather than exact an immediate punishment for every particular offence.

It is no uncommon thing with *men* not to punish for the first offence, but to give room for amendment ; and it may be the more expected of *God,* whose justice no criminal can finally escape, and whose penetration no artifice can impose upon. Had human magistrates more knowledge and more power, they might, in that proportion, give greater scope to men to form and to shew their characters, by deferring to take cognizance of crimes. It is because criminals may impose upon them by pretences of reformation, or escape from their hands, that it is, in general, wise in them to animadvert upon crimes without much delay, and with few exceptions.

For any thing that appears, therefore, the present state of the world, notwithstanding, in some respects, *all things fall alike to all*, and a visible distinction is not always made between the righteous and the wicked; and even, notwithstanding the wicked may, in some cases, derive an advantage from their vices, may perfectly correspond to such a state of moral government as a Being of infinite wisdom and power would exercise towards mankind. And if this only *may* be the case, any independent evidence of the divine benevolence ought to make us conclude that this *is* the case, and lead us to expect that, at a proper time, (of which the Divine Being himself is the only judge,) both the righteous and the wicked will meet with their just and full recompense.

But there is not wanting *independent* and sufficient evidence of a moral government of the world, similar to the independent evidence of the benevolence of its author. For, notwithstanding what has been admitted above, respecting the promiscuous distribution of happiness and misery in the world, it is unquestionable, that virtue gives a man a better chance for happiness than vice.

What happiness can any man enjoy without *health?* And is not temperance favourable to health, and intemperance the bane of it? What are all the outward advantages of life without *peace of mind?* And, whatever be the proximate cause of it, it is a fact, and therefore must have been the intention of our Maker, that peace of mind is the natural companion of integrity and honour, and not of fraud and injustice. It is the fruit of benevolence, and of that course of conduct which arises from it, and by no means of malevolence. Do we not also see that a moderate competency, which is much more valuable than riches, is generally the reward of fidelity and industry, and that possessions acquired by dishonest arts are very insecure, if, on other accounts, a man could have any enjoyment of them. What but common observation has given rise to the common proverb, that *honesty is the best policy?*

The best definition and criterion of virtue, is that disposition of mind, and that course of conduct arising from it, which is best calculated to promote a man's own happiness and the happiness of others with whom he is connected; and to prove any thing to be really and ultimately mischievous, is the same thing as to prove it to be vicious and

wrong. The rule of temperance is to eat and drink so as to
lay a foundation for health, and consequently enjoyment;
and intemperance does not consist in the pleasure we receive
from the gratification of our appetites, but in procuring
momentary pleasure with future and more lasting pain, in
.aying a foundation for diseases, and thereby disqualifying a
man for enjoying life himself, or contributing to the happi-
'ness of others who are dependent upon him. In the same
manner we fix the boundaries of all the vices and all the
virtues. Virtue is, in fact, that which naturally produces
the greatest sum of good, and vice is that which produces
the greatest sum of evil.

In.short, the virtuous man is he that acts with the greatest
wisdom and comprehension of mind, having respect to what
is future as well as what is present; and the vicious man is
he that acts with the least just prudence and foresight,
catching at present pleasure and advantage, and neglecting
what is future, though of more value to him. It cannot,
therefore, but be, that virtue must, upon the whole, lead to
happiness and vice to misery; and since this arises from the
constitution of nature and of the world; it must have been
the intention of the Author of nature that it should be so.

Also, as from the *general* benevolence of the Deity we inferred his *infinite* benevolence, so from his general respect to
virtue, we may infer his strict and invariable respect to it;
and as it cannot but appear probable that partial evils must
be admitted by an all-powerful, and certainly a benevolent
Being, because they may be, in a manner unknown to us,
connected with, or productive of good, so there is an
equal probability that, in the administration of a Being of
infinite power and wisdom, and certainly a favourer of virtue
as of happiness, all irregularities in the distribution of
rewards and punishments are either only seemingly so or
merely temporary; and that, when the whole scheme shall be
completed, they will appear to have been proper parts of
the most perfect moral administration.

Since then, it is a fact that we are in a state justly entitled
to the appellation of *moral government,* (this being not only
presumed from the consideration of the divine benevolence
previously established, but also deduced independently from
actual appearances,) there must be a foundation for what
may be termed *natural religion,* that is, there is a system of
duty, to which we ought to conform, because there are
rewards and punishments that we have to expect.

. Our duty with respect to *ourselves* and *others* is, in general;

sufficiently obvious, because it is, in fact, nothing more than to *feel* and to *act* as our own true and ultimate happiness, in conjunction with that of others, requires. With respect to the *Divine Being*, we must be guided by analogies, which, however, are tolerably distinct.

Thus, if gratitude be due to human benefactors, it must be due in a greater degree to God, from whom we receive unspeakably more than from man ; and, in like manner, it must be concluded to be our duty to reverence him, to respect his authority, and to confide in the wisdom and goodness of his providence. For since he made us, it must be evident that we are not beneath his notice and attention ; and since all the laws of nature to which we are subject, are his establishment, nothing that befals us can be unforeseen, or, consequently, unintended by him. With this persuasion, we must see and respect the hand of God in every thing! And if every thing is as God intended it to be, it is the same thing to us whether this intention was formed the moment immediately preceding any particular event, or from all eternity.

If reverence, gratitude, obedience and confidence be our duty with respect to God, (which we infer from the analogy of those duties to men,) it is agreeable to the same analogy that we *express* these sentiments in words; and this is done in the most natural manner agreeably to the same analogy, in a direct *address* to the Author of our being, so that the principles of natural religion, properly pursued, will lead us to *prayer*.

That we should express our reverence for God, our gratitude to him, and our confidence in him, is generally thought reasonable ; but it is said that we are not authorized to *ask* any thing of him. But even this is unavoidable, if we follow the analogy above-mentioned. Considering God as our governor, father, guardian or protector, we cannot resist the impulse to apply to him in our difficulties, as to any other being or person standing in the same relation to us. Analogy sets aside all distinction in this case, and if the analogy itself be natural, it is itself a part of the constitution of nature, and, therefore, sufficiently authorizes whatever is agreeable to it.

It is no objection to the natural duty of prayer to God that he is supposed to know our wants, and to be the best judge of the propriety of supplying them. For we ourselves may have the same good disposition towards our children, and yet see sufficient reason for insisting upon their personal

application to us, as an expression of their obligation, and a
necessary means of cultivating a due sense of their relation
to us, and dependence upon us.

The idea of every thing being *predetermined* from all
eternity, is no objection to prayer, because all *means* are appointed as well as *ends;* and, therefore, if prayer be in itself
a proper means, the end to be obtained by it, we may be assured, will not be had without *this* any more than without
any other means, or other necessary previous circumstances.
No man will refrain from plowing his ground because God
foresees whether he will have a harvest or not. It is sufficient for us to know that there never has been, and therefore,
probably never will be any harvest without previous plowing.
Knowing this, if we only have the desire of harvest, plowing
the ground, and every thing else that we know to be previously necessary to it, and to be *within our power,* will be
done by us of course.

It is possible, however, that were we as perfect as our
nature and state will admit, having acquired all the comprehension of mind to which we can ever attain, and having a
steady belief in the infinite wisdom, power and goodness of God, with a constant sense of his presence
with us, and unremitted attention to us, our devotion
might be nothing more than a deep *reverence* and joyful
confidence, persuaded that all the divine disposals were
right and kind; and in their calmer moments very excellent and good men *do* approach to this state. They
feel no occasion to *ask* for any thing, because they feel
no want of any thing. But the generality of mankind
always, and the best of men not possessing themselves
at all times with equal tranquillity, must and will acquiesce in a devotion of a less perfect form. And the
Divine Being, knowing this imperfect state of our nature,
must *mean* that we should act agreeably to it, and *require*
of us expressions of devotion adapted to our imperfect
state.

This progress is also agreeable to the analogy of nature: for when our children are fully possessed of that
affection for us, and confidence in us, which was the
object and end of any formal prescribed mode of address,
&c. we do not insist upon the *form.* We are then satisfied
with their experienced attachment to us, and make them
equally the objects of our kind attention, whether they
apply to us in form for what they want or not.

In all this, you see, we must content ourselves with

following the best analogies we can find, and those are clearly in favour of a *duty to God* as well as to man ; and for the same reason, a duty and a behaviour similar to that which we acknowledge to be due to our parents, guardians and friends, but differing in proportion to the infinite superiority of the Supreme Being to every inferior being, and the infinitely greater magnitude of our obligations to him. Let us now see whether there be any analogy, from the common course of nature, that can give us any insight into the *extent* and *duration* of the system of moral government under which we manifestly are. But this I shall reserve for the subject of another letter. In the mean time,

·I am, &c.

LETTER VIII.

Of the Evidence for the future Existence of Man.

DEAR SIR,

I HAVE already observed that benevolence, once proved to be *real*, can hardly be conceived to be other than *boundless;* and this must be more especially the case with the Supreme Being, who can have no rival, or be jealous of any being whatever. Such beings as *we* are may really wish well to others, and yet may wish them only a *certain degree* of happiness; but then the desire of that limitation will be found, if it be examined, to be occassioned by something peculiar to our situation, as limited and imperfect beings, and what can have no place with the Deity. His benevolence, if real, must, as we should think, be boundless. He must, therefore, wish the greatest good of his creation, and the limitation to the present *actual happiness* of the universe must arise from *perfection of happiness* being incompatible with the nature of created, and, consequently, finite beings, and with that mixture of pain, which may be really necessary, according to the best possible general constitution of nature, to promote this happiness.

But pain, we have seen, tends to limit and exclude itself, and things are evidently in a progress to a better state. There is some reason, therefore, to expect that this *melioration* will go on without limits. And as exact and equal government arises from perfect benevolence, (and even, independent of the arguments for benevolence, does take place in some degree,) we cannot, as it should seem, but be led by this analogy to expect a more perfect retribution than we see to take place here, and, consequently, to look for a state where moral agents will find more exact rewards for virtue, and more ample punishments for vice, than they meet with in this world. I do not say that the argument from these analogies is so strong as to produce a *confident expectation* of such a future state; but it certainly, in fact, produces a *wish* for it; and this wish itself, being produced by the analogy of nature, is some evidence of the thing wished for.

1 .Other analogies, it is acknowledged, tend to damp this expectation. We see that men, whose powers of perception and thought depend upon the organized state of the brain, decay and die, exactly like plants, or the inferior animals, and we see no instance of any revival. But still, while there exists in nature a power unquestionably equal to their revival, (for it is the power that actually brought them into being at first,) the former analogies may lead us to look for this future state of more exact retribution, to which we see something like a reference, in this, and for a more copious display of the divine goodness, even beyond the grave.

On some, especially on persons conscious of great integrity, and of great sufferings in consequence of it, these analogies will make a greater impression, will produce a more earnest *longing*, and, consequently, a stronger *faith*, than others will have; and the same persons will, for the same reason, be affected by them differently at different times. This fluctuation, and degree of uncertainty, must make every rational being, and especially every good man, who rejoices in what he sees of the works and government of God, earnestly long for farther information on this most interesting subject; and this farther information we may perhaps find the Universal Father has actually given us.

I think it of some importance to observe, that the degree of moral government under which we are (the constitution of nature evidently favouring a course of virtue, and frowning upon a course of vice) is a *fact* independent of all reasoning concerning the existence of God himself, and, therefore, ought to determine the conduct of those who are not satisfied with respect to the proof of the being and attributes of God, and even of those who are properly *atheists*, believing that nothing exists besides the world, or the universe, of which we ourselves are a part.

Whether there be any *author of nature*, or not, there cannot be any doubt of there being *an established course of nature*; and an atheist must believe it to be the more firmly established, and see less prospect of any change, from acknowledging no superior being capable of producing that change. If, therefore, the course of nature be actually in favour of virtue, it must be the interest and wisdom of every human being to be virtuous. And farther, if it be agreeable to the analogy of nature, independent of any consideration of the author of it, that things are in an improving state, and, consequently, that there is a tendency to a more exact and equal retribution, it must produce an expectation that this course of nature will *go on* to favour virtue still more; and, therefore, it may be within the course of nature that men, as *moral agents*, should survive the grave, or be *re-produced*, to enjoy the full reward of virtue, or to suffer the punishments due to their vices. ...

It is acknowledged that we have no idea *how* this can come to pass, but neither have we any knowledge how we, that is, the human species, came into being; so that, for any thing we know to the contrary, our *re-production* may be as much within the proper course of nature, as our original production ; and consequently, nothing hinders but that our expectation of a more perfect state of things, and a state of more exact retribution, raised by the observation of the actual course of nature, may be fulfilled. There may, therefore, be a *future state*, even though there be no God at all. That is, as it is certainly, and independently of all other considerations, our wisdom to be virtuous in this life, it may be equally our wisdom to be virtuous with a view to a life to come. And, faint as this probability may be thought, it is however *something*, and must add something to the sanctions of virtue. Let not atheists, therefore, think themselves *quite secure* with respect to a future life. Things as extraordinary as this, especially upon the hypo-thesis of there being no God, have taken place, and therefore this, which is sufficiently analogous to the rest, *may* take place also.

Let any person only consider attentively the meanest plant that comes in his way, and he cannot but discover a wonderful *extent of view* in the adaptation of every part of it to the rest, as of the root to the stem, the stem to the leaf, the leaf to the flower, the flower to the fruit, the fruit to the seed, &c. &c. &c. He will also perceive as wonder-ful an adaptation of all these to the soil and the climate, and to the destined duration, mode and extent of propaga-tion, &c. of the plant. He will also perceive a wonderful relation of one plant to another, with respect to similarity of structure, uses and mutual subserviency. He will perceive another relation that they bear to the animals that feed upon them, or, in any other respect, avail themselves of them. In extending his researches, he will perceive an equal extent of view in the parts of the animal economy, their relation to the vegetable world, and to one another, as of the carnivorous to the graminivorous, &c. and of every thing belonging to them, to their rank, place and use, in the system of the world.

After this, let him consider this world, that is, the earth, as part of a greater system, (each part of which, probably, as perfect in its kind,) with the probable relation of the solar system itself to other systems in the visible universe. And then, whether he supposes that there is any *author of nature*, or not, he must see that, *by some means or other*, nothing is ever wanting, however remote in time or place, to render every thing *complete in its kind*. And if his mind be sufficiently impressed with these *facts*, and the consideration of the many events that daily take place, of which he could not have the least previous expectation, and of the efficient or proximate causes of which he is wholly ignorant, and he will not think it impossible, that, if any other particular event, of whatever magnitude, even the reproduction of the whole human race after a certain period, will make the system *more complete*, even that event may take place, though he be ever so ignorant of the proximate cause of it. That there is both a *power* in nature, and an *extent of view*, abundantly adequate to it, if he have any knowledge of *actual existence*, he must be satisfied. In proportion, therefore, to his idea of the *propriety* and *importance* of any future state of things, in that proportion will be his *expectation* of it. Our ignorance of the *means* by which any particular future state of things may be brought about, is balanced by our acknowledged ignorance of the means in other cases, where the result is indisputable ; though we are continually advancing in the discovery of these means, in our investigation of the more general laws of nature.

A retrospective view to our former ignorance in other cases will be useful to us here. Time was, when the total solution of a piece of metal in a chemical *menstruum* would seem to be as absolute a *loss* of it, as the dissolution of a human body by putrefaction, and the recovery of it would have been thought as hopeless. And, antecedent to our knowledge of the course of nature, the burying of a seed in the earth would seem to have as little tendency to the re-production of the plant. Where there certainly exists a power equal to any production, or any event, any thing that is *possible in itself* may be, and the difference in ante-cedent probability is only that of greater and less.

I am, &c.

LETTER IX.

An Examination of Mr. Hume's DIALOGUES ON NATURAL RELIGION.

DEAR SIR,

I AM glad to find that you think there is at least some appearance of weight in what, at your request, I have urged, in answer to the objections against the belief of a God and a providence; and I am confident the more attention you give to the subject, the stronger will those arguments appear, and the more trifling and undeserving of regard you will think the cavils of atheists, ancient or modern. You wish, however, to know distinctly what I think of *Mr. Hume's posthumous Dialogues on Natural Religion;* * because, coming from a writer of some note, that work is frequently a topic of conversation in the societies you frequent.

With respect to *Mr. Hume's metaphysical writings* in general, my opinion is, that, on the whole, the world is very little the wiser for them. For though, when the merits of any question were on his side, few men ever wrote with more perspicuity, the arrangement of his thoughts being natural, and his illustrations peculiarly happy; yet I can hardly think that we are indebted to him for the least real advance in the knowledge of the human mind. Indeed, according to his own very frank confession, his object was mere *literary reputation*.† It was not the *pursuit of truth*, or the advancement of virtue and happiness; and it was much more easy to make a figure by disturbing the systems of others, than by erecting any of his own. All schemes have their respective weak sides, which a man who has nothing of his own to risk may more easily find, and expose.

In many of his *Essays* (which, in general, are excessively wire-drawn) Mr. Hume seems to have had nothing in view

---

* "Dialogues concerning Natural Religion. By David Hume, Esq." 1779. Ed. 2.

† See his Life, written by himself, 1777, pp. 32, 33. *(P.)*

but to *amuse* his readers, which he generally does agreeably enough ; proposing doubts to received hypotheses, leaving them without any solution, and altogether unconcerned about it. In short, he is to be considered in these *Essays* as a mere *writer* or *declaimer*, even more than Cicero in his book of Tusculan Questions.

He seems not to have given himself the trouble so much as to read *Dr. Hartley's Observations on Man*, a work which he could not but have heard of, and which it certainly behoved him to study. The doctrine of *association of ideas*, as explained and extended by Dr. Hartley, supplies materials for the most satisfactory solution of almost all the difficulties he has started, as I could easily shew if. I thought it of any consequence ; so that to a person acquainted with this theory of the human mind, *Hume's Essays* appear the merest trifling. Compared with Dr. Hartley, I consider Mr. Hume as not even a child.

Now, I will frankly tell you, that this last performance of Mr. Hume bas by no means changed for the better the idea I had before formed of him as a metaphysical writer. The dialogue is ingeniously and artfully conducted. *Philo*, who evidently speaks the sentiments of the writer, is not made to say all the good things that are advanced, his opponents are not made to say any thing that is very palpably absurd, and every thing is made to pass with great decency and decorum.

But though *Philo*, in the most interesting part of the debate, advances nothing but common-place objections against the belief of a God, and hackneyed declamation against the plan of providence, his antagonists are seldom represented as making any satisfactory reply. And when, at the last, evidently to save appearances, he relinquishes the argument, on which he had expatiated with so much triumph, it is without alleging any sufficient reason ; so that his arguments are left, as no doubt the writer intended, to have their full effect on the mind of the reader. Also, though the debate seemingly closes in favour of the theist, the victory is clearly on the side of the atheist. I therefore shall not be surprised if this work should have a considerable effect in promoting the cause of atheism, with those whose *general turn of thinking* and *habits of life* make them no ill-wishers to that scheme.

To satisfy your wishes, I shall recite what I think has most of the appearance of strength or plausibility, in what Mr. Hume has advanced on the atheistical side of the question, though it will necessarily lead me to repeat some things that I have observed already ; but I shall endeavour to do it in such a manner, that you will not deem it quite idle and useless repetition.

With respect to the general argument for the being of God, from the marks of design in the universe, he says, " Will any man tell me, with a serious countenance, that an orderly universe must arise from some thought and art, like the human, because we have experience of it ? To ascertain this reasoning, it were requisite that we had experience of the origin of worlds, and it is not sufficient, surely, that we have seen ships and cities arise from human art and contrivance." Pp. 65, 66.

Now, if it be admitted that there are marks of design in the universe, as numberless fitnesses of things to things prove beyond all dispute, is it not a necessary consequence, that if it had a cause at all, it must be one that is capable of design ? Will any person say that an eye could have been constructed by a being who had no knowledge of optics, who did not know the nature of light, or the laws of refraction ? And must not the universe have had a cause, as well as any thing else, that is finite and incapable of comprehending itself ?

We might just as reasonably say, that any particular ship, or city, any particular horse, or man, had nothing existing superior to it, as that the visible universe had nothing superior to it, if the universe be no more capable of comprehending itself than a ship, or a city, a horse, or a man. There can be no charm in the words *world* or *universe*, so that they should require no cause when they stand in precisely the same predicament with other things that evidently *do* require a superior cause, and could not have existed without one.

All that Mr. Hume says on the difficulty of stopping at the idea of an uncaused being, is on the supposition that this uncaused being is a *finite one*, incapable of comprehending itself, and, therefore, in the same predicament with a ship or a house, a horse or a man, which it is impossible to conceive to have existed without a superior cause. " How shall we satisfy ourselves," says he; "concerning the cause of that Being whom you suppose the author of nature ? If we stop and go no farther, why go so far ? Why not stop at the material world ? How can we satisfy ourselves without going on *in infinitum ?*—By supposing it to contain the principle of its order within itself, we really assert it to be God, and the sooner we arrive at that Divine Being, so much the better. When you go one step beyond the mundane system, you only excite an inquisitive humour, which it is impossible ever to satisfy." Pp. 93—95.

It is very true, that no person can satisfy himself with going backwards *in infinitum* from one thing that requires a superior cause, to another that equally requires a superior cause. But any person may be sufficiently satisfied with going back through finite causes as far as he has evidence of the existence of intermediate finite causes; and then, seeing that it is absurd to go on *in infinitum* in this manner, to conclude that, whether he can comprehend it or not, there *must* be some *uncaused intelligent Being*, the original and designing cause of all other beings. For, otherwise, what we *see* and *experience* could not have existed. It is true that we cannot conceive *how* this should be, but we are able to acquiesce in this ignorance, because there is no *contradiction* in it.

He says, " Motion, in many instances from gravity, from elasticity, from electricity, begins in matter without any known voluntary agent; and to suppose always in these cases an unknown voluntary agent, is mere hypothesis, and hypothesis attended with no advantages." P. 147. He also says, " Why may not motion have been propagated by impulse through all eternity ?" P. 148.

I will admit that the powers of gravity, elasticity and electricity, might have been in bodies from all eternity, without any superior cause, if the bodies in which we find them were capable of knowing that they had such powers, of that *design* which has proportioned them to one another, and of combining them in the wonderful and useful manner in which they are actually proportioned and combined in nature. But when I see that they are as evidently incapable of this as I am of properly producing a plant or an animal, I am under a necessity of looking for a higher cause; and I cannot rest till I come to a being *essentially different* from all visible beings whatever, so as not to be in the predicament that they are in, of requiring a superior cause. Also, if motion could have been in the universe without any cause, it must have been in consequence of bodies being possessed of the power of *gravity*, &c. from eternity, without a cause. But as they could not have had those powers without communication from a superior and intelligent being, capable of proportioning them in the exact and useful manner in which they are possessed, the thing is manifestly *impossible.*

What Mr. Hume says with respect to the *origin of the world* in the following paragraph, which I think unworthy of a philosopher, and miserably trifling on so serious a subject, goes entirely upon the idea of the supreme cause resembling such beings as do themselves require a superior cause, and not (which, however, *must* be the case) a being that can have no superior in wisdom or power. I, therefore, think it requires no particular animadversion.

" Many worlds," he says, " might have been botched and bungled throughout an eternity, ere this system was struck out, much labour lost, many fruitless trials made, and a slow, but continued improvement, carried on during infinite ages in the art of world making." P. 107.

" A man who follows your hypothesis, is able perhaps to assert, or conjecture, that the universe some time arose from something like design ; but beyond that position he cannot ascertain one single circumstance, and is left afterwards to fix every point of his theology by the utmost licence of fancy and hypothesis. This world, for ought he knows, is very faulty and imperfect, compared to a superior standard, and was only the first rude essay of some infant deity, who afterwards abandoned it, ashamed of his lame performance. It is the work only of some dependent inferior deity ; and is the object of derision to his superiors. It is the production of old age and dotage, in some superannuated deity, and ever since his death has run on at adventures, from the first impulse and active force, which it received from him." Pp. 111, 112.

In reading *Mr. Hume's Life,* written by himself, one might be surprised to find no mention of a *God,* or of a *providence,* which conducted him through it ; but this cannot be any longer wonderful, when we find that, for any thing he certainly believed to the contrary, he himself might be the most considerable being in the universe. His maker, if he had any, might have been either a careless playful infant, a trifling forgetful dotard, or was, perhaps, dead and buried, without leaving any other to take care of his affairs. All that he believed of his maker was, that he was capable of *something like design,* but of his own comprehensive intellectual powers he could have no doubt.

Neither can we think it at all extraordinary that Mr. Hume should have recourse to *amusing books* in the last period of his life, when he considered the Author of nature himself as never having had any serious object in view, and when he neither left any thing behind him, nor had any thing before him that was deserving of his care.   How can it be supposed that the man, who scrupled not to ridicule his maker, should consider the human race, or the world, in any other light than as objects of ridicule or pity?   And well satisfied might he be to have been so fortunate in his passage through the world, and his easy escape out of it, when it was deserted by its maker, and was continually exposed to some unforeseen and dreadful catastrophe. How poor a consolation, however, must have been his *literary fame* with such gloomy prospects as these !

What Mr. Hume says with respect to the deficiency in the proof of the *proper infinity* of the divine attributes, and of a probable *multiplicity of deities*, all goes on the same idea, viz, that the ultimate cause of the universe is such a being as must himself require a superior cause ; whereas, nothing can be more evident, how incomprehensible soever it may be, than that the Being which has existed from eternity, and is the cause of all that does exist, must be one that *cannot* have a superior, and, therefore, must be infinite in knowledge and power, and consequently, as I have endeavoured to shew before, can be but *one*.

" As the cause," he says, " ought only to be proportioned to the effect, and the effect, so far as it falls under our cognizance, is not infinite ; what pretensions have we —to ascribe that attribute to the Divine Being ?—By sharing the work among several we may so much farther limit the attributes of each, and get rid of that extensive power and knowledge which must be supposed in one deity." Pp. 104, 105, 108.   This I think unworthy of a philosopher on so grave and interesting a subject.

It is owing to the same inattention to this one consideration, that, in order to get rid of the idea of a supreme intelligent cause of all things, Mr. Hume urges the superior probability of the universe resembling a *plant*, or an *animal*. " If the universe," says he, " bears a greater likeness to animal bodies and to vegetables, than to the works of human art, it is more probable that its cause resembles the cause of the former than that of the latter ; and its origin ought rather to be ascribed to generation or vegetation, than to reason or design." P. 129.

On this, *Demea*, the orthodox speaker, very properly observes, " Whence could arise so wonderful a faculty but from design, or how can order spring from any thing which perceives not that order which it bestows?" P. 137. In reply to which, *Philo* contents himself with saying, " A tree bestows order and organization, on that tree which springs from it, without knowing the order; an animal, in the same manner, on its offspring." Ibid. And " Judging by our limited and imperfect experience, generation has some privileges above reason; for we see every day the latter arise from the former, never the former from the latter." P. 140.

Manifestly unsatisfactory as this reply is, nothing is advanced in answer to it by either of the other disputants. But it is obvious to remark, that, if an animal has marks of design in its construction, a design which itself cannot comprehend, it is hardly possible for any person to imagine that it was originally produced without a power superior to itself, and capable of comprehending its structure, though he was not himself present at the original formation of it, and, therefore, could not see it. Can we possibly believe that any particular *horse* that we know, originated without a superior cause? Equally impossible is it to believe, that the *species of horses* should have existed without a superior cause.

How little then does it avail Mr. Hume to say, that " reason, instinct, generation, vegetation,—are similar to each other, and are the causes of similar effects;" p. 135, as if *instinct, generation* and *vegetation*, did not necessarily imply *design* or reason as the cause of them. He might with equal reason have placed other powers in nature, as *gravity, elasticity*, &c. in the same rank with these; whereas, all these must equally have proceeded from reason or design, and could not have had any existence independent of it. For design is conspicuous in all those powers, and especially in the proportion and distribution of them.

Pursuing the analogy of plants and animals, he says, " In like manner as a tree sheds it seeds into the neighbouring fields and produces other trees, so the great vegetable, the world, or this planetary system, produces within itself certain seeds, which, being scattered into the surrounding chaos, vegetate into new worlds. A comet, for instance, is the seed of a world, and after it has been fully ripened by passing from sun to sun, and star to star, it is at last tossed into the unformed elements, which every where surround this universe, and immediately sprouts up into a new system." P. 132.

" Or, if—we should suppose this world to be an *animal* ; a comet is the *egg* of this animal ; and in like manner as an ostrich lays its egg in the sand, which, without any farther care, hatches the egg, and produces a new animal ; so, does not a plant or an animal, which springs from vegetation or generation, bear a stronger resemblance to the world, than does any artificial machine, which arises from reason and design ?"   Pp. 132—134.

Had any friend of religion advanced an idea so completely absurd as this, what would not Mr. Hume have said to turn it into ridicule ! With just as much probability might he have said that Glasgow grew from a seed yielded by Edinburgh, or that London and Edinburgh, marrying, by natural generation, produced York, which lies between them.   With much more probability might he have said that *pamphlets* are the productions of large *books*, that *boats* are young *ships*, and that *pistols* will grow into great *guns ;* and that either there never were any first towns, books, ships, or guns, or that, if there were, they had no makers.

How it could come into any man's head to imagine that a thing so complex as this world, consisting of land and water, earths and metals, plants and animals, &c. &c. &c. should produce a seed, or egg, containing within it the elements of all its innumerable parts, is beyond my power of conception.

What must have been that man's knowledge of philosophy and nature, who could suppose for a moment, that a comet could possibly be the seed of a world ?   Do comets spring from worlds, carrying with them the seeds of all the plants, &c. that they contain ?   Do comets travel from sun to sun, or from star to star ?   By what force are they tossed into the *unformed elements*, which Mr. Hume supposes every where to surround the universe ?   What are those elements ; and what evidence has he of their existence ? Or, supposing the comet to arrive among them, whence could arise its power of vegetating into a new system ? What analogy is there in any of those wild suppositions to any thing that actually exists ?

What Mr. Hume objects to the arguments for the *benevolence* of the Deity is such mere cavilling, and admits of such easy answers, that I am surprised that a man, whose sole object was even *literary reputation,* should have advanced it.

" The course of nature tends not to human or animal felicity, therefore it is not established for that purpose."

P. 186. He might as well have said that *health* is not agreeable to the course of nature, as that enjoyment and *happiness* is not, since the one is the necessary consequence of the other. It " is contrary," he says, in fact, " to every one's feeling and experience" to " maintain a continued existence in this world—to be eligible and desirable.—It is contrary to an authority so established as nothing can subvert." P. 193. And yet almost all animals and all men *do* desire life, and, according to his own account, his own life was a singularly happy and enviable one.

" You must prove these pure unmixed and uncontroullable attributes from the present mixed and confused phenomena, and from these alone. A hopeful undertaking!" P. 195. If *evil* was not, in a thousand ways, necessarily connected with, and subservient to *good*, the undertaking would be hopeless, but not otherwise.

" It seems plainly possible to carry on the business of life without any pain. Why then is any animal ever rendered susceptible of such a sensation?" P. 205. But pain, *as such*, we have seen to be excellently useful, as a guard against more pain and greater evils, and also as an element of future happiness; and no man can pretend to say that the same end *could* have been attained by any other means.

" The conducting of the world by general laws—seems no wise necessary to a very perfect being." P. 206. But without general laws there could have been little or no room for *wisdom* in God or man ; and what kind of happiness could we have had without the exercise of our rational powers? To have had any *intellectual enjoyments* in those circumstances (and the sensual are of little value in comparison with them), we must have been beings of quite another kind than we are at present, probably much inferior to what we are now.

" Almost all the moral as well as natural evils of human life arise from *idleness;* and were our species, by the original constitution of their frame, exempt from this vice, or infirmity, the perfect cultivation of land, the improvement of arts and manufactures, the exact execution of every office and duty, immediately follow ; and men at once may fully reach that state of society which is so imperfectly attained by the best regulated government. But as industry is a power, and the most valuable of any, nature seems determined, suitable to her usual maxims, to bestow it on men with a very sparing hand." P. 213. And yet this writer can say, that there is not " any of mind so happy as the calm and equable." P. 259. But would not more industry and *activity* necessarily disturb this calm and happy temperament, and be apt to produce quarrels, and, consequently, more unhappiness?

" I am sceptic enough," he says, " to allow that the bad appearances, notwithstanding all my reasonings, may be compatible with such attributes as you suppose; but surely they can never prove these attributes." P. 219. But if present appearances prove *real benevolence*, I think they will go very near to prove *unbounded* benevolence, for reasons that I have alleged before, and which I shall not repeat here.

It is pretty clear to me, that Mr. Hume was not sufficiently acquainted with what has been already advanced by those who have written on the subject of the being and attributes of God. Otherwise he either would not have put such weak arguments into the mouth of his favourite *Philo*, or would have put better answers into those of his opponents. It was, I imagine, his dislike of the subject that made him overlook such writers, or give but little attention to them; and I think this conjecture concerning his aversion to the subject the better founded, from his saying, that there is a "gloom and melancholy remarkable in all devout people.". P. 259.

No person really acquainted with true devotion, or those who were possessed with it, could have entertained such an opinion. What Mr. Hume had seen must have been some miserably low superstition, or wild enthusiasm, things very remote from the calm and sedate, but cheerful spirit of rational devotion.

Had he considered the nature of true devotion, he must have been sensible that the charge of gloom and melancholy can least of all apply to it. Gloom and melancholy certainly belong to the system of atheism, which entirely precludes the pleasing ideas of a benevolent Author of nature, and of a wise plan of Providence, bringing good out of all the evil we experience; which cuts off the consoling intercourse with an invisible, but omnipresent and almighty protector and friend; which admits of no settled provision for our happiness, even in this life, and closes the melancholy scene, such as Mr. Hume himself describes it, with a total annihilation.

Is it possible to draw a more gloomy and dispiriting picture of the system of the universe than Mr. Hume himself has drawn in his tenth dialogue? No melancholy religionist ever drew so dark a one. Nothing in the whole system pleases him. He finds neither *wisdom* nor *benevolence.* Speaking on the supposition of God being omnipotent and omniscient, he says, " His power we allow infinite ; whatever he wills is executed ; but neither man nor any other animal is happy ; therefore he does not will their happiness. His wisdom is infinite ; he is never mistaken in choosing the means to any end ; but the course of nature tends not to human or animal felicity ; therefore it is not established for that purpose." Pp. 185, 186.

" Look round the universe," says he, " what an immense profusion of beings, animated and organized, sensible and active ! You admire this prodigious variety and fecundity. But inspect a little more narrowly these living existences, the only beings worth regarding. How hostile and destructive to each other ! How insufficient all of them for their own happiness ! How contemptible, or odious, to the spectator ! The whole presents nothing but the idea of a blind nature, impregnated by a great vivifying principle, and pouring forth from her lap, without discernment or parental care, her maimed and abortive children." Pp. 219, 220.

Compare this with the language of the pious writers of the Scriptures. " Thou art good and doest good. The Lord is good to all, and his tender mercies are over all his works. The earth is full of the goodness of the Lord. The eyes of all wait upon thee, and thou givest them their meat in due season. Thou openest thine hand, and satisfiest the desires of every living thing. The Lord reigneth : let the earth rejoice, let the inhabitants of the isles be glad thereof. Clouds and darkness are round about him ; righteousness and judgment are the habitation of his throne."

In the Scriptures, the Divine Being is represented as encouraging us to cast all our care upon him who careth for us. The true Christian is exhorted to *rejoice evermore,* and especially to *rejoice in tribulation,* and persecution for righteousness' sake. Death is so far from being a frightful and disgusting thing, that he triumphs in it, and over it. *O death, where is thy sting ? O grave, where is thy victory ?*

Would any person hesitate about choosing to *feel* as these writers felt, or as Mr. Hume must have done ? With his views of things, the calmness and composure with which, he says, he faced death, though infinitely short of the *joyful expectation* of the Christian, could not have been any thing but affection.   If, however, with his prospects, he really was as calm, placid and cheerful as he pretends, with little reason can he charge any set of *speculative principles* with a tendency to produce gloom and melancholy. If *his* system did not produce this disposition, it never can be in the power of *system* to do it.

Notwithstanding I have differed so much from Mr. Hume with respect to the principles of his treatise, we shall, in words, at least, agree in our conclusion.   For though I think the being of a God, and his general benevolence and providence, to be sufficiently demonstrable, yet so many cavils may be started on the subject, and so much still remains that a rational creature must wish to be informed of concerning his maker, his duty here, and his expectations hereafter, that what Mr. Hume said by way of cover and irony, I can say with great seriousness, and I do not wish to say it much otherwise or better.

" The most natural sentiment," he says, " which a well-disposed mind will feel on this occasion, is a longing desire and expectation, that heaven would be pleased to dissipate, at least alleviate, this profound ignorance, by affording some more particular revelation to mankind, and making discoveries of the nature, attributes and operations of the divine object of our faith.   A person seasoned with a just sense of the imperfections of natural reason will fly to *revealed truth* with the greatest avidity.—To be a philosophical sceptic is, in a man of letters, the first and most essential step towards being a sound believing Christian."   P. 263.

I am, &c.

LETTER X.

An Examination of Mr. Hume's Essay on a Particular Providence, and a Future State.

DEAR SIR,

You tell me you have been a good deal staggered with the eleventh of Mr. Hume's *Philosophical Essays,** " Of a *Particular Providence* and of a *Future State*," thinking his reasoning, if not conclusive, yet so plausible, as to be well entitled to a particular reply ; I shall, therefore, give it as

---

* " Philosophical Essays concerning Human Understanding, Ed. 2, with Additions and Corrections." 12mo. 1750.

much consideration as I flatter myself, after what I have already advanced on the same subject, you will think sufficient.

In the character of an Epicurean philosopher, addressing an Athenian audience, he says, " Allowing the gods to be the authors of the existence, or order of the universe, it follows, that they possess that precise degree of power, intelligence and benevolence which appear in their workmanship. But nothing farther can be proved, except we call in the assistance of exaggeration and flattery to supply the defects of argument and reasoning." P. 216. He farther says, " You have no reason to give *distributive justice* any particular extent, but only so far as you see it at present extend itself." P. 223.

This is the sum of his argument, which he has only repeated in his posthumous Dialogues, and the reasoning of which you will find obviated in the preceding letters. He himself makes a friend, whom he introduces as discussing the question with him, reply to it, that intelligence once proved, from our own experience and observation, we are necessarily carried beyond what we have observed to such unseen consequences as we naturally expect from such intelligence in similar cases.

" If you saw," says he, " a half-finished building, surrounded with heaps of bricks and stones, and mortar, and all the instruments of masonry, could you not infer, from the effect, that it was a work of design and contrivance; and could you not return again, from this inferred cause, to infer new additions to the effect, and conclude that the building would soon be finished, and receive all the farther improvements which art could bestow upon it?—Why then do you refuse to admit the same method of reasoning with regard to the order of nature?" &c. P. 225.

This reply appears to me to be satisfactory. But Mr. Hume refuses to acquiesce in it, on account of a supposed total *dissimilarity* between the Divine Being and other intelligent agents, and of our more perfect knowledge of man than of God. The substance of his answer is, that we know man from various of his productions, and, therefore, from this experience of his conduct, can foretell what will be the result of those of his works of which we see only a part. Whereas " the Deity," he says, " is known to us only by his productions, and is a single being in the universe, not comprehended under any species or genus, from whose experienced attributes or qualities we can, by analogy, infer any attribute or quality in him.   As the universe shews wisdom and goodness, we infer wisdom and goodness.   As it shews a particular degree of these perfections, we infer a particular degree of, them, precisely adapted to the effects we examine.   But farther attributes, and farther degrees of the same attributes, we can never be authorized to infer, or suppose, by any rules of just reasoning." Pp. 227, 228. He therefore says, " No new fact can be inferred from the religious hypothesis, no event foreseen or foretold, no reward or punishment expected or dreaded, beyond what is already known by practice and observation." P. 230.

But if the Deity be an intelligent and designing cause (of which the universe furnishes abundant evidence), he is not, in Mr. Hume's sense, an *unique*, of a genus or species, by himself, but is to be placed in the general *class* of *intelligent and designing agents*, though infinitely superior to all others of that kind ; so that, by Mr. Hume's own concession, we are not without some *clue* to guide us in our inquiries concerning the probable tendencies and issues of what we see.

Besides, admitting the Deity to be an *unique* with respect to intelligence, it is not with *one* of his productions only that we are acquainted. We see innumerable of them ; and, as far as our experience goes, we see that all of them advance to some state of perfection.   Properly speaking, nothing is left *unfinished*.   It is true that particular plants and animals perish before they arrive at this state, but this is not the case with the *species;* and all individuals, perish in consequence of some *general laws*, calculated for the good of the whole species, that is, of the greater part of the individuals of which it consists.   Consequently, without regard to the productions of other intelligent agents, we are not destitute of *analogies*, from which to infer a future better state of things, in which there may be a fuller display of the divine attributes both of justice and benevolence.

On the whole, therefore, if we see things to be in a progress to a better state, we may reasonably conclude that the melioration will continue to proceed, and, either equably or accelerated, as we have hitherto observed it.   Whatever be the *final object* of a work of design, yet, from what we know of such works, we can generally form a tolerable guess whether they be *finished* or *unfinished*, and whether any scheme be near its beginning, its middle, or its termination.   We are, therefore, by no means precluded from all reasoning concerning a future state of things by the consideration of the infinite superiority of the author of the system of the universe to all other intelligent beings. Notwithstanding his superiority to any of them, he may be said to be *one of them ;* and, without any information from the Scriptures, we might have discovered that in this sense, at least, *in the image of God has he made man.* Or, though God should not be considered as of the same class with any of his creatures, his productions, having the same author, supply abundance of analogies among themselves.

In the same manner, the benevolence of the Deity (which, in this place, Mr. Hume does not deny, but suppose) being simply admitted, we are at liberty to reason concerning it, as well as concerning the benevolence of any other being whatever. And therefore if, in any nearly parallel case, we can see no reason why benevolence should be limited, or why a *less* and not a *greater* degree of good should be intended, it must appear probable to us, that the greatest is intended ; though, for sufficient but unknown reasons, it cannot take place at present. Just as, if we are once satisfied that any particular *parent* has a just affection for his child, we conclude that, though he does not put him into immediate possession of every thing that he has in his power to bestow upon him, it is because he is persuaded that, for the present, it would not be for his advantage ; but that, in due time (of which we also naturally presume the parent himself to be the best judge) he will do much more for him, even all that his knowledge and ability can enable him to do. And though we may presume envy, and jealousy to prevent this in natural parents, we cannot possibly suppose any thing of this kind to affect the *Universal Parent*, because we cannot imagine any interference of interest between this parent and his offspring.

We always argue in the same manner concerning the conduct of a *governor.* If we are once fully satisfied with respect to his *love of justice,* and have also no doubt of his *wisdom* and *power*, we immediately conclude, that every incorrigible criminal in his dominions will be properly punished ; and though, for the present, many criminals walk at large, we conclude that their conduct is duly attended to, and that their future treatment will be made to correspond to it.

In like manner, if the present state of things bear the aspect of a scene of *distributive justice,* it may reasonably be considered as only the beginning of a scheme of more exact and impartial administration ; so that, in due time, virtue will be more adequately rewarded, and vice more exemplarily punished, than we now see it to be. Every thing, therefore, that I have advanced on this subject in the preceding *Letters* may be perfectly well founded, notwithstanding this particular objection of Mr. Hume, and notwithstanding the great stress he lays upon it, both in this work, and in his *posthumous Dialogues*.

I am, &c.

LETTER XI.

Of the SYSTEME DE LA NATURE.

DEAR SIR,

IT would be tiresome to you, as well as irksome to myself, to go over *all* the atheistical writers that have been admired in their time; but there is one work much more celebrated abroad than that of Mr. Hume will probably ever be with us, that you wish me not to pass unnoticed. This is the *Systéme de la Nature.**

After what I have already observed in my six first letters, and my animadversions on Mr. Hume's Dialogues, &c. it will hardly be in my power to select any thing from this work that I have not noticed already. However, as this performance is considered by many persons as a kind of *Bible of Atheism*, and the manner in which it is written, though far from being closely argumentative, is often excellent in the mode of *declamation*, and the writer is much more bold and unreserved than Mr. Hume, I shall make such extracts as I am confident you will acknowledge contain the essence of his argument, and will be, at the same time, a pretty just specimen of the composition of the whole, with short remarks.

This writer admits of nothing but what is the object of our senses, and, in the common sense of the word, *material;* and concerning the origin of matter, and all the present laws of it, he expresses himself as follows :

" If we ask whence came matter, we say it has existed always. If we be asked whence came motion in matter, we

---

* " Systéme de la Nature, ou des Loix du Monde physique et du Monde moral. Par M. Mirabaud, Secretaire perpétuel, et l'un des Quarante de l'Académie Françoise." *Londres*, 1770, 2 vols. 8vo. See Vol. III. p. 214. *Mirabaud* died 1760, aged 86. By the following passage it appears that the *Systéme* was unjustly ascribed to him : " On a mis sous le nom de cet académicien, après sa mort, un cours d'athéisme, sous le titre de *Systéme de la Nature*, 1770, en 2 vol. en 8vo, qui n'est qu'un réchauffé du Spinosisme. Il est inutile d'avertir que cette insolente Philippique contre Dieu, attribuée peut-être témérairement à un académicien de Berlin, n'est pas de *Mirabaud*." Nouv. Dict. Lyons, 1804, VIII. p. 308.

answer that, for the same reason, it must have been in motion from all eternity ; since motion is a necessary consequence of its existence, of its essence and its primitive properties, such as extension, gravity, impenetrability, figure, &c.* These elements, which we never find perfectly pure, being continually in action on one another, always acting and re-acting, always combining and separating, attracting and repelling, are sufficient to explain the formation of all the beings that we see. Their motions unceasingly succeed each other. They are alternately causes and effects ; and thus form a vast circle of generations and destructions, combinations and decompositions, which never could have had any beginning, and can never have an end. To go higher, for the principle of action in matter, and the origin of things, is only removing the difficulty, and wholly withdrawing it from the examination of our senses."†

I will acknowledge, with this writer, that matter cannot exist without *powers*, as those of attraction, repulsion, &c. more or less modified, as in the form of gravity, elasticity, electricity, &c. ; for take away all the powers, that is, all the *properties* of matter, and the substance itself vanishes from our idea. Consequently, if matter has been from eternity, these powers, and the motions which are the effects of them, must also have been from eternity. But then, in the *adjustment* of these various powers, and, consequently, in *imparting* them, there must evidently have been a knowledge, comprehension and foresight, of which the bodies possessing, and subject to those laws, are altogether incapable. I therefore conclude with certainty, that a Being superior to every thing that is the object of our senses must have imparted those powers, and have adjusted them to their proper uses ; that is, that he must have *created matter itself*, which could have no existence without its powers. I am unable

---

* " Lorsqu'on demandera d'où est venu la matière ᵎ Nous dirons qu'elle a toujours existé. Si l'on demande d'où est venu le mouvement dans la matière ᵎ Nous répondrons que par la même raison elle a dû se mouvoir de toute éternité, vû que le mouvement est une suite nécessaire de son existence, de son essence et de ses propriétés primitives, telles que son étendue, sa pesanteur, son impénétrabilité, sa figure," &c. *Système*, I. p. 27.

† " Ces élémens, que nous sens ne nous montrent jamais purs, étant mis continuellement en action les uns par les autres, toujours agissant et réagissant, toujours se combinant et se séparant, s'attirant et se répoussant, suffisent pour nous expliquer la formation de tous les êtres que nous voyons ; leur mouvemens naissent sans interruption les uns des autres ; ils sont alternativement des causes et des effets, ils forment ainsi un vaste cercle de générations et de destructions, de combinaisons et de décompositions, qui n'a pu avoir de commencement et qui n'aura jamais de fin.— Vouloir remonter au de là pour trouver le principe de l'action dans la matière et l'origine des choses, ce n'est jamais que reculer la difficulté, et la soustraire absolument à l'examen de nos sens." *Ibid.* p. 30.

to account for what is *visible* without having recourse to a power that is *invisible;* and this invisible power I distinguish by the name of GOD.

"What does the word God," says he, "mean, but the impenetrable cause of the effects which astonish us, and which we cannot explain?* In this God nothing is found but a vain phantom, substituted for *the energy of nature,* which men are always determined to mistake.† Men have filled nature with spirits, because they have been almost always ignorant of true causes. For want of knowing the force of nature, they have thought it to be animated by a great spirit. For want of knowing the energy of the human machine, they have supposed that, in like manner, animated by a spirit; so that we see the word *spirit* means nothing but the unknown cause of the phenomena that we cannot explain in a natural manner."‡

To this I can only say that, if nothing that is visible *can* account for what I see, I must necessarily have recourse to something that is invisible. Just as if I hear a voice which, I am convinced, does not proceed from any thing in the room in which I am, I cannot help ascribing it to some cause without the room, unless I could believe that such a thing as *sound* could originate without any cause at all. Now men, animals, plants, and even metals and stones, are things that we can no more suppose to have existed without a cause, than a mere sound.

I am not solicitous about the term *spirit*, but I must have some name by which to distinguish that to which I ascribe such *powers* as cannot belong to any thing that I am able to see. A human body may be, and probably is, the seat of all the powers that are exerted by man; but there is in the constitution of man (of whatever materials he may consist) marks of a design and intelligence infinitely superior to any thing that is found in man. He, therefore, *must* have some superior cause, and so must every thing else that, like man, is finite. Proceeding in this manner, we must come at last to a Being whose intelligence is properly *infinite*, and then

* " Le mot *Dieu* ne désignera Jamais que la cause inconnue des effets que les hommes ont admirés ou redoutés." *Système*, II. p. 94.

† " Dans ce Dieu l'on ne trouvera qu'un vain phantôme, substitué à l'énergie de la nature que l'on s'est toujours obstiné à méconnoître." *Ibid.* p. 102.

‡ " Les hommes ont rempli la nature d'*esprits*, parce qu'ils ont presque toujours ignoré les vraies causes. Faute de connoître les forces de la nature on l'a cru animee par un *grand esprit :* faute de connoître l'energie de la machine humaine on l'a supposée pareillement animée par un *esprit*. D'où l'on voit que par le mot *esprit* l'on ne veut indiquer que la cause ignoree d'un phénomène qu'on ne sçait point expliquer d'une façon naturelle." *Ibid.* I. p. 102.

(besides that we are under a *necessity* of resting there) it ceases to be in the predicament of a man, or a plant, which must necessarily be dependent upon something superior to themselves; though, for that very reason, it ceases to be the object of our conceptions.

It is not properly our ignorance of the energy and secret powers of nature, that is, of what is visible in nature, that makes us ascribe them to something that we call a spirit, but rather a perfect comprehension and knowledge that such beings as we see, could not have existed without some superior cause distinct from themselves. This writer might just as well say, that it is because I am ignorant of the secret energy of nature, that I inquire for the cause of a sound that I hear, or of a watch that I meet with.

It is true that, because men cannot account for the power of thinking in themselves, they have had recourse to an invisible spirit; and, likewise, because they cannot account for the order of the universe, they have recourse to another, but greater, invisible spirit. So far the two cases resemble each other; but, in fact, they are very different. I discover the fallacy of the popular opinion concerning the supposed invisible spirit called the *soul,* or the seat of perception and thought in man, when I consider that all the phenomena of perception and thought depend upon the organization of the brain, and that therefore, whatever those powers are, they *must,* according to the received rules of philosophizing, be ascribed to that organization. We are not to multiply causes without necessity. And when I reflect farther, I see that no difficulty is, in fact, removed by ascribing the powers of perception and thought to an invisible or immaterial spirit, because there is no more perceivable connexion between what is *invisible* than what is *visible,* and those *powers.* It is true that I have no distinct idea of *any* proper seat of those mental powers, with what they can connect, or on what they may depend. But, for any thing that appears to the contrary, they may just as well connect with, and depend upon, the *brain,* as upon any invisible substance within the brain.

But when I pass from the immediate cause of thought in man to the cause of that cause, or the cause of this organization of the brain, I must necessarily look for it in something that is at least capable of understanding that organization; and this I know must be a being of intelligence infinitely superior to that of any *man,* and, therefore, certainly very different from any thing human. For the same reason it is in vain that I look for this intelligence in the earth, the sun, the moon, or the stars, or in all those bodies combined.

There is, indeed, in the universe, that kind of *unity* which bespeaks it to be *one work*, and, therefore, probably the work of one being; but we by no means see that *continuity of substance*, which we find in the brain, so as to conclude from that analogy, that the parts of the visible universe do themselves constitute a thinking substance. What is visible belonging to man *may*, for any thing we know to the contrary, be the seat of all his powers, and, therefore, according to the rules of philosophizing, which teach us not to multiply causes or substances without necessity, *must be concluded* to be so. But what is visible in the universe *cannot* be the seat of the intelligence that belongs to *it*, according to any analogy that we are acquainted with. Besides, allowing, impossible as it must be, that so disjointed a system as the material universe is, to have a *principle of thought* belonging to it, it has, however, so much the appearance of other works of design, that we must still look out for *its* author, as much as for that of a man.

Concerning the origin of the human race, this writer says, " The contemplator of nature will admit that he sees no contradiction in supposing that the human race, such as it is at present, has either been produced in time, or from all eternity. But some reflections seem to give a greater probability to the hypothesis, that man is a production in time, peculiar to the globe that we inhabit; who, consequently, has no higher origin than the globe itself, and is a result from the particular laws that govern it."* To those who, to cut the difficulty, " pretend that the human race is descended from a first man and first woman, created by the Divinity, we will say that we have some idea of *nature*, but that we have none of the *Deity* or of *creation;* and that to make use of these terms, is to say, in other words, that we are ignorant of *the energy of nature*, and that we do not know *how* it has produced the men that we see."†

---

* " Le contemplateur de la nature dira qu'il ne voit aucune contradiction à supposer que l'espèce humaine, telle qu'elle est aujourd'hui, a été produite soit dans le tems, soit de toute éternité.—Cependant quelques réflexions semblent favoriser ou rendre plus probable l'hypothèse que l'homme est une production faite dans le tems, particulière au globe que nous habitons, qui par conséquent ne peut dater que la formation de ce globe lui même, et qui est un résultat des loix particulières qui le dirigent." *Systême*, I. p. 82.

† " Nous dirons à ceux qui, pour trancher les difficultés, prétendent que l'espèce humaine descend d'un premier homme et d'une première femme, ciées par la Divinité, que nous avons quelques idées de la nature et que nous n'en avons aucune de

It is, I acknowledge, equally reasonable to suppose the race of men to have existed from eternity without any superior cause, as to have begun to exist in time without one; but yet the latter supposition, which this writer thinks the more probable of the two, by removing the origin of man out of the obscurity of eternity, appears more glaringly absurd, being more directly opposite to every thing that we observe or experience. Had we ever seen any thing come into being in this manner, we might conclude that man *might* have done so; but having no experience of any such thing, and, on the contrary, seeing every man, animal and plant, to be descended from pre-existent parents; we necessarily conclude that every individual of the species must have come into being in this manner, till we come to the first of the species; and this first we see no difficulty in supposing to have been formed by a being of sufficient power and skill. In the same manner, we trace back a number of *echoes*, or reverberations of sound, to something that, without being itself a sound, has a power of exciting it. But the primary cause of *man* can no more be a man, than the primary cause of a *sound* can be a sound.

As this writer ascribes every thing that exists to the energy of *nature*, he seems sometimes to annex the same ideas to that word that others do to the word *God;* so that, from some passages in his work, one would imagine that he was an atheist in name only, and not in reality.

" We cannot doubt," says he, " of the power of nature to produce all the animals that we see, by the help of combinations of matter, which are in continual action."* " Nature is not a work. It has always subsisted of itself. It is in its bosom that every thing is made."† " We cannot deny but that nature is very powerful, and very industrious."‡ " Nature is not a blind cause. It does not act at random. Nothing that it does would appear *accidental* to him who should know its manner of acting, its resources and ways."§

la Divinité ni de la création, et que se servir de ces mots c'est ne dire qu'en d'autres termes que l'on ignore l'énergie de la nature et qu'on ne sçait point comment elle a pu produire les hommes que nous voyons." *Ibid.* I pp. 88, 89.

* " Nous ne pouvons douter de la puissance de la nature; elle produit tous les animaux que nous voyons à l'aide des combinaisons de la matière qui est dans une action continuelle." *Ibid.* II. pp. 153, 154.

† " *La nature n'est point un ouvrage;* elle a toujours existé par elle-même: c'est dans son sein que tout se fait." *Ibid.* II. p. 156.

‡ " Nous ne pouvons douter que la nature ne soit très puissante et très industrieuse." *Ibid.* II. pp 157, 158.

§ La nature n'est point une cause aveugle; elle n'agit point au hazard; tout ce qu'elle fait ne seroit jamais fortuit pour celui qui connoîtroit sa façon d'agir, ses ressources et sa marche." *Ibid.* II. pp. 160, 161.

" It is nature that combines, according to certain and necessary laws, a head so organized as to make a poem. It is
nature that gives a brain proper to produce such a work."*
" Nature does nothing but what is necessary. It is not by
accidental combinations, and random throws, that it produces the beings that we see."† " Chance is nothing but
a word of imagination, like the word *God*, to cover the ignorance we are under, of the acting causes in nature, whose
ways are often inexplicable."‡

If what this writer here calls *nature* be really capable of all
that he ascribes to it ; if it be thus powerful and industrious,
if it does nothing at random, and produces beings of such
intelligence as men, &c. it is indeed no bad substitute for a
deity, but then it would be, in fact, only another name for
the same thing. It is the *powers*, not the *substance*, that we
reverence ; and a power like this, capable of producing men
and animals, without pre-existent parents, is a power not to
be overlooked. I should even think it capable of occasion-
ing as much superstitious dread as this writer imputes to the
belief of a God. Also, if the powers of this nature favour
virtue, as this writer strongly contends, it might be even
apprehended that, being capable of producing men at first,
it might be capable of *re-producing* them after they had been
dead and buried ; so that an atheist who had been very
wicked, could not be quite sure of escaping the punishment
of his crimes even in the grave.

But, notwithstanding all that this writer ascribes to nature,
and though it does not act at random, he imagines it has no
intelligence or object ; which I think is not a little para-
doxical. " Nature," says he, " has no intelligence or object.
It acts necessarily, because it exists necessarily. It is we
that have a necessary object, which is our own preserva-
tion."§ This writer, however, supposes man to act necessarily ; so that merely acting *necessarily* is not incompatible

* " C'est la nature qui combine d'après des loix certaines et necessaires une tête
organisée de manière à faire un poëme : c'est la nature qui lui donne un cerveau
propre à enfanter un pareil ouvrage." *Ibid.* II. p. 161.
† " La nature ne fait donc rien que de nécessaire ; ce n'est point par des combinaisons fortuites et par des jets hazardés qu'elle produit les êtres que nous voyons."
Ibid. II. p. 164.
‡ " Le hazard n'est rien qu'un mot imaginé, ainsi que le mot Dieu, pour couvrir
l'ignorance où l'on est des causes agissantes dans une nature dont la marche est
souvent inexplicable." *Ibid.* II. p. 165
§ " La nature n'a point de but ; elle existe nécessairement ; ses façons d'agir
sont fixées par des loix qui découlent elles-mêmes des propriétés constitutives des
êtres variés qu'elle renferme, et des circonstances que le mouvement continuel doit
nécessairement amener. C'est nous qui avons un but nécessaire, c'est de nous
conserver nous-mêmes." *Ibid.* II. p. 177.

with having an *object*. Consequently, nature, though acting necessarily, *may*, according to his own mode of reasoning, have an object; and that nature, or the Author of nature, *has* had various objects, is just as evident as it is that man has ob_ jects. The power that formed an *eye* had as certainly something in view, as he that constructed a *telescope*.

I am unable to pursue the inconsistencies of this cele_ brated writer any farther; and yet, taking the whole work together, it is the most plausible and seducing of any thing that I have yet met with in support of atheism; and the author is to be commended for writing in a frank and open manner, without the least cover or reserve, which is not the case with Mr. Hume.

I am, &c.

LETTER XII.

An Examination of some fallacious Methods of demonstrating the Being and Attributes of GOD.

DEAR SIR,

IT is, in some respects, to be regretted, that all the friends of religion do not agree in the principles on which they defend it; because it gives their common adversaries the advantage of various important concessions from some or other of them. This has, in fact, proceeded so far, that, in the opinion of some theists, the principles of professed atheists are not more dangerous than those of their particular adversaries, though equally declared theists with themselves. Also, *human passions* interfering, the enemies of atheism are apt to dispute with too much anger and rancour about their several modes of attack and defence, and to represent those who have the same ultimate object with themselves, *as favourers of atheism*, though they may hesitate to call their principles directly *atheistical*.

But, on the other hand, this very circumstance, though unfavourable in these respects, is not without some advantage; as different persons may be impressed by different modes of reasoning. And provided the great *moral purpose* be attained, which undoubtedly is an inward reverence for an invisible Being, whom we consider as the maker of us, and of all things, who is our moral governor here, and will take cognizance of our conduct hereafter, the real friends of religion, and especially those of the most truly enlarged minds, will rejoice.

Nor do we need to be alarmed at any future discovery of the weakness of any principles of religion by those who have built the most upon them. ' For if the superstructure itself be valued, a man will always look out for some better supports rather than let it fall altogether. There are few persons of a speculative turn of mind but must have observed this in themselves, with respect to various other valuable objects.

On how very different and opposite principles has the general doctrine of *morals* been founded, and how often have speculative persons changed their views of this seemingly momentous business? And yet it is not at all probable, that the *practice of morals* has ever suffered from this cause. On what different principles, also, have the civil and religious rights of men been founded, by persons who have been equally ready to lay down their lives in defence of them, and who change their speculative opinions without becoming advocates for slavery?

Why then should any friend of religion be alarmed because one person thinks that the being of God, and the great truths of natural religion, are to be proved in one way, and another person in a different way? If, as we must all acknowledge, it would be most injurious to call any person an atheist, merely because he could not prove the being of a God at all, much more, certainly, must it be injurious to call a person an atheist who does it satisfactorily to himself, though not so to us.

It is very rarely that thinking and speculative persons are convinced of any mistake of consequence; but let the confutation be ever so clear and undeniable, if the disputant be a man of virtue, I should not be apprehensive that even principles the most indisputably (yet, in fact, only *consequentially*) atheistical would ever make him an atheist.

What would become of the advocates of the doctrine of the *Trinity*, if those only should be allowed to be Trinitarians, who explained and defended it in the same manner? To say nothing of the general difference between ancient and modern times in that respect, few societies, I apprehend, of that denomination of Christians at this day, would, on this principle, hold communion with each other.

In general, the truth of any particular proposition may be so firmly assented to, and may be so intimately connected with, numberless other tenets, that a man's *whole system of opinions* must give way before that one doctrine can be rooted out of his mind ; and so total a revolution in the principles of men, who really think at all for themselves, so seldom happens, that it is no reasonable object of apprehension. It is happy for us that we are so constituted. Without this, we should be in a state of endless fluctuation ; and it is almost better to have any principles, and any character, than no fixed principles, no proper character at all.

With respect to the subject of these letters, I shall hope to derive this advantage from the discussion, that those persons who are atheistically inclined, and who have been confirmed in their disbelief of the principles of religion by the injudicious manner in which some of its friends have defended it, may find their triumph premature ; and that the system of theism is not overturned, though they should have succeeded in their refutation of some principles which have been *imagined* to be essential to it, and necessary supports of it.

With this calm, and I hope just view of the subject, I shall, in this letter, endeavour to explain the fallacy of some of the speculative principles on which real friends of religion have, at different times, endeavoured to support the doctrines of a God and of a Providence. And, in doing this, I shall have no fear of increasing, but, on the contrary, some hope of lessening, the number of atheists.

1. I shall not detain you long with the opinion of those who maintain that the belief of a God is an *instinctive principle ;* because I presume it will, at this day, be generally acknowledged, that there is no evidence of *any* idea, or principle, being properly instinctive or *innate.* We come into the world furnished with proper senses to receive the various impressions to which we are exposed ; and the traces in the mind, left by those impressions, appear to be the elements of all the ideas, and all the knowledge we ever acquire. Being then possessed of a natural capacity of acquiring to a certain degree every kind of valuable knowledge, and the knowledge of God and of religion, as well as of other things, it is not agreeable to the analogy of nature to have the same things impressed upon us in another, and quite different manner.

Besides, had the idea of God been originally impressed upon the minds of all men, the character would, no doubt, have been the same, and would not have been liable to so great variation, and perversion, as we find it to have been. Nor could we imagine it could have been so nearly, if not entirely effaced, as it appears to have been in some whole nations; if, indeed, it can be suppossed possible, on that hypothesis, for *any* person to have been an atheist.

This very unphilosophical opinion, that the belief of a God is an instinctive principle, not to be deduced by reasoning from any appearances in nature, has, however, been asserted very lately, and every other mode of defending the primary truths of religion has been most arrogantly exploded and ridiculed, by Dr. Beattie and Dr. Oswald, on principles before advanced by Dr. Reid; and yet of the good *intentions* of these writers, in this singular conduct, I never entertained a doubt, though such absurd principles, so haughtily advanced, and so weakly supported, in this enlightened age, deserve, in my opinion, every other censure. See my *Examination of these Writers.* (Vol. III.)

2. Descartes thought that the very *idea* of a God was a sufficient proof of his existence. This opinion, if defensible at all, implies the former. For unless the idea of God be of such a nature as that it could not have been acquired by any impressions to which we are exposed, it must be impossible to say but that it may have been so formed. What is there in our idea of God but human perfections magnified; and what is our idea of *infinity* itself, but the mere negation of bounds?

3. There is another mode of reasoning concerning the being of God, which, I believe, originated with Dr. Clarke, and is, I imagine, peculiar to this country, but it does not appear ever to have given general satisfaction; though some very eminent metaphysicians are still strongly attached to it. To me, however, the fallacy of it seems very obvious.

According to this author, there must be a God, or an original designing cause of all things, because it would be as much a contradiction to suppose the contrary, as to suppose that *two and two* are not equal to *four.* He also says, that the idea of God cannot be excluded from the mind, any more than the ideas of *space* or *duration*, though we use every effort we can for that purpose.

Now a *contradiction* is saying and unsaying, affirming and denying a thing at the same time, or in the same sentence; so that there is a manifest *contrariety*, or *incompatibility*, between those ideas that are asserted to coincide; and this must appear without any reasoning on the subject, just as if we should say *white is black*, and yet retain the ideas usually annexed to those terms. We immediately perceive, without any reasoning, that *black* cannot be *white*, or *white*, *black.* If we say that *two and two* are *five*, it is a contradiction, though in form one step short of a *direct* one. To make it a direct contradiction, we should first say that *two and two* are *four*, and then that *four* is *five*, which only is a direct, or proper contradiction.

Now where is the proper contradiction, direct or indirect, in saying *there is no God?* If we reduce it to a formal proposition, it is, *the universe exists without a cause.* Now, false as the proposition is, it is no more a contradiction (i. e. *in terms,* and there is no other proper contradiction) than to say that *God exists without a cause,* which is a truth. Because neither is the idea, annexed to the term *universe,* the direct reverse of the idea annexed to the term *uncaused,* nor does the idea annexed to the term *God* coincide with it.

As to the impossibility of excluding from our minds the idea of a Deity, it is altogether an affair of *consciousness;* and with respect to myself, I have no scruple to say, that I find no difficulty at all in excluding the ideas of every thing in nature, except those of *space* and *duration,* and I cannot help being surprised that the contrary should ever have been asserted.

It is true that the belief of what actually exists compels us to the belief of a God, or an uncaused being, different from mere space. But exclusive of the consideration of *an existing universe,* from which I infer the belief of a God, as the necessary cause of it, there is nothing in the mere *idea* of a Deity (as there evidently is in the idea of space) that prevents a possibility of its being excluded from the mind. But it is proper that so respectable a writer as Dr. Clarke should be heard in his own words.

" The only true idea of a self-existent, or necessarily existing Being, is the idea of a being, the supposition of whose non-existing is an express contradiction. The relation of equality between *twice two* and *four* is an absolute necessity, only because it is an immediate contradiction in terms to suppose them unequal. This is the only idea we can frame of an absolute necessity ; and to use the word in any other sense, seems to be using it without any signification at all. If any one now ask what sort of idea, the idea of that Being is, the supposition of whose non-existing is thus an express contradiction, I answer, it is the first and simplest idea we can possibly frame,—which (unless we forbear thinking at all) we cannot possibly extirpate, or remove out of our minds, of a most simple Being, absolutely eternal and infinite, original and independent."* Yet, as I have said before, I cannot imagine any difficulty in excluding this idea. But he argues the same thing in a different manner.

" That he who supposes there may possibly be no eternal and infinite Being in the universe, supposes likewise a contradiction, is evident from hence,—that when he has done his utmost in endeavouring to imagine that no such being exists, he cannot avoid imagining *an eternal and infinite nothing;* that is, he will imagine eternity and immensity removed out of the universe, yet that, at the same time, they still continue there." P. 18.

Here I think is a manifest fallacy. If, by an *eternal and infinite nothing*, he meant that nothing will be eternal and infinite but *space*, it is *false*, but surely no *contradiction;* and though an eternal and infinite Deity be removed, an eternal and infinite space will not. If there be no reference to the idea of space (which, indeed, is not mentioned), the inconclusiveness of the argument is too obvious to have escaped the observation of any person.

I acknowledge, with Dr. Clarke, that a finite being cannot be self-existent; but I do not feel the force of his reasoning on the subject, because it is the same with the preceding. " To suppose a finite being to be self-existent, is to say, that it is a contradiction for that being not to exist, the absence of which may yet be conceived without a contradiction, which is the greatest absurdity in the world." P. 44. Here he takes it for granted, that the idea of the self-existence of any being implies its being a contradiction for that being not to exist.

But though Dr. Clarke advances thus far *a priori*, that is, without any reference to an *existing universe*, in proof of the being of a God, he does not pretend to prove the divine *intelligence* in this manner, nor yet his *power*. " That the self-existent Being, is—an *understanding*, and really *active* being, does not indeed appear to us by considerations *a priori*, because—we know not wherein *intelligence* consists, nor can we see the immediate and necessary connexion of it with *self-existence*." P. 51. " The self-existent Being, the supreme cause of all things, must of necessity have infinite power," because " all things in the universe were made by him, and are entirely dependent upon him; and all the powers of all things are derived from him." P. 73.

But, what is more extraordinary, this writer thinks he can

* Demonstration, &c. Ed. 8, p. 17.

prove the *moral attributes of God* from his intelligence only. This, however, considering that he does not pretend to prove intelligence itself *a priori*, is not, strictly speaking, an argument *a priori*.

That " the supreme Cause and Author of all things must of necessity be a being of infinite goodness, justice and truth, and all other moral perfections," he proves from this consideration, that a being of infinite intelligence must perceive those *necessary fitnesses of things*, on which, according to him, morality depends ; and, " having no want of any thing, it is impossible his will should be influenced by any wrong affection," and, therefore, " he must of necessity—do always what he knows to be fittest to be done, i. e. he must act always according to the strictest rules of infinite goodness, justice and truth, and all other moral perfections." Pp. 114—116.

As the idea concerning the *foundation of morals*, on which this argument proceeds, is another subject of discussion, I shall not enter into it here, except just observing, that I perceive no necessary connexion between *intelligence*, as such, and any particular *intention* or *object* whatever ; and, therefore, nothing can prove actual *benevolence*, in preference to *malevolence*, but the actual production of *happiness*, in preference to *misery*, or, at least, a manifest tendency to it, in what is actually produced.

Dr. Clarke's mode of reasoning is not very different from that of Descartes and others, who maintain that we can prove the existence of a self-existent being from the very *idea* we have of it.   That the reader may see how he distinguishes in this case, I shall just recite what he says on the subject.

" I must have an idea of something actually existing without me, and I must see wherein consists the absolute impossibility of removing that idea, and consequently of supposing the non-existence of the thing, before I can be satisfied, from that idea, that the thing actually exists.   The bare having an idea of the proposition, *there is a self-existent being*, proves, indeed, the thing not to be impossible (for of an impossible proposition there is properly no idea), but that it actually *is* cannot be proved from the idea, unless the certainty of the *actual existence* of a necessarily existing being follows from the *possibility* of the existence of such a being ; which that it does, in this particular case, many learned men have indeed thought, and their subtle arguings upon this head are sufficient to raise a cloud not very easy to be seen through.   But it is a much clearer and more convincing way of arguing, to demonstrate, that there does actually exist without us a being whose existence is necessary and of itself, by shewing the evident contradiction contained in the contrary supposition,—and, at the same time, the absolute impossibility of destroying or removing some ideas, as of eternity and immensity, which, therefore, must needs be modes or attributes of a necessary being actually existing." P. 21.

Since, however, *mere space*, as I have observed before, may easily be conceived to have existed *infinite* and *eternal*, without any thing to occupy it, it certainly cannot be necessary to suppose it the attribute of any other being. This is manifestly very unlike the case of *black, white, long, broad,* or other *mere properties*, which cannot be conceived without some *subject* to which they belong. The dispute whether space be a *substance*, or a *property*, is, in fact, merely, or little more than verbal ; because we know nothing of any thing but its properties. But if *a capacity of subsisting, in idea, by itself* be a characteristic of *substance*, as opposed to *property*, space, undoubtedly, ought to be denominated a substance, and not a mere property ; though, when occupied by any other substance, it may assume the appearance of a property belonging to that substance. For, take away the substance, and the space it occupied will not, in idea, go with it. Nay, in that sense, it is more of the nature of substance than any thing else, because it is impossible, even in idea, to suppose it not to be permanent.

If the whole of what Dr. Clarke has advanced, on the proof of the being of a God, be attentively considered, it will not be very easy to say what his idea of God, as proved *a priori*, is. It is that of a being self-existent, eternal, and co-extended with infinite space, but not space. It is the cause of all things, but without *power, intelligence,* or *moral attributes ;* for these he makes to depend upon the perceived relation of things. Consequently, they pre-suppose intelligence, which he acknowledges cannot be proved *a priori*.

In fact, therefore, he proves nothing *a priori* but *mere being,* without any proper *powers* whatever. But the terms, *being* or *substance*, give no ideas at all when divested of powers or properties. So that, in reality, notwithstanding his assertion of the contrary, it is nothing but *empty space* that he is capable of proving *a priori*. And, with respect to this, I perfectly agree with him, because, do what we will, we cannot so much as *suppose* infinite and eternal space not to have existed.

Far, however, am I from saying that a Deity, an *efficient Deity*, with all his attributes, is not, properly speaking, *necessarily existent*, or that his existence is not, in reality, as necessary as that of space itself.   But then we come to the knowledge of this necessity, with respect to him, in a different manner.   It is by beginning *a posteriori*, finding that, in consequence of the *actual existence* of beings that must have had a cause, there must have been some being that could not have had a cause, though we are altogether at a loss to conceive, *a priori*, *how* or *why* he should exist without a cause, and can, in idea, easily imagine him not to have existed, which is not the case with respect to space. Then, the necessary existence of a supreme cause once supposed, there are various attributes, as those of *eternity*, *immensity* and *unity*, that may either with certainty, or with the greatest probability, be deduced from the consideration of *necessary existence*.

But though to us, and our conceptions, there be this difference between the idea of the existence of space, and of that of the Deity, there may not be any in reality.   Indeed, the Deity could not have been *necessarily existent*, if there had not been, in the nature of things, if we may use the phrase, (which, however, can only be improperly applied in this case,) as much reason for his existence, as for that of. space.   But neither the term *reason*, nor any thing equivalent to it, ought, in strictness, to be used in this case, lest it should imply, contrary to the supposition, that there is some proper *cause* of the divine existence; whereas, he cannot have had any cause.

On this account, I dislike the phraseology of Dr. Clarke, when he sometimes speaks of *necessity being the cause of the divine existence*.   Indeed, the whole of our language is so appropriated to *finite* and *caused* beings, that it is hardly possible to use any part of it in speaking with strict propriety of a Being *infinite* and *uncaused*.   We should, therefore, forgive one another any oversights of this nature that we inadvertently fall into.

I am, &c.

LETTER XIII.

Of the Ideas of CAUSE *and* EFFECT, *and the Influence of Mr. Hume's Opinion on this Subject, in the Argument for the Being of a* GOD.

DEAR SIR,

As some persons have imagined that the cause of atheism has derived considerable advantage from Mr. Hume's ideas concerning the nature of *cause and effect*, I shall, in this letter, endeavour to shew that the apprehension is without foundation.

Mr. Hume says, that all we can pretend to know concerning the connexion of cause and effect, is their constant *conjunction ;* by the observance of which the mind is necessarily led from the one to the other. From this the friends of religion have supposed that if this representation be just, the connexion is merely *arbitrary,* and, therefore, that such things as we have usually called *effects may* take place without any thing that we have usually observed to correspond to them, as their *causes.* Consequently, that, for any thing that we know to the contrary, the universe itself may have existed from eternity without any superior cause.

To guard against this, some of the friends of religion deny that our idea of *power* or *causation* is derived from any thing that we properly observe. But, imperfect as Mr. Hume's ideas on the subject are, (notwithstanding his laborious and tiresome discussion of it, and its being evidently a favourite topic with him,) I think I have sufficiently shewn in the third of the *Essays* prefixed to my edition of *Hartley's Theory of the Mind,* (Vol. III. p. 189,) that there is nothing in the idea of *power* or *causation,* (which is only the same idea differently modified,) that is not derived from the impressions to which we have been subject, this being to be ranked in the class of *abstract ideas,* where it does not appear that Mr. Hume ever thought of looking for it. In the Essay I here refer to, p. 191, I have shewn that the idea of *power* is far from being, what some take it to be, a simple idea, but that, on the contrary, it is one of the most complex ideas that we have, consisting of what is common to numberless impressions of very different kinds.

Besides, if the idea of power be any thing that cannot be acquired by *experience,* it comes under the description of other *innate principles* or *ideas*, which have been so long, and, I think, so justly exploded, that I think myself at liberty to take it for granted that there is no such thing.

But I shall proceed to observe that, in whatever manner we come by the idea of power or causation, it is an idea that all men have, and corresponds to something *real* in the relation of the things that suggest it. It is true that all we properly *see* of a *magnet*, and a *piece of iron*, is that, at certain distances, they approach to one another, and of a *stone*, that, in certain circumstances, it invariably tends towards the earth and we cannot give any proper or satisfactory *reason* why either of these effects should take place in these circumstances. Yet we have always found that in a similar constant conjunction of appearances, we have never failed to discover, whenever we have been able to make any discovery at all, that the event could not have been otherwise. And though, in these cases, we have only discovered a *nearer*, and never the *ultimate* cause of any appearance, yet there is an invariable experience in favour of *some* real and sufficient cause in all such conjunctions.

In consequence of this experience, it is indelibly impressed upon the minds of all men, that all events whatever, and all productions whatever, must have a necessary and adequate cause, so that nothing can begin to be without a cause foreign to itself. And let any person pretend what he will, he must himself (in consequence of the impressions to which he, together with the rest of mankind, has uniformly been exposed) have come under the influence of it, and of course, have the same persuasion.

Though, therefore, by means of some secret bias, and sophistical argumentation, a man may come to be persuaded that the universe has had no superior cause, he cannot deny but that all other things, (which the theist must shew to be in the same predicament with the universe,) must have had such a cause, so that nothing is to be apprehended from his idea of *the nature of causation in general*. Whatever that idea be, (and, in fact, it will be the same with that of the rest of mankind, let any person give whatever account of it he pleases,) he will necessarily expect a superior cause in those circumstances in which mankind in general will be satisfied that a cause is requisite.

Different persons *feel*, and are *persuaded* differently enough in some cases; but where the influences, to which their minds have been subject, have necessarily been nearly the same, the impressions made on them cannot be materially different. In this case, I should sooner imagine that the ideas annexed to the words *hunger* and *thirst,* should be different in different persons, than the ideas annexed to the words *power* and *causation,* or that they should have different effects in their serious argumentations.

I am, &c.

LETTER XIV.

An Examination of Mr. Hume's Metaphysical Writings.

DEAR SIR,

You are surprised, you tell me, that Mr. Hume, so great a master of reasoning, so cool and dispassionate a writer, and so subtle a metaphysician, should have written so loosely and unguardedly, as you are now convinced he has done in this *posthumous work* of his, a work of which, it is evident, he made great account, by his taking such effectual measures for its publication after his death. But you cannot well suppose, having always entertained a different idea, that I can be sufficiently well-founded in the censure I have passed on his *metaphysical writings in general* in my ninth letter, and, therefore, you wish I would enter on the proof of what I have advanced, by a distinct exhibition of *all* that Mr. Hume has done in this way; that when all the observations he has advanced shall be seen without the imposition of his style and manner, its real merit, its solidity or futility, may plainly appear.

Now I am ready to give the fullest satisfaction on this subject, and I should not have ventured to throw out that *general censure,* without being prepared to justify it in all the particulars, if you should call upon me to do it. Besides, I am not without hopes, that when you see on how narrow a foundation Mr. Hume's fame as a metaphysician stands, his authority as *a reasoner* will not weigh, so much as it has hitherto done, with you and others who have only a general and indistinct notion of his being *a great philosopher,* and an acute and guarded writer. This I shall do in as succinct a manner as I can, in a regular analysis of all his *Essays* that are in the least to our present purpose.

In the first of his *Philosophical Essays,* ",Of the different Species of Philosophy," which is only an introduction to the rest, it appears that he had no idea of the connexion of the different faculties of the mind, and their dependence upon one principle, as that of *association*. For he says, " The mind is endowed with several powers and faculties," and " these powers are totally distinct from each other." P. 14. But we may "hope that philosophy—may carry its researches still farther, and discover, at least, in some degree, the secret springs and principles by which the human mind is actuated in its operations." P. 15. He says, however, " it is probable that one operation and principle of the mind depends on another, which again may be resolved into one more general and universal." P. 16. What that principle is, it is evident Mr. Hume had no idea.

In his second Essay, " Of the Origin of our Ideas," I find nothing that could have been *new*, but an ill-founded suspicion, " that the simple ideas are not always, in every instance, derived from the corresponding impressions," p. 27 ; merely because, having had ideas from actual impression of the extremes of any particular *colour*, we are able, without any farther assistance from actual impressions, to raise the idea of the intermediate shades of the same colour ; not considering that this amounts to nothing more than a difference of *greater* or *less*, and, therefore, is not properly any new idea at all. It is no more than forming an idea of a middle sized hill, after having seen small hillocks and large mountains.

Let a tender eye be strongly impressed with a luminous object of white, or any other colour, and if the eye be immediately shut, the impression will of itself change into various other colours, as well as shades of the same colour ; and there can be no doubt but that this would have been the case originally, though no such colours had been known before. Now the substance of the brain being the same with that of the *retina*, and of the other nerves, it must be capable of such changes of affection as these, from causes within itself, but still the necessary consequence of external impressions.

In the third Essay, he reduces all the cases *of the connexion* or association *of ideas* to three, viz. *resemblance, contiguity* in place or time, and *cause and effect*, without attempting at a conjecture how ideas, thus related to each other, come to be associated, or what circumstances they have in common ; though it was so easy to perceive that in all of them, the immediate cause is nothing more or less than *joint impression ;* the universal and simple law of association being this, that two sensations or ideas present to the mind at the same time, will afterwards recall each other, which was well understood by Mr. Locke, and all who had treated of association before Mr. Hume. Let us now see how easily this observation will explain Mr Hume's three cases.

Things connected in *time* and *place* are generally considered together, or so near to each other, that the remains of one of the ideas is not gone out of the mind before the other has entered it. This is the reason why we so readily repeat numbers in their progressive order, and are not so well able to do it in a retrograde order. We have been most accustomed to repeat them in that order.

Resemblance is a *partial sameness*, and when that part of any idea which is the very same with part of another, is excited, it is evidently in consequence of a former joint impression that the remainder of the same idea is revived also.

Mr. Hume says, that *contrariety* may perhaps be considered as a species of *resemblance*, for a reason for which I must refer the reader to the Essay itself.* But things opposed to one another are frequently *compared* and *considered together*. It is, therefore, from frequent joint impression that their easy association is most naturally to be accounted for.

Things that are *causes and effects* to each other are also often contemplated together, and by habit we do not consider our knowledge of any thing to be complete, without knowing the cause, if it be an effect, or the effect, if it be a cause. We think the idea to be as incomplete as that of the head of a man without his body, or of his body without his head. We feel them as different parts of the same thing.

Little and imperfect, as what Mr. Hume has advanced on this subject manifestly is, he seems to have imagined that he had done something very great, when he concludes the Essay with saying, " the full explication of this principle, and all its consequences, would lead us into reasonings too profound and too copious for these Essays. It is sufficient at present to have established this conclusion, that the three connecting principles of all ideas are the relations of resemblance, contiguity and causation." P. 46.

---

* " Contrast or contrariety is a species of connexion among ideas, which may, perhaps, be considered as a species of resemblance. Where two objects are contrary, the one destroys the other, i. e. is the cause of its annihilation; and the idea of annihilation of an object implies the idea of its former existence." Essay III. p. 44. *Note.*

The fourth Essay, entitled "Sceptical Doubts," relates to our inferring an effect from a cause, asserting, that it is by a process that is not properly *reasoning*, because all that we observe is the two separate ideas, and we are altogether ignorant of their connexion; and in his fifth Essay, entitled, quaintly enough, "Sceptical Solution of these Doubts," he says, p. 73, that we make the inference by the *principle* of "Custom or Habit," which comes to this, that the two ideas have always been associated together, so that, as he expresses it, the mind is naturally led from one of them to the other, or, as he should have said more properly, one of them will necessarily introduce the other.

Leaving the question in this state, he may, with superficial readers, have weakened the foundation of our reasoning from effects to causes, as if it was properly no *reasoning* at all (which is language that he frequently uses), but only an arbitrary, and perhaps ill-founded, association of ideas. Whereas he would only have done justice to his subject, to have added, that, having found, in all such *constant* conjunctions of ideas, with respect to which we have been able to make any discovery at all, that the conjunction was really *necessary*, we conclude that the conjunction, if constant, is equally necessary, even when we are not able distinctly to perceive it. We, therefore, *presume* it, and securely act upon it. Indeed, without having made any discovery at all, we could not but be sensible, that if two events always follow one another, there must be some sufficient reason for it.

As almost every pretension to *discovery*, or *novelty*, is contained in this observation of Mr. Hume's, I shall consider it a little more strictly. When we say that two events, or appearances, are *necessarily connected*, all that we can mean is, that some more general law of nature must be violated before those events can be separated. For example, I find that the sounding of one musical string will make another string that is in unison, &c. with it, to sound also; and finding this observation invariable, I call the sounding of the first string the *cause*, and that of the second the *effect*, and have no apprehension of being disappointed in my expectation of the consequence. But I do not see what should make this conjunction necessary, till I discover that sound consists of a vibratory motion of the air, and that the air being put into this vibratory motion by the first string, communicates the same to the second by its pulses, in the same manner as the first string itself was made to vibrate.

In like manner, it was always known (and mankind have always acted on the persuasion) that respiration is necessary to animal life, and that air frequently breathed, &c. is fatal to it, though it is only of late that we have discovered the connexion of those effects with the cause. In due time we may discover the cause of this cause, &c.

The idea annexed to the term *cause* or *necessary agency*, is not a simple idea, or what could originally have been formed in the mind by the perception of any two other ideas,· as Mr. Hume seems to have expected (and which notion alone could suggest any difficulty in the case), but it represents the impression left in the mind by observing what is common to numberless cases in which there is a constant conjunction of appearances or events, in some of which we are able to see the proximate cause of the conjunction, but with respect to the rest we only *presume* it from the similarity of the cases. Notwithstanding, therefore, a definite idea, corresponding to the words *cause*, or *power*, does not occur to the mind on the original comparison of any two particular ideas, the inference from effects to causes, whether Mr. Hume will call it *reasoning* or not, is, in many cases, as safe as any reasoning whatever, so that no sceptic can derive the least advantage from this consideration.

The latter part of this Essay (which I dare say Mr. Hume considered as the first in importance in the whole work) contains a very imperfect and manifestly false account of the difference between *belief* and *imagination*. " Belief," he says, " is nothing but a more vivid, lively, forceable, firm, steady conception of an object, than what the imagination alone is ever able to attain." P. 82. And to account for this *manner* of conception, he says, that whenever we are led from one idea to another, by the connexion of *resemblance* or *contiguity*, and therefore, probably, by that of *causation* too, we at the same get a *stronger* conception of it than we should otherwise attain. Unable to account for this, he ascribes the fact to an *instinct of nature*. But he might just as well have done what Drs. Reid, Beattie and Oswald, did afterwards, viz. ascribe the sentiment of *belief itself*, as well as that which is the *cause of belief* to an arbitrary instinct of nature.

In reality, nothing can be more evidently false than what

he here supposes. For how often does it happen that we are more affected by a representation of fictitious distress, in a novel, or on the theatre, than by instances of real distress in common life? It is true that, *cæteris paribus, reality* makes a stronger impression than *fiction;* and, therefore, when an impression is, by artificial means, made stronger than usual, it sometimes imposes upon us for truth. But the idea annexed to the word *truth* is of a very complex nature, and is the impression that is left in the mind by thousands of cases in which *real existence* has been discriminated from that which has none.

A child hears a tale of distress, and having always had the truth told him, he, of course, believes it, and, according to his previously acquired sensibility, is affected with it; but he inquires farther, and finds that he has been imposed upon. Either no such person existed, or such and such things did not happen to him. He also reads tales of distress, &c. in books, but finds, by comparing them with other books, and other accounts, that they had no existence. From much observation of this kind, a complex idea, formed by a number of circumstances, is left in the mind, and to this he gives the name of *truth*, an idea which he learns to respect more and more every day, and which he acquires a habit of affixing, with all its *secondary ideas* of respect, with justness and effect, as he advances in life; so that, independently of the *strength of our feelings*, or imagination, we act very differently, according as we see reason to annex this idea of *truth* to a story, or not.

Mr. Hume says, " When a sword is levelled at my breast, does not the idea of wounds and pain strike me more strongly than when a glass of wine is presented to me, even though, by accident, this idea should occur after the appearance of the latter object?" P. 90. But let an executioner, whom he believes to have a commission to run a sword through his body, be at the distance of a hundred miles from him, and though there be neither a sword, nor the figure of a sword, near him, he would, I doubt not, by only *thinking* of a sword, in those circumstances, feel very differently, and more strongly, than if he should take a real sword in his own hand, and hold the point of it to his naked breast, when he had no apprehension of any design to hurt himself with it. But how does this tally with Mr. Hume's account of the difference between belief and fiction?

It is evident that Mr. Hume had no idea of the extent

of the power of association in the human mind, by means of which a single idea may consist of thousands of parts, being a miniature of numberless *trains of ideas,* and of whole successive *states of mind,* and yet be perfectly distinct from other ideas, consisting of as many parts, every such complex idea retaining its separate character and powers. The very *names* of persons famous in history excite in our minds an epitome of all that we know concerning them, the particulars of which we may have forgotten. How complex also are the ideas belonging to words expressive of *national customs, ranks* and *orders of men,* which, however, when pronounced ever so slightly, excite ideas perfectly distinct from each other, as much as those denoting the most simple ideas.

Now the ideas of *cause, effect, reason, instinct, probability, contingency, truth, falsehood,* &c. &c. &c. are of this nature, requiring definitions of some extent; and the ideas they in fact excite are miniatures of much more than enters into the shortest possible description of them; for they were not attained in that manner; and yet all the parts perfectly coalesce, and form distinct and permanent ideas. I have endeavoured to give some account of this business in the third of the *Essays* prefixed to my edition of *Hartley's Theory of the Mind.* (Vol. III. p. 189.)

Mr. Hume, in his sixth Essay, " Of Probability," says, that the " concurrence of several views in a particular event begets immediately, by an inexplicable contrivance of nature, the sentiment of belief." P. 94. " Let any one try," he says, " to account for this operation of the mind upon any of the received systems of philosophy, and he will be sensible of the difficulty." P. 97. On the system of Hartley there is no difficulty in it at all.

In the seventh Essay, " Of the Idea of Power," he only more particularly insists upon it, that we know of no connexion between the idea of any cause and that of any effect, though we suppose there *is* some connexion. Of this I have given, I presume, a sufficient account already.

In his eighth Essay " Of Liberty and Necessity," he very clearly illustrates some of the arguments in favour of Necessity; but not having any comprehension of the *great system,* of which that doctrine is a part, he, without the least reason, and without the least concern, abandons it to the most shocking immoral consequences.* Whereas, in rea-

---

* Such, however, as a *Necessarian,* expecting no future retribution, can scarcely refuse to admit. See *Essay* VIII., the Second *Objection,* and the *Answer,* pp. 159, 162.

lity, nothing is more favourable to the most sublime sentiments of virtue, in all its branches, as I have shewn at large
in my *Illustrations of that doctrine.*

His ninth Essay, " Of the Reason of Animals," contains
very little indeed. He only asserts, that " it is custom
alone which engages animals, from every object that strikes
their senses, to infer its usual attendant, and carries their
imaginations from the appearance of the one, to conceive
the other, in that strong and lively manner which we denominate belief." P. 169. This, unable to give any better
account of, he calls *instinct*, and says, that man avoids fire
by instinct also. Whereas, if by instinct be meant any
thing different from the association of ideas (which certainly
were not born with us), nothing is more contrary to fact.
A child knows nothing of a dread of fire, but acquires it in
consequence of the sensation of pain from it. He can even
hardly be prevented from putting his finger into the flame
of a candle. How Mr. Hume could reconcile this well-
known fact with a proper *instinctive dread of fire*, is not
easy to say.

The tenth Essay, " Of Miracles," is intended to support a
principle, according to which the relation of no appearance
whatever, not evidently similar to former appearances, can
be credible; a principle which we see refuted every day in
experimental philosophy, and which nothing could have
given the least countenance to, or have entitled to any consideration, but its affecting the credit of the miracles recorded in the Scriptures. On this account it has been
refuted by many persons, and I have considered it in my
" Institutes of Natural and Revealed Religion." (Vol. II.
pp. 114—116.)

The eleventh Essay, " Of a Particular Providence and of
a Future State," I have examined in my tenth Letter.

In his twelfth Essay, " Of the Academical or Sceptical
Philosophy," Mr. Hume maintains that, because all we
know of any object is the idea of it in our minds, we can
never prove, that those ideas, or perceptions, " could not
arise from the energy of the mind itself, or from the sug-
gestion of some invisible and unknown spirit, or from some
other cause still more unknown to us." P. 241. And that the
supposition of a connexion between those perceptions of
the mind and external objects is without any foundation in
reasoning; not considering that we have just the same reason for believing the existence of external objects, that we

have for the truth of the Copernican system. They are *the easiest hypotheses for acknowledged facts*, as I have shewn at large in the *Introduction* to my *Examination of the Writings of Drs. Reid, Beattie* and *Oswald*. (Vol. III. pp. 22—24.)

His observation, p. 243, that. *all sensible qualities*, (and, therefore, *extension* itself,) are in the mind, and not without us, is trifling. He might as well have said, that because *sound* is a thing formed within a musical instrument, and not without it, there is nothing without it that produces the sound.

To his objection to the infinite divisibility of matter, p. 246, to some angles being infinitely less than others, and those again divisible *ad infinitum*, which he allows to be *demonstrable*, and yet says, is *big with contradiction and absurdity*, at the same time that he acknowledges that " nothing can be more sceptical, or more full of doubt and hesitation, than this scepticism itself," I surely need say nothing. This does not amount to so much as a *sceptical solution of a sceptical doubt*. It may rather be called *the sceptical proposal of a sceptical doubt*.

In the conclusion of this last Essay, we find the outline of all the scepticism of his posthumous work, with the same paltry *cover*, viz. that " all reasoning from the relation of cause and effect" is founded on " a certain instinct of our nature, which—may be fallacious and deceitful." P. 251. That we can never " satisfy ourselves concerning any determination we may form with regard to the origin of worlds, and the situation of nature from and to eternity." P. 255. That " divinity or theology, as it proves the existence of a Deity, &c., has a foundation in reason, so far as it is supported by experience," (which support in a former Essay he absolutely denies it to have,) " but its best and most solid foundation is *faith* and divine revelation." P. 259.

In the first of these Essays, Mr. Hume had said, " We have, in the following Essays, attempted to throw some light upon subjects, from which uncertainty has hitherto deterred the wise, and obscurity the ignorant." P. 18. How very small is the light that he has thrown, and mixed with how much darkness, I need not repeat. " Happy," says he, " if we can unite the different species of philosophy, by reconciling profound inquiry with clearness, and truth with novelty; and still more happy, if, reasoning in this easy manner, we can undermine the foundations of an abstruse philosophy, which seems to have served hitherto only as a shelter to superstition, and a cover to absurdity and error." Pp. 18, 19.

Now, I neither see the *profundity* nor the *clearness* of his reasoning, except in things with respect to which he is far from being *original*, notwithstanding his advantage of a command of language and a great power of perspicuity, where his argument would admit of it. As to the *abstruse philosophy* which he meant to undermine, it could be nothing but the doctrine of *certainty*, and a steady persuasion concerning *truth*, and especially the truths of natural and revealed religion ; and what kind of a mind must that man have had, to whom *this* could give any satisfaction !

All men by no means judge of the value of publications by the same rules with Mr. Hume, or perhaps his own Essays would be in more danger than he himself imagined. " When we run over libraries, persuaded of these principles," says he, " what havock must we make ? If we take in hand any volume ; of Divinity, or School Metaphysics, for instance ; let us ask, *Does it contain any abstract reasonings concerning quantity or number ?* No. *Does it contain any experimental reasonings concerning matter of fact, or existence ?* No. Commit it then to the flames. For it can contain nothing then but sophistry and illusion." P. 259. It is happy for us all, that we are not judges for one another in these cases, but that a wise Providence over-rules all things. The *Scriptures* were certainly not meant to come under either of Mr. Hume's characters of *books to be saved from the flames.*

In the preceding observations, I think I have descanted upon every thing of Mr. Hume's, in which it can be pretended, or in which he himself would have pretended, that he had made any advances in the knowledge of the human mind. I need not now say how inconsiderable those advances were. All that he has observed relates to the power of association, and his ideas on that subject were much confined, going very little, if indeed, on the whole, any thing at all, beyond those of Mr. Locke, and others who had preceded him.

Mr. Hume had not even a glimpse of what was at the same time executing by Dr. Hartley, who, in an immense work of wonderful comprehension and accuracy, has demonstrated, that this single principle of *association* is the great law of the human mind, and that all those which Mr.

Hume, as well as others, had considered as *independent faculties*, are merely different *cases* or *modifications* of it; that *memory, imagination, judgment,* the *will,* and the *passions,* have the same, and no other origin ; so that by means of this one property, and the circumstances in which we are placed, we all of us come to be every thing that we are.

In his *Inquiry concerning the Principles of Morals,* Mr. Hume very well illustrates what I fancy he himself would not pretend to be *new,* though, I believe, it had not been sufficiently attended to by metaphysicians, viz. that " utility is the foundation of virtue ;" and this being the most considerable and the most elaborate work of Mr. Hume's, I have referred to it as a specimen of analytical reasoning, in my *Lectures on Criticism.* But in this work Mr. Hume refers the pleasing *feelings,* annexed to the perception of virtue, to *an instinct of nature,* confessedly unable to trace them any farther. " It is needless," he says, " to push our researches so far as to ask why we have humanity, or a fellow-feeling with others. It is sufficient that this is experienced to be a principle in human nature. We must stop somewhere in our examination of causes, and there are in every science some general principles beyond which we cannot hope to find any principle more general." P. 85. Dr. Hartley, however, not resting where Mr. Hume did, has, with wonderful sagacity, discovered the origin of benevolence, of the moral sense, and of every other principle before thought to be *instinctive,* shewing how they are derived from association, affecting us in our infant state, and as we advance in life ; and he has shewn the diversity that we find in human affections to arise from a diversity of influences, operating on us in the same general manner.

In this work, Mr. Hume classes *humility* among the *vices,* with no other view, that I can perceive, but to shew his contempt for the christian system, in which it makes a principal figure as a virtue. And he has wholly overlooked all the virtues of the *devotional kind,* when, in fact, they may be shewn, by arguments independent of the peculiar doctrines of revelation, to be, in their own nature, the most truly *valuable,* as well as the most *sublime* of all others, and to form what may be called the *key-stone* of every truly great and heroic character. Without the virtues of this class (though Dr. Smith considers Mr. Hume as " approaching as nearly to the idea of a perfectly wise and virtuous man as perhaps the nature of human frailty will permit" *), his character must have been as imperfect as his views (looking to nothing beyond the grave) were narrow.

I have thus given you my reasons, as briefly as I well could, for placing Mr. Hume so low as I do in the class of *metaphysical writers*, or *moral philosophers*. As to *Natural Philosophy*, or *Mathematics*, I never heard that he had any pretensions to merit; and of that which constitutes an *historian*, you will not, I imagine, think that much remains to him, besides that of a *pleasing compiler*, after reading Dr. Towers's judicious *Observations* on his *History of England*.† His *Miscellaneous* and *Political* Essays always pleased me, but they by no means entitle him to the *first* rank among writers of either class. As to his *style*, notwithstanding its excellence in some respects, I have shewn in my *English Grammar* (and, as I have been informed, to Mr. Hume's own satisfaction) ‡ that he has departed farther from the true idiom of the English language, than perhaps any other writer of note in the present age.

Submitting all my observations to your own judgment, and sincerely wishing the happiest issue to your laudable pursuit of truth, I remain,

Dear Sir,

Your very humble Servant,

J. PRIESTLEY.

Calne, March, 1780.

* Conclusion of Adam Smith's Letter annexed to Hume's Life. See p. 325. " In support of this high encomium no proper evidence has ever been produced. Of Mr. Hume's fortitude in adversity, of great generosity displayed by him, or of any uncommon benevolence, no instances are recorded; but these virtues have been eminently and illustriously conspicuous in many Christian characters. If the character of *David Hume* be compared with that of *Bernard Gilpin*, a country clergyman, or with that of *Thomas Firmin*, a tradesman of London, but both acting under the influence of the great truths of Christianity, the striking inferiority of this celebrated sceptic will be apparent to every impartial man. But these men were formed by the sublime views of Christianity; and such men were never produced by scepticism or infidelity." *Essay* on Johnson's Life, 1786, in Tracts, 1796, III. pp. 417, 418, by *Joseph Towers*, LL.D. He died in 1799, after having maintained through life, a christian and truly independent character. Dr. Towers's ardour, in advocating the great interests of mankind, I have often witnessed.

† First published, 1778. See Dr. Towers's *Tracts*, 1796, I. p. 233.

‡ " He acknowledged it to Mr Griffith, the bookseller." Mr. J. Priestley's Note to the *Memoirs.* See also Mr. Tytler's Strictures on the Style of Hume's Essays, in Mem. of Lord Kames, 8vo. I. pp. 236, 237.

ADDITIONAL LETTERS

TO A

𝔓𝔥𝔦𝔩𝔬𝔰𝔬𝔭𝔥𝔦𝔠𝔞𝔩 𝔘𝔫𝔟𝔢𝔩𝔦𝔢𝔳𝔢𝔯.*

[1782.]

[Re-printed from the Second Edition 1787.]

———◆◆◆———

THE

P R E F A C E.

············

IT is certainly to be wished, that every man was at full liberty not only to publish his real opinions on any subject whatever, but also to urge them with the greatest force, and to recommend them by the strongest arguments that he can produce in support of them. No *lover of truth* will wish to stand on any other ground. For my own part, I rejoice that a *professed atheist* has thought proper to stand forth in defence of his principles, though it is not with all the consistent boldness that may be expected from one who believes in a God, a providence, and a future state. I myself have no opinions that I wish to shelter behind any *authority* whatever ; and should rejoice to see the time, (and that time, I doubt not, as the world improves in wisdom, will come,) when the civil powers will relieve themselves from the attention they have hitherto given to all matters of speculation, and religion amongst the rest, an attention which has proved so embarrassing to the governors, and so distressing to the governed; and when no more countenance will be given to any particular mode of *religion* than is given to particular modes of *medicine,* or of *philosophy.*

Individuals are much better situated for providing for themselves, in this respect, than any *representatives* can do for them ; and the religion that men would voluntarily adopt

---

* Occasioned by a pamphlet entitled, " Answer to Dr Priestley's Letters to a Philosophical Unbeliever, Part I. London, 1782." *No publisher.*

for themselves would make them the best subjects to any government, and especially to one that should allow them all, without distinction, this perfect and equal liberty. This would be an attachment much stronger, and more valuable, than any that can be secured by *hire*, as is that of the members of an established church. However, till *nations* get wisdom, *individuals* must bear with their folly, and endeavour to instruct them ; and this is most effectually done by the explicit avowal, and the fearless defence, of whatever we apprehend to be true, and to be conducive to the good of society and of mankind.

That our readers may form a just idea of the subject of the present controversy, it may be proper to inform them, that Mr. Hammon,* though a declared atheist, is far from asserting, with the Epicureans of old, and the generality of atheists before him, that .there are no marks of *design* in the visible universe. Besides what I have quoted from him in the course of these Letters, he considers it as undeniably true, that " atoms cannot be arranged in a manner expressive of the most exquisite design, without competent intelligence having existed somewhere." *Answer*, p. 4.

He says farther, " The *vis naturæ*, the perpetual industry, intelligence and provision of nature, must be apparent to all who see, feel or think. I mean to distinguish this active, intelligent and designing principle, inherent as much in mat- ter as the properties of gravity, or any elastic, attractive or repulsive power, from any extraneous foreign force and design, in an invisible agent, supreme, though hidden lord, and master over all effects and appearances that present them- selves to us in the course of nature. The last supposition makes the universe, and all other organized matter, a machine, made or contrived by the arbitrary will of another being, which other being is called *God;* and my theory makes a God of this universe, or admits no other God, or designing principle than matter itself, and its various organi. zations." *Pref. Ad.* p. xxviii.

Such is the fair state of this controversy. It is my business, therefore, to shew, in the first place, that the visible universe is not, and cannot be, that *uncaused being* which Mr. Hammon supposes ; and, secondly, that the seat of that intelligence, which is acknowledged to be in the universe, cannot be in the visible universe itself, but must

---

* The name signed to a *Prefatory Address* to an anonymous " Answer from a Philosophical Unbeliever," of which Mr. H. *professes* to be merely the editor.

reside in, and belong to, some being distinct from it. One of these hypotheses must be true, for a third cannot be imagined.

These, then, are the principal subjects of the following Letters. But I have also taken some notice of what Mr. Hammon has observed with respect to the moral attributes of the Deity, the moral influence of religion, and other subjects of a miscellaneous nature.

Mr. Hammon is also so far from reprobating, as other atheists have done, the idea of a *future life*, that he not only considers it as desirable, but even as not impossible or incredible. For he places it among the things *inadmissible* and *inconclusive*, that " an atheist believes himself to be at his death for ever excluded from returning life." P. 10.

Atheism, so qualified, certainly loses much of the horror with which it has hitherto been regarded, and affords room to hope that it will soon give place to the system which gives us the fullest and most satisfactory assurance of that *future life*, to which Mr. Hammon looks with *desire*, and, seemingly, not without some degree of *hope*. This, certainly, ought to be a motive with the world to give him a patient hearing ; they have so much reason to expect a favourable issue to the debate. What occasion can there be for *terror* or *violence* of any kind, when there is so little reason to distrust the natural power of *truth ?* If I fail, let abler champions be called in ; but let atheism triumph rather than religion, by the help of force.

To conclude this preface with enforcing the sentiments with which it began : let those weak Christians, who are for calling in the aid of the magistrate to suppress heresy, learn to respect their religion more, and not act the part of the *moles,* (in the excellent comparison made use of. by a worthy baronet, in the late debate on the Dissenters' bill,) who thought that the mountain at the foot of which they were at work, was in danger of falling, and consulted how to provide some better foundation for it. Let them be assured, that its own natural basis is abundantly sufficient for its support.

If this comparison does not strike them, let them consider the instructive fable of *the horse and the stag.* What the horse lost by calling in the aid of the man, is but a faint emblem of what Christianity has lost by calling in the aid of the magistrate. They have both of them, by this means, got *masters,* who, on all occasions, make use of them for their own purposes, without any regard to them.

This I now urge in favour of my adversary ; but it is language that I may have learned from standing in the same predicament myself. For, as I have observed in the course of these Letters, if the laws of this country were strictly executed, we should both be involved in the same fate. And, perhaps, while my antagonist and myself, like *the mouse and the frog*, are assaulting each other with our weapons of pointed straw, the great *eagle* of *civil power* may seize upon us both, and crush us, without distinction, and without mercy.*

I make no apology for making no difference between the author of the *Prefatory Address*, and the body of the work to which I am replying, as Mr. Hammon, the writer of the former, approves of, and adopts the latter ; and to have distinguished them from one another would have been rather embarrassing. All the letters are addressed to Mr. Hammon.

---

* It is not easy to say how the civil power could have reached *Mr. Hammon*, who had no publisher, and could never be found. Nor, indeed, except for the purpose of still farther discussing an important subject, was such a pretender to *courage*, in a condition of the most complete *security*, worthy of my author's serious attention. It was remarked, on the first appearance of the *Additional Letters*, " that Mr. Hammon had no just claim to so much distinction, and that he has been treated by his learned antagonist, with a respect which he by no means deserved." New Ann. Reg. 1782, III p. 214

ADDITIONAL LETTERS

TO A

PHILOSOPHICAL UNBELIEVER.

——◆——

LETTER I.

Of Mr. Hammon's *Professions and Conduct, &c.*

Sir,

When I wrote my *Letters to a Philosophical Unbeliever,* I certainly wished that some person of that character would calmly and seriously discuss the arguments which I there advanced, for the belief of a God and a benevolent Providence, and give me an opportunity of perceiving what it was that really determined his mind to a conclusion so different from my own; though I did not, as you seem to have imagined, undertake to answer all the objections that might be made to what I had advanced on the subject. There is, however, something so peculiar in your Answer, that I have thought proper to take notice of it, and on that account to add a few more *Letters* to those that I published before.

There is a great appearance of *ingenuousness,* and also of *courage,* in your conduct, which does you honour; and in this country, and in these times, I am confident it will not bring you into any inconvenience. You say that you " will be looked upon as a miracle of hardiness for daring" to put your name to what you have published. *Advertisement,* p. viii. And, whereas, some have doubted whether there ever was such a person as a proper atheist, you say, " To put that matter out of all manner of doubt, I do declare, upon my honour, that I am one. Be it, therefore, for the future remembered, that in London, in the kingdom of England, in the year of our Lord one thousand seven hundred and eighty-one, a man hath publicly declared himself an atheist." P. xvii. You even profess your readiness to *suffer* martyrdom in this cause, and to *glory* in it. P. xxi.

You must allow me, however, to observe, that I have not found in your conduct that perfect ingenuousness and courage to which you pretend. You charge me (p. 61) with sending no answer to the *letter* which you have published in your *postscript*, or none that " ever came to your hand." But whether this was *my* fault or *yours*, let our readers judge from the following facts. That letter I received (only dated September 23d, and not October the 23d, 1781) on the 25th of September; and on the 27th of the same month, I sent the following answer, addressed, according to your own subscription, to Mr. *William Hammon, jun. Liverpool.* The post-mark also of your letter was *Liverpool.*

Sɪʀ,

I shall be very happy to do every thing in my power to make you perfectly easy with respect to the part you wish to take. But this can only be by giving you my real opinion that you have nothing at all to fear, especially if you write with decency, as a serious inquirer after truth. I am myself as obnoxious to the laws of this country as you can be, and at this day a *heretic* is, I should think, in more danger than an *unbeliever*.

If, contrary to my expectations, any prosecution should be undertaken against you, I can promise the most earnest interposition of myself and my friends in your favour; but farther than this, I do not think it right to engage myself.

I do not recollect that I have any where undertaken to answer all my opponents: but this is of no consequence. If what you write be deemed worthy of an answer, you need not fear having one, and from an abler hand than mine.

Sincerely wishing you may proceed in your purpose, and meet with no obstruction in it, I am,

Sir,

Your very humble servant,

J. PRIESTLEY.

Birmingham,
September 27th, 1781.

Four days after this I received the following :—

Rev. Sir,

I wrote you a letter on a philosophical subject this day se'nnight, since which I have had no answer. I only want now to know whether that letter reached you, and whether you intend to send me any answer or not. I am,

Rev. Sir,

Your most obedient and humble servant,

WILLIAM HAMMON, Jun.

Liverpool, September 30, 1781.

The post-mark of this letter was also *Liverpool*.

I cannot say that the *tone* of this letter was pleasing to me; nor indeed is it of a-piece with the *civility* of the former letter; besides that, the complaint contained in it must, upon the slightest reflection, have appeared unreasonable. For I received your letter on the 25th, and, omitting only one single day, answered it on the 27th; and though it was possible that you might have received an answer before the 30th, it was barely so; and allowing for common accidents, such as my being out of the way, or very particularly engaged at the time of its arrival at my house (which is not in Birmingham, but only near it), it was not to he expected.

No person, however, of your name could be found in Liverpool, though several persons, some of them my particular friends, and at my request, made diligent inquiry concerning you. My own letter was returned to me, and it is now at your service, with the proper post-marks upon it, and shall be sent to you without delay, if you will inform me where it will really find you.

Your *Prefatory Address* is dated Oxford-street, No. 418; but at that place no such person could be heard of. There is also no name of a *publisher* annexed to your work. How then can you say, as you do, that you have "ventured to subscribe your publication with your name, as well as I do my *Letters*, to which your publication is an answer"? P. xxi. If you inquire for me at Birmingham, as I did for you at Liverpool, I have no doubt but you will readily find me, and I assure you I shall be very glad to see you there.

As to your readiness to suffer *martyrdom* in the cause of atheism, I hope you will never be put to the trial. But you must allow me to observe, that this ostentatious profession of your courage before-hand, together with your deficiency in point of *ingenuousness of mind*, in the instance above-mentioned, gives me no expectation that you would really stand it.

You seem to be apprehensive of the *laws of this country*; but I know of no law that can affect you, except *one*, which equally affects myself. I mean the act of King William,[*] which makes it *blasphemy*, punishable by confiscation of goods, and, if persisted in, imprisonment for life, either to deny that "any of the Three Persons, the Father, Son, or Holy Spirit, is God; or to maintain that there are more Gods than one." Of these three, I have not scrupled, on many occasions, to deny the divinity of one, and the separate existence of another; so that, if the law were executed, I should suffer just the same as you, who deny the divinity of one of them, and the existence of the other two.

I would not be understood to boast of my courage, though I have lived in the open violation of this law, even citing it, and censuring it about twenty years; because I should not have ventured to walk at large, as I have done, and now do; by the mere connivance of my countrymen, unprotected by any law, if I had not thought that I had sufficient reasons to confide in their good will, and to presume on the improving *spirit of the times*. Without this secret persuasion, if I had published at all (in opposition to an article of faith, so guarded by laws and penalties), it would probably have been without my name; but I think I should not have used any *false pretences*, or have made a parade of courage which I really had not. I hope you will find that the people of this country, at least, have made so much progress in that *melioration* of which you profess yourself to be a believer, as that an avowed *Atheist* has nothing more to fear than an avowed *Socinian*.

The religion that I profess hath never been more than barely *tolerated* by the civil power of any country, and very seldom so much as that. But in this circumstance it more resembles the kingdom of my Master, which he declared to be *not of this world*.

I own I am so much impressed by this consideration, that I do not wish that my religion may ever be in any other circumstances, so as to receive any thing that can be called *aid*, or *countenance*, from worldly power. We have seen enough of a pretended *alliance between Church and State*. It has only contributed to debase the one, and enslave the other.

---

* Repealed, 1813, on the motion of Mr. W. Smith, M.P. for Norwich.

2 E 2

It is also not perfectly of a-piece with the *courage* to which you pretend, to endeavour to divert the resentment of *Christians*, by intimating, that *they* are not concerned in the question. You say, " Revealed knowledge is not descanted upon.; therefore Christians at least need take no offence. Doubts upon natural religion have not hitherto been looked upon as attacks upon revelation, but rather as corroborations of it." *Adv.* pp. v. vi. And again, " The religion established in this country is not the religion of nature, but the religion of Moses and of Jesus, with whom the writer has nothing to do. He trusts, therefore, he shall not be received as a malevolent disturber of such common opinions as are esteemed to keep in order a set of low wretches, so inclinable to be lawless." Ib. p. vii.

All this is manifestly disingenuous. Do you really believe that Christianity is not affected by the belief or disbelief of a God? What becomes of the divine mission of Moses, or of Christ, if there be no such being as that *God* from whom they pretended to be sent? You must know very well, that they are not such doubts as these that were ever thought to be any corroboration of revealed religion.

What could it be but *timidity*, and to avoid giving umbrage to the ruling powers, that led you to declare that you have " no desire of making converts"? Ib. p. vi. And to say, " I declare I am rather pleased there are so few atheists, than at all anxious to make more. I triumph in my superior light." I and " my friend—are so proud, in our singularity of being atheists, that we will hardly open our lips in company, when the question is started, for fear of making converts, and so lessening our own enjoyment by a numerous division of our privilege with others!" Pp. xv. xvi.

Now I am at a loss how to reconcile this either with your publishing any thing on the subject, or with the *benevolence* to which you likewise pretend in this publication, as an attempt " to substitute better foundations for morality," *Adv.* p. vii., and with the idea of that *debasement of mind* which you frequently ascribe to the belief of religion. If atheism be a good thing, with respect to yourself and your friends, why should it not be equally good with respect to others; and from what good principle can you wish to confine the benefit to yourselves only; and why should you not both *speak*, as well as *write*, and *suffer martyrdom* in the cause? If, on the other hand, religion be a thing valuable to society at large, though it should happen not to be so with respect to yourself, why do you not forbear to write as well as to speak against it? You say, that you are resolved to make no reply to any answer I shall make to you; and that, if I should have the advantage in the argument, you will hear my " triumph without repining!" Pref. Add. p. xv. Yet, in the same page, you promise an answer to my intended letters in behalf of *revelation.* I really see no sort of consistency either with respect to *sense,* or to *courage,* in this conduct of yours.

In general, I have no reason to complain of uncivil treatment from you; but it is not very handsome in you to put the interpretation that you do upon my saying, that I shall proceed with my *Letters to a Philosophical Unbeliever,* provided that those which I have published be *well received,* when you say, " It is then, in the sum total, just as much as if you had said, *provided this book sells well, I will write another.*" Ib. p. xiv.

It is true, as you say, that I have written many books, and if life and health be continued to me, I shall probably write more; but I can truly say (and the nature and complexion of my publications will not contradict it), that I have never yet written any thing solely, or principally, with a view to any advantage that might accrue from it; and several things, with a certainty of being a loser. Not one of them was written to please a patron, to court the populace, or to recommend myself to any sect of Christians; certainly not those of the established church, and, if possible, still less those of the same denomination with myself. It was even contrary to my own expectation, that, after some of my publications, I should have met with any countenance from them. But they have had much more liberality than I had presumed upon. And my theological writings are certainly ill calculated to gain the applause of those who are usually styled philosophers. My object, I trust, is the simple pursuit of truth, from the full persuasion that the consequence of this will be ultimately friendly to society.

The sale of a book is certainly one means of judging of its success; but of this I can assure you, Sir, I have no reason to boast; for, instead of the *number of editions* you speak of, not one, and that a very moderate one, hath yet been sold. In other respects, also, the event has been as little flattering. I do not know that my book has converted a single unbeliever; and if, as I hope, it has confirmed the faith of some, you say it hath contributed to the unhinging and overturning of yours. On no account, therefore, have I, as yet, any encouragement to proceed with this work, as

I once intended. You have, however, no need to wait for the *continuation* of those *Letters*, to which you promise an answer. I have really nothing material to add to what I have already advanced on the subject in my *Intsitutes of Natural and Revealed Religion*. I could only expect to state some parts of the evidences of revelation in a clearer and more unexceptionable light, and to reply with advantage to some particular objections. I beg, therefore, that you would reply to that work in the first place ; and if you advance any thing that I shall think to be material, whether I write with more or less difficulty, you may depend upon an answer from me. I shall be happy to contribute any thing in my power to excite a more general attention to a subject of so much importance ; being perfectly satisfied that *truth*, which is all my object, will be a gainer by the discussion.

I am, &c.

LETTER II.

Of the proper Proof of the Existence of a GOD, *as an uncaused Being.*

SIR,

As you do not discuss any of my arguments at large, but only deliver your own opinion, in a desultory, but striking manner, I do not know that I can reply to you in any better way, than by first bringing into a short compass, and exhibiting in one connected view, the principal steps in my former arguments, to which you do not appear to me to have given sufficient attention, notwithstanding I am satisfied, from your quotations, that you have read my book. The *principles and modes of argumentation* are equally known to us both. I have endeavoured to explain them in my former *Letters*, and our *data* are contained in the same *face of nature*, which is equally open to our inspection. Let us then consider the different conclusions that we draw from the same premises.

To instance in some one part of the system of nature, as a specimen of the whole, I have observed, that from whatever reason we are led to conclude that a *telescope* required a maker, an *eye* must have required a maker also ; since they are both of them equally mere *instruments* adapted to answer a particular purpose. They, therefore, prove the existence of what we call a *mind*, capable of perceiving that end or purpose, with a power of providing that means, and of adapting it to its end.

This mind must be a thing entirely foreign to the telescope, and consequently to the eye; it being as contrary to appearances that the eye should make any part of this mind as that the telescope should.

In the same manner we are necessarily led to conclude, that the *animal* whose eye it is, is the production of some mind, or intelligent being (for every *power* is referred to some *substance*) foreign to itself, and also the *system* of which that animal is a part, comprehending the whole *visible universe;* each part of which bears a relation to the rest, and therefore must derive its origin from a Being whose intelligence is capable of comprehending the whole.

The supposed *eternal generation* of one plant, or one animal, from another, does not in the least remove the difficulty of conceiving how any plant, or animal, should have no foreign cause; because there is nothing in any plant or animal that is even capable of comprehending its own structure; and much less have they the additional power of properly *producing* any thing like themselves, and of enabling one of the species to produce another. This has been the effect of an intelligence much superior to theirs. How any thing that they do contributes to this end, is altogether unknown to them.

We are, therefore, in this train of speculation, necessarily led to *one great intelligent Being,* capable both of *comprehending,* and of *producing* all the visible universe. This Being must have existed from all eternity, without any foreign cause; for, if it had had a beginning, it must have had a prior cause. We cannot, indeed, conceive *in what manner,* or *on what principles,* as we may say, such a Being exists; or why it might not be, that he should not have existed. But this does not affect the certainty, that such a Being *does* exist, drawn from the certain existence of what necessarily requires and proves it.

Nor is there any thing peculiar in this particular argument. In many other cases we admit general *facts,* without pretending to have any idea of the *mode* or *manner* of their existence. We have no idea at all how the principles of sensation and thought should depend upon, or result from, the contexture of the brain; but as we know, from undeniable facts, that these properties, or powers, do result from that organization, we necessarily believe it, without having any farther distinct idea on the subject. In like manner we

firmly believe, that there must have been an eternally existent and intelligent Being, capable of producing the visible
universe, without having any farther idea how this should
be. This is not, strictly speaking, believing what is *incomprehensible*, but what we *do* perfectly comprehend, though
we perceive it is connected with something that we are not
able to comprehend. But as you lay particular stress on this
subject, 1 shall enter a little farther into the discussion of it.

You say, " It is impossible for an intellectual being to
believe firmly in that of which he can give no account, or of
which he can form no conception. I hold the Deity, the
fancied Deity at least, of whom, with all his attributes, such
pompous descriptions are set forth, to the great terror of old
women, and the amusement of young children, to be an
object of which we form (as appears when we scrutinize into
our ideas) no conception, and therefore can give no account." P. xxxii. You also say, " All that Epicurus and
Lucretius have so greatly and convincingly said, is swept
away in a moment by these better reasoners, who yet
scruple not to declare, with Dr. Priestley, that what they
reason about is not the subject of human understanding.
But let it be asked, is it not absurd to reason with a man
about that, of which that same man asserts we have no
idea at all ? Yet, will Dr. Priestley argue, and say it is of
no importance whether the person with whom he argues has
a conception or not of the subject ? *Having no ideas includes
no impossibility ;* therefore, he goes on with his career of
words, to argue about an unseen Being, with another whom
he will allow to have no idea of the subject ; and yet it shall
be of no avail in the dispute, whether he has or no, or whether he is capable or incapable of having any. Reason fail-
ing, the passions are called upon," &c. Pp. 48, 49.

Let us now see whether the *career of words, without ideas,*
be more justly laid to my charge or yours. In order to this,
I wish, Sir, you would consider what conception you have,
or what account you can give of an uncaused and eternally
existent universe, every separate part of which bears undeniable marks of a design and intelligence, of which itself is
not capable. If you only attend to the case, I think you
will soon find that your ideas are far from being clear or
satisfactory ; notwithstanding you say in general, that " to
suppose an infinite succession of finite causes," is " so far
from being difficult," that " a mind not afraid to think, will
find it the most easy contemplation in the world to dwell
upon. Pp. 37, 38. " It is probable," you say, " if one

horse had a cause, all horses had.   But will not the argument be more consonant to itself, in supposing all horses
had the same cause ; and as one is seen to be generated from
a horse and a mare, so all were, from all eternity ?"   P. 38.

How this conclusion can appear *clear* and *satisfactory* to
your mind, is to me not a little extraordinary, as it gives
me no satisfaction at all.   To me it is the very same thing
as if, knowing nothing historically about the matter, a man
should find such a city as *London*, and conclude that it had
existed from eternity, just as it is, and had no foreign cause ;
or as if, without knowing any thing concerning the production of *horses*, or of *men*, he should conclude that any *particular horse*, or *man*, had existed from eternity, without any
foreign cause.   I do not see how these cases differ ; because
the whole *race of animals* shews the same marks of design,
in the relation they bear to other parts of the system, that
the several parts of any individual being bear to the rest of
its particular system ; and of a design of which they are
themselves incapable.   Yet should any person affirm, concerning London, or concerning any particular horse or man,
what you do not hesitate to affirm concerning the *whole
species*, and concerning the *universe,* you would not scruple
to say, that he talked without having any distinct conception
or ideas, or without reasoning consequentially from them.
For there is no objection against the independent existence
of the *individuals*, that does not equally lie against that of
the *whole species*.

I am ready enough to acknowledge, that there is something relating to an *independent first cause*, of which I can
form no proper idea, that is, of which I have no knowledge.
But this certainly implies no *contradiction*, any more than
my ignorance concerning many other things, of the *existence*
of which I have no doubt.   Every thing that I see I suppose
to have a cause foreign to itself, because it is not capable of
comprehending itself ; and the whole *visible universe*, in this
respect, comes under the same description with any plant or
animal that is a part of it.   But there is not this objection
against the supposition of a being that is capable of comprehending itself, and all things else, having existed without
cause from all eternity, whatever other difficulties may attend
the speculation.   If, then, you adopt that opinion which is
pressed with the least difficulty, and is farthest removed from
a manifest absurdity, you must abandon that of the independent existence of the *visible universe*, and have recourse

to an *invisible first cause;* which is the only alternative left you, in order to avoid the most palpable absurdity.

As you may, perhaps, still object (though you do not urge it very particularly), that the visible universe itself, though bearing marks of design, may as well be conceived to have had no foreign cause, as that the cause of the universe should have had none; I shall endeavour to state more distinctly why I conceive that there is a very great difference in the two cases.

The obvious reason why an *eye*, which is properly an instrument, or a means to gain a particular end, and also why the *animal* that is possessed of it, which is a *system of means* adapted to various ends, cannot have been uncaused, is, that they are not capable of comprehending themselves. They are properly *contrivances*, and therefore necessarily suppose a *contriver*, just as much as a *telescope* does, which comes under the same description with the *eye;* being an instrument adapted to answer a particular purpose.

Consequently, the mind can never rest till it comes to a being possessed of that wonderful property, but of which we can have no distinct ideas, because we are not possessed of it ourselves, viz. *self-comprehension.* And this being must be so essentially different from all others, that, whereas they *must* be derived, this *may* be underived; and if it *may*, it will follow from other considerations, it absolutely *must.* For the mind will always revolt at the idea of going back *ad infinitum*, through an infinite succession of mere finite causes, whatever you may pretend to the contrary.

It is not pretended, as I have said, that we can conceive, *a priori*, that a being possessed of self-comprehension, must have been uncaused : but as the mind cannot rest till it arrives at such a being, and this is a circumstance essentially different from that in which we find every other intelligent being, it *may* be capable of self-existence, of which the others are not. Any real difference in the condition of these beings may be sufficient to interrupt the analogy between them, so that we cannot be authorized to conclude concerning the one, what we do concerning the other. But these beings differ in that very circumstance on which the inference, that a *superior cause is wanting*, depends. There must be some external cause of whatever is *limited* or *finite.* We cannot conceive the possibility of its independent existence. But whatever other difficulty attends the speculation, we cannot say the same concerning a Being *unlimited* and *infinite.*

If any being whatever bear marks of *design*, there must exist somewhere a *mind* capable of that design ; and if it be not capable of it itself, we must look for it in some other being. But if that being has within itself that perfect comprehension of itself, as well as of all things else that depend upon it, we have no longer the same motive to make any farther inquiries. Such a being as this may, for any thing we can prove to the contrary, have existed without cause, and from eternity. At the same time it must be acknowledged, as before, that, supposing no visible universe to have existed, it is absolutely inconceivable by us, on what principles, as we may say, such a being as the Author of this visible universe should exist. But being sensible of the one, we are necessarily led to infer the other.

I am, &c.

LETTER III.

Concerning the Seat of that Intelligence which is conspicuous in the visible Universe.

SIR,

IN former times, those who denied the being of a God, denied also that there was any proof of *intelligence* or *design*, in the visible universe. This, however, you readily admit; but you insist upon it, that the *seat* of this intelligence and design, is in the visible universe itself, and not in any being foreign to it. On this subject you are sufficiently explicit. " The *vis naturæ*," you say, " the perpetual industry, intelligence and provision of nature, must be apparent to all who see, feel, or think. I mean to distinguish this active, intelligent and designing principle, inherent as much in matter as the properties of gravity, or any elastic, attractive or repulsive power, from any extraneous foreign force and design in an invisible agent, supreme though hidden lord, and master over all effects and appearances that present themselves to us in the course of nature. The last supposition makes the universe and all other organized matter, a machine, made or contrived by the arbitrary will of another being, which other being is called *God;* and my theory makes a God of this universe, or admits no other God or designing principle, than matter itself, and its various organizations." P. xxviii.

I cannot help thinking, that when you attend to this hypothesis, you must be satisfied that, on your own principles, it is absolutely untenable.   If it be the *marks of design* in the visible universe, that compel you to admit there is *a principle of intelligence* belonging to it, this principle must be the *cause* of those marks of design.   But can you think this to be even *possible*, when you maintain, that every *cause* must necessarily be prior to its *effect ?*   Here an orderly system pre-supposes intelligence, and yet this intelligence arises from the order.   If this be not what is called *arguing in a circle*, I do not know what is.

You may say, that the *universe*, and the *order* belonging to it (from which its principle of intelligence arises) were equally from eternity, and therefore, that the one is not prior to the other.   But still, independent of any *priority*, you make the same thing to be, at the same time, *cause* and *effect* with respect to itself.   The cause of *intelligence* is still that very *order*, or that *system* which is produced by it.

To say that the whole visible system always existed as it now does, the *cause of its own order*, i. e. of itself, is a very different thing from saying that an invisible author of nature had an eternal and necessary existence.   This is merely a thing of which we have no *idea* or *comprehension*, but what implies no more *contradiction* than that *space* or *duration* should have been from eternity, and have been uncaused; though in this case we cannot exclude the idea of them, or suppose them not to exist, and in the other, we can.

Besides this capital defect in your hypothesis, and which obliges us to have recourse to that of an intelligent uncaused being, as the author of the visible universe, I have no objection to examining the two hypotheses by your own favourite test.

You say, as I have quoted before, p. 424, " that it is impossible for an intellectual being to firmly believe in that of which he can give no account, or of which he can form no conception."   You believe, however, that this visible universe, and the present course of nature had no beginning; and as an atheist (believing nothing foreign to the system of nature) you *must* believe it.   But look a little into your own mind, and say, whether you have any clearer idea of *nature*, than you have of the *author of nature* having had no beginning.   If you be ingenuous, you must acknowledge, that you have no more conception of your own hypothesis, than you have of mine; and therefore, that, in the very first instance, you gain nothing at all by it; being as much embarrassed as ever with the necessary belief of something, which, in some respects, is absolutely incomprehensible to you.

Again, though you believe that there is a principle of intelligence and design in the visible universe, can you say that you have any proper idea *how* this exquisite design, that we see in the formation of plants and animals, &c. can possibly result from the conjoined action of such things as the sun, moon and stars, earth, air and water, &c. of which the visible universe consists, any more than of its belonging to a being that is not the object of our senses? In what respect, then, do you believe in things less incomprehensible than I do? We must both equally acknowledge, that we are led by the most undeniable facts to believe what we clearly comprehend to be necessary to the existence of those facts, though we are both of us unavoidably led to speculate farther on the subject, till we get into regions far beyond our clear conception.

Exclusive of all *matter*, and of *deity* also, can you even say, that you have a distinct idea of *duration* itself having had no beginning; or of a whole eternity being actually expired at the present moment? This, you say, (p. 30,) is *an odd notion* of my own. But certainly that must be a proper *eternity*, or an *infinite duration*, which *exceeds all finite bounds*. Is it not thus that mathematicians always define *infinity?* Now, can you name, or write down, any number of *years*, or *periods of time*, that is not even infinitely exceeded by that *great period*, which is actually terminated by the present moment?

That the intelligence and design, which is apparent in the visible universe, should result from the several parts of this visible universe in conjunction, is so contrary to any analogy in nature, that whatever else we have recourse to, in order to account for it, this must be wholly inadmissible. And if a regular confutation of such a notion be at all difficult, the difficulty is of that kind which always attends the proving or disproving of such things as are almost self-evidently true or false.

The brain of a man, or of any other animal,. is a homogeneous connected mass, and may as well be endued with the properties of *sensation and thought*, as a stone with that of *gravity*, or a load-stone with that of *magnetism;* there being only an equal difficulty in conceiving *how* such powers can belong to, or depend upon, their respective substances. But in the visible universe there is no such homogeneity, or connexion of parts.

The *universe* at large, consisting of the different stars and their respective systems of planets, have less apparent connexion than the *solar system*; and the parts of this have a less intimate connexion than those of any one of the planets, for instance, the *earth*, to which we belong, and which we have the best opportunity of examining. And yet, that the *earth*, consisting of land, water and air, fossils, plants and animals, should compose *one thinking substance*, is more incredible than that a collection of buildings, called a *town*, should have a principle of intelligence, with *ideas* and *thoughts*, such as, by your own confession, must have been in that which comprehended and produced this system. For whatever is capable of *design*, is universally termed *mind*, and must have *ideas* and *thoughts*, whether it be material or immaterial. There is an end of all our reasoning concerning effects and causes, concerning marks of design and a principle of intelligence, if this conclusion may not be depended upon.

That principle of thought and intelligence, therefore, the marks of which cannot be denied to abound in the visible universe, must belong to something else than that universe. For, difficult as it may be to conceive, that there should be an *invisible being* pervading the whole system, and attentive to all things in it, and that this Being should have existed without any foreign cause, the supposition, though ever so confounding to the imagination, is less difficult than the contrary; and one or other of them *must* be admitted.

You allow that there is in nature a principle of *production*, as well as of *destruction*; so that, "whenever the globe shall come to that temperament, fit for the life" of any *lost species* of animals, "whatever energy in nature produced it originally, if ever it had a beginning, will most probably be sufficient to produce it again. Is not," you say, "the reparation of vegetable life in the spring, equally wonderful now, as its first production? Yet this is a plain effect of the influence of the sun, whose absence would occasion death, by a perpetual winter. So far is this question from containing, in my opinion, a formidable difficulty to the Epicurean system, I cannot help judging the continual mutability of things, as an irrefragable proof of this eternal energy of nature." P. 42.

To me the conclusion which you think so very probable, appears to be drawn directly contrary to all the known rules of philosophizing. Supposing, as you do, the cause of destruction to any species of animals, to be a change of temperature in the climate, still the re-production of those animals, when the country should have recovered its former temperature, would be as proper a *miracle* as any thing to which a believer in revelation gives that name, (and would, therefore, prove the existence of a power distinct from any thing in the visible universe, and superior to it,) because we see nothing similar to this in any similar circumstances of things at present. Take a vessel of water, with fishes and insects in it. You may freeze that water, and consequently destroy all the animals that it contains. But though you may thaw that water again, you might wait long enough before you would find any more such fishes or insects in it, provided you excluded the spawn, or eggs, of others.

If there be any such thing as the reproduction of any lost animal, as of those, the bones of which you speak of, * and there be no such thing as a being distinct from the visible universe, it must be produced by what now exists, and is visible to us ; but how this should be done by any *law* or *power of nature*, with which we are acquainted (and beyond this we are not authorized to form any judgment at all), though within your creed, is beyond my conception. As the animal you speak of was an inhabitant of the *earth*, I should imagine that you would think some power residing in, and belonging to, the earth itself might be sufficient for this purpose, without calling in the aid of the sun, moon, or stars. But how the earth, with all the animals and men upon it, are to go to work, in order to re-produce this animal, I have no knowledge. I know that I should be able to contribute very little towards it. " The energy of nature,—with which," you say, " every difficulty vanishes," p. 41, is a fine expression ; but when we come to realize our ideas, and to conceive in what manner this energy of nature is to be exerted, we are just as much at a loss how to connect it with the things to be produced by it, as if no such energy existed.

You say that " the reparation of vegetable life in the spring," is " equally wonderful now, as at its first production," and that this " is a plain effect of the influence of the sun." P. 42. I am really surprised that you can, even for a moment, suppose these two cases to be at all similar: We can only judge of *powers* by *observation* and *experience:* Now, whenever did you see any plant produced when the

* " Bones of animals have been dug up, which appertain to no species now existing, and which must have perished, from an alteration in the system of things taking place, too considerable for it to endure." *Answer*, &c., p. 41.

seed was properly destroyed? In this case, what can the *sun* do to produce it? If the sun has this power, why is it not sometimes exerted, so that we should see plants spring up by means of *heat* only, without their proper seeds? That there is a Being distinct from the visible universe, possessed of the power of controulling its laws, is not a random sup_ position, like this of yours, but is sufficiently proved by *fact,* as the history of revelation shews.

I am, &c.

LETTER IV.

Of the Proof of the Being and Attributes of GOD, *from Revelation.*

SIR,

I SHALL now venture to urge another argument, hinted at, in the conclusion of the last letter, for the belief of a Deity, as a being distinct from the visible universe, which you will not deny to be adapted to affect the minds of the *vulgar;* and if it be attended to, it cannot, I think, fail to give satisfaction even to philosophical persons, and must contribute to remove any doubts that may have been occa- sioned by metaphysical speculations on the subject. The evidence I mean, is that of *miracles,* which, if they be un- deniable, clearly prove the existence of a Being distinct from what is visible in nature, and a Being who can controul the laws of it; and this can be no other than the *Author of nature.*

The evidences of revealed religion are generally considered as *subsequent* to those of natural religion, and both of them are generally treated of as altogether independent of each other. But as revelation supposes the being of a God, whose will is revealed to us, so the historical proof of actual in- terruptions in the usual course of nature, in the visible universe, is a distinct proof of the existence of a power foreign to the visible universe itself, and capable of con- troulling it. And if there be marks of *design* in such inter- positions, if they be intended to answer some purpose, and some benevolent purpose, they are distinct proofs of the *intelligence* and *benevolence* of that foreign power. And that there have been such interruptions in the course of nature, we have, in my opinion, abundantly sufficient evidence. It is clear to me, that, all things considered, the man who disbelieves this evidence, must believe things much more extraordinary, and even more contrary to present appearances (as I think I have shewn in my *Institutes of Natural and Revealed Religion)* than those which he rejects.

Such interpositions, in which the Author of nature is exhibited as communicating his will to men, by the use of *language*, &c. is better adapted to give us an idea of a *character*, of *a disposition of mind*, and even of *design*, than the settled and regular course of nature ; though to a reflecting mind, this does not fail to suggest the same thing. Let any man, the most sceptical in the world, be supposed to have been present when Moses heard the voice distinctly pronouncing the words, *I am the God of Abraham, Isaac and Jacob*, &c. promising to bring his people out of Egypt, &c. and then to have passed through the Red Sea along with them, and also to have heard an audible voice pronouncing every word of the ten commandments from Mount Sinai ; or let a person be supposed to have heard the words which, in the course of the evangelical history, were three times audibly pronounced, but proceeding from no visible Being, *This is my beloved Son, hear ye him ;* let him have heard Jesus invoke that invisible Being, and immediately afterwards raise Lazarus from the dead ; and especially let him have conversed with Jesus after he had been publicly crucified and buried : I say, let us suppose any person whatever to have been present at any of these extraordinary scenes, so as not to be able to deny that astonishing changes in the laws of nature had really taken place; and then let us suppose it possible for him to deny the existence of a Being distinct from what we call *nature*, or the *visible universe*, and capable of controulling its laws, if we can.

Moreover, if this great invisible Being, who at his pleasure controulled the laws of nature, and thereby proved himself to be equal to the establishment of them, announced himself to be the *Author of nature*, and always assumed that character ; can we suppose it possible that any person, who really believed such miraculous interpositions, should entertain a doubt that there was an invisible Author of nature, distinct from any thing that he could see in it ? It is evident, therefore, that the miracles recorded in the Old and New Testaments are naturally adapted to give the fullest satisfaction concerning the being of a God, as well as of the truth of revelation ; and, therefore, that in order to disprove the being of a God, a person must likewise disprove the evidences of the Jewish and of the Christian revelations, which I think

he will find it difficult to do, consistently with his retaining
faith in any history whatever. But this is not my present
business, farther than to point out the connexion between
the evidences of natural and revealed religion, and to shew
what you have to do before you can effectually refute either
of them.

I shall conclude this letter with shewing, that, admitting
what you profess to do concerning the visible universe, the
intelligence, and the *energy of nature*, you may admit the
whole system of revelation ; so that, in fact, you have con-
ceded rather more than you intended.

If you admit an *intention*, or *design*, in nature, you cannot exclude the idea of what we call *character*, and proper
personality, whether it belong to a being distinct from the
visible universe, or to the visible universe itself; and admitting this, the whole system of revelation may follow. And
this, in fact, is all that I am solicitous about, because it is
all that I am affected by, as it implies every thing on which
my hopes or fears are founded.

The power, or principle, that formed the eye, with a view
to enable us to see distant objects, and which for excellent
purposes established all the laws of nature, may also, for the
best of purposes, have occasionally controulled them. That
power which formed the organs of speech, may itself have
spoken from Mount Sinai, and have given mankind an
assurance of a resurrection from the dead by Jesus Christ.

It is this *power* or *principle*, in whatever it resides, that
commands my homage and obedience. It is *properties* and
powers, and not *substance*, that I pretend to have any concern
with. But I think it contrary to analogy, and the rules of
just reasoning, to suppose these powers to reside in the visible
universe; and therefore I prefer the hypothesis which ascribes
them to an invisible Being, distinct from it.

If you admit a principle of intelligence, and a power of
production and *reproduction* in nature, you are prepared to
admit all the facts on which the system of revelation is
founded; and whether they be true or false, is a thing to be
determined by *historical evidence*. If, as you say, " a future
state" be certainly desirable ; if you " firmly wish" for it,
and " are resolved to live as if such a state were to ensue,"
p. xxx ; if " immorality," as you also say, p. x. " has not
preceded" your unbelief, and will not follow it, I have no
doubt but that, by giving due attention to this evidence,
you will again become a believer and a Christian. But then,
I think, you will not long retain your present hypothesis, of

a principle of intelligence and design residing in, and properly belonging to, the visible universe; as there will then be no conceivable reason why you should not believe, and rejoice in the belief of a Supreme Being, or a maker and a moral governor of the universe, as well as myself.

I am, &c.

LETTER V.

Of the Moral Attributes of the Deity.

Sir,

As to the *moral attributes* of the Deity, viz. his *benevolence* and his *justice*, I shall not enter very far into the argument at present, not thinking that what I advanced before is at all invalidated by your merely asserting the contrary.

You say, "Take a view of human existence, and who can even allow that there is more happiness than misery in the world?" P. 22. I should think that you yourself allow it, when you speak, p. 27, of a future life (expecting it, I suppose, to resemble this) as *desirable*. However, the bulk of mankind, I doubt not, enjoy, and value their present existence. I do for one. You allow that " the condition of mankind is in a state of *melioration*," p. 4; and if this be the case, though happiness should not preponderate over misery at present, it is sure to do so in due time; so that, looking forward to the whole of things, the argument for the goodness of God, with respect to mankind at least, is quite satisfactory. "Who," you say, "will ever resolve the question if evil and pain are good and necessary now, why they will not always be so?" P. 22. I answer, this may be the case in some degree, and yet be consistent enough with the proper meaning of the figurative descriptions of a future life in the Scriptures. If you admit the doctrine of *melioration*, you must admit that, if we continue to exist, all evil will gradually vanish; and I think that, on the principles of Dr. Hartley's Theory of the Mind, I could shew, in some measure, *why* it will be so; but the discussion would be too long for this place.

Your argument against the belief of a God, at least of a just and righteous Being, on account of his not interposing to punish vice, and especially those who deny his existence, seems to me very unworthy of any person pretending to reason. " If that wished-for interposition of the Deity is put off to a future existence," you say, I cannot help observing, that future day has been already a long while waited for in vain, and any delay destroys some one attribute or other of the Deity. He wants justice, or he wants the power, or the will, to do good and be just." P. xxx. " Shall then such a tremendous Being," you say, " with such a care for the creatures he has made, suffer his own existence to be a perpetual doubt? If the course of nature does not give sufficient proof, why does not the hand divine shew itself by an extraordinary interposition of power? It is allowed miracles ought not to be cheap or plenty. One or two, at least, every thousand years might be admitted. But this is a perpetual standing miracle, that such a being as the depicted God, the author of nature, and all its works, should exist, and yet his existence be perpetually in doubt, or require a Jesus, a Mahomet, or a Priestley, to reveal it. Is not the writing of this very answer to the last of those three great luminaries of religion, a proof that no God, or no such God, at least, exists? Hear the admirable words of the author of " The System of Nature :" *Comment permet il qu'un mortel comme moi ose attaquer ses droits, ses titres, son existence même ?"* P. 49.

This, Sir, I think to be as weak as (if I may be allowed one harsh expression) it is arrogant. You, and the author of the work you quote, must have a very high opinion, indeed, of your own importance, and of the force of your writings, to imagine that a *miracle* is requisite to confute them. I trust that something far short of this will be abundantly sufficient for the purpose, with respect to mankind at large ; and, as to your own particular conviction, it may be no very great object with the Author of the universe. His wise general laws, and the excellent maxims of his government, may admit a much greater partial evil than that, and make it subservient to good. The wisdom of God will, I doubt not, appear most conspicuous when it shall be seen that sufficient provision was made, two thousand years ago, for remedying all the evils which, from foreign causes, have been introduced into the system of religion since that time. Christianity, I am confident, will be able, without the aid of any more miracles, to free itself from all its impurities, and command the assent of all the world, even the learned and most sceptical not excluded.

As to your calling upon the Divine Being to vindicate himself from your impiety, any wise and merciful sovereign,

---

* " How can he suffer a mortal like me to question his rights, his titles, and even his existence?" (P.)

who should allow his subjects a proper time for forming their characters and conduct, before he thought proper to interpose, in order to reward or punish them, might be insulted in the same manner by weak and impatient minds. If there be any such thing as a *state of trial* and *discipline*, some *delay* in administering justice must be admitted; and of what continuance that ought to be, there may be better judges than you, or the author of the *Système de la Nature*.

If you meant to pay me any compliment by classing me with *Jesus* and *Mahomet*, I must observe, that, to say nothing farther, it is a very awkward one. They (the one justly, and the other unjustly) pretended to divine communications, which you must know I never did.

I am, &c.

LETTER VI.

Of the moral Influence of Religion.

SIR,

You greatly misconceive, or mis-state, the influence of religion, when you say, " all which the knowledge of a God and the belief of a providence can in reality produce, scarce goes beyond some exterior exercises, which are vainly thought to reconcile man to God. It may make men build temples, sacrifice victims, offer up prayers, or perform something of the like nature; but never break a criminal intrigue, restore an ill-gotten wealth, or mortify the lust of man. If no other remedy were applied to vice than the remonstrances of divines, a great city, such as London, would in a fortnight's time fall into the the most horrid disorders. Religion may make men follow ceremonies: little is the inconvenience found in them. A great triumph truly for religion to make men baptize, or fast! When did it make men do virtuous actions for virtue's sake, or practise fewer inventions to get rich, where riches could not be acquired without poverty to others? The true principle most commonly seen in human actions, and which philosophy will cure sooner than religion, is the natural inclination of man for pleasure, or a taste contracted for certain objects by prejudice and habit. These prevail in whatsoever faith a man is educated, or with whatever knowledge he may store his mind." Pp. 43, 44.

Confident as you seem to be of your advantage on this

head, I have no doubt but that, if I may oppose one assertion to another, religion has gained the end that you propose,
viz. to *do virtuous actions for virtue's sake,* far more generally,
and much more effectually, than philosophy has ever done;
and that it hath carried men much higher in the path of virtue than you have even an idea of, if by the man who does
virtuous actions *for virtue's sake,* you mean that " great and
good man," described in your *Prefatory Address,* p. 33, who
" loves virtue because he finds a pleasure in it." For this is
far from being any heroic or noble principle. It is only a
more refined selfishness. Whereas, religion teaches men to
love others as themselves, and implicitly to obey God and
their consciences, as such, without any sinister view whatever. However, notwithstanding this, it is with the greatest
wisdom that the hope of reward, and the fear of punishment,
are proposed to us. If you have made any observations on
the human mind, you must know that, with or without the
belief of a God, men always begin to act from the simplest
and lowest motives; and that it is only by degrees, and the
force of habit, that these motives lose their influence, and
that men become capable of acting from more generous and
disinterested principles. If you be ignorant of this, you
have much to learn ; but you will find it admirably explained
by Dr. Hartley, to whom I refer you on the subject.

It is by slow degrees that a child comes to love even his
nurse or his parents. At first, he loves his food and his
play much more ; but in time he becomes capable of sacrificing both, and even his life, and not only to serve them,
but also his country and mankind. Though, therefore, religion begins with the *fear of God,* and the *hope of heaven,*
at length *perfect love casteth out fear,* and the true Christian
loves the Lord his God with all his heart (being wholly devoted
to his will), *and his neighbour as himself.*

Religion, if I have any idea of its nature and practical
tendency, is a very different thing from what you suppose it
to be. By extending our views to the certain prospect of a
future and better life, it must, in proportion as its principles
are attended to, give a man a higher idea of his *personal importance,* and of the *consequence of his actions;* and, in fact,
will make him a superior kind of being to the man who believes that his existence will close in a few years, and may
terminate to-morrow. You say, that " an atheist, feeling
himself to be a link in the grand chain of nature, feels his
relative importance, and dreads no imaginary being." P. 46.
But a theist, and a believer in revelation, conceives himself

to be a much more important link in the same grand chain of nature, and therefore will feel himself more concerned to act a part worthy of his rank and station. If he *fears*, it is only that great Being, who is the proper object of fear, and then only when his righteous will is not obeyed ; and his *hope*, which is certainly a delightful and valuable principle, must be allowed to be infinitely superior to any thing that an atheist can pretend to.

Besides, upon your own principles, you cannot deny that religion *must* have great practical influence, if it be really believed, so long·as mankind are governed by hopes and fears. Why is it that the *laws* and the *gallows*, as you say, keep in order such a city as London, but that men fear detection, and dread pain and death ? But a real believer in revelation well knows that if he act wickedly he can never escape detection, and that he has much more to fear than man can inflict upon him. How is it possible, then, that men should not be influenced by it ? I make no doubt but that its practical influence is very great, and even that it weighs something with those who profess to disclaim it. Indeed, human nature must be a thing very different from what we know it to be, if the principles of religion, firmly believed, (as, no doubt, they are by many,) have no real influence. No man, acquainted with history, or with common life, can deny the influence either of *enthusiasm* or of *superstition*, which are only perversions of religion.

You do not hesitate to say, that " whatever advantage religion has had in the enumeration of its martyrs, the cause of atheism may boast the same," p. xxi ; and you " mention *Vanini** as a martyr for atheism." I will not dispute the point with you, but I think I have read an account of Vanini, which represents him as not having been properly an atheist, as not having had the power of recantation at the stake, and as suffering with more reluctance than has been sometimes given out ; all which circumstances make his case much less to your purpose. But, admitting all that you can wish with respect to it, very little, we know, is to be inferred from the conduct of any *single person*, because he may be influenced by motives which will have little weight with the generality of mankind.

On the contrary, it must be something adapted to in-

. * An Italian imprisoned in England, on a charge of irreligion, in 1614, and burnt at Toulouse, in 1619, at the age of 34, the executioner having first cut off his tongue. His *atheism* has been justly questioned.

fluence *human nature in general*, and cannot but have real
moment in the conduct of men, that can produce such lists
of ready and cheerful martyrs as Christianity can boast;
men of all countries, of all ages, and of every rank and
condition in life, and differing from one another in as many
circumstances (and especially in the belief of particular
doctrines) as you can name; while they have agreed in
nothing besides the simple *profession of Christianity*, and the
belief of *a future life of retribution.* There can be no doubt,
therefore, but that, since the same causes will always produce the same effects, a time of persecution would now call
forth: as many martyrs as ever. Surely, then, if we may
judge from observation, as philosophers ought to do, we must
be convinced, that there is something in *this belief* that is
adapted to affect the hearts and lives of men, and that in
the greatest and happiest manner.

. Should you yourself suffer martyrdom in the cause of
atheism, as you express your readiness to do, p. xxi, (but in
which few will believe you to be in earnest, because, with
your prospects, they will think you a fool for so doing,) it
will contribute very little to impress mankind in general in
favour of your principles; and though you may possibly
have some admirers, I will venture to say you will have
few followers. . Unbelievers, of my acquaintance, make no
scruple of conforming to any thing that the state requires;
and, I am confident, would be the first to laugh at you, if
they were to see you going to the stake.

I am, &c.

LETTER VII.

Miscellaneous Observations.

Sir,

I do not care to animadvert upon all those passages in
your answer, in which you seem to have mistaken my
meaning; but I must take notice of one or two of them.

It is not fair in you to say, as you seem to do, that because I have endeavoured to prove that an atheist cannot
be quite sure that there will be no future state, I therefore
allow that " the course of nature may be as it is without a
God, and that there is, therefore, no natural proof of a Deity."
P. 25. What then, Sir, was my object in those Letters, to
which you have made a reply? Was it not to unfold and

exhibit the natural proof of a Deity? Do you infer whatever you please from my writings, but do not insinuate that I myself infer or allow it.

You charge me very unjustly with giving up " the reality of a *particular providence*," and you say you " give it up too ;" p. xxix ; whereas, I only deny those *frequent miraculous interpositions*, which some have supposed. But, notwithstanding this, I believe that every thing, and every event, in the whole compass of nature, was originally appointed to fit its proper place ; and this you yourself must also admit, if you acknowledge a principle of *intelligence* and *design* in the universe. For this cannot be limited to some things only, but must extend to all. Besides, the greatest things have the strictest connexion with, and dependence upon, the smallest.

If, which you allow, there was a real *design* in the original production of things, and in the establishment of the laws of nature, there must likewise have been *a foresight* of whatever would happen in consequence of those laws, and, therefore, a proper adjustment of all events to one another ; so that you cannot admit a proper intelligence in nature, without admitting the doctrine of a particular providence. Indeed, Sir, you should not have abandoned the old atheistical principle of *chance*, and admitted of *design* in nature, without attending to all the consequences of this principle. Only pursue that principle consistently, and you will soon come to believe all that I do.

You consider it as a false assertion, that " a cause needs not be prior to its effect." P. 5. Now many *secondary causes* cannot be conceived to exist a moment without producing their proper effects, as the sun, without giving light, a magnet, without attracting iron, &c. This, therefore, *may* be the case with the *original cause* of all things ; so that his works, as well as himself, may have been from all eternity.

This, however, I have only mentioned, as what may perhaps be a more probable supposition, than that the Divine Being should have existed a whole eternity without creating any other being. But this opinion is not necessarily connected with the simple proof of the being of a God.

It may not be amiss to take some notice of what you say with respect to *authority*, in the question we are discussing. I am as far as you can be from laying much stress on mere authority in matters of *speculation* and *reasoning*, though it is impossible for any man not to be more or less influenced by it. But I can by no means think with you, that " mo-

dern philosophers are nearly all atheists." P. xxiv. Indeed,
if this be the case, there must, by your account, be very few
in this country, at least you are not acquainted with many
of them ; and therefore, from your personal knowledge, can
have no authority for the assertion.   For you say, p. xvi.
you, know of none besides *yourself* and *your friend*,. the
joint authors of this answer to my Letters.   I am ready,
however, to allow that what you say may be nearly true
with respect to France and Italy, though I believe it is by
no means the case, as yet, in England ; and if you confine
yourself to those who have really advanced the bounds of
natural knowledge, and who have distinguished themselves
the most in the character of *philosophers*, you will not, I
think, find so many atheists among them, in any country, as
you may have supposed.

   You mention Hume, Helvetius, Diderot and D'Alem-
bert ; but I do not remember to have heard of any discoveries in natural or moral science made by any of them.   This
I do not say to insult them, or to insinuate that they are not
entitled to the reputation they have gained, though I scruple
not to avow this with respect to Mr. Hume.*   They have
their excellencies, but they are of a different kind.   Some
of them are mathematicians, but, properly speaking, I do
not know that any of them are to be allowed a rank, at least
any high rank, among philosophers.   In a general way of
speaking, indeed, it may be proper enough to call any person
a philosopher, who only gives his attention to the subject
of philosophy, and is acquainted with the discoveries of
others ; but when you mentioned particular names, as those
of persons known to the world in the character of philosophers, and especially so few as *four*, you should have
selected those who had made important discoveries of their
own.   You can hardly think it sufficient ·to entitle a man
to the rank of a *philosopher*, that he is merely *an unbeliever
in natural or revealed religion.* ·

   As to what you are pleased to say I myself might have
been, if I had not from my " first initiation into science,
been dedicated to what is called the immediate service of

---

* As what I have observed concerning Mr. Hume, in this place, may be misunderstood, and be thought to be invidious, I shall add what I have taken several
opportunities of saying before, viz. that I am far from thinking that it requires
great mental powers to make discoveries in natural philosophy.   They have generally been made by accident.   But as Mr. Hammon seemed willing to avail himself
of the authority of *philosophers*, I have only observed that, be their merit what it
may, that kind of authority, 'strictly speaking, and when the term is properly
defined, makes very little for him, not many of those who have distinguished themselves in that way having been atheists. *(P.)*

God," p. xxiv. it is a thing that cannot be known, except to my Maker. It is evident that you have little knowledge of my history, nor is it of any importance to the world that it should be known. I have, however, been more than once, and for a considerable length of time, near fourteen years in all, out of what you, in ridicule, call the *immediate service of God*, after I had been several years engaged in it; and now, without having any reason to complain of age or infirmity, and in preference perhaps to more lucrative pursuits, I have, from pure choice, resumed it; and I hope to continue in it as long as I shall be capable of doing the duties of it.

Sincerely wishing that you may come to see the subject of our discussion in the same light with myself, and thereby attain to the same perfect satisfaction in your pursuits and prospects that I have in mine,

I am,

Sir,

Your very humble Servant,

J. PRIESTLEY.

Birmingham, May, 1782.

LETTERS

TO A

𝔓𝔥𝔦𝔩𝔬𝔰𝔬𝔭𝔥𝔦𝔠𝔞𝔩 𝔘𝔫𝔟𝔢𝔩𝔦𝔢𝔳𝔢𝔯.

◆◆◆

PART II.

CONTAINING

A State of the Evidence of revealed Religion, with Animadversions on the two last Chapters of the First Volume of Mr. Gibbon's History of the Decline and Fall of the Roman Empire.

——— Ne te auferat ebrius ardor,
Neu clausos radiis oculos opponat apertis.
Utere mente tua.   Procul anticipata repelle
Judicia ; et recto librans examine lances,
Hanc demum, audita causa, complectere partem,
Quam mens, et ratio veri studiosa, probabit.
ANTI-LUCRETIUS.

[1787.]

◆◆◆

THE

PREFACE.

⁓⁓⁓⁓⁓⁓

IT is with much satisfaction that I have now completed this series of *Letters*, in which I have advanced what appears to me to be the best calculated to remove the objections of philosophical persons to the evidences of natural and revealed religion.

In this discussion, I flatter myself, that I have some advantage over those who have hitherto treated the same subject, both with respect to what I have undertaken to defend, and the mode in which the defence is conducted.   The articles that I undertake to defend are more consonant to reason, and my proof of them rests on the same principles on which all philosophical investigations proceed, so that, if I do not deceive myself, I have brought the questions concerning the being of a God, the truth of his moral government here, and the certainty of a life of retribution to come, (which are the great principles of all religion,) into a state in which it will be more easy to come to a fair issue with unbelievers, and to decide whether there be sufficient ground for our faith in them, or not.

With respect to both natural and revealed religion, all that we have to do is to consider whether *actual appearances*, and known *facts*, can be accounted for on any other hypothesis. In natural religion, the appearances to be accounted for are *the constitution and laws of nature*. In revealed religion, they are certain *historical facts* as indisputable as any natural appearances. They are the belief of the miracles of Moses and of Christ, and that of his resurrection, in given circumstances. As appearances in nature cannot, I apprehend, be accounted for without admitting an intelligent Author of nature, distinct from nature itself, and also that this Author of nature is a benevolent and righteous Being; so the simple fact, of the belief of the great events on which depends the truth of the divine missions of Moses and of Christ, cannot, I apprehend, be accounted for, without admitting the reality of those events.

To this particular state of the question, I have endeavoured to confine myself in this second series of Letters, referring the reader for the discussion of many things relating to the evidence of revelation to more systematical works, and to that short view of the whole compass of it, which will be found in my *Institutes of Natural and Revealed Religion*. (Vol. II. pp. 123—190.)

In this second part of my work, I have considered the divine missions of Moses and of Christ as proved by exactly similar arguments, but with little regard to their connexion; and to this *similarity of arguments* I earnestly wish to draw the attention of learned and candid *Jews*, being confident that, when once they shall truly understand the ground on which they ought to receive, and must defend, the divine mission of Moses, they will be convinced that they must also admit the truth of the divine mission of Christ; and this being admitted, they will soon acknowledge that every other objection to Christianity, on which they have laid any stress, must fall to the ground.

Those Jews with whom I have conversed or corresponded, though they firmly believe what they have been taught concerning the truth of their religion, do not appear to me to have a sufficiently distinct apprehension of the true ground of their own faith, or what arguments they must allege in order to convince an unbeliever that Moses had a divine mission, and that he worked real miracles in proof of it. A previous controversy with unbelievers would shew them the ground on which they must stand, and then, I think, they must clearly perceive that the truth of the divine mission of Christ stands more firmly and unexceptionably on the same ground, in consequence of the origin of Christianity being nearer to our own times, and more within the compass of acknowledged history.

I therefore wish that the Jews, to whom I have addressed a series of *Letters*,* would consider this work as an appendage to them, having the same object with respect to *them*, viz. as unbelievers in Christianity. They will, I flatter myself, receive some satisfaction from seeing in them a clear state of the evidences of their own religion; and I am not acquainted with any writings of their own in which this is given or attempted. Being well grounded in this, they will soon be satisfied that it is impossible for them to defend their own faith, without, at the same time, admitting what will be sufficient to vindicate ours also. Both the systems are, in effect, but one, and must stand or fall together.

It is also earnestly to be wished that the attention of *Christians*, as well as that of Jews, might be drawn to this subject, that having a clearer idea of the *certainty*, as well as of the *value* of their faith, they might both be able to defend it, whenever they hear it attacked, and also prize it the more, and be more careful to govern their lives by it. Without this, men are but *nominal Christians*, which is in reality much worse than being no Christians at all. Better would it be for any man never to have heard the name of Christ, than be his disciple in *name only*.

To be Christians to any purpose, we should always keep in view the great practical principles of our religion. It ought not to be in the power of business, or of pleasure, to make us lose sight of them. Christianity will be no obstruction to any thing that is truly rational, and becoming a man, with respect to either; and whatever is not rational, ought to be abandoned on principles that are even not Christian.

---

* " Inviting them to an amicable discussion of the evidence of Christianity." 1786.

It is because I consider the principles of Christianity as properly *practical* ones, that I am less solicitous about the conversion of any unbelievers who are much advanced in life, at least for their own sakes, since their dispositions and habits are already formed, so that it can hardly be supposed to be in the power of new and better principles to change them. But I wish it for the sake of *younger persons*, on whom their opinions have influence, and on whom good principles might have the greatest effect.

To unbelievers of a certain age, a conviction of the truth of Christianity would only be the acquisition of a new speculative truth, the magnitude and value of which would never be fully felt, or make much impression on them. Having heard it from their infancy, ·having in general believed it for some time, and not coming to disbelieve it, till they had long disregarded it, it will not have the effect of *absolute novelty,* as it had with the heathen world at the time of the promulgation of Christianity, when it produced a wonderful change in the lives and manners of persons of all ages. With respect to those unbelievers of the present times who are hackneyed in the ways of the world, their minds are already so occupied, that they would give but little attention to the principles of Christianity, if they should come to believe in it.

But, be the advantage more or less to such unbelievers themselves from their conversion to Christianity, there are others to whom it might be the greatest benefit. We see every day how men of reputed sense, and general knowledge, are looked up to by those who are young, and entering upon the busy scenes of life, and whose minds are not yet so much occupied, but that they might feel the full force of new truth. If they only perceive a person of acknowledged ability, and general good character, to smile when the subject of religion or Christianity is mentioned, they will suspect, perhaps conclude at once, that there is nothing in it that deserves their attention, and having this persuasion, however hastily formed, they may go without restraint into that career of vicious indulgence, to which their age prompts, and which they know Christianity forbids.

Whereas, were all persons of respectable characters, on other accounts, believers in Christianity, though they might not have much zeal for it, they would at least behave and speak in such a manner, when the subject was mentioned, as would lead young persons to consider it as a serious business, and not to be trifled with ; and this might lead to the most desirable consequences. What young persons embrace, they embrace with ardour, and their minds are not so much engrossed with the things of this world, but that they might attend to those of another; and, notwithstanding the impetuosity of passion, there is in uncontaminated youth, an ingenuous modesty, a sense of honour, and a dread of vice, almost peculiar to that early period of life, which, aided by good principles, may be more than equal to the restraint of their passions, and render them capable, as we frequently see them to be, of the most heroic acts of virtue.

But the greatest advantage that I look to is, that, when the parents are Christians, their children will be in the way of receiving a religious and christian education, in consequence of which they will be brought acquainted with the Scriptures from their earliest years; and without this, it is hardly possible that they should ever acquire a true relish for them. The phraseology of the Scriptures, notwithstanding the noble simplicity, and true sublimity of many parts of them, is (at least according to our present translation) so uncouth to an European ear, and both the customs, and the popular opinions of the oriental nations, which were adopted by the pious Jews, as well as others, appear so strange, that persons, whose taste has been formed by the modes of modern education, will often be more struck with such circumstances as will tend to make them smile, than with those that ought to make them serious. This will more especially be the case with those whose minds have got a tinge from reading the profane jests of such writers as Voltaire. There are many persons whose minds are in such a state, that it is not even in their own power to make the allowance that they ought to do, and which they are even sensible they ought to do, for the circumstances above-mentioned, so as to read the Scriptures with the same satisfaction and advantage, that one who has been educated a Christian, and been brought up with a reverence for those sacred books, habitually does. Our feelings are far from so readily following our opinions.

Not that I consider the books of Scripture as *inspired*, and on that account entitled to this high degree of respect, but as authentic records of the dispensations of God to mankind, with every particular of which we cannot be too well acquainted. The sacred writers, as we justly call them, were, moreover, in general, persons of such exalted piety, and disinterested benevolence, (the most genuine and affecting marks of which abound in their writings,) and the histories themselves are so valuable and improving, that no other reading can supply the place of this. It is in vain that we look in profane history, for a narrative so instructive, for characters so excellent, or forms of devotions so pure. What is there in all the remains of heathen antiquity comparable to the book of Psalms ? There never existed among the Greeks or Romans that knowledge of one God, the maker and preserver of all things, and that persuasion concerning his universal and righteous government, which alone can inspire such sentiments, and dictate such compositions.

My principal object in this work will easily be perceived to have been to give a just view of the circumstances in which Christianity was promulgated ; since, from the consideration of these alone, can it be demonstrated that the origin of it was divine ; and in describing those I have been much assisted by *Dr. Lardner's Jewish and Heathen Testimonies,** a work of singular value, and which, in my opinion, no unbeliever, who has heard of it, can hold himself excusable in rejecting Christianity, till he has read and considered. From this work only have I given the view of ancient objections to Christianity, in the 14th and 15th Letters. I have lately had occasion to peruse the authors from which he has collected them, but I know of nothing of much importance that can be added to what he has produced, and I thought it of some use and consequence to bring into one view, what is dispersed through four quarto volumes. I have chosen his translations, in preference to any that I might have given of my own, as no person will question his fidelity, his diligence, or his universal impartiality.

. Great benefit would accrue to Christianity, if it be founded in truth, (and on no other supposition would I wish to have any respect for it at all,) from a calm and free discussion of its evidences with an intelligent unbeliever. This I endeavoured to procure when I animadverted upon *Mr. Gibbon's two chapters* in the conclusion to my *History of the Corruptions of Christianity.* But with the invitation I then gave Mr. Gibbon, he has hitherto refused to comply. What may be inferred from his declining this discussion, it is for the public to judge, and it concerns himself, and not me.† A copy of these *Letters* will also be sent to him, and if he (or any other unbeliever of ability and character) choose

---

* " A Large Collection of Ancient Jewish and Heathen Testimonies to the Truth of the Christian Religion, 1764." Re-published in his Works, 1788, Vol. VII.—IX.

† See the *Correspondence* annexed to the *Discourses* on *Revealed Religion*, 1794.

to answer them, he may depend upon hearing from me in reply. And, in my opinion, and that of many others, no public controversy could be more useful, or more seasonable.

In this case it will be necessary for Mr. Gibbon, if *he* should undertake the discussion, to lay aside the mask he has affected to wear, by pretending to believe in Christianity, when he evidently does not, but it is a mask by which he conceals nothing. If I treat any thing in the religion of my country as absurd, I do it openly and gravely ; and at the same time I hold myself ready to defend whatever I advance, or to retract what I may be unable to defend.

If Mr. Gibbon believes Christianity to be *mischievous* as well as *false*, let him, as becomes an honest man and a good citizen, openly disclaim and openly oppugn it. If he thinks it to be false, but *useful*, let him neither write nor speak on the subject. Nothing can justify this, but a persuasion of its being better for the world that the scheme should be exploded and abandoned.

If any man, embarked in a voyage with others, perceives that the vessel in which they sail will certainly be lost, and that it is not in his power, or in theirs, to prevent it, he ought to keep his knowledge to himself, and not give others needless alarm and distress. If he think that, by proper exertion, there is a possibility of saving the ship, he ought to give the greatest and quickest alarm that he can. But in no case can he be justified in giving his opinion in such a manner, as that some of the passengers might understand him to mean one thing, and others another ; and in amusing himself with laughing at the mistakes that were made about his real sentiments. Such, however, has been the conduct of Mr. Gibbon with respect to a subject of infinitely more moment than the danger of a shipwreck.

If Mr. Gibbon be, as he pretends, a believer in Christianity, and a future life, let him write on the subject in such a manner, as that no person shall entertain a doubt of it ; and so that their faith may be strengthened, and not weakened by his writings. If he be an unbeliever, let him no longer trifle with the world, and use the language of deceit, without deceiving.

By replying to Mr. Gibbon, in these *Letters*, I am far from meaning to insinuate, that I think lightly of what others have done in the same controversy. On the contrary, every answer to him that I have yet seen, contains a sufficient refutation of every thing of any consequence that he has advanced against Christianity,* and the defence that he has made of *himself* against Mr. Davis, is far from amounting to a defence of the *cause* that he has espoused, which is all that the public is concerned with.   The reply of the learned Bishop of Landaff is particularly valuable, but I am sorry to see him affect to believe Mr. Gibbon to be sincere in the regard that he professes for Christianity.†   This I think to be unworthy of a christian bishop, as I think Mr. Gibbon's pretences are unworthy of a man: I treat Mr. Gibbon as unquestionably an unbeliever, and in that character I wish him to make his defence.

———

Since this preface was sent to the press, I have seen *Dr. Toulmin's* ‡ *Essay on "The Eternity of the World."*   But after what I have said in reply to Mr. Hammon, I see no reason to take particular notice of it.

He is far from denying *design*, or a principle of *intelligence*, in the universe, and sincerely wishes " to confirm mankind in the belief of the existence of what is *great, powerful* and *good.*" P. 130.

" So far," says he, " are the arguments which I have made use of from having the smallest tendency to damp the expectations of future being and felicity, that they open the most brilliant prospects to the imagination ; they enforce the excellence of moral rectitude, and the existence of infinite wisdom and intelligence, inseparable from, and pervading, an eternal universe." P. 133.

He asserts the eternity of the human race.   But, in my opinion, only proves a state of the earth anterior to the period of the Mosaic account of the creation, which I be-

* I shall take this opportunity of acquainting my reader with the satisfaction I have just received from an Essay in *Mr. Cumberland's Observer*, Vol. I. No. 11, in answer to what Mr. Gibbon has said concerning the darkness at our Saviour's crucifixion.   His remarks appear to me to be very judicious, and well expressed.   I have some doubts, however, whether that darkness was preternatural, as well as whether it was very considerable   (*P.*)

Mr. Wakefield expresses "some doubt whether the *Evangelist* (Matt. xxvii. 45,) himself designed to point out this *darkness* as a proper *miraculous* event."   He adds, that " many circumstances of the crucifixion evidently prove the *darkness* to have been slight, so as not to have prevented the standers by from distinctly seeing each other " *St. Matthew*, 1782, p. 399.   See also Lardner's Works, VII. pp 372, &c. and Watson's *Apology*, Letter V.

† See in the Bishop's *Life*, by himself, just published, the account of his correspondence with Mr Gibbon, &c. in 1776, on the publication of the *Apology*.

‡ *George Hoggart Toulmin*, M. D. Wolverhampton.   This author published " The Antiquity and Duration of the World, 1780;" " The Eternity of the World, 1785 ," " The Eternity of the Universe, 1789."   See the introduction to the latter volume.

lieve is the general opinion of philosophical Christians. He descants on the pretensions to high antiquity by the Hindoos, as those which he thinks to be the best founded, but he says nothing of the writings of Moses, who was so near to the origin of the present race of man, as (independent of other considerations, not noticed by Dr. Toulmin) makes it highly probable that his account is very near the truth.* But the belief of revelation does not absolutely require a belief of any events prior to the age of Moses, or such as himself and his contemporaries could not but have had the means of being well informed of.

---

* My author was led farther to consider this subject in Section II. of his " Comparison of the Institutions of Moses with those of the Hindoos," printed at *Northumberland* (America) in 1799, and which will, I hope, appear among the later volumes of this edition. Much light has been thrown on the same subject by Sir W. Jones, in his Dissertations, especially the *Ninth,* " On the Chronology of the Hindûs, written in January, 1788." He thus enters on an Inquiry, in which he was so well prepared to engage:—" The great antiquity of the *Hindûs* is believed so firmly by themselves, and has been the subject of so much conversation among *Europeans,* that a short view of their chronological system, which has not yet been exhibited, from certain authorities, may be acceptable to those who seek truth without partiality to received opinions, and without regarding any consequences that may result from their inquiries: the consequences, indeed, of truth cannot but be desirable, and no reasonable man will apprehend any danger to society from a general diffusion of its light; but we must not suffer ourselves to be dazzled by a false glare, nor mistake enigmas and allegories for historical verity." He then declares himself " attached to no system, and as much disposed to reject the *Mosaic* history, if it be proved erroneous, as to believe it if it be confirmed by sound reasoning from indubitable evidence." Thus he proceeds to inquire whether the system of *Indian* chronology " is not in fact the same with our own, but embellished and obscured by the fancy of their poets and the riddles of their astronomers." *Dissertations,* 1792, I. pp. 279, 280.

LETTERS

TO A

PHILOSOPHICAL UNBELIEVER.

PART II.

LETTER I.

Of the Nature of Testimony.

DEAR SIR,

I AM happy to find that, in my former *Letters*, I have been able to suggest to you such considerations as, by the help of your own just reflections, have removed the difficulties that lay in your way with respect to the belief of the being of a God, and of his moral government of the world. But you think that the arguments from the light of nature, in favour of a *future life*, amount to little more than to shew that the thing is *not impossible*, not being, upon the whole, repugnant to the observed course of nature; and that the striking *fact* of our seeing men die just like brutes or plants, without any symptom of revival, wears so different an aspect, that you cannot think we are sufficiently authorized to indulge so much as what may be called the *hope* of a resurrection. For as to the opinion of an *immaterial soul*, distinct from the body, which makes its escape at death, we are both agreed that no appearance in nature favours the supposition. Whatever the powers of *perception* and *thought* be in themselves, they evidently depend upon the organization of the brain ; and, therefore, according to all the received rules of philosophizing, must be ascribed to it, so that they cannot subsist without it.

Acknowledging, however, as you do, that a future life, and an endless continuance of being, (in which we shall make continual advances in knowledge and virtue, enlarging our comprehension of mind without limits,) affords a flattering prospect ; and as this is strongly, and with the greatest confidence, held out to us in the Christian, if not in the Jewish revelation, in which you know I am a believer, you wish that I would explain to you, as distinctly as I can, and from the first principles of *assent*, the proper ground of this faith in revealed religion, in the same manner as, in my former correspondence, I explained the principles of natural religion.   In other words, you wish me to inform you on what foundation it is that I believe that the Maker of the world, and of man, has at any time revealed his will to any part of the human race, so as to promise eternal life and happiness to those who obey it.

Encouraged by the success of my former attempt, I am very ready, on this, as on that occasion, to give you all the satisfaction in my power, and I earnestly wish that it may be with the same effect, as I am confident that, disposed as you are to the practice of virtue, a belief in revelation will make you a still better and much happier man even in this life. You will look with unspeakably more pleasure on every thing around you, and quit this scene of things, not only without regret, but with a satisfaction far exceeding that which you have ever had in it.

I shall begin with observing, that the evidence of revelation is necessarily of the *historical* kind, and rests upon *testimony;* and, though, I hardly need to explain the foundation of our faith in testimony, I shall, by way of introduction to the disquisition I am undertaking, observe that, philosophically considered, it arises from our *experience* that it may be depended upon; it having been found that there is generally a correspondence between what is asserted by men, and the things or events, which their assertions respect.   Thus, if one person tells me that another said or did so or so, and I find by any other evidence, (for instance that of my own senses,) that he actually *did* say or do what I was informed of, I am satisfied that the assertion I heard was true.   If I find by repeated experience, that the same person never does deceive me, I conclude that there must be a sufficient *cause* for this *constant appearance*, and that, in the same circumstances, the same effect may be depended upon.   In common language, I say that my informer is a *man of veracity*, and that he will not deceive me.   In the same manner, if, notwithstanding a number of impositions, I find that among mankind at large, a regard to truth greatly prevails over falsehood, I conclude that there is in general sufficient ground for *faith in testimony*.

Examining this interesting appearance more closely, I find in what cases testimony is most apt to be fallacious, as those in which men either have not sufficient opportunity of being well-informed themselves, or those in which they have an interest in deceiving others ; and separating these from other cases of human testimony, I find a still stronger ground of assent in the remaining cases.

It is true, that *single persons* may be so circumstanced, as that though to appearance, they may have had sufficient opportunity of being well informed themselves, and we can discover in them, no design to impose upon others, yet, through some unknown cause, their testimony may be defective on one or both of these accounts. But when we have the concurrent testimony of *different persons*, unconnected with each other, equally competent judges of what they relate, and to appearance equally impartial, that defect in the evidence is removed; it being to the last degree improbable that the same, or different unknown influences should affect many different persons, no way connected with each other. Accordingly, in many cases, we do not entertain the least sensible doubt of the truth of testimony, as that there exists such a city as Rome, or that Alexander conquered Darius. Our faith in a mathematical truth cannot be perceived to be stronger than our faith in such historical propositions as these.

I am, &c.

LETTER II.

Of the Evidence of Revelation.

DEAR SIR,

As human testimony is a sufficient ground of faith, it is applicable to every thing of which men can be said to be *witnesses*, that is, of whatever comes under the cognizance of their senses, as seeing, hearing, &c. and there is no fact so extraordinary, or unexpected, but may safely be admitted on this ground ; there being no limit in this case, but that of absolute *impossibility*.

Now, it cannot be denied but that it is in the power of God, the maker of the world, to signify his will to men, in the manner described in the history of the Jewish and Christian revelations, to perform all that is there advanced as a proof of his interposition in the case, and likewise to fulfil every thing that is there promised ; the most important article of which is, the raising of all mankind from the dead, and enduing them with a power of immortal life : because there is nothing in all this that implies a greater degree of power than must have been exerted in the creation of such a system as this of which we are a part. Whatever power it was that *established*, the same, no doubt, can *change* the laws of nature, or suspend the operation of them ; and I must now take it for granted, that there is a *cause*, or *author* of nature, and that this is a *designing* cause.

Whether this Being established the present order of nature from eternity, so that it be coeval with himself, or this part of the system had a beginning, from an exertion of power independent of any thing that preceded it, it must be in itself *possible*, that the same Being may exert a similar power whenever he pleases. There is no conceivable difference between this case and that of a man capable of erecting any particular engine, and retaining the power of stopping the motion of the engine, or altering the construction of it. All that can be said is, that no *motive* could exist, which should induce the Author of nature to interpose in this manner. But who can be authorized to say that the Divine Being, the Author of nature, must necessarily leave the present system to the operation of the present laws of it, and that there could never be any *propriety* or *use* in suspending them ? It must be extreme arrogance in any man to pronounce in this manner concerning his Maker.

Some interruption of the course of nature is the only proper evidence of the interposition of the Author of nature, and every other kind of evidence must necessarily be equivocal. Now there is an account of a great variety of such interpositions in the historical books of Scripture, facts, of which great numbers of persons, in some cases whole nations (by no means in circumstances in which it can be supposed that they could be deceived themselves, or be willing to deceive others) were witnesses. These interpositions were not confined to one age of the world, but distinguished several ages, to the time of Christ and the apostles.

The reality, however, of these events, is that which must be called in question by those who do not believe in the Jewish or Christian revelations. They must suppose, that the evidence alleged for the miraculous interpositions on the truth of which these revelations rest, is, in some respect or other, *insufficient;* and what a philosophical believer replies to them is, that there is a *law* respecting the validity of human testimony, as well as other things ; and that this particular testimony is so circumstanced, as that it will be more extraordinary, if it be not true, than if the things related should have happened. For such *testimony* is itself to be considered as a *fact* or *appearance*, which requires to be accounted for, as much as any other fact whatever. The most idle report cannot be raised without a *cause*. The unbeliever, therefore, should consider how he can account for the *existence* of the Jewish and Christian religions, as themselves *indisputable facts*. The cause of these facts, the believer says, is clearly found in the histories of those religions ; and he challenges the unbeliever to account for the facts on any other principle. Such I apprehend to be the true and philosophical state of the question which you wish me to discuss.

The generality even of Christians have been too apt to consider *christian faith* as something of a different nature from that which relates to other things, and unbelievers have, as might have been expected, taken their advantage of this circumstance. But the philosophical Christian forms his judgment concerning all similar propositions on similar principles, and makes no exception with respect to matters of religion. Thus, in all abstract propositions, that may be reduced to *number* or *quantity*. the evidence of truth is the coincidence of ideas belonging to the subject and predicate of any proposition. If, for example, three things, as three plants, three animals, or three men, cannot be one thing, one plant, one animal, or one man ; neither can three Divine Beings, or persons, (for in this case they must be the same thing) be only one God.

With respect to *hypotheses*, to explain appearances of any kind, the philosophical Christian considers himself as bound to admit that which, according to the received rules of philosophizing, or reasoning, is the most probable ; so that the question between him and other philosophers is, whether his hypothesis or theirs will best explain the *known facts*, such as are the present belief of Judaism and Christianity, and also the belief of them in the earliest ages to which they can be traced.

The unbeliever must say that these facts, and all that we certainly know to have been fact, may be admitted, without supposing that Moses or Christ had any divine mission, or were authorized by God to teach any doctrine at all ; and, consequently, that no miracles were ever wrought in proof of their mission. Whereas, the philosophical Christian says, that such facts as all persons in the least acquainted with history *must* admit, necessarily lead us to conclude, that Moses and the subsequent prophets, and also that Christ and the apostles, had a divine mission, and that miracles must have been wrought in attestation of them.

The philosophical Christian farther says, that the state of things could never have been what it is universally acknowledged to *be*, and *to have been*, without miracles ; and that the miracles which the unbeliever must have recourse to, besides answering no conceivable good purpose, must have been infinitely more numerous, and of a more extraordinary nature, than any that *he* has occasion to admit. For he maintains that, if the men who lived in the time of Moses, and also those who lived in the time of Christ and the apostles, were constituted as men *now* are (which must be taken for granted), they could not have believed the miracles recorded in the books of Moses, and in the New Testament, without either such sufficient evidence of their reality, as the writers of these books relate that they had (which he thinks most probable), or without a supernatural influence on their minds, disposing them to receive as true what was at the same time totally destitute of such evidence, and likewise manifestly contrary to their interest, and wishes, to receive ; so that great numbers of men must have been what we commonly call *infatuated*, or partially *deprived of their senses*, a thing which no person, who considers the circumstances of the case, can possibly admit.

They must also have been thus miraculously infatuated for the sake of building upon their belief of a series of events which had never happened, a system of religion, which of course could not be true, and therefore with a view to lead a great part of mankind, to this time, and probably to the end of all time, into a great mistake, and a mistake which they had no means of ever rectifying.

Now it can never be imagined that any miracles, and particularly so many, and of so extraordinary a kind, as this scheme requires, should have been wrought for such a purpose as this. And yet, the philosophical Christian maintains, that there is, in reality, no alternative between admitting such miracles as these, and for such a purpose as this, and the truth of those recorded in the books of Moses, the gospels, and the book of Acts, the credibility of which he submits to the most rigorous examination.

All that is necessary, therefore, to the proper discussion of the evidence of the divine mission of Moses, or of Christ, among philosophers, is to attend carefully to the circumstances which accompanied the promulgation of their respective religions, to consider the persons by whom they were received, and the influences to which they were exposed. And it appears to me, that this due attention has never yet been given to these circumstances by any unbelievers.

1 am, &c.

LETTER III.

Of the Antecedent Probability of Divine Revelation.

DEAR SIR,

To the state of the question in the preceding letter, an unbeliever will perhaps say, that the idea of divine interposition is so very extraordinary, from nothing of the kind having been known in our own times, that no evidence can authorize us to admit it; it being more easy to suppose that any testimony, however circumstanced, may be false, than that such accounts should be true.

But, besides observing that no experience of one age can be any contradiction to that of another* (and all history shews that there are a variety of events peculiar to certain periods; so that it by no means follows, that because we see no miracles in the present age, there never were any formerly), I shall, in this letter, endeavour to shew that, when the proper use of miracles, and the great object of revelation, are considered, it will not be at all incredible or improbable, that there may have been divine interpositions in former ages, though now they are not necessary, and therefore not to be expected.

Admitting the Author of nature to have had the kindest and greatest design respecting man, the rational part of his creation here (which, considering that God has been proved to be a benevolent Being, is certainly far from being improbable), viz. to lead him to the true knowledge of himself, of his duty here, and of his expectations hereafter, to lead him to cultivate proper affections respecting his Maker, and his fellow-creatures; thereby to exalt his nature, and train him for a higher sphere of existence hereafter; and admitting the nature of man always to have been what we now observe it to be, let us consider what method is best adapted to gain

---

* The objection to miracles as contradicted by present experience, is particularly considered in my *Institutes of Natural and Revealed Religion. (P.)* See Vol. II. pp. 113—117.

the end above-mentioned. With these views, would it be the wisest method to leave mankind to collect the knowledge requisite for this high moral improvement from their own observations on the course of nature, or to assist them by extraordinary communications or interpositions? That the latter, and not the former method, would be more *effectual*, and therefore preferable, may, I think, be concluded from the following considerations.

1. The knowledge necessary for this great object, viz. that of the being and unity of God, the extent of his providence and moral government, even that of several moral duties, the beneficial tendency of which is not apparent, and especially that of a future life (the demonstration of which seems, indeed, to be impossible from any appearances in nature), could never have been discovered by man.

It is true that some part of the human race have been destitute of this knowledge, and will probably remain so for many ages. But they were once in possession of it, though they have now lost it; and by subsequent revelations, things are put into such a train, as that, in due time, without any farther interposition, they must again come to the knowledge of all the useful truths above recited. It is also agreeable to the course of nature, that great things have small beginnings, and great excellence is always the produce of long time.

2. If it had been possible for men to have discovered the above-mentioned salutary truths by the light of nature, yet their attention might never have been drawn to any thing of the kind, without some direction. The bulk of mankind, at least, are not apt to attend to the causes of any uniform constant appearances, such as the rising and setting of the sun, the annual returns of summer and winter, seed-time and harvest, &c. They are only the more thoughtful and inquisitive, that endeavour to trace the causes of such phenomena as these. Whereas, if the sun should not rise, or should rise an hour later than usual, the attention of all mankind would be immediately excited; and from inquiring into the cause of a thing so *unusual*, they might be led to reflect upon the cause of what was *usual* and *regular*.

If it was of importance, therefore, that the attention of mankind should be drawn to the *Author of nature*, and that they should pay him any *homage*, there is not (as far as we can judge from our observation of human nature) any method so well calculated to produce the effect, as the exhibition of what we call *miracles*, or an interruption of the usual course of nature. So far, therefore, are miracles, which have so great an object, from being in themselves incredible, that we might even have expected them, on the idea of the Author of nature giving constant attention to the works of his hands, and being willing to engage the attention of his rational offspring to himself, as the means of exalting their natures, and fitting them for their proper happiness.

·How many are there, even of philosophers, who spend their lives in the investigation of the laws of nature, without ever raising their thoughts to the Author of nature, and even maintaining that there is no proper, that is, no intelligent Author of nature at all? If this be the case in the present highly enlightened age, what could we expect from an age destitute of all instruction? In these circumstances, it appears highly probable to me, that the idea of an intelligent Author of nature, at least of there being only *one*, infinitely great, wise and good author, would never have occurred to them at all.

Here then is a *nodus Deo vindice dignus*, a great end to be obtained, and no sufficient *natural means* to attain it. Consequently, *miracles*, having so important an use, are neither impossible nor improbable; and, therefore, the evidence of them is by no means to be rejected without serious examination. Very circumstantial evidence is, no doubt, requisite to establish their credibility, as that of any *unusual facts*, not analogous to any that we have observed. But human testimony, that of persons who have the perfect use of their senses, and under no prejudice, is abundantly competent to it.

The king of Siam, according to the story, had never seen water in any other form than that of a *fluid*, and, therefore, could have no idea, from his own experience, of the possibility of such a thing as *ice;* but, notwithstanding this, he might think it more probable that it should even become so hard as to bear men and carriages, than that the Dutchmen, who told him that it was actually sometimes so, in their country, should deceive him. In like manner, though no person now living has seen a river divide, and men walking across its channel, or any person come to life again after he had been unquestionably dead, yet, the testimony of past ages, to events of this kind, may be so circumstanced, as that it shall be naturally more probable that these things should have *then* taken place, than that the men of those ages should have combined to deceive both their contemporaries, and a posterity, by their relation of them; and in this case only, do I say that we ought to admit them.

I am, &c.

LETTER IV.

Of the Nature of Prejudice FOR, *or* AGAINST, *Revelation.*

DEAR SIR,

BEFORE I proceed any farther in this correspondence, you wish me to account for what appears to you to be a remarkable fact, viz. the great prevalence of infidelity among persons of a philosophical turn of mind. There must, as you justly observe, be a *cause* of this, as well as of every other *fact*, and though the history of revelation be true, there must be some adequate cause of its not always having been seen, or acknowledged to be so.

As I, who am myself, a believer in revelation, cannot think that the cause of infidelity in any person, is a want of sufficient evidence of its truth, I must account for it, by supposing that there is in all unbelievers, a state of mind which pre-disposes them either to give too little attention to the evidence of it, or to see that evidence, or the doctrines of revelation, in some unfavourable point of light; and in most, I think, it is owing to a want of attention to the subject, and this appears to arise very often from a secret wish that Christianity may not be true.

To be absolutely indifferent to the subject of religion and the doctrine of a future life, is hardly possible. A bad man cannot wish Christianity to be true, as a good man, especially one who has made considerable sacrifices to his integrity, cannot help wishing that it may be so. The suspicion only of its being well-founded must fill the mind of the former with painful apprehensions, and that of the latter with the most pleasing of all prospects. It might seem, therefore, that a good man is as likely to be biassed in favour of the evidences of revelation as the bad man is to be against them, did there not appear to be a considerable difference in some circumstances of the two cases.

A man has no motive to inquire into the foundation of his fears, unless he be previously determined to do every thing in his power to avoid the impending evil: because if he be previously determined to pursue a certain course *at all events*, he will think himself a gainer by troubling himself as little as possible about the risk that he runs in pursuing it; and this I apprehend to be the case with very many unbelievers. They are men of pleasure, or of ambition, to a considerable degree, though they may distinguish themselves by various liberal pursuits. Their habits and plans of life are fixed, and not being disposed to change them, they are disinclined to any *inquiry*, the issue of which might be a conviction of the importance of changing them. They are conscious to themselves that they have no reason to wish Christianity to be true, and, therefore, they think as little about it as possible.

On the other hand, the influence of the world around us is such, as that no man can have perfect confidence in his virtue and integrity. He may *hope* that a future life will be to his advantage, but this will not be such as to indispose him to inquire into the evidences of it.

Besides, every truly good man makes many sacrifices to his integrity, and, therefore, cannot but wish to know on what grounds he does this. A Christian refrains from many gratifications, for indulging in which, the world in general would not greatly blame, but rather applaud him. He has, therefore, sufficient motives to inquire whether he does not submit to these inconveniences without reason, and whether he has sufficient ground to expect an equivalent for his present sufferings, which, in time of persecution, may be very great.

It is said of the apostles, after the resurrection of our Saviour, that when they first heard of it, *they did not believe through joy.* The event was so far beyond their expectations, that they hesitated a long time before they could really believe it, and did not do it at last without the most satisfactory evidence. In the same manner will many virtuous and pious persons be affected with respect to the truth of that religion which promises them the glorious reward of a resurrection to immortal life and happiness, a thing of which they could not have any assurance from the light of nature.

Whether I have satisfactorily accounted for it or not, it is, I apprehend, indisputably true, that the generality of unbelievers are averse to inquire into the evidence of revelation. Few have taken the trouble even to read the Scriptures, which contain the history of it, though they would have read, with the greatest eagerness, any other writings of equal antiquity, and as remarkable for the peculiarities of their style and composition, &c. This can only arise from such a dislike of Christianity, as (whether they be distinctly aware of it or not) will necessarily lay an undue bias upon their minds against it.

On the other hand, believers in Christianity not only take a singular pleasure in reading the Scriptures, and every thing in favour of the evidence of it, but those of them who have a turn for reading and speculation, peruse with the greatest care whatever is written against Christianity; a proof that their wish to find Christianity true does not operate so unfavourably to freedom of inquiry with them, as a wish that it may *not* be true does with unbelievers.

These facts, I presume, will not be controverted. My own acquaintance with unbelievers is pretty extensive, and I know very few of them, though men of letters, (for others are out of the question on both sides,) who have read any thing in favour of Christianity, and most of them know little or nothing of the Scriptures.

If there be any truth in these observations, the rejection, or rather the non-reception of Christianity, by ever so many men of sense, who have not taken the trouble to inquire into the evidence of it, cannot be allowed to have much weight. It may be founded in truth, though they who made no search into it have not found it out.

I am, &c.

LETTER V.

Of the Causes of Infidelity in Persons of a speculative Turn of Mind.

DEAR SIR,

THERE is no class or description of men but what is subject to peculiar prejudices; and every *prejudice* must operate as an obstacle to the reception of some truth. It is in vain for unbelievers to pretend to be free from prejudice. They may, indeed, be free from those of the vulgar, but they have others peculiar to themselves; and the very affectation of being free from vulgar prejudice, and of being wiser than the rest of mankind, must indispose them to the admission even of truth, if it should happen to be with the common people.

The suspicion that the faith of the vulgar is superstitious and false, is, no doubt, often well founded; because they, of course, maintain the *oldest opinions*, while the speculative part of mankind are making new discoveries in science. Yet we often find that they who pride themselves on their being the farthest removed from superstition in some things, are the greatest dupes to it in others, and it is not universally true, that all old opinions are false, and all new ones well-founded. An aversion to the creed of the vulgar may therefore mislead a man, and from a fondness of singularity, he may be singularly in the wrong.

Besides, the creed of the vulgar of the present day is to be considered not so much as *their* creed, for they were not the inventors of it, as that of the thinking and inquisitive in some former period. For those whom we distinguish by the appellation of *the vulgar*, are not those who introduce any new opinions, but who receive them from others, of whose judgment they have been led to think highly. And where *science* is not concerned, but merely *historical events*, an old opinion is certainly not improbable on account of its being old; and all that Christianity rests upon is the reality of certain historical events.

They who are now Christians without inquiry, received their faith from those who did inquire, who distinguished themselves from the vulgar of their day by the novelty and singularity of their opinions, and who had the courage to defy danger and death in the cause of what they apprehended to be new and important truths. Unbelievers of the present age, therefore, ought not to consider Christianity as the belief of the vulgar of this period, but inquire whether their faith, as held by those who first embraced and propagated it, be well-founded.

But if we exclude all consideration of the illiterate, and confine our views to men of letters, it may be expected, from the very great numbers of unbelievers in the present age, that this source of prejudice against Christianity must diminish. Among those who are called *philosophers*, the unbelievers are *the crowd*, and the believers are those who have the courage to dissent from them. If we take into our view men of rank and fortune, as well as men of letters, it must be acknowledged that there are among unbelievers great numbers from whose understanding and knowledge, in other respects, the cause of infidelity can derive but little honour. From these circumstances I begin to flatter myself, that the evidences of Christianity will meet with a more impartial examination at this day than they have done in the course of the last fifty years.

Another great cause of infidelity with philosophical and speculative people is likewise happily ceasing, and in time it must be entirely removed ; and for this we are, in a great measure, indebted to unbelievers themselves. I mean the many corruptions and abuses, which, in a course of time, have been introduced into Christianity from foreign sources, and especially from the philosophy of the times in which it was promulgated. That philosophy has been exploded, but the remains of it, in the christian system, are still but too apparent; and being manifestly absurd, they expose it to many objections. The principal of these, besides the doctrines that are peculiar to the Roman Catholics, are those of a trinity of persons in the godhead, original sin, arbitrary predestination, atonement for the sins of men by the death of Christ, and (which has perhaps been as great a cause of infidelity as any other) the doctrine of the plenary inspiration of the Scriptures.

The objections of unbelievers have been a principal means of leading learned Christians to consider these supposed doctrines of Christianity ; and the consequence of this examination has been a clear discovery that those long received articles of faith (professed in all the established churches in Christendom) are no part of the system of revelation, but utterly repugnant to the genuine principles of it. This I must take for granted at present, contenting myself with appealing to the writings of learned Christians on the subject, and to my *History of the Corruptions of Christianity*.

You will naturally ask me, what is there left of the system of revelation, when the above-mentioned spurious doctrines are cut off from it ; and it may be proper, before I proceed any farther in this correspondence, to give you satisfaction on that head, that you may be fully apprized what it is that I call *Christianity*, for the truth of which I think it of so much consequence to contend. I therefore answer your question by saying, that christian faith implies a belief of all the great historical facts recorded in the Old and New Testament, in which we are informed concerning the creation and government of the world, the history of the discourses, miracles, death and resurrection of Christ, and his assurance of the resurrection of all the dead to a future life of retribution ; and this is the doctrine that is of the most consequence, to enforce the good conduct of men.

Admitting the truth of all the doctrines which have been abundantly proved to be spurious, their *value* (estimated by their influence on the morals of men) cannot be supposed, even by the admirers of them, to be of any moment compared to this ; and in the opinion of those who reject them, they have a very unfavourable tendency, giving wrong impressions concerning the character and moral government of God, and such as must tend, if they have any effect at all, to relax the obligations of virtue. This doctrine, there-'fore, viz that of the resurrection of the human race to a future life of retribution, I consider as the great doctrine of revelation, to which every thing else belonging to the system is introductory, or in some other respect subservient.

If you wish to know what, in my opinion, a Christian is bound to believe with respect to *the Scriptures*, I answer, that the books which are universally received as *authentic*, are to be considered as faithful records of past transactions, and especially the account of the intercourse that the Divine Being has kept up with mankind from the beginning of the world to the time of our Saviour and his apostles. No Christian is answerable for more than this.

The writers of the books of Scripture were *men*, and, therefore, *fallible;* but all that we have to do with them is in the character of *historians,* and *witnesses* of what they heard and saw. Of course, their credibility is to be estimated like that of other historians, viz. from the circumstances in which they wrote, as with respect to their opportunities of knowing the truth of what they relate, and the biasses to which they might be subject. Like all other historians, they were liable to mistakes with respect to things of small moment, because they might not give sufficient attention to them ; and with respect to their *reasoning*, we are fully at liberty to judge of it, as well as of that of any other men, by a due consideration of the propositions they advance, and the arguments they allege. For, it by no means follows, that because a man has had communications with the Deity for certain purposes, and he may be depended upon with respect to his account of those communications, that he is, in other respects, more wise and knowing than other men. Such is the Christianity that I profess to defend, and by no means what has too generally been considered as such.

I am, &c.

LETTER VI.

Of the History of the Jewish Religion.

DEAR SIR,

As few of the *facts* which I shall have occasion to mention will be contested, I shall not dwell so much upon the proof of them, as upon the connexion they have with the divine mission of Moses and the prophets, and that of Christ and the apostles. For this is the circumstance that appears to me to have been chiefly overlooked by unbelievers. They sometimes readily acknowledge the facts, but they do not attend to the necessary consequences of that acknowledgment. This has arisen from their want of attention to the principles of human nature, and the well-known feelings and affections of all men in similar situations.

As the Jewish religion has been more objected to than the Christian, I shall begin with the facts on which the truth of the divine mission of Moses is founded, before I proceed to that of Christ; and I hope to satisfy you that, even in this case, unbelievers are far from having any advantage in the argument, and that they ought to have attended to the *facts* and the circumstances of them more closely than they have yet done.

It has been much the custom with unbelievers, such as Voltaire, &c. to divert themselves and their readers with the history of the Jews,* with some of the peculiarities of their religion, and especially with their stupidity, obstinacy and ignorance, compared with the more polished nations of anti-quity. But it has been without considering that all these latter charges are highly unfavourable to their own object in advancing them, if it be admitted (which surely cannot be denied) that Jews, stupid and ignorant as they have been, were nevertheless *men*, and not a species of beings totally different from that of other men.

For it is obvious to remark, that so obstinate and intract-able as unbelievers describe them to have been, (as indeed their own history shews that they were,) it must have been peculiarly difficult to impose upon them, with respect to any thing to which they were exceedingly averse.

Also, from a people so unpolished and ignorant, so far behind other nations in the arts of peace and war, we should

* See a curious blunder of *Voltaire*, Vol. II. p. 212.

not naturally expect *doctrines* and *sentiments* superior to any
thing of the kind that we find in the most improved nations.
And yet the bare inspection of their writings proves that,
with respect to religion, and the doctrines concerning God
and providence, the Jews were in a high degree *knowing*,
and all other nations ignorant and barbarous. In these respects, therefore, the Jews must have been possessed of
advantages superior to those of other nations ; and if these
advantages were not *natural*, they must have been of a supernatural kind.

It must be allowed as a striking fact, that the religion of
the Jews was most essentially different from that of any other
nation in the ancient world. They had, indeed, in common
with them sacrifices, certain modes of purification, a temple,
an altar, and priests, which seem to have been almost essential to all the modes of ancient religious worship. But the
object of their worship was quite different, and infinitely superior to any thing that other nations looked up to. Also
what we may call the *morality* of their worship, the character
of the rites of it, and the temper and disposition of mind
promoted by it, were still more different. In all these
essential particulars, the religion of the Jews was so strikingly
different from that of any of their neighbouring nations, that
it could never have been derived from any of them, and an
attachment to the one must have created an aversion to the
other.

The objects of worship with the Egyptians, Babylonians,
Tyrians, Syrians, Assyrians, Philistines and Arabians, under
all their different denominations, as Edomites, Moabites,
Ammonites, &c. were the sun, moon and stars, and other
visible objects, which they supposed to be animated, and on
the influence of which they supposed their good and bad
fortune depended.* But in the religion of the Jews, the
maxims of which are clearly laid down in their sacred writings, we find that all their worship was confined to one invisible and omnipresent Deity, the maker and governor of all
things, from whom the sun, moon and stars, with every thing
else, visible and invisible, derived their existence, and at
whose disposal they all constantly are.

Now as the Jews, though an ancient nation, were not so
ancient as the Egyptians, or any of the other nations mentioned above, by whom they were completely surrounded ;
and as, with respect to natural science, it is acknowledged

* See " On the Corruption of Theology," Vol. II. pp 78—80

that they were much behind them, how came they possessed of such just and sublime conceptions with respect to the subject of *religion*, and of whom could they have learned such rational worship? This *effect*, as well as every other, must have had an adequate *cause*, and, the circumstances of the Jews considered, I see no adequate cause of so great an effect besides those divine communications, which are recorded in the books of Moses ; which shew that the Universal Parent made choice of that nation, obstinate and stupid as it always was, to be the means of preserving in the world the true knowledge of himself, and the purity of his worship, amidst the universal degeneracy of the rest of mankind.

That this was an object worthy of the interposition of the Parent of mankind, who had at heart the happiness of his offspring, we must be convinced, if we consider the moral character, as we may say, of the religious worship of the Jews, and that of their neighbouring nations. All these nations, without exception, connected with their worship (on principles which I have no occasion to examine at present, but they *did* universally connect with it, and incorporate into it) ceremonies, some of which were most horribly barbarous, and others of a most impure nature. Their priests cut and mangled themselves, and practised the most dreadful mortifications in the course of their worship. Human sacrifices were authorized in all those religions, and were very frequent in some of them. Parents did not spare their own children, but madly devoted them to death, and even the most dreadful of all deaths, that of burning alive, to appease the wrath, or secure the favour of their gods, and they gloried in thus sacrificing still greater numbers of their enemies, with every circumstance of insult and barbarity. For this we have not only the testimony of Jewish writers, but the most unexceptionable evidence of Greeks and Romans, who themselves, even in a pretty late period, were not entirely free from the same horrid rites. The Carthaginians sacrificed at one time three hundred youths of the best families in the city ;* and their religion was that of the Tyrians, one of the most distinguished nations in the neighbourhood of Judea.

All these neighbouring nations also, without exception, practised the most impure, as well as the most cruel rites, in honour of their gods, and their public festivals were, in general, scenes of riot and debauchery. Besides many shocking indecencies, which cannot be recited, women, in

* See Vol. II. p. 85.

other respects chaste, thought prostitution (in which the choice of a partner was excluded) a necessary mode of recommending themselves to the favour of their deities, and in some cases, even sodomy and bestiality were thought to be proper. *

If the severe and cruel rites above-mentioned, did not deter men from the practice of these religions, we may be well assured that the lasciviousness and debauchery which they encouraged would not do it. Accordingly we find, in all nations, a kind of rage for the ceremonies of these religions. The family of Abraham had been idolaters in Chaldæa, the Israelites had conformed to the religion of Egypt, and their whole history afterwards shews, that they had a proneness to the religious rites of their neighbours, which even astonishes us, when we consider the awful and repeated warnings of their prophets, and the dreadful calamities which, agreeably to their predictions, never failed to overtake them in consequence of their idolatry.

Now, how can we account for Abraham abandoning the religion of his country (to say nothing of his removing to so great a distance from it) and the Israelites, when they were become a nation, relinquishing the rites of the Egyptians, and adopting a religion and ceremonies of so very different a nature ? This is what no nation ever did of a sudden voluntarily, or could ever be brought to do involuntarily, by ordinary means ; and that this was involuntarily on the part of the Israelites, is most evident from their frequent relapses into their former superstitions, from which they were with great difficulty reclaimed.

The only possible explanation of this wonderful *fact*, I will venture to say, is to be found in the books of Moses, and other writings of the Old Testament, in which we have an authentic account of the frequent interpositions of the Divine Being to bring about so great an event, by miracles, which the obstinacy and incredulity of that nation, great as they always were, were not able to withstand. What could have restrained this people when they so often relapsed into idolatry, but those frequent interpositions, an historical account of which is preserved in their writings, and which at length fully convinced them, that the eye of God was in a more particular manner upon their nation ; and that though he thought proper to connive at the idolatry of other nations, which had not been distinguished by him as theirs had been, he would not bear with *them;* but that, at all events, by

* See Vol. II. p. 89.

their prosperity or adversity, they were to be a lesson to the whole world ; to teach all nations the great doctrine of the unity of God, the universality of his dominion, and the purity of his worship. This is a clear and satisfactory account of the fact, and without this supposition it is absolutely inexplicable.

If we consider the miracles of which we have an account in the books of Moses (which were unquestionably written at the time when they are said to have been performed), we see them to have been wonderfully calculated to produce this effect ; and they were of such a nature, as that no nation whatever could have been deceived into the belief of them, even if they had been as well disposed, as we know they were ill-disposed, towards the object of them.

When the great scene opens, the Israelites were in the most abject state of slavery in Egypt, without the least prospect of relief, their oppressors being a warlike nation, themselves unused to arms, and no foreign power to take their part. Yet, though these warlike Egyptians, who derived the greatest advantages from their servitude, did every thing in their power to detain them, they actually marched out of the country, without leaving any part of their property behind ; they passed forty years in a wilderness, from which so great a multitude could not have derived sufficient sustenance ; and they took possession of a country occupied by several numerous and warlike nations. Such are the *facts*, and I see no probable method of accounting for them, but upon the supposition of the truth of those miracles, which are recorded in the writings of Moses, and which explain the whole in the most satisfactory manner.

According to this account, the Israelites entirely dispirited, and, though oppressed, yet become Egyptians in their worship and inclinations, are brought with great difficulty to conceive some hope of their deliverance by the assurances of Moses, one of their brethren, who had fled from Egypt, and had been forty years settled in Arabia. He told them, that the God of their fathers had appeared to him, and notwithstanding his reluctance to undertake the commission, had enjoined him to demand their release of Pharoah ; and as a proof of his divine mission, had empowered him to work several miracles, a specimen of which he was commissioned to exhibit before them.

Pharoah, as was natural, received the proposal with great indignation, and increased his oppression of the people ; but by the infliction of the most extraordinary judgments, and those of the most public nature (with respect to which his own magicians confessed that the finger of God was in them, and the last of which was the death of the first born in every Egyptian family, in one night) he was brought to comply with the demand. Repenting of this concession, he pursued the unarmed multitude, encumbered with all their cattle and baggage, with a large army, determined to force them to return. While the Israelites were in the utmost consternation, having Pharoah and his army behind them, and the Red Sea before them, the sea opened, and made a way for their escape, and Pharoah and his army, who pursued them into the sea, were all drowned.

Presently after this, many illustrious miracles having been wrought for their relief, particularly supplying them with food and water in a miraculous manner, to suffice so great a multitude, God, in an audible voice from Mount Sinai, in the hearing of all the people, which must have exceeded three millions, standing at some distance from the foot of the mountain, so as to be far out of the hearing of any human voice, or any instrument in aid of articulation, delivered all the words of the ten commandments, with the preamble to them. This was accompanied with thunder and lightning, and a cloud covering the mountain; and of this awful appearance the people had regular notice some time before. The rest of the law was delivered to Moses himself, whose commission was so abundantly attested, that though there were several formidable conspiracies against him (in one of which his own brother Aaron, who must have been in the secret of all his measures, was concerned), and though his conduct often gave the greatest offence to all the people, and he was himself of a meek and placid nature, and so unqualified for command in war, that another was always employed whenever they had occasion to take the field, his authority was fully supported.

After the expiration of forty years, the Israelites crossed the river Jordan in the same manner as they had crossed the Red Sea, marching through the channel on dry ground; the walls of the first city which they besieged, fell down of their own accord, and in a short time, notwithstanding the opposition of the numerous and warlike inhabitants of the country, the Israelites took possession of it.

Such is the account that the books of Moses and of Joshua give of these things, and to say nothing of the internal marks of credibility in the writings of Moses, which bear as evident traces of authenticity, as any narrative or journal of events that was ever written, the miracles introduced into the history supply the only possible hypothesis to account for the rest. A fact which cannot be denied, is the *belief* of all the Israelitish nation, from that time to the present, that such events did take place, that the history we now have of them was written by Moses himself, till near the time of his death, and that the narrative was continued by other persons who recorded the events of their own times.

If the antiquity of the books of Moses, &c. be denied, it still remains to be accounted for, how all the nation could, at any period of time, be made to believe that their ancestors had come from Egypt, through the Red Sea and the river Jordan, and that such a *law* as theirs had been delivered in an audible voice from Mount Sinai, when none of those things had ever happened. This is not more probable, than that the English nation should at this time be brought to believe that their ancestors originally came from France, and that they crossed from Calais to Dover without ships. An attempt to impose upon a whole nation such an account as this, and especially a history of the events said to have been written at the time, when nothing of the kind had been heard of before, would at any period be treated with ridicule and neglect. No people ever were, or ever can be, so imposed upon, especially when the things proposed to them are so disagreeable and burthensome as the laws of Moses certainly were to the Jewish nation.

The belief of the fabulous histories of the Greek and Roman divinities, and of their intercourse with mortals, such as we read of in Ovid's Metamorphoses, &c. can bear no comparison with the belief of all the contents of the books of Moses by the nation of the Jews. It was never pretended that there was any history of the heathen gods, and of their intercourse with mankind, written at the time of the events, of which copies were ordered to be taken, and which was to be recited annually in the presence of all the people, which was the case with respect to the laws of Moses. All the stories of the heathen mythology are related with irreconcileable varieties, and the belief of them had probably never much hold of intelligent persons, and kept decreasing till, in a course of time, the stories were supposed to be in a great measure allegorical, contrived to express some mystical or moral truth ; and, at length, this whole system of heathenism was effectually discredited, and sunk into universal contempt.

On the contrary, the whole body of the Jewish nation,

attached as they formerly were to the superstitions of their neighbours, never entertained a doubt with respect to any of the contents of the books of Moses. That there were such persons as Abraham, Isaac and Jaccb, Moses and Aaron, &c. and that the things recorded of them were true, they always believed, as firmly as we do the history of Julius Cæsar or William the Conqueror; and though the nation has continued several thousand years, and has been nearly two thousand years dispersed among all other nations, their belief in the ancient history of their nation, and their respect for the books which contain it, are not in the least diminished.

There is no example of any other nation suffering as the Jews have done, without being utterly lost and confounded with the common mass of mankind, and their religious customs disappearing with them. The small remains of fire worshipers in one corner of Indostan,* where they are suffered to live unmolested, and who find little inconvenience from their religion, is not to be mentioned with the attachment of the Jews to theirs, without considering this as a fulfilment of a prophecy delivered so early as the time of Moses, and frequently repeated in later periods. This alone, I will venture to say, is a fact which no philosopher can account for, without admitting the authenticity of the books which contain the principles of the Jewish religion, and the truth of the miracles by which it was proved to be divine.

I am, &c.

LETTER VII.

Of the Historical Evidence of the Truth of Christianity.

Dear Sir,

The proof of the truth of *Christianity* from the reception it met with in the world, is similar to that of the Jewish religion, but something clearer, as falling within the compass of authentic history, so that the great facts are the more easily ascertained. Indeed, all that is requisite to establish the truth of it is universally acknowledged; the rise and progress of Christianity being as well known as that of the

---

* "In the country about *Surat*"—and "in Bombay"—according to *Prideaux*, who adds, that "although they perform their worship before fire and towards the rising sun, yet they utterly deny that they worship either of them." The reputed *fire-worshipers* or *Gaurs* "have a suburb at *Hispahan*, the metropolis of *Persia*—but the bulk of them is in *Kerman*." Connect. Pt. I. B. IV. L pp 330, 331.

Roman empire. Consequently it is only necessary to attend to the circumstances of known facts, which are themselves as easily ascertained as any other facts in history, to obtain as complete satisfaction with respect to it, as it is in the power of· historical evidence to give. If, therefore, any person continue an unbeliever, it must, in my opinion, be owing either to his not having taken proper pains to inform himself concerning facts, or to his having such a state of mind as incapacitates him for judging concerning the nature and force of the evidence. ·

·That the gospels and the book of Acts, which contain the history of the rise and first progress of Christianity, are genuine productions of the age to which they are ' usually ascribed, viz. some time before the destruction of Jerusalem, or within less than forty years after the death of Christ, and that some of· the epistles of Paul were written several years before that time (the first of them about twenty years after the death of Christ), whilst the chief actors in the scene and many of the witnesses of·the great facts were living, I must take for granted, because this does not appear ever to have been disputed ; and there·is as much evidence of it as there is of the genuinenes of any histories that were ever published. It could not, therefore, but have been well known at the time of the publication, whether the transactions recorded in those books really happened ; and so great was the attention that was given to the subject, ·and the credit that was given to the books, that innumerable copies were immediately taken, they were soon translated into various foreign languages, and they were quoted and appealed to in the earliest ages by the different sects into which' Christians were soon divided. It is a fact, therefore, that these histories were esteemed as true by great numbers, who were more competent judges in the case than any persons now living in England can be of the Revolution under King William.

To say nothing of the universal reception of the epistles of Paul, as really *his*, I will venture to say that, it is as impossible for any impartial person to peruse them without being as well satisfied with respect to their genuineness, as to those of Cicero ; the mention of particular events,· persons and places, being so frequent in them, so consistent with each other and with the history of the time.

According to the tenor of these writings, there were thousands of Jews in Jerusalem itself, as well as great ·numbers in. other places, who became Christians, in consequence of entertaining no doubt concerning ·the truth of the miracles, the death and resurrection of Christ, and also the miracles wrought by the apostles afterwards. The facts were such as no person then living expected, so as to be previously prepared to receive; and the converts were so far from gaining any thing by their belief, that they were thereby exposed to every possible inconvenience, loss of property, disgrace, every mode of torture and death. Paul himself was at the first a zealous persecutor of the Christians, and had the greatest prospect of preferment and advantage from persisting in his opposition to them. Yet even *he* was so fully convinced of the truth of Christianity, and was so sensible of the importance of it, that he became one of its most zealous preachers, and for a period of about thirty years he actually went through the greatest labours and hardships in the propagation of the gospel, uniformly declaring that he had no expectation of any thing better in this life; and at length he, together with innumerable others who had the same persuasion, cheerfully laid down his life rather than abandon his profession.

Now what kind of beings must the writers of the gospels and of the book of Acts have been, and what kind of beings must have been the thousands of that generation who received their accounts as true, and especially at such a risk, (which abundantly implies that they had every motive for making inquiry, and satisfying themselves concerning the facts,) if, after all, there was no truth in the accounts?

What should we think of a set of writers, who should uniformly relate, that, in the war of 1755, the French completely conquered all North America, the whole of Ireland, and a great part of England, which at length was reduced to be a province of France? Would it be possible for a thousand such writers to gain the least credit? Or, if they did, would not the tens of thousands who well knew that the story was very far from being true, and that the present state of things proves it to be so, say, that they were under some strange infatuation; and if, in a course of time, such histories should gain any credit, would there not be many more writers to confute the account, and would not the truth soon prevail over all the arts of falsehood?

We may therefore safely conclude, that since the history of the miracles, the death and the resurrection of Christ, and also that of the miracles wrought by the apostles, were received as true by such numbers of persons in the age in which they were published, and the account was never confuted, but Christianity kept gaining ground from that time

to the present, the great *facts* on which its credit stands
were unquestionably true. A falsehood of this nature could
never have been propagated as this was. They who first
received those books must have been previously acquainted
with the history which they contained. The histories were,
in fact, an appeal to the evidence of those into whose hands
they were put, and their reception of them is the most express sanction that could be given to them.

. That the history of Christ and the apostles could not have
established itself without the most rigid inquiry into its truth,
is evident from the persecution of Christians, which began
immediately after its first promulgation, and in Jerusalem
itself, the very scene of the transactions. In these circumstances men had every motive, and every opportunity, for
inquiring whether they sacrificed their reputation, their properties and their lives, for an idle tale, or for a truth of the
greatest certainty and importance. All these things being
considered, it appears to me that no facts, in the whole compass of history, are so well authenticated as those of the
miracles, the death and the resurrection of Christ, and also
what is related of the apostles in the book of Acts.

As to the resurrection of Christ, on which so much depends, the evidence of it is so circumstanced, as to be most
wonderfully adapted to establish itself in the remotest periods
of time. That Christ really *died*, cannot be doubted, when
it is considered that he was put to death by his enemies,
and that in the most public manner. The same persons
also, who were most nearly interested in his not appearing
any more, had the care of his sepulchre; and, being apprized
of his having foretold that he should rise again, would, no
doubt, take effectual care to guard against all imposition in
the case. Had there been any tolerably well-founded suspicion that the guards of the sepulchre had been overpowered,
or frightened away, by the friends of Christ, and that the
body had been secreted by them, they would certainly have
been apprehended and examined; and, whether the body had
been found or not, the very possibility of its having been
conveyed away would have prevented any credit being given
to their account of the resurrection.

No person can reasonably object to the *number*, or the
quality, of those who were the witnesses of Christ's resurrection, as they were persons who, without any hope of seeing him again, were the most perfectly acquainted with him,
and had sufficient opportunity of satisfying themselves that it
was the same person. He was seen at first, when he was

not at all expected, and afterwards by particular appointment, and especially in Galilee, when more than five hundred
persons were present, and in the sight of a great number of
them he went up into heaven.

Paul, one of the greatest enemies of his cause, one whom
the Jews in general would probably have chosen, if they
had been required to name any person whose conversion they
thought the least probable, was satisfied, by the evidence
of his own senses, that Jesus was really risen, he having
appeared to *him*, as he had done to others, before his ascen-
sion. Besides, all the miracles wrought by the apostles,
which are as well attested as those of our Saviour himself,
are a proof of the fact of the resurrection. For had Christ
died as a common malefactor, and there had been nothing
extraordinary in his previous history, it cannot be supposed
that any persons would have been empowered by God to
work miracles in proof of their divine mission, which evidently depended upon his.

Had Christ, after his resurrection, appeared in public,
discoursing in the temple, and confronting his judges and
Pilate, many more, no doubt, would have been satisfied
that he was really risen from the dead. But Divine Providence is abundantly vindicated in affording men only reasonable evidence of truth, sufficient to satisfy all that are
truly impartial, who really wish to know the truth, and in
withholding what is superfluous for that purpose And had
the demand of unbelievers in this respect been granted, and
the effect which they suppose would have followed from
it, really taken place, it would have been a circumstance
exceedingly unfavourable to the credit of the story in the
present, and much more in any future age.

Had the Jews of that age in general been converted, and
consequently there had been no persecution of Christians in
Judea, it would certainly have been said, that Christianity
was a contrivance of the heads of the nation, and such as we
have now no opportunity of detecting. Upon the whole,
therefore, to those who consider the nature of evidence, the
history of the resurrection of Christ is much better authenticated by such evidence as is now existing, than it would
have been in any other circumstances that we can at present
devise to strengthen it. For whatever we might add to it in
some respects, we must take from it in others. So far does
the wisdom of God exceed that of man.

Next to our having ourselves sufficient opportunity, and
likewise sufficient motives to examine into the truth of this

important fact, is the certainty that those who were then present had both the opportunity and the motive. As things
are now circumstanced, it will never be in the power of the
enemies of Christianity to say (what they might have said,
if their demands with respect to the resurrection of Christ
had been granted), that his religion was aided by the powers
of this world. On the contrary, from the very beginning
it encountered all the opposition which the power and policy
of man could bring against it, and had nothing but its own
proper evidence to support it. But this alone was such as
to enable it to do what all the power and wisdom of man
was altogether unequal to, viz. to establish itself, through
the whole extent of the Roman empire, and even beyond
the bounds of it, and finally to triumph over all the various
systems of idolatry and superstition which for ages had prevailed in it.

I am, &c.

LETTER VIII.

Of the Causes of Infidelity in early Times.

DEAR SIR,

You say, that if the facts on which the truth of Christianity depends were true, if Christ really wrought miracles,
and the apostles after him ; if he really died, and rose again
from the dead ; and if the evidence of these facts was sufficient to satisfy such great numbers as the history of the
book of Acts represents ; it is extraordinary that it did not
convince *all*, and that all mankind did not immediately become Christians. All the world, you say, was soon convinced of the truth of such events as the death of Cæsar
in the senate-house, and the defeat of Marc Antony by
Augustus. But a consideration of the principles of human
nature, and our daily observation of the history of opinions,
and the progress of truth, will satisfy all who are truly philosophical and attentive, that what you suppose must have
taken place, was not to be expected.

Two things are requisite to any person's giving his assent
to a proposition of any kind, independent of its evidence,
viz. an attention to that evidence, and also an impartial
mind, free from any bias that might indispose him to receive
and acknowledge it ; and one or other of these appears to
have been wanting in the generality of mankind, with respect

to the truth of the gospel at the time of its promulgation, and for a considerable period afterwards.

With respect to all common events, such as the deaths of particular persons, an account of battles and their consequences, &c. there is nothing so improbable in their nature, but that all mankind must be satisfied that any thing of this kind may well happen, and the immediate consequences of the deaths of great men, and of great victories, are very soon and universally felt; so that it is absolutely impossible that any doubt should long remain with respect to them. But this could not be the case with respect to such events as that of the miracles and resurrection of Christ; these having no such connexion with the state of public affairs, as that they could not but have been immediately known to every body. There was nothing to excite attention to them but the interest which each person, individually considered, had in them, and the zeal of those who were converts themselves to make converts of others.

Admitting the zeal of the first believers to have been ever so great, those to whom they addressed themselves would not believe what they heard, till they had an opportunity of inquiring into the truth of it. They would also compare the accounts of others, and in many cases this would be a process which would necessarily take a considerable *time*, even with respect to the town or village in which the transactions took place, and much more time would be requisite before the belief of such extraordinary things could become general, and well established, in distant places.

Besides, the belief of Christianity is not merely the belief of certain extraordinary *facts*, but includes likewise *inferences* from those facts, and many persons might admit the former without proceeding to the latter. That Christ had a divine mission, and was authorized by God to teach the doctrine of a future state, we justly think to be the necessary consequence of his working real miracles, and of his resurrection from the dead; and there are few persons, I imagine, in the present age, who will admit these facts, and hesitate to draw this conclusion. But we find that the facts were admitted, and yet the conclusion not drawn, by many persons at the time of the promulgation of Christianity.

The unbelieving Jews ascribed the most extraordinary of our Saviour's miracles to the agency of demons, and the heathen world in general had great faith in *magic;* really believing that the most extraordinary effects might be produced by pronouncing certain words, and performing certain ceremonies; these having, in their opinion, some unknown, but necessary connexion with the interposition of invisible powers. For it was by no means the firm belief of mankind in that age, (though it will now be considered as an incontrovertible truth,) that real miracles, or a deviation from the established laws of nature, can be produced by no other power than the great Author of nature himself, or, which comes to the same thing, by some superior Being authorized by him. They might therefore admit the miracles of Christ, and those of the apostles, without being immediately satisfied that what they taught was true; and still less that they were under obligation to make a public profession of Christianity, at the risk of all that was dear to them in life, and even of life itself. There are many steps in this progress, and many persons would stop in all of them, so that the number of declared Christians might bear but a small proportion to what it would have been, if their becoming so had depended upon nothing but the simple evidence of the truth of those facts, which, it will now be acknowledged, necessarily implies the truth of Christianity. When the number of its declared converts is considered, and compared with the situation of things in the age of the apostles, it will be found to be fully equal to what might have been expected, upon the supposition of the truth of every thing which is recorded in the gospels, and the book of Acts.

Of those persons to whom the facts were previously known, so that it was not necessary to produce any *evidence* of them, three thousand were converted in one day, on the speech of Peter, on the day of Pentecost, in which he could say to them, Acts ii. 22, 32, " Ye men of Israel, hear these words, Jesus of Nazareth, a man approved of God among you, by miracles, and wonders, and signs, which God did by him, in the midst of you, as ye yourselves also know, &c. This Jesus hath God raised up, whereof we all are witnesses." And the persons then present with him were a hundred and twenty. After the first miracle performed by Peter and John, viz. the sudden cure of a man who was well known to have been lame from his birth, the number of male converts was five thousand, so that, including women, they may be supposed to have been about ten thousand. This was in Jerusalem only, the scene of the great transactions.

In distant places, the preaching of the apostles, and of their disciples, as might be expected, had no such sudden effect. A few converts in any particular place, were made at first, and their numbers kept increasing gradually. But within the age of the apostles, (who did not preach without the limits of Judea, or to any Gentiles, till about ten years after the death of Christ,) there were christian churches in all the great cities of the Roman empire, and many of them were very numerous, so as to be full of factions among themselves, as appears by the epistles of Paul to several of them. In the villages there were fewer Christians than in the towns, the inhabitants of them being more out of the way of receiving intelligence concerning what had passed at so great a distance. This, it must be acknowledged, was agreeable to the natural course of things.

Beside the assertion of a divine mission, Jesus laid claim to the character of the *Messiah* foretold in the Jewish prophecies; and the persuasion of the whole body of the Jewish nation concerning the temporal reign of their Messiah, was so deeply rooted in their minds, that whatever miracles Jesus had wrought, it could not be expected that many of them would receive such a person as he was, in that character, especially after his ignominious death. They might think that there was something very extraordinary in the case, and what they could not satisfactorily account for, without receiving him as their Messiah. Besides, the manner in which Christ had exposed the vices of the scribes, pharisees and chief priests, who were the leading men among the Jews, must have provoked the ambitious and worldly-minded among them to such a degree, as that no evidence, or reason whatever, could reconcile them to his pretensions, so as to make them ready to lay down their lives for their adherence to him whom they themselves had put to death.

Such a revolution in the state of men's minds, will not be expected by any who have a knowledge of mankind; and considering the great number of those who may be called the personal enemies of Christ, and their influence with others, together with their attachment to the notion of a temporal deliverer, and their opinion of the power of demons, the number of Jewish converts in the age of the apostles, was certainly as great as could reasonably be expected. We find a considerable body of them in all the cities of the Roman empire in which Jews were resident. To them we always find the apostle Paul preached in the first place, and he never failed to convince some of *them* before he particularly addressed himself to the Gentiles; and it cannot be doubted, but that the number of Jewish as well as of Gentile Christians kept increasing, though it is but little that we know of the former, on account of the latter having little intercourse with them, and they are the writings of the Gentile Christians only that are come down to us.

After the second century, it is probable that there was no great addition made to the number of Jewish converts. But we shall the less wonder at this, when it is considered, that, besides the preceding causes, which must have indisposed all Jews to receive Jesus as their Messiah, the doctrines of the pre-existence and of the divinity of Christ, which (being directly contrary to what they had been taught in the prophets concerning the Messiah) were in the highest degree offensive to them, were advanced. These doctrines, so foreign to the genuine principles of both Judaism and Christianity, were generally received by the learned Christians, who were the preachers and writers of the age; and some time after the council of Nice, they were the general belief of the whole christian world. Such doctrines as these, which were represented as essential to Christianity, a Jew might think himself not obliged even to consider or examine. This has continued to be the state of things with the Jews to this very day, as I find by their writings and conversation.

The heathen world in general were strongly attached to their several superstitions. Their religion entered into all their civil transactions, so that the business of every day bore some traces of it; every festivity to which they had been accustomed, and every thing connected with pleasure and the enjoyment of life was connected with it, and a part of it.* To abandon all this, implies much more than the mere reception of new truth. It was almost equivalent to making men over again. In fact, there is no example in the history of the world before the time of Christ, of any nation or considerable body of men changing their religion, except the primitive one, for the idolatry and superstition which then universally prevailed. Conquests had frequently been made, and the greatest revolutions in the state of empires, and of arts and sciences, had taken place, but these were all easy things compared to a revolution in matters of religion. This, therefore, could not be expected to be accomplished in a short time. That it did take place so completely as it

* "The religion of the nations," says Mr. Gibbon, "was not merely a speculative doctrine, professed in the schools, or preached in the temples. The innumerable duties and rites of polytheism were closely interwoven with every circumstance of business or pleasure, of public or of private life, and it seemed impossible to escape the observance of them without at the same time renouncing the commerce of mankind, and all the offices and amusements of society," many particulars of which he proceeds to enumerate. Ch. xv. Ed. 4, 4to. I. p. 553. (P.)

afterwards did in all the ancient world, that it was in time effected by Christianity, when philosophy had not been able to contribute any thing towards it, is the most wonderful event in the history of mankind, and what nothing could have produced, but the fullest evidence of the miracles and resurrection of Christ ; and this being of the historical kind, necessarily required *time* to establish itself.

When the magnitude of this effect is considered, we see a reason for all the miracles of Christ, and also for those that were wrought by the apostles afterwards. For, we may easily imagine that in Greece or at Rome, no evidence of miracles wrought in Judea, would have been much attended to, if the inhabitants of those distant places had not been witnesses of similar miracles wrought before their own eyes. But these were so numerous, and the knowledge of them extended so far, that, great as the effect was, they were sufficient at length to accomplish their purpose.

As to the more learned among the Gentiles, whether they had been used to treat all religion with contempt, which in that age, was the case with many, or to reverence the establishment under which they lived, which continued to be the case with others, we may easily imagine how they would be affected at the first hearing of miracles wrought in a distant country, and to support the claim of a divine mission by a crucified malefactor. By such persons it cannot but be supposed that the preaching of Christianity would be treated with ridicule, and nothing but the knowledge and evidence of it, being *obtruded* upon them, (which could only happen in very peculiar circumstances,) could induce them to make any inquiry about it. And what effect can evidence produce without *attention* and a due *examination* of it ?

Some have expressed their surprise that such persons as Seneca, Pliny and Tacitus, did not become Christians. But can we be sure that either Seneca or Tacitus took any pains to inform themselves about Christianity ? It is pretty evident that Pliny did not.* But his case, and that of other

---

* According to his own account, in the well-known epistle to Trajan, he had never attended any judicial proceedings against the Christians, except as they were brought before his own tribunal. He then merely demanded if they were *Christians,* without inquiring what Christianity was; and on a confession, thrice repeated, commanded their execution. "Interrogavi ipsos, an essent Christiani confitentes iterum et tertio interrogavi, supplicium minatus· perseverantes duci jussi." *Ep.* xcvii. See also *Lardner,* VII p 299, his reflections on *Pliny* and the Christians, pp. 318 and 330, and on the "Importance of Inquisitiveness in Things of Religion," p. 342. Also *Bryant* "Upon the Authenticity of the Scriptures." Ed. 2d, 1799, pp. 143—149.

speculative heathens, will be considered more largely in a subsequent letter. Seneca was contemporary with the apostle Paul, but do we know that he ever conferred with Paul, or any other Christian, upon the subject: and without this, what could he know or believe, more than other men, who had never heard the name of Christ?

Tacitus appears to have been shamefully ignorant of the history of the Jews, which he might have learned from the books of Scripture, or the works of Josephus, which were extant in Greek in his time. Had he taken the trouble to read them, he could never have given such a crude and absurd account of the Jews as he has done.* He had evidently heard nothing but vague reports, derived originally from the Scriptures, but at such a distance, as to retain very little resemblance to the truth. And can it be supposed that a man who took no pains to inform himself concerning the Jews, (a remarkable ancient nation, many of them dispersed in all parts of the Roman empire,) whose history he undertook to write, would take any more pains to inform himself concerning the Christians, who in his time were generally confounded with the Jews, whose history he did *not* undertake to write?

As to a later period, notwithstanding Christianity kept gaining ground in spite of all opposition, its progress must have been retarded by the many divisions among Christians, and the absurd doctrines held by some of them, in consequence of which many persons, not ill-disposed with respect to Christianity, might decline joining any particular denomination of Christians. This we see to be the case with respect to the Catholics abroad, and many members of the established church in this country. They are sensible enough of the errors of their respective systems, but they see those who dissent from them divided among themselves, and hating and despising one another ; and not feeling themselves sufficiently interested to examine which of them is in the right, they continue where they are. This must have been the case with many of the Gentiles in the early ages of Christianity.

Besides, whilst Christianity was exposed to persecution, great numbers of a timid disposition may have been well convinced of the goodness of the cause, without being able to relinquish their possessions, and especially to lose their

* See his *History,* B. v. *ad init.*

lives for it, which, however, Christianity absolutely requires. This we find to have been the character of Nicodemus and others, in our Saviour's time, and there were many such in all ages. Nay, many professed Christians renounced their profession in the severity of persecution. And if this was the case with those who, no doubt, still continued to believe it, well it may be supposed that many might by the same means be prevented from making any profession of it at all.

That this was the actual state of things in the second and third century; that besides a great number of professed Christians, there were at least as many who secretly thought better of it than they did of the established religion, was abundantly evident in the revolution made by Constantine; who could not with safety have declared himself a Christian, have given such open encouragement to Christians, and have discountenanced the idolatry which had prevailed before, if the minds of the great mass of the people had not been sufficiently prepared for so great a change. And this preparation could consist of nothing but a general profession, or at least a general good opinion of Christianity. Had the popular opinion at that time been very violently against Christianity, many competitors for the empire would, no doubt, have availed themselves of it: and indeed some of Constantine's rivals did endeavour to avail themselves of the zeal that remained for the popular superstitions, but without effect. This change could not have been made by Marcus Aurelius, or any of the earlier emperors, if they had been Christians. This remarkable fact therefore, viz. the easy establishment of Christianity, and the extinction of Heathenism by Constantine,[*] and his successors, is of itself an abundant proof of the progress that Christianity had made in the preceding period.

The emperor Julian bore as much good will to Heathenism, as Constantine had done to Christianity, but what was he able to effect? He did not choose to attack the new religion openly, but he discouraged the profession of it by every method in his power.[†] In this, however, he met with nothing but disappointment, and presently after his death, the establishment of Christianity returned like a tide in the ocean ; and had any other emperor, half a century after the time of Julian, attempted as much as he did, the genera[l]

---

* See *Lardner*, IV. pp. 168, 180.
† Ibid. VIII. pp. 370—372. De La Blèterie, *Julien*, 1746, p. 261.

opinion would, no doubt, have been so much against him, that he must have abdicated the empire ; so strong was the general attachment to Christianity in that age, notwithstanding all the unfavourable circumstances attending the rise and progress of it. Had it been in the power of men of learning and inquiry, after the attention of mankind was sufficiently excited to the subject, to have exposed the pretensions of Christ, as we can those of Mahomet, it would certainly have been done before the age of Julian or that of Constantine.

There is no writer from whom this might have been expected so much as from Josephus, who, on account of his being contemporary with the apostles, and even with Christ himself, and passing a great part of his life in Judea, which was the great theatre of their miracles, must have had the best opportunity of examining into the foundation of Christianity, and consequently of detecting any fraud or imposture that might have been employed about it. That he could not want any *inclination* to do this, is evident from his not being a Christian. As he gives so particular an account of the Jewish sects, the Pharisees, Sadducees and Essenes, why did he give no account of the Christians, whose origin was among the Jews, and who, he must have known, were very numerous in Judea, in all the provinces of the Roman empire, and in Rome itself, where he finally resided, so that some account of them might naturally be expected in such a history as his ? The most probable account of his remarkable silence concerning the Christians is, that for some reason or other, he disliked Christianity, so as not to choose to make profession of it, and yet was not able to allege any thing of consequence against it, and therefore, chose to make no mention at all of the subject. There is no other motive for the silence of this writer concerning Christ and the affairs of Christians, that appears to me to be in the smallest degree probable. As to the testimony concerning Christ which is found in the present copies of his history, it has been sufficiently proved to be spurious, being inconsistent with the other parts of his writings and with his own conduct and profession.*

* See Josephus *Antiq. Jud.* L: xviii. Ch. iii. Sect. iii. *Lardner,* VII. pp. 120—129, 273—285, where he decides against the *testimony.* In favour of its authenticity, see Whiston's *Josephus,* Dissert. i., **Dr. Chandler** and the Abbé du *Voisin* in the Appendix to Lardner's *Life,* pp. clv—clxviii., Mr. Jacob Bryant's *Vindiciæ Flavianæ,* 1780, *Ecclesiastical Researches,* by Rev. Dr. John Jones and his Letters in Mon. Repos. 1818, XIII. pp. 38, 101.

Upon the whole, it must certainly appear to any person who is sufficiently acquainted with the history of Christianity, that it had no countenance from *power*, and that even the *learning* of the age was as hostile to it as the civil government. What then but *truth*, under every disadvantage, external and internal, could have procured it that establishment which, in about three centuries, it acquired through the whole extent of the Roman empire, and even among many of the barbarous nations beyond the bounds of it, to the extermination of all the other modes of religion which had prevailed in them before ?

I am, &c.

LETTER IX.

A more particular Account of the Nature of those Prejudices to which the Heathens were subject with respect to Christianity.

Dear Sir,

They who express any surprise that Christianity did not make a more rapid progress in the world, besides not being acquainted with the real state of things in the age in which it was promulgated, do not appear to me to have given sufficient attention to the doctrine concerning *assent to truth* in general, whether natural, moral or historical.

Nothing is more observable, than that when the mind is prepossessed in favour of any particular opinion, the contrary one will not always be admitted on the authority of its proper *evidence* only. We see every day that men are *silenced* without being *convinced*. They may see nothing to object to a new set of principles, but they may justly suspect that every consideration necessary to form a right judgment in the case, may not be present to their minds, and think that when they shall have time to recollect themselves, things may appear in a very different light, and therefore may suspend their assent. Or, perceiving an utter inconsistency between the new opinion proposed to them, and those which they have hitherto held, and being persuaded that they once saw sufficient reason for what they have been accustomed to maintain, they may think themselves excusable if, without taking the trouble to re-examine the subject, they content themselves with their former sentiments upon it. They may think that there must be some latent fallacy in the arguments for the new principle, though they are not able to detect it.

When we consider propositions with their proofs, as mere logicians, we are apt to think that nothing more is requisite to secure a full assent to them, than a perception of the agreement of ideas; but in reality there are many other causes of assent besides this; and some of the very strongest with respect to the great bulk of mankind, are of a very different nature. In their minds there is such an established connexion between the ideas of *truth* and *right*, and those of the opinions and practices of their parents, their countrymen, their party, their teachers, &c. (a connexion formed in the earliest years of infancy, and receiving additional strength in every period of life,) that it is not in the power of any thing that we call *evidence*, to separate them. In this case, persons who are not of an inquisitive and speculative turn, that is, the great mass of mankind, will hardly ever listen to any attempt to separate them. What is more common than to hear the charge of heresy, impiety and blasphemy, thundered out against particular opinions, by persons who are so far from pretending to have examined them, that they will even declare they think it wrong to examine, or deliberate in the case; such examination and deliberation implying at least a *doubt*, which they dread to entertain, even for a moment.

Besides, we all know that a regard to ease, reputation and interest, imperceptibly biasses the judgments of men; so that if it be for a man's ease, reputation or interest, to maintain a particular opinion, how well disposed soever he may be in other respects, he is not to be trusted with the discussion. He is no judge of his own impartiality; as the same arguments will appear to him in a very different light from what they would have done, if his ease, interest, reputation, &c. had been on the other side. The degree of this influence would not be suspected, except by persons who know mankind well, and who have attended to the history of controversy. Can any Protestant imagine, that there would ever have been so many ingenious defences of the doctrine of transubstantiation, or that so many persons would have really believed in it, if, besides the influence of education and authority, it had not been part of a system which it was inconvenient, disreputable or hazardous, to abandon? All Unitarians must see the force of the same influences on the minds of those who defend the doctrine of the Trinity.

We see the effect of the same causes of error, in civil life. For we shall certainly deceive ourselves, and think too ill of mankind, if we should imagine that they always act contrary to their judgment, when they assert and maintain what we most clearly see to be false. Their connexions and interests, &c. impose upon their judgments. When nations go to war, both sides, I doubt not, in general, seriously think themselves in the right. They think they are only returning injuries received, or preventing the effects of the most hostile intentions ; and they read with indignation the manifestos of their adversaries, which always breathe the spirit of peace.

Did every man, as an individual, really judge for himself, without the interference of any undue influence, we should not see the same opinions and maxims prevail, as they generally do, in particular families, schools, and communities of any kind. Whenever great bodies of men, connected as they must be by interest, or some other equally strong bond of union, profess the same opinion, there can be no doubt but that their interest, or other principle of union, had a considerable influence, in forming their judgments and that had they not been under that influence, they would have thought as variously as any other equal number of men, who are not so connected.

On account of some of these undue influences, by means of which the proper effect of evidence is precluded, we are not to expect that any arguments will have much weight with the generality of persons who are far advanced in life. By one means or other they have, as we usually say, *made up their minds*, and notwithstanding all that can be proposed to them, if they should be prevailed upon to give any kind or degree of attention to a new opinion, they will frequently only remain the more confirmed in their former way of thinking. We may wonder that reasons which appear so clear and convincing to ourselves, should have no weight with others. But universal experience shews that, in many cases, they have even less than none. For considerations which we think to make for us, they often think to make against us ; and where *conduct* is concerned, the mildest expostulations will often only exasperate ; so that, instead of persuading men to act as we wish them to do, we often leave them more obstinate in their own way.

If any person doubt the truth of this observation, let him make the experiment himself, which it will not be difficult to do. If he be a Christian, let him propose a conference with a Jew ; if he be a Catholic, let him have an interview with a Protestant ; or if a Protestant, with an old Catholic ;

if. he be a Trinitarian, let him propose his arguments to an Unitarian; if an Unitarian, let him argue with a Trinitarian; if a Whig in this country with an old Tory; or if a Tory with a staunch Whig. I do not say that in such conferences as these no man will ever gain his point; but it appears to me, from the course of my observation, that if the parties be turned forty or, fifty years of age, and if by reading, think-ing or conversation, they have been long settled in their opinions, it is not one case in a hundred in which any change of opinion will be produced by this means. There are many Jews, many Catholics, many Trinitarians, many Arians, many Deists and many Atheists, on whom I am sensible that no arguments, or mode of address, that I, as an *Unitarian Christian* could make use of, would have any effect whatever.

Let a man go into Spain and Portugal, and, if it were pos-sible, even work miracles, to shew them that the Protestant religion is true; if they were not more in number than those which we have reason to think were wrought by the apostles; and if after a certain time they were discontinued, as those of the apostles were, a great proportion of the inhabitants would probably, for a long time at least, continue to think as they now do. How many persons are there who would have no patience to hear such preachers, or any thing that could be said about them; and whatever reports they could not avoid hearing concerning their *miracles*, they would, without any examination, conclude them to be all tricks and imposi-tions; and when these workers of miracles were gone off the stage, the conversion of this Popish nation to the Pro-testant religion, would probably proceed no faster than that of the heathen world to Christianity.

How little disposed some persons of the best understand-ing may be to give any attention to those who are of a party or profession different from their own, we have a pretty remarkable example of in the late Dr. Johnson, who was so bigotted a churchman, that when he was in Scot-land, and would gladly have heard Dr. Robertson preach, he would not go into a church, though established by law, because it was a Presbyterian one.* Supposing the prin-ciples of this despised Presbyterian church to have been ever so right and clear, can any person imagine it to have been possible for such a man as Dr. Johnson to have been a convert to them? But the contempt with which the philo-sophers, and men of learning among the Heathens, con-

* See Boswell's *Tour*, 1786. Towers's Tracts, III. p. 429.

sidered Christianity, probably far exceeded that which Dr. Johnson entertained for the tenets or practices of the Presbyterians.

How little also is it that many of the learned clergy of the church of England know of the dissenters, or their writings! Great numbers of them have no more knowledge of what is transacted in a conventicle, than in a pagoda, and would sooner, I dare say, be persuaded to enter the latter, than the former. By this we may judge of the reluctance with which the proud and learned Gentiles would receive any proposal to go into a Christian church, in the first, or even the second century. Let the principles of any set of men, who are much despised, and little known, be ever so *true* or *evident*, there can be no chance of their becoming generally prevalent, except in a long course of time. Let no person then wonder at the *time* which the great revolution effected by Christianity took up, and at the remains of Heathenism in many villages, and remote parts of the world, which had but little intercourse with strangers. The change was *rapid*, considering all the circumstances of the case, and what could never have been effected at all but by the force of truth.

Philosophical truth seems to be better calculated to make its way in the world than truth of a religious nature, because men are not so much interested in opposing it. But it must not be forgotten, that Galileo was put into the Inquisition for maintaining one of the first principles of modern philosophy.* The doctrine of Newton made but little progress abroad in the first half century after its publication in England, and at this very day it is not received (or has not been received till very lately) in *all* the foreign universities. Can any person attend to these facts (and many others of a similar nature might be mentioned), and wonder that the gentile world was not sooner converted to Christianity?

I am, &c.

* *Milton,* speaking of his travels in Italy, in 1637, says, " there it was that I found and visited the famous *Galileo,* grown old, a prisoner to the Inquisition, for thinking in astronomy otherwise than the *Franciscan* and *Dominican* licensers thought." *Areopagitica.* Galileo was imprisoned in 1633, when in his 70th year, as a *relapse,* for publishing his *Dialogues* in 1632, having, in 1615, been discharged, on a promise of not teaching the philosophical *heresy* of Copernicus He was sentenced to repeat the seven penitential psalms once a week during three years. He, however, submitted to a prescribed recantation in 1634, and was allowed to be a prisoner *at large* in a small town in the territory of Florence, where Milton visited him. See Nouv. Dict. Hist. III. pp. 18, 19. " Some expressions in Paradise Lost have led an Italian biographer of the poet to suppose that—he caught from Galileo, or his disciples, some ideas approaching to the Newtonian philosophy." *Hayley,* p. 37.

LETTER X.

*Of the different Foundations on which the Belief of Judaism
or Christianity, and that of other Religions stands.*

DEAR SIR,

MANY persons content themselves with saying, they
have no occasion to inquire into the origin of the Jewish or
Christian religions.   Mankind, they say, have always been
credulous, and vulgar errors are innumerable.   What could
be more firmly believed than the fabulous histories of
Apollo, Diana, and the rest of the Grecian and Roman
divinities, by the Greeks and Romans, the story of Mahomet's journey to heaven by the Mahometans, the transfor-
mations of Wishnou by the Indians, or the legendary tales
of the church of Rome by the generality of the Catholics?
All these things are, or were, most firmly believed by whole
nations, so that it would have been hazardous for any
person to intimate the least doubt with respect to them;
and yet what man of sense will say that they even deserve
any examination? Why then may not this be the case
with the Jewish and Christian religions?

But those who satisfy themselves with this light manner
of treating the subject, have not sufficiently considered the
essential difference between the circumstances of a mere
tradition and those of a *history written at the time*, not to
mention other circumstances of the greatest importance in
the case; and, therefore, though I have mentioned this difference in my introductory letters, I shall enter into a fuller
discussion of it here, with an application to the case in
hand.

We know that when any thing is told from one person to
another, it never fails to be altered; and if it be of an extraordinary nature (such as most persons take great pleasure
in telling and hearing), it will be enlarged in almost every
hand through which it passes, so that in a short time, the
original relater shall not know the story that he himself first
told; and it is often impossible to trace the rise and progress of reports, which in length of time gain the greatest
credit. Of this we have frequent examples, especially in
time of war, and public disturbances of any kind; so that
wise men pay little regard to the belief of the multitude in
things of this nature, especially if no persons have been

interested to inquire into the origin of the reports, and to detect the errors that might be in them. In these very circumstances are the stories in the Heathen Mythology, the Popish Legends, &c. so that they might gain great credit, and in time get recorded in writing, without any foundation in truth. But in all these cases it will be easy to ascertain whether the history was committed to writing by an eye-witness, and whether it was propagated and recorded by unprejudiced persons.

The case of a history written at the time of any transactions, or so near to it, that the memory of them was fresh in the minds 'of those into whose hands the accounts came, and especially the history of such things as no person was previously disposed to believe, and such as would not be admitted without inquiring into their truth, is essentially different from that of a mere tradition, which it was no body's interest to reject. And such was the history of the transactions on which the truth of the Jewish and Christian religion depends. The former is contained in the books of Moses, recited by himself, in the hearing of all the people for whose use they were written, and the latter in the gospels and the book of Acts, probably all written by eye-witnesses of the facts recorded in them, and received without objection by eye-witnesses; and it can never be said that either the religion of Moses, or that of Jesus, was such as the people to whom they were delivered, were at all predisposed to receive, or to relish.

Neither of these histories stole upon the world insensibly, so that it might be said that a small matter might grow to a great magnitude before it was committed to writing, and that then it was too late to examine into its truth. On the contrary, the accounts were published while the events were fresh in the memory of those into whose hands the books came, and who would never have given their sanction to them, but have immediately rejected them, as fabulous, if they had not known them to be true; so that their credit must have been blasted at once, and they would never have been transmitted to posterity as authentic narratives of facts. This will be more evident if it be considered how deeply interested were both those who embraced, and those who rejected the doctrines of these books, to examine into their authenticity.

Where neither life, property, nor reputation are concerned, accounts of transactions may get into the world without much examination. But this was not the case with respect

to the history of Moses, or that of Christ, especially the
latter. Every man who embraced Christianity, considered
himself as bound to maintain the truth of it at the hazard of
his life, and of every thing dear to him. And surely those
who died a violent death for their adherence to Christianity
(which was the case with most of the apostles, and many
other primitive Christians, themselves witnesses of the
miracles and resurrection of Christ) would not have done it
but upon grounds that to them appeared sufficient. They
must certainly have been fully persuaded that the cause in
which they suffered so much, and so long, was a good
one ; and, living at the time, they had the best opportunity
of knowing it.

This argument will apply to the martyrs of the next and
following ages. And it is remarkable, that the persecution
continued as long as an inquiry into the truth of the facts
was tolerably easy, viz. about three hundred years, after
which time the value of martyrdom, considered as an evidence of the truth of the facts, would be much diminished ;
but during this period, the evidence they afforded was in
some views acquiring additional strength. For, if the first
set of martyrs, those who were our Saviour's contemporaries, could be supposed to have been under a kind of
infatuation, and have sacrificed their lives without sufficient
reason, those of the next generation had sufficient time to
recollect themselves, and would hardly have followed them
in the same course, without examination ; and they still
had sufficient opportunity for the purpose. The gospels
were then recent publications, and it might easily have
been inquired, in the very scene of the transactions, whether
the things had been as they were related or not.

If even the second generation should have been blinded
to their destruction, which is beyond measure improbable,
the third was not wholly destitute of the means of inquiry,
and they would certainly have availed themselves of it,
rather than have suffered what we know they did in the
cause of Christianity. In this manner, successive generations of martyrs bore their testimony to the truth of those
facts, for their faith in which they suffered, till no reasonable doubt could remain but that, if the history of the
gospels and of the book of Acts, had not been in the main
authentic, the falsehood would have been detected.

On the other hand, as the martyrs for Christianity were
deeply interested to inquire into the truth of that for which
they suffered, their enemies, who were as much exasperated

as men could be at the progress of Christianity, had motives sufficient to detect and expose the imposture of it, if it had been in their power. The umbrage that was taken at Christianity, in Judea, the scene of the transactions, began with itself. Christ himself was never without the most bitter enemies. The same was the case with the apostles; and certainly they who imprisoned them, and *charged them to preach no more in that name*, Acts iv. 17, would have exposed their artifices and pretended miracles, if it had been in their power; and they wanted no opportunity for the purpose, having every thing in the country, at their command.

In these remarkable circumstances Christianity was preached, and its professors were persecuted in Judea itself for the space of forty years, without its being pretended that the most watchful eye had discovered any imposture in the case. The activity of Paul, while he was a persecutor, was only employed in *haling men and women, and committing them to prison*, Acts viii. 3, and *persecuting them into strange cities.* He himself was afterwards a prisoner for his profession of Christianity, two years in Judea, where forty men entered into a bond *that they would neither eat nor drink till they had killed him*, Acts xxiii. 12; but nothing is said of their attempt to find out his artifices to deceive the people; though this, as they could not but know, would have answered their purpose infinitely better than killing him.

Another theatre of Christian miracles was in Gentile countries, where the preachers of Christianity had always adversaries as well as friends. But here also we hear of no detection of their frauds; even though every other method was taken to prevent the spread of Christianity. In the time of Julian, no writings, or records of any kind, had been destroyed; and if *he* could have discovered any thing respecting the origin or propagation of Christianity, that would have been to its prejudice, would he have spared any pains to bring it to light? He had evidently no hopes of being able to do any thing of the kind, and, therefore, he attacked Christianity in other ways.

Similar observations may be applied to the history of the Jewish religion. All the articles of it were formed at once, and committed to writing by Moses himself; and the books were not kept secret, but express orders were given, and provision was made, for frequent copies to be taken of them. Nothing essential to this religion rests upon tradition. If any alteration or innovation had been attempted, it might easily have been detected, and no fraud in the establishment of it could possibly have been concealed. The body of the people, to whom this law was given, frequently rebelled against Moses, and would even have gone back to Egypt. Aaron, Moses's own brother, and Miriam, his sister, who could not have been out of the secret of any of the means of deceiving the multitude, that he might have employed, took umbrage at his pre-eminence, and therefore wanted no motive to detect any imposition they knew him to have been guilty of.

Though there were not, properly speaking, any martyrs to the Jewish religion in that early period, the institutions themselves were many of them so burdensome, especially that of circumcision, and others of them so hazardous, as those of the sabbath, the sabbatical year, &c. and all of them so contrary to the rites to which the people had been accustomed, and for which they had contracted a fondness, which they never wholly lost, that they must have been sufficiently disposed, in every period of their history, to detect any imposition they could have found in it. Their own idolatrous kings, and the priests of Baal would, no doubt, have been glad to have justified their desertion of the religion of Moses, by the discovery of any thing that would have been to its prejudice. They were with respect to Judaism, what Julian was with respect to Christianity.

When these things are considered, how can it be said that the case of the Jewish and Christian religions bear any resemblance to the fabulous mythology of the Greeks and Romans, the metamorphoses of the Indian *Wishnou*, the journey of Mahomet to heaven, or the legendary tales of the church of Rome, all of which are founded on mere tradition, none of the pretended facts having been committed to writing at the time, and all of them received by those who suffered nothing for their faith in them, who were previously disposed to receive them, and add to them; and when no unbelievers had any opportunity of examining into the truth of them, and when there do not appear to have been any persons, like the persecutors of Christians, interested to expose their falsehood? Nothing, therefore, can be less entitled to credit than these stories, and nothing more worthy of it, than those Jewish and Christian histories, to which they have most injudiciously been compared.

I am, &c.

LETTER XI.

The Evidence of Judaism and Christianity compared with that of Mahometanism, and of the Religion of Indostan.

DEAR SIR,

SOME have compared the rise and progress of Christianity to that of Mahometanism, and that of Judaism to that of the religion of Indostan. But they certainly never attended to several very remarkable differences in both the cases.

1. There is no fact, of an historical nature, on which the truth of the Mahometan religion is said to be founded, that could be subjected to examination, because all the miracle that Mahomet himself pretended to was the revelation of the Koran made to himself only. However, any person may judge at this day whether the composition of it be such, as that human ability (that of Mahomet himself, for instance, assisted by some confidential friend) could not have been equal to it. Let any man of sense now read the Koran, and give his opinion on the subject.*

2. Mahometanism never did gain any converts in consequence of an examination into the grounds of it, among persons not interested in the reception of it. In what country was this religion ever generally received, in which the ruling powers opposed it, and persecuted it, or in which the ruling powers were not previously Mahometans?

The first Mahometans were all native Arabs, who were universally gainers by the propagation of their religion. But though they conquered many countries, their religion never became that of the generality of the ancient inhabitants, if they had been Christians before. Notwithstanding all the hardships to which they subjected those of that religion, and especially the contempt with which they treat them, all the countries of the East are still full of Christians of various denominations. The far greater part of Asia Minor, where the Turks were long settled before they invaded Europe, and also the greatest part of Turkey in Europe, of which they have been possessed three hundred years, is Christian, Constantinople itself at least half so.† The greatest part of

---

* See *Dr. Addison* and *Sir W. Jones* in *Note*, Vol. II. p. 50.

† " The inhabitants are said to amount to 900,000, of which 800,000 are *Greeks*, nearly 200,000 *Armenians*, the rest Turks or other Europeans." Crutwell's *Gazetteer*, 1798. In 1669, the *Greek* Christians had " about six and twenty churches in

Spain was once in the possession of Mahometans, and some parts of it near eight hundred years ; but we read of few or no Mahometans in it, beside native Moors from Africa.

In Indostan the governors only are Mahometans, though it is three hundred years since they conquered the country, so that whenever the government shall cease to be Mahometan, the profession of that religion in it will cease of course.

That many persons have, in a course of time, become firm believers in Mahometanism, cannot be doubted ; and, therefore, many will probably continue so, especially in Turkey and Arabia, though the government of these countries should become Christian. But we may safely prophecy that, whenever the government shall be changed, a death blow, a blow from which it will never recover, will be given to that religion, and all the remains of it will vanish in due time.

The Tartars, who at length conquered the Saracens, and put an end to the Caliphate, adopted their religion in preference to Heathenism ; but it by no means appears to have been done upon an inquiry into the historical evidence of it. Those Tartars who first conformed to the Mahometan religion, were those who had served under the Mahometan princes. They acquired power and influence by degrees, and many of them, no doubt, thought it necessary to make profession of that religion in order to establish themselves the better among a people who would not have any other. Thus Mahometanism, from being the religion of the *chiefs* among the Tartars, became in time that of the common people, and was afterwards adopted by other tribes of Tartars. If in any manner similar to this, or in any other in which the first converts were *princes*, the Christian religion came to be professed by any of the northern nations of Europe, I would lay no stress on such conversions as a proof of the truth of Christianity, or as any recommendation of it.

3. There never has been any period in which the merits and evidence of the Mahometan and Christian religions were freely debated by learned men. In all Mahometan countries it is death to make a proselyte, or to conceal one. Let this important circumstance be changed, and let a free intercourse be opened between Mahometans and rational,

---

Constantinople," besides " six churches at *Galata,*" and " the churches belonging to the town's and villages near Constantinople, on either side of the Bosphorus." See an account of the Greek Church, by Thomas Smith, B. D. 1680, pp. 53, 55, 56. Mr. S. had been chaplain to the English embassador at Constantinople.

that is, Unitarian Christians, and I shall have no doubt with respect to the consequence.*

4. Mahomet began with converting his own family, in which he met with difficulty, though they were interested in his success, and afterwards his nearest relations derived the greatest advantage from the scheme. On the contrary, Christ does not appear to have addressed himself particularly either to his own family, or to the ruling powers of the country, and no person connected with him ever derived any advantage from his undertaking. Two of his brothers were apostles, but they died martyrs, as well as most of the other apostles. The posterity of Moses derived no advantage from their relation to him, but continued in the rank of common Levites. None of Mahomet's first followers died voluntary martyrs to their faith in his divine mission. To risk one's life in battle with the hope of victory, is a very different thing from calmly submitting to a cruel death, without any hope but in a future life.

5. That the divine mission of Mahomet was firmly believed, and pretty early too, may be accounted for without supposing it to be true. His own family and acquaintance might be taken by his austerities and confident assertions, and the success of his enterprize would soon give them a notion that he had the countenance of heaven. His enthusiasm would pass for inspiration, and at length he might even himself imagine that a particular providence attended him. But had Mahomet died in battle, and consequently all the effects of his *arms* had ceased, where would have been his religion?

The religion of Christ was propagated in very different circumstances. No man having pretensions to a divine mission, could have died in circumstances more unfavourable to the credit of it than he did; and yet his religion gained ground, and notwithstanding every mode of opposition, is firmly believed, in all revolutions of empires, by

---

* There are some passages on this subject at the close of Sir W. Jones's Anniversary Discourse at Calcutta, 1784, in reading which it is not very easy to discover *all* the author might intend to express. He says, "the *Muselmáns* are already a sort of heterodox *Christians:* they are *Christians,* if Locke reasons justly, because they firmly believe the immaculate conception, divine character, and miracles of the *Messiah;* but they are heterodox in denying vehemently his character of Son, and his equality, as God, with the Father, of whose unity they entertain and express the most awful ideas." He adds, "that neither *Muselmáns* nor *Hindús* will ever be converted by any mission from the church of *Rome* or from any other church." *On the Gods of Greece, Italy and India.* Dissertations, 1792, I. pp. 63, 64.

those who derive no worldly advantage from the profession of it, to this day.

It should also be considered, that what is most reputable in the religion of Mahomet, is derived from the Jewish and Christian religions, the corruptions of which he began with undertaking to reform ; and he had a particular advantage in addressing the Arabs, as the descendants of Abraham. His doctrine of the *divine unity*, gave him great advantage over the generality of Christians of that age, who had most miserably bewildered themselves with their notions of a trinity in the Godhead, of which it was impossible that they should give any rational account.

It has been said that *the religion of Indostan* is contained in written books, as well as that of Moses, and may be of as great, or greater antiquity, and that the belief of the people in it is no less firm than that of Jews or Christians in theirs. But I beg leave to make the following observations on the subject.

· 1. The books which contain this religion are not, as far as appears, of an historical nature, giving an account of miracles wrought in proof of the divine mission of those who wrote them, or who published the religion contained in them, but consist only of doctrines concerning God, the creation, the destination of the human race, &c. and in themselves utterly irrational, so that every thing the books contain might have been composed without any supernatural assistance.* And there is nothing that we can now examine by the rules of history and testimony. Consequently, the Vedas cannot be brought into comparison with the books of Moses, the gospels, and the book of Acts.

2. The age of the books is very uncertain, as there has not yet been discovered any authentic history of the country, giving an account of the authors of those books, and con-

---

* See on the Religion of *Indostan*, Vol III. pp. 391—396, also the author's communication, in 1787, under the signature *Scrutator*, to *Theol. Repos.* VI. p. 408.

We have just now a very unexpected and gratifying opportunity of acquiring more correct information respecting the sacred books of the *Hindoos*, from the labours of *Rammohun Roy*, " a learned, eloquent and opulent Brahmun," who " has publicly taught the doctrine of the divine unity and perfection, to the native Hindoos," for whose use " he has translated the *Vedant*, one of their most sacred books, (a compendium of the *Veds*,) from the *Sungskrit*, into the *Bengalee* and *Hindostanee*, and circulated those translations free of expense. He has translated an abridgment. of this work into English," from which, says Mr. Belsham, " it appears that Christianity itself does not teach a purer theism than that of the Vedant and the Veds." See " An Introduction by the Rev. Thomas Belsham," prefixed to " A Letter to the *Unitarian Society*, by a Native Unitarian Christian of Madrass," 1818, pp. xviii. —xxv.

tinuing the history from that time to the present, which is the case with the books of Moses.

3. The religious books of the Hindoos are confined to one class of people in the country, who support their rank and privileges by keeping the common people in ignorance of them. It is even death by the laws of the country, for persons of a lower cast to read those books, or to hear them read by another person,* which is certainly a very suspicious circumstance. And though, by this means, those of the inferior casts are kept in subjection to their superiors, they are all taught to believe that they are of a higher rank, and greater favourites of heaven than the rest of mankind; that they will be rewarded for their adherence to their religion, and punished for deserting it. It has never been said that the faith of the lower people is the result of *inquiry* and conviction, nor do the Indians attempt to convert other people.

4. The professors of this religion never suffered any persecution for it; at least not in times in which the evidence of it was open to examination, as was the case with Christianity. Their faith, therefore, is only like that of the Greeks and Romans, in their religions, a faith founded on mere tradition, and having the sanction of dark antiquity. Let the Hindoos, as well as the Mahometans, become acquainted with our literature, and have free intercourse with Unitarian Christians, and I have no doubt but that the result will be in favour of Christianity.†

I am, &c.

---

* "If a man of the *Sooder*, (the lowest original tribe of Gentoos,) read the *Beids* of the *Shaster*, (the most ancient and venerable of the Gentoo Scriptures,) or the *Pooràn*, (one of the Gentoo Scriptures upon history,) to a *Bramin*, a *Chepteree*, or a *Bice*, (the first, second and third original tribe of Gentoos,) then the magistrate shall heat some bitter oil, and pour it into the aforesaid *Sooder's* mouth, and if a *Sooder* listens to the *Beids* of the *Shaster*, then the oil, heated as before, shall be poured into his ears, and *arzeez* (tin) and wax shall be melted together, and the orifice of his ears shall be stopped up therewith. This ordination serves also for the *Arzàl* tribe (an inferior tribe of the Hindoos).

"If a *Sooder* get by heart the *Beids* of the *Shaster*, the magistrate shall put him to death." See "A Code of Gentoo Laws or Ordinations of the Pundits, from a Persian Translation made from the Original, written in the Shanscrit Language, by Mr. Halhed, under the sanction of Governor-General Hastings, 1777," pp. 261, 262, and the *Glossary*. The very learned translator complains that "the customs and manners of these people, to their great injury, have long been misrepresented in the western world." P. xi. That his representations, which possess every claim to authenticity, have served to improve our opinions of these *customs and manners*, as discovered in the *Gentoo Laws*, may be reasonably doubted.

† May we not hope that the dawn of that day, which my author gladly anticipated, has arrived? See the *Letter* from William Roberts, a *native* of Madras, mentioned in the *Note*, p. 502. Also *Christian Reformer*, IV. p. 1.

LETTER XII.

Of the Nature of Idolatry, and the Attachment of the Heathens to it, as a principal Cause of their hatred of Christians.

DEAR SIR,

You acknowledge that cases may be supposed, in which the most sufficient evidence would not produce its natural effect on the minds of men; that numbers might remain unconvinced, in circumstances in which we think that we ourselves could not hesitate to declare ourselves converts to an opinion. You are sensible that, in cases of this nature, we either do not sufficiently consider the difference between the previous state of our minds and that of theirs, or that we do not place ourselves precisely in the same circumstances, and that, on these accounts, it must be impossible to argue justly from the persuasion or feelings of any one man to those of any other. But you wish to know more particularly than I have hitherto explained it, what was the actual state of the gentile world in general with respect to Christianity, especially in what manner it appears to have been treated by those who did not receive, but continued to oppose it, and what kind of objections were in those early ages made to it.

As this is a very reasonable request, I shall give you all the satisfaction in my power with respect to it; and I am confident that a just exhibition of those ancient times will convince you, that the opposition which Christianity then met with, can supply no valid argument against it at this day. The objections which were then made to Christianity were of such a nature, that they can have no weight with any modern unbelievers, so that if it had been possible for any person in those times to have enjoyed the superior light of the present age, he must have been ashamed of almost every thing which was alleged against the gospel by the ancient opposers of it. Indeed, so very absurd were the notions of the Heathens, philosophers as well as others, that it is even difficult for us at this day to suppose they could ever have existed, at least so generally, as universal history shews that they did. On this account, though I might content myself with shewing the *fact*, I shall descant a little on the causes of it.

. So little connexion do we see or can imagine, between the religious ceremonies of the Greeks and Romans,(such as sacrifices, processions, games, &c.) and the *welfare of a state*, that we can hardly bring ourselves to believe that any men of sense could ever have entertained the idea. Yet nothing was so deeply fixed in the minds of the gentile world in general.

The whole system of false religion or idolatry, arose from the notion of a connexion between good or bad fortune, and certain acts or *ceremonies*, which, for some reason or other, were supposed to gain the favour or incur the displeasure of those divinities which had the dispensation of good or evil in the world.

In the infant state of the world, when the *true* causes of things were not known, it is not to be wondered at that men should fix upon *wrong* ones ; for they are never easy without imagining some hypothesis for every phenomenon. And since the best concerted plans were often unsuccessful, for reasons which the wisest men could not foresee or comprehend, they concluded that besides those causes of the events of life, which might be traced to the power and policy of men, there must be other and invisible ones, and such as were independent of the regular operation of the laws of nature. We may see the same propensity among ignorant people at this day: for *superstition* is always in proportion to *ignorance*. But, whereas, the ignorance and superstition of the present day have no resource but in a blind *fate*, or capricious *fortune*, residing in they know not what; mankind in the early ages fixed upon the great visible objects in nature, such as the sun, moon and stars.

Being sensible of their power in some respects, mankind easily imagined that it extended to other things, and this influence not being subject to any known regular laws, so that events might be predicted, or guarded against, they concluded that their power was not a *necessary influence*, but a *voluntary agency*. Then concluding, that there must be a sentient and intelligent principle in the heavenly bodies, they might easily go on to imagine that there was a similar sentient principle in the earth, and even in the separate parts of it, as seas, rivers, mountains, &c. also in animals, and especially in man, whose passions and affections they could not explain by what was visible in his frame. This invisible principle they would easily suppose to be, like that in the heavenly bodies, incorruptible and immortal.

In this train of thinking, mankind were soon provided with a prodigious number of invisible beings, whose favour it behoved them to court, and whose displeasure they had to avoid. And prosperous or adverse events having actually followed certain actions, they would naturally imagine that the same actions, or others similar to them, had an influence with the beings who had the power over those events.

This mental process was not peculiar to ancient times. We see the same thing in the practice of many gamesters now, who will even imagine that good or bad fortune depends upon a particular place at the table, and that it may be changed by turning round their chair, &c. ; and when once any opinion, though of this most ridiculous kind, has got the sanction of *general belief*, on however insufficient grounds, it is not easily eradicated. For if the expected event do not follow the usual circumstances, the blame will be laid on a thousand unperceived causes, rather than it will be supposed that those circumstances had no real tendency to produce the desired effect. Consequently the same things will continue to be practised with the same expectations, and a single coincidence of the usual preliminary preparations with the expected event will be talked of and magnified, while numberless failures will be forgotten or accounted for. And the longer any superstitious rite had been practised, the more would its efficacy be depended upon, and the less regard would be paid to the cases in which it had failed.

From such causes as these, it cannot be denied that, in the age of Christ and the apostles, the religious customs of the heathen world had got the firmest hold on the minds of men. No person was able to trace the origin of any rite of importance, so that the veneration bestowed on every thing that was *ancient* was attached to them; and it was taken for granted, that the well-being of all states absolutely depended upon the observance of the religious rites which had been from time immemorial practised in them.

Hence every person who suggested an idea of the insignificance of such things, and much more one who protested against them, was considered as a dangerous member of society, and treated as an *atheist*, because he was an enemy to such gods as his fellow-citizens acknowledged, and promoted the discontinuance of those rites on which, in their opinion, the safety of the commonwealth depended:

On these principles, and without any farther inquiry, such a person was thought unworthy of protection or of life. Consequently Christians, as dissenters from the established worship were hated, so that the very *name* was sufficient to condemn them, and the most patriotic magistrates thought it their duty to exterminate them. Such was the prejudice against Christianity on this account only, that it was thought unnecessary to inquire into the ground of their faith; and persons of the most excellent characters in other respects, and of the most cultivated minds, such as Trajan, Pliny and Marcus Aurelius,* made no scruple to condemn to death and even to torture, all who only acknowledged themselves to be Christians.

It was, however, the belief of all the ancient Heathens, that different kinds of worship were proper for different people. Indeed, they could not but see that different nations had been prosperous, notwithstanding their different religions, and, therefore, the greatest conquerors tolerated the nations that were subject to their empire in their peculiar rites. On this principle the Jews had obtained a toleration for themselves wherever they were dispersed through the Roman empire; and, under the idea that Christianity was a sect among the Jews, this was also for a long time tolerated by the Romans. But as soon as, by the increase of proselytes, the nature of Christianity began to be perceived, and the national religion was apprehended to be in danger from it, the most violent measures were taken to exterminate it. The same, no doubt, would have been the case with Judaism, if the progress of it had been equally alarming.

We perceive the extreme veneration for the ancient customs of nations, and the offence that was taken at Christianity, as a *novel* religion, upon all occasions. Celsus upbraids the Jewish Christians with deserting the law of their country.† " The Jews," he says, " having the proper laws of their country, act like other men; forasmuch as all follow the institutions of their country whatever they are. And that is reasonable enough, because different laws have been framed by different people; and it is fit that those things should be observed which have been established by public authority."‡ Julian also thought more favourably of the Jews than of the Christians, because the former had sacrifices and priests, &c. in common with the Gentiles. This was "a popular argument against the Christians," their customs being peculiar to themselves, and different " from those of all other people."§

---

* M. Antoninus, the philosopher. See *Lardner*, VII. p. 433.
† *Lardner*, VIII. p. 44.   ‡ Ibid. p. 47.   § Ibid. p. 406.

The anciént religions being established by the laws of the countries in which they were observed, Christianity was considered as an *illegal* thing ; and the assemblies of Christians not being *authorized by law*, all those who frequented them were considered as liable to punishment on that account only, and *assembling in secret* was always thought dangerous in well-regulated states.   Celsus objects " that Christians secretly hold assemblies together contrary to law."[*]

On this account, Christians, not denying, but avowing these practices, were considered as obnoxious to the law. Among others, Athenagoras complains that Christians were " persecuted for the name only ;"[†] and when a man was thought well of on other accounts, it was an objection to him that he was a Christian.   According to Tertullian, it was usual with them to say, such a one " is a good man, only he is a Christian."[‡]

That the Heathens really believed that the welfare of the state depended upon the observance of their ancient religious ceremonies, and that public calamities were occasioned by the omission of them, there is the most abundant evidence.   I shall only mention a few of the proofs, such as will shew that not the vulgar only, but the most enlightened of the Heathens, and persons in the highest authority, held the same opinion, and that they considered Christians as the cause of all the calamities of the empire.   Maximin, in one of his rescripts, speaking of the hurricanes and earthquakes of those times, says, " there is no man that does not know, that all these, and worse calamities, have heretofore often happened, and that they have befallen us because of the pernicious error and empty vanity of those execrable men, which has so spread as to cover almost the whole earth with shame and dishonour."[§]   Porphyry, a philosopher, who wrote against Christianity, said, " since Jesus has been honoured, none have received any public benefit from the gods."[||]

When some of the senators petitioned the emperors Valentinian, Theodosius and Arcadius, to replace the altar of victory which had been taken from the door of the senate-house, they said, in the person of Rome, " This way of worship has brought all the world into obedience to my laws.   These rites drove Hannibal from my walls, and the Gauls from the capitol."[¶]   It was more particularly ima-

---

* *Lardner*, VIII. p. 45.   † Ibid. VII. p. 410.   ‡ Ibid. VIII. p. 92.
§ Ibid. p. 315. || Ibid. p. 220.   ¶ Ibid. IX. p. 139.

gined that " the public welfare" depended upon the vestal virgins.*

Zozimus, a heathen historian, says, that from the time of ¡ " the public sacrifices ceasing, and all other things received from ancient tradition being neglected, the Roman empire has gradually declined till it has become the habitation of barbarians," &c.† Also, speaking of the prosperity of the empire, during the observance of the secular games, he says, " in the third consulship of Constantine and Licinus, the time of a hundred and ten years was completed, when the festival ought to have been observed according to custom. And not having been then observed, there was a necessity that affairs should sink into the distress and misery in which they now are."‡

Libanius, a distinguished heathen philosopher of the fourth century, speaking of the sacrifices which were then permitted at Rome, but suppressed in other places, says, " if in the sacrifices there performed consists the stability of the empire" (which he took for granted), " it ought to be reckoned beneficial to sacrifice every where."§ Again, " neither," says he, " is it at Rome only that the liberty of sacrificing remains, but also in the city of Serapis, that great and populous city" (meaning Alexandria), " which has a multitude of temples, by which it renders the plenty of Egypt common to all men. This plenty is the work of the Nile. It therefore celebrates the Nile, and persuades him to rise, and overflow the fields. If those rites were not performed, when and by whom they ought, he would not do so, which they themselves seem to be sensible of, who willingly enough abolish such things, but do not abolish these, but permit the river to enjoy his ancient rites, for the sake of the benefit he affords."‖ The temple and statue of Serapis being at length demolished, " it was given out by the gentile people, that the Nile would no longer overflow. Nevertheless, it rose the following year to an uncommon height."¶

When Rhadagaisus, a Goth, invaded the Roman empire, " the Pagans" gave out that " they could by no means withstand such an enemy, who had the assistance of the gods, to whom he sacrificed every day;" whereas " *they* had none to help them, now the gods and their rites were

---

* *Lardner*, IX. p. 141.   † Ibid p. 50.   ‡ Ibid. p 34.   § Ibid. VIII. p. 449.
‖ Ibid.   ¶ Ibid. IX. p. 162.

banished.—The Christian religion," they said, "had quite ruined the state, and brought them into this miserable condition." This barbarian, however, was conquered, and in a most complete manner. " Rome did afterwards fall into the hands of another enemy, but he was a Christian," and the Romans found him to be a merciful conqueror.* Notwithstanding all this, the Pagans still attributed all the misfortunes of the empire to the progress of Christianity; and in answer to this, Austin wrote his famous book *De Civitate Dei.*

In consequence of the Heathens ascribing all prosperous events to the favour of their gods, they considered temporal prosperity as a proof of their power, and therefore naturally concluded that religion to be a bad one, which exposed its votaries to temporal evils. - Hence Celsus objects to Christians their not being delivered by Christ when they were condemned to death.† Hence, also, arose part of the prejudice against Christ himself, viz. his being *put to death*, independent of the mode of his death, which marked him to be a low and mean character. Celsus, in particular, did not fail to object to Christians the miserable death of Christ.‡

Many of the Heathens, instead of admiring the courage of the christian martyrs, as dying in the cause of truth, reproached them for their folly and obstinacy on that account. Porphyry, alluding to Christians, speaks of them as " mean people, who, having embraced rules different from their former way of life, will endure to be torn limb from limb, rather than return to their old course."§ Tertullian shews how inconsistently the Heathens reasoned on this subject, who could allow, that to die for one's country was honourable, but could think that " to die for God and truth" was " reproachful and dishonourable."||

It is obvious to remark, with Lardner, on this occasion, that certainly men who were so much despised and hated, and who were exposed to so much misery in consequence of being Christians, must have thought that they had good reasons for becoming such; and since many of them were men of good understanding in other respects, they would, no doubt, take proper pains to inquire into the ground of that faith to which they sacrificed so much.

I am, &c.

* *Lardner,* IX. p. 178.   † Ibid. VIII. p. 46.   ‡ Ibid. p. 41.
    § Ibid. p. 225. || Ibid. VII. p. 404.

LETTER XIII.

The Attachment of the Heathens to their Religion more particularly proved.

DEAR SIR,

ABSURD as the heathen religion was, there is the most indisputable evidence of several of the wisest of the Heathens, long after the time of our Saviour, being the most firmly attached to it, and especially of their practising the rites of *divination* prescribed by it, whenever they wished to pry into futurity. This was always a great article in the heathen religions; and the promises they held out of giving men information of this kind was, in all ages, one of the greatest inducements to follow them. Nor shall we wonder at this, when we consider how many persons, of whose good sense in other respects, better things might be expected, do even now secretly listen to the idle tales of the lowest fortune-tellers, and what numbers never fail to flock to any person who gives out the most absurd public advertisement for this purpose. In all these things the philosophers of antiquity, who might have been expected to know better, " did little or nothing," as Lardner observes, " to improve the senti-ments of mankind ;" but, on the contrary, " they confirmed the prejudices of the common people, and made them still worse than they otherwise would have been."*

Philosophers " gave credit to the Pythagorean fables,"† and in particular entertained the most ridiculous idea of *inspiration*, and of an intercourse between the gods and men. This " superstition and credulity," Dr. Lardner apprehends to have been the " common dispositions in heathen people, of all ranks, high and low, learned and unlearned."‡ " It does not appear," he observes, " that Pliny, or Tacitus, did admit any doubts about the grounds of the ancient worship, or make any serious inquiries about religious truth."§

Pliny was an augur, and greatly valued the office. Every Roman emperor was *Pontifex maximus.* Marcus Aurelius was introduced into the college of priests called *Salii*, at the age of eight years, and was complete master of all the rules of the order, so as to be able to discharge, himself, the func-tions of that priesthood. It is probable, therefore, that he

---

* *Lardner*, VIII. p. 286,   † Ibid. p. 285.   ‡ Ibid. IX. p. 30.
§ Ibid. VII. p. 343.

gained in his childhood a deep tincture of superstition, which grew up with him, and was retained by him afterwards. He was indeed, extremely superstitious, and a rigid perse-cutor ; and he disliked the Christians because " they outdid the Stoics themselves," in bearing pain and death. *

Julian, another philosophical emperor, was so " supersti-tious, so addicted to sacrificing, that it was said, the race of bulls would be destroyed if he returned victorious from Persia.   And such was the multitude of his victims, that his soldiers who partook of them were often much disordered by excess in eating and drinking."† " On festivals to the honour of Venus," he " walked in procession with lewd women, and others of the worst characters, followed by his horse and guards."‡ Sacrificing on some occasion to Mars, and " the omens not being favourable, he—called Jupiter to witness, that he would never more offer a sacrifice to Mars "§

That the doctrine of *demons*, and of their intercourse with men, and also that of the gods in general, and the notion of *inspiration* by them, really obtained among the Heathens, long after the promulgation of Christianity, absurd as all modern philosophers will think them to be, there is the most abundant evidence.   Damascius wrote that, the wife of Hierocles " became possessed," and " as the demon would not be persuaded to depart by good words, his disciple Theosebius compelled him by an oath, though he did not understand magic or theurgy ; but he abjured him by the rays of the sun, and the god of the Hebrews.   Whereupon the demon departed, crying out, that he reverenced the gods, and him in particular.   " This," adds Dr. Lardner, is a " story of a gentile philosopher, told by a gentile histo-rian."‖

Marinus, speaking of Proclus, says, " how dear he was to the goddess, president of philosophy," (meaning Minerva) " appeared from the great progress which he made in that study, to which he had been directed by the goddess herself." Among other superstitions of this Proclus, Marinus says, that " once a month he purified himself, according to the rites of the mother of the gods."¶ Of Ædesius, Eunapius says, that he " became little inferior to his master Jamblichus, setting aside the inspiration which belonged to Jambli-chus."**

* *Lardner*, VII. p. 399.   † Ibid. VIII. p. 361.   ‡ Ibid. p. 366.   § Ibid. p. 362.
‖ Ibid. IX. p. 65.   ¶ Ibid. pp. 70, 71.   ** Ibid. IX. p. 3.

As it was imagined that the gods had the knowledge of future events, and often communicated it to men in their oracles, and by other modes of divination, it was pretended that, among other things, the progress of Christianity (which was certainly a most interesting event to the heathen world in general) was foretold by them. Eunapius, speaking of the philosopher Antoninus, says, " At that time he was not accounted more than a man, and conversed among men. Yet he foretold to all his disciples, that, after his death, there would be no temples, but that the magnificent and sacred temple of Serapis would be laid in ruinous heaps, and that fabulous confusion and unformed darkness would tyrannize over the best parts of the earth. All which things time has brought to pass, and his prediction has obtained the credit of an oracle."* It was generally believed among the Heathens, that there was " an oracle wherein it was declared that the Christian religion should subsist for three hundred and sixty-five years;" and many were converted when they found that there was no truth in that oracle. †

The most remarkable thing in the history of Paganism, after Christianity came to be the established religion of the Roman empire, was a solemn consultation, and divination, of the heathen philosophers, in the year 374, to find out who should succeed the Emperor Valens.‡ They were extremely uneasy at the great progress of Christianity, and were very desirous that the next emperor might be a Heathen. This consultation being discovered, those who were concerned in it, and especially Maximus, who had been a great favourite of Julian, were put to death.§

The true spirit of the heathen religion, as held by the

* *Lardner*, IX. p. 4.   + Ibid. pp. 171, 172.   ‡ Ibid. p. 116.

§ That the reader may have some idea of the nature of this solemn *divination*, at which the gravest of the heathen philosophers assisted, I shall copy the following account of it by Ammianus Marcellinus: " A tripod made of laurel was artificially prepared, and consecrated, with certain prescribed secret charms and invocations. It was then placed in the middle of a room, perfumed with Arabian spices. The charger upon which it was set, had upon its utmost brim the four and twenty letters of the alphabet, neatly engraved, and set at due distances from each other. Then a person clad in linen vestments, with linen socks upon his feet, and a suitable covering upon his head, came in with laurel branches in his hands, and, after some mystic charms performed, shaked a ring, hanging at a curtain, about the edge of the charger, which, jumping up and down, fell upon such and such letters of the alphabet, where it seemed to stay, the priest also then composing certain heroic verses, in answer to the interrogatories that had been proposed The letters which' the ring pointed out in this case were four, ΘΕΟΔ, which being put together composed these two syllables, Theod, whereupon one that stood by presently cried out, that the oracle plainly intended *Theodorus*. Nor did we make any farther inquiries, being all well satisfied that he was the person intended." (*P.*) Ibid. p. 117.

most eminent philosophers in this age, may be seen in a story concerning this Maximus, related by Eunapius, who says that, " Soon after Julian's arrival at Constantinople— he sent a messenger with letters to Maximus and Chrysanthius, inviting them to come to him. They thought proper to ask counsel of the gods, but the tokens which they received were discouraging ; whereupon Chrysanthius plainly told Maximus, there can be no thoughts of going to seek preferment. We must stay where we are. Perhaps it may be needful for us to hide ourselves. On the contrary, Maximus urged, we are not to content ourselves with a single refusal ; we ought rather to force the gods till they give us a favourable answer suited to our wishes. Chrysanthius replied, that he dared not to disobey the first admonitions which had been received, and went away. Maximus renewed his inquiries till he obtained such an answer as he wanted." *

. Innumerable other things might be related of many of the heathen philosophers, equal to any thing in the popish legends. Nothing could exceed their superstition and credulity. Far, therefore, is it from being true, as some moderns, and especially Mr. Gibbon, have pretended, that the belief in Paganism was nearly worn out, and that it was an easy thing for Christianity to step in, and take its place.

At this day good sense teaches men toleration with respect to religion, and apprehends no inconvenience from it to the state. But considering the notions and maxims which we have seen to have been adopted by the wisest of the Heathens, we cannot wonder that they were no friends to toleration, but, from principle, the most rigid persecutors. This was the case with those who, in other respects, were the very best of the emperors. But they really thought that they were promoting the welfare of the empire, by the extermination of Christians out of it.

Trajan, justly celebrated for his wisdom and justice in other respects, was a persecutor of the Christians. His edict against them " was never abrogated" till the time of Constantine ; and, according to this, " the presidents" of the provinces " were required to pronounce sentence of death upon all who were brought before them, and accused of Christianity, unless they denied themselves to be Christians." †

The elegant and philosophical Pliny thought that those who obstinately refused to sacrifice to the gods were justly

<hr>

* *Lardner,* IX. pp. 130, 131.   † Ibid. VIII. p. 338.

deserving of death; though he acknowledges, that when he had made inquiry by torture, of some who had abandoned the profession of Christianity, he could not find that they were guilty of any thing else; and that, in their private assemblies, they bound themselves by an oath to the practice of virtue.

Marcus Aurelius, the most philosophical of the emperors, and who is famed for his moderation, was a more bigotted Heathen than Trajan, and a more violent persecutor of the Christians.

Hierocles, who wrote against the Christians, was himself " a persecutor, and an adviser of persecution."* " When prefect of Alexandria," he insulted " the Christians who were brought before him in the most opprobrious manner, though they were men of great gravity; and he delivered women, some of which were devoted to virginity, into the hands of bawds," for the purpose of prostitution.†

Julian wanted no good-will to extirpate Christianity, but he had seen the little effect of the more violent kind of persecution in the former reigns, when Christians were far less numerous than they were in his time. He did not choose, therefore, to adopt the same measures, but he omitted no opportunity of shewing his malevolence to Christianity, and the professors of it, in every method that he thought safe, and likely to be successful. Lardner truly observes, " that he was intent upon extirpating Christianity with the greatest dispatch;" and " that, with all his pretensions to right reason, and all his professions of humanity, moderation, tenderness and equity, he has not escaped the just imputation of being a persecutor."‡

In his letter to the prefect of Egypt, Julian says, " It concerns me extremely, that all the gods are despised."§ Libanius, speaking of the severities of former reigns, says, that " Julian dissented from those who had practised such things, as not obtaining the end aimed at," and that " he was sensible that no benefit was to be expected from such violence.—Considering, therefore, these things, and that their affairs had been increased by slaughters, he declined what he could not approve of."|| He connived, however, at a tumult, in which George, the Arian bishop of Alexandria, was murdered; and he banished " Athanasius, Eleusis of Cyzicum, and Titus of Bostra, all of them men of great distinction," on very slight pretences.¶ He " not only de-

---

* *Lardner,* VIII. p. 257.　　† Ibid. p. 260.　　‡ Ibid. p. 423.
§ Ibid. p. 415.　　|| Ibid. pp. 438, 139.　　¶ Ibid. p. 423.

prived the Christians of magistracy, and all honours and dignities, but likewise," it is said, " of equal rights of citizenship." * But what particularly distinguishes his reign is, his forbidding all Christians the benefit of human literature. " That," says Ammianus, a heathen historian, " was an unmerciful law, and ought for ever to be buried in silence, which forbade the Christians to teach grammar or rhetoric." †

As a reason for this law, Julian, in an ironical manner, unworthy of a prince, alleged that it was absurd to teach the heathen writers, and at the same time not to espouse their religion. With the same cruel sneer he stripped the church of Edessa of its wealth, saying, that Christianity promised the kingdom of heaven to the poor.

That Julian would have extirpated Christianity, if it had been in his power, is evident from what he says of the books which had belonged to George, the Arian bishop, mentioned before, which he ordered to be seized for his own use. Writing on the subject to the governor of Egypt, he says, " he had a large number of books, many philosophical and rhetorical, and also many concerning the doctrine of the impious Galileans, which I could wish to have utterly destroyed; but lest books of value should be destroyed with them, let these also be carefully sought for." ‡   Damascius, Lardner observes, appears to have " approved of any attempts against Christians and the Christian religion." §

It is remarkable that, during all the persecution of Christians, which from the decree of Nero was never wholly intermitted, no heathen philosopher ever pleaded the cause of humanity and toleration, which was grossly violated in their persons; though Libanius commended Jovian for his toleration of the Pagans. On the whole, it is most evident, that the Heathens did every thing in their power to extirpate the Christian religion, but were not able to do it.

We shall the less wonder at the unbelief of the most learned adversaries of Christianity, and of the unrelenting violence with which they persecuted the Christians, when we consider how ignorant they were of the principles of Christianity. Lardner justly observes that, though we have so many letters of Pliny to Tacitus, and other learned men, his contemporaries, and it appears from his own evidence, that Christians were numerous in Bythinia, the province in which he resided, he never mentions to them the subject of Christianity; ‖ so that it is most probable, he had never

---

* *Lardner*, VIII. p. 371.   † Ibid. p. 470.   ‡ Ibid. pp. 413, 414.
§ Ibid. IX. p. 78.   ‖ Ibid. VII. p. 343.

had the curiosity even to look into their books.   The same
is probable also concerning Marcus Aurelius.*   This emperor says, " from Diognetus I learned not to busy myself
about vain things, nor to give credit to wonder-workers and
stories of incantations and expelling demons, and such like
things."†   Of Libanius also, who wrote in a late period,
Lardner observes, that he did " not perceive that he had
read the books of the New Testament,—nor the Old." ‡

It is possible, however, that he and other learned Heathens
might think it beneath them to mention Christian writers,
though they *had* read their books, hoping perhaps to extin-
guish the memory of them by their silence.   Lardner observes, that " Epictetus and others may have suppressed
their own thoughts, and have been reserved in their discourses, lest they should excite inquisitiveness in their
hearers, and occasion doubts about the popular deities, and
the worship paid to them."§   A similar reason might also
occasion the silence of Josephus.   Celsus also, though he
appears to have read the New Testament, never mentions
the names of any of the writers.‖

. I am, &c.

LETTER XIV.

*Of the Objections to the Historical Evidence of Christianity
in early Times.*

DEAR SIR,

HAVING shewn in what manner the Heathens were
affected towards Christianity, I shall now proceed to shew
what it was that they actually objected to it ; and though
none of their writings against Christianity are now extant,
it is not difficult to collect this from those of the Christians
who have noticed them, from the many fragments which
have been preserved of them, and from the history of the
times in general. · This has been done with great care by
Dr. Lardner, in his *Jewish and Heathen Testimonies*, and for
your use I shall abridge and digest what he has collected.

Unbelievers of the present day may complain that the
writings of Heathens against Christianity are now lost ; but
Christians lament this loss much more than they do, and

---

* *Lardner,* VII. p. 406.   † Ibid. p. 409.   ‡ Ibid. VIII. p. 437.
§ Ibid. p. 96.   ‖ Ibid. p. 56.

in all ages have paid more attention to them than the
Heathens themselves did.   Chrysostom says, " the books
written against Christianity were so contemptible, that
they had been all in a manner lost long ago.   Many of
them perished almost as soon as they appeared.   But if
they are still to be found any where, it is among the Christians." *   It is not denied, however, that there were edicts
of christian princes for the suppression of these books of
the Heathens, as there had been similar edicts of heathen
emperors for suppressing the books of the Christians.   But
the different effect of these edicts is itself a proof of the
different degree of attachment that was had to these books,
and, consequently, of the different degree of *credit* that was
due to them.   Had the objections of these heathen writers
to Christianity been solid, it may well be presumed that,
since they had all the powers of government in their favour,
for near three hundred years, they would have effected their
purpose, and of course have preserved themselves.

The most valuable, however, of all the writers against
Christianity, was undoubtedly Celsus, the earliest of them;
and it can hardly be doubted but that every thing of consequence in him is preserved in Origen's answer to him, as
the arguments of Porphyry and Hierocles are preserved in
Eusebius, and those of Julian in Cyril; besides that we
have several of Julian's own works, in which he reflects
upon Christianity.   Upon the whole, therefore, every impartial person must be satisfied, that we are at this day able
to see a very clear state of the objections to Christianity in
all the early ages; and I shall now fairly exhibit them,
without omitting any that can be thought by any unbeliever to be worth mentioning, beginning with those that
relate to the *credibility of the facts* in the gospel history,
which indeed are all that are worthy of much consideration.
For if the books be genuine, and the facts recorded in them
be true, all other objections signify nothing.   It will then
be indisputable, that the scheme has the sanction of the
Divine Being, and, therefore, that we must reconcile to
ourselves the particular difficulties we meet with in revelation, as we do those that we find in the works of nature and
the course of providence, that is, as well as we can.

It is remarkable that not one of the writers against Christianity in the early ages disputed the genuineness of any of
the historical books of the New Testament, or of the

* *Lardner*, VIII. p. 3.

Epistles of Paul. On the contrary, this important circumstance is tacitly allowed by Celsus, Hierocles and Julian,
who quote the Gospels of Matthew, Mark and Luke, as
written before the death of John, and that of John as written
by himself. In short, not one of these heathen writers expresses any opinion on this subject different from that
which was held by all Christians, in all times, viz. that the
books were written by the persons whose names they bear,
and that they were published before their deaths. Celsus,
indeed, says that the writers had altered some things, but of
this he does not appear to have brought any proof. * And
" Hierocles—endeavoured to disparage" the writers, by
" calling them *illiterate, liars and impostors.*"† But these
also are mere terms of reproach, without proof or probability. With more assurance, he said, "that Jesus had
been expelled from Judea, and after that committed robbery, accompanied by a band of nine hundred men."‡ But
he might as well have said, that he took Jerusalem by
storm, and made himself king of it. Such assertions as
these, without any circumstances to make them probable,
are deserving of nothing but contempt.

It does not appear whether Celsus admitted the miracles
of Jesus or not. But as he did not expressly deny them, or
endeavour to refute the account of them in the gospels, it is
probable that he had no great objection to any of them,
except to that of the resurrection. He " pretends to grant
that the things related of Jesus are true, such as healing
diseases, raising the dead, feeding multitudes with a few
loaves.—And then adds, ' Well, then, let us grant, that all
these things were done by you.' After which he instanceth
in the tricks of the Egyptians, and other impostors ; and
then asketh this question : ' because they do such things,
must we therefore esteem them to be God's sons?'"§ He
insinuates that the apostles and other Christians might
work miracles by the same means. For, he " says that he
had seen, with some presbyters, books, in a barbarous language, containing the names of demons, and other charms."‖
Both this writer, and the unbelieving Jews said, farther,
that Jesus " learned magical arts in Egypt."¶

But to say nothing of the time when Jesus was there,
which, according to the common opinion, was only in his
infancy, it is well observed by Dr. Lardner (after Grotius),

---

* *Lardner*, VIII. p. 62.   † Ibid. p. 262.   ‡ Ibid. p. 263.   § Ibid. p. 24.
‖ Ibid. p. 48.   ¶ Ibid. VII. pp. 28, 151. VIII. p. 19.

that if diseases could have been cured by any art then known in Egypt, we should certainly have heard more of the effects of it; and the emperors, and others, would, no doubt, have learned it, as well as Jesus.*

. Of the same nature with this, and equally undeserving of any serious answer, is the assertion of some Jews, that Jesus worked his miracles by means of the name of God, which he stole out of the temple. As to the power of magic, it was always supposed to be derived from the heathen deities, and therefore it would have been extraordinary indeed, if they had permitted Jesus and his disciples to employ it to the destruction of their own empire.

It was also said by the Heathens, that, allowing Christ to have wrought miracles, things of as wonderful a nature had been done before. " Celsus—laid hold of old Greek stories to oppose to the miracles of Jesus, and those of the Jewish prophets."† Hierocles did not deny the miracles of Christ, but he said that even greater things had been done by Apollonius." ‡ And Marcellinus, in his letter to Austin, says, the Heathens " are continually talking of their Apollonius, Apuleius, and other magicians, whose miracles, they say, are greater than our Saviour's." §

As the miracles of Apollonius will not be contended for by any modern unbeliever, it is sufficient to say upon this subject with Dr. Lardner, " Some will ask how came it to pass that many heathen people were supposed to equal Apollonius to Jesus, or even to prefer him before our Lord. I answer, the reason was, that they were willing to lay hold of any thing that offered, to save the sinking cause of polytheism, and the rites belonging to it; as shipwrecked men catch at every twig, or straw, that comes in their way, to save themselves from drowning." ||

How ready the Heathens were to cavil at the gospel history, and how much we may depend upon it, that they would have detected any imposition with respect to it, if it had been possible for them to do it, we may clearly infer from the apparent insignificance of many of their objections. Thus " Celsus pretends, that the disciples did not believe in Jesus, because they forsook him in his last sufferings."¶ He also says of the resurrection of Christ, " But who saw all this? Why, a distracted woman, and one or two more of the same imposture, and some dreamers, who fancied

* Lardner, VIII. p. 26. † Ibid. p. 276. ‡ Ibid. p. 257. , § Ibid. IX. p. 187.
|| Ibid. VIII. p. 275.   ¶ Ibid. p. 32.

they saw things as they desired to have them; the same that had happened to innumerable people." * This dis-tracted woman was Mary Magdalene, a person of character and fortune, who had been insane, but was then in her sober senses; and neither she, nor any of the disciples, expected to see Jesus again. This writer does not even take notice of the great number who did see him repeatedly, or, of the opportunity they had of examining at leisure the person of Jesus, and of their being, in consequence of this, fully satisfied, that he was risen from the dead; so far was he from choosing to enter into a critical examination of the evidence of this remarkable fact.

With respect to his resurrection, Celsus also says, "If he would make manifest his divine power, he should have shewn himself to them that derided him, to him that con-demned him, and indeed to all. For surely he had no reason to fear any mortal, now after he had died, and, as you say, was a God." † I have already considered this objec-tion, which derives no force from the time in which it was made, and 1 have shewn the futility of it.

The most important circumstance relating to the evidence of Christianity, is the number of the converts to it near the time of the facts on which it was founded. Both the num-ber and the rank, as well as character of these converts, were much misrepresented by Julian. He says, " Jesus having persuaded a few among you, and those the worst of men, has now been celebrated about three hundred years, having done nothing in his life-time worthy of remembrance; unless one thinks it a mighty matter to heal lame and blind people, and exorcize demoniacs in the villages of Bethsaida and Beth-any." ‡ These few converts, on the day of Pentecost only, which was the first day of the publication of the gospel, amounted to three thousand, and presently after they may be computed to have been about ten thousand, and in a few years they must have been many times that number, in Judea itself. And no sooner was the gospel preached in gentile countries, but the number of converts, as has been shewn, became very considerable. That these converts were the *worst of men*, was notoriously false, unless by this phrase, Julian meant what he appears to have done by similar phrases in other places, viz. men who set themselves to overturn the religion of the Roman empire. But this they might have done, and yet have been men of the most exalted piety and virtue.

* *Lardner,* VIII. p. 33.   † Ibid. p. 34.   ‡ Ibid. p. 399.

Porphyry also, willing to stigmatize the apostles, charges them, but without any proof, with being deceivers, influenced by worldly views.

In answer to such charges as these, Origen, who must have known who the Christians were, and what kind of people they had been, and whose veracity was never called in · question, (except in modern times, by Mosheim * and Dr. Horsley, who, on being called upon to do it, has not been able to make good his charge against him,)† says, there were more christian converts " from no very bad life, than of such as were abandoned."‡

Indeed, from the nature of the case, it may be supposed that the first christian converts were persons of an inquisitive turn of mind, which is seldom the character of those who are very profligate; and their readiness to abandon their vices, and to embrace a doctrine which required the strictest purity and rectitude of conduct, and even to sacrifice their lives in the cause of truth (a temper of mind not acquired all at once), shews that they could not have been ill-disposed with respect to moral virtue, even before their conversion to Christianity. Some of them, no doubt, had been men of immoral characters, and the excellency of Christianity appeared by its reclaiming them.

As to the miracles of our Saviour, which Julian ridicules, but the truth of which he does not dispute, any one of the things which he mentions, such as curing the lame and the blind, and exorcizing demoniacs (though he passes over in silence all the more conspicuous and splendid miracles) was a sufficient proof of a divine mission; since it is manifestly above the power of man to do any of them. This objection, however, to our Lord's miracles, as inconsiderable things, we hear of in a later period. Thus, in Austin's time, it was said that the " dispossessing demons, healing sick people, and raising men to life, which," (it was said, but without truth,) " some others have done, are only small matters to be performed by the Deity." §

Julian farther says, the first Christians " were contented with deceiving maid-servants and slaves, and by them some men and women, such as Cornelius and Sergius. If

---

* Yet, in the *History*, Mosheim appears to call in question " the justness of his judgment" rather than his *veracity;* acknowledging " the fervour of his piety," and that " his virtues and his labours deserve the admiration of all ages." *Ecc. Hist.* Cent. III. Pt. ii. Sect. vii. I. p. 219.

† See "Controversy with Bishop Horsley,' Pt. ii. Letter iv. and Pt. iii. Letter i.

‡ *Lardner*, VIII. p. 14.   § Ibid. IX. p. 190.

there were then any other men of eminence brought over to you, I mean in the times of Tiberius and Claudius, when these things happened, let me pass for a liar in every thing I say." *

The conversion of Cornelius and Sergius Paulus, Julian had from the book of Acts, the truth of which he did not dispute. But the same book, and also the Epistles of Paul (the genuineness of which was never questioned), shew clearly that, besides Cornelius and Sergius, there were several other men of rank and eminence who became Christians. If a great number of the gentile converts had not been opulent, they could not have made the liberal contributions which they did to the poor in Jerusalem; and though many of *these* were in low circumstances, their wants had been relieved by the sale of estates belonging to the richer among them.

Besides this, Julian takes advantage of the little that was then certainly known of the age of the apostles, and also confines his observations to the times of Tiberius and Claudius. For presently after this, it is notorious that there were many Christians, in every distinguished rank in life. Christian writers very soon equalled in numbers and ability those among the Heathens, and before the time of Constantine far exceeded them. With respect to *wealth*, the revenues of some of the churches, even during the time of persecution, were complained of as exorbitant. As to *rank*, it appears from the Epistles of Paul, that there were Christians even in the family of the emperor; and Tertullian seems to intimate that, when he wrote his Apology, which was at the close of the second century, " there were some considerable numbers of Christians in the Senate." †

With respect to the spread of Christianity, it may be proved that it went on uniformly gaining ground, from the time of its promulgation to the establishment of it by Constantine; which fact alone is, as I have shewn, a sufficient proof of the progress which it had made before that time; and without appealing to the writings of Christians, and the facts mentioned by any of them. This may be abundantly proved from the testimony of the Heathens themselves.

The number of Christians must have been very great in the time of Pliny, about eighty years after the death of Christ, and about seventy after the first preaching of the

* *Lardner*, VIII. p. 402.   † Ibid. IX. p. 150.   Reeves's *Apologies*, I. 324.

gospel to the Gentiles, as appears from his own letters to Trajan on the subject. As a magistrate, Pliny was much embarrassed what to do with the number of Christians who were brought before him, in whom he found no other crime than that they were Christians. A part of one of his letters I shall copy.

Having related what he had heard of what was transacted in their private assemblies, which will be mentioned here-after, he says, " After receiving this account, I judged it the more necessary to examine, and that by torture, two maid-servants, which were called ministers; but I have discovered nothing beside a bad and excessive superstition. Suspend-ing, therefore, all judicial proceedings, I have recourse to you for advice. For it has appeared unto me a matter highly deserving consideration, especially upon account of the great number of persons who are in danger of suffering. For many of all ages, and every rank, of both sexes likewise, are accused, and will be accused. Nor has the contagion of this superstition seized cities only, but the lesser towns also, and the open country. Nevertheless, it seems to me that it may be restrained and corrected. It is certain that the temples, which were almost forsaken, begin to be more frequented, and the sacred solemnities, after a long inter-mission, are revived. Victims likewise are every where bought up, whereas for some time there were few pur-chasers. Whence it is easy to imagine what numbers of men might be reclaimed, if pardon were granted to those who shall repent." *

This letter alone is a sufficient proof of the astonishing progress that Christianity had made, in a short space of time after the promulgation of it, and at a considerable distance from the place of its rise. What progress it had made in the time of Julian, in whose reign it was no man's interest to be a Christian, appears from many passages in his own writings, and especially from what passed, when he " went on a feast-day to pay his homage to the temple of Apollo and Daphne, in the neighbourhood of Antioch : but there were neither people nor sacrifices ; the priest had only a small victim, of his own preparing. Of this Julian complains grievously, that so large a city had not provided some bulls for a sacrifice on that solemnity."†

These are proofs of such a spread of Christianity as might have been expected from its being founded on truth, having

* *Lardner*, VII. pp. 293, 294.   † Ibid. VIII. p. 419.

had to struggle with deep-rooted prejudices of various kinds, but still making its way by its own evidence, till idolatry was every where finally exterminated. It were to be wished, that it had had no aid of any other kind. However, as the progress it had made by its own strength, in the face of all oppositions, had been uniform, in the course of near three hundred years, there can be no doubt but that the same end would have been effected (and, I believe, sooner, at least more completely) without any aid from civil power at all.

These are all the objections that I can find to have been advanced, by any of the ancient writers against Christianity, with respect to the proper, or historical evidence of it ; and I dare say you will be surprised that they are so few, and so insignificant. They certainly amount to no proof of imposture in the founders of Christianity.

That it was not in the power of persecution to stop the progress of Christianity, was sufficiently proved. It was even acknowledged and lamented by its adversaries, that it had a contrary effect. Maximin, in one of his rescripts, says, " It is, I am persuaded, well known to yourself, and to all men, how that our lords and fathers, Dioclesian and Maximian, when they saw that almost all mankind were forsaking the worship of the gods, and going over to the sect of the Christians, did rightly ordain, that all men who had forsaken the worship of their immortal gods, should be called back again to the worship of the gods by public pains and penalties. But when I first of all happily came into the east, and perceived that great numbers of men, who might be useful to the public, were for the fore-mentioned cause banished by the judges into several places, I gave orders, that for the future, none of them should be severe toward the people of their province, but rather endeavour to reduce them to the worship of the gods by fair words and good usage."*

In another rescript concerning the Christians, he says, " Forasmuch as it has been manifestly found, by the experience of a long course of time, that they cannot by any means whatever be induced to depart from this obstinacy of disposition, you are therefore to write to the curators and other magistrates, and to the governors of the villages of every city, that they are no longer to concern themselves in this affair."†

The firmness with which Christians bore persecution and death, in all forms, was so far from being denied by their

* Lardner, VIII. p. 317   † Ibid. p. 311.

adversaries, that it was, as I have shewn, the subject of complaint, and even of reproach among them. On the other hand, the Heathens shewed no such resolution when their religion was discountenanced by the state. Austin says, " Who of the Pagans has been found sacrificing, since sacrifices have been prohibited by the laws, and did not deny it? Who of them has been found worshipping an idol, and did not cry out, ' I have done no such thing,' dreading to be convicted? On the other hand, the disciples of Christ, by his words, and by his example in dying and rising again, have been raised above the fear of death."*

The Heathens themselves made a merit of their compliance with the laws in this respect. Libanius says, " I appeal to the guardians of this law : who has known any of those whom you have plundered, to have sacrificed upon the altars, so as the law does not permit? What young or old person what man, what woman?" &c.† Some weak christian emperors threatened with death several acts of the heathen superstition, but we do not find that the threatened punishment was ever inflicted. In general, indeed, as Dr. Lardner observes, those severe edicts were never carried into execution ; and the Heathens were permitted to write in defence of their religion, and against Christianity, without any molestation.

Julian dissembled his strong attachment to Heathenism ten years, conforming in the strictest manner to the rites of a religion which he inwardly detested, and which he was determined, if ever it should be in his power, to suppress. This is the known conduct of most of the unbelievers of modern times. They are so far from making any difficulty of appearing as Christians, and even solemnly subscribing to their belief of it, that they would laugh at the scruples of any man who should refuse to do it, if his interest required it. Most Catholic countries abound with such christianized unbelievers. It is no secret, that many cardinals, and some popes, have had no real belief in Christianity, and have even been atheists. The generality of writers against Christianity are so far from risking any thing in the cause of what they deem to be truth, that wherever there has been the shadow of danger, they have always done it in a mean and covert manner, pretending to believe what they really wish to undermine. This has been the conduct of, I believe, every unbeliever who has put his name to his work, as that of

* *Lardner*, IX. p. 203.   † Ibid. VIII. p. 446.

Voltaire and others abroad, and of Mr. Hume and Mr. Gibbon in this country.

I am, &c.

LETTER XV.

Of other Objections to Christianity in early Times.

DEAR SIR,

HAVING fairly stated to you all the objections that I can find to have been made to the proper, that is, the historical evidence of Christianity, by any of its ancient adversaries, I now proceed to mention their objections of other kinds. But I must observe, that none of these can amount to a refutation of the scheme, unless the things objected to either imply a contradiction, or inculcate gross immorality. But nothing of this kind has ever been proved: In things of small consequence, it may safely be allowed that christian historians, as well as others, may have been mistaken, and also that christian writers may, like other writers, have reasoned ill. But this is mere *humanity*, and cannot affect that revelation which they had from God, and which was proved by miracles. It is not, however, foreign to my purpose to shew what kind of objections were really advanced against Christianity in early ages, that we may form some judgment concerning the state of mind and turn of thinking, in the unbelievers of those times.

It is remarkable, that one of the strongest objections to Christianity that we meet with was occasioned by the mistake of Christians, who, with a view to magnify the person of their Master, exalted him first into a demi-god, and afterwards into a God, equal to his own God and Father. And it was just, that what had been done with a view to remove the objection that had been made to Christianity, on account of the meanness and ignominious death of Christ (in which they, like the apostles, ought to have gloried), should be thus turned to their disadvantage.

In Celsus, the Jewish objector says to Christ, " What occasion had you, when an infant, to be carried into Egypt, lest you should be killed ? A God has no reason to be afraid of death."* Celsus himself says, " that Christians argue miserably when they say, that the Son of God is the Word.

* *Lardner*, VIII. p. 21.

himself;" and after all " shew him to be but a miserable man, condemned, scourged and crucified."* Ridiculing the doctrine of the incarnation, he says, " Was the mother of Jesus handsome, that God should be in love with her beauty ? It is unworthy of God to suppose him to be taken with a corruptible body, or to be in love with a woman, whether she be of royal descent or otherwise."† And again, " If God would send forth a spirit from himself, what need had he to breathe him into the womb of a woman ? For, since he knew how to make men, he might have formed a body for this spirit, and not have cast his own spirit into such filth."‡

It is with a view to the doctrine of the divinity of Christ, that Celsus says, " Never any man betrayed another man with whom he sat at table : and how much less would any man who was so favoured by a God, betray him ?"§ Christ's sufferings and death could not be painful and grievous to him, " he being a God and consenting to them."‖ He also ridicules the idea of a God eating " the flesh of lambs," and drinking " gall and vinegar."¶

Alluding to the same doctrine, Porphyry says, " If the Son of God be Word, he must be either outward word or inward word. But he is neither this, nor that."**

Julian, who was better acquainted with the true principles of Christianity, charges the Christians with introducing a *second God*, contrary to Moses and the prophets ;†† and says, that " neither Paul, nor Matthew, nor Luke, nor Mark, have dared to call Jesus God, but honest John," after the death of Peter and Paul.‡‡ Other philosophers, however, continued to repeat the same objection. Libanius, speaking of Julian, says, " By the guidance of philosophy he soon wiped off the reproach of impiety, and learned the truth, and acknowledged those for gods who were such indeed, instead of him who was only thought to be so."§§

Volusian, in his correspondence with Austin, says, " I cannot conceive that the Lord and Governor of the world should be lodged in the body of a virgin, and lie there ten months, and then be brought forth, without prejudice to the virginity of his mother."‖‖ Also Marcellinus, a Christian, tells Augustine, that " the doctrine of the Lord's incarnation—was indeed a subject of common discourse, and was much disliked, and censured by many," and that " Augustine therefore would do well to clear it up."¶¶

---

* *Lardner,* VIII. p. 15. † Ibid. p. 19. ‡ Ibid. § Ibid. p. 30.
‖ Ibid. ¶ Ibid. p. 31. ** Ibid. p. 211. †† Ibid. p. 396.
‡‡ Ibid. p. 400. §§ Ibid. p. 438. ‖‖ Ibid. IX. p. 185. ¶¶ Ibid. p. 186.

In the preceding articles, the Christians themselves gave but too much occasion to the objection that was made to their religion, and the same was the case with respect to some others. Porphyry, for example, objected to the doctrine of *everlasting punishment*, as contrary to our Saviour's own maxim, " with what measure you mete, it shall be meted to you again."* The language in which the fathers often express themselves, leads us to think that many of them, at least, did hold the doctrine of the proper eternity of hell torments, though nothing can be more contrary to reason, or be less countenanced by the true sense of Scripture, in which the duration of future punishment is expressed in terms of an indefinite signification ; and which abounds with maxims utterly irreconcileable with that doctrine, representing the government of God as perfectly equitable, and approving itself to the reason of men.

The superstition of the primitive times gave but too much reason for Julian's saying to the Christians, " you worship the wood of the cross, and make signs of it upon your foreheads."† He also charged Christians " with having killed some who persisted in the ancient religion" (which, however, does not appear to have been the case) and some heretics ; but he adds, " these are your own inventions ; for Jesus has no where directed you to do such things ; nor yet Paul."‡ We may add, in this place, that the monks were a just object of ridicule to the Heathens, as idle people, and burthensome to the community.

In many other cases, however, neither Christianity itself, nor the professors of it, gave any just occasion to the objections that were made to it, and least of all to that of Celsus, that the doctrine of Christ " contains in it nothing weighty and new."§ The doctrine of a resurrection, and of a future life, was certainly new to the heathen world ; and if any thing be *weighty*, this is. Notwithstanding this, it was commonly ridiculed by the Heathens in general, and by Celsus in particular.‖ They said the thing was impossible, and therefore incredible. They thought the body unworthy of being raised, and that the soul would do better without it. That the thing is *impossible* to that Power which originally made man, will hardly be advanced at this day ; and modern unbelievers will not readily join their predecessors in their

* *Lardner,* VIII. p. 223. † Ibid. p. 402. ‡ Ibid. IX. p. 210.
§ Ibid. VIII. p. 36 ‖ Ibid. p. 38.

doctrine concerning the peculiar happiness of a soul disen-
gaged from the incumbrance of a body.

It was an ancient, as well as a modern objection to Christianity, that the knowledge of it is not universal. This was
urged by Celsus,[*] by Porphyry,[†] and by Julian.[‡] To this
it is sufficient to say, that the Divine Being may have good
reasons for distributing all his favours very unequally. He
has given to men more understanding than to brutes ; he has
given to some men a better understanding than to others ;
and he gives to some ages, and to some nations, advantages
which he denies to others. But in this his equity cannot be
impeached, so long as no improvement is required of what has
not been bestowed ; and as to his *wisdom* in these unequal
distributions, it must certainly be great presumption in man
to arraign that.[§]

There is no end of the objections that have been made to
Christianity, in ancient or modern times, from the mistakes
of the objectors, or their cavilling at things of no moment.
Thus Celsus objects to Christians the sentiments of the
Gnostics.[‖] Porphyry charged Peter with imprecating death
on Ananias and Sapphira, when, in reality, he only foretold
what the Divine Being would do.[¶] Porphyry also said, it
was improbable that Nebuchadnezzar should shew that
respect to Daniel which is asserted in his book.[**] He ridiculed the queen, mentioned in the account of Belshazzar's
feast, supposing her to have been his wife, " for knowing
more than her husband ;"[††] and he confounds Darius the
Mede, with Darius the son of Hystaspes.[‡‡]

The Pagans in the time of Austin said, " how could the
same God reject the old sacrifices, and institute a new way
of worship?"[§§] But it does not appear that God has rejected
the old sacrifices, though, the Jewish temple being destroyed,
the service of it cannot now be performed, as it may be at
the restoration of the Jews to their own country ; when,
according to the prophecies of Ezekiel, the temple will be
rebuilt, and the service of it resumed. Besides, admitting the
principles of those who object to the restoration of sacrifices,
as only adapted to the infant state of the world, it is not
contrary to the analogy of nature, that things should be

* *Lardner*, VIII. p. 42.   † Ibid. p. 221.   ‡ Ibid. p. 395.
§ See Young's " Dissertation on Idolatrous Corruptions in Religion," II. pp. 250
—254. Law's *Theory*, Part I.
‖ *Lardner*, VIII. p. 51.   ¶ Ibid. p. 212.   ** Ibid. p. 188.
†† Ibid. p. 189.   ‡‡ Ibid. p. 191.   §§ Ibid. IX. p. 187.

in a progressive state, always approaching nearer to perfection.

In the time of Austin it was said, that Christianity " was inconsistent with good order among men and the welfare of society," in consequence of the passive conduct which it recommended.* But the only pretence for this are some proverbial expressions of our Saviour, which some have understood too literally.

Hierocles said, " that the Scriptures overthrow themselves by the contradictions with which they abound.† But it does not appear what kind of contradictions he meant. They could not be any that affect the credibility of the principal facts, and it is on these alone that the truth of Christianity depends.

Porphyry inferred the falsehood of Christianity from the disputes between Paul and Barnabas, and other circumstances of a similar nature. But may not honest men see things in different lights, and sometimes give way to intemperate heat? As they differed, it is the more probable that, if there had been any thing sinister in the conduct of either of them, it would have come to light. Men that differ are not disposed to screen or favour one another.

The " eighteen arguments of Proclus" against Christianity, did not affect " the Christian religion in general, but only, or chiefly, that one opinion of the Christians, that the world had a beginning."‡ This, however, may easily be proved to have been true, by arguments that have no dependence on revelation.

" Julian objects against the Mosaic account of the creation of the world, the fall of man, and the confusion of languages. He finds fault also with the decalogue."§ Intelligent Christians also object to some of these things, concerning which Moses himself could have had no information, except from tradition. But this does not affect the credibility of what he writes as having passed under his own eyes, and those of his contemporaries, the account of which was published in his own life-time. Julian's objections to the decalogue, could only shew his ignorance or his malice.

The subject of *prophecy* has always been acknowledged to be attended with much difficulty, and therefore we do not wonder that unbelievers, in all ages, have urged their objections to it. Celsus says, that " the prophecies may be

* *Lardner,* IX. p. 187.   † Ibid. VIII. p. 255.   ‡ Ibid. IX. p. 68.   § Ibid. VIII. p. 396.

applied to many others with more probability than to Jesus."*
This is readily acknowledged to be the case with respect to
many of the prophecies of the Old Testament, which have
by some Christians been applied to Christ.   But there are
also some of them, which can apply to no other person ; and
it cannot be denied that they were delivered some hundreds
of years before he was born.   The destruction of Jerusalem,
and the desolation of Judea, were clearly foretold by our
Saviour himself.   The present dispersed state of the Jews is
the subject of a whole series of prophecy, beginning with
Moses.   And if this remarkable people should be restored
to their own country, and become a flourishing nation in it,
which is likewise foretold, few persons, I think, will doubt
of the reality of a prophetic spirit,

The prophecies of Daniel are so clear, that Porphyry says,
he " does not foretel things to come, but relates what had
already happened."†   He also said that the book of Daniel
could not be genuine, because it was written in Greek, as
he argued from the story of Susannah.   It is very evident,
however, that some of the prophecies of Daniel relate to the
Roman empire, which is described under various images,
and this certainly did not exist at the time that the book of
Daniel was first translated into Greek.   The decay of the
Roman empire is also mentioned in the book of Daniel, and
this had not taken place in the time of Porphyry himself.
As to the story of Susannah, it is no part of the book of
Daniel, but a spurious work, probably written in Greek.

I have already observed that the great offence that was
given by Christians, was their drawing people from the
worship of the heathen gods, on which it was imagined the
prosperity of the state depended.   On this account they
were treated as atheistical and profane persons, and dangerous
in a community.   And it is well known that when persons
go under an ill name, and are on any account, generally
odious, every thing bad is readily believed of them.   Thus,
because Christians were often obliged to meet for religious
worship in the night, they were charged with putting out
the lights, and committing " promiscuous lewdness ;" and
probably their eating bread and drinking wine in the celebra-
tion of the Lord's Supper, might give occasion to its being
said, " that they killed a child and ate it," as we find in
Celsus.‡

* *Lardner*, VIII. p. 42.   † Ibid. p. 185.   ‡ Ibid. p. 54.

Besides, that every thing of this nature is in the highest degree incredible, no proof was ever pretended to be brought of
such practices; and whenever any inquiry was made into their
conduct, nothing was ever discovered to their discredit.   All
that Pliny could find upon the strictest scrutiny, and from
those who had deserted them, was (as we find from his
epistle to Trajan) as follows : " The whole of their fault, or
error, lay in this, that they were wont to meet together on a
stated day, before it was light and sing among themselves,
alternately a hymn to Christ, as a god, and bind themselves
by an oath, not to the commission of any wickedness," (with
which they had been often charged,) " but not to be guilty
of theft, or robbery, or adultery, never to falsify their word,
nor to deny a pledge committed to them, when called upon
to return it.   When these things were performed, it was
their custom to separate, and then to come together again
to a meal, which they ate in common, without any disorder.
But this they had forborne since the publication of my edict,
by which, according to your commands, I prohibited assemblies.   After receiving this account, I judged it the more
necessary to examine, and that by torture, two maid-servants,
who were called *ministers*.   But I discovered nothing besides
a bad and excessive superstition."*

On occasion of the vague and groundless accusation of
Christians, and the odium they unjustly lay under, Justin
Martyr gives a simple and natural account of what was transacted in their assemblies, and then challenges their heathen
adversaries in a very proper manner on the subject.   " On
the day called Sunday," he says, " we all meet together, &c.
&c. &c.   On which day Jesus Christ our Saviour rose from
the dead," and " appeared to his apostles and disciples, and
taught them those things which we have set before you, and
refer to your consideration.   If these things appear agreeable
to reason and truth, pay a regard to them.   If they appear
trifling, reject them as such.   But do not treat as enemies,
nor appoint capital punishment to those who have done no
harm.   For we foretel unto you, that you will not escape the
future judgment of God, if you persist in unrighteousness,
and we shall say, " *The will of the Lord be done.*"†

Julian more than once reproaches the heathen priests with
the better morals of the Christians.   In his letter to the
high-priest of Galatia, he says, " If Hellenism does not

* *Lardner,* VII. p. 293.   See also Bryant's *Authenticity,* &c. pp. 142—150.
† Ibid. VII. p. 344.   Reeves's *Apol.* I. p. 127.

prosper according to our wish, it is the fault of those who profess it.—Why do we not look to that which has been the principal cause of the augmentation of impiety, humanity to strangers, care in burying the dead, and that sanctity of life of which they make such a show, all which things I will have to be really practised by our people ?   It is a shame, when there are no beggars among the Jews, and impious Galileans relieve not only their own people, but ours also, that our poor should be neglected by us, and be left ·helpless and destitute."*

Ammianus Marcellinus also, who censures the bishops of Rome, says, " they might be happy indeed, if, despising the grandeur of the city, which they allege as an excuse for their luxury, they would imitate the life of some country bishops, who, by their temperance in eating and drinking, by the plainness of their habit, and the modesty of their whole behaviour, approve themselves to the eternal Deity, and his true worshippers, as men of virtue and piety."†

Such were the objections that were advanced against Christianity in early ages, when there was the best opportunity of inquiring into the grounds of it; and it is easy to see that they affect nothing on which its credibility at all depends.   Admitting what the unbelievers of those ages urged against the facts on which the truth of Christianity depends, it is evident that they had no pretence for rejecting it which a modern unbeliever would not be ashamed to avow.   And whatever may be ·said of the good sense of the early writers against Christianity, it is evident that it was no guard against the most despicable superstition, and the most unjust and cruel treatment of those who differed from them on the subject of religion.   Whatever were the virtues of Marcus Aurelius or Julian, they did not teach them toleration or humanity, where religion was concerned ; and so far were they from being the *esprits forts* of the present age, that they gave into the most ridiculous credulity in divination, and all the other absurd pretences of the heathen philosophers and priests.

I am, &c.

---

* *Lardner*, VIII. pp. 416, 417.   † Ibid. p. 474.

LETTER XVI.

Of the Two last Chapters of the First Book of Mr. Gibbon's History of the Decline and Fall of the Roman Empire.

Dear Sir,

Though it is not my intention, in this correspondence, to animadvert upon particular writers, yet, as you say that the *Two last Chapters* (xv. xvi.) *of Mr. Gibbon's History* have made more unbelievers than any thing that has been published of late years; and have greatly contributed to confirm many in their unbelief, I shall, at your request, take notice of such of his observations as more properly affect the *historical evidence* of Christianity, and which I have not already noticed in the *Conclusion** *of my History of the Corruptions of Christianity*, in which I made some observations on what he has been pleased to call the secondary causes of its growth.

There I shewed how inadequate all the *five causes* he mentions are to account for the fact, without the *primary cause*, " the convincing evidence of the doctrine itself," which he contents himself with indistinctly mentioning, in part of a sentence, as wishing to keep it out of sight as much as possible. For in what that *convincing evidence* consisted he does not say, whether in the nature of the doctrines themselves, or in the truth of the great facts in the Christian history. As to what he says of " the ruling providence of its great Author," it might be equally a proof of the truth of Paganism or Mahometanism, and no doubt he thought so.

Indeed, strange as it may seem, Mr. Gibbon himself appears to have entirely overlooked the necessary connexion between his *secondary* and the *primary* causes†of the growth of Christianity, though the former imply so firm a persua-

---

* Part I. "Considerations addressed to Unbelievers, and especially to Mr. Gibbon."

† Mr. Gibbon professes to inquire " not indeed what were the first, but what were the secondary causes of the rapid growth of the Christian church." He then states the five following causes —

. " I. The inflexible, and if we may use the expression, the intolerant zeal of the Christians, derived, it is true, from the Jewish religion, but purified from the narrow and unsocial spirit, which, instead of inviting, had deterred the Gentiles from embracing the law of Moses. II. The doctrine of a future life, improved by every additional circumstance which could give weight and efficacy to that important truth. III The miraculous powers ascribed to the primitive church. IV. The pure and austere morals of the Christians. V. The union and discipline of the Christian republic, which gradually formed an independent and increasing state in the heart of the Roman Empire." *Decline and Fall*, Ch. xv. 4to. Ed. 4. I. p. 536.

sion of the truth of it, in the minds of its professors, as could
never, in the natural course of things, have been produced
without the real existence of the great facts, which were the
object of their faith.　For, without mentioning any more of
his causes, to suppose that the inflexible or intolerant zeal of
the primitive Christians, and their firm belief in a future life,
could have been produced without there being any truth in
the history of the miracles, death and resurrection of Christ,
is to suppose that a pile of building must be supported by
pillars, but that those pillars may stand in the air, without
touching the ground, or with the Indians, that the world is
supported by an elephant, and the elephant by a tortoise,
but the tortoise by nothing.

What is most remarkable in Mr. Gibbon's conduct of his
argument, (for such these two chapters of his history ought
to be termed,) is that, without pretending to consider the
proper evidence of the miracles of Christ, and those of the
apostles, the firm belief of which, by those who were in circumstances the most proper for the examination of them,
must have produced all his secondary causes,) he takes
every opportunity of insinuating, in the course of his narrative, every thing that he can to take from the effect of that
evidence, which he carefully keeps out of sight.　And
though it is by gross misrepresentation of facts, and giving
them colours that by no means belong to them, they are such
as the unwary reader will not suspect.　Some of these only,
I shall, in this letter, point out to you, that you may be
upon your guard against others of a similar nature.　In his
account, in particular, of the conduct of the heathen magistrates in the persecution of Christians, and of the behaviour
of the Christians under persecution, he never fails to mention
or suppress every thing that could make the former appear to
advantage, and the latter to disadvantage.

I have noticed the strange concession of Mr. Gibbon, that
the Jews acted " in contradiction to every known principle
of the human mind," in yielding " a stronger and more ready
assent to the traditions of their remote ancestors, than to the
evidence of their own senses," (*Hist. of Corruptions, General
Conclusion,*) without being aware that no such proposition,
relating to the sentiments and conduct of *men* can be true.　I
shall now quote another very extraordinary assertion of his,
relating to that *singular people*, as he calls them, and as they
must indeed be, if they could *feel* and *act* as he supposes
them to have done.

" The contemporaries of Moses and Joshua," he says,

" had beheld with careless indifference the most amazing
miracles" (p. 559); by which he would insinuate that those
miracles were never performed. But the only authority on
which Mr. Gibbon could assert any thing concerning the
miracles to which the Jews were witnesses, says, that they
were far from being beheld with careless indifference. The
Israelites were so much terrified with the appearances at
Mount Sinai, that they requested that God would not speak
to them any more in that manner, but by Moses. And so
far were the miracles which they saw from making no impression on them, that notwithstanding their strong propensity
to idolatry, their influence continued all that generation, and
that which immediately succeeded it. We read, Joshua
xxiv. 31, " And Israel served the Lord all the days of
Joshua, and all.the days of the elders that outlived Joshua,
and which had known all the works of the Lord, that he had
done for Israel."

An insinuation that most nearly affects the credibility of
the gospel history, in Mr. Gibbon's account, is contained in
the following paragraph : " The Jews of Palestine," he says,
" who had fondly expected a temporal deliverer, gave so cold
a reception to the miracles of the divine prophet, that it was
found unnecessary to publish, or at least to preserve any
Hebrew gospel. The authentic histories of the acts of
Christ were composed in the Greek language, at a considerable distance from Jerusalem, and after the gentile converts
were grown extremely numerous." I. p. 603.

This must have been intended to insinuate that the authentic gospels were not published in the country where the
facts were known, and that they were not much credited in
Judea itself; whereas nothing is more certain than that the
most zealous of all Christians, notwithstanding the disappointment of their fond hopes of a temporal Messiah, were
the Jewish converts, and that by them only was the gospel
propagated in distant countries. These Jewish Christians
also had a gospel of their own,* which was published as
early, and was as much regarded as any other; and whether
Mr. Gibbon will call it *authentic* or not, there was no material difference between it and the other gospels, all containing an account of the miracles, death and resurrection of
Christ. This Hebrew gospel was preserved as long as the

---

* See F. *Simon.* C. H. Pt. i Ch. v.—ix.   *Michaelis,* Introd. Lect. 1750, Sect.
lxxxix. xc. and *Lardner,* Index, *St. Matthew.*

Jewish Christians existed, and some of them remained till after the time of Austin.

The other gospels, though written in Greek, for the use of those who understood that language, and at a distance from Judea, were all written by Jews, and while the transactions were recent; and it was nothing but a well-grounded persuasion of their authenticity, that could have procured this remarkable history that firm credit which was given to it in all parts of the world. Let Mr. Gibbon say how this effect could have been produced, if the gospel history had not been attended with every circumstance requisite to establish its credibility in that age, and consequently in all future ages.

Mr. Gibbon insinuates an objection to the evidences of Christianity from its not having recommended itself to some wise and virtuous Heathens in the early ages. "We stand in need," says he, in his ironical manner, " of such reflections, to comfort us for the loss of some illustrious characters, which in our eyes might have seemed the most worthy of the heavenly present. The names of Seneca, of the elder and the younger Pliny, of Tacitus, of Plutarch, of Galen, of the slave Epictetus, and of the Emperor Marcus Antoninus, adorn the age in which they flourished, and exalt the dignity of human nature. They filled with glory their respective stations, either in active or contemplative life. Their excellent understandings were improved by study. Philosophy had purified their minds from the prejudices of the popular superstition, and their days were spent in the pursuit of truth and the practice of virtue. Yet all these sages (it is no less an object of surprise than of concern) overlooked or rejected the perfection of the Christian system. Their language, or their silence, equally discover their contempt for the growing sect, which in their time had diffused itself over the Roman empire. Those among them who condescend to mention the Christians, consider them only as obstinate and perverse enthusiasts, who exacted an implicit submission to their mysterious doctrines, without being able to produce a single argument that could engage the attention of men of sense and learning." I. p. 616.

In this there can be no doubt but Mr. Gibbon gives his own opinion in the form of that of the ancients; and afterwards, affecting to lament that the cause of Christianity was not defended by abler advocates, he says, that " when they would demonstrate the divine origin of Christianity, they insist much more strongly on the predictions which announced, than on the miracles which accompanied the appearance of the Messiah."

If this had been the case, and if, with such miserable advocates, and such insufficient arguments, Christianity had, as Mr. Gibbon says, " diffused itself over the Roman empire," so early as the time of Seneca, it will not be very easy for him to account for so extraordinary a fact. Here is a great *effect* without any adequate *cause.* Yet this does not appear to have struck our philosopher as any thing extraordinary. It satisfies him that some thousands of people took it into their heads, without any reason at all, that Christ and the apostles wrought miracles, that they madly devoted their labours, their fortunes, and their lives, to the propagation of their groundless opinion, and that by their inflexible zeal and obstinacy, they forced the belief of it on the rest of the world. Such is the philosophy of Mr. Gibbon, and of other unbelievers.

If Mr. Gibbon had read the New Testament with care, he would have seen that the first preachers of Christianity had no *mysterious doctrines* to teach. Hear what Paul says in the Areopagus at Athens. Acts xvii. 30, 31 : " The times of this ignorance God winked at, but now commandeth all men every where to repent. Because he hath appointed a day in the which he will judge the world in righteousness, by that man whom he hath ordained, whereof he hath given assurance unto all men, in that he hath raised him from the dead ;" and of this he himself, and " above five hundred brethren," as he says, 1 Cor. xv. 6, were witnesses.

What is there *mysterious* in all this ? Is it less intelligible, or in itself less probable than the elegant mythology of Greece and Rome ? If in that age the *miracles* were less particularly insisted on, it was because they were not disputed. They were not *things done in a corner*, but such as whole countries were witnesses of. The arguments from prophecy, which Mr. Gibbon ridicules, had their weight chiefly with the Jews, but were not improperly urged upon the Gentiles, who, seeing a wonderful correspondence between the predictions and the events, would be sensible of the divinity of the whole system of revelation, begun in Judaism, and completed in Christianity.

I am far from being disposed to detract from the merit of Seneca, and the other distinguished Heathens here mentioned by Mr. Gibbon ; though with respect to the younger Pliny and Marcus Antoninus, he is far from being justified in saying that their minds were purified " from the prejudices of the popular superstition." For it has been shewn that they, as well as Julian, were bigots to it. But let Mr. Gibbon pro‑ duce what evidence he has of these men, of such excellent understandings, and freedom from prejudice, having made any proper *inquiry* into the nature and truth of Christianity, and say what arguments they opposed to those of the Chris‑ tian teachers. Otherwise their overlooking or rejecting Christianity implies no reflections upon *it*, but upon them‑ selves.

Notwithstanding what Mr. Gibbon here says, that the christian preachers could not produce " a single argument that could engage the attention of men of sense and learn‑ ing," (p. 617,) yet it is unquestionable, that, whether it was by *argument*, or any other means, men of sense, and learning too, did embrace Christianity ; and that, in a very reasonable space of time, there was not a man of sense or learning that did not. It should also be considered that none of the persons mentioned by Mr. Gibbon, ran any risk by continuing Heathens, whereas, in that age, a man hazarded every thing by becoming a Christian. Which of them, then, was more likely to inquire into the truth of Christianity, and by whose verdict shall we be best justified in abiding ?

" How shall we excuse," says Mr. Gibbon, ": the supine inattention of the pagan and philosophic world, to those evidences which were presented by the hand of Omnipotence, not to their reason, but to their senses ? During the age of Christ, of his apostles and of their first disciples, the doctrine which they preached was confirmed by innumerable prodi‑ gies. The lame walked, the blind saw, the sick were healed, the dead were raised, demons were expelled, and the laws of nature were frequently suspended for the benefit of the church. But the sages of Greece and Rome turned aside from the awful spectacle ; and pursuing the ordinary occupa‑ tions of life or study, appeared unconscious of any alterations in the moral or physical government of the world. Under the reign of Tiberius, the whole earth, or at least a cele‑ brated province of the Roman empire, was involved in a preternatural darkness of three hours. Even this miraculous event, which ought to have excited the wonder, the curio‑ sity, and the devotion of mankind, passed without notice, in an age of science and history." I. p. 618.

This was, no doubt, meant to insinuate, that the mira‑ cles Mr. Gibbon recites were never performed, since they did not engage the attention of the sages of Greece and Rome. But their *inattention*, I presume has been suffi‑

ciently accounted for ; and if they did not give proper *attention*, and did not trouble themselves to make the necessary *inquiries*, their unbelief reflects no discredit on Christianity.

As to the *darkness* about which Mr. Gibbon makes so great a parade, it was not very likely to attract the notice of historians, as it was not so great, but that the persons who attended the crucifixion could see to give Jesus vinegar on a spear, and he could distinguish his mother and his disciple John. (See p. 451, *Note*.)

With a view no doubt to insinuate that much credit was not given to the account of the miracles, death, and resurrection of Christ, by the inhabitants of Judea, Mr. Gibbon says, " A more accurate inquiry will induce us to doubt whether any of those persons who had been witnesses to the miracles of Christ were permitted, beyond the limits of Palestine, to seal with their blood the truth of their testimony." I. p. 635.

Admitting all this, it is not denied but there were martyrs to Christianity, of those who were witnesses to the miracles of Christ, *within the bounds of Palestine;* and these were of more value than any others. And whether any of them suffered *without* the bounds of Palestine, or not, converts were made in other countries ; and· this must have been by the credit that was given to the accounts of the miracles of Christ, whether the testimony was sealed with blood, or not. But the epistles of Paul are a sufficient evidence of the great hardships to which himself, and many other Christians, were exposed in *distant countries.* Mr. Gibbon cannot deny the reality of the persecution under Nero, in Rome at least ; and in that persecution, according to the testimony of the ancients, to which there is no reason to object, both Peter and Paul were put to death. It is likewise the general opinion, that, except the two James's, (both of whom suffered at Jerusalem,) and John, who lived to a great age at Ephesus, all the other apostles died martyrs without the bounds of Palestine. And it must be acknowledged, that the testimony of the apostles thus *sealed*, as Mr. Gibbon says, *with their blood*, was of more value than any other, as they had the most perfect knowledge of the history and character of Christ.

In order to suggest that it was a long time before the Christians suffered any legal persecution from the Romans, Mr. Gibbon says, " We may assure ourselves, that when he" (Pliny) " accepted the government of Bythinia, there were no general laws, or decrees of the Senate, in force against the Christians;* that neither Trajan, nor any of his virtuous predecessors, whose edicts were received into the civil and criminal jurisprudence, had publicly declared their intentions concerning the new sect; and that whatever proceedings had been carried on against the Christians, there were none of sufficient weight and authority to establish a precedent for the conduct of a Roman magistrate." I. p. 647.

On this I would observe, that when Pliny arrived in his province, it was evidently the custom to condemn Christians to death, merely *as such;* and whether this was done by a proper *law,* or otherwise, it was no less a trial of the faith of those who suffered death. But both the letters of Pliny, and the answer of Trajan, shew that the proceedings had been upon an existing law, whether enacted by Trajan himself, or any of his predecessors. His answer clearly implies that he did not send the governor any *new law,* but only informed him how he ought to act with respect to convictions on a former law, instructing him to condemn those who were proved to be guilty, but not to seek for proofs of guilt. A strange and inconsistent proceeding, as was justly remarked by Tertullian. If the profession of Christianity was deserving of death, why might not the guilty be sought for, as well as other criminals? And if it was not, why condemn to death those who professed it?

The probability is, that the law by which the Christians had been persecuted was one of Nero, or Domitian; and to say nothing of the inscription† found in Spain (which, however, Lardner supposes may be genuine), Orosius says, that the edict of Nero extended to the provinces. It is certainly highly probable, that he who put so many Christians to death, and in so shocking a manner, would think the whole sect deserving to be extirpated in all parts of the empire.

Mr. Gibbon appears to have been sufficiently sensible of the value of such a testimony to the truth of the gospel history, as is furnished by the *early martyrdoms,* and, therefore, he takes great pains to diminish their number; and when the facts cannot be denied, he endeavours to exhibit them in the most unfavourable light, as either a criminal obstinacy, or a mad and ridiculous contempt of life. And

---

* See Mr. Melmoth's note, in his *Translation,* B. x. line 98, and Mr. Bryant's strictures on his opinion, *Authenticity,* &c. pp. 166—176.

† " On a monument found in Portugal, *To Nero Claudius Cæsar, Augustus, High Priest, for clearing the Province of Robbers, and those who taught Mankind a new Superstition.* None can doubt that by a new superstition is here intended Christianity." *Lardner,* VII. p. 248, where see the original from *Gruter,* pp. 238, 239.

yet, though this is evidently his object, he cannot avoid mentioning such circumstances as shew the shocking cruelty and injustice of the persecutors, and the noble constancy of the persecuted. " Punishment," he says, " was not the inevitable consequence of conviction; and the Chrisians whose guilt was the most clearly proved, by the testimony of witnesses, or even by their voluntary confession, still retained in their own power the alternative of life or death. It was not so much the past offence, as the actual resistance, which excited the indignation of the magistrate. He was persuaded that he offered them an easy pardon, since, if they consented to cast a few grains of incense upon the altar, they were dismissed from the tribunal in safety, and with applause. It was esteemed the duty of a humane judge to endeavour to reclaim, rather than to punish, those deluded enthusiasts. Varying his tone, according to the age, the sex, or the situation of the prisoners, he frequently condescended to set before their eyes every circumstance which could render life more pleasing or death more terrible ; and to solicit, nay, to entreat them, that they would shew some compassion to themselves, to their families and to their friends. If threats and persuasions proved ineffectual, he had often recourse to violence. The scourge and the rack were called in to supply the deficiency of argument ; and every act of cruelty was employed to subdue such inflexible, and, as it appeared to the Pagans, such criminal obstinacy." I. p. 650.

No doubt, the humanity of some of the Roman magistrates led them to favour the Christians in the manner that Mr. Gibbon has described. But others took every advantage that the laws, and the temper of the times, gave them, and indulged themselves in acts of the most wanton barbarity.

With respect to the number of the martyrs, Mr. Gibbon seems to triumph, p. 653, in the confession of Origen, who says that it was *inconsiderable*. But this term is comparative, and the real value of it must be estimated by a regard to *the whole*, of which it was *a part*; and then it may be inferred, that many hundreds, or even thousands, might be said to be inconsiderable. Origen says, that " the providence of God restrained the violence of the persecutors, lest the whole race of Christians should be extirpated ;" and then adds, " that they who suffered death were few, and easily numbered." *Contra Celsum*, Lib. iii. p. 116. From this it is evident, that, in the idea of Origen, the number of martyrs was few, when compared to the whole number of

Christians, which, no doubt, consisted of many hundreds of thousands in his time; and he could hardly have imagined there was any danger of the extirpation of the whole race of them, by the death of a much greater number than that to which Mr. Gibbon seems willing to reduce them.

Besides, it was not by *death* only, that the faith and con-stancy of the Christians was shewn.   As Mr. Gibbon him-self says, the Roman magistrates " were far from condemning all the Christians who were accused before their tribunal, and very far from punishing with death all those who were convicted of an obstinate adherence to the new superstition; contenting themselves, for the most part, with the milder chastisements of imprisonment, exile, or slavery in the mines." I. p. 652.

These things Mr. Gibbon mentions as milder chastise-ments.   But does not the suffering of such punishments as these (some of them, in my opinion, far more trying than the prospect of immediate death) sufficiently evidence the firmness of the faith of the Christians in the cause for which they suffered; and could so many thousands have suffered in this manner without having taken some care to inform themselves concerning the truth for which they suffered? Would Mr. Gibbon himself be content to be imprisoned, or to go to work in the mines for life, or with the prospect of " a general pardon" at some future, but uncertain time, p. 653, without being well satisfied that he had good reason for submitting to it? And were there not among the Chris-tiáns, who *did* suffer these things, and all that the utmost malice of their enemies could suggest, men who valued life, and the enjoyments of it, as much as Mr. Gibbon can do, and who had as much to lose as he can have?

" The general assertion of Origen," Mr. Gibbon says, " may be explained, and confirmed, by the particular testi-mony of his friend Dionysius, who, in the immense city of Alexandria, and under the rigorous persecution of Decius, reckons only ten men and seven women who suffered for the profession of the christian name." I. p. 654.   But if the account of Dionysius be examined, it will be found that, besides some horrid violences before this persecution, in which many lost their lives, the deaths of these seventeen persons are mentioned only on account of there being some-thing remarkable in them.   He is far from saying, with Mr. Gibbon, that these were *all* that suffered death; and he says that many professed their readiness to die, insomuch that the judges shuddered, and the Christians went out of the tribunal in triumph. He adds, that many were torn to pieces by the Gentiles in other cities and villages.

Mr. Gibbon also says, that " from the history of Eusebius it may be collected that only nine bishops were punished with death; and we are assured by his particular enumeration of the martyrs of Palestine, that no more than ninety-two Christians were entitled to that honourable appellation," p. 701 ; and from this he draws what he calls " a very important and probable conclusion," viz. that " the multitude of Christians in the Roman empire, on whom a capital punishment was inflicted by a judicial sentence, will be reduced to somewhat less than two thousand persons," p. 702 ; whereas, " more than a hundred thousand are said to have suffered, in the Netherlands alone, by the hand of the executioner." I. p. 703.

Even this number would be abundantly sufficient for all the purposes for which martyrdoms are alleged, by the advocates for Christianity; considering *who* those martyrs were, how capable they were of satisfying themselves concerning the truth of Christianity, and how interested they were in the inquiry. But by looking into Eusebius, it will appear that Mr. Gibbon was no more authorized to assert that the ninety-two were the *only* martyrs in Palestine, than that the seventeen were the only ones in Alexandria. The probability is, that it was very far short of the whole number.

Mr. Gibbon proceeds to relate the particulars of the martyrdom of Cyprian, and, as usual with him, in a manner as favourable to the persecutors, and as unfavourable to the martyr, as possible ; as if he might have submitted to death, in those circumstances even without any real belief in Christianity, from the mere honour of suffering, and the infamy of shrinking from it. " Could we suppose," says he, p. 659, " that the Bishop of Carthage had employed the profession of the Christian faith only as the instrument of his avarice or ambition, it was still incumbent on him to support the character he had assumed ; and if he possessed the smallest degree of manly fortitude, rather to expose himself to the most cruel tortures, than by a single act to exchange the reputation of a whole life for the abhorrence of his christian brethren, and the contempt of the gentile world. But if the zeal of Cyprian was supported by the sincere conviction of the truth of those doctrines which he preached, the crown of martyrdom must have appeared to him as an object of desire rather than of terror!" I. p. 659. But what made it so infamous to decline martyrdom, and so honourable to suffer it, but a general persuasion of the truth, and the infinite importance of the truth, of Christianity, for which they suffered? Whence arose this general and strong persuasion of this truth, our historian does not investigate. He here says, that, had Cyprian not suffered, he would have incurred the contempt of the gentile world. In a passage quoted above, he said that, on throwing a few grains of incense into the fire, the Christians went from the tribunals of the magistrates with safety, and with applause. Let it then be one or the other, as Mr. Gibbon's changing purpose may require.

Whatever was the *motive*, Mr. Gibbon does sufficient justice to the readiness of the primitive Christians to suffer martyrdom, in its most frightful forms. " The sober discretion of the present age," he says, " will more readily censure than admire, but can more easily admire, than imitate, the fervour of the first Christians, who, according to the lively expression of Sulpicius Severus, desired martyrdom with more eagerness than his own contemporaries solicited a bishopric." I. p. 661.

In this, I trust, Mr. Gibbon judges from his own feelings only. The present christian world in general holds the primitive martyrs in as high veneration, as did their contemporaries, (though neither they, nor the more judicious in the primitive times, approved of the zeal of any in courting martyrdom,) and would be ready, I doubt not, if they were in the the same manner called to it, to follow their example. In what age of the christian church have there not been those who may with propriety be called *martyrs* to what they held to be the truth of the gospel? Mr. Gibbon does not, he cannot deny, that there were thousands of such at the time of the reformation; and cannot he suppose that the same men would have been as ready to die for the profession of Christianity, as for the doctrines of Protestantism?

The only use that a defender of Christianity makes of the martyrdoms of Christians in early times, is as a proof of the firmness of their faith in the cause for which they suffered; such a faith requiring an adequate *cause*. But this firm faith is as evident in the readiness to suffer, as in the actual suffering, provided there be no doubt of the sincerity of that professed readiness. But this was then so far from being doubted, with respect to the generality of those who proposed themselves, that it was ridiculed, as madness and infatuation, by the Heathens of those times. And Mr. Gibbon, in the following account, evidently joins the Heathens in this ridicule.

" The Christians sometimes supplied by their voluntary declaration, the want of an accuser, rudely disturbed the public service of Paganism, and rushing in crowds round the tribunals of the magistrates, called upon them to pronounce, and to inflict, the sentence of the law. The behaviour of the Christians was too remarkable to escape the notice of the ancient philosophers. But they seem to have considered it with much less admiration than astonishment. Incapable of conceiving the motives which sometimes transported the fortitude of believers beyond the bounds of prudence or reason, they treated such an eagerness to die, as the strange result of obstinate despair, of stupid insensibility, or of superstitious phrensy. ' Unhappy men,' exclaimed the pro-consul Antoninus, to the Christians of Asia, ' unhappy men, if you are thus weary of your lives, is it so difficult for you to find ropes and precipices ?' He was extremely cautious, as it is observed by a learned and pious historian, of punishing men who had found no accusers but themselves, the imperial laws not having made any provision for so unexpected a case. Condemning, therefore, a few, as a warning to their brethren, he dismissed the multitude with indignation and contempt." I. pp. 661, 662.

To what purpose can it be to any man to endeavour, as Mr. Gibbon does, to reduce the number of christian martyrs, when their *readiness to suffer* martyrdom is not only acknowledged, but ridiculed ; so that the *number* was a circumstance that did not depend upon themselves, but upon their adversaries. This willingness to suffer martyrdom I own to be censurable, since our Saviour exhorts his followers not to court persecution, but to avoid it, if it can be done with honour. But certainly this courting of suffering, is no argument of a less firm faith ; and it is this firm faith that is alone of any use in proving the truth of those facts which were the objects of it. That the faith of Christians in the truth or the gospel history in those early times (when it was not difficult for persons who were sufficiently in earnest to discover the truth) was real, and not to be shaken by torture or death, Mr. Gibbon sufficiently acknowledges. Let him then account for this fact on the supposition of there being no truth in the gospel history, if he can.

The inefficacy of persecution to extirpate Christianity,

is abundantly confessed by Mr. Gibbon, in his account of the conduct of Galerius, who was the prompter to what was called the Diocletian persecution. " But when Galerius had obtained the supreme power, and the government of the East, he indulged in their fullest extent his zeal and cruelty, not only in the provinces of Thrace and Asia, which acknowledged his immediate jurisdiction, but in those of Syria, Palestine and Egypt; where Maximin gratified his own inclination, by yielding a rigorous óbedience to the stern commands of his benefactor. The frequent disappointments of his ambitious views, the experience of six years of persecution, and the salutary reflections which a lingering and painful distemper suggested to the mind of Galerius, at length convinced him, that the most violent efforts of despotism are insufficient to extirpate a whole people, or to subdue their religious prejudices." I. p. 695.

Is it not extraordinary that Mr. Gibbon should be able to write this, if he reflected at all on what he wrote, without believing that the faith of Christians stood on no very slight foundation?

I have now, I think, explained myself as fully as I have been able, on every article relating to the evidence of revealed religion, to which you wished that I would give particular attention; and submitting all that I have advanced to your own calm and serious consideration, I subscribe myself.

Dear Sir,

Yours sincerely,

J. PRIESTLEY.

———

END OF VOLUME IV.

———

G. SMALLFIELD, PRINTER, HACKNEY.